Wissenschaftliche Untersuchungen
zum Neuen Testament · 2. Reihe

Herausgeber / Editor
Jörg Frey (München)

Mitherausgeber / Associate Editors
Friedrich Avemarie (Marburg)
Markus Bockmuehl (Oxford)
Hans-Josef Klauck (Chicago, IL)

259

Jonathan Marshall

Jesus, Patrons, and Benefactors

Roman Palestine and the Gospel of Luke

WIPF & STOCK · Eugene, Oregon

JONATHAN MARSHALL: Born 1978; 2008 PhD; taught courses at Biola University (La Mirada, CA) and Eternity Bible College (Simi Valley, CA); currently Associate Pastor in the Camarillo Evangelical Free Church (EFCA; Camarillo, CA).

Wipf and Stock Publishers
199 W 8th Ave, Suite 3
Eugene, OR 97401

Jesus, Patrons and Benefactors
Roman Palestine and the Gospel of Luke
By Marshall, Jonathan
Copyright©2009 Mohr Siebeck
ISBN 13: 978-1-4982-2455-0
Publication date 3/25/2015
Previously published by Mohr Siebeck, 2009

For Kimi:
I understand God better because of my delight in you.

"You shall be a crown of beauty in the hand of the LORD, and a royal diadem in the hand of your God. You shall no more be termed Forsaken, and your land shall no more be termed Desolate, but you shall be called My Delight is in Her, and your land Married; for the LORD delights in you, and your land shall be married. For as a young man marries a young woman, so shall your sons marry you, and as the bridegroom rejoices over the bride, so shall your God rejoice over you." Isaiah 62:3–5

Acknowledgements

In a work on patrons and benefactors it goes without saying that debts of gratitude must be acknowledged. The present book is a nearly unaltered version of a dissertation presented to Trinity Evangelical Divinity School which I wrote while enjoying a private writer's study afforded by the generosity of my in-laws, Bob and Donna King. Peace and quiet enabled me to speedily work through mounds of materials and I am grateful to them for encouragement and for ignoring me long enough to let me focus. It wasn't easy on any of us, so I thank you for your patience. The dissertation was supervised by Eckhard Schnabel whose expertise in primary and secondary literature refined my thinking and opened up new doors of insight. I am grateful for constant encouragement and support, and especially for pushing me to continue on in the process. David Pao, my second reader, assisted me greatly in first developing the subject of this study and through several conversations got me to think in new (profitable) directions. Willem VanGemeren also deserves recognition for countless graces. I believe we would still be in Chicago slaving away had it not been for his constant work on our behalf.

Several scholars opened random emails from an unknown student and graciously assisted me in this journey. I can only list them here, but their influence on this book runs deeply: Zeba Crook, Jonathan Reed, Mark Chancey, Seth Schwartz, John Nicols, Koenraad Verboven, Stephan Joubert, and Peter Nelson. Thank you for graciously answering sometimes insignificant questions from a complete stranger. Seth Schwartz and John Nicols also allowed me to see some of their work pre-publication which enhanced my thinking. Ron Fay's help with inscriptions is also greatly appreciated.

I should also express gratitude to Jörg Frey, editor of the WUNT II series, for his invitation to publish this dissertation. Henning Ziebritzki, Ilse König, Ilka Waetzoldt, and the editorial staff of Mohr Siebeck Publishing house assisted with details and deadlines. I am humbled to have been helped by such capable people and to be included in the series.

Friends, family, and colleagues collaborated on the editing and formatting of this work and I am grateful for their expertise and generosity. Appreciation goes out to Prof. Peter Balla, Dr. Suzanne Marshall, Kevin Compton, Stefan Lauxtermann, Cara Shelton, and Chris Kelleher. Andy Wilkinson deserves special recognition for teaching a novice everything he now knows about formatting tricks. I would still be struggling through the process without their help, so I am grateful. Kevin Compton and the library staffs of Trinity International University, Biola University, and Fuller Theological Seminary came to my aid in various ways. They saved me many hours of labor.

Kimi and I got to experience true community and fellowship while I worked on this project because of faithful and funny friends. Thanks to Matt and Sharon Tebbe, Paul and Christy Penley, and Adam and Ann Gustine for making life better. Thanks to my parents, Jay and Suzanne Marshall. I would not be here without their encouragement and many forms of support throughout my life. Thanks to my brothers, Chris and Zac, who have helped me in many ways. Thanks also to my in-laws, Bob, Donna, and Mark King. Their many acts of generosity gave me a place to write, think, and grow.

I thank my wife Kimi for countless gifts and acts of kindness. She brings joy to my life and lightened the burden of a project like this. She helps me to keep sight of reality. I dedicate this book to her because she sacrificed a lot with a smile and a skip in her step that continually brought me out of the fog and into the light. Our wedding Scripture still rings true.

Camarillo, October 2008   Jonathan Marshall

Table of Contents

Acknowledgements VII

List of Abbreviations XIII

Chapter 1. Introduction 1

    1.1 Preliminary Definitions Discipleship, Benefactor, Patron-Client 3
    1.2 Appropriateness of the Study 7
    1.3 Scholarly Setting for the Current Study 11
    1.4 Methodology 15
    1.5 Aims of This Study. 23

Chapter 2. Benefaction and Patrocinium
in First-Century Palestine 24

    2.1 Benefaction and Patronage According to Ancient Sources 25
        2.1.1 Reciprocity in Ancient Greece 27
        2.1.2 Benefaction and Patronage in Hellenistic and Roman Times 32
        2.1.3 Defining *Patrocinium* and Benefaction 44
        2.1.4 Criteria for Detecting *Patrocinium* or Benefaction 49
        2.1.5 Methodology and Focus of Study 52
    2.2 Benefaction and Patronage in Palestine 53
        2.2.1 Hellenization and Romanization in Palestine:
            Recent Developments 54
        2.2.2 Archaeology and Methodological Developments 57
        2.2.3 Galilee: Benefaction and *Patrocinium* 59
            Cana 68
            Nazareth 71
            Capernaum 73
            Tiberias 76
            Sepphoris 85
            Summary: Galilee, Benefaction, and *Patrocinium* 91
        2.2.4 Jerusalem: Benefaction and *Patrocinium* 92
        2.2.5 Outside of Galilee and Jerusalem:
            Benefaction and *Patrocinium* 106
            Caesarea Maritima 106

	Samaria	110
	Smaller Cities in Philip's Tetrarchy	112
	Gamla	116
	Bethsaida	117
	Tyre	118
2.2.6	Conclusions of the Regional Perspective	121

Chapter 3. Benefaction *and* Patrocinium *and the Herodian Rulers* 125

3.1 Herod I 125
   3.1.1 Education 126
   3.1.2 Relationship to the Emperor and Rome 126
   3.1.3 Public Perception 128
   3.1.4 Construction Projects 130
   3.1.5 Coins 133
   3.1.6 Benefactions 134
3.2 Herod Antipas 136
   3.2.1 Education 137
   3.2.2 Relationship to the Emperor and Rome 137
   3.2.3 Public Perception 139
   3.2.4 Construction Projects 142
   3.2.5 Coins 143
   3.2.6 Benefactions 145
3.3 Herod Philip 149
   3.3.1 Education 150
   3.3.2 Relationship to the Emperor and Rome 150
   3.3.3 Public Perception 151
   3.3.4 Construction Projects 152
   3.3.5 Coins 153
   3.3.6 Benefactions 154
3.4 Agrippa I 155
   3.4.1 Education 156
   3.4.2 Relationship to the Emperor and Rome 157
   3.4.3 Public Perception 160
   3.4.4 Construction Projects 162
   3.4.5 Coins 163
   3.4.6 Benefactions 165
3.5 Summary of Personality Perspective 170
3.6 Conclusion 172

Chapter 4. Reciprocity, Patrocinium, and Benefaction in the Sermon on the Plain (Luke 6:17–38) 174

4.1 Modes of Cultural Transmission in the Ministry of Jesus 176
    4.1.1 Evidence from Jesus' Travels and Encounters 177
    4.1.2 Evidence from Herodian Family 184
    4.1.3 Summary 191
4.2 The Sermon on the Plain (Luke 6:17–38) 191
    4.2.1 Introductory Summary (6:17–19): 193
        Literary Context 193
        Linguistic Evidence 196
        Cultural Matters 199
        Conclusion 201
    4.2.2 Blessings and Woes (6:20–26) 202
        Literary Context 202
        Linguistic Evidence 203
        Cultural Matters 204
        Conclusion 210
    4.2.3 Loving Enemies (6:27–38) 211
        Literary Context 211
        Linguistic Evidence 216
        Cultural Matters 225
        Conclusion 243
4.3 Conclusions for The Sermon on the Plain (Luke 6:17–38) 245

Chapter 5. Reciprocity, Benefaction, Patrocinium, and Friendship at Table (Luke 14:1–24) 248

5.1 Healing the Dropsical Man (14:1–6) 250
    5.1.1 Literary Context 250
    5.1.2 Linguistic Evidence 252
    5.1.3 Cultural Matters 253
    5.1.4 Conclusion 255
5.2 Wedding Seat Arrangements (14:7–11) 256
    5.2.1 Literary Context 256
    5.2.2 Linguistic Evidence 257
    5.2.3 Cultural Matters 259
    5.2.4 Conclusion 264
5.3 Banquet Guest List (14:12–14) 264
    5.3.1 Literary Context 264
    5.3.2 Linguistic Evidence 265
    5.3.3 Cultural Matters 269

5.3.4 Conclusion 272
5.4 Refused Invitations and New Guests (14:15–24) 273
    5.4.1 Literary Context 273
    5.4.2 Linguistic Evidence 275
    5.4.3 Cultural Matters 276
    5.4.4 Conclusion 282
5.5 Conclusions for the Table Discussion (Luke 14:1–24) 284

Chapter 6. Benefaction and Patrocinium *at the Last Supper (Luke 22:14–34)* 286

6.1 A Passover to Remember (22:14–23) 288
    6.1.1 Literary Context 288
    6.1.2 Linguistic Evidence 291
    6.1.3 Cultural Matters 294
    6.1.4 Conclusion 299
6.2 Leaders and Disciples (22:24–34) 300
    6.2.1 Literary Context 300
    6.2.2 Linguistic Evidence 303
    6.2.3 Cultural Matters 310
    6.2.4 Conclusion 314
6.3 Conclusions for the Last Supper (22:14–34) 320

Chapter 7. Conclusion 324

7.1 *Patrocinium* and Benefaction in First-Century Palestine 324
7.2 Patrons, Benefactors, and Discipleship in
    Luke 6:17–38; 14:1–24; 22:14–34 328
7.3 Fulfillment of the Aims of Research 333
7.4 Prospects for Further Research 334

Bibliography 339
Index of Ancient Sources 375
Index of Modern Authors 379
Index of Subjects and Key Terms 381

List of Abbreviations

Translations of Greek and Latin texts are taken from the Loeb Classical Library, unless otherwise noted. Most translations have been taken from a standard authority except for those occasions in which such authorities were not immediately available. In those situations the author has facilitated the translation himself. New Testament quotations follow the Nestle-Aland 27th edition. The bibliography, footnotes, and abbreviations follow *The SBL Handbook of Style* (ed. P. H. Alexander et al., 3rd edition 2003). The following list mentions those materials not included in the *SBL Handbook*'s list of abbreviations.

CEG	*Carmina epigraphica Graeca*
CEJL	Commentaries on Early Jewish Literature
CIIP	*Corpus Inscriptionum Iudaeae/Palestinae*
GDI	*Sammlung der griechischen Dialekt-Inschriften*
GrB	*Grazer Beiträge*
IGLS	*Inscriptions Grecques et Latines de la Syrie*
IGR	*Inscriptiones Graecae ad res Romanas pertinentes*
ILS	*Inscriptiones Latinae Selectae*
JSHJ	*Journal for the Study of the Historical Jesus*
P.Abinn.	*The Abinnaeus Archive: Papers of a Roman Officer in the Reign of Constantine*
PKöln	*Kölner Papyri*
PCairZen	*Zenon papyri*
P.Mert.	*A Descriptive Catalogue of the Greek Papyri in the Collection of Wilfred Merton*
P.Ryl.	*Catalogue of the Greek Papyri in the John Rylands Library at Manchester*
RPC	*Roman Provincial Coinage*

Chapter 1

Introduction

Benefactors and patrons were a well-known group in the Roman Empire whose presence could not fail to be noted by many of the early Christians. Their monuments could be found scattered throughout major and minor cities or alongside roads as visible reminders of their generosity and the consequent public glory due to them. They were heralded in public at festivals, games, and other ceremonies. Another form of public acclaim could be found in the entourages which loyally followed patrons throughout cities telling of their generosity in part to remain in the group who directly benefited from their benevolence. Much of daily life depended upon their generosity since they built gymnasia, roads, theaters, aqueducts, and temples in addition to providing food and protection against enemies. Christians who inhabited cities like Athens, Ephesus, and Rome would have been exposed to a number of these projects and posses. Inscriptions which outlined the public worth of the giver were set in prominent locations available to be read and evaluated by any literate Christian. Announcements of patronal generosity would likely have been heard by Christian passers-by.

By the second century the ideology[1] which supported this practice had penetrated the ranks of Christianity quite thoroughly.[2] F. W. Danker mentions several passages in second century Christian literature which adopt the ideology of benefaction in their instruction (1 *Clem* 19:2; 20:11; 21:1; 23:1; 38:3; cf. *EpDiog* 8:11; *EpDiog* 9:5; 10:6; *IgnRom* 5:1). C. A. Bobertz and B. E. Daley explain how patronage transformed and was transformed by the Lord's Supper in Christian communities during the first half-millennium of Christian history.[3] A. B. Wheatley addresses the same time

---

[1] "Ideology" will be used throughout this book according to the fourth definition in the Oxford English Dictionary: "A systematic scheme of ideas, usu. relating to politics or society, or to the conduct of a class or group, and regarded as justifying actions, esp. one that is held implicitly or adopted as a whole and maintained regardless of the course of action." *OED* (2nd ed.; vol. 7; Oxford: Clarendon Press, 1989), 7.622.

[2] Frederick W. Danker, "Bridging St. Paul and the Apostolic Fathers: A Study in Reciprocity," *CurTM* 15 (1988): 84–94.

[3] Charles A. Bobertz, "The Role of Patron in the *cena Dominica* of Hippolytus' Apostolic Tradition," *JTS* [NS] 44 (1993): 170–184; Brian E. Daley, "Position and Patronage

frame, but expands his study to include other facets of patronage and benefaction which influenced Christian identity.[4] Christians had found a way to function as benefactors and patrons within their own community.

Since benefaction and patronage pervaded the Roman Empire and patronage ideology came early into the Christian community, it comes as no surprise that scholars have turned to the Gospels to discuss their interaction with patronage and benefaction. Palestine was a part of the Roman Empire, so it is natural for some to suppose that its citizens adopted this way of life. J. B. Green claims that patronage had thoroughly penetrated all Mediterranean societies, so, for example, "debt" in Luke "must be understood within the framework of patronal relationships."[5] F. W. Danker and H. Moxnes have contributed extensively to discussions of benefactors and patrons especially in Luke-Acts.[6] Danker describes God and Jesus as benefactors par excellence whose generosity, even to the point of suffering, fulfilled a Greco-Roman ideal and simultaneously challenged the system. Moxnes finds in Luke-Acts the adoption of patronage as a model for discipleship. God's people, following a transformed version of patron-client relationships, live in a godly way by imitating and overturning com-mon conceptions of patronage. The Pharisees are critiqued because they accepted patronage without any modifications.[7] After offering a general description of patron-client relationships and discipleship in Luke-Acts, Moxnes suggests that further exegesis would be beneficial for scholars in order to more thoroughly understand these relationships and early Christian appropriation of these Greco-Roman practices.[8]

---

in the Early Church: The Original Meaning of 'Primacy of Honour,'" *JTS* [NS] 44 (1993): 529–53.

[4] Alan Brent Wheatley, "The use and transformation of patronage in early Christianity from Jesus of Nazareth to Paul of Samosata" (PhD diss., University of California at Los Angeles, 1999).

[5] Joel B. Green, *The Theology of the Gospel of Luke* (NTT; Cambridge: Cambridge University Press, 1995), 114–115.

[6] Frederick W. Danker, *Benefactor: Epigraphic Study of a Greco-Roman and New Testament Semantic Field* (St. Louis: Clayton, 1982); idem, *Jesus and the New Age: A Commentary on St. Luke's Gospel* (Philadelphia: Fortress, 1988); idem, *Luke* (Proclamation Commentaries; Fortress: Philadelphia, 1987); idem, "The Endangered Benefactor in Luke-Acts," in *The Society of Biblical Literature 1981 Seminar Papers* (Society of Biblical Literature Seminar Papers 20; Chico: Scholars Press, 1981), 39–48; Halvor Moxnes, "Patron-Client Relations and the New Community in Luke-Acts," in *The Social World of Luke-Acts* (ed. Jerome H. Neyrey; Peabody: Hendrickson, 1991), 241–268; idem, *The Economy of the Kingdom: Social Conflict and Economic Relations in Luke's Gospel* (Philadelphia: Fortress Press, 1988); idem, *Putting Jesus in His Place: A Radical Vision of Household and Kingdom* (Louisville and London: John Knox Press, 2003).

[7] Moxnes, *Economy*, 101–108.

[8] Moxnes, "Patron-Client," 268.

1.1 Preliminary Definitions – Discipleship, Benefactor, and Patron-Client

It is important to begin with some preliminary definitions of major terms adopted in this study (discipleship, benefactor, patron-client). "Benefactor" and "patron" will be expanded upon at length in the next chapter and final definitions will be given (see section 2.1.3). Here some comments will establish a general meaning as well as potential points of distinction.

One of the key terms for this monograph, "discipleship," can be approached in a variety of ways, but the one adopted in this study is broad and somewhat non-technical. Works on discipleship might approach the subject from a linguistic vantage point. These survey Greek terms such as μαθητής/μανθάνω, οἱ ἀκολουθοῦντες/ἀκολουθέω, ἀπόστολος or μάρτυς.[9] One might limit the era to include only the time of Jesus,[10] or one may not so limit the discussion.[11] One might adopt a redactional approach comparing and contrasting Luke's presentation with his purported sources or near contemporaries (Mark, Q, L, Matthew, John).[12] P. K. Nelson follows H. Crouzel in his preference for a definition of disciple which includes any person with a relationship and loyalty to Jesus.[13] This is the sense in which "discipleship" is used in this monograph. According to this use of "disci-

---

[9] Nelson provides a good survey of works on discipleship. Peter K. Nelson, *Leadership and Discipleship: A Study of Luke 22:24–30* (SBLDS 138; Atlanta: Scholars Press, 1994), 233–235. Those who adopt a linguistic approach include, Brian E. Beck, *Christian Character in the Gospel of Luke* (London: Epworth Press, 1989), 93–94; Paul Kariamadam, "Discipleship in the Lucan Journey Narrative," *Jeevadhara* 16 (1980): 111–130, 113–114; Rosalie Ryan, "The Women from Galilee and Discipleship in Luke," *BTB* 15 (1985): 56–59, 56–58; M. Sheridan, "Disciples and Discipleship in Matthew and Luke," *BTB* 3 (1973): 235–255, 252–254.

[10] Hans Dieter Betz, *Nachfolge und Nachahmung Jesu Christi im Neuen Testament* (Beiträge zur historischen Theologie 37; Tübingen: Mohr, 1967), 40–41.

[11] C. F. Evans, *Saint Luke* (TPINTC; London: SCM, 1990), 99–104; J. A. Fitzmyer, *The Gospel According to Luke I-IX: Introduction, Translation, and Notes* (AB; Garden City: Doubleday, 1981), 1:235, 241–251; Heinz Schürmann, "Der Jüngerkreis Jesu als Zeichen für Israel," *Geist und Leben* 16 (1963): 21–35, 27–34; C. H. Talbert, "Discipleship in Luke-Acts," in *Discipleship in the New Testament* (ed. Fernando F. Segovia; Philadelphia: Fortress Press, 1985), 62–75, 62.

[12] Richard N. Longenecker, "Taking Up the Cross Daily: Discipleship in Luke-Acts," in *Patterns of Discipleship in the New Testament* (ed. Richard N. Longenecker; Grand Rapids: Eerdmans, 1996), 50–76.

[13] H. Crouzel, "La imitation et la 'suite' de Dieu et du Christ dans les premiers siècles chrétiens, ainsi que leurs sources gréco-romaines et hébraique," *JAC* 21 (1978): 7–41, 19–21; Nelson, *Leadership*, 234–236. R. N. Longenecker adopts a similar definition of discipleship though he starts with occurrences of the word-group, proceeds primarily from a redactional standpoint, and transitions into a broader definition once the text has opened that opportunity. Longenecker, "Discipleship."

pleship", specific vocabulary which can be translated as "disciple" need not be present for the discussion to proceed. A description of protocol commensurate with joining the Jesus movement must be present. By investigating the teachings of Jesus given to disciples and potential disciples I hope to discover the particular way that Jesus adopted and/or transformed notions of benefaction and patronage into his expectations of allegiance to him.

Benefactors expressed their ἀρετή through generous acts and were publicly recognized by the beneficiaries of their generosity. P. Veyne defines euergetism (civic benefaction) as "private munificence for public benefit."[14] Building on Veyne, K. Lomas and T. Cornell explain euergetism as "a means of harnessing the wealth of the elites of the Roman empire to provide the public amenities needed by cities and to provide entertainment for their citizens."[15] Benefactors built roads, stadia, gymnasia, and temples for the public. In Homeric times, a benefactor might go to battle on behalf of a city. If victorious, he would be publicly lauded as a εὐεργέτης or σωτήρ. Public expression of ἀρετή later developed in the private sphere as benefactors showered their generosity upon smaller groups and individuals. Though terms like ἀρετή, εὐεργέτης, and σωτήρ are common in inscriptions which identify benefactors these are not technical terms for "benefactor."[16] Rather there is a semantic and thematic field of terms and ideas which connote the activity of benefactors (see section 2.1).[17] Benefactors could inscribe their own merits for public viewing (autobiographical; *OGIS* 383; *IGR* 3.159; *SIG* 814), or they could be heralded by the people (biographical; *OGIS* 90, 458, 666; *SIG* 760; *SEG* 6.672; *IGLS* 5.1998). Inscriptions served as public reminders of the benefactor's gene-rosity or as reminders to the benefactor that this public appreciated the generosity. Benefactors would be motivated to continue their generosity after recognizing that they would be publicly praised for it.

Patronage can be used in two different yet related ways. In the Roman world *patrocinium* described a relationship between a patron (*patronus*;

---

[14] Paul Veyne, *Le pain et le cirque: sociologie historique d'un pluralisme politique* (L'Univers historique; Paris: Seuil, 1976); ET, *Bread and Circuses: Historical Sociology and Political Pluralism* (trans. and abridged Oswyn Murray and Brian Pearce; London: Penguin Press, 1990).

[15] Kathryn Lomas and Tim Cornell, "Introduction: Patronage and Benefaction in Ancient Italy," in *Bread and Circuses: Euergetism and Municipal Patronage in Roman Italy* (ed. Kathryn Lomas and Tim Cornell; London: Routledge, 2003), 1–11, 1.

[16] Danker, *Benefactor*, 323; cf. C. Bradford Welles, *Royal Correspondence in the Hellenistic Period* (repr. Chicago: Ares, 1974), only 10 of 75 documents investigated contain εὐεργ- terms; F. von Gaertringen, *Inschriften von Priene* (Berlin: Georg Reimer, 1908), only 18 of the first 247 documents contain εὐεργ–terms.

[17] Danker, *Benefactor*, 26–28.

1.1 Preliminary Definitions – Discipleship, Benefactor, and Patron-Client

κηδεμών, πάτρων, πατρώνης) and a client (*cliens*; κλίενς or πελάτης). Patrons provided legal and financial aid to their clients and received public honor and loyalty in return. Patrons and clients entered a relationship through the initiative, usually, of the clients who sought from the patron protection and help. Clients could be Roman or non-Roman, but the title *patronus* was preserved for Romans in positions of authority who entered this specific relationship. Building from this practice and these terms, social historians and anthropologists have created the socio-historical category of patronage with respective patrons and clients. For the past twenty-five years R. P. Saller has provided the most prominent definition for both the Roman and socio-historical practice of patronage.[18] As a classicist, Saller builds from investigations of the Roman world, but his definition became a standard definition by which social historians identify patronage in both ancient Roman and non-ancient, non-Roman societies.[19] Saller identifies three descriptions of patron-client relationships: (1) reciprocal in the sense of exchange of goods/services; (2) relational in the sense of a long term relationship, not simply a marketplace transaction; and (3) asymmyetrical in the sense of a social distance between the two parties. This definition has been adopted by social historians to describe ancient and modern societies and by New Testament scholars to describe early Christian practices (section 2.1.3).[20]

Confusion has entered these discussions because of differences in definition between socio-historical patron-client relations and Roman *patrocinium*. K. Verboven clarifies that the *patronus-cliens* relationship which developed *sui generis* in Roman society falls under the "heading" of (socio-historical) patronage, but cannot be fully explained by that category.[21] The *patronus-cliens* relationship involved specifically Roman prac-

---

[18] Saller, *Personal Patronage*, 1.

[19] Andrew Wallace-Hadrill, *Patronage in Ancient Society* (London and New York: Routledge, 1989); Peter Garnsey and Richard P. Saller, eds., *The Roman Empire: Economy, Society, and Culture* (Berkeley: University of California Press, 1987); Luis Roniger, "Modern Patron-Client Relations and Historical Clientelism: Some Clues from Ancient Republican Rome," *Archives Europeennes de Sociologie* 24 (1983): 63–95; S. N. Eisenstadt and Luis Roniger, *Patrons, Clients and Friends: Interpersonal Relations and the Structure of Trust in Society* (Cambridge: Cambridge University Press, 1984).

[20] Moxnes, "Patron-Client," 243–244; D. A. DeSilva, *Honor, Patronage, Kinship and Purity: Unlocking New Testament Culture* (Downers Grove: InterVarsity Press, 2000); Jerome H. Neyrey, "God, Benefactor and Patron: The Major Cultural Model for Interpreting the Deity in Greco-Roman Antiquity," *JSNT* 27 (2005): 465–492.

[21] Koenraad Verboven, *The Economy of Friends: Economic Aspects of* Amicitia *and Patronage in the Late Republic* (Brussels: Latomus, 2002), 12. Unfortunately for NT scholars Verboven decides to address Roman *amicitia*, but not *patrocinium*. His patronage study aligns more closely with the sociological category and he suggests an elaborate study on *patrocinium* is still needed.

tices (e.g., often, though not always, the *salutatio*) that do not obtain in other societies. In order to employ the socio-historical category in other societies, social historians drop some of the necessarily Roman traits of the practice.

Based upon Saller's work it has become commonplace to use socio-historical categories to study Roman society, and for social historians to include Roman society in studies of ancient societies. This has created some confusion because the socio-historical categories of patron and client are not synonymous with the Roman categories of *patronus* and *cliens*. "The [socio-historical] concepts of 'patronage' and 'clientage' indicate a general type of personal relationship that may occur in any society under widely different names and appearances and which is characterised by reciprocity, asymmetry and personal loyalty. *Patrocinium* and *clientele* on the other hand were typically Roman concepts that can only be fully understood within the context of Roman history and culture."[22] H. Moxnes, following A. Blok, provides a good example of a socio-historical understanding of patron-client relationship to describe non-Roman relationships.[23] Blok mentions "father-son, God-man, saint-devotee, godfather-godchild, lord-vassal, landlord-tenant, politician-voter, [and] professor-assistant" as patron-client relationships.[24] Socio-historical patronage can describe many relationships, but this is quite different than Roman *patrocinium* which described one type of (Roman) relationship.

C. Eilers, in a thorough study of *patrocinium* in the Roman east, confirms Verboven's concern over the confusion of the Roman and socio-historical definitions of patronage.[25] He advances this critique by claiming that social historians and anthropologists misunderstand *patrocinium*. For example, social historians misunderstand the specifically Roman nature of *patrocinium*, the criteria which confirm its practice, its transferability to other cultures, and its relationship to other practices (specifically *suffragium* and so-called "literary patronage"). This misunderstanding leads social historians to derive an errant understanding of socio-historical patron-client relationships (see section 2.1.2; 2.1.3). For example, Eilers insists that *patrocinium* was not the relationship through which kingdoms were conferred (*suffragium*), nor did endowed authors identify the en-

---

[22] Verboven, *Economy*, 51. On *patrocinium* and *clientes* see also, Hans-Joachim Gehrke, "Patronus," in *Brill's New Pauly* (ed. H. Cancik and H. Schneider; Leiden: Brill, 2004), 5:154–156; Jens-Uwe Krause, "Patrocinium I. Political," *BNP* (2007), 10:618–620; Andrew W. Lintott, "Cliens, clientes," *BNP* 3 (2003), 3:450–452.

[23] Moxnes, "Patron-Client," 242.

[24] Blok, "Variations," 366.

[25] Claude Eilers, *Roman Patrons of Greek Cities* (Oxford Classical Monographs; Oxford: Oxford University Press, 2002), 2–18.

dower as a literary patron.[26] Additionally, *patrocinium* did not begin with an overt act of generosity on the part of the superior (a benefaction), but could only begin with an intentional effort by the inferior party to enter a patron-client relationship.[27] J. Harrison confirms the confusion created by social historians when they use the "more Roman-sounding" patron-client terminology.[28] The use of patron-client terminology in a broad sense is problematic because it may cause the inadvertent importing of a specific aspect of Roman culture which may or may not have been present among the authors and audiences of the NT literature.

Socio-historical patron-client categories can describe a multitude of relationships among which might be *patronus*, *cliens*, or *euergetism*. But it is imperative to properly define and distinguish between socio-historical and Roman forms of patronage. The confusion created by these overlapping definitions motivates the present study to properly define terms and differentiate definitions. To the extent that patron-client relations are in view, this study focuses on Roman *patrocinium*.[29] Nevertheless, it will offer suggestions about socio-historical patron-client relations at times. At a certain level socio-historical patron-client relations can be assumed of almost any society because the definition is so general and flexible. *Patrocinium*, on the other hand, cannot be assumed of many cultures. It must be shown to have existed through evidence. It is hoped that by distinguishing the two practices confusion can be mitigated and NT investigations into, especially, the culture of Jesus and the early church in Palestine can be advanced.

1.2 Appropriateness of the Study

There are several reasons which justify a new investigation of patrons, benefactors, and discipleship in Luke. This study will focus on *patrocinium* and benefaction rather than the socio-historical patron-client relationship. As mentioned above, the only work which develops the theme of patron-client relationships and Luke-Acts urges at its end the need for more detailed exegesis of Luke to better substantiate the claim.[30] Since Moxnes made that request almost two decades ago no scholar has devoted

---

[26] Eilers, *Roman Patrons*, 2–4, 6, 17.

[27] Eilers, *Roman Patrons*, 31–33.

[28] Harrison, *Language*, 15.

[29] Cf. the approach of John Nicols, "Patrons of Greek Cities in the Early Principate," *ZPE* 80 (1990): 81–108, 81.

[30] Moxnes, "Patron-Client," 268.

extended attention to its resolution. A monograph devoted to patron-client relationships and discipleship appropriately responds to Moxnes' request.

In a similar vein, the work which focuses on Luke-Acts and benefactors is in need of up-dating. Danker devoted three works to benefactors and Luke-Acts, *Benefactor* (1982), *Jesus and the New Age* (1988), and *Luke* (1976; 1987). His is the only extended treatment of benefactors and Luke available. It has now been two decades since the completion of his last work and no monograph has appeared to improve upon his work. Articles by NT scholars which appear during this interval rarely bring new primary source information into discussion,[31] and related works which cite Danker do so typically without bringing in newer secondary sources.[32] There is need for a focused study on the topic once again in order to evaluate the sustainability of Danker's studies and to assess their applicability to Luke's Gospel.

Advances in scholarly understanding of patrons, clients, and benefactors in the early Roman empire can improve our grasp of these relationships and how they potentially operated in first-century Palestine. At the time of Danker's efforts only one unpublished dissertation had been devoted to the inscriptions of Hellenistic benefactors (Mott 1971).[33] Danker did not incorporate the work of Veyne (1976).[34] Moxnes builds largely off of the work of R. P. Saller (1982), S. N. Eisenstadt and L. Roniger (1984), E. Gellner

---

[31] E.g., Ian Sloan, "The Greatest and the Youngest: Greco-Roman Reciprocity in the Farewell Address, Luke 22:24–30," *Studies in Religion* 22 (1993): 63–73. Lull adds some literary evidence to his discussion. D. J. Lull, "The Servant-Benefactor as a Model of Greatness (Lk 22:24–30)," *NovT* 28 (1986): 289–305.

[32] E.g., Joel B. Green, "'Salvation to the End of the Earth' (Acts 13:47): God as Saviour in the Acts of the Apostles," in *Witness to the Gospel: The Theology of Acts* (ed. I. Howard Marshall and David Peterson; Grand Rapids: Eerdmans, 1998), 83–106, 87; Nelson, *Leadership*, 150–152; Darrell L. Bock, *Luke* (BECNT 3; 2 vols. Grand Rapids: Baker, 1994), 2.1737; Fitzmyer, *Luke*, 2.1417; Philip F. Esler, *Community and Gospel in Luke-Acts: The Social and Political Motivations of Lucan Theology* (SNTSMS 57; Cambridge: Cambridge University Press, 1987), 256.

[33] Charles Mott, "The Greek Benefactor and Deliverance from Moral Distress" (PhD diss., Harvard University, 1971); idem, "Greek Ethics and Christian Conversion: The Philonic Background of Titus II 10–14 and III 3–7," *NovT* 20 (1978): 22–48. He also mentions Hendrik Bolkestein, *Wohltätigkeit und Armenpflege im vorchristlichen Altertum. Ein Beitrag zum Problem "Moral und Gesellschaft"* (Utrecht: Oosthoek, 1939). Eiliv Skaard, *Zwei Religiös-Politische Begriffe: Euergetes-Concordia* (Avhand-linger utgitt av Det Norske Videnskaps-Akademi i Oslo; Vol 2; Hist.-Filos. Klasse. 1931; No 2. Oslo: Jacob Dybwad, 1932). But Bolkestein focuses on "concern for the poor" and does not deal with epigraphical evidence. Skaard "discusses a few terms and phrases, but shows little interest in Hellenistic inscriptions." Danker, *Benefactor*, 49. Danker apparently overlooked Veyne, *Le pain et le cirque* (1976).

[34] Veyne, *Le pain et le cirque*.

1.2 Appropriateness of the Study

and J. Waterbury (1977), and A. Blok (1969).[35] These works depend upon earlier classical scholarship including T. Mommsen (1864–1879), E. Badian (1958), M. Gelzer (1969), R. Syme (1939), A. von Premerstein (1937), and L. Harmand (1957).[36] These works also depend on the socio-historical and anthropological work of M. Mauss (1967), M. D. Sahlins (1972), K. Polanyi (1968), and P. Bourdieu (1977).[37] It appears that Moxnes (1991) overlooked some important classical works that were published just prior to his article,[38] but it is also clear that several important works by classicists have appeared after Moxnes and improved our understanding of *patrocinium* and benefaction.[39] Responding to the works on patronage by

---

[35] Saller, *Patronage*; Eisenstadt and Roniger, *Patrons, Clients and Friends*; Ernest Gellner and John Waterbury, eds., *Patrons and Clients in Mediterranean Societies* (London: Duckworth, 1977); A. Blok, "Variations in Patronage," *Sociologische Gids* (1969): 365–378.

[36] T. Mommsen, "Das römische Gastrecht und die römische Clientel," in *Römische Forschungen* (2 vols.; Berlin, 1864–1879), 1.355–390; E. Badian, *Foreign Clientelae* (Oxford: Oxford University Press, 1958); Matthias Gelzer, *The Roman Nobility* (trans. Robin Seager; Oxford: Blackwell, 1969); R. Syme, *The Roman Revolution* (Oxford: Oxford University Press, 1939); A. von Premerstein, *Vom Werden und Wesen des Prinzipats* (Abhandlungen der bayerischen Akademie der Wissenschaften, philologische-historische Abteilung; NS 15; Munich, 1937); L. Harmand, *Un aspect social et politique du monde romain: Le Patronat sur les collectivités publiques des origins au Bas-Empire* (Publications de la Faculté des Lettres de l'Université de Clermont, 2nd serv. 2; Paris, 1957).

[37] Marcel Mauss, *The Gift: Forms and Functions of Exchange in Archaic Societies* (trans. W. D. Halls; New York: Norton, 1967); Marshall David Sahlins, *Stone Age Economics* (Chicago: Aldine-Atherton, 1972); Karl Polanyi, *Primitive, Archaic, and Modern Economies: Essays of Karl Polanyi* (Garden City: Anchor Books, 1968); Pierre Bourdieu, *Outline of a Theory of Practice* (Cambridge: Cambridge University Press, 1977). Some classicists build from the classical and sociological studies which informed Saller even if they depart from Saller at points. Phebe Lowell Bowditch, *Horace and the Gift Economy of Patronage* (Classics and Contemporary Thought 7; Berkeley: University of California Press, 2001), 7; Lomas and Cornell, *Bread and Circuses*.

[38] P. A. Brunt, "Clientela," in idem, *The Fall of the Roman Republic and Related Essays* (Oxford: Oxford University Press, 1988), 382–442; J. Touloumakos, "Zum römischen Gemeindepatronat im griechischen Osten," *Hermes* 116 (1988): 304–324; N. Rouland, *Pouvoir politique et dépendance personnelle dans l'Antiquité romaine: Genèse et rôle des rapports de clientèle* (Brussels, 1979); P. M. Nigdelis, "'Ρωμαῖοι πάτρωνες και "ἀναγκαιότατοι καιροί" (παρατηρήσεις στην επιγραφή SEG 32.825 τῆς Πάρου)," *Hellenika* 40 (1989): 34–49. If Moxnes had incorporated Brunt he would have heard the critique that Mommsen created his understanding of patronage virtually *ex nihilo*, Brunt, "Clientela," 401 n. 48.

[39] Eilers, *Roman Patrons*; Verboven, *Economy*; Veyne, *Bread and Circuses*; E. Rawson, "The Eastern Clientela of Cladius and the Claudii," *Historia* 22 (1973): 219–239, reprinted in idem, *Roman Culture and Society: Collected Papers* (Oxford: Oxford University Press, 1991), 102–124; R. Duthoy, "Quelques observations concernant la mention d'un patronat municipal dans les inscriptions," *AC* 50 (1981): 295–305; idem, "Sens et

Eilers (2002), Verboven (2002), Bowditch (2001), Lomas and Cornell (2003), Nauta (2001), and De Rossi (2001), K. Verboven has recently remarked that *patrocinium* is once again "to the fore" in classical studies.[40] It behooves NT scholarship to avail itself of these advances.

It seems, however, that NT scholars have not availed themselves of the newer classical studies. For some it is not neglect of the sources, but the simple fact that these classical works were written after NT scholars produced their material. Scholars who wrote before the recent outpouring of classical works on patronage could naturally improve their reading through incorporation of this new material. J. B. Green's commentary on Luke (1997), which explains much of Luke from its "Mediterranean" context and Luke's attack of the "Roman patronal system", builds from the same resource base as Moxnes builds.[41] Hanson and Oakman (2000) develop their understanding of Palestinian "pyramids of power" (patronage) from the same socio-historical works.[42] B. J. Malina and R. L. Rohrbaugh (2003) discuss the Roman patronal system which, they claim, persisted in Jesus' Palestine building from the same literature.[43] However, some scholars have written after these recent studies and demonstrate neglect of better material. Two recent works on patronage and benefaction by NT scholars, J. H. Neyrey (2005) and Y. S. Ahn (2006), neglect to interact with any studies done in the last two decades. They derive their understanding of patronage and benefaction from the same pool of resources from which Moxnes draws.[44] Neither scholar draws upon the advances in classical

---

fonction du patronat municipal durant le Principat," *AC* 53 (1984): 145–156; idem, "Scénarios de cooptation des patrons municipaux en Italie," *Epigraphica* 46 (1984): 23–48; idem, "Le profil social des patrons municipaux en Italie sous le Haut-Empire," *AncSoc* 15–17 (1984–1986): 121–154; P. I. Wilkins, "Legates of Numidia as Municipal Patrons," *Chiron* 23 (1993): 189–206; Nicols, "Patrons of Greek Cities," 81–108; Alexander Yakobson, *Elections and Electioneering in Rome: A Study in the Political System of the Late Republic* (Stuttgart: F. Steiner, 1999).

[40] Koenraad Verboven, "Review of Claude Eilers, *Roman Patrons of Greek Cities*," *BMCR* 6.19 (2003). See also, Ruurd Nauta, *Poetry for Patrons: Literary Communication in the Age of Domitian* (Mnemosyne Supp. 206; Leiden: Brill, 2001); Filippo Canali De Rossi, *Il ruolo dei 'patroni' nelle relazioni politiche fra il mondo greco e Roma in età repubblicana ed augustea* (Beiträge zur Altertumskunde 159; München: Saur, 2001). John Nicols is currently in discussion with Brill to publish his (long-anticipated) monograph, John Nicols, *The Patronage of Communities in the Roman Empire*. Forthcoming.

[41] Green, *Luke*, 270–271; idem, *Theology of Luke*, 114–115.

[42] Hanson and Oakman, *Palestine*, 70–86. They add G. E. M. De Ste. Croix, "*Suffragium*: From Vote to Patronage," *British Journal of Sociology* 5 (1954): 33–48.

[43] Bruce J. Malina and Richard L. Rohrbaugh, eds., *Social-Science Commentary on the Synoptic Gospels* (Minneapolis: Fortress Press, 2003), 388–391.

[44] Neyrey, "God, Benefactor and Patron," 465–492; Yong Sung Ahn, *The Reign of God and Rome in Luke's Passion Narrative: An East Asian Global Perspective* (Biblical

studies which have arrived in the past few years. NT scholars have sometimes neglected the best classical works from the previous generation (Brunt, Touloumoukos, Rouland, Nigdelis), and NT scholars continue to ignore more recent classical works which have appeared in the last decade (Eilers, Verboven, Nicols, Bowditch, Lomas and Cornell, De Rossi, and Nauta). A study which incorporates the new developments in the classical study of patrons, clients, and benefactors is needed.

1.3 Scholarly Setting for the Current Study

An investigation of *patrocinium* and benefaction in first-century Palestine, and the potential appropriation of these practices by Jesus and the early Christians, joins a very active conversation about the historical Jesus and his context. The approach of this study follows the example of many recent works which broadly fall into the quest for the historical Jesus. One of the hallmarks of the so-called "Third Quest" is a desire to construct a plausible historical backdrop for the historical Jesus.[45] S. Freyne explains the problem which created the need to construct a plausible historical context for Jesus.[46] With Käsemann's criterion of dissimilarity scholarship finds itself on sure ground about the historical Jesus only when he is completely different from potential influences (e.g., Judaism) and effects (i.e. early Christianity).[47] There is then no "connecting link" between Jesus, the culture of his day, and the group which grew from his influence.[48] A new approach was needed which could incorporate points of similarity and dissimilarity between Jesus, his culture, and early Christians.

Interpretation Series 80; Leiden: Brill, 2006), 161–168. One study Neyrey draws from which was not mentioned in Moxnes, Veyne (1990), is more recent but is essentially a translation and revision of his much earlier work (1976). Veyne, *Bread and Circuses* (1990); idem, *Le pain et le cirque* (1976).

[45] Gerd Theissen and Dagmar Winter, *Die Kriterienfrage in der Jesusforschung: Vom Differenzkriterium zum Plausibilitätskriterium* (Freiburg: Novum Testamentum et Orbis Antiquus, 1997); ET, *The Quest for the Plausible Jesus: The Question of Criteria* (trans. M. Eugene Boring; Louisville: Westminster, 2002); G. Theissen, "Historical Scepticism and the Criteria of Jesus Research: My Attempt to Leap over Lessing's Yawning Gulf," *SJT* 49 (1996): 146–175; Seán Freyne, *Galilee and Gospel: Collected Essays* (WUNT 125; Tübingen: Mohr Siebeck, 2000), 20–25; Paul Foster, "Educating Jesus: The Search for a Plausible Context," *JSHJ* 4 (2006): 7–33; Stanley E. Porter, "Luke 17.11–19 and the Criteria for Authenticity Revisited," *JSHJ* 1 (2003): 201–224.

[46] Freyne, *Galilee and Gospel*, 22–24.

[47] E. Käsemann, "Das Problem des historischen Jesus," *ZTK* 51 (1954): 125–152; ET, "The Problem of the Historical Jesus," in idem, *Essays on New Testament Themes* (London: SCM Press, 1964), 15–47.

[48] Käsemann, "Historical Jesus," 37.

This need has compelled many scholars, including many from archaeological and sociological fields, to search for a plausible historical context for the historical Jesus.[49] M. H. Jensen is among the recent spate of scholars who combine archaeological research and literary investigation in order to describe the culture of Galilee and, at the broader level, Palestine, during the early Roman period.[50] Several reasons may be advanced for this de-

---

[49] Major works on this topic include: Burton L. Mack, *The Lost Gospel: The Book of Q & Christian Origins* (Shaftesbury, Dorset: Element, 1993); J. D. Crossan, *The Historical Jesus: The Life of a Mediterranean Jewish Peasant* (Edinburgh: T & T Clark, 1991); John Dominic Crossan and Jonathan L. Reed, *Excavating Jesus: Beneath the Stones, Behind the Texts* (New York: HarperCollins, 2001); L. Vaage, *Galilean Upstarts: Jesus' First Followers According to Q* (Valley Forge: Trinity Press International, 1994); F. G. Downing, *Cynics and Christian Origins* (Edinburgh: T. & T. Clark, 1992); G. Vermès, *Jesus the Jew* (London: Collins, 1973): B. Meyer, *The Aims of Jesus* (London: 1979); R. Riesner, *Jesus als Lehrer* (WUNT 7; Tübingen: Mohr, 1981); E. P. Sanders, *Jesus and Judaism* (London: SCM, 1985); Freyne, *Galilee and Gospel*; idem, *Galilee: From Alexander the Great to Hadrian 323 B.C.E. to 135 C.E.: A Study of Second Temple Judaism* (Notre Dame: University of Notre Dame Press, 1980); idem, *Jesus, a Jewish Galilean: A New Reading of the Jesus Story* (London: T & T Clark, 2004); John P. Meier, *A Marginal Jew: Rethinking the Historical Jesus* (The Anchor Bible Reference Library; 3 vols.; New York: Doubleday, 1991–2001); James H. Charlesworth, ed., *Jesus and Archaeology* (Grand Rapids: Eerdmans, 2006); Richard A. Horsley, *Jesus and Empire: Kingdom of God and the New World Disorder* (Minneapolis: Fortress Press, 2003); Mark A. Chancey, *The Myth of a Gentile Galilee* (Cambridge: Cambridge University Press, 2002); idem, *Greco-Roman Culture and the Galilee of Jesus* (SNTMS 134; Cambridge: Cambridge University Press, 2005).

[50] Morten Hørning Jensen, *Herod Antipas in Galilee: The Literary and Archaeological Sources on the Reign of Herod Antipas and its Socio-Economic Impact on Galilee* (WUNT 2.215; Tübingen: Mohr Siebeck, 2006), 3–5. Among the scholars who have approached historical Jesus studies in this manner Jensen lists, Meier, *A Marginal Jew*, 167–195; N. T. Wright, *Jesus and the Victory of God* (Minneapolis: Fortress Press, 1996), 85–86; Theissen and Winter, *Die Kriterienfrage*; Tom Holmén, "Doubts about Double Dissimilarity: Restructuring the Main Criterion of Jesus-of-History Research," in *Authenticating the Words of Jesus* (ed. Bruce Chilton and Craig A. Evans; New Testament Tools and Studies 28.1; Leiden: Brill, 1999), 47–80; Freyne, *Galilee and Gospel*, 20; idem, "The Geography, Politics, and Economics of Galilee and the Quest for the Historical Jesus," in *Studying the Historical Jesus: Evaluations of the State of Current Research* (ed. Bruce Chilton and Craig A. Evans; Leiden: Brill, 1994), 75–122, 75; Jonathan L. Reed, *Archaeology and the Galilean Jesus: A Re-Examination of the Evidence* (Harrisburg: Trinity Press, 2000); Douglas R. Edwards and C. Thomas McCollough, eds., *Archaeology and the Galilee: Texts and Contexts in the Graeco-Roman and Byzantine Periods* (Atlanta: Scholars Press, 1997). After Jensen's 2006 publication, several new studies have arrived. Markus Cromhout, *Jesus and Identity: Reconstructing Judean Ethnicity in Q* (Matrix: The Bible in Mediterranean Context 2; Eugene: Cascade Books, 2007); Douglas E. Oakman, *Jesus and the Peasants* (Matrix: The Bible in Mediterranean Context; Eugene: Cascade, 2008); Amy-Jill Levine, Dale C. Allison, and John Dominic Crossan, eds., *The Historical Jesus in Context* (Princeton Readings in

velopment. Jensen identifies two. (1) Sean Freyne's monumental work, *Galilee: From Alexander the Great to Hadrian 323 B.C.E. to 135 C.E.: A Study of Second Temple Judaism*, for the first time laid out a quasi-comprehensive depiction of the political, social, economic, and cultural milieu of Galilee.[51] His work became a foundation for many to build upon. (2) Recent developments in archaeology, specifically in regard to methodology and extended access to sites, have produced a situation in which the lives of the non-elite, among whom Jesus matured, may be described. This "New Archaeology," as it is commonly referred to, puts emphasis on ordinary, daily life rather than monumental features (see section 2.4.2).[52] There is, however, an inherent danger in the process because constructions of Galilee tend to create consequent pictures of Jesus (see next paragraph).[53] Aware of this danger, scholars continue to make more precise geographical and chronological distinctions in their investigation of Palestine's cultures. Rather than broad-brush painting of Palestine as a "Mediterranean," "Roman," or "Hellenistic" culture, many have attempted to provide nuance and distinction in terms of the eras and regions investigated and the relative influence of Jewish and non-Jewish cultures. M. Goodman notes the awareness historians and archaeologists now have over the problems of generalizing about the cultures, economies, societies, and religions of regions as vast and variegated as the Mediterranean world.[54] Advances on many levels provide a remedy to this problem since archaeologists now have access to information about not just regions but sub-regions within the larger provinces. Nuancing and specification in regard to the culture of early Roman Galilee can now be undertaken properly.

Within this new facet of the quest for the historical Jesus several major issues have arisen. M. H. Jensen and J. Reed identify four issues which have been central to the debates, have aroused polarized opinions, but have recently moved toward consensus.[55] The issues can be summarized as fol-

---

Religions; Princeton: Princeton University Press, 2006); Jürgen Zangenberg, H. W. Attridge, and D. B. Martin, eds. *Religion, Ethnicity and Identity in Ancient Galilee: A Region in Transition* (Tübingen: Mohr Siebeck, 2007).

[51] Freyne, *Galilee: From Alexander the Great to Hadrian*.

[52] Jensen, *Antipas*, 3, 126–135; Sean Freyne, "Archaeology and the Historical Jesus," in Freyne, *Galilee and Gospel*, 160–182.

[53] Reed, *Archaeology*, 8; Freyne, "Geography, Politics, Economics," 76; Sean Freyne, "Galilee and Judea: The Social World of Jesus," in *The Face of New Testament Studies: A Survey of Recent Research* (ed. Scot McKnight and Grant R. Osborne; Grand Rapids: Baker Academic, 2004), 21–35.

[54] Martin Goodman, "Foreword," in *Religion and Society in Roman Palestine: Old Questions, New Approaches* (ed. Douglas R. Edwards; New York and London: Routledge, 2004), xiii—xvii, xiii. He cites P. Hordern and N. Purcell, *The Corrupting Seas: A Study of Mediterranean History* (Oxford: Blackwell, 2000).

[55] Jensen, *Antipas*, 5–9; Reed, *Archaeology*, 8–9.

lows, with important contributors to each debate in parenthesis (see section 2.4.3): (1) the ethnic identity of the Galileans (R. Horsley, A. Alt, S. Freyne), (2) the cultural and religious climate of Galilee (A. Overman, E. M. Meyers, R. Batey, J. D. Crossan, F. G. Downing, B. L. Mack, M. A. Chancey, J. L. Reed, R. Horsley), (3) the economic situation (H. Moxnes, K. C. Hanson, D. E. Oakman, D. A. Fiensy, J. Pastor), and (4) the political atmosphere (S. Freyne, L. H. Feldman, R. Horsley, S. Zeitlin). It is the second of these questions which is the central concern of the present study. Galilee, and Palestine, has been described as a hotbed for Hellenization or an enclave of Jewish zealots. Either extreme lends itself to a quite different interpretation of the ministry and message of Jesus. Jensen describes this particular issue as "the most intensively debated" among the four, but, as will be argued in the following chapter, material and textual evidence have "largely settled the issue" in favor of those who espouse a more Jewish climate.[56]

Scholarship is concerned with the question of the early Christians and their relationship with Jesus. This question develops because of a deficiency left by the criterion of dissimilarity. Scholars recognized a second problematic result of Käsemann's criterion of dissimilarity, namely, it left no ground for understanding the movement which emerged from Jesus' influence. As scholars began to understand the social world of Jesus they were able to understand the movement which developed from his influence. Jensen explains, "One key area of investigation, therefore, is the nature and development of the earliest Palestinian Jesus movement which the historical Jesus is likely to have impressed most with his stamp"[57] This trend can be seen in numerous works which examine the rise and development of early Christianity from socio-historical and archaeological vantage points.[58] A study of patrons, clients, and benefactors in first-century Pales-

---

[56] Jensen, *Antipas*, 7–8.

[57] Jensen, *Antipas*, 73.

[58] E.g., L. Michael White and O. Larry Yarbrough, eds., *The Social World of the First Christians: Essays in Honor of Wayne A. Meeks* (Minneapolis: Fortress Press, 1995); Ekkehard W. Stegemann and Wolfgang Stegemann, *Urchristliche Sozialgeschichte: die Anfänge im Judentum und die Christusgemeinden in der mediterranen Welt* (Stuttgart: Kohlhammer, 1995); ET, *The Jesus Movement: A Social History of Its First-century* (trans. O. C. Dean, Jr.; Minneapolis: Fortress Press, 1999); E. A. Judge, *Social Distinctives of the Christians in the First-century: Pivotal Essays* (ed. David M. Scholer; Peabody: Hendrickson Publishers, 2007); Andrew E. Arterbury, *Entertaining Angels: Early Christian Hospitality in Its Mediterranean Setting* (NTM 8; Sheffield: Sheffield Phoenix, 2005); Richard L. Batey, *Jesus and the Forgotten City: New Light on Sepphoris and the Urban World of Jesus* (Grand Rapids: Baker, 1991); Ismo Dunderberg, Kari Syreeni, and Christopher Tuckett, eds., *Fair Play: Diversity and Conflicts in Early Christianity: Essays in Honour of Heikki Räisänen* (Leiden: Brill, 2002); Richard A. Horsley and Neil Asher Silberman, *The Message and the Kingdom: How Jesus and Paul Ignited a*

tine should improve our understanding of the culture of Jesus and his earliest followers. An investigation of three pericopes in Luke's gospel, wherein Jesus instructs his disciples, should provide insight about their response to their culture and appropriation of his message.

1.4 Methodology

Luke-Acts has been studied from many angles.[59] Scholars have approached it from literary,[60] theological,[61] historical,[62] and socio-historical[63] vantage

---

Revolution and Transformed the Ancient World (Minneapolis: Fortress Press, 1997); Neyrey, *Social World*.

[59] For bibliography on various approaches to Luke-Acts undertaken before 1994, see Joel B. Green and Michael C. McKeever, *Luke-Acts and New Testament Historiography* (IBR Bibliographies 8; Grand Rapids: Baker, 1994).

[60] Mikeal C. Parsons, *Luke: Storyteller, Interpreter, Evangelist* (Peabody: Hendrickson, 2007); Daniel Marguerat, *First Christian Historian: Writing the "Acts of the Apostles"* (Cambridge: Cambridge University Press, 2002); C. M. Tuckett, ed., *Luke's Literary Achievement: Collected Essays* (JSNT 116; Sheffield, England: Sheffield Academic Press, 1995); William S. Kurz, *Reading Luke-Acts: Dynamics of Biblical Narrative* (Louisville: Westminster/John Knox Press, 1993); Loveday Alexander, *The Preface to Luke's Gospel: Literary Convention and Social Context in Luke 1.1–4 and Acts 1.1* (Cambridge: Cambridge University Press, 1993); idem, *Acts in Its Ancient Literary Context: A Classicist Looks at the Acts of the Apostles* (Early Christianity in Context; New York: T & T Clark International, 2005); Robert J. Karris, *Luke, Artist and Theologian: Luke's Passion Account As Literature* (Theological Inquiries; New York: Paulist Press, 1985); Richard I. Pervo, *Profit with Delight: The Literary Genre of the Acts of the Apostles* (Philadelphia: Fortress Press, 1987); Bruce W. Winter and Andrew D. Clarke, eds., *The Book of Acts in Its Ancient Literary Setting* (BAFCS 1; Grand Rapids: Eerdmans, 1993).

[61] François Bovon, *Luke the Theologian: Fifty-Five Years of Research (1950–2005)* (Waco: Baylor University Press, 2006); I. H. Marshall, *Luke: Historian and Theologian* (Exeter: Authentic Paternoster, 2006); Marshall and Peterson, *Witness to the Gospel*; Green, *Theology*; Jacob Jervell, *The Theology of the Acts of the Apostles* (New Testament Theology; Cambridge: Cambridge University Press, 1996).

[62] C. J. Hemer, *Luke the Historian* (Manchester, England: John Rylands University Library, 1977); Clare K. Rothschild, *Luke-Acts and the Rhetoric of History: An Investigation of Early Christian Historiography* (WUNT 175; Tübingen: Mohr Siebeck, 2004); Alexander Mittelstaedt, *Lukas als Historiker: zur Datierung des lukanischen Doppelwerkes* (TANZ 43; Tübingen: Francke, 2006); Héctor Sánchez, *Das lukanische Geschichtswerk im Spiegel heilsgeschichtlicher Übergänge* (Paderborner theologische Studien 29; Paderborn: Ferdinand Schöningh, 2001); Gregory E. Sterling, *Historiography and Self-Definition: Josephos, Luke-Acts, and Apologetic Historiography* (NovTSupp 64; Leiden: Brill, 1992).

[63] Esler, *Community and Gospel*; Malina and Rohrbaugh, *Social-Science Commentary*; Neyrey, *Social World of Luke-Acts*.

points often with a considerable amount of overlap in the approaches. In particular, the literature which approaches Luke from historical, or sociohistorical, perspective has brought forth many new insights which have been challenged, refined, and sometimes overturned. These approaches are of central importance for the present study since both have ventured into discussion of benefaction, patronage, and reciprocity in Luke-Acts.

Those scholars who focus primarily on historical Galilee tend to shy away from the typical redaction critical approaches to determining the historical Jesus, and instead they prefer a focus on "historical plausibility." W. R. Telford identifies the discussion of broader historical, social, and political issues rather than the interrogation of specific sayings as the growing trend in historical Jesus studies.[64] In general this approach uses archaeological and literary sources to construct a legitimate picture of first-century Galilee (or Palestine) which is then compared to the sayings and actions of Jesus as they are depicted in the Gospels. They then pose a broader question on their findings. Does the portrait of Jesus in the Gospels correspond with what a first-century Galilean villager could have said or done if one accepts the version of the historical Galilee (or Palestine) determined from the archaeological and literary sources? Into what kind of political and social climate did Jesus enter and what kind of response to this climate, if any, did he make? The approach usually does not seek to determine the authenticity of specific sayings, although that is often a part of the study, but instead keeps itself at the more general level.

This study follows the path proposed by E. M. Meyers, S. Freyne, J. L. Reed, and M. H. Jensen who urge interpreters of biblical texts to employ both archaeological and literary evidence toward the construction of a nuanced portrait of the culture in which the biblical texts are set. Meyers has written extensively in an effort to bring archaeology and literary studies into better communication. He emphasizes the need for "regionalism", the idea that one should set out to describe a particular area (e.g. city, village, or tetrarchy) in its distinct form rather than simply assuming a monolithic culture for a larger vicinity (e.g. "the Mediterranean," "the Roman Empire," or "Hellenistic society").[65] In studies of patrons, benefactors, and

---

[64] William R. Telford, "Major Trends and Interpretive Issues in the Study of Jesus," in *Studying the Historical Jesus: Evaluations of the State of Current Research* (ed. Bruce Chilton and Craig A. Evans; New Testament Tools and Studies; Leiden: Brill, 1998), 33–74.

[65] Eric M. Meyers, "Galilean Regionalism as a Factor in Historical Reconstruction," *BASOR* 221 (1976): 93–101; Reed, *Archaeology*, 3–4, 23, 109; Jensen, *Antipas*, 126–127; Jürgen Zangenberg, "Opening Up Our View: Khirbet Qumran in a Regional Perspective," in *Religion and Society in Roman Palestine: Old Questions, New Approaches* (ed. Douglas R. Edwards; New York and London: Routledge, 2004), 170–187; Oakman, *Jesus and the Peasants*, 245–279; Sean Freyne, "Galileans, Phoenicians, and Itureans: A Study of

1.4 Methodology

clients there has been a tendency to assume that since these practices flourished elsewhere in the early Roman Empire they must have been present, or flourished, in Palestine during the same era. Others forego this assumption but accuse Luke of importing the practice from his own culture into the culture of Jesus and his earliest followers. Following Meyers' lead, focused attention on Palestine and the various smaller regions within it will be investigated in an attempt to discern whether or not these Hellenistic/Roman ways existed and/or flourished in that area during the early Roman empire.

The call to identify regional differences in discussions of ancient cultures drives the second chapter of this study. Evidence from both archaeological and literary sources will be categorized according to region (city, village). An assessment of the culture of that specific city or village in light of the archaeological data will then be compared with the accompanying portrait of the specific city or village as described in the literary sources. Cities and villages are categorized into broader regions to summarize aspects of culture in that particular region. Archaeological data for several of these regions is rather sparse. It would not be prudent to describe cultures too confidently from sporadic remains, so in those instances where evidence provides a relatively slim picture of the culture this study hesitates to draw firm conclusions. Since this study is focused on patronage and benefaction discussion will be limited to those pieces of evidence which directly address these realities. Though each of the four issues mentioned above (section 1.2) has an impact, whether explicitly or implicitly, on the topic, these issues will not be addressed either directly or thoroughly in the study. Specifically, no attempt is made to substantiate a complete portrait of economic or political life in any of the regions examined.

Freyne, Reed, and Jensen have succeeded in developing and working out an approach to the biblical texts which appreciates both archaeological and literary data without giving overdue priority to either. Freyne's groundbreaking work (mentioned above) began his journey toward an ac-

---

Regional Contrasts in the Hellenistic Age," in *Hellenism in the Land of Israel* (ed. John J. Collins and Gregory A. Sterling; Notre Dame: University of Notre Dame Press, 2001), 182–215; idem, "Archaeology and the Historical Jesus," in Charlesworth, *Archaeology*, 64–83; James H. Charlesworth, "Conclusion: The Historical Jesus and Biblical Archaeology: Reflections on New Methodologies and Perspectives," in idem, *Archaeology*, 692–695; Rafael Frankel, Nimrod Getzov, Mordechai Aviam, and Avi Degani, eds., *Settlement Dynamics and Regional Diversity in Ancient Upper Galilee: Archaeological Survey of Upper Galilee* (IAA reports 14; Jerusalem: Israel Antiquities Authority, 2001). Moxnes, *Economy*, 24–26 suggests that such distinctions are unnecessary when describing patronage in the Mediterranean since such cultural values did not fluctuate frequently in that era.

curate description of the culture of Jesus and he has continued on that journey with many articles and monographs.[66] In the process he began to work with socio-historical models which forced him to rethink some of his earlier positions.[67] Although he admits that no single "wedding" of literary and archaeological evidence has gained a scholarly consensus, in general there is a need for "text and spade" to commence an "inter-textual" dialogue where each challenges the reading of the other.[68] The "text" of the spade, because of advances in archaeological method, would not usually be written sources (e.g. inscriptions) but the descriptions of the first-century world which arise from the collection and interpretation of mundane material (e.g. bowls, tools, coins).[69] In this study, however, inscriptions, however sparse, will be invaluable as they give explicit evidence of patronage and benefaction. The "text" of the spade, in this study, will thus combine mundane materials and written archaeological evidence to create a story of first-century society. Archaeological evidence will not be used as "proof" of the biblical text as if the material remains and its interpretation are somehow objective attestation of the "biased" text. It will instead be used as another voice which describes life in Palestine during the early Roman Empire.

I rely upon Jensen's methodology in advocating a slower adoption of socio-historical models.[70] Freyne's change from seeing Antipas' role in Galilee in terms of harmony to identifying conflict which paralleled his implementation of socio-historical models warns of the impact that models

---

[66] See the recent *Festschrift* to Freyne, Werner G. Jeanrond and Andrew D. H. Mayes, eds., *Recognising the Margins: Developments in Biblical and Theological Studies: Essays in Honour of Seán Freyne* (Blackrock, Co. Dublin: Columba Press, 2006).

[67] Jensen notes Freyne's transition from a harmony to conflict model for understanding Galilee, which Jensen argues is dependent upon his adoption of sociological models. Jensen, *Antipas*, 9–34.

[68] Freyne, "Archaeology and the Historical Jesus," 163–164. Miriam Peskowitz uses the terminology of "dual interpretation," suggested by Martin Goodman, "Foreword," in *Religion and Society in Roman Palestine: Old Questions, New Approaches* (ed. Douglas R. Edwards; New York and London: Routledge, 2004), xiii-xvii, xv. For the admitted difficulties see Eric M. Meyers and James F. Strange, *Archaeology, the Rabbis and Early Christianity* (London and Nashvillle: SCM and John Knox Press, 1981).

[69] This is particularly suitable for first-century Palestine which has relatively few inscriptional remains and even less related to benefaction and/patronage. See Seth Schwartz, "Euergetism in Josephus and the Epigraphical Culture of First-Century Jerusalem," in *From Hellenism to Islam: Cultural and Linguistic Change in the Roman Near East* (ed. Hannah Cotton, David J. Wasserstein, Jonathan Price, and Robert Hoyland; Cambridge: Cambridge University Press, forthcoming). I am grateful to Dr. Schwartz for allowing me to view this article in a rough form before its publication.

[70] Jensen, *Antipas*, and idem, "Josephus and Antipas: A Case Study of Josephus' Narratives on Herod Antipas," *Making History: Josephus and Historical Method* (ed. Zuleika Rodgers; JSJSupp 110; Leiden: Brill, 2007), 289–312.

may have on one's reading of the text. M. Sawicki notes that models can be mistakenly used as evidence when in fact they are not.[71] The approach of the social historian is preferable who begins with the particulars of a specific group and lets models arise from the evidence. This approach seems to be a better choice in light of the minimal evidence, inability for live observation, questions of how representative that evidence is of society at large, potentially biased sources, and the deterministic danger of models.[72] This monograph is more interested in historical *realia* than in a socio-historical description of society. In this regard, I am more concerned to identify or exclude the presence of benefaction or *patrocinium* in first-century Palestine. A socio-historical model may adequately summarize these relations, but this study primarily hopes to discern whether these historical practices prevailed in the culture. Jensen provides a good example of this approach.[73] He advocates a "contextualized source-oriented approach, which focuses on the sources available and thereafter applies an appropriate model, since the models otherwise seem to have a deterministic influence on the results."[74] He divides Palestine into regions and sub-regions. He then addresses the archaeological data on each sub-region building an understanding of that area solely from the archaeological data. He then investigates literary data, primarily but not exclusively Josephus. When multiple sources (e.g. Josephus and another author, or Josephus in two writings) attest an incident or description he attempts to discern a motive behind both descriptions and to filter out apparent bias or coloring. Jensen eventually challenges the models advocated by S. Freyne, M. Moreland, and J. D. Crossan for understanding Antipas and Galilee. Jensen concludes that the conditions developed by the social historians necessary to substantiate their models are lacking in the archaeological and literary record.[75] It is indeed a possibility that the models advocated for the subject of this monograph will not find sufficient support from the data, but the substantiation or refutation of these models is not the first priority of the study. My primary goal is to discern the historical picture of early Roman Palestine and specifically the adoption, rejection, or modification of *patrocinium* and benefaction by Jesus and his earliest followers. Whether these historical practices can be summarized adequately by socio-historical

---

[71] Marianne Sawicki, *Crossing Galilee: Architectures of Contact in the Occupied Land of Jesus* (Harrisburg: Trinity Press, 1998), 80.

[72] Carolyn Osiek, "The New Handmaid: The Bible and Social Sciences," *Theological Studies* 50.2 (1989): 260–278, 270, in Jensen, *Antipas*, 31.

[73] One might also suggest Reed, *Archaeology*, or the contributions to Edwards, *Religion and Society*, as other good examples of this approach.

[74] Jensen, *Antipas*, 34.

[75] Jensen, *Antipas*, 248–250.

models and whether this is indeed a helpful way forward will be addressed briefly in the second chapter.

Following the regional perspective an examination of four main personalities which governed early Roman Palestine will be undertaken in the third chapter. Herod I, Antipas, Philip, and Agrippa I each had a role in influencing the culture in which Jesus and his earliest followers lived. Again both archaeological and literary evidence can be adduced to develop a picture of these historical characters. Naturally, more evidence is available for Herod I, but there is sufficient information provided to give an adequate description of the latter three. Since archaeological evidence usually cannot offer interpretations of euergetistic inscriptions it will be used primarily to attest the presence of euergetistic practices. Literary evidence can begin the critique of the practice and sometimes corroborates the conclusions derived from archaeology.

A purpose of the study is to provide a plausible description of first-century Palestine. Jensen thinks it possible to distinguish between plausible, implausible, and wrong readings and therefore seeks to find a plausible reading that cannot be proven to be wrong. At the same time he admits that the source material may be insufficient to answer the question he has set out to investigate.[76] The same disclaimer seems appropriate for this study. While a plausible context may be surmised it is unwise to suggest that our reading cannot be modified and improved on account of future discoveries and revised methodologies. Furthermore, one can provide a plausible context for the life of Jesus without being able to "prove" that he must have interacted with the specifics of that context.

Some justification may be necessary for the selection of Luke and three specific passages (6:17–38; 14:1–24; 22:14–34). Luke-Acts has been the subject of a few studies on benefactors and patrons. Danker, whose work on benefactors has proven to be a foundational work for subsequent NT studies on the subject, has written two commentaries on Luke in which he attempts to demonstrate the importance of benefactor ideology for the interpretation of Luke's two volume work.[77] In summarizing the importance of his study of benefactors he suggests that Luke, above all other NT authors, interpreted Jesus and explained his importance in terms of benefaction which would have been well understood by his Gentile audience.[78] Moxnes has approached Luke-Acts in reference to patron-client relationships. He explains redactional changes (e.g., Matt 8:5–13; Luke 7:1–10) made by Luke which draw out his understanding of patron-client relationships and their importance for understanding early Christianity. He sug-

---

[76] Jensen, *Antipas*, 47–48.
[77] Danker, *Benefactor*; idem, *New Age*; idem, *Luke*.
[78] Danker, *Benefactor*, 27–28.

1.4 Methodology

gests that the paradigm of patron-client illuminates much of Luke-Acts.[79] Commentators have drawn from Danker and Moxnes especially in the interpretation of a few passages.

Three passages in Luke (6:17–38; 14:1–24; 22:14–34) have been selected for this study because they involve specific teaching of Jesus and have been interpreted in terms of patronage and benefaction. J. B. Green probably draws most heavily from Danker and Moxnes among commentators. He contends that the ideology of patronage and benefaction had so penetrated Mediterranean culture that Jesus' instruction in the Sermon on the Plain (Luke 6:17–38) is best interpreted in reference to these Greco-Roman relationships.[80] The "reversal speech" (6:20–26) is a benefaction to the poor.[81] Others see in Jesus' discussion of reciprocity reason to assert that God supersedes prevailing notions of benefaction and patronage.[82] Jesus may transform or overturn these practices.[83] The healing of the dropsical man, and the teaching that follows, have also been interpreted in terms of patronage and benefaction (Luke 14:1–24).[84] This generosity beyond the "in-group" mirrors benefactors whose generosity often stretched outside of their social group.[85] It is argued by K. C. Hanson and D. E. Oakman that since patrons often maintained good relations with clients through meals the passage should be interpreted in terms of patronage.[86] Jesus' instruction at the Last Supper is a natural candidate for discussions of benefactors and patrons since Luke refers to εὐεργέτης (22:14–38). L. T. Johnson, J. B. Green, D. L. Bock, J. A. Fitzmyer, Y. S. Ahn, and others draw from Danker and Moxnes in their interpretation of the passage.[87] These three

---

[79] Moxnes, "Patron-Client," 241–242.

[80] Green, *Luke*, 270–271; idem, *Theology of Luke*, 114–115.

[81] Moxnes, *Economy*, 20; idem, "Patron-Client," 257–258; Johnson, *Luke*, 111; Lull, "Servant-Benefactor," 289.

[82] deSilva, *Honor, Patronage*, 129–131.

[83] François Bovon, *Luke 1: A Commentary on the Gospel of Luke 1:1–9:50* (trans. Christine M. Thomas; Minneapolis: Fortress Press, 2002), 1.237, 241; idem, *Das Evangelium nach Lukas* (EKK 3.1; Benziger Verlag: Zürich, 1989), 1.276; idem, *L'Évangile selon Saint Luc 1,1–9,50* (Commentaire du Nouveau Testament 3a; Labor et Fides: Geneva, 1991), 269 n. 35. Cf. Danker, *Luke*, 33–34; W. C. van Unnik, "Die Motivierung der Feindesliebe in Lukas VI,32–35," *NovT* 8 (1966): 284–300.

[84] Green, *Luke*, 547–548; idem, *Theology*, 114–116.

[85] Danker, *Benefactor*, 339.

[86] K. C. Hanson and Douglas E. Oakman, *Palestine in the Time of Jesus: Social Structures and Social Conflicts* (Minneapolis: Fortress Press, 1998), 74–76.

[87] L. T. Johnson, *The Gospel of Luke* (SacPag; Collegeville: Liturgical Press, 1991), 343–350; J. B. Green, *The Gospel of Luke* (NICNT; Grand Rapids: Eerdmans, 1997), 260–281, 767–770; D. L. Bock, *Luke* (BECNT; Grand Rapids: Baker, 1994), 2.1737; Fitzmyer, *Luke*, 2.1416–1417; Ahn, *The Reign of God*, 161–168; Esler, *Community and Gospel*, 208; Nelson, *Leadership*, 150–152.

passages are therefore a good starting point for an investigation of patronage and benefaction in Luke. Since they each contain instruction from Jesus toward potential disciples they are particularly suited for a discussion of patronage, benefaction, and discipleship.

Based upon the purported cultural origins of Luke (Gentile God-fearer) and the susceptibility of his work to interpretation in terms of benefaction and patronage, it would be easier to study Luke as a theologian, but this study aims to investigate the historical Jesus. As scholars comment on the relationship between Luke, patrons, and benefactors a charge is frequently made against Luke that he has not described Jesus' culture faithfully but has instead merely described his own. Sometimes this charge has no bite; Luke simply translated the message to make it understandable to his audience.[88] But others seem to disparage Luke's trustworthiness on account of his apparent adoption of benefaction and/or patronage in description of first-century Palestine.[89] Part of the burden of this study is to determine whether Luke has errantly adopted a custom of Greco-Roman life which did not persist in first-century Palestine.

Since this study evaluates whether Luke's presentation of Jesus "fits" with the historical picture of Palestine which is developed, the exegetical portion of this study must advance in two stages. First, it must precisely determine the content of what is set forth in Luke's Gospel to see if Luke in fact employs *patrocinium* and benefaction as interpretive paradigms. In this stage of the exegesis typical exegetical approaches are adopted. The literary context is established to situate the particular passage under review. Linguistic analysis next identifies terminology which may support a reading in terms of *patrocinium* or benefaction. The content of the teaching is then compared to Hellenistic Jewish and Greco-Roman culture to determine the best "fit" for the teaching. At different points, redaction and source analyses will further clarify the content of Luke's presentation. The purpose of these analyses is to clarify and distinguish the particular content of Luke's presentation of Jesus in order to substantiate or discredit the claim that he does in fact employ *patrocinium* and benefaction.

Second, after determining whether or not *patrocinium* and benefaction serve as interpretive paradigms for Jesus' teaching, the content of Luke's presentation is compared to the historical *realia* of first-century Palestine. At this stage the first part of the study (chs. 2–3) will be brought to bear on

---

[88] Danker, *Benefactor*, 26–28.

[89] E.g., Willi Braun, *Feasting and Social Rhetoric in Luke 14* (SNTSMS 85; Cambridge: Cambridge University Press, 1995), 99; Richard L. Rohrbaugh, "The Pre-Industrial City in Luke-Acts: Urban Social Relations," in Neyrey, *Social World*, 125–149, 141; Moxnes, "Patron-Client," 256–257, but see Moxnes, *Economy*, 36–47 where he seems to assume the presence of patron-client relationships in Palestine.

the second part of the study (chs. 4–6). The first part of the study determines whether or not *patrocinium* and benefaction prevailed in various parts of Palestine and the likelihood of a Galilean villager becoming aware of their practice. Drawing together the two parts of this study it is possible to determine if Luke describes Jesus as adopting categories which were unavailable for someone of his provenance. Likewise, the results of the first part of the study demonstrate what someone of Jesus' provenance could have known. No attempt is made however to establish conclusively whether the historical Jesus said what Luke reports he said. In this regard the study builds a picture of historical plausibility.

1.5 Aims of This Study

This study has five interrelated aims. First, it hopes to provide insight about life in first-century Palestine. This has become a very fruitful field in scholarship in the past decade and this study attempts to cull from the best resources on that investigation while advancing new information on the specific topic of benefactors and patrons. Second, by investigating the historical *realia* of first-century Palestine this study seeks to provide insight into the historical Jesus. Advancing new angles on the culture of Palestine will potentially provide for a more robust and accurate understanding of the historical Jesus. Third, related to the question of the historical Jesus, it is hoped that this investigation will provide another angle from which the early Christians may be described. The relationship between Jesus and early Christianity is an important topic and this study carries the potential to move forward the discussion of Jesus' relationship to the movement connected to him. Fourth, the exegetical investigation of Luke's Gospel undertaken in the third chapter will hopefully open new avenues of thought and challenge currently held opinions. Precision in the interpretation of the Third Gospel should be a product of this study. Fifth, since socio-historical and anthropological models continue to have a prominent position in NT scholarship, it is important to evaluate the worth of the social scientific category "patron-client." This study should challenge certain conceptions of the construct and provide for a better evaluation of its value.

Chapter 2

Benefaction and *Patrocinium* in First-century Palestine

Before considering Luke-Acts and the use of benefaction or patronage to describe discipleship, it is imperative to (1) describe these social relationships and (2) investigate first-century Palestine to see if these relationships were actually in operation during the ministry years of Jesus and the earliest Christians. Since descriptions of patronage and benefaction typically begin with reference to sociological studies, a brief review of this literature and its followers in NT scholarship has been provided. Criticisms launched against this approach were then laid out. The primary criticism offered against the sociological category of patron-client is that it does not first dig deeply into the specific culture being described (here, Palestine), but rather draws from cross-cultural analysis and more or less assumes the universality of cultures. A second major criticism is that the sociological language of "patron-client" is easily confused with the Roman category of *patrocinium*. Adoption of the sociological category can imply the presence of Roman modes of thought which may or may not have been historical *realia*. This project hopes to ground itself more concretely in first-century Palestinian culture. So rather than accepting the conclusions of cross-cultural analysis it explores the various regions within which the earliest Christians would have operated. Chapter 2 provides a regional perspective which surveys Galilee, Jerusalem, Caesarea, Samaria, some smaller cities in Philip's tetrarchy, and Tyre. Chapter 3 provides a "personality perspective," which examines Herod I, Herod Antipas, Philip, and Agrippa I. In the process an attempt is made to discern the possibility or actual practice of benefaction or *patrocinium* in villages, cities, or persons. Since no specific attempt has been previously made to identify and describe these relationships in Palestine this survey charts new territory but admits at the outset the impossibility of exhausting such a vast subject.[1] The reader should consider this investigation an attempt to lay out the evidence and to suggest plausible

---

[1] There have been several attempts by sociologists to describe first-century Palestine through their models (e.g., Hanson and Oakman, *Palestine*), but no monograph which specifically addresses benefaction and *patrocinium* from a historical perspective has been attempted.

readings without claiming comprehensiveness. Two broad conclusions have been reached: (1) benefaction was relatively more well-known than *patrocinium*, though it did not penetrate every region investigated, and (2) sociological patron-client terminology confuses historical study and would be best replaced with the general Greco-Roman category of reciprocity.

2.1 Benefaction and Patronage According to Ancient Sources

As scholars progress deeper into the subject they tend to move away from sociological models and toward descriptions of society from primary sources (literary and archaeological evidence). Often these studies attempt to justify, qualify, or nullify the models set forth by sociology. The first source traditionally turned to among the primary witnesses is Seneca's *De beneficiis*.[2] A natural selection, Seneca (4 B.C.–A.D. 65) articulates his understanding of proper and improper forms of beneficence through seven, often repetitive, books. Dio Chrysostom (A.D. 40–120) and Cicero (106–43 B.C.) usually receive attention after Seneca. Dio's discourses on kingship offer insights about proper rule, and, in this regard, the appropriate form of generosity hoped for from a good ruler (e.g., *De regno* 1.12–26). Cicero's letters open windows into the day to day affairs of patrons and clients. His position in the upper strata of society puts him in a prime spot to describe *patrocinium* for his readers. A few other scholars have approached patronage and benefaction from the side of epigraphy and inscriptions. These give access, we are told, to the common knowledge level spanning a broader band of social classes. F. W. Danker introduces this tack with his *Benefactor: Epigraphic Study of a Graeco-Roman and New Testament Semantic Field*. He surveys fifty-three inscriptions (mostly ancient, but several modern)[3] and provides four insightful essays about the

---

[2] For example, Stephan Joubert, "Coming to Terms with a Neglected Aspect of Ancient Mediterranean Reciprocity: Seneca's Views on Benefit-Exchange in *De beneficiis* as the Framework for a Model of Social Exchange," in *Social Scientific Models for Interpreting the Bible: Essays by the Context Group in Honor of Bruce J. Malina* (ed. John J. Pilch; Leiden: Brill, 2000), 47–63; cf. idem, *Paul as Benefactor: Reciprocity, Strategy, and Theological Reflection in Paul's Collection* (WUNT 2.124; Tübingen: Mohr Siebeck, 2000). For a critique of Joubert, see Zeba A. Crook, *Reconceptualising Conversion: Patronage, Loyalty, and Conversion in the Religions of the Ancient Mediterranean* (BZNW 130; Berlin/New York: Walter de Gruyter, 2004), 59–66.

[3] Danker selects epigraphic sources primarily from the fifth century B.C. to the third centuries A.D., but also includes two from the 20th century (nos. 14, 40) to show how the ideology has continued into the present. He also includes four documents from the LXX (nos. 13, 25, 49A, 49B) which show the adaptation of Hellenistic motifs. On sources, see Danker, *Benefactor*, 29–30.

implications of his study for New Testament research.⁴ J. R. Harrison agrees with Danker that inscriptions should be valued for their ability to attest to what the non-elite had access to more so than (elite) literary works.⁵ He uses them to establish the prominence of χάρις language in benefaction.

One central question which has interested scholars in this field has been the question of differences, if any, between what is perceived to be "Greek" benefaction and "Roman" patronage. Many proceed from the assumption that though some difference might exist between these two, the differences were not substantial enough or would not have been recognized as such by the ancients and therefore need not be emphasized in our day.⁶ Others disagree.⁷ In this section a survey of the development of thought will hopefully shed light on this central question as well as offer a sufficient description of the historical practices of benefaction and patronage. The survey, which begins long before Cicero, Seneca, and Dio Chrysostom, is an often treaded path which needs only to be reiterated at this point.⁸

Literature on Hellenistic and Roman culture, with particular attention toward benefaction and patronage, has developed broadly agreed upon lines of thought with an occasional dissenting voice. Rather than attempting to rewrite the history of reciprocity from the seventh century B.C. to first-century A.D., the results of three recent and substantial works on the subject will be set forth. *Reciprocity in Ancient Greece*, as its name helpfully expresses, discusses reciprocity (in its various expressions) with a focus on 8th–3rd century B.C. Greece.⁹ At times this work also provides

---

⁴ The four essays can be understood in part by their topics and the brief description of each: Profile – terminology relating to "personal characteristics of benefactors"; Benefits – "principle types of contributions"; Endangered benefactor – "conferment of benefits from the perspective of life that is hazarded to the uttermost"; Response – gratitude and "the various directions that are taken in reaction to benefactions," Danker, *Benefactor*, 45–46.

⁵ Danker, *Benefactor*, 28–29; Harrison, *Language*, 24.

⁶ E.g., Crook, *Conversion*, 59–66; H. Hendrix, "Benefactor/Patron Networks in the Urban Environment: Evidence from Thessalonica," *Semeia* 56 (1991): 39–58; David W. Pao, *Thanksgiving: An Investigation of a Pauline Theme* (NSBT 13; Downers Grove: InterVarsity Press, 2002), 165–172.

⁷ Esp. Joubert, *Benefactor*; idem, "Ancient Mediteranean Reciprocity"; Alan C. Mitchell, "'Greet the Friends by Name': New Testament Evidence for the Greco-Roman topos on Friendship," in *Greco-Roman Perspectives on Friendship* (ed. John T. Fitzgerald; RBS 34; Atlanta: Scholars Press, 1997).

⁸ For many of the details of this path and its twists and turns see Joubert, *Benefactor*; Crook, *Conversion*; Verboven, *Economy*.

⁹ C. Gill, N. Postlethwaite, and R. Seaford, eds., *Reciprocity in Ancient Greece* (New York: Oxford University Press, 1998).

insight into the trajectory which reciprocity eventually took in the Hellenistic era. Two works focusing on Hellenistic and Roman culture between the second century B.C. and first-century A.D. bring the debate up to date despite differing at points. Stephan Joubert's *Paul as Benefactor* and Zeba Crook's *Reconceptualising Conversion* have extensive treatments of benefaction and patronage with particular attention on their studies' bearing on NT texts.[10] These studies provide a general description of patronage and benefaction. A few recent works by classicists will provide nuance and clarification to these descriptions.

2.1.1 Reciprocity in Ancient Greece

Before the advent of its specialized forms (benefaction/patronage), reciprocity had a more general tenor which surfaced quite clearly in Ancient Greece. "Reciprocity is the principle and practice of voluntary requital, of benefit for benefit (positive reciprocity) or harm for harm (negative reciprocity)."[11] In pre-industrialized and pre-state Greece reciprocity should be expected. Reciprocity (both positive and negative) thrives in environments lacking a state political structure and commercial exchange. Homeric society provides a good example.[12] But as states and commercialization develop popular attitudes toward reciprocity grow somewhat hostile. Reciprocal exchange may even be viewed as bribery. Plato and Socrates critique both positive and negative reciprocity (*Seventh Letter* 336e, 332a4, 333e, 325d, 334b, 332c, 567, 568d, 571c-d, 574c).[13] Socrates goes so far as to say that it does not amount to justice if a person returns insult for insult to enemies or gift for gift to friends. Reciprocity muddles with the purity of commercial exchange and the structures of the political system.[14] Anna Missiou demonstrates just such differences of opinion among major city-states.[15] Missiou studies Athens and Sparta concluding that "because of their contrasting socio-political systems during the fifth century, Athens and Sparta held divergent views about the notion of reciprocal generos-

---

[10] Joubert, *Benefactor*; Crook, *Conversion*.

[11] Richard Seaford, "Introduction," in Gill, Postlethwaite, and Seaford, *Reciprocity in Ancient Greece*, 1–11, 1.

[12] Seaford, "Introduction," 4–7. This point emphasizes the impropriety of using modern sociological research to create categories which will be applied to ancient cultures. There never was a Greek "state" in antiquity which approximated a modern state, so the social constructs created would have been different than those created in modern cultures.

[13] Whether Plato wrote this letter or not is still debated, cf. Seaford, "Introduction," 8.

[14] Seaford, "Introduction," 8–11.

[15] Anna Missiou, "Reciprocal Generosity in the Foreign Affairs of Fifth-Century Athens and Sparta," in Gill, Postlethwaite, and Seaford, *Reciprocity in Ancient Greece*, 181–197.

ity."¹⁶ Reciprocity failed to function as a sufficient basis upon which to make political arguments in Athens whereas Sparta frequently appealed to reciprocity in political matters.¹⁷ This difference actually played an important role, according to Herodotos, in justifying the Spartan aggression toward Athens. They had been ungrateful (*Herodotos* 5.90; cf. 5.91.2).¹⁸ Missiou distinguishes the two more clearly as representing two views toward benefaction.¹⁹ Athenians gave benefits because of "the intrinsic merit of actions freely undertaken."²⁰ The beneficiary, needing not to reciprocate, feels "indefinite gratitude." Other Greeks (notably some Spartans) demanded repayment which leads the beneficiary to feel not gratitude but rather the burden of a debt.

It may seem that monetization might hinder the reciprocal exchange system because benefits and gifts can be paid for with an agreed upon price and no margin exists for a debt to remain. It will not perpetuate the cycle of "owing" a debt. But this is not always true. Hans van Wees, in a cross-cultural anthropological study, maintains that certain societies persisted in reciprocal systems even when monetization had penetrated fairly thoroughly (e.g., the Maring and the Siane).²¹ Van Wees goes on to define euergetism, the specific form of reciprocity which grew prominent as Hellenism developed, as a system in which "public benefactions, often on a grand scale, and often repaid with collectively granted honours, serve to legitimate the wealth and power of elites, at all levels, from local to imperial."²² The practice was pervasive and prominent in antiquity. It is also significant that, at this point, all parties involved seem to consistently deny "that a relation of power exists."²³

Questions of benefaction and patronage tend to be enmeshed with definitions and descriptions of friendship, so a brief discussion of reciprocity and friendship should be added. In Ancient Greece reciprocity was a fundamental component of friendship, but at times Greeks appear to have chosen their friends for more than simply utilitarian reasons. Aristotle (*Nic. Eth.* 8.2) "specifies three conditions for friendship: (1) mutual good will; (2) consciousness that the good will is reciprocated; and (3) desiring the

---

[16] Missiou, "Foreign Affairs," 182.
[17] Missiou, "Foreign Affairs," 184–185.
[18] Missiou, "Foreign Affairs," 186–187.
[19] Missiou, "Foreign Affairs," 186–191.
[20] Missiou, "Foreign Affairs," 191.
[21] Hans van Wees, "The Law of Gratitude: Reciprocity in Anthropological Theory," in Gill, Postlethwaite, and Seaford, *Reciprocity in Ancient Greece*, 13–49, here 48.
[22] Van Wees, "Law," 45.
[23] Van Wees, "Law," 47.

good for the sake of the other."[24] Though one may enter a friendship for emotional or utilitarian reasons, Aristotle maintains that true affection still exists in the predominately utilitarian relationship. Here the parties emotionally appreciate the usefulness of the other. Friends may thus involve the consistent balance of loans and debts.[25] Konstan notes that "[b]etween the classical democracy and the Hellenistic monarchies, there is a change in the treatment of friendship.... [I]n the texts that survive the dominant note is that of mutual help between equals in time of crisis rather than the asymmetrical exchange of protection and support between great men and their entourage."[26] In Athens, friendship between equals effectively warded off patronage by invoking an "ethic of mutual assistance among peers in times of need." Such a system kept "social dependency" at bay.[27]

Reciprocity was not confined to mundane matters alone, but instead it became an integral part of Ancient Greek religious expression which carried over into a few Roman authors.[28] Reciprocity, for the most part, enjoyed a positive place in Greek religion, though it also endured critique by some authors. Seaford claims that the problems with reciprocity encountered in human relations were mirrored in human-deity relations. The gods need nothing including reciprocal thank offerings, exchanges can become commodified and thus lose the relational aspect, or the human side may scorn the distance implied by the necessity of animal sacrifice.[29] In human-deity relationships χαρίς takes a central place in descriptions of the actions of both the deity and human agents even if reciprocity itself receives a critique. Robert Parker elaborates upon this theme. According to him, χαρίς is the central word of the religious reciprocal exchange and is used on "both sides of the relationship" (giver and receiver).[30] He goes through many different levels of interaction between gods and mortals which sup-

---

[24] David Konstan, "Reciprocity and Friendship," in Gill, Postlethwaite, and Seaford, *Reciprocity in Ancient Greece*, 279–301, 284.

[25] Konstan, "Friendship," 285–286.

[26] Konstan, "Friendship," 298.

[27] Konstan, "Friendship," 299. See, P. Millett, "Patronage and Its Avoidance in Classical Athens," in *Patronage in Ancient Society* (ed. Andrew Wallace-Hadrill; London and New York: Routledge, 1989), 15–47, 43.

[28] Crook devotes much attention to the use of reciprocity in Greek and Roman religion, Crook, *Conversion*. In addition to several authors in this edition see also Andrew Erskine, "The Romans as Common Benefactors," *Historia* 43 (1994): 70–87, esp. 71–76, 79–81; R. F. Price, *Rituals and Power: The Roman Imperial Cult in Asia Minor* (Cambridge: Cambridge University Press, 1984); A. D. Nock, "Soter and Euergetes," in *Essays on Religion and the Ancient World* (ed. Z. Stewart; Oxford: Oxford University Press, 1972), 2.75; M. Nilsson, *Geschichte der griechischen Religion* II^2 (Munich: 1961), 183.

[29] Seaford, "Introduction," 10.

[30] Robert Parker, "Pleasing Thighs: Reciprocity in Greek Religion," in Gill, Postlethwaite, and Seaford, *Reciprocity in Ancient Greece*, 105–125, here 108.

port this statement. Humans respond with χαρίς to the χαρίς of the gods. Often the response of χαρίς is meant to arouse even more χαρίς from the gods. The human response might be pleasing (χαρίετα, κεχαρισμένα) and the return might also have this descriptor (χαρίεσσα). "That is to say, the ideas of reciprocity and repayment are associated with *khari*-words, but not in a direct semantic way. One gift or act endowed with *kharis*, power to please, will call forth another which will in turn evoke yet another; but a *kharis* even when given in return for a *kharis* is not in meaning a recompense, however much it may be so in function."[31] For example, Mantiklos commends his generosity and receives an appropriate epithet (Ϝεχαβόλοι ἀργυροτόξοοι) for his good deeds (*CEG* 326; cf. 227, 332, 275).[32]

Μάντιχλός μ' ἀνέθεκε Ϝεχαβόλοι ἀργυροτόξοοι τᾶς {δ}δε
κάτας τὺ δέ Φοῖβε δίδοι χαρίϜετταν ἀμοιβ[άν] *CEG* 326
"Mantiklos dedicated me to the far-shooting Lord of the Silver Bow, a tithe. You, Phoibos, give some pleasing favor in return" (*CEG* 326; Steiner)[33]

The use of χάρις and χαρίϜετταν ἀμοιβ[άν] "supports a chain of reciprocity based on gratitude (χάρις) for the previous favor (χάρις)."[34] Χάρις typically worked to force the hands of the gods into benefiting the people, but some saw χάρις as a problem.[35] Χάρις as an integral part of Greek religious expression which could be viewed in both positive and negative light persisted at least until the second century B.C.[36] This situation is true of ancient Greece, but Parker points out that in subsequent times the χάρι-word transitions to refer specifically to gratitude.[37] Jan-Maarten Bremer agrees by identifying two words which act as "technical terms for actions

---

[31] Parker, "Thighs," 108.
[32] See Parker, "Thighs," 110–111. Cf. *CEG* 227: Φαρθένε ἐν ἀχροπόλει Τελεσῖνος ἄγαλμ' ἀνέθεκεν Κέτιος ἠοι χαίροσα διδοίες ἄλο ἀναθέναι
[33] Deborah Tarn Steiner, *Images in Mind: Statues in Archaic and Classical Greek Literature and Thought* (Princeton: Princeton University Press, 2001); Margherita Guarducci, *Epigrafia Greca: Caratteri e Storia della Disciplina La Scrittura Greca dale Origini all'età Imperiale* (Istituto Poligrafico Dello Stato: Rome, 1967), 145–146; Georg Karo, *Greek Personality in Archaic Sculpture* (Martin Classical Lectures 11; Cambridge: Pub. for Oberlin College by Harvard University Press, 1948), 70. R. M. Burrows and P. N. Ure, "Excavations at Rhitsóna in Boeotia," *Annual of the British School of Athens* 14 (1907–08): 226–318, plates vii-xv; Joseph W. Day, "Interactive Offerings: Early Greek Dedicatory Epigrams and Ritual," *Harvard Studies in Classical Philology* 96 (1994): 37–74, 41–42.
[34] Day, "Interactive Offerings," 56–57.
[35] Parker, "Thighs," 114–118.
[36] Parker, "Thighs," 112–113; See Richard Seaford, *Reciprocity and Ritual: Homer and Tragedy in the Developing City-State* (Oxford: Clarendon Press, 1994).
[37] Parker, "Thighs," 112–113.

of religious gratitude: χαριστήριον and εὐχαριστηρία."[38] The terms grow in importance as expressions of gratitude in the Hellenistic and Roman periods. The majority of uses of χαριστήριον surfaces among "Greek authors living and writing under Roman control, and with special frequency in those authors who as orators or historians deal with Roman affairs: Dionysios of Halikarnassos (15 instances), Flavius Josephus (21), Plutarch (9), and Themistios (27!)." Εὐχαριστεῖν and χαριστήριον occur in the "late Hellenistic and Roman period[s] ... as technical terms for public manifestations of gratitude" to both men and gods.[39] He provides the example of Hadrian, Roman emperor and philhellene, expressing hope to the gods in (Greek) reciprocal terms (*IG* 7, 1828).[40]

While the gods reciprocate quite regularly, the exchange is not one of matching values (a sacrifice for an equal value favor), but of "voluntary, if socially prescribed, expression of a relationship of friendship."[41] Furthermore it is not that one meets the level of the gift with a proper valued return, but rather that the person assumes the proper attitude in response (Aristotle *Nic. Eth.* 1163b15–18; Hesiod *Works and Days* 335–340). In Aristotle and Plato the ability of a human to actually repay adequately the χαρίς of the gods is considered ridiculous. What counts is the effort to respond properly.[42] Asymmetry marks the relationship between man and god, and thus reciprocity between these parties is not performed between equals. Socrates' student, Euthydemos, bemoans his inability to repay the gods fully (*Mem.* 4.3.15). The critical terms in this exchange (χάρις, ἀμείβεσθαι) denote his desire to repay adequately the benefits of the gods.[43] Symmetry cannot be approached, but a "voluntary return for benefit" (Seaford) is certainly possible by man who builds temples or statues, or offers sacrifices and offerings. In these reciprocal exchanges it must be emphasized that no contract binds the two parties, no exchange of equal values (market) takes place, and the preservation and improvement of the human-god relation takes precedence.[44]

Reciprocity in religious settings, with its inherent asymmetry, serves as a foundation for some increasingly asymmetrical forms of reciprocity in both Hellenistic and Roman society. The public benefactor, with seemingly boundless resources, provided for entire cities and could not, indeed did not desire to, be repaid. The patron cherished his access to first-order

---

[38] Jan-Maarten Bremer, "The Reciprocity of Giving and Thanksgiving in Greek Worship," in Gill, Postlethwaite, and Seaford, *Reciprocity in Ancient Greece*, 127–137, 128.
[39] Bremer, "Greek Worship," 128–129.
[40] Bremer, "Greek Worship," 133.
[41] Parker, "Thighs," 118–119.
[42] Parker, "Thighs," 119.
[43] Bremer, "Greek Worship," 127.
[44] Bremer, "Greek Worship," 133.

goods which the client could only attain through him. Both relished in the fact that they could not be reciprocated fully. Additionally, reciprocity continued to play a prominent role in religious expressions in both Hellenistic and Roman cultures.

2.1.2 Benefaction and Patronage in Hellenistic and Roman Times

In Hellenistic and Roman times, reciprocity took on more specific forms. In the Hellenistic world benefaction was a prominent form of reciprocity.[45] In the Roman world *patrocinium* was a more particular type of reciprocity.[46] Focusing especially on the third century B.C. to the first-century A.D., Stephan Joubert (2000) and Zeba Crook (2004) provide current descriptions of these forms of reciprocity in correlation with NT studies, though they differ at one significant point. These two debate how much overlap exists between the two concepts and whether or not they are but one social relationship with different vocabulary to describe it. Joubert dis-

---

[45] Some works relevant to benefaction include: Veyne, *Bread and Circuses*; Danker, *Benefactor*; idem, "Reciprocity in the Ancient World and in Acts 15:23–29," in *Political Issues in Luke-Acts* (ed. Richard J. Cassidy and Philip J. Scharper; Maryknoll: Orbis Books, 1983), 49–58; Bolkestein, *Wohltätigkeit*; Phillipe Gauthier, *Les cités grecques et leurs bienfaiteurs* (Paris: Boccard, 1985); Erskine, "Common Benefactors"; Arthur Robinson Hands, *Charities and Social Aid in Greece and Rome* (Aspects of Greek and Roman Life; Ithaca: Cornell University Press, 1968); Mott, "The Greek Benefactor"; W. Donlan, "Reciprocities in Homer," *Classical World* 75 (1982): 137–176; Bonnie MacLachlan, *The Age of Grace: Charis in Early Greek Poetry* (Princeton: Princeton University Press, 1993); Albrecht Dihle, *Die goldene Regel: eine Einführung in die Geschichte der antiken und frühchristlichen Vulgärethik* (Studienhefte zur Altertumswissenschaft, 7; Göttingen: Vandenhoeck & Ruprecht, 1962).

[46] Some works relevant to patronage include: Eiler, *Roman Patrons*; Nicols, "Pliny and Patronage"; idem, "Patrons of Provinces"; idem, *The Patronage of Communities in the Roman Empire*; Touloumoukos, "Zum römischen Gemeindepatronat"; Verboven, *Economy*; Brunt, "Clientelae"; De Rossi, *Il ruolo dei 'patroni'*; Yakobson, *Elections and Electioneering*; Rouland, *Pouvoir politique*; Mommsen, "Das römische Gastrecht und die römische Clientel"; Gelzer, *The Roman Nobility*; Syme, *The Roman Revolution*; Lily Ross Taylor, *Party Politics in the Age of Caesar* (Berkeley: University of California Press, 1949); Lomas and Cornell, *Bread and Circuses*; de Ste. Croix, "*Suffragium*: From Vote to Patronage"; Badian, *Foreign Clientelae*; Saller, *Personal Patronage*; Wallace-Hadrill, *Patronage in Ancient Society*; Jean-Louis Ferrary, "The Hellenistic World and Roman Political Patronage," in *Hellenistic Constructs: Essays in Culture, History, and Historiography* (ed. P. Cartledge, P. Garnsey, and E. S. Gruen; Hellenistic Culture and Society 26; Berkeley: University of California, 1997), 105–119; Joseph Hellegouarc'h, *Le vocabulaire latin des relations et des partis politiques sous la République* (Paris: Les Belles lettres, 1963); Harold Mattingly, *The Emperor and His Clients* (Sydney: Australasian Medical, 1948); A. J. Dunston, ed., *Essays on Roman Culture: The Todd Memorial Lectures* (Toronto: Stevens, 1976); Fergus Millar, *The Emperor in the Roman World, 31 BC-AD 337* (Ithaca: Cornell University Press, 1977).

tinguishes the two more strongly, while Crook holds them more closely together. By laying out Joubert's case first the potential differences can be seen more clearly. Crook's critique will next be set out. Crook and Joubert provide a substantially accurate description of the practices, so several lines of description, shared by both authors, will be traced.[47] However, neither author had the opportunity to incorporate the works of Eilers (2002) and Verboven (2002) and they seem to have preferred the descriptions of patronage provided in socio-historical studies (e.g., Wallace-Hadrill; Eisenstadt and Roniger; cf. Saller) above those given by classicists which were available at the time of writing (e.g., Brunt, Touloumoukos, Nicols). Therefore, a brief discussion of classical descriptions of *patrocinium* will be given. A few paragraphs which bring into the discussion the clarifications advanced by classicists will provide reason to prefer, in general, Joubert's reading above Crook's. In short, Joubert is correct that *patrocinium* and benefaction are different, but for slightly different reasons than he proposes.

Stephan Joubert understands patronage and benefaction to be two distinct, though related, forms of reciprocity. Patronage stems from the Roman world. He follows (the Roman historian) Richard Saller's definition of patronage which has gained wide acceptance.[48] Though admittedly difficult to define, Saller gives three components of patron-client relations: reciprocal in the sense of exchange of goods/services, relational in the sense of a long-term relationship not a simple marketplace transaction, and asymmyetrical in the sense of a social distance between the two parties.[49] Joubert also follows Boissevain who distinguishes first order (land and wealth directly controlled by patron) from second order (access to patron with first order goods, strategic contacts) resources.[50]

Joubert begins his description of Greek/Hellenistic benefaction with a discussion of Aristotle's *Nicomachean Ethics* and Seneca's *De beneficii*. According to Joubert's reading, Aristotle critiques benefactors as "lovers of honour (φιλότιμοι), and beneficiaries, as lovers of money (φιλοχρή-

---

[47] For much more detail on the descriptions see, Eilers, *Roman Patrons*, 1–108; Joubert, *Benefactor*, chs. 1–2, Crook, *Conversion*, 53–249, Danker, *Benefactor*, 317–488, also Harrison, *Language*, 1–24; Zeba A. Crook, "Reciprocity: Covenantal Exchange as a Test Case," in *Ancient Israel: The Old Testament in Its Social Context* (ed. Philip F. Esler; Minneapolis: Fortress Press, 2006), 78–91.

[48] Joubert, *Benefactor*, 23.

[49] Saller, *Patronage*, 1.

[50] Joubert, *Benefactor*, 28; Jeremy Boissevain, *Friends of Friends: Networks, Manipulators and Coalitions* (New York: St. Martin's Press, 1974), 147–148.

µατοι; *Rhet.* 1361a43–1361b3)."⁵¹ Aristotle would rather the giver give altruistically without recompense in mind (*Nic. Eth.* 4.1.7). This falls in line with the discussion of reciprocity in Ancient Greece noted above. Joubert then argues that Seneca's presentation of exchange goes against the normal ethic of reciprocity inherent in Greco-Roman society.⁵² "Shameful self-centred motives, such as the wealth or exalted social position of the recipient (IV.3, 1–2), should be very far removed from the benefactor's mind."⁵³ Seneca also opposed agonistic battles (*Ben.* 1.1.8).⁵⁴ Rejecting a benefit is rejecting a relationship, asking for a benefit is asking for a relationship (*Ben.* 1.2.1; 6.42.1). Two broad categories of benefactor surface in Seneca's portrait: benefactors to individuals and groups. In the first category a benefit only qualifies as such (rather than being understood as a gift or something else) if it is given specifically to one person and is not simply the random blessing of being in the right group. The second kind of benefactor, however, bestowed "collective benefits upon his community."⁵⁵ This is called euergetism. Benefits were "edifices and pleasures to the citizens rather than alms to the poor."⁵⁶ It was assumed that a benefactor maintained his reputation by repeated benefactions and thus, "[g]enerally, euergetism was a long-term reciprocal relationship between a benefactor and his/her community."⁵⁷ Joubert concludes that most benefactors gave benefits to increase their own honor more than to alleviate troubles of the poor.⁵⁸

For this reason benefactors often preferred the "glamorous" benefits like games, festivals, monetary handouts, and spectacles. Joubert mentions Lucius Gastricus Regulus who acquired many offices (*aedile, prefect iure dicundo, duovir,* and *quinquennial duovir*) and was honored as ἀγωνοθέτης of the Tiberea Caesarea Sebastea, Ishmian and Caesarean games, and for

---

⁵¹ Joubert, *Benefactor*, 39–40. Aristotle does not belong to the Hellenistic era and this is one argument against Joubert's use of Aristotle. Crook's critique of Joubert's use of Aristotle will be presented below.

⁵² Joubert, *Benefactor*, 41. For the Greco-Roman ethic of reciprocity he refers to Hands, *Charities*, 26–48.

⁵³ Joubert, *Benefactor*, 43.

⁵⁴ Joubert, *Benefactor*, 44.

⁵⁵ Joubert, *Benefactor*, 51. See Danker, *Benefactor*; F. Quass, *Die Honoratiorenschicht in den Städten des griechischen Ostens: Untersuchungen zur politischen und sozialen Entwicklung in hellenistischer und römischer Zeit* (Stuttgart: Steiner Verlag, 1993), 26ff; Gauthier, *Les cités grecques et leurs bienfaiteurs*. Gauthier discusses the shift in emphasis that took place in the second century B.C. from benefactors to patrons of cities.

⁵⁶ Veyne, Murray, and Pearce, *Bread and Circuses*, 20; in Joubert, *Benefactor*, 53.

⁵⁷ Joubert, *Benefactor*, 55.

⁵⁸ Joubert, *Benefactor*, 57–58. For a summary of benefits conferred and their relationship to the New Testament, see, Danker, *Benefactor*, 393–416.

"his introduction of poetry contests, an athletic contest for girls, his renovation of buildings and the holding of a banquet for the people of the colony, etc."[59] He adds an inscription honoring Moschion who four times gave money to his city to alleviate financial burdens. Moschion also helped build a gymnaisium, fixed Alexander the Great's sanctuary, and "assumed the priesthood of Olympian Zeus."[60] These benefactors earned reputations for lavish expenditures for extreme projects. One may rescue a people from financial distress or provide entertainment facilities.

One example of a benefaction decree will show the ways that benefactors lavished gifts and how beneficiaries expressed their gratitude. Ptolemy V had done many great things for the benefit of the people of Egypt, so they responded with a lengthy declaration of his generosity and the honor due to him (27 March 196 B.C.). Benefits included "declarations of amnesty and pardon; some remission of taxes, rents, and debts; certain tax and public service exemptions for the priests; and generous gifts to the temples."[61] Since the decree spans several pages of written text, only pertinent excerpts will be reproduced here, followed by Danker's translation (*Sammelbuch* 8299; Danker, no. 31; *SEG* 8232; *OGIS* 90; *CIG* 3.4697):

Βασιλεύοντος τοῦ νέου καὶ παραλβόντος τὴν βασιλείαν παρὰ τοῦ πατρὸς κυρίου βασιλειῶν μεγαλοδόξου τοῦ τὴν Αἴγυπτον κατραστησαμένου καὶ τὰ πρὸς τοὺς θεοὺς εὐσεβοῦς ἀντιπάλων ὑπερτέρου τοῦ τὸν βίον τῶν ἀνθρώπων ἐπανορθώσαντος κυρίου τριακονταετηρίδων καθάπερ ὁ Ἡφαιστος ὁ μέγας βασιλέως καθάπερ ὁ Ἥλιος... Ἐπειδὴ βασιλυὲς Προλεμαῖος αἰωνόβιος ἠγαπημένος ὑπό τοῦ φθᾶ θεὸς Ἐπιφανὴς Εὐχάριστος ὁ ἐγ βασιλέως Προλεμαίου καὶ βασιλίσσης Ἀρσινοης θεῶν φιλοπατόρων κατὰ Πολλὰ εὐεργέτηκεν τά θ' ἱερὰ καὶ τοὺς ἐν αὐτοῖς ὄντας καὶ τοὺς ὑπὸ τὴν ἑαυτοῦ βασιλείαν τασσομένους ἄπαντας ὑπάρχων θεὸς ἐκ θεοῦ καὶ θεᾶς καθάπερ Προς ὁ τῆς Ἴσιος καὶ Ὀσιριος υἱός ὁ ἐπαμύνας τῶι πατρὶ αὐτοῦ Ὀσίρει τὰ πρὸς θεοὺς (ll. 1–2, 9–10)[62]

"In the reign of the young (King) – who has received the rule from his father – Glorious Lord of the Royal Crowns, who brought stablility to the land of Egypt and showed his piety in everything that pertains to the Gods, supreme over his enemies, who improved the people's lot, Lord of the Thirty Years' Festival; like Hephaistos the Great; a king like Helios ... Whereas Ever-Living King Ptolemy Beloved-of-Phtah God Epiphanes Eucharistos, son of King Ptolemy (IV) and Queen Arsinoe, the Gods Philopatores, has in many ways showed generosity to the temples and to those who dwell in them and to all who are

---

[59] Joubert, *Benefactor*, 52. He refers to J. H. Kent, *The Inscriptions 1926–1950* (Corinth: Results of Excavations VIII/3; Princeton: Princeton University Press, 1966), no. 153. I could not locate this resource in any library or online catalog.

[60] Carl Johann Fredrich and Friedrich Hiller von Gaertringen, eds., *Inschriften von Priene* (Berlin: Walter de Gruyter, 1968), no. 1.

[61] Danker, *Benefactor*, 206.

[62] Emil Kiessling, ed., *Sammelbuch Griechischer Urkunden aus Ägypten* (im Auftrag der Strassburger Wissenschaftlichen Gesellschaft von Friederich Presigke und Friedrich Bilabel; Selbstverlag in Kommission bei Otto Harrassowitz: Wiesbaden, 1955), 5.8299.

under his scepter, being a god, son of a god and a goddess – as is Horus, the son of Isis and Osiris, who avenged his father Osiris...."

The decree goes on to describe the various acts of generosity bestowed by the king upon the people. Feasts and festivals celebrating the king were established in his honor in this decree. The decree itself was then reproduced on "a stele of hard stone in sacred and demotic and Greek letters" and placed in "each of the temples comprising the first [and second and third rank, near the image of the immortal King]."[63] This decree follows most of the standard features of benefaction decrees. It begins by establishing the date and the authoritative body who initiated the decree, follows with a problem which was resolved by the benefactor and an elaborate recitation of the great deeds of the benefactor, and ends with a resolution to publicly honor the benefactor in various ways.

Joubert identifies a few important points where he thinks that patronage and benefaction depart in their meaning and the social perception of them.[64] In these two reciprocal relationships he finds differences in the content (goods and services) of what is exchanged and in the nature of the relationship inaugurated in the exchange. According to Joubert, Roman patronage focused on "landlords and peasant farmers, the *patronus-libertus* relationship, patronage of communities, the role of the emperor, client-friendships, brokerage, and the clienteles of individual Roman patrons." The social nature of the relationships also differed in that Roman patrons increased status differentials by their gifts. Greek benefactors would lose honor if they did not continue benefits or if they failed to return a gift that had been given in response to a previous benefit.[65] Greeks also had civic benefaction which provided for all people without distinction, not just on the fortunate few. "The basic character of euergetism was its *collective nature*," but in the case of individual exchanges or small group exchanges "the social relationship between individuals was instituted and kept in tact by *face-to-face exchanges* of services and counter services." According to Joubert, benefactors did not entrench status differentials with their benefit-exchanges.[66] It is possible that certain gifts and relationships could be seen under both terms (like the emperor's role). While "Patron" was a Roman title and "Savior" a Greek title, a worthy emperor could be called both by

---

[63] Danker, *Benefactor*, 211.

[64] Joubert cites a couple of authors as generally in line with his reading. John Nicols, "Pliny and the Patronage of Communities," *Hermes* 108 (1980): 365–385; Mitchell, "Greet the Friends." Batten follows Joubert and Ferrary in maintaining this distinction, cf. Alicia Batten, "God in the Letter of James: Patron or Benefactor?" *NTS* 50 (2004): 257–272; Ferrary, "Roman Political Patronage,"110.

[65] Joubert, *Benefactor*, 67.

[66] Joubert, *Benefactor*, 68.

the people.⁶⁷ In short, according to Joubert, benefaction is a group-oriented, non-exploitative relationship which did not perpetuate status differentials. Patronage, on the other hand, was primarily an individual-focused, exploitative relationship that entrenched status differentials.

Zeba Crook disagrees at this point with Joubert. He thinks that distinguishing between the two in the primary literature is nearly impossible since their different vocabularies are used in reference to both practices. First, he argues against Joubert's use of Aristotle to define benefaction because Aristotle does not claim to describe benefaction, but to provide the mean between two extremes. As was discussed above, in Aristotle's day reciprocity was still quite generalized and had not as yet become full-fledged benefaction. Second, Joubert's use of the term "benefaction" to describe giving between equals fits better under the category of balanced reciprocity since benefaction presumes that one party will assume a subservient position in the relationship (general reciprocity).⁶⁸ Third, he challenges Joubert's use of Seneca for two reasons. (1) Joubert takes from Seneca's *De Beneficiis* the notion that benefaction was not exploitative but was rather generous and selfless. But because Seneca appears to be writing prescriptively rather than descriptively one should not conclude that the ideal he desires is the reality he encounters. (2) In order to establish Joubert's case that *De Beneficiis* describes "Greek" benefaction which is non-exploitative and not "Roman" patronage which does exploit, Joubert must show for certain that Seneca intends only to describe the former and not the latter. It seems however that this cannot be proven, but instead that Seneca describes reciprocal exchanges between unequal parties (including benefaction and patronage) in general. "After all, Seneca is writing in Latin (thus the term euergetism would have been foreign to him) and as one firmly ensconced within the practices and institution of Roman patronage."⁶⁹ Crook also takes issue with Joubert's notion that in benefaction the recipient of the benefaction would return it with a benefaction and thus put the original giver in debt to him. "This is a puzzling interpretation of something that can be understood very differently, namely that the public discharging of one's reciprocity was intended to show that giving to the person/association in question was a risk-free and worthwhile endeavour."⁷⁰ Therefore, Crook contends, Joubert should not describe Paul's relation to the Jerusalem church as benefaction; it is instead gift exchange. "The recipient of a gift is obligated to return another *gift of equal or greater value*; the recipient of a benefaction or act of patronage is obli-

---

⁶⁷ On this see Joubert, *Benefactor*, 63–66; Cicero, *Verr.* 2.2.154.
⁶⁸ Crook, *Conversion*, 61–62.
⁶⁹ Crook, *Conversion*, 62.
⁷⁰ Crook, *Conversion*, 63.

gated to reciprocate by conferring honour, praise, gratitude and loyalty to a patron or benefactor."[71]

Crook claims that patronage and benefaction are not the exact same thing, but that they cannot be distinguished quite so clearly in the primary literature. Many NT scholars agree with Crook's stance,[72] but recent classical studies suggest that Joubert is probably closer to the truth. Joubert is correct to claim that *patrocinium* and benefaction are different. However, his assessment of how the two practices differ needs revision. Before identifying the differences between the two practices it will be beneficial to identify reasons for the difficulty in reading sources and differentiating the practices.

Differentiating between the two concepts is complicated by Roman fascination with Hellenistic culture and their general approach to foreign peoples. In his description of "Romanization in the East," Ramsay MacMullen suggests that Roman leaders, spokesmen, and common businessmen embraced Hellenism more than enforced their own culture.[73] He finds in Augustus and Cicero examples of the Roman imposition (or, better, non-imposition) of culture. He opens with reference to Cicero and Augustus and their belief that in Hellenism true civilization could be found. They did not impose Roman culture on the peoples, but rather took from them poetry, proverbs, art, and ways of living. This blurs the line between "Roman" and "Greek."[74] He finds examples in Miletus and other eastern cities of Romans inclining toward "fitting in" to the point that they even "deny their ancestral culture if not the advantages of their Roman citizenship and connections."[75] He thinks the Greeks in these regions were willing to receive more aggressive cultural change than the Romans attempted. Even though Latin names "appeared increasingly in the public record and might be called a form of Romanization...the customs, social or political, which accounted for their appearance were entirely Hellenistic."[76] He goes on to suggest that Rome did not seek to impose a uniform Roman law in the provinces, relatively low numbers of Romans immigrated to these areas,

---

[71] Crook, *Conversion*, 64. On this passage Danker and Joubert have a stronger case than Crook allows.

[72] E.g., Moxnes, "Patron-Client," 249; Neyrey, "God, Benefactor and Patron," 471 n. 22; Green, *Luke*, 270–271; idem, *Theology of Luke*, 114–115; Pao, *Thanksgiving*, 165; Parsons, *Luke*, 175–176.

[73] Ramsay MacMullen, *Romanization in the Time of Augustus* (New Haven: Yale University Press, 2000), 1–29.

[74] MacMullen, *Romanization*, 1–3. MacMullen refers to M. Denti "La scultura ellenistica delle regioni transpadane nel I secolo a. C.: problemi e prospettive di ricera," *Dialoghi di archeologia* 37 (1989): 9–26.

[75] MacMullen, *Romanization*, 5.

[76] MacMullen, *Romanization*, 5–6.

and Latin shrank from importance (in this era) without concerted efforts by new generations to reinforce it. These suggestions, which will be referred to in more detail below (section 2.2), point toward a low amount of Romanization in the east.

In regard to benefaction and patronage, R. MacMullen and A. Erskine argue that the conquered peoples continued to interact in Hellenistic ways (benefaction) and actually influenced their Roman rulers to do likewise. For example, Herod's Hellenistic love of honor (φιλοτιμία) compelled him to impress both those above and those below him. This thoroughly Hellenistic motivation actually infiltrated Roman ranks (Lucullus, Pompey, Aulus Gabinius, Caesar, Antony, Augustus) and they expressed themselves through euergetism to several Greek cities in properly Hellenistic ways.[77]

When Roman emperors took control of the east, Greek speakers responded quite often by describing them as the ultimate expression of the Hellenistic "benefactor." The role of the benefactor was "fundamental to the Greek conception of a king" (Arist. *Pol* 1310b34ff, 1286b10f; Polybius 5.11.6.).[78] The cult of the monarch attributed this role, in addition to savior, to the king.[79] Greeks had a vocabulary to describe great people and gods, but the Roman empire created a new phenomenon. Erskine contends that when Rome took control of the East the Greeks responded not primarily by adopting their vocabulary (*patrocinium*), but by adjusting the categories of benefaction. Rather than identifying an individual as a benefactor of a city, the Greeks developed the notion that Rome (collectively) was the benefactor to all (collectively). The phrase repeated throughout the inscriptions is Ῥωμαῖοι οἱ κοινοὶ εὐεργέται.[80] They surpassed previous notions of power by being insuperable and without rival. During the imperial period, Greeks began to identify powerful individuals (Julius Caesar, Augustus) as capable of benefiting all.[81] These individuals were thus described as "common benefactors." The phrase almost always comes in contexts in which Rome is not the subject. Mention is made of Rome being a common benefactor to

---

[77] MacMullen, *Romanization*, 22–24 esp. n. 86 for references.

[78] Erskine, "Common Benefactors," 71.

[79] Antiochus III and Attalus I receive these titles (*OGIS* 239 [Delos]; 291 [Pergamum]), Erskine, "Common Benefactors," 72.

[80] For examples among the local ruler cults see: Lysimachus *SIG*^{3} 372; Eumenes *OGIS* 267; Ptolemy III *OGIS* 75–78.

[81] Erskine identifies the following important works for each personality, "Common Benefactors," 81–87. Julius Caesar: A. E. Raubitschek, "Epigraphical Notes on Julius Caesar," *JRS* 44 (1954): 65–75. Augustus: Jeanne Robert and Louis Robert, "Bulletin Épigraphique," *Bull. Épigr.* 83 (1970): 362–488, 422–423, no. 422; Klaus Tuchelt, *Frühe Denkmäler Roms in Kleinasien: Beiträge zur archäologischen Überlieferung aus der Zeit der Republik und des Augustus* (Istanbuler Mitteilungen 23; Tübingen: Wasmuth, 1979), 62.

emphasize that whatever benefaction might come from an individual it has derived ultimately from the generosity of Rome.[82] Between Ancient Greece and imperial Rome notions of benefaction developed and eventually were employed to describe the new power.

Romanization, including *patrocinium*, did enter the Greek east, but it is necessary to make chronological and geographical distinctions. In describing the reign of Augustus, MacMullen comments, "The currents of influence, however, flowed in both directions, east and west." Three areas of Roman influence "stand out": notions of superiority (*maiestas*), favors (*fides, gratia, amicitia, patronus, clientele, patrocinium*), and triumphal display (*philotimia*).[83] Nicols concludes that it is imperative, however, to make a chronological distinction. These Roman concepts, including *patrocinium*, flourished in the time of Augustus, however at the end of his reign Augustus (possibly with the influence of Tiberius) regulated the ascription of honorific titles (including *patronus*, but not euergetes) among peregrine (foreign) communities (Cassius Dio, 56.25–26).[84] The following table illustrates Nicols' point:

Table 1: Epigraphical Attested Cases of Civic Patronage

	90 B.C–A.D. 11/12	A.D.13–117
Eastern Provinces	72	11
Western Provinces	22	61
Italy	27	44

Patrocinium consequently virtually disappeared in the eastern peregrine communities around A.D. 11/12 and did not come back into the mainstream until approximately A.D. 117. Nicols argues that Augustus saw in the bestowal of titles like πάτρων, σωτήρ, κτίστης, and θεός to senators a challenge to "the uniqueness of his own achievement and could not be allowed."[85] "Euergetes" did not present such a challenge since it carries a retrospective rather than prospective tense. It reflects an actual gift rather than the future relationship which inheres in *patrocinium*. Further, because neither patron nor client could take the other to court (Dionysos Halicarnassus 2.10.3) an evil senator may accrue clients and have a legal upper-

---

[82] Erskine, "Common Benefactors," 78–79.

[83] MacMullen, *Romanization*, 24.

[84] Nicols, "Patrons of Greek Cities," 81–108. Augustus himself does not have the title *patronus* attributed to him after 2 B.C., Nicols argues, because he preferred the title *pater patriae* with its universal connotations, ibid., 82.

[85] Nicols, "Patrons of Greek Cities," 86. Eilers contests Nicols' reason for the decline (edict of Augustus), but recognizes the same trend. Eilers, *Roman Patrons*, 164–165.

2.1 Benefaction and Patronage According to Ancient Sources

hand wherein he could not be brought to justice. "For both patron and client it was impious and immoral to accuse each other in court" (DionHal 2.10.3). Therefore one, like Verrus, who takes the title of πάτρων and σωτήρ is considered a "usurper" (Cicero *Verrines* 2.2.114, 154).[86]

Nicols claims that classicists widely acknowledge the decrease of civic patronage in the east at the same time that it "dramatically increases in the West."[87] He cites two areas of broad agreement which correspond with this general statement: (1) "the bulk of the Greek evidence on civic patronage is Late Republican or Augustan." (2) Greek speakers honored Roman magistrates with "traditional Hellenistic titles (euergetes, soter, theos, etc.) ... more frequently than they extended the imported title 'patron'." He claims euergetes and soter occur approximately four times more than patron in epigraphical data.[88] "Beginning with Tiberius, however, the traditional Hellenistic titles, with the exception of euergetes, cease to be used in respect to Roman magistrates."[89] Εὐεργέτης continued as an ascribed title, but πάτρων and σωτήρ ceased to be ascribed to rulers in foreign communities.

The necessary geographical distinctions correspond with the chronological distinction. During Augustus' reign there were many patrons of cities in the east. But no inscriptional evidence identifies any city patron in Palestine from Augustus to Trajan. Eilers identifies five inscriptions relevant to the topic of civic patrons in Syria and Palestine (C150–154).[90] These constitute the closest link to Palestine, but there is reason to question their attestation to the practice of *patrocinium* in the area. The reference to a patron in Laodiceia (*SEG* 27.976 = Eilers, *Roman Patrons*, C150) is questionable because in that inscription πάτρωνα is "heavily restored and the date and identities are uncertain."[91] There is attestation of an anonymous patron in Laodicea (Syria) which dates to the late Republic (C151 = *IGLS* 4.1258). Another inscription identifies a patron of Tyre under Nero (C153 = *PIR*² 1.139), too late for our investigation. Another inscription which is in close proximity to Palestine, but predates our period is a decree honoring M. Aemilius Scaurus from approximately 63–61 B.C. (C152 = *IGR* 3.1102; see section 2.2.5 *Tyre*). No inscriptions can be found from our period in Palestine or Syria which describe a city patron. This

---

[86] Nicols, "Patrons of Greek Cities," 86.
[87] Nicols, "Patrons of Greek Cities," 81.
[88] Nicols, "Patrons of Greek Cities," 81.
[89] Nicols, "Patrons of Greek Cities," 81–82.
[90] Four of these inscriptions will be discussed (C150–153), the fourth is excluded because its provenance is highly questionable (C154). Nicols was unable to locate any patrons in Egypt, Palestine, Syria, or mainland Greece between A.D. 11–117 with possible exception of Laodicea (*SEG* 27.976), Nicols, "Patrons of Greek Cities," 84.
[91] Nicols, "Patrons of Greek Cities," 84 n. 12; Eilers, *Roman Patrons*, C150.

corresponds with Nicols' larger point that *patrocinium* virtually disappeared in peregrine communities from A.D. 11 to 117.

A final point is necessary to mention which both Nicols and Eilers emphasize. In the inscriptions which Eilers surveys Greeks in the east have many labels for foreign benefactors (σωτήρ, εὐεργέτης, πρόξενος), but it is only the Romans for whom they transliterate the title πάτρων.[92] This suggests that Greeks in the east did not fully embrace the title, but saw in it something foreign and particularly Roman.[93] There is no example of a non-Roman being identified as a city patron in Eilers' study.

Though previous Roman historians equated the titles patron and benefactor this is not appropriate.[94] Eilers provides four arguments against equating the two titles.[95] (1) Latin did not have a direct equivalent to εὐ 'εργέτης (*ILS* 6633; 6744; *CIL* 10.416). (2) Εὐεργέτης describes an action more than a relationship (contra *patrocinium*). (3) Σωτήρ (providing safety) more closely approximates the action of a *patronus*.[96] (4) Benefaction could be bestowed, but patronage had to be requested and granted. Eilers provides an example of how patron and benefactor differ in his interpretation of *IGR* 4.305 (= C74). Julius Caesar was patron and benefactor of Pergamum, but savior and benefactor of all Greeks.

Ὁ δῆμος Γάϊον Ἰούλιον Γαίου υἱὸν Καίσαρα τὸν αὐτοκράτορα καὶ ἀρχιερέα ὕπατον τὸ δεύτερον τὸν ἑαυτοῦ πάτρωνα καὶ εὐεργέτην τῶν Ἑλλήνων ἁπάντων σωτῆρα καὶ εὐεργέτην εὐσεβείας ἕνεκα καὶ δικαιοσύνης
"The people (honoured) Gaius Iulius Caesar, son of Gaius, imperator and pontifex maximus, consul for the second time, their patron and benefactor, savior and benefactor of all Greeks, because of his piety and justice." Eilers, *Roman Patrons*, no. 74.

According to Eilers, Pergamum had asked for Caesar's patronage, but "all Greeks" could not make this request. Therefore the inscriber claims that Julius Caesar was patron of Pergamum but had provided safety (savior) and generosity (benefactor) to all Greeks.[97]

---

[92] His study includes "150 specific examples ... . in the epigraphy and literature of the late Republic and early empire," Eilers, *Roman Patrons*, 17–18.

[93] Eilers, *Roman Patrons*, 18. One of Nicols' conclusions involves the restoration of inscriptions in the east for this period (A.D. 11–117). Rather than "casually" restoring "πάτρωνα" one should prefer εὐεργέτην or κηδέμωνα (in, e.g., *BCH* 50.1926.443 n. 80 [for Memmius Regulus] and *IGR* 4.125 [for Hirrius Fronto Neratius Pansa]), Nicols, "Patrons of Greek Cities," 91.

[94] E.g., Bowersock, *Augustus and the Greek World*, 13.

[95] Eilers, *Roman Patrons*, 110–111.

[96] W. Ameling, "Lucius Licinius in Chios," *ZPE* 77 (1989): 98–100, 100 n. 18.

[97] Eilers, *Roman Patrons*, 184–185.

Excursus: *A Classicist Critique of Saller's Definition of Patronage*

In discussions of patron-client relationship in the NT it is common to use Saller's three-fold definition in order to identify patrons, but Eilers has recently demonstrated the error which inheres in this process. Saller takes a cue from Proculus' description of Rome expressing authority over other regions through the metaphor of the patron-client relationship (Ulp. *Digest* 49.15.7.1).[98] But Eilers disputes the conclusion which he draws from this. Saller suggests that Proculus gives the "determinants" of patron-client relationships as *auctoritas*, *dignitas*, and *vires*, and that these three therefore substantiate the presence of *patrocinium*. This leads to Saller's often cited three-fold definition of the determinants of patronage: (1) asymmetry, (2) long term relationship, and (3) reciprocal. Eilers objects. It is not the case that when asymmetry and authority are mentioned a patron-client relationship is in view, but rather that when a patron-client relationship is in view there must also be issues of authority and asymmetry. Saller tries to argue from the general (description) to the specific (relationship), but Eilers insists that one can only legitimately argue from the specific (relationship) to the general (description).[99] "Proculus is not saying that relationships of inequality are by their nature patron-client, but that patron-client relationships – like Rome's relations with its weakest subjects – were marked by significant inequality."[100] Social scientists have adopted the terminology of patron-client from Saller's definition and reapplied it to modern cultures. Eilers suggests that they have not always understood the Roman world from which the term derives. In the process of taking the definition into the social sciences the definition of patron-client changes from its Roman expression. Also, when socio-historians reapply the socio-historical model derived from the Roman sources back onto other Roman sources the new model is not always helpful. In the process of becoming a social science model it has lost its specificity and no longer can contain only relationships which fall under the category of *patrocinium*, but may now include *suffragium*, literary patronage, and most other relationships as long as they are asymmetrical, long term, and reciprocal (as in Saller's definition).[101] Confusion about terminology, specifically for English speakers, has crept in because of our dependency on the Romantic languages. We employ, for example, the term "literary patronage" to describe a writer who receives financial support from a patron. The Romans had such an endowment as well, but literary writers did not see themselves as clients. Precision is necessary in such an environment because of the risk of importing foreign elements into relationships which did not exist in the ancient culture. Moderns call patronage the practice of appointing someone special authority in public service, and the Romans practiced such appointing as well. But they never called the parties involved *patronus* and *cliens* respectively, nor did they refer to the practice as *patrocinium* or *patronatus*. When Romans did such things they called it *suffragium*. No evidence assumes that patrons were expected to provide *suffragium* for

---

[98] Saller, *Patronage*, 52, 60–61.

[99] Eilers, *Roman Patrons*, 12–13.

[100] Eilers, *Roman Patrons*, 13. Eilers also goes against the common assumption that the term *cliens* is sparse in the ancient sources because it was offensive to be identified as inferior. He interprets the passage typically cited in this vein as not supporting this conclusion (Cicero, *Off.*, 2.69; Seneca, *Ben.* 2.23.3). He rather thinks it refers to a class of people for whom clientage itself was abhorrent (not just the title "client"). Statues erected by clients in honor of patrons suggest to him that some clients took great pride in being connected to the honorable men of their day, Eilers, *Roman Patrons*, 15–16.

[101] Eilers, *Roman Patrons*, 5–7.

cliens, nor that those who provided *suffragium* were referred to as *patroni*.[102] Eilers details a few different understandings among classicists of what patrons did for their cities.[103] Two basic approaches emerge. (1) Patrons were a "part of the apparatus of the government of the empire" (J. M. Reynolds, J. Touloumakos, W. Eck, M. Gelzer, T. Wiedemann).[104] (2) Patrons functioned as civic benefactors (Harmand, Nicols).[105] Spitzl connects both aspects.[106] Early in the Republic *patronus* could mean advocate (in a legal sense) without implying a patron-client relationship.[107] Patrons could provide mediation for provinces with Rome (*IG Bulg.* i². 314a = C31). After going through several examples (esp. *Aphrodisias and Rome*, doc. 3) Eilers concludes that patronal responsibilities were varied and cannot be confined to a "list of the specific responsibilities that patrons were expected to fulfil for client cities and allow it to define for us the extent of a patron's obligations. Patronal responsibility was by nature general and non-specific."[108]

2.1.3 Defining Patrocinium *and Benefaction*

A broad level of agreement unites descriptions of *patrocinium* and benefaction despite continuing debate whether they are one or two modes of interaction. In the following paragraphs areas of overlap and distinction will be given. I begin with areas of similarity between *patrocinium* and benefaction. There are seven main areas where patronage and benefaction generally overlap: asymmetrical relationship; disparity between parties in access to certain goods and services; non-legal/contractual relationship; reciprocity and relationship expected; increase in honor intended; potentially viewed with either favor or distaste by the general population; relationship to gods can be expressed in these terms; and the language of grace predominates.

The areas of overlap between patronage and benefaction are significant and fairly consistent though it is necessary to nuance at points. To begin with, both patronage and benefaction involve asymmetrical relationships.[109] It is assumed that the patron/benefactor is a person full of fine attributes (ἀρετή, σπουδή, ἀνήρ ἀγαθός, εὐεργέτης, σωτήρ, χρηστός, εὐσέβεια, δἰ καιοσύνῃ, *liberalitas, benignitas, gratia, fides, beneuolentia, amor, existi-*

---

[102] Eilers, *Roman Patrons*, 3–4.

[103] Eilers, *Roman Patrons*, 84–108.

[104] J. M. Reynolds, "Review of Harmand, *Un aspect social et politique*," *RBPh* 37 (1959): 1149–1151; Touloumakos, "Gemeindepatronat"; W. Eck, *Die staatliche Organisation Italiens in der hohen Kaiserzeit* (Vestigia 28; Munich, 1979), 15 n. 27; Gelzer, *Roman Nobility*, 86–101; T. E. J. Wiedemann, *Adults and Children in the Roman Empire* (London: Routledge, 1989), 132.

[105] Harmand, *Aspect*, 358–385; Nicols, "Pliny"; idem, *The Patronage of Communities* (forthcoming), ch. 4.

[106] T. Spitzl, *Lex Municipii Malacitani* (Vestigia 36; Munich: Beck, 1984), 76.

[107] Eilers, *Roman Patrons*, 88–89; Brunt, "*Amicitia* in the Late Roman Republic," 372–376, 405.

[108] Eilers, *Roman Patrons*, 94–95.

[109] Here, correctly, Eisenstadt and Roniger, *Patrons*, 55.

matio, dignitas).¹¹⁰ The recipient (beneficiary or client) may possess these qualities as well, but they lack the means to express them. The benefactor or patron can meet the needs of the less fortunate by expressing his greatness. Benefactors thus receive titles like κηδεμών, εὐεργέτης, σωτήρ, κτίστης, or πρόξενος.¹¹¹ Disparity exists, though the distance between the parties can vary. Earlier studies questioned whether anyone other than the emperor could be called "patron", but now it is agreed that though he is the epitome of the patron others can be so named.¹¹² The major means by which needs are met is the patron/benefactor's access to certain goods and services unavailable to the recipients. Goods held at the fingertips of patrons and benefactors differ, but they are similar in their special privilege to regularly unavailable resources.

Both benefactors and patrons expect a relationship to begin with their generosity, but both could also be viewed as exploitation. These relationships are entered into voluntarily and for the most part they can be disbanded voluntarily as well. No contracts tie the parties together, only social obligation and the inner force of honor binds them. There were thoughts, at times, of legalizing reciprocity which probably tells us all we need of the gut reaction toward those who did not follow proper procedure (cf. Seneca *Ben.* 3.6.1–3.7.1). Neither patrons nor benefactors give from pure altruism, but rather they expect to receive something in return. Reciprocity is the norm, and society frowns when it is withheld. Some form of honor should be bestowed upon the patron or benefactor in light of the show of generosity. Recipients of benefactions typically erected public monuments declaring the generous act.¹¹³ By doing so they showed their own honor and worthiness to be so treated by other benefactors. Reciprocity toward patrons was also expressed publicly. Clients were expected to show loyalty (*fides*; πίστις) over the long term. This became public when clients followed the patron into various spheres (political, economic, and social), assisting where possible (Horace *Ep.* 1.7.9; Martial 2.18; 2.57; 6:48).¹¹⁴ As the network of clients increased so did the reputation of the pa-

---

[110] The Greek terms come from Danker, *Benefactor*, 317–331, and the Latin from Verboven, *Economy*, 35–48. These lists could be expanded.

[111] Ferrary, "Hellenistic World," 105–106; Eilers, *Roman Patrons*, 17–18.

[112] Both Nicols and Eilers produce lists of patrons other than the emperor in Greek cities in the east. Nicols, "Patrons of Greek Cities"; Eilers, *Roman Patrons*, 191–292; cf. the lists in G. Chiranky, "Rome and Cotys: Two Problems," *Athenaeum* 60 (1982): 461–481; Tuchelt, *Frühe Denkmäler*, 61–63, 196–232.

[113] For details see Bradley H. McLean, *An Introduction to Greek Epigraphy of the Hellenistic and Roman Periods from Alexander the Great Down to the Reign of Constantine (323 B.C.–A.D.337)* (Ann Arbor: University of Michigan Press, 2002), 218–225.

[114] Crook, *Conversion*, 71.

tron. Reputation often translated into political power.[115] Clients sometimes erected statues in honor of their patrons as well.[116] Nevertheless, both patrons and benefactors could be looked on favorably or unfavorably by the general population (e.g., patron – Dionysos Halicarnassus 2.10.3; Cicero *Verrines* 2.2.114, 154; benefactor – Albinus, Ptolemy II).[117] Exploitation is not one of the differences between benefactors and patrons as Joubert suggests since both patrons and benefactors could exploit their position. Seneca was compelled to write seven books outlining the right attitudes and motivations for generosity and reciprocity probably because of its abuse in his day. Both patronage and benefaction could be exploited.

Patronage and benefaction surface in religious expression. Seneca and Dio Chrysostom remark upon the role of the gods as benefactors hoping that humans would aspire to that greatness. Different authors use the language of benefaction to describe the activity of the gods (Asclepius *Sacred Tales* 2.294.8; 4.323.14; 4.337.11; 4.329.16; *Speech of Asclepius* 39.19; Philo *Plant*. 90).[118] The role of χάρις in the Greco-Roman reciprocity system has only recently been investigated, but the findings have been significant. Harrison argues that "by the first-century A.D. χάρις had become the central leitmotiv of the hellenistic reciprocity system."[119] In numerous inscriptions and literary works the language of grace is ubiquitous. In a similar manner as was discussed in regard to the Ancient Greek reciprocity system, grace was used on all sides of the exchange (e.g., giver, receiver, attitudes, gift, nature of gift). This general description gives the major areas of overlap between the two practices. More specific expressions of patronage or benefaction will be inserted, where appropriate, in subsequent chapters.

---

[115] Eisenstadt and Roniger, *Patrons*, 60.

[116] Eilers, *Roman Patrons*, 15–16.

[117] The following have been adduced as examples of men/tyrants desiring to be called benefactors with the commentator who identified the man in parenthesis. Albinus in Josephus *Ant*. 20.253 and security officials in Hieropolis in A.D. 100 (Danker, *Benefactor*, 294); Ptolemy II (Luce, *Luke*, 333; Danker, *New Age*, 348); cf. kings generally without tyrannical undertones in Dio Chrysostom *Or*. 66.2; 75.7–8 (Nock, "Soter and Euergetes," 2.724–725). Self-proclamation as a benefactor was common among both the tyrannical and the benevolent. "Autobiographical" inscriptions in which the rich broadcasted their generosity were quite common (e.g., *OGIS* 383; *IGR* 3.159; *SIG* 814), Danker, *Benefactor*, 42–44. On the exploitation of patronage, Nicols builds his case for the decline of *patrocinium* in the east in part because of the legal problems entailed with corrupt patrons who took advantage of the fact that they could not be brought to court by clients. They would exploit this aspect of *patrocinium* to their advantage so Augustus responded by outlawing *patrocinium* in the peregrine communities, Nicols, "Patrons of Greek Cities," 86–87.

[118] Crook, *Conversion*, 78; Neyrey, "God, Benefactor and Patron," 473.

[119] Harrison, *Language*, 2.

2.1 Benefaction and Patronage According to Ancient Sources

The discussion of Joubert and Crook allows for the similarities and differences between benefaction and patronage to come to light, but there is further differentiation which is necessary because of the heavy dependence upon Saller's definition of patronage and recent classical studies on *patrocinium*. More recent works on *patrocinium* clarify the nature of the Roman practice. It appears that classical scholars separate benefaction from *patrocinium* quite clearly.[120] There are five main differences between patron and benefactor. (1) Benefactor is an honorary title given to one who expressed a significant amount of generosity toward an individual or, usually, group. A relationship ensued, but "benefactor" does not in itself describe a relationship. *Patrocinium* describes a specific relationship between two individuals or an individual and a group which did not necessarily entail expressions of generosity. It primarily involved legal protection, but included any sort of activity on behalf of the client.

(2) There is a difference in the nature of the benefits. Daily survival matters (food, jobs, etc.) were given by patrons, but occasional luxury items (buildings, streets, games, etc.) came from benefactors.[121] Patronage tended to deal with necessities of life (food, jobs, legal protection, advice, etc.) while benefactions tended to look more like luxury goods (stadiums, amphitheaters, roads, temples, etc.). A patron might provide a daily food allowance to a client or offer legal help in a time of crisis. Patrons had access to what sociologists call "first-order" goods, namely "land, jobs, goods, funds, power ... information," and access to the highest authorities.[122] Benefactions might be described as a bit more "over-the-top." When Herod built "Apollo's temple at Rhodes, at his own expense," Josephus describes this as one of Herod's benefactions (εὐεργεσίας; *Ant.* 16.147). When a benefactor offered the people salvation (e.g., military defeat of an enemy), εὐεργεσία would be used to describe the rescue (*SIG* 174; cf. *IG* II² 110):

[M]ενέλαος Πελαγῶν εὐεργέτ[ης]
Ἐπὶ Χαριχλείδου ἄρχοντες ἐπὶ τῆς Οἰνηΐδος ἕχτης πρυτανείας
῎δοξεν τῆι βουλῆι καὶ τῶι δήμωι Οἰνεῒς ἐπρυτάνευεν Νιχι[ό]στραρος ἐγραμμάτευεν Χαριχλῆς Λευχονοεὺς ἐπεστάλ[τ]ει Σάτρρυρος εἶπεν ἐπειδὴ Τιμόθεος ὁ στρατηγὸς

---

[120] E.g., Eilers, *Roman Patrons*, ch. 4; J. Nicols "Civic Patronage in Ancient Rome," (Department of History, University of Oregon, typescript, 1995), 11; Bowditch, *Horace*, 15.

[121] Crook, *Conversion*, 65.

[122] Bruce Malina, "Patron and Client," *Forum* 4 (1988): 2–32, 12. Access to such goods stemmed from the legal position held by most patrons before the Augustan era. Ferrary shows that the title patron was largely, but not exclusively, held by magistrates and senators before Augustus since they could protect cities and hold back harsh treatment of citizens. This changed with Augustus because of the monarchical, as opposed to oligarchical, character of the new empire. Ferrary, "Hellenistic World," 110–113.

ἀποφα[ί|νε]ι Μενέλαον τὸν Πελαγόνα καὶ αὐτὸν συνπολεμο[ῦ|ντα] καὶ χρήματα παρέχοντα εἰς τὸν πόλεμον τὸν πρ|ὸς] Χαλχιδέας καὶ πρὸς ᾿Αμφίπολιν ἐψηφίσθαι τῆι β|[ουλ]ῆι προσάγειν αὐτὸν εἰς τὸν δῆμον εἰς τὴν πρώ|[την] ἐκκλησίαν γνώμην δὲ Ξυνβάλλεσθαι τῆς βουλῆ|ς ε]ἰς τὸν δῆμον ὅτι δοχεῖ τῆι βουλῆι ἐπαινέσαι μὲ|[ν αὐ]τὸν ὅτι ἀνὴρ ἀγαθός ἐστιν καὶ ποιεῖ ὅτι δύναται| ἀγ]αθὸν τὸν δῆμον τὸν ᾿Αθηναίων ἐπιμ̣ λεῖσθαι | [δὲ] αὐτοῦ καὶ τοὺς στρατηγοὺς τοὺς ὄντας περ|[ὶ Μα]κεδονιαν ὅπως ἄν ἐάν του δέηται τυνχά|[νηι]. εἶναι δὲ καὶ εὐρέσθαι αὐτῶι παρὰ τοῦ δήμο|[υ ἐ]άν τι δύνηται καὶ ἄλλο ἀγαθόν Καλέσαι δὲ [καὶ| Με]νέλαον ἐπι ξένια εἰς τὸ πρυτανεῖον εἰς [αὔριον. | Σάτυ]ρος εἶπεν τὰ μὲν ἄλλα καθάπε[ρ τῆι βουλῆι | ἐπει]δὴ [δ]ὲ καὶ οἱ πρόγονοι οἱ Με[νελάου εὐεργέται ἦσαν] τοῦ δήμο τοῦ ᾿Αθη[ναίων εἶναι καὶ | Μενέλαον εὐεργέ]τη[ν --]

"Menelaos of Pelagonia, Benefactor in the archonship of Charikleides, in the sixth prytaneia of Oineis. Resolution of the Council and the People. The tribe of Oineis was presiding, | Nikostratos was clerk, Charikles of Leukonia was chairman. Satyros made the motion: WHEREAS General Timotheus proposes Menelaos of Palagonia, who campaigned with him and furnished material for the war against the Chalkidians and against Amphipolis, be it resolved by the Council | to bring him before the next assembly of the People and to present to the People the decision of the Council: that the Council resolves to commend him as a good man, who does whatever good he can for the people of Athens, | and also decrees that the generals in Macedonia are to show their concern for him, so that he receives whatever he needs; and (be it further resolved) that the People give consideration to other ways in which they can reward him and that they invite Menelaos to meals at the magistrates' hall, beginning on [the morrow].|(Amendment)[Saty]ros made the motion: All other matters shall be dealt with as determined by [the Council]. And whereas all the forbears of Menelaos were benefactors of the people of Athens, be it resolved that [Menelaos be considered benefactor - - -]." (Danker, *Benefactor*, 87–88, no. 15; capital letters original)

In the inscription (362–363 B.C.), the people praise Menelaos for aiding in the battle against the Chalkidians and Amphipolis and eventually attaining victory. The council agrees to reciprocate the valor with special privileges including the bestowal of εὐεργέτης as an honorific title. Benefactors often sought to relieve their people from the trials they endured by providing liberation and salvation. This sometimes took the specific form of forgiveness of debts (Esther 8:12 LXX; *CIL* III^2, 769–799; *IGR* III, 739).[123]

(3) The recipient of a benefaction could ascribe the title of benefactor to the bestower of the benefit (thereby inspiring further generosity). *Patrocinium* must be entered by approaching a potential patron and requesting his

---

[123] Danker, *Benefactor*, 401–402, nos. 49B (Esther 8:12 LXX), 43 (*CIL* III^2, 769–799), 19 (*IGR* III, 739); Hans Volkmann, *Res Gestae Divi Augusti: Das Monumentum Ancyranum* (Kleine Texte für Vorlesungen und Übungen 29–30; Berlin: De Gruyter, 1969); E. Loewy in *Reisen im Lykien, Milyas und Kibyratis* (ed. Eugene Petersen, Adolf Hermann, and F. von Luschan; Reisen in südwestlichen Kleinasien 2; Vienna: Gerold, 1889), 76–133, no. 161.

patronage. Aulus Gellius appears to give a concise definition of *patrocinium* in his description of the initiation of the relationship.[124]

Qui sese ... in fidem patrociniumque nostrum dedierunt
"those who have committed themselves to our trust and patronage" (Gellius *NA* 5.13.2; trans. Eilers)

A difference probably exists between civic and personal patronage in this regard since the initiation of a personal patronage relationship may have been less formal.[125] *Patrocinium* is a Roman relationship that must be entered into by an initiatory act usually on the part of the client.[126]

Two other differences have been treated above and only need reiterating here. (4) Greeks ascribed the title benefactor to both Greeks and Romans, adopting the expanded version "common benefactors" for the emperor, but both Greeks and Romans reserved the title *patronus* to Romans. This is understandable since the primary role of the patron in its early forms was representation before Roman authority and one expects a Roman (usually a senator) to have such connections. (5) *Patrocinium* declined sharply in the east with the end of Augustus' reign and did not return until Trajan (A.D. 11–117).[127] Euergetism, however, remained a commonly employed category of description in the east throughout this era.

2.1.4 Criteria for Detecting Patrocinium or Benefaction

If it is assumed that these two expressions of reciprocity are equally likely to surface in any given society unfortunate results may follow. Much of our knowledge of patronage derives from sources in the western empire. It must be emphasized again that significant differences exist between the Latin west and the Greek east during the early Roman Empire. Recent works by Ramsay MacMullen, Warwick Ball, and Fergus Millar caution that the east in the early Empire continued to be quite Hellenistic and had not (yet) been fully overcome by Romanization.[128] Cultural influences

---

[124] Eilers, *Roman Patrons*, 19. *Aphrodisias and Rome* doc. 3 provides an extended case for Eilers, but cannot be treated here because of its length and the complexity of the argument. See ibid., 23–25.

[125] Verboven, "Review of Eilers, *Roman Patrons*."

[126] This is one burden of Eilers, *Roman Patrons*, 19–83.

[127] Nicols claims that *patrocinium* changed character in this interval as it morphed to become practically synonymous with benefaction, Nicols, "Patrons of Greek Cities," 93.

[128] MacMullen, *Romanization*; Ball, *Rome*; Fergus Millar, *Rome, the Greek World, and the East* III: *The Greek World, the Jews and the East* (ed. Hannah Cotton; Chapel Hill: University of North Carolina Press, 2006); idem, *Rome, the Greek World, and the East* II: *Government, Society and Culture in the Roman Empire* (with Guy M. Rogers; Chapel Hill: University of North Carolina Press, 2004); idem, *Rome, the Greek World, and the East* I: *The Roman Republic and the Augustan Revolution* (with Guy M. Rogers;

went both ways, and often Hellenism won out. MacMullen provides a succinct statement for the minimal Romanization in the east.[129] Romanization in the east was very slight for three main reasons. First, Romans (from Italy) had grown accustomed to thinking that the Hellenistic way was civilized and superior. When they settled into new lands they felt no compulsion to convert a "barbarian" people to Roman ways since they would not thus judge a Hellenistic society. The Roman outlook on new cultures was relatively more relaxed and less intrusive. Second, sheer numbers forbid them from exerting any kind of majority opinion and they did not exert their legal authority to institute change. Though some Romans moved to the east they did not inhabit every city and, when they did inhabit one, they did not create a new majority culture. They were still outnumbered. Third, without concerted efforts by Roman immigrants to promote their culture it simply died out in a couple of generations. In the end, MacMullen claims, "captive Greece took Rome captive."[130]

Therefore, as one progresses further east in the Roman Empire, the likelihood of western, or Latin, cultural expressions shrinks and the presence of Hellenism or eastern influences grows more probable. With the more general concept of benefaction being Hellenistic and the more specific concept of patronage being Roman, it is intrinsically more likely that benefaction will be found. Blanket statements and assumptions must be resisted, however, because individuals and groups of people can plausibly construct pockets of Romanization regardless of how far east they live. Some of the Herodian kings discussed in the next chapter spent substantial time in Rome and could have created one such pocket of Romanization. It is also possible that neither benefaction nor patronage will be found as Palestine is investigated.

With all the ambiguity between the terms and the overlap of practice and terminology two questions must be asked: How can one determine if patronage is being practiced (self-consciously perhaps) rather than benefaction? How can one determine if benefaction is present? In order to detect and confidently identify patronage rather than benefaction, a few factors would have to converge. (1) A high level of Romanization. It might only involve a single person or a small group, but their affinity with Ro-

---

Chapel Hill: University of North Carolina Press, 2002); idem, *The Roman Republic and the Augustan Revolution* (Studies in the History of Greece and Rome; Chapel Hill: University of North Carolina Press, 2002); idem, *The Roman Near East: 31 BC – AD 337* (Cambridge: Harvard University Press, 1993). Ball would go a step further to say that the Near East still retained many of its unique cultures to a great extent. Even Hellenism had not infiltrated to the extent normally assumed (since, e.g., Hengel).

[129] MacMullen, *Romanization*, 1–29.

[130] MacMullen, *Romanization*, 29. For similar sounding statements that claim the east eventually captivated Rome see Ball, *Rome*, 1–5.

2.1 Benefaction and Patronage According to Ancient Sources

man culture would have to be quite high. (2) The superior person (potential patron) involved in the relationship must be considered "Roman" by the persons in the inferior position (potential clients). Since only Romans were ascribed the title "patron," the person who practices *patrocinium* must be considered Roman by the audience. (3) Direct verbal evidence. Beyond the general verbiage of reciprocity, one would need to find specific terminology used consistently apart from benefaction terminology. Since this study deals with Palestine, vocabulary could come in Greek, Latin, or Aramaic. Greek will be of primary importance, and so it is necessary to point out potentially important terms. H. J. Mason identifies several Greek words commonly adopted in place of Latin terms. These are not "equivalents" but they are suggestive of the Roman practice of *patrocinium* in a Greek language context. He lists as follows: κηδεμονία, πατρωνεία, and προστασία for *patronatus*; κηδεμών, πάτρων, πατρώνης, προστάτης for *patronus*; πατρ ωνεύω for *patronus esse*; κλίενς and πελάτης for *cliens*; ἐπιτροπή for *fides*.[131] (4) Evidence that the interactions line up sufficiently with the practice of *patrocinium* as detected elsewhere. Language can be a good indicator of the understanding held by the author, but the lines are blurred when authors conflate the sets of terminology. Since both Hellenists and Romans have used both *patrocinium* and benefaction vocabulary to describe either practice, it is necessary to show that *patrocinium* language is being connected to an appropriate expression of *patrocinium*. These four criteria could be combined to provide a high level of plausibility of the practice of *patrocinium* even if questions remain.

To establish the practice of benefaction may be difficult as well. Five criteria can be set forth: (1) A significant level of Hellenization would have to be established. Again this may only involve a significantly Hellenized individual or group rather than the entire population. (2) Written sources intended to be read by locals which assume or employ benefaction concepts can be another clue. When people write to their own they do not intentionally adopt foreign categories, perhaps for fear of being thought an "outsider." (3) A significant amount of material (epigraphy, governmental structure, public expressions) not necessarily aimed at the local population, but nevertheless consistently viewed by them, could indicate awareness if not practice of benefaction. Harrison compellingly argues that epigraphy gives a better insight into common knowledge than literature since it was more widely read.[132] (4) If a relational connection can be established between a person who definitely operates within the benefaction paradigm and others (in our case Jesus and the apostles), then the plausibility of the

---

[131] Hugh J. Mason, *Greek Terms for Roman Institutions: A Lexicon and Analysis* (American Studies in Papyrology 13; Hakkert: Toronto, 1974), 179, 187, 195.

[132] Harrison, *Language*, 24.

latter comprehending the practice grows. (5) The fifth point is both a disclaimer and a criterion. Following his monumental work on benefaction and epigraphy, Danker concludes that "the Graeco-Roman world had no technical generic expression for the civic-minded benefactor."[133] He suggests that the ancients worked from a "common stock" of phrases and semantic fields. Therefore, while terms like εὐεργεσία, εὐεργέτης, σωτήρ, χάρις, φιλοτιμία, εὐχαριστέω, ἀνήρ ἀγαθός, φίλος, κτίστης, κηδεμών, and προξενός have been consistently connected with benefaction, their presence is not necessary to establish the presence of the benefaction concept. As Danker puts it, this "depth-structural reality... breaks into various thematic patterns and comes to linguistic expression in numerous modes and forms."[134] Rather than looking for one or two specific terms, a confluence of terms and ideas will raise the likelihood of the presence of benefaction.

2.1.5 Methodology and Focus of Study

As we have seen it is not safe to assume the presence of *patrocinium* or euergetism in any ancient culture. Unfortunately, many NT scholars have begun with this assumption, or proceeded with the sociological category patron-client without explicitly identifying the difference. Moving forward with this assumption has the detrimental effect of importing foreign ideas and ways of interacting into a culture. For this reason, and others (see chapter 1), E. A. Judge calls for a city by city investigation before generalizations are made. M. Sawicki and M. Goodman echo this call by claiming that Palestine should not be treated as part of a monolithic "Mediterranean" society. A "regional perspective" is needed. That is, cities and smaller areas should be investigated on a case by case basis to see if they, or individuals or smaller groups within them, engaged in either *patrocinium* or euergetism. So far work has been done on Thessalonika, Corinth, Philippi, and Ephesus,[135] but at this point no extended treatment of

---

[133] Danker, *Benefactor*, 43.

[134] Danker, *Benefactor*, 27; cf. Ferrary, "Hellenistic World," 105.

[135] Citations found in Harrison, *Language*, 16–18. Thessalonika: H. Hendrix, "Benefactor/Patron Networks in the Urban Environment: Evidence from Thessalonica," *Semeia* 56 (1991): 39–58; Christoph Vom Brocke, *Thessaloniki, Stadt des Kassander und Gemeinde des Paulus: eine frühe christliche Gemeinde in ihrer heidnischen Umwelt* (WUNT 125; Tübingen: Mohr Siebeck, 2001); Corinth: Chow, *Patronage and Power*; Thomas E. Clarke, *Above Every Name: The Lordship of Christ and Social Systems* (Woodstock Studies 5; Ramsey: Paulist Press, 1980); B. Winter, *Seek the Welfare of the City: Christians as Benefactors and Citizens* (FCCGRW; Grand Rapids: Eerdmans, 1994); Philippi: Lukas Bormann, *Philippi: Stadt und Christengemeinde zur Zeit des Paulus* (NovTSupp 78; Leiden: Brill, 1995); Ephesus: G. H. R. Horsley, "The Inscriptions of Ephesos and the New Testament," *NovT* 34/2 (1992): 106–168.

Palestine has been undertaken. The following section addresses this lacuna.

Since the Mediterranean world can no longer be understood as a monolithic culture, a regional investigation of individual cultures is needed. The following investigation of Palestine proceeds in this direction. It begins in Galilee, with limits enforced by the available archaeological and literary evidence. Judea is addressed next, with special attention paid to Jerusalem. Some surrounding regions will then be treated, notably Caesarea Maritima, Samaria, some smaller cities in Philip's tetrarchy, and Tyre. After this a personality perspective will be attempted. Since Romanization or Hellenization can infiltrate through a prominent personality, and may trickle down through various relationships, it seems appropriate to examine the extent of cultural influences on important personalities in Palestine. Four members of the Herodian family, Herod I,[136] Antipas, Philip, and Agrippa I, need examination. The approach to these regions and personalities will follow Jensen's recent work on Herod Antipas.[137] He advocates a "contextualized source-oriented approach, which focuses on the sources available and thereafter applies an appropriate model, since the models otherwise seem to have a deterministic influence on the results."[138] The models he initially distances himself from are sociological models (e.g., economic-conflict) which have generally had a deterministic influence on our subject (patron-client model), too.

2.2 Benefaction and Patronage in Palestine

Before the regional and personality investigations can begin an introduction to Hellenization and Romanization in Palestine and newer approaches to source material are appropriate. For those who do not simply jump from sociological models to interpreting texts, different procedures take precedence. Sometimes if one discovers high levels of Hellenization in Palestine he suggests that benefaction can be assumed. Joubert uses this equation. He claims that being from Galilee would mean awareness of Greco-Roman benefaction based on Horsley's picture of the Hellenization of Galilee.[139] He lists as evidence for this assumption that 40% of inscriptions were in

---

[136] The title "Herod I" is preferred in this monograph rather than "Herod the Great" as is common, or "Herod the king" as in Richardson, *Herod*, 12, esp. Appendix B.

[137] Jensen, *Antipas*.

[138] Jensen, *Antipas*, 34.

[139] Joubert, *Benefactor*, 99; Richard A. Horsley, *Archaeology, History, and Society in Galilee: The Social Context of Jesus and the Rabbis* (Valley Forge: Trinity Press International, 1996), 107–130.

Greek and that there were cosmopolitan urban centers, Greek buildings, art, gymnasiums, and stadiums. This picture of Galilee will be critiqued in what follows, but here it is instructive that a connection between Hellenization and benefaction is made explicit. Hellenization can indicate the presence of benefaction, but this fact alone does not suffice to prove the point. It is a further mistake to take Hellenization as evidence for *patrocinium*. *Patrocinium* more directly derives from Roman culture so a high level of Romanization can be one component of an argument for its presence. Preceding the regional perspective, an overview of scholarly views on Hellenization in Palestine will provide a general picture of the region as a whole. So this study begins with a general look at Hellenization in Palestine before advancing to a specific look at Hellenization in individual cities and regions. The shift, which will be identified in the following section, in the understanding of Hellenization in Palestine comes in large part because of newer approaches to source material. After the brief overview of Hellenization and Romanization in Palestine a recap of these newer methodologies will be given.

2.2.1 Hellenization and Romanization in Palestine: Recent Developments

Following the trend setting works of Elias Bickerman, Victor Tcherikover, and Martin Hengel, scholars have deliberated various appraisals of the influence of Greek and Roman culture in Palestine.[140] Since Hengel, scholars have moved away from seeing "Judaism standing over against Hellenism" and toward a picture of Judaism pushing at "an active re-tailoring and re-shaping of tradition in light of their material, ideological and philosophical surroundings."[141] It is now widely acknowledged that a regional perspective is needed when assessing "Hellenization" and "Romanization." For example, it is not prudent to take evidence from Jerusalem and use it in a description of Capernaum. Since Galilee looms largest for this study, and many assume that levels of cultural influence in Galilee imply similar in-

---

[140] E. J. Bickerman, *Der Gott der Makkabäer: Untersuchungen über Sinn und Ursprung der Makkabäischen Erhebung* (Berlin: Schocken Verlag, 1937), ET, *The God of the Maccabees: Studies on the Meaning and Origin of the Maccabean Revolt* (Studies in Judaism in Late Antiquity 32; Leiden: Brill, 1979); Victor Tcherikover, *Hellenistic Civilization and the Jews* (Philadelphia: Jewish Publication Society of America, 1959); Martin Hengel, *Judaism and Hellenism: Studies in Their Encounter in Palestine During the Early Hellenistic Period* (Philadelphia: Fortress Press, 1974).

[141] Carol Bakhos, "Introduction," in *Ancient Judaism in Its Hellenistic Context* (ed. Carol Bakhos; JSJSupp 95; Leiden: Brill, 2005), 1–7, 2. Cf. Millar, *Near East*, 352. Millar mentions Feldman as a contrasting opinion, L. H. Feldman, "How Much Hellenism in Jewish Palestine?" *HUCA* 57 (1986): 83. See also, M. Hengel and Christoph Markschies, *The "Hellenization" of Judaea in the First-century After Christ* (London: SCM Press, 1989).

fluences elsewhere,[142] a representative sampling of scholars who have argued for intense Hellenization or Romanization in Galilee, D. E. Oakman, M. Sawicki, and R. Batey, should give an adequate introduction to the broader topic.

D. E. Oakman follows B. L. Mack in considering Palestine thoroughly Hellenized, Galilee "cosmopolitan," and the connection between Galilee and Jerusalem (or temple) weak.[143] Richard Batey supposes that Galilee was "occupied" by Rome in the sense that they set up a government (*Ant.* 14.91; *War* 1.170) and army which leads to the idea of large Gentile populations, pagan temples, and pig farms.[144] Sawicki postulates an extremely high level of Romanization claiming that Herod Antipas attempted to make Galilee a "little Italy."[145] She consistently employs "occupation" and "colonization" terminology, assumes the presence of many Romans (e.g., soldiers), and postulates a desire by its rulers (esp. Antipas) to increase business travel through the region via an overt Romanization program. These conclusions have been rebutted aggressively.

Many scholars, including several who previously held a "Hellenized Galilee" view, now agree that Galilee was as Jewish as Judea. Four arguments serve as the basis for this conclusion: the presence of Jewish material culture (e.g., *miqvaoth*, limestone vessels, lack of pig bones, implements of Jewish religious practice, unique burial practice including the use of *loculi* tombs, and the predominance of Hasmonean coins),[146] a lower population density than previously conjectured,[147] lack of Roman or

---

[142] Galilee serves as a microcosm of sorts for many studies, so conclusions about its Hellenization tend to be applied to Palestine as a whole.

[143] Oakman, "Models and Archaeology," 116–117; Mack, *Lost Gospel*, esp. 51–68.

[144] Richard Batey, *Jesus and the Forgotten City: New Light on Sepphoris and the Urban World of Jesus* (Grand Rapids: Baker, 1991); cf. Howard Clark Kee, "Early Christianity in the Galilee," in *The Galilee in Late Antiquity* (ed. Lee I. Levine; New York: Jewish Theological Seminary of America, 1992), 3–22. These scholars at points build off the work of Shirley Jackson Case, "Jesus and Sepphoris," *JBL* 45 (1926): 14–22.

[145] Sawicki, *Crossing*, 158.

[146] Jensen, *Antipas*, 7–8; see Eric M. Meyers and Mark A. Chancey, "How Jewish Was Sepphoris in Jesus' Time?" *BAR* 26/4 (2000): 18–33; Mark A. Chancey, "The Cultural Milieu of Ancient Sepphoris," *NTS* 47 (2001): 127–145; idem, *The Myth of a Gentile Galilee* (Cambridge: Cambridge University Press, 2002); Mordechai Aviam, "First-century Jewish Galilee: An Archaeological Perspective," in *Religion and Society in Roman Palestine: Old Questions, New Approaches* (ed. Douglas R. Edwards; New York and London: Routledge, 2004), 7–27; Reed, *Archaeology*, 100–138; Crossan and Reed, *Excavating Jesus*. For a different reading of this evidence see Douglas E. Oakman, "Models and Archaeology in the Social Interpretation of Jesus," in *Social Scientific Models for Interpreting the Bible: Essays by the Context Group in Honor of Bruce J. Malina* (ed. John J. Pilch; Leiden: Brill, 2000), 102–131, 112–115.

[147] Reed, *Archaeology*, 62–99.

Hellenistic identity markers (e.g., Roman or Hellenistic religious implements, symbols on coins, architecture, or art),[148] and emphasis on stratigraphy to date evidence (because Galilee underwent a rather significant change in the second and third centuries).[149]

Numismatic evidence is another way to account for the public identity of a region, and a recent assessment of coinage in the Roman provinces marks a distinction between the east and west in relation to Romanization.[150] Coins in the Roman provinces, especially Judea, paint a portrait of cultures largely resistant to Romanization up until A.D. 250. The period 50 B.C. to A.D. 50 marks a transition toward more dramatic Romanization throughout the empire. Judea seems to have resisted the transition as well (at least numismatic evidence leads in this direction). In reference primarily to the post-Revolt era, Howgego opines that the "strident nature of the slogans" found in Palestinian coins adds to the impression of anti-Romanization in Palestine.[151] For example, monolingual Hebrew coins of the first revolt era boldly proclaim "Jerusalem the Holy" probably in defiance of the earlier Tyrian shekel which calls that city *hieros*.[152] There is no example of a monolingual coin in a language other than Latin or Greek anywhere in the empire in the post-Tiberian era. The monolingual Hebrew coins of the Jewish revolt thus stand out quite clearly and intimate a significantly different stance toward Rome.

Exclusive use of Roman imperial coins in the west from A.D. 50 onwards coupled with the persistence of local coinages in the east till A.D. 250 suggests the persistence of cultural differences.[153] Switching to imperial coinage served the interest of leaders at all levels in the west, but allegiance to Greek heritage in the east served the same parties in the east.[154] Nuance must be maintained because certain client-kings desired to

---

[148] Meyers and Chancey, "How Jewish," 27–38; Reed, *Archaeology*, 123–131; Horsley, *Archaeology, History, and Society in Galilee*, 59.

[149] Jensen, *Antipas*, 8. Eric M. Meyers, "Jesus and His Galilean Context," in Edwards and McCollough, *Archaeology and the Galilee*, 57–66; Mark Chancey, "Galilee and Greco-Roman Culture in the Time of Jesus: The Neglected Significance of Chronology," *The Society of Biblical Literature 2003 Seminar Papers* (SBLSP 42; Atlanta: Scholars Press, 2003), 173–87; Mark Chancey, *Greco-Roman Culture and the Galilee of Jesus* (SNTSMS 134; Cambridge: Cambridge University Press, 2005), 43–70.

[150] C. J. Howgego, Volker Heuchert, and Andrew Burnett, eds., *Coinage and Identity in the Roman Provinces* (Oxford: Oxford University Press, 2004).

[151] Christopher Howgego, "Coinage and Identity in the Roman Provinces," in Howgego, Heuchert, Burnett, *Coinage*, 1–17, 13 (pl. 14.1, 1).

[152] Martin Goodman, "Coinage and Identity: The Jewish Evidence," in Howgego, Heuchert, Burnett, *Coinage*, 163–166, 165, pl. 14.1, 4.

[153] Andrew Burnett, "The Roman West and the Roman East," in Howgego, Heuchert, Burnett, *Coinage*, 171–180, 176–77.

[154] Howgego, "Coinage," 14.

strengthen the Roman connection.[155] Numismatic evidence, therefore, suggests that the public identity of Palestine should not be considered heavily Romanized, but the possibility that certain client-kings were thus directed presents itself. If Mark Chancey's proposal that coins were "organs of information" is adopted then it is plausible that the populace would have been able to gather a general impression of their message, whether they were literate or not, and the portraiture would help in this.[156] This is one way that the cultural leanings of the elite could trickle down to the masses. Whether they would embrace these leanings is another story.

A consensus seems to be building that sees less Hellenization and Romanization in Galilee than earlier scholars had maintained, and a related trend sees Judea in similar light.[157] All sides agree, however, that blanket statements assuming a monolithic Palestinian culture will not do. Detailed work on individual regions and sub-regions must take precedence. The "regional perspective" approach is one of the great turning points in cultural study developed by Eric Meyers.[158]

2.2.2 Archaeology and Methodological Developments

Several advancements and adjustments in the archeologist's methods and goals have changed the way that first-century Palestinian culture has been approached. Halvor Moxnes connects the newer approaches with the resurgence in interest for determining the culture of Jesus as a central component of recent Jesus scholarship.[159] Jensen provides the most thorough and up-to-date discussion of archaeology and Jesus studies. He discusses three phases of development in archaeological method and theory (classical, new, and post-processional [newer] archaeology).[160] The core of the

---

[155] Burnett, "West and East," 177–179.

[156] Mark A. Chancey, "City Coins and Roman Power in Palestine: From Pompey to the Great Revolt," in *Religion and Society in Roman Palestine: Old Questions, New Approaches* (ed. Douglas R. Edwards; New York and London: Routledge, 2004), 103–112, 104.

[157] See also MacMullen, *Romanization*; Ball, *Rome*.

[158] Eric M. Meyers, "Galilean Regionalism as a Factor in Historical Reconstruction," *BASOR* 221 (1976): 92–102; idem, "The Cultural Setting of Galilee: The Case of Regionalism and Early Judaism," *ANRW* 19.2.1 (1979): 686–702.

[159] Moxnes, "Construction," 65.

[160] Classical Archaeology: Stephan L. Dyson, "A Classical Archaeologist's Response to the 'New Archaeology,'" *BASOR* 242 (1981): 7–14; idem, "From New to New Age Archaeology: Archaeological Theory and Classical Archaeology—A 1990s Perspective," *American Journal of Archaeology* 97 (1993): 195–203; New Archaeology: Michael Shanks and Christopher Tiller, *Re-Constructing Archaeology: Theory and Practice* (Cambridge: Cambridge University Press, 1987); William G. Dever, "The Impact of the 'New Archaeology' on Syro-Palestinian Archaeology," *BASOR* 242 (1981): 15–30; idem,

shift amounts to a change in focus from major structures (classical) to interpretations of minor finds concerned with common, daily, and often nonelite life.[161] Reed warns that previous approaches, which focused on "public architecture, the languages on public inscriptions, or civic decorative elements ... tend to be more informative of the ruler's predilections than the populace's preferences, and are less significant for determining a region's ethnicity."[162] He suspects that "material culture inside domestic or private space" gives a better window into everyday life and is thus a more appropriate method for deciphering Hellenization in Palestine.[163] Sean Freyne adds an interesting observation. He describes how the shifting focus in archaeology (from specific artifacts as "proof" for the veracity of biblical narratives to a contextual showcase of culture in general) correlates with the rising interest in social science interpretation of the Bible. The two still have not found a consistent way to wed, but many approaches are making it increasingly possible to use archaeology and social models productively toward describing Jesus and earliest Christianity.[164] Jensen identifies the difficulty of bringing sociology and archaeology together by showing how different conclusions about Galilee (conflict or harmony) correspond rather consistently with the discipline which receives priority.[165] For this reason Jensen prioritizes archaeology and text before models. Nevertheless, scholars have grown in their capacity to keep "text and spade" together in the interpretive process. James Strange promotes a "dialogical method" where literary and archaeological evidence posit reconstructions of the social world individually before joining together for a joint reconstruction.[166] Texts and artifacts must be interpreted and neither offers an unbiased view into the first-century. Artifacts of both monumen-

---

"Impact of the 'New Archaeology,'" in *Benchmarks in Time and Culture: An Introduction to Palestinian Archaeology* (ed. Joel F. Drinkard, Gerald L. Mattingly, and Maxwell J. Miller; Atlanta: Scholars Press, 1988), 337–52; Newer archaeology: Ian Hodder, *The Archaeological Process: An Introduction* (Oxford: Blackwell Publishers, 1999).

[161] For Jensen's survey of methodology and theory see *Antipas*, 127–135.
[162] Reed, *Archaeology*, 43.
[163] Reed, *Archaeology*, 44.
[164] Freyne, *Galilee and Gospel*, 160–4.
[165] Morten Hørning Jensen, "Josephus and Antipas: A Case Study of Josephus' Narratives on Herod Antipas," in *Making History: Josephus and Historical Method* (JSJSupp 110; ed. Zuleika Rodgers; Leiden: Brill, 2007), 289–312, 289–290; cf. Jensen, *Antipas*, 9–34; idem, "Herod Antipas in Galilee: Friend or Foe of the Historical Jesus," *JSHJ* 5 (2007): 7–32.
[166] James F. Strange, "The Sayings of Jesus and Archaeology," in *Hillel and Jesus: Comparative Studies of Two Major Religious Leaders* (ed. James H. Charlesworth and Loren L. Johns; Minneapolis: Fortress Press, 1997), 291–305, here, 296–297, found in Jensen, *Antipas*, 133. This is also the approach of Crossan and Reed, *Excavating Jesus*, see Prologue.

tal and mundane importance can illuminate this study. Benefactors tended to express generosity and receive recognition through monuments, but general patterns of Hellenization and Romanization can be best detected in the mundane. In the following regional and personality perspectives, "text and spade" will interact as culture is honed in upon.

A set of criteria to determine or quantify Romanization or Hellenization should be clarified. The problem of definitions immediately comes up when trying to distinguish between something "Hellenistic" and something "Roman." To be sure these are nebulous and fluid categories to a certain degree. Perhaps it would be best to follow Ramsay MacMullen who foregoes definitions and instead looks for matches between Italy and the regions he studies. Roman in his work means "Italian."[167] He looks at immigration from Italy, the influx of Italian modes of thought or behaviors (eating, entertaining, governing, etc.), and the influence of Italian architecture in the provinces. These three main areas serve for MacMullen as indicators of "Romanization." These criteria help in the regional study, but something more may be added for the personality perspective. In that portion, education in Rome, relationship to the emperor, construction projects/style, coinage, and public perception may all lend insight into the recognition of Romanization in the individual.

2.2.3 Galilee: Benefaction and Patrocinium

The culture of Galilee has been at the heart of Jewish and Christian studies for some time now with a variety of options being offered for its description. Interest in Galilee has sprung up simultaneously in archaeological and biblical studies circles with an emphasis on regionalism.[168] Reed lists several spectrums upon which the culture of Galilee has been placed: "in terms of ethnicity, it has been described as Jewish, 'Israelite,' or even syncretistic and Gentile; in terms of cultural traditions and religion, Galilee has been portrayed as either conservatively Jewish or Hellenistic; in terms of economics, either impoverished or prosperous; in terms of its political climate, it has been portrayed as either zealously nationalistic or shrewdly acquiescent."[169] S. Freyne puts himself with M. Goodman in thinking that Galilee had a "predominantly peasant Jewish village culture" while D. Edwards, A. Overman, and J. Strange speak "confidently about the urbanisation of Galilee, particularly lower Galilee."[170] Urbanization often implies Hellenization.

---

[167] MacMullen, *Romanization*, xi.
[168] Reed, *Archaeology*, 3–4.
[169] Reed, *Archaeology*, 8–9, see bibliography in n. 25.
[170] Both citations can be found in Sean Freyne, *Galilee and Gospel*, 86; Martin Goodman, *State and Society in Roman Galilee, A.D. 132–212* (Totowa: Rowman &

Since Galilee proves more important in the upbringing and ministry of Jesus, more time will be devoted to describing its culture. With evidence both archaeological and literary being somewhat sparse and sporadic, it is beneficial to devote some time to an evaluation of the region as a whole. This can provide a framework for the village and city discussions. The following paragraphs cover the various major questions being addressed in archaeological investigations of Galilee. They are: (1) the ethnic identity of the Galileans, (2) the cultural and religious climate of Galilee, (3) the economic situation, and (4) the political atmosphere.

The ethnic identity of the people living in Galilee before the first-century can have a significant influence on the degree of loyalty to Judaism or Hellenism anticipated by the investigator. Three main options have been advanced. Some (e.g., S. Freyne, S. Klein, M. H. Jensen) hold that Galilee was "essentially Jewish in the first-century, either because it was already inhabited by Jews prior to the Hasmonean annexation, or because they colonized and populated it with Judeans."[171] As Jews they held temple and Jerusalem in high regard making pilgrimages frequently. Others (e.g., Emil Schürer, Walter, Bauer) see it as "essentially Gentile," populated by Itureans (syncretistic?) who converted to Judaism in the second century B.C. and were critical of Jerusalem and the temple's claim to centrality. Still others (e.g., A. Alt, R. Horsley, M. Sawicki) maintain that Galilee consisted of Jewish inhabitants who were not taken to Assyria in the eighth century (the so-called "leftover" theory). These Jews retained the northern prophetic tradition which called for "the revitalization of Israelite village communities and a return to covenantal principles as a means of redressing social, political, and economic injustices."[172] Though supporters of each view persist, the first option, that Galilee consisted of a repopulated Jewish demographic, is gaining momentum.[173] Reed makes the most compelling argument for this position and against the other two. Zvi Gal's surveys and stratigraphic excavations argue persuasively for "almost complete abandonment" of Galilee at the close of the Iron Age (1000–586 B.C.) thus ruling out the "leftover" Jews theory of Alt and Horsley.[174] Rising population

---

Allanheld, 1983); David J., Lull, ed., *Society of Biblical Literature 1988 Seminar Papers* (SBL Seminar Papers 27; Atlanta: Scholars Press, 1988); James H. Charlesworth and Walter P. Weaver, eds., *What Has Archaeology to Do with Faith?* (Philadelphia: Trinity Press International, 1992).

[171] Reed, *Archaeology*, 24.

[172] Reed, *Archaeology*, 24–25.

[173] Jensen, *Antipas*, 6–7. The most recent advocate of this view is Cromhout, *Jesus and Identity*, 231–256.

[174] "Zvi Gal's survey of Lower Galilee, which, when coupled with the results of stratigraphic excavations in Upper and Lower Galilee, paint a picture of a totally devastated and depopulated Galilee in the wake of the Assyrian campaigns of 733/732 B.C.E."

can be detected in the later Hellenistic period (167–63 B.C.). Material remains show a link between Galileans and Jewish identity markers which increased significantly from practically nothing before this time. He supports his position with significant literary evidence.[175]

The evaluation of the cultural and religious climate of Galilee has also had its polarities, but scholars seem to be moving toward positing a stronger Jewish presence. Some (S. E. Porter, D. E. Oakman, B. L. Mack; and the earlier works of J. D. Crossan and E. M. Meyers) suggest that Galilee was deeply Hellenistic in both culture and religion. Stanley Porter has recently claimed that Galilee, especially lower Galilee, was the "Palestinian area most heavily influenced by Greek language and culture (although these two do not necessarily need to be seen together)."[176] The extent of Hellenization in Galilee argued for by Mack leads him to conclude that Galileans felt some hostility toward the Jerusalem temple.[177]

But archaeological evidence persuades more and more scholars to think of Galilee as being as thoroughly Jewish as Judea. Reed finds four patterns of artifacts "remarkably similar to those in Judea." He emphasizes: "1) the chalk vessels, 2) stepped plastered pools, 3) secondary burial with ossuaries in loculi tombs, and 4) bone profiles that lack pork."[178] Chalk/limestone vessels are associated with ritual purity since stone wares were considered impervious to impurity (related to priestly classes, temple, and Phari-

---

Reed, *Archaeology*, 27–29; Zvi Gal, *The Lower Galilee During the Iron Age* (ASOR Dissertation Series 8; Winona Lake: Eisenbrauns, 1992); idem, "The Lower Galilee in the Iron Age II: Analysis of Survey Material and its Historical Interpretation," *Tel Aviv* 15–16 (1988–1989): 56–64. There is no occupational evidence between the 7th and 6th centuries in over 80 sites examined in the Upper and Lower Galilee. But there is evidence for occupation in the 12th to 8th centuries and subsequently in the 5th century B.C. Cf. James D. G. Dunn, "Did Jesus Attend the Synagogue," in Charlesworth, *Archaeology*, 206–222, 207–216.

[175] For a rebuttal of Horsley's "leftover theory" see Reed, *Archaeology*, 28–34 and against Schürer's Iturean hypothesis see Reed, *Archaeology*, 35–39. See also Freyne, "Geography of Restoration," 292–303.

[176] Stanley E. Porter, "Jesus and the Use of Greek in Galilee," in *Studying the Historical Jesus: Evaluations of the State of Current Research* (ed. Bruce Chilton and Craig A. Evans; Leiden: Brill, 1998), 123–154, 134. He cites A. H. M. Jones, *Cities of the Eastern Roman Provinces* (New York: Oxford University Press, 1998); Tessa Rajak, *Josephus, the Historian and His Society* (Philadelphia: Fortress Press, 1984), 46–64, now see Tessa Rajak, *Josephus: The Historian and His Society* (London: Duckworth, 2002). See also Kee, "Early Christianity," 20–21 and bibliography for evidence of Greek language in Galilee.

[177] Mack, *Lost Gospel*, 51, 58–62; cf. Oakman, "Models and Archaeology," 116–117.

[178] Reed, *Archaeology*, 44. For the same assessment see Jensen, *Antipas*, 6–9; Meyers and Chancey, "How Jewish," 18–33; Chancey, "Cultural Milieu of Ancient Sepphoris," 127–145.

sees).[179] The pools are mostly identified as *miqvaoth*, a sign of Jewish identity and purity concerns.[180] Though the final two patterns (burial, meals) have been less published or excavated, when they have been studied they follow the patterns of material culture in Judea.[181] Zooarchaeological data also shows that pig avoidance, a Jewish identity marker, was established by the Late Hellenistic Period.[182] Reed comments that "together, this fourfold cluster offers a reliable indicator of Jewish religious identity, which is the well-established pattern in Jerusalem and Judea of the period."[183]

Whereas the first two questions (ethnicity, culture) have seen a consensus developing, the latter two (economics, politics) have been described as approaching an impasse. Economics and politics work together and so a conclusion about one leads to conclusions about the other. Scholarship has vacillated between viewing Galilee as poor or severely economically stratified (therefore, unstable; S. Freyne [later works, 1992–2004], M. Moreland, R. L. Horsley, J. D. Crossan, and W. Arnal) and relatively prosperous (thus, peaceful; Freyne [earlier works 1980–1988], E. M. Meyers, D. Edwards, J. Strange, J. Reed, and M. Aviam).[184] Tension between town and country (rural-urban), Tiberius' role in relation to Roman exploitation, and the impact of Tiberius' building campaigns have been central points of debate in this discussion. Freyne's transition provides a good example of the interplay of these factors. In his earlier works he describes Herod Antipas as a buffer between oppression from Rome and the one who made stability possible. In his later works Antipas's building program and new economy

---

[179] E.g., *Kelim* 10:1. Roland Deines, "Die Abwehr der Fremden in den Texten aus Qumran. Zum Verständnis der Fremdenfeindlichkeit in der Qumrangemeinde," in *Die Heiden: Juden, Christen und das Problem des Fremden* (WUNT 70; ed. Reinhard Feldmeier and Ulrich Heckel; Tübingen: Mohr, 1994), 59–91; Roland Deines, *Jüdische Steingefässe und pharisäische Frömmigkeit: ein archäologisch-historischer Beitrag zum Verständnis von Joh 2,6 und der jüdischen Reinheitshalacha zur Zeit Jesu* (WUNT 52; Tübingen: Mohr, 1993).

[180] Smaller ones in private homes, larger ones in public, with around 300 discovered in Jerusalem, Judea, Golan, Galilee, but none so far in Samaria and sparse in the coastlands. Reed, *Archaeology*, 45–46.

[181] Reed, *Archaeology*, 47.

[182] Reed, *Archaeology*, 49; cf. Brian Hesse and Paula Wapnish, "Can Pig Remains Be Used for Ethnic Diagnosis in the Ancient Near East?" in *The Archaeology of Israel: Constructing the Past, Interpreting the Present* (JSOT 237; ed. Neil Asher Silberman and David B. Small; Sheffield: Sheffield Academic Press, 1997), 238–270.

[183] Reed, *Archaeology*, 49. Cf. 1 Macc 5:14–15; 10:25–45; 13:40; Polybius *His* 5.62; *Ant.* 13.28, 337–8, 319; 20.123; *War* 1.64; 2.238. Crossan's work with Reed has influenced him about the cultural environment of Jesus. He now sees a stronger Jewish presence. Crossan and Reed, *Excavating Jesus*.

[184] Jensen provides the most complete appraisal of these viewpoints and provides the "impasse" description. Jensen, *Antipas*, 9–34.

increase tenancy, debts, and general social unrest to the point of provoking social banditry.[185]

It seems, however, that the archaeological evidence leans toward harmony and relative prosperity (earlier Freyne) and against conflict and relative economic distress (later Freyne). Jensen's detailed and thorough work supports the harmony position by showing the lack of evidence necessary to support the conflict model and the multi-faceted evidence in support of the harmony model. The sociological models which the conflict model adherents build upon require certain factors to establish their conclusion. Freyne (following T. F. Carney), Moreland (James C. Scott), and Crossan (Lenski-Kautsky) each use these sociological models and find that societal friction and conflict exist when rapid change occurs in several areas: "specialization, monetization, attitudinal changes, urbanization, scribalization, increasing overt modes of resistance, difficulties in upholding the peasant ideology of safety-first, risk sharing and protection from urban centres."[186] Though Jensen did not directly focus on these issues he finds it noteworthy that no increase in any of those factors touched on in his study can be found. Advocates of a picture of conflict must show that monetization increased; but the evidence goes against this. Urbanization has to have a detrimental impact on rural areas, but Jensen shows the opposite. Antipas would have had to be intent on taxation, but this was not his first priority.[187] The periods before and after Antipas are more susceptible to this type of analysis, so perhaps they had the type of conflict anticipated by the sociological models.[188] Jensen's study of Galilee and the impact of Antipas yields a rather mild conclusion. Antipas had a fairly uneventful career marked by peace, moderate economic improvement, and relative prosperity in both town and country.

In addition to these four major questions there are some big picture questions which may indicate a general level of Hellenization or Romanization in Galilee. These questions fit better in an overview format and thus will be touched upon here. How much Greek was spoken? What kinds of government were in place (Hellenistic, Roman, Jewish)? How much trade occurred and did this bring Hellenization or Romanization? When Romans ruled did they impose their culture on the new society? Did they impose Latin? Did the Roman army reside in Galilee in the early first-century? When Romans took positions in government did they respect Jewish religion or force their culture upon the people? How did the Galileans view Roman presence and leadership? Debate surrounds each of these questions,

---

[185] Jensen, *Antipas*, 19–20.
[186] Jensen, *Antipas*, 249.
[187] Jensen, *Antipas*, 249.
[188] Jensen, *Antipas*, 249.

and there is not space to cover each thoroughly. Instead, a short appraisal identifies assumptions made in this study and scholars to whom one may refer for extensive treatment.

Galilee's tumultuous centuries leading up to the era of Jesus brought with them several possible Hellenistic influences. Hellenization can be detected to a certain extent in the adoption of the Greek language, but it is not a precise equation (language = culture). Assessments of the amount of Greek spoken in Jesus' Galilee differ, but it does seem that it had penetrated most levels of society even if it was not the primary language.[189] Some evidence in favor of this conclusion will be advanced in subsequent sections.

Hellenistic forms of government may be a surer source of Hellenization. The Ptolemies instituted "many different forms of Greek officialdom into Galilee."[190] The strategy of Pompey undermined much of the progress made by Jewish leaders in the Maccabee era since he freed many cities in the larger area (e.g., Dora, Strato's Tower, Arethusa, Apollonia, Joppa, Jamnia, Azotus, Anthedon, Gaza, and Raphia).[191] He preferred to leave rural peoples under the control of locally respected dynasts, so when Pompey had taken control of the area and reduced it to its "rural core, Judaea proper, Samareitis, Galilee, and Peraea," he gave Hyrcanus the high priesthood and local control.[192] Gabinius left Hyrcanus with only spiritual authority, transferring his political power into the hands of "districts ruled by councils of nobles."[193] Antony granted the Idumean Herod I jurisdiction in 40 B.C. and he retained control for several decades. During the Herodian dynasty areas were divided into toparchies and further subdivided into villages ruled by a στρατηγός and "village clerk appointed ... by the crown" (a system which remained from the Seleucid era).[194] Many different leaders had control and several cultures influenced the political climate of Palestine in the first-century before and after Jesus. Further reference to the specific types of governing undertaken in Galilee and Palestine generally will be offered below (sections 2.2.3, 2.2.4, 2.2.5).

It is possible that trade between regions also brought cultural influence so this has been one component of assessments of the Hellenization or Romanization of Palestine. Freyne's investigation of trade patterns be-

---

[189] For recent work on this subject which argues this position, see Collins and Sterling, *Hellenism*.

[190] Sean Freyne, "Galileans, Phoenicians, and Itureans: A Study of Regional Contrasts in the Hellenistic Age," in *Hellenism in the Land of Israel* (ed. John J. Collins and Gregory A. Sterling; Notre Dame: University of Notre Dame Press, 2001), 182–215, 198.

[191] Jones, *Cities*, 257. These cities were restored under the rule of Gabinius.

[192] Jones, *Cities*, 256–258.

[193] Jones, *Cities*, 258.

[194] Jones, *Cities*, 272–273.

2.2 Benefaction and Patronage in Palestine

tween Tyre and Galilee shows that trade took place when geographical realities allowed for it, but when they prevented trade it was not pursued. Coin distributions confirm this since Tyrian coins were used for trade, temple tax, and hoarding while Hasmonean coinage was valued for everyday use.[195] Freyne concludes that traders and merchants from Phoenicia did not attempt to Hellenize Galilee. Hellenism, though present in architecture, language, ceramics, and trade, was spotty and restricted to these few areas.[196] In Jesus' era Galilee was tied to Hasmonean ways.

The advent of Roman rule provided for the possibility of Roman cultural influence, but Romanization did not have deep roots. To begin with Rome did not typically impose Latin upon its conquered territories, and Galilee was no exception. Josephus mentions five administrative centers set up by Pompey (πέντε δὲ συνέδρια καταστήσας; *Ant.* 14.91; *War* 1.170), which some have interpreted as Roman led outposts for the next ninety years, but in fact they were Jewish-led and only lasted a couple of years.[197] Rome did not rule Galilee or Judea directly in the era most important for this study, but allowed kings, tetrarchs, and high priests local rule and *de facto* authority (ca. 31 B.C. to ca. A.D. 44).[198] One significant vehicle through which Romanization may have come was through the education (sometimes in Rome) and election (by Rome) of client-kings and tetrarchs for Galilee. This will be discussed in more detail in the personality perspectives. M. Sawicki envisions Roman soldiers residing in Galilee during this era, but no such military presence is likely. The Romans chose not to control their areas by putting armies in every single small territory. The army intended to protect Palestine would have been in Syria. "Rome did not station armies in the client kingdoms, and thus there were no Roman soldiers in Herod's kingdom (after he gained full control of it), or in the tetrarchies of Archelaos and Antipas."[199]

When Romans took control, they by and large attempted to keep the regions peaceful by respecting the local culture. Numismatic evidence shows how the Romans attempted to keep the peace in Judea. The first three Roman administrators (Coponius A.D. 6–9; Marcus Ambibulus A.D. 9–12;

---

[195] Reed, *Archaeology*, 142.

[196] Freyne, "Hellenistic Age," 208–210.

[197] Kee interprets this as evidence of Romanization. Howard Clark Kee, "Early Christianity in the Galilee: Reassessing the Evidence from the Gospels," in *The Galilee in Late Antiquity* (ed. Lee I. Levine; New York: Jewish Theological Seminary of America; Cambridge, Mass.: Harvard University Press, 1992), 3–22. Sanders offers the rebuttal. Sanders, "Jesus' Galilee," 6–9.

[198] For the history of the power transfers at this time see, Jones, *Cities*, 256–259.

[199] Sanders, "Jesus' Galilee," 10. On the relative paucity of military in Galilee compared to Samarea and Judea see also D. Fiensy, *The Social History of Palestine in the Herodian Period: The Land Is Mine* (Lewiston: Edwin Mellon, 1991), 21–60.

Valerius Gratus A.D. 15–26) adhered to Jewish scruples in minting coins, which circulated in Galilee. Though they did add the name of the emperor (which Philip also had done though in a non-Jewish area), they employed symbols which "closely corresponded to the Jewish tradition by using ears of corn, palm trees, lilies, the *cornucopia* with a *caduceus*, ceremonial vessels (on the coins of Gratus), palm branches and branches of a vine."[200] Pontius Pilate (A.D. 26–36), though not adding an image of the emperor to his coins, depicted articles (in A.D. 29–31) used in Roman cult (*simpulum*/ladle; *lituus*/Roman augural staff) which could have potentially agitated astute Jews.[201] This leads to the possibility that Galileans would have perhaps grown increasingly aware of the Roman authority during the ministry years of Jesus and perhaps started to see this as a source of aggravation. This will be discussed in detail in the personality perspectives.

If any Roman influence would be directly felt it would have been in the cities which tended to be "the centres of Roman rule" even if their "origin, composition or character" was more deeply indebted to another culture.[202] Rome did have some special interest in Galilee, since it was a very significant area in Israel for mainstream Diaspora Judaism.[203] Because Galilee enjoyed such a privileged position among Babylonian Diaspora Jews who sided with the Parthians against the Romans during the last part of the first-century B.C., it became important for Romans to appease Jewish interests throughout their empire (by granting freedoms) and to secure a stronghold in the region by (financially) supporting Herod's temple project.[204]

Scholars continue to debate whether Galileans despised the Roman presence or if they did not feel it as a significant burden. R. Horsley posits significant social unrest in Galilee directed largely against Rome. Recently, Peter Richardson has taken Horsley's portrait, in general, tempered it a little, but still maintains the position that Galileans took an anti-Roman stance. This stance was usually more covert than overt and subtle rather than explicit, but nevertheless it was significant.[205] He cites Antipas' aniconic coins to be a form of protest against Roman power since Herod

---

[200] Jensen, *Antipas*, 203.

[201] Jensen, *Antipas*, 202–3; Ya'akov Meshorer, *Ancient Jewish Coinage* (2 vols.; Dix Hills: Amphora Books, 1982), 2:173–174.

[202] Ball, *Rome*, 150.

[203] Etienne Nodet, "Josephus' Attempt to Reorganize Judaism from Rome," in Rodgers, *Making History*, 103–122, 105–110. Nodet claims it was the most significant province in the region, but this seems to be too difficult to establish. His arguments from the political maneuverings of Herod I do not exactly prove his point.

[204] Nodet, "Reorganize," 110.

[205] Peter Richardson, *Building Jewish in the Roman East* (JSJSupp 92; Waco: Baylor University Press, 2004), 18.

Philip and others gladly put images on their coins (but, see sections 3.2.5 and 3.3.5). He reads the coin distribution (primarily Hasmonean rather than Roman) in Galilean villages to be an expression of nationalistic fervor and anti-Roman protest,[206] interprets *miqvaoth* as a sign of unwillingness to compromise with the Romans,[207] sees the use of stone vessels as indicative of Jewish religious allegiance, and marks the switch (from Roman to Herodian) pottery as an expression of subtle resistance.[208]

His arguments, however, merit some reservation. It seems more likely that Antipas' aniconic coins should be attributed to his desire to maintain stability among his Jewish populace, since this would have pleased both Roman authorities and Jewish inhabitants (more on Antipas and Rome in section 3.2). Reading *miqvaoth* as stubborn resistance seems to go too far. There was very little Roman presence in Galilee (see below, sections 2.2.3 *Tiberias, Sepphoris*, and *Summary*), so no Roman would probably have ever seen such "resistance." It seems better to interpret the *miqvaoth* as simply an expression of Jewish identity. Andrea Berlin, from whom Richardson derives his final point, has since adjusted her own interpretation of decreasing Roman pottery. Galileans switched from Roman (*ETS – Eastern Terra Sigillata*) to less-ornate Herodian pottery not for resistance reasons, but because eating habits changed. She had earlier suggested that this push to more Jewish utensils was a form of covert resistance.[209] The disappearance of all other types of serving plates, not only the *ETS* dishes, suggested to her a simpler explanation: people were not eating in large groups as much, but instead dishing casseroles from cooking bowls into simple, smaller bowls. This was no covert resistance; it was simply a change in dining habits.[210]

Anti-Romanization no doubt increased in the years leading to the first revolt, and some signs of resistance can be detected in the literary sources (*War* 2.55–65; *Ant*. 17.269–284), but chronological distinctions should be maintained. It is probably better to suggest that at the beginning of Antipas' reign anti-Romanization was relatively low, but toward the end of this time tensions may have increased. Following Antipas and leading to the

---

[206] Danny Syon, "Tyre and Gamla: A Study in the Monetary Influence of Southern Phoenicia on Galilee and the Golan in the Hellenistic and Roman Periods" (Jerusalem: PhD diss., 2004).

[207] Cf. Oakman, "Models and Archaeology," 113–115.

[208] Richardson, *Building*, 18–20.

[209] Andrea M. Berlin, "Romanization and Anti-Romanization in Pre-Revolt Galilee," in *The First Jewish Revolt* (ed. Andrea M. Berlin and J. Andrew Overman; London and New York: Routledge, 2002), 57–73.

[210] Andrea M. Berlin, *Gamla 1: The Pottery of the Second Temple Period, The Shmarya Gutmann Excavations, 1976–1989* (IAA Reports 29; Jerusalem: Israel Antiquities Authority, 2006), in Jensen, *Antipas*, 239.

first revolt tensions really started to flare to the point that anti-Romanization would be expressed in various, explicit forms.

A closer look at Galilean villages and cities can add nuance to the questions that have been addressed in the overview above. If Romanization is thought to be quite low (or even absent) in Galilee in general, where does it surface and in what measure? If Hellenization is also considered relatively slight, where does it surface and to what extent? An investigation of several villages and cities in Galilee should provide insight into these questions. Only a small number of inscriptions have been found in Galilee so the search for evidence of benefaction or patronage must take a somewhat indirect route. It looks for Romanization and Hellenization in archaeological remains to provide a general backdrop upon which these social practices might surface. It then reads literary texts in relation to that backdrop and in dialogical form to see what may plausibly be concluded from both sources. Thus, the regional perspective first gives a picture through archaeology and then follows with a picture from the literary sources.

In this subsection three villages (Cana, Nazareth, Capernaum) and two cities (Tiberias, Sepphoris) of Galilee are assessed in terms of the impact of Hellenism and Romanism and connections to benefaction or patronage are advanced.

Cana

Recent archaeological investigations of Cana confirm the small village's predominately Jewish culture intermixed with hints of Hellenism. The Jewish component is evidenced by "Hasmonean coins, the stoneware and the stepped pools."[211] Richardson and Jensen add the necropolis and its thirteen tombs to this list of evidence favoring the point that Cana was a Jewish village.[212] Two significant, early Roman period structures have been found which demonstrate concern for Judaism and relative prosperity in the small village. A synagogue, perhaps, and a large central courtyard house have been discovered.[213] Jensen points to other evidence of thriving industry capable of supporting the population and creating a small group of

---

[211] Jensen, *Antipas*, 167.

[212] Peter Richardson, "What Has Cana to Do with Capernaum?" *NTS* 48 (2002): 314–331, 328.

[213] Richardson, *Building Jewish*, plate 15, 17; D. R. Edwards, "Khirbet Qana: From Jewish Village to Christian Pilgrimage Site," in *The Roman and Byzantine Near East* (Journal of Roman Archaeology Supplementary Series 49; ed. J. H. Humphrey; vol. 3. Portsmouth: JRA, 2002), 101–132, 111–113.

wealthier citizens.[214] These discoveries combine with a lack of evidence of any significant change in the first-century to suggest that life proceeded rather smoothly in the time of Antipas.[215]

Some evidence of Hellenistic cultural influence can be found in early first-century Cana. It is possible that the city had a quasi-Hippodamian plan for its layout.[216] Richardson is tentative about this conclusion. He questions whether the layout derives from topographical limitations or cultural imposition. He leans toward the conclusion that the layout was intentional. Several "small finds" (frescoed walls, evidence of wealth) express the differences between the "major urban centers" (Sepphoris, Tiberias, Panias) and the "rural villages" (Cana, Capernaum, Yodefat).[217] Richardson identifies this difference in terms of degrees of Hellenization with villages being noticeably less "Hellenized" than the cities. Wealth, culture, and religious diversity signal to Richardson increased Hellenization in those cities, but, without entering the discussion on his assessment of the cities here, it is critical that he does not find such marks of Hellenization in Cana. I have not read of any archaeological evidence of Romanization in architecture, coins, or inscriptions, in first-century Cana.

Since a significant component of benefaction expression comes in the form of honorary inscriptions, literacy among the lower social classes opens up the possibility that these lower classes would be able to make sense of the relationship. Esther Eshel and D. R. Edwards have identified what they believe to be the fragment of an Aramaic/Hebrew abecedary found in Cana.[218] This abecedary proves to be important because the social location of the inscriber can be determined. Eshel and Edwards suggest the inscribing of letters prior to firing, the unskilled script, and the type of fabric come from the hand of a Galilean of the artisan class.[219] The scribe must have been familiar enough with writing to practice while waiting to

---

[214] E. J. Schnabel identifies one wealthy family as the hosts of the wedding at Cana, Eckhard J. Schnabel, *Early Christian Mission: Jesus and the Twelve* (Downers Grove: InterVarsity Press, 2004), 1.232–233.

[215] Jensen, *Antipas*, 167–169.

[216] Peter Richardson, "Khirbet Qana (and Other Villages) as a Context for Jesus," in Richardson, *Building Jewish*, 55–71, 56–58, 69.

[217] Richardson, "Khirbet Qana," 69.

[218] Esther Eshel and Douglas R. Edwards, "Language and Writing in Early Roman Galilee: Social Location of a Potter's Abecedary from Khirbet Qana," in *Religion and Society in Roman Palestine: Old Questions, New Approaches* (ed. Douglas R. Edwards; New York and London: Routledge, 2004), 49–55; cf. Edwards, "Khirbet Qana," 116.

[219] Eshel and Edwards, "Abecedary," 53. Eshel and Edwards (51–53) mention several other abecedary finds spanning a number of centuries both B.C. and A.D. Most carry an Aramaic or Hebrew script, but several others have Phoenician or Greek scripts. This is the first such find in a Jewish village in Galilee.

throw a pot into the kiln.[220] They suggest from this that reading/writing may have been a bit more prevalent and socio-economically diversified than is typically assumed.[221]

Literary evidence on Cana is minimal. It is usually mentioned in passing as a location through or in which troops passed or stopped (*Ant.* 13.391; *War* 1.102; *Ant.* 15.112), but twice it is a quasi-permanent location for important figures. Herod I made a headquarters (τὸ στρατόπεδον ηὔλιστο) at Cana (*War* 1.334), and Josephus stayed in the village for a time (*Life* 86–87). If Herod spent significant time in this headquarters then he could have had some cultural influence on that village. The Arabian army had stationed themselves there (στρατιὰ τῶν ᾿Αράβων; *Ant.* 15.112), and Herod I waged war with the king of Arabia because of the latter's ingratitude (ἀγνωμονοῦντος) toward him (*Ant.* 15.108). Antony incited Herod against the king for his unfaithfulness (ἀπιστία; 15.110). Herod responds to his soldiers' zeal to fight by setting his mind not to be outdone in ἀρετή (15.114). The soldiers demonstrated great zeal (σπουδή). But Herod's Hellenization may be tempered by the fact that his army still consists of ᾿Ιουδαῖοι. In another episode, Jews side with Herod out of hatred for Antigonus and as a response to Herod's noble deeds (κατορθώμασιν; *War* 1.334–335).

Josephus does not go into much detail about the village itself. It may be significant, though not sufficiently so to build a case upon, that when Josephus has opportunity to mention a role as benefactor, savior, or patron of the village he does not (*Life* 398–401). He summarizes a story of military victory referring to his deeds (ἡ πρᾶξις), but does not develop the idea that he has been a benefactor or patron through specific vocabulary (*Life* 402).

There is the possibility from this literary evidence that villagers in Cana might have interacted with some Hellenized and Romanized individuals, but we do not know how deeply the relationship could have gone. Herod uses Hellenistic language which is typically connected to benefactors. He responds because of a lack of gratitude (more Hellenistic?) while Antony sends because of the king's infidelity (more Roman?). Herod desires to stand out as preeminent in ἀρετή and gains a reputation for glorious deeds,

---

[220] Eshel and Edwards, "Abecedary," 53.

[221] On literacy in Palestine, see Catherine Hezser, *Jewish Literacy in Roman Palestine* (TSAJ 81; Tübingen: Mohr Siebeck, 2001); Alan R. Millard, *Reading and Writing in the Time of Jesus* (New York: New York University Press, 2000); Rainer Riesner, *Jesus als Lehrer: eine Untersuchung zum Ursprung der Evangelien-Überlieferung* (WUNT 7; Tübingen: Mohr Siebeck, 1981), 119–245, 412–413.

both Hellenistic ideals.[222] If Josephus is not merely projecting his ideology upon these villagers then one might suppose that they have a hint of Hellenism among them, or at least among certain leaders.

Nazareth

Work on Nazareth tends to conclude that it was predominately a peasant Jewish village with no political importance or conclusive evidence of Hellenization or Romanization before A.D. 40.[223] Following the growing consensus mentioned above on the ethnicity of Galileans in general, Reed and Crossan argue that the people of Nazareth were most likely "Hasmonean colonizers or Jewish settlers" who had arrived within the last two centuries before the common era.[224] Material evidence confirms the picture of a small, Jewish village of approximately 5 hectares and 400 persons.[225]

Nazareth's relationship to Sepphoris has been frequently discussed with a strong likelihood that its villagers were aware of their larger neighbor. The two were only five kilometers apart. The influence of Sepphoris on Nazareth comes into discussion typically because of the Hellenization assumed of the larger city and the possible implications this might have for the culture of Jesus' hometown. In this vein, Reed contrasts the finds at Sepphoris with those at Nazareth. Although excavations at Nazareth are relatively new, the differences between it and Sepphoris are suggestive. No public buildings, central road, orthogonal layout, public inscriptions, or coins have been discovered.[226] The differences could be attributable to the lack of thorough investigation to this point, but the lack of inscriptions might also be explained by lower literacy and the absence of elite sponsors. Only one Aramaic funerary inscription has been found among the tombs (*CII* 2.988).

---

[222] *Op* 169; *Jos* 99; *Spec Leg* 1.284; *Virt* 165–66, 68–69; *Ben* 1.10.4; 3.1.1. Harrison, *Language*, 125; Danker, *Benefactor*, 27, 45–46, 436, 442; Crook, *Conversion*, 58; Van Wees, "Gratitude"; Erskine, "Common Benefactors," 87.

[223] Since Nazareth is not mentioned in Jewish sources until the third century A.D. this study must proceed on archaeological and NT evidence alone. Kee, "Early Christianity," 14–15.

[224] Reed and Crossan, *Excavating Jesus*, 32.

[225] Reed, *Archaeology*, 83–84; Bellarmino Bagatti, *Villaggi Cristiani di Galilea* (Jerusalem: Franciscan Printing Press, 1971); Bellarmino Bagatti and Eugenio Alliata, *Excavations in Nazareth* (Jerusalem: Franciscan Printing Press, 1969); Bargil Pixner, *Wege des Messias und Stätten der Urkirche: Jesus und das Judenchristentum im Licht neuer archäologischer Erkenntnisse* (2nd ed.; Giesen: Brunnen, 1994); Schnabel, *Mission*, 1.228–229.

[226] Reed, *Archaeology*, 131–132.

Of course, Reed can only determine the near complete absence of inscriptions by ruling out the Nazareth Inscription.²²⁷ This decree of Caesar forbidding tomb robbing has been the cause of much scholarly debate, no doubt in part the result of the fact that the inscription was not found *in situ*. If early (reign of Tiberias or before) and originally set up in Nazareth it would argue toward a Greek and/or Roman cultural awareness in the village during the early first-century.²²⁸ If later (Claudius, Nero, or beyond) or originally situated elsewhere than Nazareth then it has lesser (or perhaps zero) impact on this study. The inscription was written in Greek and Van Der Horst argues was likely intended to be read by the villagers. He assumes adeptness in the Greek language in addition to literacy.²²⁹ As a decree, or rescript of a decree, it would imply awareness of imperial jurisdiction and perhaps the threat of Roman intervention for law-breaking. Nevertheless, no end to the debate about the date and provenance of this inscription appears to be in sight. Including it as evidence for or against Hellenization or Romanization seems imprudent.²³⁰

More instructive for the amount of Hellenization in Nazareth could be its connection to Sepphoris as hinted at in the literary sources. For his part, Reed allows evidence, fairly unrestrictedly, from the NT to inform his answer to the question of Nazareth's relationship to Sepphoris. He claims that knowledge and use of words associated with *poleis* (e.g., πλατεῖα ἡ πύλη, ἀγορά) "lends credibility to the position that rural Galileans were aware of Sepphoris."²³¹ Their close proximity adds to this possibility. But the probability of awareness of Sepphoris does not necessarily mean a deeper Hellenization or Romanization in Nazareth. It will be argued below that Sepphoris itself was only beginning its Hellenization in the era of Jesus and that significant evidence of Jewishness litters its landscape (section 2.2.3 *Sepphoris*). Luke situates a synagogue, complete with an attendant (ὑπηρέτης) and a scroll of Scripture, in the city where Jesus was brought up (4:16, 20, 24).²³² As yet no synagogue has been found to validate Luke's

---

²²⁷ The most recent discussions of the inscription in my research were Pieter W. Van Der Horst, "Greek in Jewish Palestine in Light of Jewish Epigraphy," in Collins and Sterling, *Hellenism*, 154–174; Adalberto Giovannini and Marguerite Hirot, "L'inscription de Nazareth: Nouvelle Interprétation," *ZPE* 124 (1999): 107–132. *Editio princeps*, F. Cumont, "Un rescrit impérial sur la violation de sépulture," *Revue Historique* 163 (1930): 241–266.

²²⁸ MacMullen finds both Greek and Roman terms in the edict, *Romanization*, 11.

²²⁹ Van Der Horst, "Jewish Epigraphy," 162.

²³⁰ Giovannini and Hirt suggest that the inscription is not from Palestine though it may be from Augustus' era. Giovannini and Hirt, "L'inscription de Nazareth," 129–130.

²³¹ Reed, *Archaeology*, 132.

²³² Batey challenges the historicity of a synagogue-as-building at this stage of Israel's history. Batey, "Early Christianity."

claim, but excavations are still in the beginning stages. It must be concluded that Nazareth had little if any consistent Hellenistic or Roman influence apart from the occasional passer-by.

Capernaum

Capernaum has received various assessments, but it seems best to conclude that it was a slightly larger (relative to Nazareth) Jewish village which witnessed increasing regional trade, and thus Gentile traffic, during the reign of Antipas. Population estimates range from 25,000 (H. C. Kee) or 12–15,000 (Meyers and Strange) to 1,700 to 1,000 (Reed).[233] The smallest numbers seem to be better calculated because they derive from modern reassessments of the size of the area (6–10 hectares not 30) and a population density scale appropriate for a village. Assessments of its city-plan range from an organized polis-style (advocated by Strange, Corbo, and others) to an "organic growing village" without plan and without significant financial endowment.[234] The latter seems more accurate because of a lack of orthogonal grid planning, paved and columned roads, or public monuments surrounding an agora. Capernaum differed from Cana and Yodefat in the last regard, since no evidence of elite living has yet been found within its boundaries.[235]

Reed argues that though Capernaum did not sit on an international trade route (contra Strange), the building of Tiberias (A.D. 18/19) and the renaming of Bethsaida as Julias increased regional trade in Galilee through Capernaum. Interregional trade, including inhabitants of the Decapolis, would have increased during this time as well making it quite likely that more Gentiles would have been passing through Capernaum in the first quarter of the first-century.[236]

Though Capernaum offers fewer signs of Hellenistic and Jewish culture than other cities, the evidence which is available suggests the importance of Judaism. As a poorer village, marks of elite living (Hellenistic dwelling places and decoration) should not be as expected. The absence of decorative elements (red roofs, frescoes, plastered facades, marble, etc.) indicates this modesty and a lack of visible Hellenization.[237] The "Jewishness" of Capernaum can be established through various pieces of evidence. The presence of stone vessels in each "domestic unit" excavated parallel those

---

[233] Numbers found in Reed, *Archaeology*, 65, 152. Cf. Reed and Crossan, *Excavating Jesus*, 81; Vassilios Tzaferis, *Excavations at Capernaum* (Winona Lake: Eisenbrauns in association with Pepperdine University, 1989).

[234] Reed, *Archaeology*, 152–153.

[235] Reed, *Archaeology*, 148; cf. Jensen, *Antipas*, 172.

[236] Reed, *Archaeology*, 148.

[237] Reed, *Archaeology*, 156–157, see 139–169 for the full discussion of Capernaum.

of other Jewish sites. That no *miqwaot* have yet been found speaks toward the relatively modest economy rather than a lack of religious zeal.²³⁸ Its prominence as a Jewish and Christian pilgrimage site (in the Byzantine era) speaks of its importance to both religions. Rabbinic reference to *minim* in the region suggests that heretics stood out in a predominately Jewish area (*Midr. Qoh.* 1.8; 7.26). Capernaum was substantially Jewish, so when Jesus went from Nazareth to Capernaum he simply moved to a larger Jewish village from a smaller one. Nevertheless, Capernaum's location and size, along with interregional trade, would have made Gentile presence or interaction for Jesus' life more likely.²³⁹

Complete absence of inscriptions, both public and private, in the region betrays the relative status that Capernaum had earned at this time since benefactors and beneficiaries would typically have branded "all sorts of public surfaces: pavements, columns, fountains, and statues; they were the billboards of ancient city life."²⁴⁰ One votive inscription (*CIJ*, II, 983) had been previously attached to first-century Capernaum, but "elle appartient plus probablement au IIIe siècle."²⁴¹ Excavations have not thoroughly opened up the first-century city, so this conclusion remains tentative.

The literary evidence has been interpreted as indicating both Hellenistic and Roman influence. One group suggests that Antipas went "way over the top" in his projects in the village in large part because of Josephus' use of the phrase ἀγαπῶν τὴν ἡσυχίαν (*Ant.* 18.245):

Ὁ δὲ τέως μὲν ἀπεμάχετο ἀγαπῶν τὴν ἡσυχίαν καὶ τῆς Ῥώμης τὸν ὄχλον δι' ὑποψίας λαμβάνων ἀναδιδάσκειν τε αὐτὴν ἐπειρᾶτο
"For a while he resisted and tried to change her mind, for he was content with his tranquility and was wary of the Roman bustle." (Feldman, LCL)

The phrase is interpreted by this group as "lover of luxury" and leads to the conclusion that Antipas attempted a transformation of the village through lavish expenditures. But the text should be read "lover of rest" or "content with his tranquility," distinguished from the commotion of the Roman political struggle, rather than as lover of luxury signaling the importance of the fishing industry in the village.²⁴² Herod Antipas simply did not desire to bother involving himself in a political battle.

---

²³⁸ Reed, *Archaeology*, 157–158.
²³⁹ Reed, *Archaeology*, 161–163.
²⁴⁰ Reed, *Archaeology*, 150.
²⁴¹ Baruch Lifshitz, *Donateurs et fondateurs dans les synagogues juives, répertoire des dédicaces grecques relatives à la construction et à la réfection des synagogues* (Cahiers de la Revue biblique 7; Paris: Gabalda, 1967), 61.
²⁴² Hanson translates "lover of luxury," Jensen translates "lover of rest," and Loeb (Feldman) reads "content with his tranquility." K. C. Hanson, "The Galilean Fishing

2.2 Benefaction and Patronage in Palestine

Luke's story of the centurion in Capernaum has introduced another question and a possible insight into the presence of benefaction or patronage in this village (Luke 7:1–10). Scholars question the ethnicity of the man with Kee proposing that the centurion was Roman while Reed and Crossan argue that he may have been Jewish or another ethnicity.[243] To Kee, he was part of the "despised Roman occupying forces" and Jesus' dealings with him did not conform to the "ethnic integrity of the covenant."[244] Reed and Crossan argue against this proposal. Antipas used Roman names for his officials so the presence of an ἑκατοντάρχης does not imply Roman legionnaires being stationed there. It is historically implausible that a centurion and 100 Roman legionnaires would have been stationed in Capernaum, since troops only periodically marched through Galilee.[245] Kee's argument appears to rest on an untenable historical reconstruction (that a legion would be stationed in Capernaum) which flows from a mistaken assessment of its size (25,000 inhabitants) and a misapprehension of the positioning of Roman force.[246] It seems best to suppose that the centurion was neither ethnically Roman nor Jewish, but, perhaps, Syrian because Rome could have had a legion stationed there.[247]

Regardless of the centurion's ethnicity it is provocative that he is credited with building the synagogue for the inhabitants. In later times this would be commemorated with a benefaction inscription and the person honored as a benefactor.[248] What many have interpreted as a pre-revolt era synagogue has been discovered in Capernaum.[249] The date of the synagogue is a point of debate since early studies maintained that it belonged to a second century or later period, but subsequent studies now favor a first-

---

Economy and the Jesus Tradition," *BTB* 27/3(1997): 99–111, 103, found in Jensen, *Antipas*, 174–175.

[243] Kee, "Early Christianity," 18; Reed, *Archaeology*, 162; Crossan in Crossan and Reed, *Excavating Jesus*, 88–89.

[244] Kee, "Early Christianity," 18.

[245] Reed and Crossan, *Excavating Jesus*, 88–89; Reed, *Archaeology*, 162.

[246] See Sanders, "Jesus' Galilee," for a better historical reconstruction.

[247] Millar, *Near East*, 32; Sanders, "Jesus' Galilee," 10; A. N. Sherwin-White, *Roman Society and Roman Law in the New Testament* (Oxford: Clarendon, 1963), 123–124.

[248] Examples of which can be found in Lifshitz, *Donateurs*.

[249] Donald D. Binder, *Into the Temple Courts: The Place of the Synagogues in the Second Temple Period* (Atlanta: Society of Biblical Literature, 1999), 189 n. 61; Stanislao Loffreda, *Recovering Capharnaum* (Jerusalem: Edizioni Custodia Terra Santa, 1985), 46–49. These two references found in Jensen, *Antipas*, 170–171 and Schnabel, *Mission*, 1.230–231. See also, John S. Kloppenborg, "The Theodotus Synagogue Inscription and the Problem of First-Century Synagogue Buildings," in Charlesworth, *Jesus and Archaeology*, 236–282, 249 n. 44.

century date.²⁵⁰ Luke's narrative includes details which bespeak a benefactor/beneficiary relationship.²⁵¹ The zeal (σπουδαίως; 7:4) of the recipients to plead with Jesus to save (διασῴζω; 7:3) the servant on behalf of the worthy (ἄξιός; 7:4) centurion combines with the centurion's love for the nation (ἀγαπάω τὸ ἔθνος η'μῶν; 7:5) and his use of mediator/friends (φίλους; 7:6) to suggest an awareness of benefaction.²⁵² All these terms surface frequently in benefaction situations. The nature of the gift, a one-time, large non-necessity, resembles more closely a benefaction. Admittedly, Jews would have considered the synagogue very important to daily life, but it is a relatively expensive project that benefits an entire community. It is not necessary for survival itself like the donations of patrons tend to be. If the centurion had come from outside Israel, as Luke suggests (7:9), then he brings benefaction ideology into this small village and the villagers apparently pick up on it.²⁵³

Capernaum witnessed little in the way of overt Hellenization or Romanization in architecture, inscriptions, or coins, but it did experience increasing amounts of Gentile traffic which could no doubt have made its inhabitants aware of the ways in which others interacted. To date archaeologists have not found tangible evidence that benefaction had entered, at least not to the point that an inscription commemorated a benefit. This corresponds quite well with the low level of Hellenization. Josephus and the NT do not improve upon the archaeological record with other information about its cultural make-up, but Luke's story of the centurion's benefit suggests that benefaction could enter with Gentile traffic through the village. This centurion interacted as a benefactor more than patron to the Jews.

Tiberias

A range of opinions about the depth and pervasiveness of Hellenization and Romanization in Tiberias has been proposed, but it seems most accu-

---

[250] Jensen briefly describes the discussion of its date with reference to Loffreda, *Capharnaum*; Virgilio Corbo, "Capernaum," *ABD* 1.866–869; M. Avi-Yonah, "The Foundation of Tiberias," *IEJ* 1 (1950–1951): 160–169; Binder, *Temple Courts*; Jodi Magness, "The Question of the Synagogue: The Problem of Typology," in *The Special Problem of the Synagogue* (ed. Alan J. Avery-Peck; Leiden: Brill, 2001), 1–48. Loffreda and Corbo offered the first suggestion of a second century or later date, but subsequently changed opinions after Avi-Yonah had laid out his argument.

[251] Cf. De Silva, *Honor, Patronage*, 123–124; Moxnes, "Patron-Client," 252–253.

[252] "Friends" is probably a reference to those of equal status (beneficiaries) though it could be a euphemism for (lower-status) clients. Brunt, Eilers, and Nicols are skeptical of connecting "φιλὸς" with "client." Brunt, "Clientela," 392–395; Eilers, *Roman Patrons*, 14.

[253] Moxnes mixes sociological patron-client and historical benefaction language in his description of this scene. Moxnes, *Economy*, 59–60.

rate to conclude that the newly founded city only entered the initial stages of Hellenization in the time of Antipas and Romanization was more superficial than authentic. Antipas instituted a "Hellenistic pattern" to the Jewish-Hellenistic city, but Jewish culture dominated Tiberias in the first half of the first-century in regard to ethnicity, government, and religious expression.[254] Tiberias does have a few indicators of benefaction (and, later, patronage).

Many factors have been proposed to support the notion that Tiberias was deeply Hellenistic, but several of them may be disputed leaving a slightly less Hellenized portrait. Four main features contribute to the case for Hellenization in Tiberias: government, monumental structures, foundation upon unclean ground with consequent Gentile population, and the possibility of Greek *paideia*. In this discussion of the four potential signs of Hellenization or Romanization, literary and archaeological evidence will be combined in each section.

The Hellenistic institutions and offices of Tiberias are most closely connected to the War period, though they may reflect situations earlier in the century (βουλή *War* 2.641; *Life* 64, 169, 284, 300, 313, 381; a mayor – ἄρχων *Life* 134, 278, 294; *War* 2.599; ten principal men – πρώτους δέκα, *Life* 69, 269; governors – ὑπάρχοις *War* 2.615). The ἀγορανόμος is one office confidently connected to the time of Jesus (*Ant.* 18.149). Two lead weights have inscriptions telling of an agora and the office of *agoranomos* in Tiberias in the first-century A.D. (one dates to A.D. 31), thus confirming Josephus' description.[255] They read:

ΕΠΙ ΗΡΩΔΟΥ
ΤΕΤΡΑΧΟΥ
ΛΔΛ ΑΓΟΡΑ
ΝΟΜΟΥ ΓΑΙ
ΟΥ ΙΟΥΛΙΟΥ
ΕΤΑΛΕΝΤΟ
"In the 34th year of Herod the tetrarch,
[in the term of office as] *agoranomos* of Gaius Julius ..."

But Meyers and Reed both find archaeological evidence to suggest that the political and administrative form of Tiberias was Jewish in the era of Jesus.[256] Mark Chancey contends that it was not until the third quarter of the

---

[254] Jensen, *Antipas*, 136.

[255] Jensen, *Antipas*, 138, text and Shraga Qedar's translation, 146; Shraga Qedar, "Two Lead Weights of Herod Antipas and Agrippa II and the Early History of Tiberias," *Israel Numismatic Journal* 9 (1986–1987): 29–35; Chancey, *Culture of Jesus*, 87–88; cf. Zeev Weiss, "Josephus and Archaeology on the Cities of the Galilee," in Rodgers, *Making History*, 385–414.

[256] E. M. Meyers, "Jesus and His Galilean Context," in *Archaeology and the Galilee: Texts and Contexts in Graeco-Roman Galilee in the Graeco-Roman and Byzantine Peri-*

first-century that rule in Tiberias resembled an "eastern Hellenistic (not western Roman) city" complete with ten *protoi*, a *boule* of six hundred men, and public assemblies to address serious issues.[257] Antipas did take up Tiberias as his northern headquarters, after founding it around A.D. 18/19,[258] which opens the possibility of Hellenistic and Roman influence in governing approach.[259] If chronological distinctions are maintained then government will not support strong Hellenization in Tiberias in the era of Jesus, but a cultural shift may have started to take form with the inception of some Hellenistic offices and the more frequent presence of Antipas.

The second factor, monumental structures, argues for slightly more Hellenization in Tiberias. It has been said that Antipas attempted in vein to emulate his father's passion for construction. His monumental structures could imply an effort to be considered one of the Hellenistic kings, a title he eventually desired (*Ant.* 18.242–246; see section 3.2.2). Antipas perhaps built a stadium (*War* 2.618; *Life* 92, 331),[260] a palace (destroyed by Jews for artistic depictions of animals), and a gate complex which "may have been a free-standing arch, serving more to signify Tiberias' status as a city than to defend it."[261] The stadium probably dates to the first-century, but scholars cannot confidently narrow this down to the first half of the century.[262] It could just as easily date to the period of Roman administration (A.D. 44–55/60) as to the period of Antipas. The gate may not have been built until the second century, but Foerster, its excavator, argues for a first-century date.[263] That is to say, it is difficult to tell how much monumental construction Antipas attempted in Tiberias, or at least how much of his

---

ods (ed. D. R. Edwards, M. Aviam, and C. Thomas McCollough; Atlanta: Scholars Press, 1997), 57–66, here 64; Reed, *Archaeology*, 122. Cf. Jones, *Cities*, 275–276.

[257] Chancey, *Culture of Jesus*, 88.

[258] The precise date of Tiberias' foundation is disputed. In favor of A.D. 19, Meshorer, *Treasury*, 81–82. For A.D. 18, *Tabula Imperii Romani Iudaea*, 249. For ca. A.D. 20, see, Chancey, *Galilee*, 47.

[259] M. Avi-Yonah, "The Foundation of Tiberias," *Israel Exploration Journal* 1 (1950–1951): 160–169.

[260] Jensen discusses this stadium as the discovery of Moshe Hartal; cf. Jensen, *Antipas*, 144–145. Jensen hesitates to be more precise than to ascribe a first-century date to the stadium, even though it is possible that Antipas built it. See also, Chancey, *Culture of Jesus*, 87 who refers to "Roman Stadium Found at Tiberias," *Jerusalem Post*, June 17, 2002.

[261] Chancey, *Culture of Jesus*, 87. He refers to Monika Bernett, "Der Kaiserkult als Teil der politischen Geschichte Iudeas unter den Herodianern und Roemern (30 v.–66n. Chr.)," (Habilitationsschrift, Munich, 2002), 202.

[262] Jensen, *Antipas*, 144–48.

[263] Second-century: Chancey, *Culture of Jesus*, 87; Bernett, "Kaiserkult." First-century: Gideon Foerster, "Beth-Shean at the Foot of the Mound," *NEAHL*, 1:1471. This discussion is summarized in Jensen, *Antipas*, 139–140.

2.2 Benefaction and Patronage in Palestine

construction has yet been discovered. Josephus does give Antipas credit for many substantial projects, a practice which resembles the Hellenistic kings' thirst for largesse, but archaeologists have not yet been able to identify and assess them.

The third factor which signals Hellenization to many is a significant Gentile population in consequence of unclean living conditions. This conclusion has been reached from both literary and archaeological evidence, but it has recently been objected to quite strongly by Jensen. He argues that evidence of a Gentile population in Tiberias cannot be found in either the literary or archaeological evidence. Antipas built Tiberias upon a cemetery which would mean an unclean dwelling place for Jews (*Ant.* 18.36–38).

Ἡρώδης δὲ ὁ τετράρχης ἐπὶ μέγα γὰρ ἦν τῷ Τιβερίῳ φιλίας προελθὼν οἰκοδομεῖται πόλιν ἐπώνυμον αὐτῷ Τιβεριάδα τοῖς κρατίστοις ἐπικτίσας αὐτὴν τῆς Γαλιλαίας ἐπὶ λίμνῃ τῇ Γεννησαρίτιδι θερμά τε οὐκ ἄπωθέν ἐστιν ἐν κώμῃ Ἀμμαθοὺς ὄνομα αὐτῇ σύγκλυδες δὲ ᾤκισαν οὐκ ὀλίγον δὲ καὶ τὸ Γαλιλαῖον ἦν καὶ ὅσοι μὲν ἐκ τῆς ὑ'π' αὐτῷ γῆς ἀναγκαστοὶ καὶ πρὸς βίαν εἰς τὴν κατοικίαν ἀγόμενοι τινὲς δὲ καὶ τῶν ἐν τέλει ἐδέξατο δὲ αὐτοῖς συνοίκους καὶ τοὺς πανταχόθεν ἐπισυναγομένους ἄνδρας ἀπόρους (*Ant.* 18.36–37)

"The tetrarch Herod, inasmuch as he had gained a high place among the friends of Tiberius, had a city built, named after him Tiberias, which he established in the best region of Galilee on Lake Gennesaritis. There is a hot spring not far from it in a village called Ammathus. The new settlers were a promiscuous rabble, no small contingent being Galilaean, with such as were drafted from territory subject to him and brought forcibly to the new foundation. Some of these were magistrates. Herod accepted as participants even poor men who were brought in to join the others from any and all places of origin. It was a question whether some were even free beyond cavil."

Several scholars assume that Josephus references a Gentile population by his use of the term σύγκλυδες.[264] Jensen suggests that this assumption stems from Whiston's influential, and outdated, translation of Josephus. He translates the Greek word as "strangers" (*Ant.* 18.37), but Jensen suggests the term is better translated "mob."[265] Josephus uses the term three other times (*Ant.* 19.243; *War* 5.27, 443).

ἴστε μὴν στρατόν ὃς ὑπὲρ Κλαυδίου μαχεῖται πλήθει χρόνου ὁ πλιτεύειν μεμελετηκότα τὰ δ' ἡμέτερα συγκλύδων ἀνθρώπων πλῆθος δ' ἔσται καὶ τῶν παρὰ δόξαν τῆς δουλείας ἀπηλλαγμένων δυσκράτητα πρὸς δὲ τεχνίτας μαχούμεθα προαγαγόντες ἄνδρας μηδ' ὅπως σπάσαι τὰ ξίφη εἰδότας (*Ant.* 19.243)

---

[264] Avi-Yonah, "Foundation," 163; Yizhar Hirschfeld and Katharina Galor, "New Excavations in Roman, Byzantine and Early Islamic Tiberias," in *Religion, Ethnicity and Identity in Ancient Galilee* (ed. Jürgen Zangenberg, H. W. Attridge, and D. B. Martin; Tübingen: Mohr Siebeck, 2007), in Jensen, *Antipas*, 135.

[265] Jensen, *Antipas*, 135–136.

"You know, of course, that the army that will fight for Claudius has been long trained to bear arms, while ours will be a motley rabble consisting of men who have unexpectedly been released from slavery and who are consequently hard to control."

Πανταχόθεν δὲ τῆς πόλεως πολεμουμένης ὑπὸ τῶν ἐπιβούλων καὶ συγκλύδων μέσος ὁ δῆμος ὥσπερ μέγα σῶμα διεσπαράσσετο (*War* 5.27)

"The city being now on all sides beset by these battling conspirators and their rabble, between them the people, like some huge carcase, was torn in pieces."

οἵ γε τελευταῖον καὶ τὸ γένος ἐφαύλιζον τῶν Ἑβραίων ὡς ἧττον ἀσεβεῖς δοκοῖεν πρὸς ἀλλοτρίους ἐξωμολογήσαντο δ' ὅπερ ἦσαν εἶναι δοῦλοι καὶ σύγκλυδες καὶ νόθα τοῦ ἔθνους φθάρματα (*War* 5.443)

"Indeed they ended by actually disparaging the Hebrew race, in order to appear less impious in so treating aliens, and owned themselves, what indeed they were, slaves, the dregs of society and the bastard scum of the nation."

It is translated, respectively, as "motley rabble," "rabble," and "bastard scum of the [Hebrew] nation."[266] It is better to understand the "mixed" adjective as a description of the socio-economic status of the various groups brought in.[267] Feldman's "promiscuous rabble" captures the idea well. Though σύγκλυδες cannot be used to suggest greater Hellenization in Tiberias, Josephus does indicate that Antipas operated as a benefactor on behalf of the σύγκλυδες he brought to Tiberias. Josephus describes Antipas as a benefactor to the new inhabitants of Tiberias when he provided for them out of his own means (εὐηργέτησεν; *Ant.* 18.37–38).

ἔστι δ' οὓς μηδὲ σαφῶς ἐλευθέρους πολλά τε αὐτοὺς κἀπὶ πολλοῖς ἠλευθέρωσεν καὶ εὖ 'ηργέτησεν ἀνάγκασμα τοῦ μὴ ἀπολείψειν τὴν πόλιν ἐπιθείς κατασκευαῖς τε οἰκήσεων ·τέλεσι τοῖς αὐτοῦ καὶ γῆς ἐπιδόσει (*Ant.* 18.38)

"These latter he often and in large bodies liberated and benefited (imposing the condition that they should not quit the city), by equipping houses at his own expense and adding new gifts of land. For he knew that this settlement was contrary to the law and tradition of the Jews because Tiberias was built on the site of tombs that had been obliterated, of which there were many there. And our law declares that such settlers are unclean for seven days."

Antipas did not inhabit Tiberias with large numbers of Gentiles, but he did function as a benefactor himself with respect to the new residents.

The fourth feature which suggests high levels of Hellenization could be the possibility of *paideia* in Tiberias. Josephus ascribes Greek *paideia* to many in his narratives, including Justus of Tiberias, the Jewish writer.[268]

μέτριον γὰρ ἰδιώτης ὢν ἦγεν αὐτὸν καὶ τοῖς πᾶσιν ἀρκῶν ἦν παιδείᾳ τε συνιὼν καὶ μάλιστα τῇ Ἑλληνίδι (*Ant.* 19.213)

---

[266] Feldman, *LCL*. Or "rude [multitude," "wicked crowds," and "scum" (of the Hebrew nation) in Sanders, "Jesus' Relation," 76–77.

[267] Jensen, *Antipas*, 136.

[268] Cf. *Life* 40, 336–59; *Apion* 1.73; Tessa Rajak, "Greeks and Barbarians in Josephus," in Collins and Sterling, *Hellenism*, 244–262, 257.

"For in private life he bore himself modestly and was satisfied with what he had. He pursued his studies, especially in Greek."

An obvious consequence of this is that Justus of Tiberias (and Josephus) spoke and wrote in Greek (*Life* 34–42, 65, 336–360).[269] Gymnasia were the typical locus of *paideia* so one may wonder where the instruction took place since no gymnasium has yet been discovered in Tiberias. Collins argues, in regard to Jerusalem's gymnasium, that the education could consist of classic Greek works without offending Jewish sensibilities, but whether this happened or not is another question.[270]

It appears that some Hellenization had penetrated the culture of Tiberias, but it was not as pronounced as some have supposed. Hellenistic forms of government had just been introduced in the time of Jesus, some monumental structures were constructed, Greek language and education had made some inroads, and perhaps a few Greeks had come to live there. But the majority of the Hellenization took place in the century after Jesus.

Some have suggested that Antipas brought intense Romanization to Tiberias, but a more judicious reading of the sources downplays but does not dismiss the presence of Roman culture. At a later time Josephus could accuse the Tiberians for loving neither Rome nor the king (*Life* 345), but it appears that Antipas made some effort to give a different impression. Antipas founded and named the city in honor of the newly appointed emperor (*Ant.* 18.36). Renaming cities was a common practice among the Hellenistic kings desiring to be seen as benefactors. Suetonius explains that friendly kings created cities in honor of Augustus (Suetonius *Aug.* 60):

Reges amici atque socii et singuli in suo quisque regno caesares urbes condiderunt.
"His friends and allies among the kings each in his own realm founded a city called Caesarea." (J. C. Rolfe, LCL)

Antipas expressed his allegiance to and potentially advanced his friendship with Tiberius by naming the city in his honor.

Josephus also describes his relationship to the Tiberians in a blend of patronage and benefaction terminology, but he refers to a period after the era under discussion. During the time of John, Josephus' abode was in Cana and John apparently had the Tiberians switch allegiance (ἀφίσταμαι and προστίθημι) from fidelity to Josephus to John (*Life* 86–88). Josephus describes the fidelity the Tiberians had toward him (τῆς πρός με πίστεως) and how John had persuaded the men to leave him (πειθε τοὺς ἀνθρώπους ἀποστάντας) and be joined to John (προστίθεσθαι αὐτῷ). There are two men in particular, Justus and Pistus, who revolted (ἀποστάντες ἐμοῦ) from

---

[269] Porter, "Jesus and the Use of Greek," 141.
[270] John J. Collins, "Cult and Culture: The Limits of Hellenization in Judea," in Collins and Sterling, *Hellenism*, 38–61.

Josephus and joined John (προσθέσθαι τῷ 'Ιωάννῃ). If the story reflects how Josephus conceptualized his relationships at the time, and is not simply a later reconceptualization, then the ideology of patronage eventually entered Tiberias (cf. προστάτης of the Galileans; *Life* 1.250).

Tiberias differed considerably from villages in Galilee according to the archaeological evidence. Its palace and other monumental structures, along with white plastered walls, and "typical Roman city layout" would have distinguished it from those smaller places.[271] Antipas overlooked Jewish scruples building on a cemetery and the construction of a stadium and theater (if indeed from his era) show the dominance of Roman culture among the elite who would have mimicked him. At the same time these monuments probably only suggest "a provincial 'Roman urban overlay.'"[272] Horsley finds little evidence for a cosmopolitan culture in the first few decades after the creation of Tiberias.[273]

Some authors suggest that the stadium was the location of gladiatorial games, but this oversteps the capabilities of this smaller venue. Gladiatorial games required the proper venue. Vitruvius commends rectangular Roman style forums with a particular spacing of columns (Vitruvius *On Architecture*, 5.1.1).

Graeci in quadrato amplissimis et duplicibus porticibus fora contituunt crebrisque columnis et lapideis aut marmoreis epistyliis adornant et supra ambulationes in contignationibus faciunt. Italiae vero urbibus non eadum est ratione faciendum, ideo quod a maioribus consuetudo tradita est gladiatoria munera in foro dari. Igitur circum spectacula spatiosiora intercolumnia distribuantur circaque in porticibus argentariae tabernae maenianaque superioribus coazationibus conlocentur; quae et ad usum et ad cevtigalia publica recta erunt disposita.
"The Greeks plan the forum on the square with most ample double colonnades and close-set columns; they ornament them with stone or marble architraves, and above they make promenades on the boarded floors. But in the cities of Italy we must not proceed on the same plan, because the custom of giving gladiatorial shows in the forum has been handed down from our ancestors. For that reason more roomy intercolumniations are to be used round the spectacle; in the colonnades, silversmiths' shops; and balconies, rightly placed for convenience and for public revenue, are to be placed on the upper floors." (Frank Granger, LCL)

For this reason, MacMullen differentiates the stadium at Tiberias from those in Caesarea and Jerusalem. Tiberias' oval shaped race-track might

---

[271] Jensen, *Antipas*, 148.

[272] Horsley, "Jesus and Galilee," 63. He cites James F. Strange, "Some Implications of Archaeology for New Testament Studies," in *What Has Archaeology to Do with Faith?* (ed. James Charlesworth and Walter Weaver; Philadelphia: Fortress, 1992), 31–35.

[273] Richard A. Horsley, "Jesus and Galilee: The Contingencies of a Renewal Movement," in *Galilee Through the Centuries: Confluence of Cultures* (ed. Eric M. Meyers; Winona Lake: Eisenbrauns, 1999), 57–74.

2.2 Benefaction and Patronage in Palestine

work, but was less than ideal for gladiatorial games. The stadia in Caesarea and Jerusalem were well-suited for them.[274] Chancey challenges H. A. Harris who claims that Simon Peter grew up watching bloody gladiator shows since he finds no evidence for such shows in first-century Galilee.[275] It is not that such games were impossible to hold in the stadium, but that archaeological (and literary) evidence of such games is lacking.

Others have made much of the fact that Tiberias had been pronounced a *polis* which may indicate a level of affinity between inhabitants and Roman administration.[276] Warwick Ball responds that though many assume that Rome "consciously encouraged the development of settlements into cities" not one example of a completely newly founded city can be found in the East.[277] Becoming a *polis* in the east did not indicate colonization, but simply autonomy.[278] He goes on to argue that the establishment of cities says qualitatively little about the city's (or its citizens') "consciousness" or attraction to Roman ways since the majority of these established cities derived their status from imperial whim. An emperor was praised in a certain place so the settlement received appropriate recognition by the ruler. Furthermore, Tiberias did not even have the complete autonomy which was traditionally granted.[279] That Nero, before the Jewish revolt, could give Tiberias to Agrippa II indicates that the city did not have full autonomy, but rather a "merely municipal autonomy."[280] It had a tradition of allegiance to the Herodian family (Antipas to Agrippa II), and its farmlands were controlled by them as well. Since in a typical polis farmers who farmed outlying regions were included among the citizens and it seems that in Tiberias the Herodian ruler ruled these lands and excluded residents from citizenship, Tiberias functioned as a toparchic capital. "Tiberias was formally a polis, but was a polis of a modified Herodian sort that made it

---

[274] MacMullen, *Romanization*, 16–17.

[275] Chancey, *Culture of Jesus*, 87–90; H. A. Harris, *Greek Athletics and the Jews* (Cardiff: University of Wales Press, 1976), 106. Chancey simply states that no evidence can be found for gladiatorial games. He allows for the possibility of footraces in the stadium, and for the assemblage of crowds (*War* 2.599; *Life* 132–133).

[276] E.g., Mack, *Lost Gospel*, 58–61. At a later time Sepphorites definitely expressed affinity toward the Roman administration, Weiss, "Cities of the Galilee," 386–387.

[277] Ball, *Rome*, 149. Ball quotes John D. Grainger, "Village Government in Roman Syria and Arabia," *Levant* 27 (1995): 179–195, 180. Ball refers also to Greg Woolf, "Urbanization," in *The Early Roman Empire in the East Oxford* (Oxbow Monograph 95; ed. S. E. Alcock; Oxford: Oxford University Press, 1997), 1–14. Cf. Sanders, "Jesus' Galilee," 27.

[278] Ball, *Rome*, 149, quoting A. H. M. Jones, *Cities of the Eastern Roman Provinces* (Oxford: Oxford University Press, 1971), 247.

[279] Sanders, "Jesus' Galilee," 26–28.

[280] A. H. M. Jones and Michael Avi-Yonah, *Cities of the Eastern Roman Provinces* (Amsterdam: Gieben, 1983), 276, in Sanders, "Jesus' Galilee," 27.

not much different from a toparchic capital, controlled by a ruler or his appointees. It lacked many of the features of a true polis."[281] Some Roman culture had entered Tiberias with Antipas, but it appears to have been not much more than a veneer. The general populace could have been aware of benefaction and patronage through the naming of their city after the new emperor. But so naming the city and being named a *polis* by the emperor does not necessitate that the general population saw themselves as more "Roman" than their neighbors. Josephus expresses how things developed over time. He gives evidence that in subsequent decades benefaction and patronage were categories he could use in reference to interpersonal relationships in Tiberias (*Life* 86–88). But he can also rebuke the people for not being friendly to Rome or the king.

Hellenization and Romanization had not overtaken Tiberias, but rather the newly founded city consisted of a strong Jewish element. This can be seen through a number of factors. Reed locates the same Jewish identity markers in Tiberias that had been found in other parts of Galilee (stone vessels, a *miqveh*, and ossuaries).[282] Though Antipas lured people from other villages and the countryside to Tiberias and Sepphoris, "[t]here is no archaeological evidence for large numbers of non-Jews living in the new Herodian cities."[283] Josephus does mention some Greeks in Tiberias, but this refers to a period just after the era under discussion (*Life* 66–67). The evidence that Jews controlled many of the administrative and political offices also attests to the strength of the Jewish hold on this city. The destruction of Antipas' palace by the Jews for its depiction of animals shows the religious fervor evident in this city. The palace was discovered covered in ash which possibly confirms Josephus' tale (*Life* 64–69).[284]

Though no explicit mention of visits to Tiberias is made in the gospels, there are several hints of knowledge (either first or second-hand in the gospels). Jesus and the disciples go to cities (Matt 10:11; Luke 10:8), a royal palace is mentioned (Tiberias? Luke 7:25), an agora and plaza are talked about (Luke 7:32, 10:10; 13:26; 14:21), and also a bank, gate, court, and prison are mentioned (Matt 13:29; Luke 7:12; Luke 19:23; Luke 12:57–59).[285] Perhaps Jesus had more contact, or his disciples had contact,

---

[281] Sanders, "Jesus' Galilee," 28.

[282] Reed, *Archaeology*, 50.

[283] Reed, *Archaeology*, 84.

[284] Jensen, *Antipas*, 142–143; Yizhar Hirschfeld, "Tiberias," *Excavations and Surveys in Israel* 16 (1997): 35–42; Yizhar Hirschfeld and Katharina Galor, "New Excavations in Roman, Byzantine and Early Islamic Tiberias," in Zangenberg, Attridge, and Martin, *Religion*, forthcoming.

[285] Schnabel, *Mission*, 1.238.

with these cities, but it is suggestive that no polemic is launched against them but rather against Capernaum, Chorazin, and Bethsaida.[286]

Tiberias in the early first-century was fairly Jewish with hints of Hellenistic and Roman influence. Its government later resembled Hellenistic governments, but it is not certain that this same scenario existed in the time of Jesus. Antipas built some monumental structures which indicate a level of Hellenization, but he did not import large numbers of Gentiles to inhabit the new city. Greek paideia was possible in the city, but it is difficult to identify where it might have taken place. Antipas attempted some cultural influence, specifically through naming the city in honor of the emperor and constructing monumental works. These actions, however, tell more of his personal sentiments than those of the population at large. Tiberias held a strong Jewish element that revolted when Antipas breached religious commands. Finally, though no specific mention of a visit to Tiberias is mentioned in the NT, there are hints that its characters were familiar with the city.

Sepphoris

Cultural analyses of Sepphoris still maintain polar extremes in regard to Hellenization and Romanization. H. C. Kee, in his latest effort to describe the city, urges that in Sepphoris "[a]ll the features of a Hellenistic city were there, including a theater, hippodrome, and temples" during the time of Jesus.[287] To deny awareness, or interaction, with strong Hellenism is, for Kee, "historically untenable." At the other extreme stands E. P. Sanders who argues for minimal Hellenistic and Roman influence. A main point in his argument is the denial of the early first-century presence of a theater or temples and the conclusion that no one in Sepphoris would have used them even if they had existed.[288] There are several main points of debate in regard to Hellenization and Romanization in Sepphoris: the administrative center mentioned by Josephus (*Ant.* 14.91; *War* 1.170); the presence of temples, a theater, cardo, and basilical building in the first half of the first-century; Roman colonists or soldiers in the city and the ethnic make-up of the inhabitants; the nature of this "polis"; and the presence of an elite class. Several recent works on Sepphoris conclude that it was a predominately Jewish location in its urban infancy that had adopted a Hellenistic overlay. It seems that more scholars today posit less Hellenism in Sepphoris. In the following discussion the literary evidence for a "Roman administrative center" will be addressed first. Following this, archaeological

---

[286] Reed, *Archaeology*, 98–99.
[287] Kee, "Early Christianity," 15.
[288] Sanders, "Jesus' Galilee," 32.

evidence will be examined to discern the various features which may or may not have been present during the ministries of Jesus and the apostles (temples, theater, cardo, basilical building; ethnic make-up of inhabitants; elite class).

Josephus' reference to a potentially Roman administrative center in Sepphoris, if true and if it persisted for around a century, would suggest a significant amount of Romanization in the city, but this reading of government in Sepphoris should be rejected. Josephus mentions five centers which Pompey set up in Palestine: Jerusalem, Gadara, Amathus, Jericho, and Sepphoris (*Ant.* 14.91; cf. *War* 1.170).

πέντε δὲ συνέδρια καταστήσας εἰς ἴσας μοίρας διένειμε τὸ ἔθνος καὶ ἐπολιτεύοντο οἱ μὲν ἐν Ἱεροσολύμοις οἱ δὲ ἐν Γαδάροις οἱ δὲ ἐν Ἀμαθοῦντι τέταρτοι δ' ἦσαν ἐν Ἱεριχοῦντι καὶ τὸ πέμπτον ἐν Σαπφώροις τῆς Γαλιλαίας καὶ οἱ μὲν ἀπηλλαγμένοι δυναστείας ἐν ἀριστοκρατίᾳ διῆγον

"He also set up five councils (synhedria), and divided the nation into as many districts; these centres of government were: first, Jerusalem, next, Gadara, third, Amathus, fourth, Jericho, and fifth, Sepphoris in Galilee. And so the people were removed from monarchic rule and lived under an aristocracy."

Kee[289] and Sanders differ on the reading and implications of this statement. In Kee's construction Romans held control of the city and comprised its governing body for nearly a century (from Pompey through Christ). But Kee's construction falters for several reasons. First, Romans were not the staff of this government, but rather it was a Jewish led center. Both E. P. Sanders and Stuart Miller have shown this to be the case.[290] The government was a Jewish aristocracy (τὴν ἄλλην πολιτείαν ἐπὶ προστασίᾳ τῶν ἀρίστων; *War* 1.169). Peitholaus, "second in command at Jerusalem," was Jewish (*War* 1.172, 180; *Ant.* 14.84). Before leaving for Syria, Gabinius altered the government to align with Antipater's wishes (*War* 1.178) thus leaving Hyrcanus II and Antipater in authority (*War* 1.87; *Ant.* 14.127–132; c. 48–47 B.C). Second, Kee neglects the distinction between senatorial and imperial provinces, of which the latter had only indirect Roman rule either through client kings or local administration. The proposed government of Kee could not have endured through the time of Jesus because Galilee became a part of an imperial Roman province in the reign of Herod I. Third, being an "administrative center" did not last indefinitely, but actually ended after only one or two years, not the ninety or so proposed by

---

[289] Kee, "Early Christianity."

[290] Sanders, "Jesus' Galilee," 7 n. 14; Stuart S. Miller, "Hellenistic and Roman Sepphoris: The Historical Evidence," in *Sepphoris in Galilee: Crosscurrents of Culture* (ed. Rebecca Martin Nagy, Carol L. Meyers, Eric M. Meyers, and Ze'ev Weiss; Winona Lake: Eisenbrauns, 1996), 21–27. For other details see S. Herbert and A. Berlin, "A New Administrative Centre for Persian and Hellenistic Galilee: Preliminary Report of the University of Minnesota Excavation of Kadesh," *BASOR* 329 (2003): 13–59.

Kee.[291] For these reasons it seems best to conclude that no direct Roman rule of Sepphoris took place from Gabinius' rule (63 B.C.) through the time of Jesus. Richard Horsley has recently argued that even three decades after Jesus, Tiberias and Sepphoris did not show great cosmopolitan flare. Though the language of administration would have been Greek, Hellenization was superficial.[292] A Roman or Hellenistic form of government in the time of Jesus would be one factor contributing to the possibility of patronage or benefaction in Sepphoris, but it is historically unlikely.

Debate about the presence of monumental buildings in Sepphoris during the time of Jesus also has implications for the amount of Hellenization or Romanization in the city, but increasingly scholars push the dates for the major structures into the later first and early second centuries. Kee and Batey provide the impetus for viewing Sepphoris as a richly Hellenistic or Roman city in the early first-century mainly by contending that the major structures discovered in Sepphoris began or were completed by the time of Jesus' ministry. Batey argues that Sepphoris would have had many amenities consistent with Roman life including a theatre and a temple to Roma and Augustus.[293] The renaming of Sepphoris around this time as *Autocratoris* (as a synonym of *Imperatoria*) has been read as confirmation that such a temple corresponded with the presence of the imperial cult.[294] By itself the new name would suggest a tangible tie to Rome, but this does not necessitate that the inhabitants themselves felt the same allegiance as Antipas. Renaming the city is a typical benefit given by Hellenistic kings to honor others (cf. Suetonius *Aug* 60).

Nevertheless, there are respective major problems with the use of the theater and temples to support notions of heavy Hellenization and Romanization in Sepphoris. For many reasons it seems best to conclude that the theater was not constructed until after the time of Jesus. The Hebrew University team that completed the excavation of the theater bases its later date (late first or early second century) "on a range of archaeological factors: material culture, building construction, building plan, architectural ornamentation, and – looking at the broader picture – how the theater fits

---

[291] Sanders, "Jesus' Galilee," 7.

[292] Richard A. Horsley, "Jesus and Galilee: The Contingencies of a Renewal Movement," in *Galilee Through the Centuries: Confluence of Cultures* (ed. Eric M. Meyers; Winona Lake: Eisenbrauns, 1999), 57–74, 63–64.

[293] Batey, *Forgotten City*, 56; cf. idem, "Jesus and the Theatre"; idem, "Sepphoris: An Urban Portrait of Jesus," *BAR* 18 (1992): 50–63.

[294] *Autocratoris* has also been interpreted as "autonomous." Louis H. Feldman, "The Term 'Galileans' in Josephus," *Jewish Quarterly Review* 72 (1981–82): 50–52, 51.

into Sepphoris's new urban infrastructure."[295] Several ceramic vessels (A.D. 70–80) provide a *terminus post quem* for the theater's construction since they were found covered in thick fill below its outer wall.[296]

Several of the other monumental constructions posited by Kee and Batey for early first-century era Sepphoris do not appear to belong to that era. No (pagan) temple has yet been found in Sepphoris, though excavations continue, so these should not yet be assumed to have been a part of early first-century life.[297] Some have attempted to use the Dionysiac mosaic as evidence that fascination and participation in this cult spanned the centuries before and after Christ, but Freyne has recently made a strong case that this mosaic belongs to the second or third century A.D.[298] Other scholars attempt to locate the cardo and basilical building in early first-century Sepphoris. Various dates for these structures have been offered, but even if they belong to the period of Jesus they would only signal the "urban infancy" of Sepphoris.[299]

Details in the archaeological remains also do not indicate high levels of Hellenization. Reed examines the decorative elements and the material culture of Sepphoris and Tiberias concluding that neither "shows the same kind of appetite for materials, buildings, and particularly decorative elements that symbolized Greco-Roman culture, compared to Caesarea Maritima or Scythopolis, the major cities in Palestine."[300] Tiberias had the feel of a Roman polis more so than Sepphoris for it, unlike its neighbor, contained monumental structures and public buildings. Sepphoris had a rural feel because it lacked Roman or Hellenistic style public buildings.[301]

It seems that Herod I and Antipas neglected Sepphoris in their building programs. The rebuilt wall is the only project mentioned in Josephus (*War* 2.574).[302] Evidence from archaeology and Josephus suggests that no monumental structures existed in early first-century Sepphoris and this minimizes the presence of Hellenization or Romanization in the city. The discovery of an agora in Sepphoris (and *agoranomoi*, see below, section

---

[295] Zeev Weiss, "Josephus and Archaeology on the Cities of the Galilee," in *Making History: Josephus and Historical Method* (ed. Zuleika Rodgers; JSJSupp 110; Leiden: Brill, 2007), 385–414, here 402–404.

[296] Weiss, "Cities," 402.

[297] Jensen, *Antipas*, 91.

[298] Sean Freyne, "Dionysos and Herakles in Galilee: The Sepphoris Mosaic in Context," in Edwards, *Religion and Society*, 56–69.

[299] Jensen, *Antipas*, 162.

[300] Reed, *Archaeology*, 94–96.

[301] Zeev Weiss, "Josephus and Archaeology on the Cities of the Galilee," in Rodgers, *Making History*, 385–414, 407.

[302] Weiss, "Cities," 393–4; S. S. Miller, "Josephus on the Cities of Galilee: Factions, Rivalries and Alliances in the First Jewish Revolt," *Historia* 50/4 (2001): 453–67, 454.

2.2.3 *Sepphoris*) gives a hint of Hellenization in the era, but this should not be overemphasized.

The ethnic make-up of Sepphoris has also been used to support a view of Sepphoris as Hellenized or Romanized, but increasingly scholars suggest it was predominately Jewish. Fergus Millar describes Sepphoris and Tiberias as comprised of "mixed gentile and Jewish" populations.[303] Assessments like Millar's typically flow from a broad chronological reading of the material culture and hints in the primary literature. The increasing use of stratification to more precisely date material culture challenges these broad brush portraits and paints a different picture. In the early first-century little or no Romans inhabited Sepphoris on a consistent basis, a situation which dramatically changed in the post-revolt era. Precision in regard to the dating of the temple and theater diminishes the likelihood of Roman inhabitants. Antipas stationed no Roman army in the city, but rather soldiers in this period would have been Jewish.[304]

Comparing material cultures throughout Galilee one can see that Sepphoris was significantly Jewish. The four major material parallels (lack of pig bones, *miqvaoth*, stone vessels, and burial) show this. In fact, the largest swath of evidence for Jewish identity comes from Sepphoris (100 stone vessel fragments, twenty *miqvaoth*, no pig bones, Second Temple Jewish tombs).[305] Two inscriptions found in Sepphoris support the notion that Jews participated in the highest civic positions in the city during the first-century.[306] The first is an inscription on a jar handle (first-century B.C.) with the Greek office ἐπιμελητής transliterated in Hebrew letters.[307] The term may mean governor, commander, or military leader.[308] The second is a lead weight (first-century A.D.) with Latin measurement on it (half litra), a drawing of an agora, and two Jewish names in Greek letters described as *agoranomoi* (market inspectors who sold permits).[309] These show Jews in positions of authority in Sepphoris,[310] and also multiple languages in use.

---

[303] Millar, *Near East*, 343.

[304] Sanders, "Jesus' Galilee," 10; Zeev Safrai, "The Roman Army in the Galilee," in Levine, *Late Antiquity*, 103–114; Eric M. Meyers, "Sepphoris on the Eve of the Great Revolt (67–68 C.E.): Archaeology and Josephus," in Meyers, *Centuries*, 109–122, 114, 120–122; Milton Moreland, "The Galilean Response to Earliest Christianity: A Cross-cultural Study of the Subsistence Ethic," in Edwards, *Religion*, 37–48, 42–43.

[305] Reed, *Archaeology*, 49.

[306] Reed, *Archaeology*, 134.

[307] Meyers, "Sepphoris on the Eve of the Great Revolt," 112–113.

[308] Meyers, "Sepphoris on the Eve of the Great Revolt," 112–113.

[309] Reed and Crossan, *Excavating Jesus*, 64–65.

[310] Eric Meyers claims the *epimeletes* would "no doubt" have been Jewish, Meyers, "Sepphoris on the Eve," 112–113; Meyers cites J. Naveh, "Jar fragment with inscription in Hebrew," in Nagy, et al., *Sepphoris in Galilee*, 170.

Reed concludes that elite Jews in Sepphoris would have interacted in Greek, but this would have made them only relatively more Hellenistic, while the rural folk would definitely have conversed in Aramaic.[311] If the inhabitants of Sepphoris were just as Jewish, they were perhaps also slightly more Hellenized.[312] They could visit the agora and one of their own had responsibility over it. In some measure at least they would have been learning how to function in a Hellenistic culture.

Though Sepphoris developed into a Roman or Hellenistic style *polis* toward the end of the first-century, in the era of Jesus it lacked many essential features of autonomous cities. Typical cities had temples, gymnasia, gridded roads, theaters, and other public buildings. They also minted coins and were protected or surrounded by gates. While not all of these features need be present to qualify as a true *polis*, it is noteworthy that for the first third of the first-century Sepphoris most likely had none of them. By the end of the first-century and spilling over into the second, Sepphoris acquired these elements, but one should not confuse its later form with its earlier form.[313] Sanders describes Sepphoris in Jesus' day as a Herodian-style *polis*, lacking pagan temples and gymnasia out of deference to Jewish scruples.[314] In the second half of the first-century things changed. It was not until A.D. 67/68 that Sepphoris minted its widely known "Neronias-Sepphoris, city of peace" coins.[315] The gate is the single feature which garners the most attention for being established in Antipas' time because of the citation by Josephus (*Ant.* 18.27). But a gate alone does not a Hellenistic or Roman *polis* make. While no public buildings have been uncovered, a well-decorated house indicates relative wealth. No elite wares have been found which tempers this description.[316] Moreland suggests the friction between rich and poor has been exaggerated, in conjunction with the finding that the rich in Sepphoris were not all too wealthy.[317] In Jesus' day Sepphoris was not a Hellenistic or Roman city. But social change toward Helleni-

---

[311] Reed, *Archaeology*, 134. Reed refers to G. W. Bowersock, *Hellenism in Late Antiquity* (Cambridge: Cambridge University Press, 1990), 1–13.

[312] Reed, *Archaeology*, 217.

[313] Eric M. Meyers, "The Early Roman Period at Sepphoris: Chronological, Archaeological, Literary, and Social Considerations," in *Hesed Ve-Emet: Studies in Honor of Ernest S. Frerichs* (ed. Jodi Magness and Seymour Gitin; Atlanta: Scholars Press, 1998), 343–355; Ehud Netzer and Zeev Weiss "Architectural Development of Sepphoris During the Roman and Byzantine Periods," in Edwards and McCollough, *Archaeology*, 117–129.

[314] Sanders, "Jesus' Galilee," 29–31.

[315] Ya'aḳov Meshorer, *A Treasury of Jewish Coins from the Persian Period to Bar Kokhba* (Jerusalem: Yad ben-Zvi Press, 2001), 102–105.

[316] Jensen, *Antipas*, 152–53; Reed, *Archaeology*, 126.

[317] Moreland, "Subsistence Ethic," 43. See Reed, "Galileans, 'Israelite Village Communities,' and the Sayings Gospel Q," in Meyers, *Centuries*, 93–96.

zation was afoot. Antipas had started the process and Sepphoris may have been viewed as indicative of this move.[318]

Though some have thought patronage and/or benefaction existed in Sepphoris at the time of Jesus, the evidence minimizes its likelihood. Freyne thinks patronage operated at Sepphoris, but he does not describe how it operated or give evidence for this assertion.[319] He most likely refers to sociological patronage since elsewhere he downplays Romanization in this city. Low levels of Romanization make adoption of *patrocinium* unlikely. A major hurdle to overcome for anyone desiring to espouse patronage or benefaction in Sepphoris, or in Galilee in general, is the overall lack of honorary inscriptions. These would be the most likely place to find evidence of patronage or benefaction and they are ubiquitous in those regions which adopted the practice(s).[320] More recently, Chancey has offered a sweeping statement that denies the presence of any honorary inscriptions in Galilee.[321] Low levels of trade with more Hellenized and Romanized parts of Palestine (the coast and Decapolis) also reduce the likelihood of patronage and benefaction since cultural exchange would be minimal.[322]

Summary: Galilee, Benefaction and Patrocinium

In this survey of villages and cities of Galilee a few important insights have been discovered. In general, both villages and cities in Galilee were predominately Jewish as far as ethnicity and culture. Jewish identity markers present a fairly consistent picture of Galilean life as significantly involved in the Jewish religious world. Hellenistic and Roman influence can be seen in some public monuments in Tiberias, but nowhere else in the region. When these monuments have been discovered and described it has been found that the construction materials and style attempt a balance between "looking Greco-Roman" and not offending Jewish sensibilities. Antipas did not always strike this balance, as in his palace which was destroyed by offended Jews. Some materials and architectural pieces conform to Roman tastes and the general practice of constructing monumental structures flows from the standards of the Hellenistic kings. But it is noteworthy that throughout the region not a single honorary inscription has been found. This would be quite odd if Galilee were as deeply entrenched in Hellenism as earlier scholars suggested because such inscriptions were

---

[318] Freyne, *Galilee and Gospel*, 93.

[319] Freyne, *Galilee and Gospel*, 175.

[320] See below, sections 3.1.6; 3.2.6; 3.4.6, the many euergetistic inscriptions to Herod I, Antipas, and Agrippa I found in Athens. *OGIS* 414, 415, 427; cf. *OGIS* 417, 428.

[321] Chancey, *Culture of Jesus*, 150; Reed, *Archaeology*, 113–114, 121, and private correspondence.

[322] Reed, *Archaeology*, 215–216.

commonplace. This lack leads Chancey to question whether Galileans consciously rejected this part of Greco-Roman culture.[323] Chancey can of course only speak of the general populace in this way since Antipas renamed two cities in honor of the emperor. This practice conforms to an ideal found among Hellenistic benefactors elsewhere. Very few if any Romans inhabited Galilee. Herod I or Antipas may have brought some Roman influence (see chapter 3). It was shown, however, that neither government officials nor soldiers in Galilee were likely to be ethnically Roman. This probably indicates that any trickling down of Hellenism or Romanism must proceed along a fairly direct path from the Herods. Some interregional trade in Capernaum and Tiberias (but apparently not Sepphoris) makes it possible that cultural exchange could happen between regions and thus inhabitants of those Galilean locations could learn of benefaction or patronage apart from the Herods. The centurion's synagogue possibly indicates the practice of benefaction among Jews in Capernaum. Toward the end of the century patronage and benefaction made definite inroads into Galilee as a few stories from Josephus relate.

2.2.4 Jerusalem: Benefaction and Patrocinium

When turning from Galilee to the other regions in Palestine different possibilities arise and significantly different conclusions may be reached. The two main cities under investigation in this section and the next (2.2.5), Caesarea and Jerusalem, contain substantial amounts of Hellenistic and Roman influence. They also have inscriptional evidence that directly bears upon this study. Both Caesarea and Jerusalem have honorary inscriptions that conform to benefaction patterns. Less debate surrounds the extent of Hellenization in these cities though there still remains some disagreement. A look at Samaria and Philip's tetrarchy in general will also shed light on our subject. As locations with significantly smaller Jewish populations, the rulers of these areas engaged with less caution in the social practices of Hellenism and Romanism. It is intrinsically more likely that this study will discover evidence of the practice of benefaction and/or patronage in these places, but this must nevertheless be demonstrated.

The influence of Hellenistic and Roman thought was considerably more pronounced in Jerusalem than it was in Galilee. Jerusalem experienced different waves of Hellenistic influence from the Hasmonean era to the post-revolt era. Residue from each era remained so that Jerusalem's inhabitants would have been relatively familiar with non-Jewish ways. The particular expression of Hellenism important for this study, benefaction, has attestation in both literary and archaeological sources. Romanization, on the other

---

[323] Chancey, *Culture of Jesus*, 150.

2.2 Benefaction and Patronage in Palestine

hand, was not as pronounced in the first half of the first-century. In small ways Herod and the prefects attempted to import some Roman culture into the city, but it was minimal, sporadic, and overshadowed by both Jewish and Hellenistic culture. Its concomitant social expression, *patrocinium*, was likewise less familiar than benefaction. This section investigates three main topics: Hellenistic and Roman culture, Jewish culture, and benefaction and patronage. In the following discussion, when both archaeological and literary evidence are available I will present the archaeological evidence before the literary. When only one type of evidence is present then only that type will be discussed.

Hellenism infiltrated Jerusalem long before Jesus, and though the people had points of objection they willingly incorporated many of the less offensive components. One of the recurring conclusions in the recently written volume *Hellenism in the Land of Israel* is that the Jewish people did not object to Greek culture itself but rather to affronts and compromises to their religion.[324] Use of the Greek language does not necessarily mean the adoption of Greek culture, but it does suggest that the culture has a presence and some influence. A person could speak the language without embracing a "Greek" way of life. The Greek-speaker would, however, recognize that some others operated in "Greek" ways. Arguments in favor of widespread use of Greek in first-century Jerusalem come from both archaeological and literary evidence.

One specific way that several of the contributors to *Hellenism in the Land of Israel* argue for widespread use of Greek is by examining the languages of the inscriptions. Since 36% of inscriptions and 46% of ossuaries use Greek in Jerusalem, Gregory Sterling concludes that "the common residents of Jerusalem used Greek from Herod I to the end of the First Revolt."[325] He means that they could carry on a business transaction or conversation, though they would not have had literary skills. Pieter W. Van Der Horst makes a similar case.[326] His main argument is the simple fact that between Frey's study of 530 inscriptions (*CIJ*) and Price's estimate of 1800 (*Corpus Inscriptionum Iudaeae/Palestinae* [*CIIP*]) the percentage of Greek inscriptions is still above 50%. These inscriptions range from educated to non-educated, good Greek to bad, and thus do not represent only the elite class.

---

[324] Collins and Sterling, *Hellenism*.

[325] Gregory E. Sterling, "Judaism between Jerusalem and Alexandria," in Collins and Sterling, *Hellenism*, 263–301, 273, contra Jan Nicolaas Sevenster, *Do You Know Greek? How Much Greek Could the First Jewish Christian Have Known?* (NovTSupp 19; Leiden: Brill, 1968); Saul Lieberman, *Greek and Hellenism in Jewish Palestine* (Jerusalem: Bialik Institute, 1962).

[326] Pieter W. Van Der Horst, "Greek in Jewish Palestine in Light of Jewish Epigraphy," in Collins and Sterling, *Hellenism*, 154–174.

Josephus' comment in *Ant.* 20.264 has been taken to mean that not many attempted to learn Greek among the Jews, but this does not seem to be the best way to read the text.

παρ' ἡμῖν γὰρ οὐκ ἐκείνους ἀποδέχονται τοὺς πολλῶν ἐθνῶν διάλεκτον ἐκμαθόντας διὰ τὸ κοινὸν εἶναι νομίζειν τὸ ἐπιτήδευμα τοῦτο μόνον οὐκ ἐλευθέροις τοῖς τυχοῦσιν ἀλλὰ καὶ τῶν οἰκετῶν τοῖς θέλουσι μόνοις δὲ σοφίαν μαρτυροῦσιν τοῖς τὰ νόμιμα σαφῶς ἐπισταμένοις καὶ τὴν τῶν ἱερῶν γραμμάτων δύναμιν ἑ'ρμηνεῦσαι δυναμένοις (*Ant.* 20.264)

"For our people do not favour those persons who have mastered the speech of many nations, or who adorn their style with smoothness of diction, because they consider that not only is such skill common to ordinary freemen but that even slaves who so choose may acquire it. But they give credit for wisdom to those alone who have an exact knowledge of the law and who are capable of interpreting the meaning of the Holy Scriptures."

Josephus depreciates Greek learning not because it is ill-regarded, but because it is so common as to have gone down even among the slave class (*Ant.* 20.262–265). What Josephus perceives to be well-regarded among his peers is not the frills associated with elegant pronunciation because anyone can do that, but the wisdom associated with understanding the legal system.[327]

Nevertheless use of the Greek language does not equal thorough Hellenization. Seth Schwartz suggests that the use of Greek among those considered staunchly pro-Jewish (e.g., Qumran, priests), and therefore assumed to be anti-Hellenistic, was evident and therefore argues against the language-equals-culture equation.[328] Thus, Jerusalem Jews could pick up the language as a component of Hellenization without much inner turmoil.

A second major way that contributors to this volume support the idea of significant Hellenization is by arguing for the availability of Greek education in Jerusalem. According to Josephus, Jason and Herod I teamed up to bring more Hellenistic culture to Jerusalem with a gymnasium, games, a hippodrome, and an amphitheater.[329] The gymnasium may have fallen out of use in the time of Herod (Josephus does not again mention it in this capacity), but it appears it still functioned as an oratory location. Though the

---

[327] Flavius Josephus *Life of Josephus* (trans. and comm. Steve Mason; Leiden: Brill Academic Publishers, 2003).

[328] Seth Schwartz, "Hebrew and Imperialism in Jewish Palestine," in Bakhos, *Hellenistic Context*, 53–84.

[329] Sterling, "Jerusalem and Alexandria," 274–275. There is some debate about how many structures were actually constructed. Was there a separate theater from the amphitheater? Is the hippodrome the same construction as the amphitheater? Netzer considers the hippodrome and amphitheater to be the same structure. Netzer, *Architecture*, 281. Cf. *Ant.* 12:239–241.

Jews naturally responded with resentment to statues[330] and anything else that offended their religion in Jerusalem (e.g., going to the theater), other purposes of the gymnasium did not offend. The gymnasium "was multifaceted, a military school, a school of civic preparation, a philosophical and literary school, a school for physical culture, a school in piety toward the gods."[331] Many cities taught their individual histories and traditions in their gymnasia (sometimes adding Greek history/traditions) and it seems Jerusalem would have done the same.[332] R. Doran argues that because Sirach, written ten years before the gymnasium's construction, is not averse to Greek language, philosophical argumentation, pedagogy, or literature (Sir 39:4), it seems probable that educators in Jerusalem's gymnasium would have done much the same. J. Collins adds three examples of Jews writing in Greek (with Eupolemes the only one within Judea) and adopting Greek rhetorical style (Philo, 4 Macc, and Eupolemes).[333] T. Rajak concludes that on account of this education the Jews could have been accurately "classed among the Hellenes, even if they were more readily incorporated on the barbarian side."[334] In general, Jewish revulsion against Hellenism did not focus on language, pedagogy, stories, or the use of philosophy, but instead on the proscription of their religion.[335]

The monumental structures briefly mentioned above lend another piece of evidence in support of Hellenization in Jerusalem. Herod's grandiose structures served to build his reputation, in Rome and elsewhere, as a notable Hellenistic king. Large structures intended primarily for pleasure and to augment one's reputation were a staple of these kings. A. Lichtenberger has recently argued that two of the structures (theater and amphitheater) have not been found by archeologists because of Herod's focus on being ranked among the Hellenistic kings.[336] His argument proceeds as follows. Josephus describes a theater and an amphitheater in the vicinity of Jerusalem. He constructed them in honor of Augustus, but did not desire them to be used subsequently since this might be perceived to mean that he had not built them solely for Augustus. He could display his opulence, and direct it solely toward Augustus, if the theaters did not last past the games. So he built them with wood, a practice not uncommon in those days (and even

---

[330] Schwartz, "Euergetism in Josephus."

[331] Robert Doran, "The High Cost of a Good Education," in Collins and Sterling, *Hellenism*, 94–115, 95.

[332] Doran, "High Cost," 96–97.

[333] Collins, "Cult," 38–61.

[334] Tessa Rajak, "Greeks and Barbarians in Josephus," Collins and Sterling, *Hellenism*, 244–262, 258.

[335] Collins, "Cult."

[336] Achim Lichtenberger, "Jesus and the Theater in Jerusalem," in Charlesworth, *Jesus and Archaeology*, 283–299.

mentioned at points by Josephus). Their disintegration over time explains why archeologists have not found the structures. Whether or not one adopts the conclusion that they were constructed out of wood (Netzer casts much doubt on the claim),[337] the argument highlights Herod's purpose in the project. Namely, he desired to lavish great gifts as an expression of his wealth and to boost his reputation with Augustus and the people. This construction mentality derives directly from Hellenistic ideals for kingship and is matched in many ways in Herod's other constructions. Though the mentality was Hellenistic the construction style and the pragmatic purpose of the theater would likely have been Roman. Ball strongly urges that all of the theaters are Roman, rather than Greek, in the east. There is not one Greek theater in the east. The presence of amphitheatres signals the presence of Latin influence since easterners tended to look upon the blood sports with disgust.[338] Jerusalem's theater has not been found (perhaps because it disintegrated), but if it followed the pattern described by Ball then it would have been in Roman style and used for Roman activities. There is archaeological reason to believe that elite inhabitants of Jerusalem, other than the local ruler, adopted some Hellenism. Collins thinks the Hellenization of the upper classes in Jerusalem "vividly shown by the archeological remains in the Jewish quarter."[339] A noteworthy example is the "palatial mansion" which N. Avigad describes in reference to its frescoes, mosaics, water installations, and "vaulted ritual bath." [340] The interior of the house attests Greek ornamentation (i.e. ashlar construction) which had "already become *passé* in the Hellenistic world and even in Italy" by the first-century.[341] Apparently the style persisted in the east much later than its place of origin. The mansion provides an example of the type of Hellenization which the elite embraced.

The literary evidence tells of two other staples of Hellenistic cities: a gymnasium and hippodrome. Gymnasia were a necessary fixture in any city desiring to be recognized as truly Hellenistic. Jerusalem would improve its reputation among Hellenes through Herod's gymnasium. It was earlier suggested that the gymnasium served as an educational center, at

---

[337] Netzer specifically attacks J. Patrich, "Herod's Theater in Jerusalem—A New Proposal," *IEJ* 52 (2002): 231–239, which he elsewhere connects to Lichtenberger's earlier work, A. Lichtenberger, *Die Baupolitik Herodes des Grossen* (Abhandlungen des deutschen Palästinavereins 26; Wiesbaden: Harrassowitz Verlag, 1999), 78–79. Netzer, *Architecture*, 135 n. 28, 280 n. 15.

[338] Ball, *Rome*, 305.

[339] Collins, "Cult," 54 n. 88; Nahman Avigad, *Discovering Jerusalem* (Nashville: Nelson, 1983), 81–202; Lee I. Levine, *Judaism and Hellenism in Antiquity: Conflict or Confluence* (Seattle: University of Washington Press, 1998), 48–51.

[340] Avigad, *Jerusalem*, 95–120.

[341] Avigad, *Jerusalem*, 102.

least for a time, in addition to many other purposes. It would be recognized as a foreign edifice, perhaps a tribute to Hellenism. Similarly, the hippodrome would signal to others that Jerusalem was a quality Hellenistic city. It brought with it foreign activities enjoyed (potentially at least) by Hellenistically inclined inhabitants or visitors. Josephus describes Herod's desire in the construction and endowment of these entertainment facilities (*Ant.* 15.271).

καὶ πάνθ' ὅσα κατὰ πολυτέλειαν ἢ σεμνοπρέπειαν παρ' ἑκάστοις ἐσπούδαστο φιλοτιμίᾳ τοῦ διάσημον αὑτῷ γενέσθαι τὴν ἐπίδειξιν ἐξεμιμήσατο
"And whatever costly or magnificent efforts had been made by others, all these did Herod imitate in his ambition to see his spectacle become famous."

He went overboard to elevate his status and out of a love of honor (φιλοτιμίᾳ) he took great pains to publicly display his grandeur. Such expression was the supreme focus of the Hellenistic benefactor.

A story from Philo also suggests that upper class Jews at times consorted with the Hellenistic authority figures. Philo gives an account of Herodian and Sanhedrin collaboration on political matters that may have provided an opportunity for cultural influence (*Legatio Ad Gaium* §261–329). The story indicates a close connection and willingness to work together between Antipas and the Jewish leaders "to spearhead a major delegation sent to approach Pilate."[342] The dispute was religious in nature with possible offense coming from the inscription of Tiberius' full name (including the religious titles *divi filius* and *pontifex maximus*)[343] and political in nature as the groups attempted to maintain the balance of power in Jerusalem.[344] The story does not imply that Jews and Romans interacted openly and without qualm, but rather that Jews were offended by the operations of some Roman officials (here, Pilate) while they were able to find support (whether this support was genuine on the part of the Romans is still up for consideration) from others (here, Antipas). It also suggests that Antipas was significantly involved in matters taking place among the Jewish populace in Jerusalem, though he had no official role in that city. If this pattern of relationship is more than a one-time affair then one could argue that Hellenism potentially percolated directly through its staunchest advocates toward those who might benefit most from adopting it.

The presence of Romans in Jerusalem would provide opportunity for Romanization, but it seems that the number of Roman "colonists"[345] or

---

[342] Jensen, *Antipas*, 108.

[343] Helen K. Bond, *Pontius Pilate in History and Interpretation* (SNTSMS 100; Cambridge: Cambridge University Press, 1998), 24–48, esp. 39.

[344] Jensen, *Antipas*, 108.

[345] "Colonist" implies the intrusion of non-natives to permanently inhabit a new area for the purpose of establishing or promoting the non-native culture or rule. Sawicki uses

even long-term visitors would have been remarkably low. Roman colonists or long-term visitors can be found in armies, governments, vacationers, or pilgrims. Millar shares a different opinion than Safrai and Sanders on this issue. He thinks it probable that Rome permanently stationed an army in Jerusalem perhaps because of the tendency of the temple-related festivals to get out of hand.[346] But a closer examination by Safrai draws a different conclusion. No Roman army would have been stationed in Palestine during the first-century because of the way that Rome controlled its provinces and border regions. He concludes that there were only a few locally raised Roman soldiers in the Antonia of Jerusalem (*War* 5.244). Roman legions were stationed in Judea and Galilee in the second century, but not in the first.[347] Sanders continues in this debate by confronting the view expressed by Sawicki and Crossan in regard to "colonization." Those authors propose that Rome colonized Galilee and Judea by sending immigrants (displacing locals), setting up governments, and turning the places into reproductions of their homeland. But this did not happen. Rome may have treated other provinces in this way, but they did not colonize Palestine.[348] Apart from the few soldiers roaming around the Antonia, the occasional prefect, and temporary visitors there were not that many Romans (or Gentiles for that matter) in Jerusalem during this period.[349]

Both archaeological and literary evidence demonstrate that Jerusalem was a predominately Jewish city in terms of both religion and ethnicity. If

---

the term "in its modern political and economic sense, not in its ancient honorific sense, of course." Sawicki, *Crossing Galilee*, 246.

[346] Millar, *Near East*, 45.

[347] Safrai, "Army," in Sanders, "Jesus' Galilee," 10–11.

[348] Sanders, "Jesus' Galilee," 35. Alexander the Great colonized some of Syria, including Gerasa (in Samaria), Capitolias, and Dium. He put Macedonians in these cities for various reasons. The Ptolemies colonized very little in Syria, preferring instead Egypt. Their one colony in Palestine, Philoteria (on the Sea of Galilee), was destroyed by Alexander Jannaeus. Jones does not mention colonies established in Palestine between Augustus and Agrippa I. Since mention of colonization had been a consistent pattern in the previous sections it seems reasonable to conclude that colonization did not take place during this era. See Jones, *Cities*, 237–238, 240–241, 242–267. After the Jewish revolt a few Palestinian cities were referred to as colonies, E. Mary Smallwood, *The Jews Under Roman Rule: From Pompey to Diocletian* (Studies in Judaism in Late Antiquity 20; Leiden: Brill, 1976). Emmaus may have been popularly known as a colony, hence the subsequent name "Culoneih", ibid., 341 n. 42. Caesarea earned "colonial status as Colonia Prima" under Vespasian, ibid., 343. Hadrian rejuvenated Jerusalem giving it colonial status, ibid., 135, 433 n. 21, 459–461. Sebaste earned the title colony under Severus, ibid., 488, 490, 493–494.

[349] Lee makes a similar case for all of Palestine in regard to Romanization. Reuben Yat Tin Lee, "Romanization in Palestine: A Study of Urban Development from Herod the Great to AD 70," (British Archaeological Reports International Series 1180; Archaeopress: Oxford, 2003).

few Roman or Hellenistic colonists inhabited Jerusalem, the overwhelming majority would have been ethnically Jewish. This can be shown quite clearly through the ubiquitous ethnic identity markers identified earlier in Reed's study (chalk vessels, *miqvaoth*, burial tombs, and absence of pig bones). Reed remarks that this is the "well-established pattern" for Jerusalem and Judea during this period.[350] Apart from the few monumental structures built by Herod and the decorative elements identified as Hellenistic by Collins, the major portion of construction and decoration in Jerusalem was thoroughly Jewish. Even Herod knew better than to adorn his monuments with offensive material. He occasionally departed from this better judgment, but in general he kept the peace by not offending Jews in Palestine.[351]

When Herod's judgment did lapse, stories in Josephus confirm the vehemence with which many Jews protected their traditions. The golden eagle incident probably ranks among the clearest examples (*War* 1.648–55; *Ant.* 17.146–63). Herod constructed a golden eagle, put it over a temple-gate, and dedicated it to the Jerusalem temple. Breaking the second commandment, he catalyzed Jewish zeal. These men chose to die for the sanctity of the temple. Even Josephus who is often portrayed as a Roman-friendly writer evaluates Palestine's leaders based on their adherence to Jewish custom. He has political aims coordinating with this, but it is nevertheless clear that he cares about the maintenance of the traditions by those who claim to adhere to the faith.[352]

One final point supports the importance of Jews to life in first-century Jerusalem. Though a prefect could step in to control Jerusalem, high priests were its *de facto* rulers. Tcherikover earlier suggested that Jerusalem could be considered a *polis* with the Sanhedrin approximating the Greek βουλή, but Millar thinks it too difficult to conclude this with certainty.[353] Jews held the major positions of authority, especially those in charge of daily affairs.

If the ethnicity of inhabitants, style of architecture and decoration, and form of government are sufficient to establish the culture of a city then Jerusalem should be considered primarily Jewish. The presence of certain monumental structures, some Hellenistic education, and the pervasiveness of Greek language suggest a good amount of Hellenistic influence as well. The occasional Roman inhabitant, sporadic Roman style and décor, and

---

[350] See note 147.
[351] See Peter Richardson, "Law and Piety in Herod's Architecture," in Richardson, *Building Jewish*, 225–239.
[352] Jensen, *Antipas*, 54–100.
[353] Millar, *Near East*, 361. V. A. Tcherikover, "Was Jerusalem a 'Polis'?" *IEJ* 14 (1964): 61–78, 61.

lack of Roman government allow for only the faintest hint of Romanization.

The particular expressions of Hellenization and Romanization, respectively benefaction and *patrocinium*, bear witness, to a similar degree as the cultural influences in general, in the archaeological and literary records of Jerusalem. Three significant inscriptions speak to the practice of benefaction in Jerusalem. Herod was publicly known as a benefactor as is attested in a Greek inscription on a limestone weight found in Jerusalem. Meshorer considers the inscription to be a series of abbreviations. The full text (left), Meshorer's interpretation of the abbreviations (right), and his translation (below) is given here:

L ΛΒ ΒΑΣ ΗΡ ΕΝ   L ΛΒ ΒΑΣΙΛΕΩΣ ΗΡΩΔΟΝ ΕΝΕΡΓΕΤΟΝ
ΦΙΛΟΚ   ΦΙΛΟΚΑΙΣΑΡΟΣ
ΑΓΟΡ   ΑΓΟΡΑΝΟΜΟΝ
ΩΑ Ρ   ΜΝΑ ΤΡΙΑ

"Year 32 of King Herod, Benefactor, Friend of Caesar/Inspector of Markets/Three Minas."[354]

The weight comes from around the end of Herod's life, 9/8 B.C., and "is the only known Judean inscription referring to Herod as 'Benefactor' (εὐ[εργέτης]) and as 'Friend of Caesar' (φιλοκ[αῖσαρος])."[355] According to Richardson, the inscription bears witness that Herod had "no compunctions about promoting his imperial connections."[356] It should be cautioned however that the first two letters of benefactor could be read differently, perhaps as *eu[sebeia]* (pious).[357] Identifying Herod as a friend of Caesar blurs any distinction between benefaction and patronage while simultaneously suggesting involvement in those realms.

In addition to the use of *euergetes* to describe Herod, other inscriptional evidence supports the notion that Jews had some understanding of benefactions. *SEG* 1277 (18/17 B.C.) found in Jerusalem reads:

[- - -] (ἔτους) κ' ἐπ' ἀρχιερέως
[- - -] παρις 'Ακέσωνος
[- - -] ἐν 'Ρόδωι
[- - - π]ρόστρωσιν
[- - - δ]ραξμάς
[In the reign of Herod the King]/
in the 20th year, upon the high priest/
[Simon, S]paris Akeonos/
[a foreign resident] in Rhodes/

---

[354] Y. Meshorer, "A Stone Weight from the Reign of Herod," *IEJ* 20 (1970): 97–98.
[355] Richardson, *Herod*, 204.
[356] Richardson, *Herod*, 204.
[357] Richardson, *Herod*, 204. Richardson follows Meshorer in choosing εὐ[εργέτης].

[donated the] pavement/[at a cost of {?}] drachmas."³⁵⁸

Apparently a Jewish resident of Rhodes had donated some of the paving for "the platform south of the Temple Mount."³⁵⁹ Herod erected a temple to Apollo at Rhodes and there was apparently a Jewish community in the city (*Ant.* 16.147; 1 Macc 15:23; Suetonius *Tib* 32.4; *IG* 12.1.593; 12.1.11).³⁶⁰ 1 Macc 11:37 and 14:26 mention many inscriptions on the temple, but so far this is the only one which has been found which describes a donation to it. B. Isaac, S. Schwartz, and P. Richardson describe the inscription as recognition of a benefaction.³⁶¹ Apparently the donator (Sparis? Paris?) was a Jewish sympathizer, though he could also have been compelled by the many benefits Herod had conferred on Rhodes (*Ant.* 16.18, 147; *War* 1.280).

The third major inscription, the Theodotus inscription, relates a Jewish understanding of benefits in a religious setting. Though its date has been disputed, there is good reason to conclude that it derives from early in the first-century.³⁶² The text comes from *SEG* 8.170 (cf. *CIJ* II 1404):

Θεόδοτος Οὐεττηνοῦ ἱερεὺς καὶ
ἀρχισυνάγωγος, υἱὸς ἀρχισυν[αγώ]
γ[ο]υ, υἱωνὸς ἀρχισυν[α]γώγου, ᾠκο
δόμησε τὴν συναγωγ[ὴ]ν εἰς ἀν[άν]νω
σ[ιν] νόμου καὶ εἰς [δ]ιδαχὴν ἐντολῶν, καὶ
τὸν ξενῶνα κα[ὶ τὰ] δώματα καὶ τὰ χρη
σ[τ]ήρια τῶν ὑδάτων εἰς κατάλυμα τοῖ
ς [χ]ρήζουσιν ἀπὸ τῆς ξέ[ν]ης, ἣν ἐθεμε
λ[ίω]σαν οἱ πατέρες [α]ὐτοῦ καὶ οἱ πρε
σ[β]ύτεροι καὶ Σιμων[ί]δης

---

³⁵⁸ B. Mazar, *SEG* 33 (1983): 1277, p. 384–185. *Editio princeps*, B. Isaac, "A Donation for Herod's Temple in Jerusalem," *IEJ* 33 (1983): 86–92.

³⁵⁹ Isaac, "Donation," plate 9B; Richardson identifies the platform as the gift in Richardson, *Friend of the Romans*, 205.

³⁶⁰ Isaac explains these references in support of the notion that a Jewish community existed in Rhodes at this time. Isaac, "Donation," 90–91.

³⁶¹ Isaac, "Donation"; Schwartz, "Euergetism in Josephus"; Richardson, *Friend of the Romans*, 205.

³⁶² *Editio princeps* R. Weill, "La Cité de David: Compte rendu des fouilles exécutées à Jérusalem sur le site de la ville primitive. Campaigne de 1913–14 [I-IV]," *REJ* 69 (1919): 3–85[I]; 70 (1920): 1–36 [II]; 149–179 [III]; 71 (1920): 1–45 [IV] + Plates. *SEG* VIII 170; *CIJ* 1404; cf. *SEG* XLI 1841, L 1500. *SEG* 52: 557 mentions the debate about its dating. H. C. Kee's late date (post 70) has been "strongly rejected" by Leah Di Segni. Kloppenborg Verbin offers a lengthy rebuttal as well. John S. Kloppenborg Verbin, "Dating Theodotos (*CIJ* II 1404)," *JJS* 51 (2000): 243–280. See H. C. Kee, "The Transformation of the Synagogue After 70 C.E.: Its Import for Early Christianity," *NTS* 36 (1990): 1–24. For a synopsis of his argument see *SEG* 50: 505. Kloppenborg, "Dating Theodotus," 272.

"Theodotos son of Vettenus, priest and archisynagogos, son of an archisynagogos and grandson of an archisynagogos, built the assembly hall (synagogue) for the reading of the Law and for the teaching of the commandments, and the guest room, the chambers, and the water fittings, as an inn for those in need from foreign parts, (the synagogue) which his fathers founded with the elders and Simonides."[363]

It has been dated pre-70 by some, simply first-century, or as late as second-fourth century (H. C. Kee), but it is best considered early first-century. There is both archaeological and literary evidence of synagogues in the first-century (contra Kee) and the lack of customary first-to-second century transformations in lettering also rules out the later date.[364] The well-known inscription publicly praises Theodotus and his fathers for their generosity on behalf of the synagogue. In certain ways, it resembles typical euergetistic inscriptions. Generous donors had constructed the synagogue in order to promote the study of their law. It differs from typical benefaction inscriptions in that it does not adorn a statue and is rather tempered in its praise of the donor.[365] The inscription probably derives from the time of the apostles' ministry or perhaps before, and provides evidence that benefaction had not only entered Jerusalem, but that it was understood and practiced (in a tempered manner) by faithful Jews.

Richardson has suggested a possible reading of another potentially suggestive find, though he admits reservations. Reminder of Herod's benefaction of Caesarea Maritima could be offered in the coins which he struck bearing an anchor, though Alexander Jannaeus and Agrippa I also used the anchor image.[366] These inscriptions show at least some familiarity with benefaction in Jerusalem, and the erection and naming of monumental structures in the city support this finding.

Monumental structures and games and the naming of them after notable figures also tell of significant benefaction and, to a lesser extent, *patrocinium*. Since one of the distinguishing characteristics between the practices is the nature of the gifts (grandiose versus mundane), the erection of monumental structures will naturally suggest a closer affinity to benefaction than patronage. Herod made huge attempts to garner the favor of Rome through his opulence, though this certainly was not his only goal in his construction projects (see section 3.1.4). Herod rebuilt the temple to monumental proportions in part to distinguish Jerusalem as a notable Hellenistic city, but also as an opportunity to benefit his superiors. Upon completion of its fortress he named it after his friend Marc Antony. David Braund's short explanation shows that this practice is particularly Hellenis-

---

[363] Kloppenborg Verbin, "Dating Theodotos," 244.
[364] Kloppenborg Verbin, "Dating Theodotos," 244–280.
[365] Schwartz, "Euergetism in Josephus."
[366] Richardson, *Herod*, 213.

2.2 Benefaction and Patronage in Palestine

tic. Attributing new names to cities or structures in honor of superiors was a particularly eastern practice.[367] Hellenistic kings expressed allegiance to Roman rulers through Hellenistic modes of expression (starting as early as Augustus or perhaps Antony).[368] Hellenistic kings actually influenced the Romans to express themselves in these ways.[369]

According to Josephus, Herod saw Antony as a benefactor (εὐεργέτης) and so exerted himself in every way for his benefit (*Ant.* 15.189–190).

ἔλεγεν γὰρ τῷ Καίσαρι καὶ φιλίαν αὐτῷ γενέσθαι μεγίστην πρὸς Ἀντώνιον καὶ πάντα πρᾶξαι κατὰ τὴν αὐτοῦ δύναμιν ὡς ἐπ' ἐκείνῳ γενήσεται τὰ πράγματα στρατείας μὲν οὐ κοινωνήσας κατὰ περιολκὰς τῶν Ἀράβων πέμψας δὲ καὶ χρήματα καὶ σῖτον ἐκείνωκαὶ ταῦτ' εἶναι μετριώτερα τῶν ἐπιβαλλόντων αὐτῷ γενέσθαι τὸν γὰρ ὁμολογοῦντα μὲν εἶναι φίλον εὐεργέτην δ' ἐκεῖνον ἐπιστάμενον παντὶ μέρει καὶ ψυχῆς καὶ σώματος καὶ περιουσίας συγκινδυνεύειν δέον ὧν αὐτὸς ἔλαττον ἢ καλῶς εἶχεν ἃ ναστραφεὶς ἀλλ' ἐκεῖνό γε συνειδέναι καλῶς ἑαυτῷ πεποιηκότι τὸ μηδ' ἡττηθέντα τὴν ἐν Ἀκτίῳ μάχην καταλιπεῖν

"For he told Caesar that he had had the greatest friendship for Antony and had done everything in his power to bring control of affairs into his hands. He had not, to be sure, taken part in his campaign because he had been distracted there by the Arabs, but he had sent him money and grain though these were more modest contributions than he ought to have made. For when a man acknowledges himself to be another's friend and knows that friend to be his benefactor, he ought to share his danger by risking every bit of his soul and body and substance. In this he had behaved less well than he ought but in one respect at least he was conscious of having done well, namely in not having abandoned Antony after his defeat in the battle of Actium."

Herod continued this practice in Jerusalem naming a palace in Jerusalem Caesareum for Octavian.[370] The games instituted in the theater by Herod also announced his Hellenistic zeal to be known as a benefactor. No archaeological remains exist for the theater (and amphitheater if they are separate) so scholars proceed strictly from literary evidence.[371] These theaters were built to honor Augustus in festival games (27/28 B.C.). But the games appear to have only happened once, not repeated like the Actium games. Perhaps they ended because of popular protest to images and gladiator contests. The games and theaters express both Roman (inscription honoring Octavian, agitation of animals) and Hellenistic (display of

---

[367] David Braund, *Rome and the Friendly King: The Character of the Client Kingship* (London: Croom Helm, 1984), 108. See, Suetonius, *Aug.* 60. For example, cities named Caesarea include those by "Herod, Archelaus I of Cappadocia, Juba II of Mauretania, Polemo I as king in the Bosporus, and by Herod's son, Philip the tetrarch. In addition, it is quite possible that Deiotarus Philadelpus of Paphlagonia and Philopater of Cilicia also founded Caesareae." Braund continues with many other examples.

[368] Braund, *Friendly King*, 109.
[369] MacMullen, *Romanization*, 22–24 esp. n. 86.
[370] Ball, *Rome*, 51.
[371] Lichtenberger, "Theater," 283. See, *Ant.* 15.267–278; not in *War*.

wealth πολυτέλεια or τρυφή; displays of royalty) influences.³⁷² Since games express wealth and grandeur they fall closer to the notion of benefaction than patronage. Through these structures and games the Jewish population of Jerusalem would have become aware of Greek notions of benefaction and its grandiose expression. They may or may not have picked up the subtle hints of Romanization, and perhaps *patrocinium*, included.

Other literary evidence also bears witness to the practice of benefaction in Jerusalem. Two main pieces of literary evidence paint a portrait of Jerusalem Jews functioning as benefactors. The first can be found in 1 Macc 14:25–49 and has been described as an "Honorary Decree for Simon the Maccabee" (13 Sept 140 B.C.).³⁷³ Van Henten describes the decree which follows the benefaction structure, was placed in the temple in a conspicuous place, and honors the Maccabees for great works. With only minor disagreement, Krentz affirms Van Henten's reading and refers to Danker's work on benefaction inscriptions. The people of Jerusalem wonder how they will return a favor (χάριν ἀποδώσομεν) to Simon for warding off Israel's enemies (14:25–26; cf. *Ant.* 13.124). They propose gifts and a decree to honor him publicly.

It is remarkable how the Maccabee decree parallels the form of benefaction decrees found in McLean.³⁷⁴ It begins by establishing the date of the decree (18 Elul Year 172). After listing the body presenting the decree (14:28), it announces the reason for honoring the honorand (14:29). Beginning with ἐπεὶ is standard form for such decrees and benefactors were typically honored for going out of their way to the point of endangering their lives.³⁷⁵ The creed belabors the great works done by Simon and the relationship of honor he incurred in the process with both Jews and Romans (14:38–40). In light of these things the Jews and high priests resolved (εὖ 'δόκησαν) to grant Simon honor. Such resolution is another structural com-

---

[372] Lichtenberger, "Theater," 286–288.

[373] Gregg Gardner, "Jewish Leadership and Hellenistic Benefaction in the Second Century B.C.E.," *JBL* 126.2 (2007): 327–343, 332–337; Jan Willem Van Henten, "The Honorary Decree for Simon the Maccabee (1 Macc 14:25–49) in Its Hellenistic Context," in Collins and Sterling, *Hellenism*, 116–145; Edgar Krentz, "The Honorary Decree for Simon the Maccabee," in Collins and Sterling, *Hellenism*, 146–153; Danker, *Benefactor*, 80–83, no 13. Goldstein inserts 1 Macc 15:15–24 at 14:24 which helps clarify the chronology, but is not a necessary conclusion for the present argument, Jonathan A. Goldstein, *1 Maccabees* (AB 41; Garden City: Doubleday, 1976), 485 n. b., 492–494. Goldstein does not expand upon Hellenistic or Semitic parallels to this decree at length, but makes a few brief references especially to Nehemiah 9–10, ibid., 488–509, esp. 501–504.

[374] McLean, *Introduction to Greek Epigraphy*.

[375] Frederick W. Danker, "The Endangered Benefactor in Luke-Acts," in *The Society of Biblical Literature 1981 Seminar Papers* (SBLSP 20; Chico: Scholars Press, 1981), 39–48.

monplace of benefaction inscriptions and dedications. Simon receives the typical gold and purple adorned on benefactors as a display of honor (14:43–44). The decree will be inscribed on bronze and placed prominently so that all will be reminded of Simon's honor in the community (14:48). Jews in Jerusalem during the Hasmonean period apparently knew how to treat their leaders in typical Hellenistic ways.[376] They were understood to be benefactors. Onias III was so entitled by the people (2 Macc 4:2–4). In this context the phrase benefactor of the city (τὸν εὐεργέτην τῆς πόλεως) is paralleled with the idea that Onias is the patron of his compatriots (τὸν κηδεμόνα τῶν ὁμοεθνῶν). Κηδεμών can approximate a formal title that replaces *patronus*.[377] God also provides benefactions for the people (2 Macc 10:38). The authors of 1–2 Maccabees thus ascribe the practice of benefaction to Jerusalem's Jewish leaders (and God).

The second piece of evidence comes from Josephus who uses benefaction terminology in relation to some Jerusalemites. Josephus describes John and ten evil men who profess to be benefactors and saviors of Jerusalem (ὡς εὐεργέται καὶ σωτῆρες τῆς πόλεως; *War* 4.145–146). Their pretensions to the titles derived from a spurious relation to the Romans and a consequent slaying of several men. Josephus does not agree that they had this relationship or deserved these titles. In a later story Simon is accused of being unfaithful to his benefactors (πρὸς εὐεργέτας ἄπιστος; *War* 5.536). Simon had betrayed the Romans by killing those Jews that joined their side. Judas son of Judas, who makes the comment about Simon's change of fidelity, desires to submit to Roman protection since it is surer. A third episode describes the wicked people of Jerusalem opening the gates "to admit Cestius as their benefactor" (*War* 2.538). In the midst of the Roman attempt to burn down the temple gate, some Jews aided the Roman intrusion. In these stories Josephus assumes familiarity with the language of benefaction among the people of Jerusalem from the time of Jesus to the revolt.

Jerusalem's residents had several avenues through which they could become familiar with benefaction (and *patrocinium*), and some evidence suggests that they did learn the practice. It is impossible to conclude how pervasive the practice was among Jews through the proposed evidence, but it is plausible that a typical, lower-class resident or pilgrim could have been exposed to the ideology. It is significant that commemoration of benefactors were not made with statues (as in other cities).[378] Inscriptions

---

[376] Gardner, "Jewish Leadership," 327–343; Nigel M. Kennell, "New Light on 2 Maccabees 4:7–15," *JJS* 56 (2005): 10–24, 19.

[377] *AE* 1906.1; *IG* 5.1.380; *IG* 2².3596; *IG* 2².4217; *SEG* 20.681; *SEG* 11.923; cf. Mason, *Greek Terms*, 152.

[378] Schwartz, "Euergetism in Josephus."

in the temple and perhaps a synagogue were open for all to see. The small literate class could easily read these inscriptions and begin to understand the practice of benefaction. If literacy and socio-economic status do not always go hand in hand (as was suggested above) then these inscriptions may have been viewed by several economic strata of Jerusalem (or pilgrims). Some of Herod's grander projects and his naming of them after notable Romans would have created some buzz that could potentially educate the lower and illiterate classes about his Hellenistic motivations. Josephus' stories of renegade Jews tell of lower status Jerusalemites capable of using this form of cultural expression. These accounts seem to be the extension of a practice begun in the Hasmonean period and attested to by 1 Macc 14. Relationships between Jewish and Roman or Hellenistic officials provide another likely conduit of cultural education. Governors were not cut-off from their constituents, and it seems probable that their interaction would inform the Jews of Hellenistic and Roman ways. After the initial conversation it does not seem improbable that the Jews would discuss the implications of this way of life and assess its compatibility with their religion. Perhaps some reflection on Jewishness and benefaction and patronage had begun even before the time of Jesus.[379] Certainly some Jews had already incorporated this mode of public praise, as 1 Macc 14 indicates.

2.2.5 Outside of Galilee and Jerusalem: Benefaction and Patrocinium

Outside of Judea and Galilee the likelihood of benefaction and patronage increases, though one is still more likely to find benefaction since Hellenism had more sway than Romanism. The following section focuses on a few cities which are mentioned as sites visited by Jesus and his apostles or as hometowns for important personalities. The study investigates Caesarea, Samaria, a few smaller cities of Philip's tetrarchy, and Tyre.

Caesarea Maritima

While the vast majority of Palestine should be understood primarily as Jewish, small pockets of Hellenistic and Roman influence did exist. The most prominent example of this is certainly Caesarea Maritima, the city created by Herod to express his allegiance to Augustus. Herod rebuilt and renamed an earlier town in honor of Augustus between 22 and 10 B.C. The construction of Caesarea and Sebaste in honor of Augustus are the only examples of such a practice during the reign of Augustus in the Near East (*War* 1.156, 414).[380] His Romanization efforts included the erection of a

---

[379] Schwartz describes the reflection on benefaction made by Josephus. Schwartz, "Euergetism in Josephus."

[380] Millar, *Near East*, 355.

Temple to Rome and Augustus, forum, baths, theater, hippodrome, wall, promontory palace, and an amphitheater which generally followed Roman rather than Near Eastern architectural techniques.[381] Caesarea was a pagan *polis* with amenities available for pagan worship and ways of life. Even if the religion of the inhabitants was not as purely pagan as in other cities of the empire and devotion to Zeus a thinly veiled dedication to a Semitic deity, it is still quite different for its syncretization of Jewish and Roman piety.[382] Herod tried more earnestly to make this a Roman city with "Roman entertainment, Roman gods, and even Roman concrete," a freedom he did not enjoy in Jerusalem.[383] By the time of Pilate part of the non-Jewish population would have been the prefect and the Roman soldiers sent to support the prefect's institution in Caesarea (*Ant.* 18.55–64; *War* 2.169–175).[384]

Caesarea provided rich soil for Herod to maintain his program of establishing a name for himself among the Hellenistic kings through lavish gifts and pompous affairs. He continued naming structures for Roman leaders and creating/dedicating games in their honor. Herod named the large tower of the harbor after Caesar's son-in-law Drusus (*War* 1.412).[385] Construction of the harbor itself is a monument to Herod's largesse making Caesarea a notable Hellenistic city. Josephus describes Herod's constructions and the honors he directed through them (*War* 1.414–415).

καὶ τοῦ στόματος ἀντικρὺ ναὸς Καίσαρος ἐπὶ γηλόφου κάλλει καὶ μεγέθει διάφορος ἐν δ' αὐτῷ κολοσσὸς Καίσαρος οὐκ ἀποδέων τοῦ Ὀλυμπίασιν Διός ᾧ καὶ προσείκασται 'Ρώμης δὲ ἴσος "Ηρᾳ τῇ κατ' "Αργος ἀνέθηκεν δὲ τῇ μὲν ἐπαρχίᾳ τὴν πόλιν τοῖς ταύτῃ δὲ πλοϊζομένοις τὸν λιμένα Καίσαρι δὲ τὴν τιμὴν τοῦ κτίσματος Καισάρειαν γοῦν ὠνόμασεν αὐτήν τά γε μὴν λοιπὰ τῶν ἔργων ἀμφιθέατρον καὶ θέατρον καὶ ἃ γοράς ἄξια τῆς προσηγορίας ἐνιδρύσατο καὶ πενταετηρικοὺς ἀγῶνας καταστησάμενος ὁ'μοίως ἐκάλεσεν ἀπὸ τοῦ Καίσαρος πρῶτος αὐτὸς ἆθλα μέγιστα προθεὶς ἐπὶ τῆς ἑκατοστῆς ἐνενηκοστῆς δευτέρας ὀλυμπιάδος ἐν οἷς οὐ μόνον οἱ νικῶντες ἀλλὰ καὶ οἱ μετ' αὐτοὺς καὶ οἱ τρίτοι τοῦ βασιλικοῦ πλούτου μετελάμβανον

---

[381] For the latest archeological overviews of Caesarea see Netzer, *Architecture*, 94–118; Ball, *Rome*, 177; Jensen, *Antipas*, 182–184; Avner Raban and Kenneth Holum, eds., *Caesarea Maritima: A Retrospective After Two Millennia* (Leiden: Brill, 1996). Netzer identifies one point of divergence, the temple followed some features of Greek and Hellenistic temples, *Architecture*, 273. Netzer doubts that Herod could have learned much about architecture while in Rome since it was under construction and he was under duress. He does, however, show some imitation.

[382] Ball, *Rome*, 317.

[383] Ball, *Rome*, 177. He quotes from Kenneth G. Holum, Robert L. Hohlfelder, and Roberta Blender Maltese, eds. *King Herod's Dream: Caesarea on the Sea* (New York: Norton, 1988), 105.

[384] Sanders, "Jesus' Galilee," 10; cf. Safrai, "Roman Army."

[385] Josephus describes Caesarea in *War* 1.408–415; *Ant.* 15.331–341.

"On an eminence facing the harbour-mouth stood Caesar's temple, remarkable for its beauty and grand proportions; it contained a colossal statue of the emperor, not inferior to the Olympian Zeus, which served for its model, and another of Rome, rivaling that of Hera at Argos. The city Herod dedicated to the province, the harbour to navigators in these waters, to Caesar the glory of this new foundation, to which he accordingly gave the name of Caesarea. The rest of the buildings – amphitheatre, theatre, public places – were constructed in a style worthy of the name which the city bore. He further instituted quinquennial games, likewise named after Caesar, and inaugurated them himself, in the hundred and ninety-second Olympiad, offering prizes of the highest value; at these games not the victors only, but also those who obtained second and third places, participated in the royal bounty."

Herod erected a temple to Augustus, dedicated the city to the province (ἀνέθηκεν δὲ τῇ μὲν ἐπαρχίᾳ τὴν πόλιν), and the harbor to the sailors (τοῖς ταύτῃ δὲ πλοϊζομένοις τὸν λιμένα). He named the entire city to honor Octavian (τὴν τιμὴν τοῦ κτίσματος). The other buildings, including a hippodrome/amphitheater,[386] market place, and theater, were also worthy of the same name (ἄξια τῆς προσηγορίας). Herod instituted games to be held every fifth year called Caesar's Games (ἐκάλεσεν ἀπὸ τοῦ Καίσαρος). These might include "classic Roman games associated with the imperial cult."[387] Again the creation of games follows the pattern of Hellenistic kings offering benefactions to their superiors to express their magnanimity and to solidify the relationship with Rome. Josephus describes Herod's motivation as a love of honor, a thoroughly Hellenistic impetus (φιλότιμος; *War* 1.408–409). The descriptions given by Josephus highlight the lavish nature of Herod's most glorious project. He speaks of its white stones and brightly adorned palaces in which Herod ἐν ᾗ μάλιστα τὸ φύσει μεγαλόνουν ἐπεδείξατο (*War* 1.408). Through great expense and a love of honor Herod overcame nature's obstacles to create the harbor (*War* 1.410). Clearly, Herod desired to be counted among the Hellenistic kings as a supreme benefactor to Caesarea.

Euergetistic inscriptions can be found confirming the adoption of the practice not only by Herod, but also by other local rulers like Pilate.[388] The well-known Pilate Inscription appears to be a euergetistic dedication to Tiberius in Caesarea. Hanson and Oakman reconstruct the inscription with translation as follows (*AE* 1963 no. 104):[389]

---

[386] Properly identifying this discovery has been difficult. Netzer follows Porath and Humphrey in identifying it as a "hippodrome-stadium" which housed "Roman spectacles." See Netzer, *Architecture*, 118.

[387] Netzer, *Architecture*, 279.

[388] Reed, *Archaeology*, 123. Reed mentioned the Pilate inscription as of central importance to euergetism in private correspondence.

[389] C. M. Lehmann and K. Holum, *The Joint Expedition to Caesarea Maritima: Excavation Reports V: The Greek and Latin Inscriptions of Caesarea Maritima* (Boston: American Schools of Oriental Research, 1999), 68–71; G. Alföldy, "Pontius Pilatus und

[DIS AUGUSTI]S TIBÉRIUM	To the honorable gods (this) Tiberium
[....PO]NTIUS PILATUS	Pontius Pilate,
[...PRAEF]ECTUS IUDA[EA]E	Prefect of Judea,
[..FECIT D]É[DICAVIT]	had dedicated

The fragmentary nature of the remains prevents strong conclusions about the nature of the inscription. Further difficulty arises because the inscription was not found *in situ*. It is possible, following Lémonon, that the inscription is not a dedication to Tiberius but merely a description of the building to which the inscription was attached.[390] However, J. E. Taylor suggests that the recreation of the final line as *dedicavit* might be expected because of grammar and other inscriptions of a similar nature.[391] She then compares "Tiberium" with Hadrianeum which, in Latin, indicates the erection of an honorary structure.[392] Outside evidence on Pilate supports the reading of this inscription as a dedication to Tiberius and promotion of the Roman imperial cult. Taylor surveys Pilate's coins and investigates the story of the Roman shields (Philo, *Leg ad Gaium*, 299–305) to construct this picture of Pilate. Although certainty cannot be gained, it seems more likely that this inscription is a dedication which accompanied the benefaction of a small structure to honor Tiberius.

It seems best to conclude that benefaction would have been familiar to many in the city, though it is unclear how widely understood *patrocinium* might be. With the stronger Hellenistic expressions of opulence and the presence of euergetistic inscriptions the general populace would have been surrounded by the culture of benefaction in most of the city. *Patrocinium*, being a bit more private and deriving directly from Romans themselves, would have spread sporadically. An individual influenced by Roman ways may have taken a client and instructed him. That client in turn could have informed others, but the social relationship by nature was not broadcast in the same way that a public inscription or monument broadcast a benefactor's generosity and relationship to the city. Roman soldiers or perhaps the prefect himself may have interacted with others to educate or involve them in Roman patronage, but this would have been on a smaller scale than the open proclamation of benefaction made through Herod's grand construction projects.

---

das Tiberium von Caesarea Maritima," *Scripta Classica Israelitica* 18 (1999): 85–93; Hanson and Oakman, *Palestine*, 78.

[390] J. P. Lémonon, *Pilate et le gouvernement de la Judée: texts et monuments* (Études Bibliques; Paris: Gabalda, 1981), 26–32, in Bond, *Pilate*, 11–12.

[391] Joan E. Taylor, "Pontius Pilate and the Imperial Cult in Roman Judaea," *NTS* 52 (2006): 555–582, 565.

[392] Taylor, "Pilate," 567.

Samaria

Samaria presents a host of problems when assessments of its culture begin.[393] The stigma of "syncretistic Jews" though perhaps an accurate description of a few inhabitants should not be thought to cover all residents of the region. Demarcations between pagan and Samaritan (or even Jewish) religion existed. Samarians and Samaritans should also be distinguished from one another with the former referring to constituents of the geographical area and the latter referring to adherents to a form of religion.[394] Archaeology accentuates these problems since no major excavation and/or publication of finds for its villages has been done. To date only its largest cities have been investigated.[395] Apart from these problems, however, it is still possible to discern the general nature of this region and some of its ways.

Successive intrusions of immigrants caused various levels of fluctuation in the cultural, ethnic, and religious make-up of Samaria. Zangenberg summarizes many of these intrusions by foreigners (Macedonians, Sidonians, Assyrians, etc.).[396] The Hasmoneans changed this. They destroyed Samaritan holy cites and repopulated the land with Jews (*Ant.* 14.87–91). One exception would have been Sebaste (at this point still named Samaria, the city) which they practically ignored. At this time Samaria had a mixed population of Jews, pagans, and Samaritans. Herod was not content with this situation, so when he took power he attempted to recreate Samaria, and especially Sebaste, as a Hellenized city. The culture created by Herod remained intact in the time of Jesus and the apostles and progressed toward deeper Hellenization before thorough Romanization in the second and third centuries.

---

[393] Jürgen Zangenberg, "Between Jerusalem and Galilee: Samaria in the Time of Jesus," in Charlesworth, *Jesus and Archaeology*, 393–432; idem, *Frühes Christentum in Samarien: Topographische und traditiongeschichtliche Studien zu den Samarientexten im Johannesevangelium* (TANZ 27; Tübingen: Francke, 1998); idem, "Simon Magus," in *Religionsgeschichte des Neuen Testaments* (ed., A. v. Dobbeler, K. Erlemann, and R. Heiligenthal; Festschrift Klaus Berger; Tübingen: Francke, 2000), 519–540; A. Lindemann, "Samaria und die Samaritaner im Neuen Testament," *Wort und Dienst* 22 (1993): 51–76; D. Hamm, "What the Samaritan Leper Sees: The Narrative Christology of Luke 17:11–19," *CBQ* 56 (1994): 273–287; J. P. Meier, "The Historical Jesus and the Historical Samaritans: What Can Be Said?" *Biblica* 81 (2000): 202–232; Martina Böhm, *Samarien und die Samaritai bei Lukas: Eine Studie zum religionshistorischen und traditionsgeschichtlichen Hintergrund der lukanischen Samarientexte und zu deren topographischer Verhaftung* (WUNT 2:111; Tübingen: Mohr Siebeck, 1999).

[394] Meier, "Historical Samaritans," 204.

[395] Zangenberg, "Samaria," in Charlesworth, *Jesus and Archaeology*, 408.

[396] Zangenberg, "Samaria," 402–404.

2.2 Benefaction and Patronage in Palestine

For a few reasons it is quite likely that Samarians (Samaritans, pagans, and Jews) interacted or were familiar with benefaction. This is especially so in Sebaste. The newly refounded city of Sebaste was Herod's attempt to reinvigorate the land with Hellenism. He kept strong ties with the city (*Ant.* 14.408; *War* 1.299, 166) and gave it a "Greek style" constitution.[397] He intended to proclaim the magnificence of his name in the construction of Sebaste and to secure connection to the emperor he renamed it (τὸ φιλότιμον ἐπετηδεύετο τήν τε προσηγορίαν ὑπήλλαττε Σεβαστὴν καλῶν; *Ant.* 15.296). *Sebaste* is the Greek equivalent of *imperator*. Many signs of wealth, including royal palaces, a wall, and frescoes have been found.[398] By lavishing great wealth on the city, Herod purposed to leave a monument to his beneficence (μνημεῖα φιλανθρωπίας; *Ant.* 15.298).

ἔν τε τοῖς κατὰ μέρος διὰ πάντων ἐκόσμει τὴν πόλιν τὸ μὲν ἀναγκαῖον τῆς ἀσφαλείας ὁρῶν καὶ τῇ τῶν περιβόλων ἐρυμνότητι φρούριον αὐτὴν ποιούμενος ἐπὶ τῇ μείζονι τὸ δ' εὐπρεπὲς ὡς ἂν ἐκ τοῦ φιλοκαλεῖν καὶ μνημεῖα φιλανθρωπίας ἀπολιπεῖν ἐν ὑστέρῳ
"The various parts of the city he also adorned in a variety of ways, and seeing the necessity of security, he made it a first-class fortress by strengthening its outer walls. He also made it splendid in order to leave to posterity a monument of the humanity [μνημεῖα φιλανθρωπίας] that arose from his love of beauty."

According to Josephus, then, Herod had the motivations of a Hellenistic benefactor in the re-foundation of the city. The construction of temples attests various expressions of benefaction. The Samarians in requesting favor from Antiochus to be dissociated from the Jews refer to him as benefactor and Savior (τὸν εὐεργέτην καὶ σωτῆρα; *Ant.* 12.258–261). Their request as interpreted by Antiochus was a plea to be reckoned Greeks, so their temple was appropriately re-titled Temple of Greek Zeus (*Ant.* 12.263). Apparently, the Samarians were able to articulate their desires in the language of Hellenistic benefaction before the era of Herod.

But Herod takes Antiochus' assumption one step further. His new temple was dedicated directly to Rome and Augustus.[399] Herod had to assume a significantly Hellenized and pagan population in order to go ahead with this project since he typically refrained from offending religious sensibilities. As suggested previously, naming monumental structures in honor of a superior was a quintessential expression of Hellenistic benefaction. Herod's Romanizing of Sebaste was somewhat intentional since he built

---

[397] Zangenberg, "Samaria," 428.
[398] Zangenberg, "Samaria," 412–413; cf. Jensen, *Antipas*, 179–85 who discusses several cities including Scythopolis.
[399] The most recent archaeological description of this temple is found in Ehud Netzer with Rachel Laureys-Chachy, *The Architecture of Herod, the Great Builder* (Tübingen: Mohr Siebeck, 2006), 85–92.

his Temple to Rome and Augustus in Roman style.[400] Herod also, apparently, constructed a stadium (not mentioned by Josephus) which could have been the location of games or a training ground for chariot races. Netzer interprets the erection of this stadium as a "gesture" to the pagan and Hellenistically influenced populace of Sebaste who would have desired such activities.[401] The stadium incorporates mostly Greek, with some Roman, styles. Romanism may have entered when Archelaos was banished in A.D. 6 and Roman procurators took over, but this would have been slight compared to the overwhelming presence of Hellenism.

It can be argued that Herod's influence was only felt in the new Hellenistic city, but the discovery of a tomb in a somewhat distant village challenges that view. Several inscriptions found in a tomb in Gitta (hometown of Simon Magus) show the use of Greek in the village even among Jews. Many of the inscriptions mention Herodians, Marcus and Agrippa, and Tiberius. It has been proposed that the tomb belongs to a Jewish family "somehow related to the Herodian dynasty."[402] Indeed, it would be incorrect to assume that cities only housed pagans and villages only housed conservatives (Samaritans or Jews). Villages contained both segments of society and it is even possible that some were ethnically and religiously mixed.[403]

The pervasiveness of Hellenism, the depth of pagan religious practice, and the presence of monumental structures dedicated to Roman superiors in addition to the renaming of the entire city after the emperor all argue for familiarity with the ideology of benefaction in Samaria. This is confirmed in a few narratives from Josephus where the populace articulates its desires from this vantage point.

Smaller Cities in Philip's Tetrarchy

It is not easy to describe Philip's tetrarchy. It contained one of the most overtly pagan cities in the region (Paneas) which became a center for Roman culture (Caesarea Philippi).[404] In some of its smaller villages and cit-

---

[400] Netzer gives this description, Netzer, *Architecture*, 270–271, while Ball claims it was in eastern style, Ball, *Rome*, 177.

[401] Netzer, *Architecture*, 92–93, 277–280, 284.

[402] Zangenberg, "Samaria," 419–420. He quotes Y. Porath, E. Yannai, and A. Kasher, "Archaeological Remains at Jatt," *Atiqot* 27 (1999): 1–78 and 167*-171*, 170.

[403] Zangengerg, "Samaria," 411.

[404] On Caesarea Philippi, John Francis Wilson, *Caesarea Philippi: Basias, the Lost City of Pan* (London and New York: I. B. Tauris, 2004), 1–37. Also see, Schnabel, *Mission*, 1.253–254, who identifies the following sources: Benzinger, "Caesarea Nr. 9," *PW* 3 (1899): 1291–1292; G. Hölscher, *PW* 13.3 (1949): 594–600; C. Colpe, "Caesarea 2," *KP* 1:1004; J.-P. Rey-Coquais, "Paneas," *PECS* 2:670; John Kutscko, "Caesarea," *ABD* 1:803; Z. U. Maoz, "Banias," *NEAEHL* 1:136–143; Steveno Menno Moors, "De Decapo-

ies strong allegiance to Judaism surfaces (e.g., Gamla). In still other areas, a recent description refuses to admit much Hellenism or Romanism at all, but instead maintains the persistence of "Arab" culture.[405] A monolithic perspective of Philip's territory will not do, but space prohibits the type of analysis necessary to do the region full justice. Instead a brief review of each of these cultural components must suffice, and the admission that only the surface has been scratched will qualify later connections and conclusions drawn from this part of the study.[406] Archaeological evidence will be brought forth first, and literary evidence will follow. Literary evidence for Philip's tetrarchy is rather slim, so emphasis rests on archaeology.

Much archaeological evidence suggests that Hellenism and Romanism had established a solid foothold in Philip's tetrarchy before the time of Jesus. The region passed through many hands from Pompey to Herod I to Philip.[407] Each brought a different political center-point (Rome, Jerusalem, Syria respectively). Several of the Greek cities of the Decapolis were "equipped with various public institutions such as theatres, monumental gates, temples, etc."[408] In Hippos, granted the status of polis by Pompey, a second century B.C. temple's *temenos* has been uncovered which "corresponds with coins minted in 37 B.C. with the image of Tyche."[409] Gadara also had a second century B.C. temple complex. Coin finds confirm the practice of the Greco-Roman cult in Gadara.[410] Scythopolis was the largest city in the first-century and it had a theater, two temples, coins confirming allegiance to Tyche and Nike, and an amphitheater. Scythopolis was a polis with "several of the institutions connected with this status."[411] It contains euergetistic inscriptions consistent with a Greek polis and the practice of benefaction.[412] Public architecture far surpasses that found in Galilee for

---

lis Steden en dorpen in de Romeinse pronciecies Syria en Arabia" (Diss. Rijksuniversiteit, Leiden, 1992), 211–217; Strickert, "Coins"; Dan Urman, "Public Structures and Jewish Communities in the Golan Heights," in *Ancient Synagogues: Historical Analysis and Archaeological Discovery* (ed. Dan Urman and Paul V. M. Flesher; 2 vols.; StPB 47; Leiden: Brill, 1995), 389–390.

[405] Ball's comments on the Decapolis, Ball, *Rome*, 181.

[406] Moxnes suggests that more attention needs to be paid to Galilean relations to Decapolis, Gadara, Gaulanitis, and Batanea. Cf. Moxnes, "Construction," 74.

[407] Jensen, *Antipas*, 179.

[408] Jensen, *Antipas*, 179. For a thorough analysis of the Decapolis see Achim Lichtenberger, *Kulte und Kultur der Dekapolis* (Abhandlungen des deutschen Pälastina-Vereins 29; Wiesbaden: Harrassowitz Verlag, 2003).

[409] Jensen, *Antipas*, 180.

[410] Jensen, *Antipas*, 180.

[411] Jensen, *Antipas*, 181.

[412] Reed, *Archaeology*, 123. He mentioned the Dionysos altar as important in this regard in private correspondence.

the same period which suggests stronger Hellenization and provides opportunity for benefaction.

Philip followed in his father's footsteps naming cities in honor of his Roman superiors. He took the cultic religious site of Paneas, transformed it slightly, and renamed it in honor of Caesar and himself. Apparently Philip desired to connect himself to Rome quite openly. Caesarea Philippi quickly became a "center for Roman culture."[413] Freyne suggests that the cultic temple would have signaled to passersby the epochal changes taking place under Augustus' rule. They would not have needed to read *Res Gestae* to understand that a new age (of Roman salvation) was upon them.[414]

A study of coinage shows the different approach taken in Philip's tetrarchy. Whereas Herod I and Antipas abstained from images and overt connections to Rome out of deference to their Jewish constituents, Philip needed no such reserve. He happily put images of people and cultic materials on his coins apparently without fear of dissension. Even before Philip, Gadara minted a coin with an image of the emperor and an inscription of his name in 31/30 B.C.[415] Numismatic evidence points toward significant Romanization and Hellenization.

Josephus describes Philip's building activity in commendatory terms. After increasing its population size and improving it through great deeds (τῇ ἄλλῃ δυνάμει), Philip renamed Bethsaida after Caesar's wife Julias (*Ant.* 18.28).[416] He advanced it to the level of a *polis* in this process (see sections 3.3.2, 3.3.4). In some areas controlled by Philip Hellenism, and benefaction, had taken hold.

But not all agree that Hellenism truly infiltrated as thoroughly as this brief survey suggests. Warwick Ball claims that the Decapolis was not the Hellenistic neighbor of Galilee and Judea that many think. He proposes that the Decapolis should not be thought of as Hellenistic since it remained "wholly Arab."[417] Naming it such was probably an effort by Rome to pronounce its presence, but this held little water among the inhabitants who

---

[413] Kee, "Early Christianity," 19. *Life* 2, 52–57.

[414] Sean Freyne, *Jesus, a Jewish Galilean: A New Reading of the Jesus Story* (London: T & T Clark, 2004), 133–134.

[415] Mark A. Chancey, "City Coins and Roman Power," 103–112, 106. See also Rachel Barkay, *The Coinage of Nysa-Scythopolis (Beth-Shean)* (Jerusalem: Israel Numismatic Society, 2003). See section 3.3.5.

[416] For more detail see, Rami Arav and Richard A. Freund, eds., *Bethsaida: A City by the North Shore of the Sea of Galilee* (vol 2; Kirksville: Thomas Jefferson University Press, 1995). Josephus claims it was Caesar's daughter, but she was banished in 2 B.C., so it must be concluded that Augustus' wife is the Julias so honored, Strickert, "Coins of Philip," in Arav and Freund, *Bethsaida*, 165–189, 183; contra David C. Braund, "Philip," *ABD*, 5:311.

[417] Ball, *Rome*, 181.

2.2 Benefaction and Patronage in Palestine

knew better.[418] Its cities were comprised of mixed Graeco-Macedonian, Arab, and Jewish (particularly in Scythopolis) peoples with Arabs forming the bulk and Greeks filling the administrative roles. "The architecture is oriental, the temples and the cults were to local Semitic deities. To view the Decapolis as an 'island of Hellenism' or as 'unambiguously Greek' in 'public character' is untenable."[419] His discussion of a Greek inscription found in Damascus illustrates his approach.[420] The inscription should not be connected to describe all in its vicinity, but perhaps only the one who inscribed it (contra Millar). Ball brings up this inscription because many use the evidence of one Greek inscription to conclude that an area was fluent or bilingual, but they do not do the same when they find a foreign language (e.g., Palmyrene) in Britain. Greek was a lingua franca out of necessity, since the new administrators would not tolerate the old lingua franca (Aramaic) and the inhabitants could not handle any local rival language (Hebrew, Nabatean). Its use does not imply "Greek 'character' or even much culture" nor "the extinction of native languages."[421]

While Ball's argument deserves attention, and certainly adds nuance to the portrait of the Decapolis, it is also slightly overstated. Influence from the east certainly persisted and should be taken into consideration when determining the cultural make-up and indebtedness of the region. But more than a lone Greek inscription has been found in the area. Jensen and Syon have surveyed the coin distribution in the area and note a few important points. (1) Ball is correct that eastern influences persisted and this is attested in coin distribution (see Syon's percentages in section 2.2.5 *Gamla*). But, (2) Jensen shows that at least in Gamla the distribution of coins witnesses a drop off of Phoenician coins with an increase in Jewish and Greek coins during different periods (see following section). Adding to this, the majority of inscriptions found were in Greek (with some Latin). Nuance is necessary. A brief look at Gamla and Bethsaida shows some of the cultural complexity in Philip's tetrarchy.

---

[418] Ball, *Rome*, 181. Jones, *Cities of the Eastern Roman Provinces*; Julian M. C. Bowsher, "Architecture and Religion in the Decapolis: A Numismatic Survey," *PEQ* 119 (Jan-June 1987): 62–69.

[419] Ball, *Rome*, 181. The two quotes are from, respectively, Graf in Philip Freeman and D. L. Kennedy, ed., *The Defence of the Roman and Byzantine East: Proceedings of a Colloquium Held at the University of Sheffield in April 1986* (BAR International Series 297; 2 vols. Oxford: B.A.R., 1986); Millar, *Near East*, 412–13.

[420] The inscription is found in Millar, *Near East*, 318.

[421] Ball, *Rome*, 3–5.

Gamla

Not all territories in Philip's tetrarchy can be described as either Hellenistic or Arab because at least Gamla deserves to be thought Jewish and intimately connected to Antipas' Galilee. Jensen chooses to include Gamla in his survey of Galilean villages even though it properly belonged to Philip's tetrarchy. Two reasons support this decision: (1) Coin finds show a strong economic connection between Gamla and Galilee (and Judaism). In Gamla 3,964 of 6,314 coins studied were Hasmonean (62.8%) while Herodian and other Roman administration (304, 4.8%) and Seleucid (610, 9.7%) coins were even overshadowed by Phoenician (928, 14.7%).[422] Since more of Antipas' coins were found in Gamla than Philip's, M. Aviam suggests that those citizens felt stronger ties to Galilee than to Philip's territory. Remarkably high volumes of Hasmonean coins have been found in Galilee into the first-century leading to Aviam's "highly probable" conclusion that Galileans continued to use these strongly nationalistic coins for local commerce.[423] (2) Other finds express the strength of Jewishness in the village. Large houses with white plastered walls, streets beautifully paved, and two large public buildings (a synagogue and a basilica) attest that the olive oil industry in this region paid good dividends. The identification of a *miqveh* next to one olive press signals zeal to maintain ritual purity during the production process.[424] Discoveries of a synagogue and a *miqveh* point to adherence to Jewish ritual in Gamla. Richardson goes so far as to say that the combination of Hasmonean coins, synagogue, and *miqveh* suggest anti-Roman protest in the region.[425]

Some evidence in Josephus might be adduced to support this reading, and it is also slightly suggestive for a study of benefaction (*War* 2.117–118; *Ant.* 18.1–10). Judas, the Gaulanite from Gamla, and Sadduc (a Pharisee perhaps also from Gamla?) incited revolts against Roman taxation. They desired to gain honor (τιμή) and good (ἀγαθός) for their magnanimity (μεγαλόφρονος) (*Ant.* 18.5). The two, in attempting to earn freedom for the region, have vocabulary common for benefactors connected to their motivations, but Josephus does not expand upon the story long enough to confirm that they self-consciously took this social role. One need not go as far

---

[422] D. Syon, "The Coins from Gamla: An Interim Report," *Israel Numismatic Journal* 12 (1992/93): 34–55, 27, figure 1, found in Jensen, *Antipas*, 214.

[423] Mordechai Aviam, "First-century Jewish Galilee: An Archaeological Perspective," in Edwards, *Religion and Society*, 7–27, 21.

[424] Jensen, *Antipas*, 176–77; he cites, Shmaryahu Gutman, "Gamla," *NEAEHL*, 2:459–63; Danny Syon and Shlomit Nemlich, *Gamla* (Qatzrin, Israel: Golan Archaeological Museum, 2001); Danny Syon and Z. Yavor, "Gamla 1997–2000," *Hadashot Arkheologiyot-Excavations and Surveys in Israel* 114 (2005): 2–5.

[425] Richardson, *Building Jewish*, 20.

as Richardson to realize that some parts of Philip's territory still aligned themselves with Jewishness. It is possible that at least Josephus depicts the actions of some constituents along benefaction or patronage lines since he later remarks that the actions of these men forfeited the protection of their Roman friends (*Ant.* 18.7). This survey shows that Gamla connected itself to Galilee (and by implication, Judaism) in "religion, culture, and trade."[426]

Bethsaida

More concretely important for studies of Jesus and the earliest Christians must be Bethsaida. Jesus was quite familiar with Bethsaida since at least three of his disciples hailed from the city, he performed mighty deeds in it, fed a multitude there, and pronounced woes upon it (Mark 8:22–25; Luke 9:10–17; Matt 11:21; Luke 10:13). The gospel portrait of Galileans moving freely in Bethsaida corresponds with some evidence of trade between the two areas.[427] A mixture of cultures can be located in Bethsaida with some important discoveries related to Philip's reign. Jewish populations persisted from the Hasmonean through the Herodian period as is attested by limestone vessels.[428] Numismatic evidence from Bethsaida qualifies this description slightly. Neither Herod I nor Antipas elected to mint coins bearing images out of respect for their Jewish constituents, but Philip imprinted images of emperors, the emperor's wife, himself, and a Roman temple on his coins. The most common type bears the image of the emperor (Augustus then Tiberius) on the obverse and a tetrastyle temple on the reverse. He repeated this type, with slight variations, each of the eight times he minted.[429] Josephus does not tell of revolt against this practice so it seems likely that Jewish population levels were low, the form of Judaism in the city was less conservative, or a combination of these two factors existed.[430]

Several indicators of Hellenistic and Roman influence have been discovered among the remains, but R. Arav warns that the degree of Hellenization in Bethsaida was quite small and moved from the top down.[431] Arav interprets a small structure as a temple to Livia-Julia which explains why Philip renamed the city. This structure corresponds with some implements

---

[426] Jensen, *Antipas*, 175–177.

[427] Toni Tessaro, "Hellenistic and Roman Ceramic Cooking Ware from Bethsaida," in Arav and Freund, *Bethsaida*, 127–139, 137; Reed, *Archaeology*, 148.

[428] Rami Arav, "Bethsaida," in Charlesworth, *Jesus and Archaeology*, 145–166, 161.

[429] Fred Strickert, "The Coins of Philip," in Arav and Freund, *Bethsaida*, 165–189, 166, figure 1.

[430] Strickert, "Coins," 167–168.

[431] Arav, "Bethsaida," 166.

of the imperial cult discovered in the area (shovel, female figurine).[432] Five coins minted by Philip with images of Livia and a temple also connect the city and temple with the emperor's wife. "Livia-Julias was the first priestess of the cult of Augustus at Rome."[433] Strickert identifies a coin bearing the description κτίστης which has traditionally been interpreted as a reference to the foundation of Caesarea Philippi, but Strickert argues that it more properly marks the change of Bethsaida from village to city (*Ant.* 18.28).[434] Renaming the city after Herod's wife shows the political alliance which had been developing between the Herods and Rome.[435] Coins commemorating Julias' death support the idea that Philip desired to express affinity for Rome.[436]

Study of the fineware unearthed in Bethsaida undertaken by S. Fortner offers another glimpse into the cultural indebtedness of the region. She concludes that the majority of discovered fineware consists mainly of Hellenistic fineware (200 B.C. to 100 B.C.) with only a few Roman wares (first-century B.C. to first-century A.D.) that taper off considerably in the first-century A.D.[437] The low amount of Hellenistic and Roman wares in the first-century and the effusive love of Rome expressed by Philip draw out the difference between the normal populace and the governing authority. Philip intended to promote Hellenism and to advertise his relationship with Rome in coins, monuments, and cult. The people did not leave much response to this effort in the material remains nor does Josephus mention their involvement in things Hellenistic. Judaism may have differed in this region, but Philip did not (need to?) make accommodations for large numbers of imperial cult worshipers. Inhabitants could have developed familiarity with benefaction and/or patronage if they studied Philip or questioned the purpose for his constructions and coins. But no material evidence has been left of inscriptions which clearly demarcate the outright practice of either form of reciprocity.

Tyre

Tyre was strongly Hellenistic even though it maintained much of its historic cultural roots. This can be seen first in some religious remains. Freyne goes through several Phoenician inscriptions wherein the Greek

---

[432] Chancey resists this interpretation as built upon too shaky of evidence, but he seems a bit too skeptical. Chancey, *Culture of Jesus*, 90–94.

[433] Arav, "Bethsaida," 162–164.

[434] Strickert, "Coins," 182.

[435] Freyne, *Jesus*, 133–134.

[436] Strickert, "Coins," 183–184.

[437] Sandra Fortner, "Hellenistic and Roman Fineware from Bethsaida," in Arav and Freund, *Bethsaida*, 99–126, 106–107.

and Semitic gods interchange names. Similarly Phoenician people sometimes adopt theophoric names that derive from Hellenistic deities (rather than Phoenician). Because of Tyre's precarious geographical location it depended on outside sources for much of its food supply. Galilee served this purpose well.[438] Trade between Tyre and Galilee can be monitored through the distributions of coins, contrary to Horsley's somewhat minimalist postulation, and Phoenician fine wares.[439] Fluctuations in trade are evident through the centuries preceding Jesus with some tapering off in lower Galilee in the second century B.C.[440] Upper Galilee consistently contains both Tyrian and Hasmonean coinage through the first-century A.D., but lower Galilee does not. In Jodefat (for example), Hasmonean coinage takes over in the second century B.C. with Tyrian coinage dropping out. The distribution patterns of Phoenician fine wares also open up the cultural situation of Galilee in the first and second centuries B.C. During this time Galilee became rather self-sufficient and cut itself off from Tyrian dependency. It is somewhat difficult to discern whether these changes occurred for ideological or simply geographical reasons since distribution patterns fluctuate also in relation to the availability of an easy trade route. Freyne concludes from his study that Tyre did not attempt to Hellenize Galilee overtly. It involved itself in trade for utilitarian reasons, but did not force Hellenism on the region. This assumes, however, that Hellenism had strongly influenced Phoenician culture.

According to Josephus even in the time of Aristotle a Jewish resident of the region could be "Greek" not only in language but also in soul (*Apion* 1.178–180).

οὗτος οὖν ὁ ἄνθρωπος ἐπιξενούμενός τε πολλοῖς κἀκ τῶν ἄνω τόπων εἰς τοὺς ἐπιθαλαττίους ὑποκαταβαίνων Ἑλληνικὸς ἦν οὐ τῇ διαλέκτῳ μόνον ἀλλὰ καὶ τῇ ψυχῇ (*Apion* 1.180–181)
"Now this man, who was entertained by a large circle of friends and was on his way down from the interior to the coast, not only spoke Greek, but had the soul of a Greek."

---

[438] Freyne, *Galilee and Gospel*, 167. Theissen mentions several of the decrees which had implications on Tyre/Galilee relations, Gerd Theissen, *The Gospels in Context: Social and Political History in the Synoptic Tradition* (trans. Linda M. Maloney; Minneapolis: Fortress Press, 1991), 73–75: Pliny *NH* 5.17.76; Strabo *Geog* 16.2.23; 1 Kgs 5:11; *Ant.* 8.141; 8.54; Ezek 27:17; 1 Kgs 17:7–16; *Ant.* 14.190–216; *Ant.* 20.212; *Life* 71; *Y. Demai* 1.3; *Cant. Rab.* 5.14; *pp Abod. Zar* 4.39c.

[439] For some of the views see the Meiron archaeological project (Meyers and Hanson), Richard A. Horsley, *Galilee: History, Politics, People* (Valley Forge: Trinity Press International, 1995), 162; D. Barag, "Tyrian Currency in Galilee," *Israel Numismatic Journal* 6/7 (1982/83): 7–13; U. Rappaport, "Phoenicia and Galilee: Economy, Territory and Political Relations," *Studia Phoenicia* 9 (1992): 262–268.

[440] For the following see Freyne, "Galileans, Phoenicians, and Itureans," 202–209.

G. Theissen employs this background to read Mark 7:24–30. The description of the Syrophoenician woman as a Ἑλληνίς probably indicates fluency in Greek language and perhaps culture. This does not of course preclude the predominance of Aramaic in the region but supports the idea of bilinguals.[441] These stories are instructive for how thoroughly Hellenized residents of the region could become. Hellenism did not feel "invasive" to the Phoenicians, though they were simultaneously capable of maintaining "clear traces of their pre-Greek past in cultural terms."[442]

Consistent with this level of Hellenism, the description by Josephus of a decree made by Caesar and posted in Tyre and Sidon expresses the adoption of benefaction, *suffragium*, and friendship in those cities. Josephus records the public honors made by the emperors that honor the Jewish nation for their benefaction and friendship with them (*Ant*. 14.185–267). These display for all the world the loyalty (τὴν πίστιν) shown to Rome by the Jews (14.186). The important decree for this section is one made by Julius Caesar in Sidon announcing the relationship of the Jews to Rome (14.190–195). A public decree is made which follows many of the patterns of benefaction intermixed with evidence of *suffragium* (ἐπεί; πίστιν τε καὶ σπουδήν; διὰ ταύτας; φίλοις; εὐεργέτησαν 14.190, 192, 194). Hyrcanus and his family receive leadership roles (governor and high priesthood) through Caesar's decree. They are to be acknowledged as Caesar's friends (14.194). Granting leadership positions was not a necessary component of *patrocinium*, but *suffragium*, the Roman term for such appointments. The bestowal of leadership positions often came from benefactors.[443] This decree is to be set in bronze and placed publicly in Sidon, Tyre, and Askelon, in the temple and everywhere (14.197–198). Caesar assumes that benefaction, *suffragium*, and friendship were familiar enough among the populace that such a decree would not be misunderstood, but instead would provide compelling reason for the people to act appropriately toward the Jews.

Other inscriptions give evidence that Tyre identified itself as the client of certain patrons. Eilers points to an inscription in which M. Aemilius Scaurus is recognized as the patron of Tyre (*IGR* 3.1102).[444]

ἡ βουλὴ Καὶ ὁ δῆμος
Μᾶρκον Αἰμύλιον Μάρκου υἱόν
Σκαῦρον ἀντιταμίαν ἀντι
Στράτηγον τὸν ἑαυτῶν

---

[441] Theissen, *Gospels in Context*, 60–70.

[442] Sean Freyne, "Galileans, Phoenicians, and Itureans: A Study of Regional Contrasts in the Hellenistic Age," in Collins and Sterling, *Hellenism*, 182–215, 188.

[443] Eilers, *Roman Patrons*, 3–4.

[444] Eilers, *Roman Patrons*, 146 n. 6, 243, 264; C152, C153; cf. Nicols, "Patrons of Greek Cities," 84; Brunt, "Clientela," 396.

Πάτρωνα εὐνοίας ἕνεκε[ν].
"The council and the people (honoured) Marcus Aemilius Scaurus, son of Marcus, proquaestor pro praetore, their patron, because of his benevolence."

M. Aemilius Scaurus functioned in the new role, *proquaestor pro praetore*, under Pompey between 63–61 B.C. Another inscription identifies Ti. Iulius Alexander as one of only a few non-senatorial patrons of cities.[445] This inscription, still unpublished, identifies Ti. Iulias Alexander as the patron of Tyre during his tenure as procurator of Syria under Nero.[446] These inscriptions show that before and after the time of Jesus Romans were sometimes identified as patrons in Tyre.

2.2.6 Conclusions of the Regional Perspective

Before offering a summary of the regional perspective it is appropriate to cull the archaeological and literary evidence to be reminded of what it offered.

Archaeology can provide evidence of Hellenism, Romanism, and Jewishness, along with pockets of benefaction and patronage, but it simultaneously insists that regional distinctions be maintained. In Galilee, archaeology paints an overwhelmingly Jewish portrait especially in the mundane materials it exposes. Most of the four major signs of Jewish piety (limestone/chalk vessels, *miqvaoth*, Jewish burial, lack of pork bones) surface in each village surveyed in addition to the two major cities (Tiberias, Sepphoris). The predominance of Hasmonean coinage adds to this picture of Jewish allegiance. Very rarely do any signs of Hellenism arise in the villages (city plan in Cana), but Tiberias had a few monumental structures which showed some Hellenistic and Roman influence. No euergetistic inscriptions have been found in Galilee which reduces the amount of benefaction expected in this region.

Archaeology paints a different portrait in the rest of the regions surveyed. In Jerusalem monumental structures, benefaction inscriptions, and the honorary naming of structures and games all contribute to the suggestion that benefaction, and to a lesser extent *patrocinium*, operated in the early first-century. This parallels the finding of more Hellenism in the city in general. Fewer Romans and minimal signs of overt Romanization in the archaeological remains suggest a lesser likelihood of *patrocinium*. Caesarea can be described in similar terms, but Hellenism and Romanism definitely increased substantially in this city. The enormity of Herod's projects in this harbor city, the presence of Romans, and the identification of

---

[445] Eilers, *Roman Patrons*, 243.
[446] Eilers, *Roman Patrons*, 264; C153. J. –P. Rey-Coquais, "Syrie romaine, de Pompée à Dioclétien," *JRS* 68 (1978): 44–73, 71 n. 369.

euergetistic inscriptions coalesce to suggest significant adoption of benefaction. The public nature of benefaction makes its presence more likely and pervasive than the more private patronage. Some monumental (temple[s], palaces, frescoes, stadium) and inscriptional evidence in Samaria argues for the presence of benefaction in that area. Other evidence links Hellenism (and Judaism) with Samarian village culture which suggests that the ideology of benefaction spilled out of the cities. Euergetistic inscriptions, monuments constructed in honor of superiors, and numismatic evidence builds a case for the practice of benefaction and to some extent patronage in Philip's tetrarchy. Coin finds, a *miqveh*, and a synagogue argue that some parts (e.g., Gamla) of this territory remained predominately Jewish. Some small finds in Bethsaida evidence some Romanization, but this primarily took hold among the elite classes. The people of Tyre imbibed Hellenism without forfeiting their historic cultural roots, and evidence of both *patrocinium* and benefaction surface in Tyre. The archaeological evidence supports regional differences in regard to the adoption of benefaction and *patrocinium*. These differences usually conformed with the picture drawn from the literary sources.

The literary evidence brought to bear on this study also demands distinctions among the regions though it too provides evidence of Hellenistic and Roman influence as well as the adoption of benefaction and *patrocinium* (especially among the elite). One does not expect much detailed description of the Galilean villages in the sources, but they do relate stories of prominent figures (e.g., Herod, Antony, Josephus, centurion) passing through or spending some time in the villages. These occasions provide the most concrete opportunity for the transmission of benefaction or patronage in the villages. Josephus' use of specific vocabulary connected to benefaction (in e.g., Cana, Tiberias) especially in his descriptions of these events could be a window into the culture or at least its outside influences. Naming cities and structures in honor of superiors gives some insight into the practice of benefaction, and perhaps *patrocinium*, in, especially, Tiberias and Sepphoris. Literary and archaeological evidence for Galilee combine to describe the role Jews took in the nascent Hellenistic forms of government (e.g., *epimeletes*, *agoranomos*), thus providing a link between the Hellenistic superiors and the common Jewish residents. Literary evidence on Jerusalem tells of Hellenistic education as well as relationships between common Jews and Hellenistic/Roman officials (Josephus, Philo). A few descriptions of Jews functioning as benefactors in Jerusalem aligns with the archaeological evidence (1 Macc 14:25–49; 2 Macc 4:2; *War* 4.145–146; 5.536; 2.538). Josephus describes the actions of the Hellenistic leadership in Caesarea in benefaction terms and he mentions some interchanges between Jews and Hellenists which provides a vehicle for these ideas to filter into this culture (*War* 2.285–291). Josephus also employs benefaction ideology and terminology in his description of Samaria (*Ant.* 15.296; 12.258–261, 263). Philip's tetrarchy shows signs of Hellenism, Romanism, and the use of benefaction. It is noteworthy when Josephus describes the actions of two Jews (Judas of Gamla and Sadduc) in a predominately Jewish area using diction associated with benefaction as well. According to Josephus it was possible for a Jew in Tyre to be Greek in both language and soul (*Apion* 1.178–180), a fact which lends insight into the depth of Hellenization in this city. His description of decrees erected in the region gives another window into the practice of benefaction in the city (*Ant.* 14.185–267).

This survey of regions and cities critical to the ministry of Jesus and his earliest followers (and opponents) yields several important results. First, Galilee, including Sepphoris and Tiberias, was predominately Jewish though it began to experience a turn toward Hellenism around the time of Jesus. Cana, Nazareth, and Capernaum were thoroughly Jewish with only hints of Hellenization. If Luke's centurion-synagogue story is included then an expression of benefaction took place in Capernaum. Tiberias, and to a lesser extent Sepphoris, did show some signs of Hellenization and hints of benefaction. Tiberias had been more thoroughly overhauled earlier in the life of Jesus while Sepphoris was only receiving attention as Jesus began his ministry. A trajectory toward Hellenization, and Romanization, began early in the first-century, but it was not until the end of that century and into the next that the foreign cultures took complete control. Evidence of literacy among the lower classes does make these villagers capable of interpreting benefaction texts while on pilgrimage or travel to other areas, but they would not have received such education in their hometowns. No clear evidence of *patrocinium* was detected in Galilee.

Second, Jerusalem, while thoroughly Jewish, had Hellenized a little more and clear evidence of benefaction has been discovered in both literary and archaeological remains. Romanization and *patrocinium* were not as prominent. The general picture of Hellenization in Jerusalem found in architecture, education, language, and literature conforms to the evidence of benefaction in the city and the likelihood that it had penetrated multiple social strata among the Jews. Pilgrims would read euergetistic inscriptions at the temple and see monuments of a Hellenistic king dominating the landscape. Freyne suggests that Herod pushed for pilgrimage as part of a revenue generating program for his newly refurbished temple.[447]

Third, Caesarea and Samaria had been strongly Hellenized and inscriptions, monuments, and literature attest the practice of benefaction. A few

---

[447] Sean Freyne, "Behind the Names: Galileans, Samaritans, *Ioudaioi*," in Meyers, *Galilee Through the Centuries*, 39–55, 55 n. 44.

Romans lived in Caesarea which makes the practice of patronage possible if less pervasive.

Fourth, other cities in Philip's tetrarchy should be described cautiously because of the diversity of cultures. Philip mimicked his father in public monuments and an overt effort to be counted as a benefactor. Some public architecture and euergetistic inscriptions show that benefaction could be familiar to inhabitants (Caesarea Philippi, Bethsaida/Julias, Scythopolis). But with good reason the Hellenization of certain places (esp. Gamla, Bethsaida) has been deemed small. Much of the Hellenization and Romanization should be attributed to Philip's strategy of self-preservation.

Fifth, the Hellenization of Tyre was substantial which can also be seen in the practice of patronage, benefaction, and friendship. In the story related by Josephus *patrocinium* seems to be more in view than benefaction because of the nature of the gift and the ethnicity of the giver. Interestingly, the story also gives insight into the way that Jewish rulers and Jews related to Roman authority through patronage, benefaction, and friendship. Two decrees, before and after the time of Jesus, confirm that Tyrians identified certain Romans as patrons.

Chapter 3

Benefaction and *Patrocinium* and The Herodian Rulers

The regional perspective gives a general picture of culture in the cities and villages in and around Palestine, but a personality perspective may shed light on the specific practice of *patrocinium* or benefaction by individuals in those areas. This is critical for the present study because these practices could potentially pass between individuals of various social classes. At times only slight evidence can be adduced to describe an area, but a fuller picture can be developed for certain personalities. Four major figures will be studied: Herod I, Herod Antipas, Herod Philip, and Agrippa I. Again, a blend of archaeological and literary evidence will be drawn together. Specific focus rests on upbringing and education, relationship to the emperor(s), construction projects, coinage, and public perception. Naturally, those texts and artifacts which directly mention the practice of *patrocinium* or benefaction will be highlighted. It would be impossible to give a detailed description of each facet, so this section admittedly rests on and refers to the more thorough works of others.

3.1 Herod I

Herod I is a pivotal figure in a study of patronage and benefaction in first-century Palestine. His rule (40 B.C.–4 B.C.) provided opportunity for him to leave an architectural legacy which draws much attention for what it says of his relationship to Hellenistic and Roman culture. Numismatic evidence shows signs of respect toward Jews, but hints at his linkage to Roman authority. Epigraphic remains directly describe Herod as a benefactor both in Palestine and elsewhere. Josephus' view of Herod has its polarities since he both applauds him for magnanimity and scorns him for tyranny (*War* 1.400, 429–430; *Ant.* 14.377–778; *War* 2.84–86; *Ant.* 17.191). Scholars espouse various readings of Herod from outright pagan to would-be pious Jew. The wealth of material which he left behind, in both archaeological and literary records, makes assessment difficult. Nevertheless, in each of the categories investigated below Herod expresses himself in Hellenistic terms and/or specifically as a benefactor. His knowledge and exercise of *patrocinium* is overshadowed by his practice of benefaction. No extant sources attribute the title "patron" to Herod I.[1] At the same time a recent trend in studies on Herod views him as attempting, if not successfully, to please Jews both in Palestine and abroad. The following investigation examines his education, relationship to the emperor and Rome, public perception, construction projects, coins, and benefactions.

3.1.1 Education

Not much can be known with certainty of Herod's early years, but it seems that he was reared and educated in and around Palestine and Idumea. During Roman power struggles around 53 B.C. Herod was taken to the Nabataean king Malichus I for safety with his family (*Ant.* 14.122; *War* 1.181–182).[2] Herod did not receive a Roman education in his youth. Braund shows that being "educated" by Rome (in Rome) primarily referred to the establishment or development of strategic relationships with Romans and language skills (Latin and Greek).[3] Kings and elites would send their sons to Rome in order for them to make contact with the emperor. This relationship had earned the father his governing role and would ensure (or at least work toward) his son's succession. Herod I apparently did not have this privilege though he certainly sent his sons in this direction. He did not have the formal opportunity to develop friendships in Rome as other political hopefuls had, but he became acquainted with several prominent figures first through his father and then during his own tenure in power. He did eventually make it to Rome and learned Roman ways, but his primary imprint was made by the eastern rulers of Idumea, Nabatea, and Palestine.[4]

3.1.2 Relationship to the Emperor and Rome

Herod's jockeying for position with Roman emperors and other notables is well-known. Josephus' account of Herod's potential blunder in choosing between Antony and Augustus is instructive about Herod's adoption of benefaction and friendship ideology. He originally sided with Antony (*Ant.*

---

[1] One of Herod's political colleagues, M. Agrippa, had earned the title (*CIG* 3609). Herod intervened on behalf of the Ilienses when Agrippa imposed a large fine on them (Nicolaus of Damascus, *FGrHist* 90 F 134). Agrippa likely became the patron of this city at this point. Eilers, *Roman Patrons*, 223–224.

[2] Netzer, *Great Builder*, 4–5. He was approximately twenty years old at this time having been born ca. 73 B.C.

[3] Braund, *Friendly King*, 9–21.

[4] Kasher and Witztum offer a psychology of this upbringing which aligns with what will be concluded below. Aryeh Kasher and Eliezer Witztum, *King Herod: A Persecuted Persecutor; A Case Study in Psychohistory and Psychobiography* (Berlin: Walter De Gruyter, 2007), 18–19.

15.109), but upon his loss at Actium concocted a defense of this position in a plea for honor from the new emperor Octavian (*Ant.* 15.161; 15.189–193). Josephus describes Herod's posture as one of friendship toward Antony (φιλίας; *Ant.* 15.162, 189). Herod believed he would be crowned king of Judea after Antony's victory (*War* 1.226; *Ant.* 14.280), but he instead received the territory from Augustus (*War* 2.215). In the plea Herod defends his relationship to Antony as an expression of the quality of allegiance he shows to his benefactors (*Ant.* 15.193).

νῦν οὖν εἰ μὲν τῇ πρὸς Ἀντώνιον ὀργῇ κρίνεις καὶ τὴν ἐμὴν προθυμίαν οὐκ ἂν εἴη μοι τῶν πεπραγμένων ἄρνησις οὐδ' ἀπαξιώσω τὴν ἐμαυτοῦ πρὸς ἐκεῖνον εὔνοιαν ἐκ τοῦ φανεροῦ λέγειν εἰ δὲ τὸ πρόσωπον ἀνελὼν τίς εἰμι πρὸς τοὺς εὐεργέτας καὶ ποῖος φίλος ἐξετάζοις ἐνέσται σοι πείρᾳ τῶν ἤδη γεγενημένων ἡμᾶς εἰδέναι τοῦ γὰρ ὀνόματος ὑπαλλαγέντος οὐδὲν ἔλαττον αὐτὸ τὸ τῆς φιλίας βέβαιον ἐν ἡμῖν εὐδοκιμεῖν δυνήσεται.

"If now in your anger at Antony you also condemn my zeal (in his cause), I will not deny that I have acted in this way nor will I be ashamed to speak openly of my loyalty to him. But if you disregard the outward appearance and examine how I behave toward my benefactors and what sort of friend I am, you can find out about me from what you learn concerning my past actions. For with merely a change in name the very ideal of firm friendship, as exemplified in me, will no less fully win approval."

He has been a most loyal friend to his benefactor Antony, and now if Augustus will accept the request, he promises to have the same strength of friendship with him (τὸ τῆς φιλίας βέβαιον). Augustus respects this approach, restores Herod's crown, and admonishes him to keep his promise to be the same sort of friend with him as he had been with Antony (15.194–195). Right away Herod confirmed his promise by expending his energy on benefactions toward Caesar and his friends (15.196). Herod's knowledge of Hellenistic and Roman social norms saved him his position and increased his reputation. It is noteworthy that he adopts the vocabulary of benefaction and friendship and to a lesser extent (loyalty), *patrocinium*.[5]

Herod also expressed his relationship to the emperors and Rome by naming structures and cities in their honor. Cities named for the Caesars advertised well (cf. Suetonius *Aug* 60). Warwick Ball lists the monuments and cities Herod built and named after Roman superiors and family: "the citadel of Antonia in Jerusalem he named after Marc Antony, his palace named Agrippaeum after Agrippa, a tower at Caesarea named Drusium after Augustus' stepson Drussus, the towns of Antipatris named after his father and Phaeselis named after his brother. His greatest dedications, however, were named in honour of Octavian (Caesar): another palace in

---

[5] Braund remarks that the sources tend to use friendship language rather than client-language in discussions of "client kings." Thus, Josephus' use of this terminology is not unique but instead typical (*Friendly King*, 5–7).

Jerusalem called Caesareum, and two entirely new cities, one in Samaria called Sebaste (Greek for Augustus) and a complete new port for Palestine named Caesarea."⁶ All of the kings who attributed new names in honor of kings were from the "Greek east." Braund briefly explains how this practice is particularly Hellenistic. Hellenistic kings expressed allegiance to Roman rulers through Hellenistic modes of expression starting as early as Augustus or perhaps Antony.⁷

One could also show one's relationship to Rome through adoption of honorary nomenclature for oneself or by naming children in honor of a notable Roman. In a few inscriptions described below Herod identifies himself, or is so identified by his beneficiaries, as a friend of Rome or Caesar. Titulature such as φιλορώμαιος, φιλοβασιλεῖς, φιλοκαῖσαρ, φιλοσεβαστὸς, or similar variations is a particularly Hellenistic way to declare allegiance.⁸ Daniel Schwartz argues that Agrippa's three names were the result of his grandfather's, Herod, relationship with emperors and Roman notables: Marcus (for Marcus Antonius – "responsible for his enthronement"), Julius (Julius Caesar, who benefited Herod's father with citizenship and τῆς τε ἄλλης τιμῆς καὶ φιλοφρονήσεως, *War* 1.194; *Ant.* 14.137), and Agrippa (M. Vipsanius Agrippa, "Augustus' son-in-law and right-hand man and Herod's friend").⁹ Herod apparently preferred the vocabulary of friendship in describing his relationship to Rome and outsiders looking in followed suit. Herod, Josephus, and outsiders used both benefactor and friendship language to describe Herod's relationship with Rome and the emperor.

3.1.3 Public Perception

It is somewhat precarious to describe "public perception" with reference only to Josephus, but he does offer relatively nuanced descriptions of prominent figures. Jensen's work on Herod Antipas has recently shed new light on Josephus' purpose in his narratives. He critiques his main characters according to their ability to navigate between Jewish and Roman sensitivities and thereby maintain the peace. His accounts of Herod I are interspersed with both positive and negative assessments. Josephus critiques Herod I on three fronts: (1) "First, in his relations to his Hasmonean family in-laws." (2) For exhibiting an over-eager friendship with Rome (φιλορώμαιος). (3) For ruling as a tyrant.¹⁰ In general, *Antiquities* paints a

---

⁶ Ball, *Rome*, 51. For a more complete list of projects see Richardson, *Herod*, 177–191, 197–202, 272–273; Braund, *Friendly King*, 107–109.
⁷ Braund, *Friendly King*, 109.
⁸ Braund, *Friendly King*, 105–106.
⁹ Schwartz, *Agrippa I*, 40.
¹⁰ Jensen, *Antipas*, 70. See e.g., Josephus's editorial remarks in *Ant.* 14.274; 15.266–267, 328; 16.150–159; 17.180–181, 191–192; 18.127–129.

darker picture of Herod I than the *War* does, but there are some positive portrayals of him even in that longer work (*Ant.* 15.303–316, 380–425; *War* 1.401–402).

The critique which Josephus levels against Herod comes in part because he was motivated by Hellenistic passion for glory and expected Hellenistic-type reciprocation for his benefits. Josephus criticizes Herod for building out of a love of honor (φιλοτιμία) and a zeal to please the emperor and the Romans with constructions that the Jews would not tolerate (*Ant.* 15.328–330). Herod appealed to the people that he had been commanded by Caesar and desired to honor and please him (τιμῆς; χαριζόμενος). In a different passage, Josephus suggests two sides to Herod's nature (*Ant.* 16.150–59). Josephus describes him in both glowing and derogatory terms. No one can deny that he is supremely beneficent (εὐεργετικωτάτῃ) since Herod constantly lavished benefactions (τὰς εὐεργεσίας) on others (16.150). But he is simultaneously tyrannical and even sub-human when punishing and ill-treating his enemies and family (16.151). One main problem is simply that all his benefits derive from his love of honor which the Jewish tradition rejects as a proper motivation (φιλότιμος; 16.153, 158). His threats and judgments grew out of his ambition to procure all honor for himself (ἐκ τοῦ μόνος ἐθέλειν τετιμῆσθαι; 16.156). The Jewish nation could not take part in such honoring of men since they prefer righteousness to glory and cannot flatter a king through statues, temples, or any other thing (*Ant.* 16.158–159).

τό γε μὴν Ἰουδαίων ἔθνος ἠλλοτρίωται νόμῳ πρὸς πάντα τὰ τοιαῦτα καὶ συνείθισται τὸ δίκαιον ἀντὶ τοῦ πρὸς δόξαν ἠγαπηκέναι διόπερ οὐκ ἦν αὐτῷ κεχαρισμένον ὅτι μὴ δυνατὸν εἰκόσιν ἢ ναοῖς ἢ τοιούτοις ἐπιτηδεύμασιν κολακεύειν τοῦ βασιλέως τὸ φιλότιμον αἰτία μὲν αὕτη μοι δοκεῖ τῆς Ἡρώδου περὶ μὲν τοὺς οἰκείους καὶ συμ̱ βούλους ἁμαρτίας περὶ δὲ τοὺς ἔξω καὶ μὴ προσήκοντας εὐεργεσίας

"But, as it happens, the Jewish nation is by law opposed to all such things and is accustomed to admire righteousness rather than glory. It was therefore not in his good graces, because it found it impossible to flatter the king's ambition with statues or temples or such tokens. And this seems to me to have been the reason for Herod's bad treatment of his own people and his counselors, and of his beneficence toward foreigners and those who were unattached to him." (R. Marcus)

Herod's efforts did not afford him the expected response, so he chose to withhold his benefits (οὐκ ἦν αὐτω κεχαρισμένον). He was not reciprocated properly, so he would not continue in generosity. From Josephus' vantage point Herod was truly a benefactor, but his Hellenistic motivations were deplorable in Jewish eyes. His generosity did not overcome his compromise of the Jewish religion. Since the Jews did not reciprocate in Hellenistically proper ways (through statues, temples, tokens), Herod refused to benefit them more.[11]

3.1.4 Construction Projects

Herod's reputation as a builder garners the most attention among his examiners, and they give insight into his various influences, motivations, and overall political strategies.[12] In different ways they tell of a man deeply indebted to Hellenistic Judaism who desired to be seen as a first class example of a Hellenistic king while promoting his Roman connections. Different motivations probably coalesced in Herod's mind as he built what would be the most lasting tribute to his reign. Some propose that he built purely for megalomaniacal reasons. Others think he tried to mask his tyranny with generosity. A few modern observers suggest that he had the international reputation of Judaism in mind. Jewish contemporaries of Herod had mixed feelings about his projects, and this continued into the next few centuries of Jewish thought. The following paragraphs describe the style/form of his projects and his plausible motivations.

The strongest cultural influences on Herod in general (Hasmonean, Hellenistic, Roman) expressed themselves in proportional degree in his construction projects. Herod was deeply indebted to Hasmonean ingenuity since he had been reared in a culture they had created. Part of this indebtedness shows up in Herod's adherence to Jewish religious sensitivities. Several observers note that in Jewish areas Herod refrained from offenses (the golden eagle being the major exception), but he typically would not have the same caution in non-Jewish areas.[13] Josephus mentions no other detail which aroused hostility among Jews in Herod's projects (*War* 1.648–55; *Ant.* 17.146–63).[14] As was mentioned above, Herod even kept to these principles within some of his private dwellings, a fact which suggests he may have been more genuinely concerned with Jewish piety than is sometimes proposed. His overall style reflects primarily Hellenistic influences. He followed Hellenistic influences in beauty (*Ant.* 15.298), and desired in the process to leave a monument to his magnificence and beneficence (τὸ φιλότιμον; μνημεῖα φιλανθρωπίας; *Ant.* 15.296, 298). In the tradition of the Hellenistic kings, he publicly displayed opulence and grandeur with processions, symposia, "conspicuous consumption," exotic animals, and expensive materials.[15] This practice probably was augmented by his Orien-

---

[11] Schwartz, "Euergetism in Josephus."
[12] For a detailed list of Herod's construction projects in Palestine and elsewhere see Richardson, *Herod*, 197–202.
[13] Sanders, "Jesus' Galilee," 18.
[14] Richardson, *Building Jewish*, 228.
[15] Lichtenberger, "Theater," 287–88.

tal influences.[16] His indebtedness to Roman architecture is primarily in regard to technology.[17] Some components reflect Roman tastes (bathhouses, formal gardens), but cannot always be restricted to this culture since Hellenism also enjoyed these items.[18] Herod pointed toward his Roman connections by naming buildings after them and founding games in their honor. He stands out as well as a promoter of the imperial cult. Since the imperial cult spread less strongly into the Greek East, Herod's erection of temples to the emperor makes him unique (Sebaste, Caesarea, Panias).[19] Herod may be credited with introducing Romanization into the area, but this only surfaced in a few decorations and forms, some renaming, and an occasional temple.[20] Beyond this "Herod actually continued the process of Hellenization of Judaea."[21] Herod had been influenced to a greater degree by Hasmonean/Jewish and Hellenistic (and Oriental) culture and this corresponds with the style of his building projects.

Opinions about Herod's motivation for building vary and have ramifications for the understanding of benefaction. An earlier view held that Herod offended Jewish sensibilities by muffling "traditional autonomous institutions" (e.g., Pharisees), relegating Torah, and strengthening the "foreign element" in the kingdom.[22] He attempted to counterbalance the hostility aroused among Jews who saw through his program with building projects (esp. rebuilding the temple) and certain sensitivities (e.g., aniconic buildings and coins), but these thinly veiled attempts to assuage failed to attain their purpose.[23] Thus, Herod's benefactions (buildings, etc.) were an attempt to cover up his tyranny. Recent appraisals of Herod tend to be slightly more nuanced. Richardson offers a "subtler view of Herod" in his assessment of Herodian architecture. He sees Herod espousing a "complex form of piety" which included but went beyond "acceptable Judaism" and "a concern for torah that worked within its limitations."[24] One particularly strong argument in Richardson's favor is his observation that Herod refrained from offending Jewish law within his private dwellings. These were intended to be the "cutting edge" of his projects and yet he installed

---

[16] Richardson, *Building Jewish*, 226–227; Netzer, *Great Builder*, 243.
[17] Netzer, *Great Builder*, 288–292; Richardson, *Building Jewish*, 226–227.
[18] Netzer, *Great Builder*, 292.
[19] Richardson, *Building Jewish*, 5–6.
[20] Netzer, *Great Builder*, 243–269.
[21] Netzer, *Great Builder*, 292.
[22] Shimon Applebaum in *Encyclopedia Judaica*, 8:382.
[23] Peter Richardson, "Law and Piety in Herod's Architecture," *Building Jewish*, 225–239, here 226–227, 225.
[24] Richardson, *Building Jewish*, 225. Richardson cites Herod's sensitivity toward Jews as a component of most recent assessments of his religion (esp. lack of images, inclusion of *miqvaoth*), *Building Jewish*, 8.

miqvaoth and neglected images.[25] Others emphasize the difference between his projects in Palestine and those outside it, noting that he basically attempted to keep the peace with Jews by observing their religious rules, but outside of Palestine freely promoted other cults (e.g., Athens).[26] A few inscriptions on temple remains show that Herod was viewed as a benefactor of Greco-Roman cults (see below, 3.1.6). Richardson counters that Herod's projects outside of Palestine were intended to extend the reputation of Judaism in the Mediterranean world.[27] Herod did not give gifts that only promoted Judaism (this would arouse jealousy) but he also tempered the pro-Greco-Roman gifts so as not to arouse Jewish anger. This approach would improve the Jewish reputation. Along similar lines, S. Rocca argues that Herod attempted to fulfill Jewish hopes of another Solomon, a Jewish king who functioned as a benefactor to foreign cities.[28]

Opinions about his projects also differed in Herod's day and in subsequent centuries. Jewish observers had different impressions of Herod. Josephus describes Herod's benefactions as expression of piety (*War* 1.400; *Ant.* 14.377–78), but later he blasts him as a tyrant (*War* 2.84–86; *Ant.* 17.191).[29] In his account of Herod's passing authority to his sons, Josephus emphasizes Herod's blending of piety and friendship with Rome (*War* 1.457–462). Josephus mentions several of the civic benefits conferred in the Diaspora which show Herod's concern for Jews outside of Palestine as well (*Ant.* 16.146–149). Josephus praises Herod's benefactions to other cities which were in part an attempt to restore crumbling ancient Greece (*War* 1.422–28). Not only building projects and the restoration of games, Herod also provided tax-relief and distributed food to famished regions. Each of these acts of benevolence showed his generosity. He heralds Herod's magnanimity in these projects, but in the following narrative critiques Herod for being motivated by his Hellenistically-derived love of honor (see above; *Ant.* 16.150–159). The Rabbis had their own opinions. Strikingly, some applaud a few works as glorious, but not all were in agreement (*Gemara, Sukkah* 51b; cf. *b. Baba Bathra* 3b; *b. Ta'anith* 23a; *Ant.* 15.245, 387; *b. Baba Bathra* 3b). *B. Baba Bathra* 3b offers a long negative comment on Herod. *B. Buta*, a contemporary of Herod's, criticizes him at length, but praises the temple and its role.[30] If Herod was motivated by a desire to promote international Judaism then, to some extent, it

---

[25] Richardson, *Building Jewish*, 227–228.

[26] Sanders, "Jesus' Galilee."

[27] Richardson, *Building Jewish*, 174.

[28] Samuel Rocca, "Josephus and the Psalms of Solomon on Herod's Messianic Aspirations: An Interpretation," in Rodgers, *Making History*, 313–333.

[29] Richardson, *Herod*, 191–192.

[30] This analysis is taken from Richardson, *Herod*, 248–249. Another strong critique of Herod can be found in *Test Mos* 6.1–9.

seems that he failed in the eyes of his main audience. Not all Jews looked down on Herod; it appears that one Jewish group in Rome dedicated a synagogue to Herod.[31]

Nevertheless the main problem brought up by Josephus in regard to Herod's projects is his love of honor. Josephus clarifies that this motivation is offensive to Jews because it gives to man what properly belongs to God. It is thus a religious offense. Josephus appears to have few qualms with Herod's generosity. He should be praised for his benefactions. Josephus focuses on the motivation as problematic. The style and motivation of Herod's projects were probably multi-faceted, but when Herod followed his Hellenistic architectural influences into the arena of motivations he received rebuke from his Jewish observers.

3.1.5 Coins

Though each ruler in the Herodian family minted coins, differences between them must be maintained. Herod I printed only one dated coin which very plausibly connects him in gratitude to the Romans who had recently set him up as king (issued ca. 37 B.C.).[32] Its helmet and palm branches have been variously interpreted, but interpretations tend to suggest his open appeal to Rome.[33] In subsequent, undated issues from Jerusalem Herod incorporated Hasmonean and Roman symbols without explicitly condoning pagan practice. Various interpretations have been put forth for the rest of Herod's coins, but it is instructive that he did not mint names or images of emperors, and neither did he put indisputably pagan symbols on them.[34] Richardson's survey of Herod's coins leads him to conclude that Herod chose conservative symbols and titles which would not raise aggression. He used Jewish symbols and moderately Roman ones at times which could be interpreted in multiple ways by different audiences (wreath, diadem, vine, anchor, cornucopia, galley, and eagle).[35] Meshorer offers a different assessment. He focuses on the Roman symbols (winged caduceus no. 39; pomegranate between the horns of the double cornucopia no. 53; eagle no. 54) which cannot be explained compellingly in the context of

---

[31] *CIJ* 173 (Rome). Richardson's translation reads: "... synagogue/... of the Herodians/... a blessing to all." Found in Richardson, *Herod*, 209.

[32] For recent comments on Herod's coins see Jensen, *Antipas*, 194–197; Richardson, *Herod*, 211–215; Ya'akov Meshorer, *Jewish Coins of the Second Temple Period* (trans. I. H. Levine; Tel-Aviv: Am Hassefer, 1967), 64–68, 127–130.

[33] Meshorer, *Treasury*, 63 in Jensen, *Antipas*, 195.

[34] Jensen, *Antipas*, 197. Adam Kolman Marshak, "The Dated Coins of Herod the Great: Towards a New Chronology," *JSJ* 37/2 (2006): 212–240.

[35] Richardson, *Herod*, 211–215.

Jewish symbolism.[36] Herod employed some symbols which tell of his Roman aspirations, but he did avoid the most offensive practice. The coins of Herod I though sometimes provocative, ambiguous or quasi-offensive, typically refrained from images or inscriptions of emperors. He appears to have desired to please both his Jewish and Roman audiences simultaneously.[37] Herod appears to have refrained from boasting of his benefactions on coinage by following the Roman love of minting coins with pictures of buildings. He pursued a politically savvy route which minimized offense.

3.1.6 Benefactions

Herod's reputation for being a benefactor abounds in both Josephus and benefaction inscriptions. This reputation was the norm for Hellenistic kings. Braund describes the manner in which the kings related when encountering inter-state relations. "Beneficence, or euergetism, had been at the very heart of Hellenistic kingship. Nor was it absent in the West. As Veyne has recently remarked, 'donner est le geste royal par excellence.'"[38] Lists of Herod's benefactions both within Palestine and outside his realm tend to become rather lengthy. Several such lists can be found in Josephus (*War* 1.422–428; *Ant.* 16.146–149, 18–19, 23–26). Herod explicitly operated as a benefactor among benefactors. He both ascribed the title to others and was so described by his contemporaries. Josephus gives several examples of this. Herod is concerned for the welfare of his benefactor in the delegation of Phraates (*Ant.* 15.18–20). Herod saw Antony as a benefactor and expended every effort for his welfare (*Ant.* 15.190). Alexandra proclaims Herod the benefactor of all (τὸν πάντων αὐτῶν εὐεργέτην) (*Ant.* 15.232–233). Herod calls himself a benefactor and brother to Pheroras who despises him with bad accusations (*Ant.*16.209–212). Herod responds by saying he desires to avenge himself through increased benefits (μειζόνως εὐεργετῶν). Herod asks Caesar to consider how he treats benefactors in general, not just Antony (*Ant.* 15.193). Herod is praised for benefits (τὰς εὐεργεσίας) toward all mankind (πρὸς ἅπαντας ἀνθρώπους) and an attitude of beneficence (εὐεργετικωτάτη) (*Ant.* 16.150). Herod's reputation for benefaction was so pronounced that Josephus despairs of being able to describe all the honorifics which Herod had dedicated both to his friends (τῶν αὐτῶν ὠνόμασεν φίλων) and to Caesar (*War* 1.407). Herod also functioned as a benefactor in the distribution of territories in his will. Bypassing Antipas, Herod benefited (χαριζόμενος) Archelaos with the kingdom

---

[36] Meshorer, *Jewish Coins*, 65–66.
[37] Jensen, *Antipas*, 194–197.
[38] Braund, *Friendly King*, 75–76; Veyne, *Le pain*, 228.

(*Ant.* 17.188). The use of "benefactor" as a title in reference to Herod conforms to its presence in inscriptions found in Palestine and elsewhere.

Inscriptional evidence attests to Herod's role as a benefactor both in its use of the title and in attribution of credit to him for benefits. Recall the stone weight, briefly mentioned above (section 2.2.4), that was found in Jerusalem. Its inscription is the only known Judean use of the title benefactor for Herod.[39] A lead weight found in Ashdod has remarkable parallels which does cast some doubt on the reading of "benefactor" in the Jerusalem inscription. This other lead weight reads:

Βασιλε[ύ]ο
ντ[ο]ς Ἡρώ
δου Εὐσε
βοῦς καὶ φ
ιλοκαίσ(αρος)
"In the time of King/Herod/pious(eusebias)/and friend/of Caesar."[40]

Nevertheless, Richardson adopts benefactor as the original reading from the stone weight. Outside of Palestine Herod, and others, freely appended his name to benefits given or received. In Athens an inscription was found at the base of what was apparently a statue. The inscription reads: "The people to King Herod/friend of Romans/because of his good works and good will toward the city."[41] Josephus records that Athens had been filled with Herod's benefits (*War* 1.425–426), and the inscriptional evidence confirms this. Another inscription (*OGIS* 415) reads as follows:

[Βα]σιλεῖ Ἡρώδει κυρίῳ
Ὀβαίσατος Σαόδου
ἔθηκα τὸν ἀνδριάντα ταῖς ἐμαῖς δαπάναι[ς]
"To King Herod, master,/
Obiasath, son of Saodos/
placed the statue at his own expense."

This inscription apparently stood in front of a life-size statue of Herod at "the Temple of Ba'al Shamim by a member of a family associated with Si'a," but the statue was not recovered.[42] Inscriptions thanking Herod for

---

[39] Y. Meshorer, "A Stone Weight from the Reign of Herod," *IEJ* 20 (1970): 97–98.

[40] The Jerusalem weight had only the first two letters of "benefactor" on it, and these are the same first two letters as the full reading of "pious" in the Ashdod weight. Kushnir-Stein therefore reconstructs the Jerusalem weight with Εὐσεβοῦς rather than Εὐ 'εργέτης. Richardson, *Herod*, 204, #2b. Alla Kushnir-Stein, "An Inscribed Lead Weight from Ashdod: A Reconsideration," *ZPE* 105 (1995): 81–84, 83–84; *Editio Princeps* M. Dothan, ed., *Ashdod I-II: The Second and Third Seasons of Excavations* (Atiqot, Eng. Ser. IX-X; Jerusalem, 1971), 68, 72, pl. XXV: 7, fig. 30:6.

[41] *OGIS* 414; cf. Richardson, *Herod*, 207, no. 6; Braund, *Friendly King*, 428.

[42] *Editio Princeps* W. H. Waddington, ap. Lebas Inscr. III 2364; *Ant.* 16.285; Richardson, *Herod*, 207.

benefactions can be found in Masada, Jerusalem, Ashdod, Si'a, Rome, Athens, Cos, and Delos.[43] Herod had built a reputation for benefaction in many places in the empire, and the inscriptional remains attest to this.

Herod I appears to have been largely a product of his upbringing. Raised among eastern kings and Hasmonean rulers, Herod operated in ways akin to his predecessors. He constructed in Hellenistic styles, made allowance for Jewish religious observance, and promoted his reputation with Roman rulers through Hellenistic means. As other Hellenistic kings, Herod sought to be known as a benefactor. Many in his own day paid him this honor. Offense among Jews sprung up because of his motivations in this quest. His desire to steal for himself honor which rightfully belongs to God caused Josephus to castigate him. But Herod's reputation did not die when he passed. The most prominent tributes to his personality persisted through the time of Jesus and the apostles. These structures, for example the temple and Caesarea's harbor, provided a way for his reputation to continue beyond the grave. Inscriptions identifying him as a benefactor also persisted. Herod far exceeds his contemporaries in regard to public architecture and it is quite likely that he was still a topic of conversation within Palestine in the ministry years of Jesus and the apostles. His reputation as a benefactor could easily have been one such point of debate since on the one hand generosity was a laudable attitude, but on the other hand Herod's motivations undermined a central component of Jewish religion, namely that all honor belongs to God. Visits to any of the cities Herod benefited most (Jerusalem, Caesarea, Samaria) would be the most likely cause of his name, and the ideology of benefaction, being brought up. *Patrocinium* was not as important in Herod's life. Hints here and there of Romanization and of patronage may be found, but they are overshadowed by the pervasive presence of benefaction.

3.2 Herod Antipas

Compared to his father, Antipas' life was fairly calm and uneventful. He had ambitions it seems to emulate his father, but did not have the means or drive to follow through. His tenure (4 B.C. - A.D. 39) was peaceful in part because of this lack of initiative. He did spark an occasional controversy (construction of Tiberias, murder of John the Baptist, marriage to Herodias, etc.). He was known within his own realm and outside of it as a benefactor, though of a significantly less prominent form than his father. With more intentional interactions with Rome in his early years it is more

---

[43] Richardson, *Herod*, 210.

likely that he learned of *patrocinium*, but no explicit evidence affirms this. The same categories employed to describe his father (education, relationship to the emperors and Rome, public perception, construction projects, coins, and benefactions) will be taken up again to describe Antipas.

3.2.1 Education

Only a passing reference to Antipas' upbringing in Josephus informs us of his education in Rome. In detailing some of Herod's wives and children, Josephus mentions that Antipas and Archelaos were the sons of a woman of the Samarian nation (τοῦ Σαμαρέων ἔθνους). These two were reared (τροφὰς εἶχον) in Rome by a private man (*Ant.* 17.20). The phrase literally means "had a living," but it is interpreted as an education because of examples of other sons of Herod receiving education in Rome and because of the nature of education at that time.[44] Josephus provides more detail with three of Antipas' brothers who were also sent to Rome in their youth for education (Alexander, Aristobulus, Antipater; *Ant.* 15.342–343; 16.78–86). Education in Rome became a quasi-standard for Herod's sons. The purpose of the education was to develop strategic friendships. The sender hoped that the child would develop friendships and be promoted later in life through them. Maintenance of these friendships was the central part of the social promotion strategy.[45] Josephus' text does not say when Antipas came to Rome, but Batey suggests that it was as a teenager (ca. 10 B.C.– A.D. 2).[46] No matter when Antipas arrived in Rome he would have had opportunity to develop friendships and learn Roman ways. Nevertheless, it appears that his love for Rome was not as fervent as others. It will be shown in the next section that he apparently only pursued the bare minimum in the maintenance of these strategic friendships.

3.2.2 Relationship to the Emperors and Rome

Antipas ruled under three emperors, Augustus, Tiberius, and Gaius Caligula, with varying degrees of success. Antipas acquired a solid connection with Rome, even though it started poorly. Antipas was raised in Rome during the reign of Augustus, but Augustus preferred Archelaos over Antipas to take over their father's territory, even though Antipas had been the originally assigned recipient (*Ant.* 17.20, 188) and had the support of some Herodians and Jews (*Ant.* 17.224–227; Nikolaos, *FGrH* 90 frag. 136 §9). Antipas received a tetrarchy with which he was not completely content.

---

[44] Jensen, *Antipas*, 222.
[45] Braund, *Friendly King*, 9–21.
[46] Richard A. Batey, "Did Antipas Build the Sepphoris Theater?" in Charlesworth, *Jesus and Archaeology*, 111–119, 119.

The only political actions recorded under Augustus' reign were the construction of a wall in Sepphoris, making it the "ornament of all Galilee", and naming it *Autocratoris* (Greek for *Imperator*), and the construction of a wall around Betharanphtha and renaming it for Augustus' wife Julia (*Ant.* 18.27). Though on a smaller scale compared to his father's actions, these were Hellenistic ways of honoring superiors. Within Augustus' reign Antipas made at least a couple of moves as a Hellenistic benefactor. Under Tiberius, Antipas flourished. The construction of his most famous city, Tiberias, grew out of the important friendship (φιλίας) the two had developed (*Ant.* 18.36). Antipas desired to honor his friend with the new city even though he had to overcome some obstacles created by Jewish religion. A large graveyard marred the location of the new city and repulsed Jews who were brought in to inhabit the area. Antipas made it worth their while by building them nice homes and offering them land. Galileans and other Jews, including a number of poor people, were relocated to the area. Josephus describes Antipas as a benefactor (εὐηργέτησεν) to these people because of his generosity in giving away homes and granting freedom to those who were not freemen (*Ant.* 18.37–38). Antipas followed the course of Hellenistic kings by naming the new city after Tiberius. He had a great relationship with Tiberius (garnering favor over against contenders for power like Agrippa I), but met demise when Gaius (and Agrippa) took office (*War* 2.181–183; *Ant.* 18.240–255).[47] Antipas' wife urged him to approach Gaius in request to become king (like her brother Agrippa). Antipas was actually content (by this time) with his position and preferred a quiet life. So, he resisted the request. When he eventually gave in, Gaius and Agrippa were not pleased. Antipas was banished to Gaul along with his wife (*Ant.* 18.242–245).

In the course of these three emperors Antipas had varying qualities of relationship. He was overlooked by Augustus for a time but given a tetrarchy to rule. He earned the title "friend of Caesar" under Tiberius and honored his friend with the founding and naming of a city after him. Antipas lost this privileged status under Gaius under whom he was banished. It seems that he took little initiative in improving these friendships. In his own territory he did not construct temples or promote the imperial cult. He created only two fairly small cities in honor of the emperors. He certainly did not go to the same extent as his father in developing his Roman connection, but he did have the advantage of being reared in Rome and he did make some effort in the friendships.

---

[47] Jensen, *Antipas*, 90–94.

3.2.3 Public Perception

Antipas had a reputation for being too close to Rome, but some Jews regarded him as an ally. The most substantial literary evidence can be found in Josephus and the NT.[48] Josephus accuses Antipas for being too friendly with the Romans to the point that the Jewish stability was disturbed.[49] Three situations display the error of his ways, the building of Tiberias, the marriage to Herodias, and the killing of John the Baptist (*Ant.* 18.101–129). Interestingly, in Josephus' narrative of the murder of John, he refers to John as ἀγαθὸν ἄνδρα, a description which has been noted as a synonym of benefactor in many inscriptions and literary works (*Ant.* 18.117).[50] The NT picks up the last two offenses and adds its own third, responsibility in the death of Jesus (Mark 6:14–19; Matt 14:1–4; Luke 3:19; Acts 4:27). Of the NT authors Luke offers the fullest treatment of Antipas (Luke 3:1, 19–20; 8:3; 9:7–9; 13:31–33; 23:1–15; Acts 4:27).[51] The evangelists assume that the lower classes felt some impact from Antipas' reign. Jesus shows awareness of Antipas' ways with a saying that smacks of a political or economic critique (Luke 13:31–33). Though "fox" is an ambiguous metaphor it probably refers to cunning, destructiveness, and insignificance (compared to a lion).[52] The bending reed could refer to Antipas (Luke 7:24 Matt 11:17);[53] soft robes and royal palaces possibly contrast John the Baptist with Antipas and his royal palace cities (Sepphoris and Tiberias). Sepphoris (Zippori) means "little bird" in Hebrew and it is possible that Jesus contrasts himself with Antipas (fox) and Sepphoris (bird) (Luke 9:58).[54] Jesus appears to allude to the battle for power between Archelaos and Antipas in his parable of the minas (Luke 19:11–27).[55] Use of this story implies

---

[48] Jensen has a treatment of all the other literary sources on Antipas in *Antipas*, 101–109. These include: Nikolaos (*FGrH* 90, frag. 136 §§ 8–11); Tacitus (*Hist.* 5.9); Strabo (*Geogr.* 16.2.46), Dio Cassius (*LV.* 27.6), Justin (*Dial.* 103.4); Philo (*Legat.* 299–305).

[49] Jensen, *Antipas*, 99–100.

[50] Danker, *Benefactor*, 319; B. Winter, *Seek the Welfare of the City*, 34–35; *SIG* 174, 127; *GDI* 5464, 5698, 5366.

[51] For a more complete survey of Antipas in Luke-Acts see John A. Darr, *Herod the Fox: Audience Criticism and Lukan Characterization* (JSNT 163; Sheffield: Sheffield Academic Press, 1998).

[52] Jensen, *Antipas*, 116–117.

[53] Theissen, *Gospels in Context*, 26–41.

[54] Reed, *Archaeology*, 138.

[55] Brian Schultz, "Jesus as Archelaus in the Parable of the Pounds (Lk. 19:11–27)," *NovT* 49/2 (2007): 105–127; Plummer, *Luke*, 437–438; Nolland, *Luke*, 3.911; Fitzmyer, *Luke*, 2.1234–1235; Marshall, *Luke*, 703–704; N. T. Wright, *Jesus and the Victory of God* (Minneapolis: Fortress, 1996), 632–633. Schultz claims that the connection to Archelaos is almost unanimous, Schultz, "Archelaus," 109. Two commentators deny the connection, Bernhard Scott, *Hear Now the Parable: A Commentary on the Parables of Jesus* (Minneapolis: Fortress, 1989), 223; Bovon, *Luc*, 3.257–258. Denaux questions the connection,

not only his own knowledge but knowledge of this situation among his audience. It implies familiarity among the lower classes with Herodian political maneuvering.[56] The happenings in the Herodian family were not the special knowledge of the upper class, but were known and discussed by the lower classes. They perhaps reached these lower classes through the Jewish leadership that conversed with them or through the various helpers that tended to Herodian needs (e.g., Luke 8:3). In all these stories the evangelists relate that the lower classes were aware of Antipas' rule and several felt compelled to speak against it. Both Josephus and the NT attribute evil deeds to Antipas (e.g., marriage to Herodias, deaths of John the Baptist and Jesus, construction of Tiberias). They also describe him in certain events as ambivalent/inept (*Ant.* 18.101–105; Mark 6:20), offensive to Jewish scruples (*Ant.* 18.38; Luke 3:19), and in league with some Jewish leaders (*Ant.* 18.122; Mark 3:6; 8:15; 12:13; cf. Philo, *Legatio Ad Gaium* §261–329). Josephus explicitly remarks that Antipas cared too much about his Roman superiors, while Luke only hints at this.[57]

Though both sources attribute negative traits to Antipas, there is a brighter side. Despite the disparaging remarks on Antipas, Josephus does have some positive things to say. He mentions Antipas going to Jerusalem to make sacrifices at the temple (*Ant.* 18.122), he does not explicitly refer to him as a τύραννος (as he had for Herod I), he highlights the euergetism of Antipas in providing for the poor new settlers of Tiberias (*Ant.* 18.36–38), and he commends him for maintaining peace during the debacle with John the Baptist (*Ant.* 18.118). Luke also leaves room for some leniency in regard to Antipas. It is debated how active Antipas was in Jesus' trial and crucifixion, but it seems that he took a somewhat passive role.[58] Luke emphasizes the innocence of Pilate in his narrative and by pinning Antipas to Pilate (Luke 23:12) the impression arises that Antipas, too, should be thought quasi-innocent (Luke 23:4, 14–15, 32). Antipas shares responsibil-

---

A. Denaux, "The Parable of the King-Judge (Lk 19,12–28, and Its Relation to the Entry Story (Lk 19,29–44)," *ZNW* 93 (2002): 35–57, 53–54; idem, "The Parable of the Talents/Pounds (Q 19,12–27)—A Reconstruction of the Q Text," in *The Sayings Source Q and the Historical Jesus* (ed. A. Lindemann; BETL 157; Leuven: University Press, 2001), 430.

[56] Knowledge of the Herodian source and distribution of power (the Roman political machine) makes Jesus' words about his kingdom distribution more potent (Luke 22:24–30).

[57] By consistently preferring "Herod" rather than clarifying names (e.g., Antipas, Philip, Agrippa), Luke gives the impression that the family acted in one accord. He does differentiate between the tetrarch and king (Luke 3:1, 19; 9:7; Acts 13:1) and mentions Philip by name once, but more often than not members of the family are referred to simply as Herod. In this regard they appear to be condemned, as a group, of the deeds done under the single name. Schwartz, *Agrippa I*, 120 n. 50.

[58] Jensen, *Antipas*, 120–124.

ity, but Luke also shows Antipas' interest in Jesus (Luke 9:7–9; 23:8, 15).[59] Jesus does not give in to Antipas' curiosity, so the latter becomes an example of one of those who do not see or hear the message.[60] Nevertheless, it is not solely a negative portrayal.

Archaeological research leads to the conclusion that the time of Antipas was peaceful, mild, and relatively prosperous which supports the idea that Antipas' reign was somewhat uneventful. Under Antipas, Galilee developed into a "small, prosperous Jewish kingdom." This forty year period was marked by flourishing and almost "no domestic turmoil."[61] Freyne suggests that this prosperity added stress to daily life, created tension, and aroused hostility.[62] The picture of Galilean economics in Reed, Aviam, and Jensen tempers this description. It does not rule out aggression and hostility, but downplays its extent.[63] The literary and archaeological evidence combine in their description of Antipas' rule as another low time for Jewish inhabitants, though not nearly as bad as his father's era. Overall, it was rather uneventful.[64]

The public perceived that Antipas was too friendly with his Roman superiors and not faithful enough to the Jewish religion. They caught wind of his plea for power when Archelaos won Augustus' favor. Josephus records that Antipas participated in the Jerusalem festivals, but Josephus was not persuaded that this erased the errors of breaking Israel's covenant in regard to his marriage to Herodias, the murder of John the Baptist, and the construction of Tiberias on unclean ground. In addition to several critiques for his deception and luxurious lifestyle, the NT authors add the murder of Jesus to the list of wrong-doings. However, they do not place all the blame on Antipas for the crucifixion. Luke offers Antipas some leniency since he sided with Pilate in pronouncing Jesus innocent. In these stories it is possible that some of the ideology of benefaction and *patrocinium* filtered through.[65] Josephus may further his critique of Antipas by describing John the Baptist with a synonym to benefactor. It should be clarified, that the sources do not explicitly critique Antipas in relation to this ideology.

---

[59] Jensen, *Antipas*, 121; Hoehner, *Antipas*, 245; Darr, *Audience*, 211.

[60] Darr, *Audience*, 212.

[61] Mordechai Aviam, "First-century Jewish Galilee: An Archaeological Perspective," in Edwards, *Religion*, 7–27, 21.

[62] Sean Freyne, "Herodian Economics in Galilee: Searching for a Suitable Model," in *Galilee and Gospel*, 90–91

[63] Reed, *Archaeology*, 97; Aviam, "Jewish Galilee"; Jensen, "Josephus and Antipas," 290. Jensen finds in Freyne's analysis an overemphasis on sociological models. By beginning with this model Freyne stretches the evidence beyond its capacity.

[64] Jensen, "Josephus and Antipas," 309–310; idem, *Antipas*, 99–100.

[65] Those who investigated the debacle between Archelaos and Antipas before Augustus may have learned how positions of authority were given through *suffragium*

3.2.4 Construction Projects

Antipas did not match his father in construction projects. Only two cities in his region need be discussed in regard to building activity, Tiberias and Sepphoris. The difficulties involved in dating material remains in these two cities have created some controversy about the extent of Antipas' construction program. For example, in Tiberias some argue that Antipas deliberately built a stadium in Tiberias and possibly a theater ("not mentioned in the sources") to gain favor with the emperor.[66] Lämmer argues that Antipas instituted games devoid of the most offensive components of the imperial cult. It is possible that Antipas undertook these projects, but this conclusion is not yet justified based solely on the source material. The stadium discovered by Moshe Hartal may be Antipas' but as of yet it cannot be dated to his era (*War* 2.618; *Life* 92, 331). It may just as likely be from the mid-first-century.[67] The material remains do not permit a date more precise than simply first-century for the stadium in Tiberias.[68] A similar situation persists for the theater in Sepphoris.[69] Though Batey and Kee argue strenuously for an early date (early first-century), most others push just as hard for a later date (late first-early second century).[70] The final reports of several digs have only recently been published.[71] No consensus has yet been reached as to the date of this theater. Other than the theater, cardo, and an unexcavated building underneath the basilical building, no major buildings have a range of dates which overlaps with Antipas.[72] If one

---

[66] According to M. Lämmer in Jensen, *Antipas*, 145. Manfred Lämmer, "Griechische Wettkämpfe in Galiläa unter der Herrschaft des Herodes Antipas," *Kölner Beiträge zu Sportwissenschaft* 5 (1976): 37–67, 53. Lämmer is followed by Sandra Fortner, "Tiberias – Eine Stadt zu Ehren des Kaisers," in *Leben am See Gennesaret: Kulturgeschichtliche Entdeckungen in einer biblischen Region* (ed. Jürgen Zangenberg, et al; Sonderbände der Antiken Welt; Mainz: Verlag Philipp von Zabern, 2003), 86–92; Monika Bernett, "Roman Imperial Cult in the Galilee: Structures, Functions and Dynamics," in Rodgers, *Making History*. I could not locate Zangenberg in the Worldcat library database.

[67] Jensen, *Antipas*, 145–146, 148.

[68] Jensen, *Antipas*, 145. A marble floor has been proposed as the floor of Antipas' Tiberias palace ibid., 141–144, 146.

[69] The Sepphoris theater was first excavated in 1931 by L. Waterman. Leroy Waterman, et al., *Preliminary Report of the University of Michigan: Excavations at Sepphoris, Palestine in 1931* (Ann Arbor: University of Michigan Press, 1937).

[70] For history and complications in this project see Jensen, *Antipas*, 154–156. Batey published his theory most recently in Batey, "Early Christianity," in Charlesworth, *Jesus and Archaeology*.

[71] James F. Strange, Thomas R. W. Longstaff, and Dennis Groh, eds., *Excavations at Sepphoris* (Brill Reference Library of Judaism 22; Leiden: Brill, 2006).

[72] Jensen, *Antipas*, 161. Other major finds in Sepphoris, but outside of Antipas' time include: decumanus, three insulae, mansion with Dionysos mosaic, Nile festival building,

admits these three as the products of Antipas, the city still does not deserve to be considered of the same status as Caesarea, Jerusalem, or Tiberias, not to mention other major *poleis* of the empire.[73] Antipas did not litter his landscape with monumental constructions.

What stands out in this survey is the lack of honorary constructions. Even if all the monumental works attributed to Antipas by various interpreters truly derive from this Herod, they still do not amount to much in the way of honoring superiors. No temples and no dedicated games to honor the emperor are explicitly mentioned. Only two small cities commemorate rulers. In all, Antipas did very little to perpetuate and improve his relationship with Rome. He may have had the interests of his Jewish inhabitants in mind, but he was not perceived as pious by the aforementioned sources. He constructed very few projects intended to honor his Roman superiors. He did not support the imperial cult in Palestine (though he did elsewhere). This perhaps partially explains his fall from favor upon Tiberius' death.

3.2.5 Coins

Antipas differed in his approach to minting coins.[74] Philip and Agrippa I made some connection to the emperor, either by mentioning his name or depicting his image, in several of their coins, but Antipas refused this practice until his last minting (A.D. 38/39). He mimicked his father and Archelaos in his restraint. Normally, Antipas made Jewish-friendly coins. It was not until his last minting that Antipas attempted to honor the Roman emperor in a coin. Antipas minted four types of coins: (1) A small coin recently discovered by Hendin (the only one of its kind) appears to come from a very early stage in his career (before the founding of Tiberias).[75] It includes barley/wheat with TET PA_ _HΣ Δ on the obverse, and a "palm tree with seven branches, and the legend HP W" on the reverse. The images are typically Jewish and the words have been interpreted as "Tetrarch, Herod" (nominative).[76] (2) The first series of coins he minted was intended,

---

basilical building [final form], northern synagogue, and "huge cisterns just outside the city limits."

[73] Reed, *Archaeology*, 94–96. Two inscriptions likely originally connected to Greco-Roman cultic edifices outside of Palestine (Cos, Delos) show that Antipas participated in the Greco-Roman cult, at least through donation, outside his realm (see section 3.2.6). The latter was in commemoration for help in the temple of Apollo while the former does not indicate the reason for the inscription. Antipas has far fewer inscriptions commemorating his generosity outside his realm than his father.

[74] This section is deeply indebted to Jensen, *Antipas*, 203–214; Meshorer, *Jewish Coinage*, 72–75, 133–135.

[75] David Hendin, "A New Coin Type of Herod Antipas," *INJ* 15 (2003–2006): 56–61.

[76] Jensen, *Antipas*, 204.

perhaps, to recognize the founding of Tiberias (issued A.D. 19/20).[77] The reverse carries "the legend TIBEPIAC encircled by a wreath" while the obverse has the date, "Herod the Tetrarch" (genitive), and a bowing stalk (Reed? Palm branch? Laurel?). Theissen's well-known interpretation of the reed shaking in the wind comes from the image of the reed on this coin.[78] The reed was a popular symbol in Palestine and particularly Galilee. These stayed in circulation for at least nine years until Antipas delivered again. (3) Antipas may have been responding to aggressive minting by Pilate when he issued his third coin type (A.D. 28/29).[79] The reverse carries the city-name ΤΙΒΕΡΙΑΣ and the date, and the obverse has "of Herod the Tetrarch" (genitive) and a palm branch. This imagery (palm branch) is susceptible to the interpretation that Antipas wanted to be honored in Roman terms, but Jensen finds this weak and rejects the proposal that Antipas had Messianic aspirations (Horsley and Silberman).[80] Instead the coin follows the Jewish aniconic pattern and uses common imagery found in many Hasmonean coins. It may mark the maturation of Tiberias as a city. (4) His last minting witnesses some changes (A.D. 38/39). His own name is now in the nominative, but ΤΙΒΕΡΙΑΣ is replaced with ΓΑΙΩ ΚΑΙΣΑΡΙ ΓΕΡΜΑΝΙΚΩ in the dative. Use of the dative directly marks the emperor Gaius Caesar Germanicus as the object of honor.[81] Only Philip had so explicitly recognized the emperor. Antipas' restriction to the use of the name, without an image, put him in a middle ground between Philip (image and inscription) and previous Jewish rulers (neither image nor inscription). Jensen connects this minting with Josephus' story of the battle to be king between Antipas and Agrippa I (*Ant.* 18.240–255). Antipas attempted to flatter the emperor, but Agrippa's concurrent issue (see below, 3.4.5) carried not only the name but the image of the emperor and his three sisters.[82] Agrippa earned the emperor's favor; Antipas was exiled.

Jensen contrasts Antipas' coins with those of other rulers in Palestine from Herod I to Pilate. Antipas' coins adhered more closely to Jewish standards (at least until his last minting), whereas Pilate may have attempted to provoke the Jews with some of his coins. Richardson cites Antipas' aniconic coins as a form of protest against Roman power (since

---

[77] Ya'akov Meshorer, *Jewish Coins of the Second Temple Period* (Tel Aviv: Am Hassefer, 1967), 74; Meshorer, *Treasury*, 75–78.

[78] Theissen, *Gospels*, 26–41.

[79] Meshorer, *Treasury*, 79–82.

[80] Jensen, *Antipas*, 207–208. Richard A. Horsley and Neil Asher Silberman, *The Message and the Kingdom: How Jesus and Paul Ignited a Revolution and Transformed the Ancient World* (Minneapolis: Fortress Press, 1997), 22.

[81] Meshorer, *Treasury*, 91–94.

[82] Jensen, *Antipas*, 208–209.

others gladly put images on their coins), but this goes too far.[83] That the imagery adopted by Antipas has been interpreted as pro-Roman by some interpreters shows that it was ambiguous enough to offend neither Jews nor Romans. That the final issue explicitly honors the emperor shows that Antipas did not have animosity toward his superiors. He may not have shared the zeal of other rulers for Rome, but he did not protest against them. His father also shunned images, but he certainly did not do so for anti-Roman protest. It was simply a political move intended to keep his constituents and superiors happy. Jensen describes Antipas' coins as "modest, carefully adapted, and slightly insignificant" making it possible for them to enter "circulation fairly unnoticed, as just another edition of regular Jewish coinage with floral images."[84] For the purposes of this study, only the last issue enters the world of honorifics. The coin cannot be used in favor of benefaction or *patrocinium* per se, but it does show some relation to Roman superiors and a desire to honor them. The coin shows that later in life Antipas more freely functioned in the Greek and Roman world of social interaction.

3.2.6 Benefactions

Antipas did not make the same concerted effort to be known as an international benefactor as his father had made. He built few monumental buildings in his tetrarchy, and is only rarely attested outside his realm as a donator. He instituted no games in his area, and did not broadcast his relationship with Rome explicitly on his coins until later in life. Nevertheless, he did make a few attempts to bolster his reputation as a benefactor. Both Josephus and archaeological remains relate these attempts.

Josephus mentions a few benefits which Antipas gave to the people and a few scenarios in which he operated in reciprocal relations. In founding Tiberias on unclean ground Antipas ran up against an obstacle for his Jewish inhabitants. He resolved this issue by offering free homes and land for new residents. Josephus describes this action as one of benefaction (*Ant.* 18.37–38). In addition to free homes and land Antipas also granted the benefit of freedom to those who were "not quite free" (ἔστι δ' οὓς μηδὲ σαφῶς ἐλευθέρους). Antipas constructed the city because of his friendship (φιλίας) with the new emperor Tiberius. He did a similar deed by renaming Sepphoris and Betharamphtha for the emperor and his wife respectively (*Ant.* 18.27). Such projects were of central importance among those attempting to strengthen friendships and improve their political position. Favor with Tiberius won Antipas the honor of hosting a strategic meeting

---

[83] Richardson, *Building Jewish*, 19.
[84] Jensen, *Antipas*, 217.

with Artabanus and Vitellius (*Ant.* 18.101–105).⁸⁵ Tiberius, Josephus tells us, desired a political friendship with Artabanus (Τιβέριος ἠξίου φιλίαν αὐτῷ γενέσθαι πρὸς τὸν 'Αρτάβανον). Antipas held a great feast and came to peaceful terms with the two (18.102–104), but his subsequent actions created resentment and Josephus critiques Antipas as politically inept (18.105).⁸⁶ Antipas appears somewhat clumsy as a politician and perhaps also as a friend. Toward the beginning of his political career, when Augustus deliberated the merits of Archelaos and Antipas, Archelaos' dishonorable treatment of his father the great benefactor (τοιαῦτα εὐεργετήσαντος; εὐεργετεῖν) was put forth by Antipater as a central reason for his not being worthy of being king (*Ant.* 17.230–239).⁸⁷ Such dishonor would transfer to the emperor, Antipater reasoned, if he stood in the position of benefactor. Antipas is not commended as one who honors his benefactors, but at least he has not been castigated as being dishonorable to them. In the end, Nicolaus proved more persuasive to Augustus. Antipas certainly moved in circles where proper etiquette toward benefactors and as benefactors was expected. According to Josephus, Antipas operated as a benefactor and friend during his tenure as tetrarch even if he was not as savvy in those affairs as others.

A few dedicatory inscriptions found outside of Palestine show how Antipas promoted himself as a benefactor in non-Jewish contexts. The overall lack of honorific inscriptions in Antipas' territories means that one will not find written evidence of benefactions there. However, there are at least three dedicatory inscriptions found outside of Palestine which refer to Antipas in benefaction contexts (*OGIS* 416, 417; *SEG* 16.488). The first, from Cos, reads:

Ἡρώδην,
Ἡρώδου τοῦ βασιλέως υἱόν,
τετράρχην,
Φίλων 'Αγλαοῦ, φύσει δὲ Νίκωνος,
τὸν αὐτοῦ ξένον καὶ Φίλον.
"Herod,
the son of Herod the King,

---

⁸⁵ For problems with the dating of Josephus' narrative (under Tiberius or Gaius?) see Emil Schürer, *The History of the Jewish People in the Age of Jesus Christ (175 B.C. – A.D. 135)* (ed. Géza Vermès and Fergus Millar; Edinburgh: Clark, 1973), 1.350–352; Richardson, *Herod*, 305–306 n. 46.

⁸⁶ Jensen, *Antipas*, 92, 98, 228.

⁸⁷ In the counterargument Nikolaos accuses Antipater and his colleagues of ill-treating their father's benefactor (εὐεργέτου; *Ant.* 17.243). His argument thus implies that since Antipas' followers have thus treated their benefactor they will treat Caesar in the same manner. Indeed, when speaking against Archelaos they injure Caesar himself (*Ant.* 17.241).

tetrarch,
Philo, son of Aglaos, but by birth son of Nikonos,
his guest and friend"

The accusative use of Herod and an implied πρὸς τὸν or ἀνατίθημι with Philon as subject indicates that Philon inscribed an honorary inscription with, probably, an accompanying statue to commemorate Antipas' generosity to the island city. No mention is made of what Herod contributed, because it would have been obvious in its original setting, but Jensen suggests something connected to the Greco-Roman cult of that city. He posits that Antipas had no qualms with participating in the Greco-Roman cults outside of Palestine.[88] For this study, it is instructive that Antipas is treated as a benefactor and friend outside of his realm. Antipas is described in similar terms by the people of Delos in an inscription found in the "*propylon* (a monumental roofed gateway) of the temple of Apollo":

'Ο δῆμος ὁ 'Α[θηναίων καὶ οἱ]
κατοι[χ]ο[ῦντες τὴν νῆσον]
'Ηρώδην βασιλέ[ως 'Ηρώδου υἱόν]
τετράρχην ἀρετῆ[ς ἕνεκεν καὶ εὐνοί]
ας τῆς εἰς ἑαυτοὺ[ς 'Απολλωνί ἀνέθηκαν]
ἐπὶ ἐπιμ[ελητοῦ τῆς νήσου 'Απολ]
λωνίου Μ--------------------------

"The Athenian people and those/
living on the island,/
for Herod, son of Herod the King,/
Tetrarch on account of piety and good/
will shown to them/
when Apollonios, son of Apollonios of Phamnous was epimeletes."[89]

Several reconstructions of the original text (which has now been lost) have been adduced. The details do not matter to this argument, but what comes through in the inscription is that Antipas was considered a benefactor in Delos. He is known for his ἀρετή and εὔνοια, two common attributes of benefactors.[90] Antipas had a similar dedicatory inscription in honor of his benefactions at Chios (*SEG* 16.488):[91]

[- - - - - - - ἐκ τῶν ἰ]δίων ἐ[πισκευά]-
[σαντα καὶ ἄλλα τ]ε πολλὰ καὶ μεγάλα

---

[88] Jensen, *Antipas*, 209–211.
[89] *OGIS* 417. Ed. Th. Homolle Bull. De corr. Hell. III (1879) p. 365, n. 5. For the location see, Jensen, *Antipas*, 210–211; for the translation see, Richardson, *Herod*, 209; for other translations see Jensen, *Antipas*, 211.
[90] Danker, *Benefactor*, 27, 317–318, 331; Crook, *Conversion*, 205–208; Harrison, *Language*, 120.
[91] *Editio Princeps* A. P. Stephanou, 'Εθνόμαρτυς Πλάτων ὁ Χίου Nov. 1956, 131; translation from Richardson, *Herod*, 206.

[τῆι πόλει χαρισάμε]νον καὶ εἰς τὸ διηνε-
[κὲς ἐλαιοθετή]σαντα, ἀρετῆς ἕνεκεν καὶ
[εὐνοίας τῆς ε]ἰς ἑαυτὴν ἐπιμεληθέντος
[τῆς ἐπισκευῆ]ς 'Απολλωνίου Ὁ τοῦ Φιλολόγου.
"[so and so was honored for such and such]/
which he repaired with his own money/
and for all the many and great things/
he donated to the city and for his perpetually/
providing anointment oil for the athletes/
for his virtuousness and his benevolence/
toward the city. The supervisor of the repairs/
was Apollonios, son of Apollonios the Philologist."

No name has been inscribed, so it is only "plausibility which links the inscription with any Herod." This inscription shares the same name (Apollonios, son of Apollonios) which leads Richardson to connect it to *OGIS* 417. It stood in Delos "before the Temple of Apollo."[92] It speaks of several benefactions of Antipas including provision for games, reparation of the temple, and other donations to the city. These monuments were not of the same scale as Antipas' father, nor were they as pervasive in the Mediterranean world, but they do attest to his role as a benefactor. Antipas pales in comparison to his father in regard to international donations, and this was perhaps in part because he did not share the same passion for political promotion (*War* 2.182).

Herod Antipas began in a position ripe for advancing in the political world of Rome, but his reluctance to shower benefits on his superiors kept him in a lower position. His education in Rome resulted in some friendships which lasted through most of his career. He likely learned of *patrocinium* and benefaction during this time, but the sources investigated do not explicitly mention the former. He seems to have done the bare minimum to express allegiance to Rome, limiting himself to the creation/renaming of a few cities (no temples were built, no images on coins were made, etc.). He attained the title "friend of Caesar" (*Ant.* 18.36), but lost this privilege upon Tiberius' death. Even in that friendship Antipas did not extend himself fully. He minted a series of coins with Tiberius' name on them, but did not include his image. He built Tiberias for the emperor, but did not include a temple to the emperor. Outside of Palestine a few inscriptions show his involvement in providing benefactions for non-Jews. These projects appear to have been few and far between. Antipas' failure to move up the social ranks may have been, as Jensen consistently reminds, attributable to a lack of zeal in showing loyalty to Rome. Despite this apathy toward social promotion, Antipas was still viewed in his realm as overly friendly toward Rome and not strict enough in his adherence to

---

[92] Richardson, *Herod*, 206.

Jewish scruples. His luxurious lifestyle, marriage to Herodias, construction of Tiberias, and murder of John the Baptist (and Jesus) earned him a poor reputation among his people. He was able to quell major uprisings surrounding these events, but this did not overcome ill-feelings among the people. In all, Antipas should be understood as a "minor Roman client ruler" whose long reign (43 years) was not marred by any major upheaval or dramatic changes in economy.[93] He was a less extravagant benefactor for whom the ideology of friendship proved important.

3.3 Philip

With no systematic treatment of Philip available, this study can only begin to outline major points.[94] Such a study would be invaluable to understanding several of the earliest followers of Jesus (e.g., Philip, Andrew, Peter) in addition to the cultural setting of a few important episodes in the gospels (e.g., Matt 16:13–20; Mark 6:45–53; 8:22–26; 8:27–30; Luke 9:10–17). It is surprising that a companion volume, examining Philip, to the monographs on Herod I, Antipas, and Agrippa I has not been issued.[95] F. M. Strickert recently declared, "One cannot overemphasize the significance of the imagery on Philip's coins when discussing the environment of Christian origins."[96] It seems that the same could be said of Philip and his tetrarchy in general (4 B.C. – A.D. 34). Josephus only provides three descriptions of Philip's activity (*War* 2.167–168; *Ant.* 18.27–28, 106–108).[97] According to Josephus, Philip is a notable exception to the pattern of unrighteous rulers (*War* 2.167–168; *Ant.* 18.27–28, 106–108). His kindness and availability earned him a good reputation among his people. The primary archaeological evidence for Philip can be found in his coins, although he did undertake a few building projects. Philip minted images of himself, emperors, Augustus' wife Julia, and the newly refurbished Au-

---

[93] Jensen, *Antipas*, 227.

[94] Cf. Wilson, *Caesarea Philippi*, 18–23, 18.

[95] E.g., Richardson, *Herod*; Hoehner, *Herod Antipas*; Jensen, *Antipas*; Schwartz, *Agrippa I*. Richardson makes a case for such a study, ibid., 303–305. On Philip see, Wilson, *Caesarea Philippi*, 18–23; Frederick M. Strickert, *Bethsaida: Home of the Apostles* (Collegeville: Liturgical Press, 1998); Fred Strickert, "The Coins of Philip," in Arav and Freund, *Bethsaida*, 165–189; Nikos Kokkinos, *The Herodian Dynasty: Origins, Role in Society and Eclipse* (Journal for the Study of the Pseudepigrapha 30; Sheffield: Sheffield Academic Press, 1998); Arav, "Bethsaida," in Charlesworth, *Jesus and Archaeology*; David C. Braund, "Philip," *ABD* 5:310–311; Richardson, *Herod*, 301–305.

[96] Strickert, "Coins of Philip," 168.

[97] For other primary sources see, Pliny, *NH* 16.74; Ptolemy 5.15.26; Philo, *Legatio* 326; Cassius Dio 59.12; Tacitus, *Annals* 12.23.

gusteum (at Caesarea Philippi). With such slim evidence one cannot determine conclusively if Philip thought of his activity in *patrocinium* or benefaction categories. Benefaction seems slightly more likely, but his early involvement at Rome and subsequent support of the imperial cult make *patrocinium* a possibility. A brief survey of Philip's education, relationship with Rome and the emperors, public perception, construction projects, coins, and benefactions will be provided.

3.3.1 Education

Philip, like many of his brothers, was educated in Rome. The same phrase employed by Josephus to describe Antipas' education is adopted in the brief description of Philip (αὐτὸς ἐν 'Ρώμῃ τροφὰς εἶχεν; *Ant.* 17.21). In the *War* parallel Josephus exchanges the phrase for a more overt reference to (Hellenistic) education in Rome (ἐπὶ 'Ρώμης παιδευόμενοι; *War* 1.602). Again it is difficult to tell when this education began, but at the time of Antipater's education both Philip and Archelaos are described as still being youths (μειράκιά τε ἤδη; *War* 1.602). Since this education primarily consisted in the learning of languages and acquiring of strategic friendships it is quite likely that Philip learned the methods and vocabulary of *patrocinium* and benefaction during his stay. Most likely he also cultivated some friendships which later aided in his political promotion.

3.3.2 Relationship to the Emperors and Rome

The tetrarch probably initiated friendships with Rome while a youth, and he made a few important expressions of fidelity within his realm even though he rarely visited the capital. Unlike his brothers and father, Philip did not have a political motivation for abstaining from the Greco-Roman cults or public recognition of the emperor. It will be discussed below (section 3.3.5) how Philip decided to imprint the emperor's (and his family's) names and images on his coins. Each time Philip minted he included an image of the emperor, and many of the coins have multiple images in addition to words acknowledging his positive relationship with Rome. He also refurbished the temple to Caesar, constructed a small temple in honor of Livia-Julia,[98] and renamed two cities in honor of these friends (Caesarea Philippi, Julias). Unlike his brothers, but like his father in Caesarea, Philip

---

[98] Arav, "Bethsaida," in Charlesworth, *Jesus and Archaeology*, 162–164. Both Augustus' wife and daughter were honored as benefactresses by the people of Thasos, Victor Ehrenberg and A. H. M. Jones, *Documents Illustrating the Reigns of Augustus and Tiberius* (2. ed.; reprint, 1955; Oxford: Clarendon, 1976), 77; David C. Braund, *Augustus to Nero: A Sourcebook on Roman History, 31 BC-AD 68* (London: Crook Helm, 1985), 74.

supported the imperial cult.⁹⁹ He did experience some turmoil in the political realm. Antipater falsely accused Philip of indicting Herod in the murder of Aristobulus. Herod hated him for this accusation, but Philip was later cleared of the charge and regained a good name with his father (*Ant.* 17.80, 146, 189). Philip preferred to be present in his own tetrarchy (rather than traveling to Rome), but he did have one noteworthy expedition to Rome during his life. While Archelaos left for Rome to be involved in the discussion about his father's will he left Philip in charge (κηδεμών) of the territories (*War* 2.14). Κηδεμών, employed by Josephus to describe Philip's role, is among those terms attributed to benefactors and patrons. Eventually, however, Philip went to Rome under the advice of Varus, Roman governor of Syria, to be present while Augustus deliberated (*Ant.* 17.219, 303). He eventually received a tetrarchy consisting of Gaulanitis, Trachonitis, and Paneas (*Ant.* 17.189). He received 100 talents annually in tribute, whereas Antipas received 200 annually from Galilee and Perea (*Ant.* 17.318–319). He received probably the worst portion among the distribution, but he expressed a good amount of appreciation in his coins, construction projects, and renaming of cities.¹⁰⁰ Philip's education in Rome and liberty in expressing allegiance to the imperial family indicates an awareness of Hellenistic and Roman ways, and, presumably, of *patrocinium* and benefaction even though Josephus does not point this out.

3.3.3 Public Perception

Philip's long rule, thirty-seven years, could possibly derive from his likable governing style. In the paragraph which introduces Philip, Josephus describes Archelaos and Philip as being of "full dispositions" (φρονήματος μεστοί; *War* 1.602). This description fleshes itself out during his rule. In his political career, he probably gained the admiration of the people through his tax policy. Philip required only small amounts of tax from the people in Batanea and Trachonitis, and only for a little while (*Ant.* 17.27). His father had set this standard as a way to protect his territory during his reign (*Ant.* 17.23–27). Philip chose to maintain it. This liberty actually continued through Agrippa II (*Ant.* 17.28). Philip's policy of traveling around his region with selected friends to adjudicate complaints for his people also won him favor (*Ant.* 18.107). He loved to be in his own territory, so he did not travel to Rome but instead made a circuit through his territory and doled out punishments for the guilty and reprieve for the unjustly condemned. He was buried, with great pomp, at a monument he con-

---

⁹⁹ Arav, "Bethsaida," 148.
¹⁰⁰ Strickert, "Coins of Philip," 167, who refers to Ya'akov Meshorer, *Ancient Jewish Coinage* (Dix Hills: Amphora Books, 1982), 2:45.

structed for himself (ὁ μνημεῖον ὃ ἔτι πρότερον ᾠκοδόμησεν; 18.108). Josephus' perception of Philip can be detected not only in the language and description he chooses, but also in the contrast which he develops by following his short and laudable section on Philip (*Ant.* 18.105–109) with chronicles of Antipas' major shortcomings (*Ant.* 18.109–126).[101] Philip did not make the same mistakes as Antipas had. He was, rather, a person of moderation and quietness in both life and government (*Ant.* 18.106).

μέτριον δὲ ἐν οἷς ἦρχεν παρασχὼν τὸν τρόπον καὶ ἀπράγμονα ἴαιταν μὲν γὰρ τὸ πᾶν ἐν γῇ τῇ ὑποτελεῖ ἐποιεῖτο πρόοδοι δ' ἦσαν αὐτῷ σὺν ὀλίγοις τῶν ἐπιλέκτων
"In his conduct of the government he showed a moderate and easy-going disposition. Indeed, he spent all his time in the territory subject to him. When he went on circuit he had only a few select companions."

Josephus does not indict Philip for overzealousness toward Rome or for disobeying the Jewish commands.

3.3.4 Construction Projects

Philip undertook a few important construction projects in recognition of the imperial family, but no evidence exists for building outside of his tetrarchy in his name. Herod I built a temple in Paneas to honor Augustus which Philip "embellished" (*War* 1.404–406; *Ant.* 15.363–364; *Ant.* 18.28; *War* 2.168).[102] The tetrastyle form of the temple in Philip's day can be seen in the coins upon which he imprinted a picture. He then renamed the city Caesarea Philippi to mark it as a parallel to Caesarea on the coast (*Ant.* 15.363; *War* 1.404).[103] Connecting his name to Caesar could have been a strategic move to increase his own reputation by showing just how strong was his allegiance to Rome (a similar connection exists in his coins). Philip also improved Bethsaida to the status of *polis* and renamed it Julias in honor of the emperor's wife. Josephus mentions the number of inhabitants and τῇ ἄλλῃ δυνάμει which made the title

---

[101] Jensen, *Antipas*, 82 who refers to Klaus-Stefan Krieger, *Geschichtsschreibung als Apologetik bei Flavius Josephus* (TANZ 9; Tübingen: Francke, 1994), 50–51. Something of Josephus' ideal world may be detected in this contrast. Antipas had constructed no temples nor engraved coins with images, two things Josephus looks down upon elsewhere, but Philip did both. These were offenses to Jews, obviously, but Josephus does not seem to mind in regard to Philip. Jensen's proposal that Josephus is more concerned with stability between Rome and Jews expects this approach by Josephus. Since the inhabitants of Philip's territory consisted of more non-Jews, they would not be offended by the images and temples. No riots ensued because of them. Josephus cannot be upset because stability persists despite the breaking of the second commandment.

[102] Richardson, *Herod*, 302; P. Richardson, "Religion, Architecture and Ethics: Some First-century Case Studies," *HBT* 10.2 (1988): 19–49; Netzer describes the options for this building, *Great Builder*, 218–222.

[103] Strickert, "Coins of Philip," 167.

polis appropriate (*Ant.* 18.28). A small structure found in this city has been interpreted as a temple to Livia-Julia. Livia-Julias had a special role in the cult of Augustus being its first priestess.[104] Philip attempted to bolster his relationship with Rome by commemorating a city and temple in honor of the emperor's wife. But, unlike his father and Antipas, Philip did not pursue an aggressive building program, and "there is no record of Philip making benefactions" to Canatha and Bosra despite his father's involvement in nearby Si'a.[105] The large works which Philip constructed in his realm would be considered benefactions, as would be the naming of cities and temples for superiors. With such slight evidence it is impossible to tell whether Philip understood his actions along the lines of *patrocinium* or benefaction, but their affinity with the works of his father and Antipas points in favor of the latter more than the former.

3.3.5 Coins

One of the richest resources for describing Philip comes in the numismatic evidence.[106] Despite his economic shortcomings (the smallest inheritance), he began his mint twenty years before Antipas and minted twice as many coins in his lifetime. It is true, however, that the poor preservation of his coins probably derives from lower quality means of production.[107] Philip issued eight types of which several had multiple mintings. On each coin Philip put an image, whether it be his or the emperor's face, or the hand of Julia holding ears of grain. Philip's first coin aligned him with the emperor with his own image and an inscription, ΦΙΛΙΠΠΟΥ ΤΕΤΡΑΡΧΟΥ, along with Augustus' head and the inscription ΚΑΙΣΑΡ ΣΕΒΑΣΤΟΥ. Within the same year Philip replaced his face for a picture of the Augusteum (in Caesarea Philippi).[108] Strickert suggests that Philip protected himself from Jewish attack by putting a lily (Jewish symbol) in the middle of the temple picture thus leaving himself room to argue that this was not a pagan temple.[109] This coin, with the emperor's face on the obverse and tetrastyle temple on the reverse (subsequently without the lily), was repeated with slight variation each of the eight times Philip minted. He also minted images of himself, Livia/Julia (wife of Augustus), and the imperial couple (Augustus and Livia).[110] Meshorer interprets Philip's coins as expressions of grateful-

---

[104] Arav, "Bethsaida," 164.
[105] Richardson, *Herod*, 302–303.
[106] Some resources on Philip's coins include: Strickert, "Coins of Philip"; Jensen, *Antipas*, 198–200; Meshorer, *Jewish Coinage*, 76–77, 135–136.
[107] Jensen, *Antipas*, 165–166.
[108] Jensen, *Antipas*, 199.
[109] Strickert, "Coins of Philip," 167–168.
[110] Strickert, "Coins of Philip," 166.

ness for Rome's generosity towards him.[111] Strickert suggests the timing and imagery of Philip's (and Antipas' to an extent) coins was his attempt to remind inhabitants of the legitimacy of his rule in the face of the Roman procurators' monopolization of power.[112] In one issue Philip actually preempts Claudius in deifying Livia, even to the point of undermining Tiberius' explicit command to mourn her death (and thus restrict her from deification).[113] This and the renaming of Bethsaida were explicit ways that Philip expressed his friendship with the emperor's wife. His inclusion of Roman symbols at times hints at support of the imperial cult as well. Philip more explicitly promoted his connection to Rome than Herod I or Antipas had in their coins. He is the first to use imperial images and inscriptions and does not hesitate to include imagery connected to the imperial cult. His apparent reason for doing so was in gracious response to Rome's generosity with him. Philip's coins were one way that he cultivated his friendship with Rome.

3.3.6 Benefactions

With such a dearth of evidence it is practically impossible to determine whether Philip consciously adopted patronage or benefaction as an ideology. He certainly had developed friendships with Rome and honored those friends in architecture, the renaming of cities, and coins. His improvements to Caesarea Philippi and its temple, along with renaming the city, served to honor the emperor and to connect himself to that rule. These actions fall into line with typical modes of honoring among the Hellenistic kings. Such large scale gifts come closer to benefactions than expressions of gratitude found in *patrocinium*, but this cannot be determined concretely. Philip does seem more involved in Roman religious practice, e.g., the construction of temples to the emperor and his wife and depiction of one temple and cultic articles on coins, which suggests a greater awareness and participation in Roman ways of interacting. On the other hand, he did not frequent Rome and we have only a small record of his entertaining Romans in his realm. Since his tetrarchy contained many non-Roman easterners along with Jews he may just as likely have resorted to their modes of social interaction. This would decrease his expression of *patrocinium* and possibly increase the expression of benefaction or other types of reciprocity. The evidence leans slightly toward benefaction as the way Philip understood his work. No record of benefactions outside his realm exists for Philip which indicates that, if he involved himself in either mode of social ex-

---

[111] Meshorer, *Ancient Jewish*, 2:45.
[112] Strickert, "Coins of Philip," 170–173.
[113] Jensen, *Antipas*, 199–200.

pression, he should be understood as participating on a smaller scale. At this point one cannot dogmatically decide between *patrocinium* and benefaction, but must instead resolve that Philip expressed himself in reciprocal relationships and sought to honor his superiors through calling public attention to them. If Philip made a circuit around his region in a quest to rectify unjust rulings, then the disciples (Andrew, Philip, Peter) could have learned these modes of reciprocity directly from him. Perhaps a friend or acquaintance had been treated unfairly and caught the attention of Philip during one of his rounds. As pious Jews they, more than others in the tetrarchy, might have been offended by Philip's overt connection to Rome. They will certainly have seen in him the closest expression of leadership and perhaps subconsciously imbibed his manner as a model.

3.4 Agrippa I

Agrippa stands apart from Herod's progeny discussed thus far as one more comfortable in Roman environs than Jewish. For thirty formative years (c. age five to thirty-five) Agrippa lived in Rome and cultivated friendships with the imperial family. When he eventually gained some authority in Palestine he resided in Caesarea Maritima ("little Rome") making only an occasional trip to Jerusalem (A.D. 37–44). His acts of Jewish piety have been interpreted as a farce, piety, and political sagacity by various interpreters,[114] but he also kindled a relationship with Roman cults and chose pointed symbols of Roman allegiance in his coins. He built relationships with cities outside of his realm and is noted for having been identified as a patron of the Roman colony of Heliopolis (*IGLS* 6.2759; cf. *ILS* 3.2.8957). For a brief stint (A.D. 41–44) he ruled almost the entire realm (excluding Gadara, Gaza, and Hippos) of his grandfather, Herod I. Throughout his rule, Agrippa made several trips to Rome to reinforce his strategic friendships. It appears, however, that towards the end of his life Agrippa grew somewhat disenchanted with the imperial family. Since Josephus devotes more time to Agrippa than any other person besides Herod I (e.g., *Ant.* 18.126–19.366; *War* 2.178–222), it would be impossible to detail all events and nuances of his career.[115] The six categories adopted for the previous rulers will once again be taken up for Agrippa.

---

[114] Schwartz, *Agrippa I*, 133–134 sees Agrippa's Jewish acts as only for show. Josephus apparently thought Agrippa to be a pious Jew (cf. the summary in *Ant.* 19.328–334). Jensen understands Agrippa to have attained a political balance in appeasing his Jewish and Roman contemporaries, Jensen, *Antipas*, 83–86.

[115] The most comprehensive work on Agrippa I is Schwartz, *Agrippa I*, but see also Jensen, *Antipas*, 83–86, 201–202; Andrew Burnett, "The coinage of King Agrippa I of

3.4.1 Education

Herod I knew that the longevity and success of his dynasty depended upon strategic friendships, so towards the end of his life he sent Agrippa to Rome for his education. Before heading off to Rome, Agrippa received a bit of an education from his grandfather, Herod I (*Ant.* 17.12; cf. *Ant.* 15.342–343; 16.6; 18.143; *War* 1.555). He was perhaps five years old when he entered the capital, and he soon fulfilled the hopes of his father by developing friendships with Drusus (Tiberius' son) and Antonia (the wife of Drusus the Great; εἰς φιλίαν ἀφίκετο). The former friendship was so strong that after Drusus' death, Tiberius forbid Agrippa to see him because the sight of his son's close friend reminded the emperor of his sorrow (*Ant.* 18.146). It can be surmised that Drusus' love for banquets and gladiatorial games influenced his best friend (*Annals* 3.37; 1.76; cf. Gaius and Claudius *Ant.* 19.130; Suetonius *Claud.* 34).[116] Antonia's friendship with Agrippa was quite critical because she had a compelling connection with the two most important emperors of Agrippa's political tenure (grandmother of Gaius and mother of Claudius).[117] Agrippa grew up under the watch of Livia (Augustus' wife) with the future emperor Claudius, in addition to the emperor's son Drusus, and L. Pomponius Flaccus (later the legate of Syria) (*Ant.* 18.165, 146, 166, 188, 150).[118] A little later, Agrippa exploited these relationships while he was deeply in debt so that he might retain Tiberius' friendship (ἡ φιλία τοῦ Τιβερίου; *Ant.* 18.164–165; see below section 3.4).

ὁ δὲ μηδὲν τῇ ὀργῇ τοῦ Καίσαρος καταπλαγεὶς Ἀντωνίας δεῖται Γερμανικοῦ μητρὸς καὶ Κλαυδίου τοῦ ὕστερον γενομένου Καίσαρος δάνεισμα αὐτῷ δοθῆναι τῶν τριάκοντα μυριάδων ὡς φιλίας μὴ α'μάρτοι τῆς πρὸς Τιβέριον ἡ δὲ Βερενίκης τε μνήμῃ τῆς μητρὸς αὐτοῦ σφόδρα γὰρ ἀλλήλαις ἐχρῶντο αἵδε αἱ γυναῖκες καὶ αὐτῷ ὁμοτροφίας πρὸς τοὺς ἀμφὶ Κλαύδιον γεγενημένης δίδωσι τὸ ἀργύριον καὶ αὐτῷ ἀποτίσαντι τὸ χρέος ἀνεπικώλυτος ἦν ἡ φιλία τοῦ Τιβερίου

"Undismayed by the emperor's anger, Agrippa asked Antonia, the mother of Germanicus and of the future emperor Claudius, to grant him a loan of 300,000 drachmas so that he might not lose the friendship of Tiberius. Antonia, both because she still remembered Berenice his mother – for the two ladies had been deeply attached to each other – and because Agrippa had been brought up with Claudius and his circle, provided the money.

Judaea," in *Mélanges de numismatique: offerts à Pierre Bastien à l'occasion de son 75ᵉ anniversaire* (eds. H. Huvelin, M. Christol and G. Gautier; Wetteren: NR Editions, 1987), 25–38; Hans-Josef Klauck, *Magic and Paganism in Early Christianity: The World of the Acts of the Apostles* (trans. Brian McNeil; Minneapolis: Fortress Press, 2004).

[116] Schwartz, *Agrippa I*, 134 n. 117.
[117] Schwartz, *Agrippa I*, 41–42.
[118] Schwartz, *Agrippa I*, 42–43.

When he had discharged the debt, there was no longer any obstacle to his friendship with Tiberius."

Agrippa most likely took up an education in Greek and Latin (Cassius Dio, *Roman History* 60.8.3; *Leg.* 276–329), and though he could speak in Hebrew/Aramaic (*Ant.* 18.228), Schwartz emphasizes that this was not an education in "being Jewish" but only in a language necessary to rule properly.[119] It was Augustus' desire to groom future rulers in Roman ways by bringing them to the capital at a young age.[120] It therefore seems quite likely that Agrippa learned not only how "friendships" worked, but also about *patrocinium* and benefaction. Learning about these practices would likely have been a significant component of his education.

3.4.2 Relationship to the Emperors and Rome

On a deeper level, probably, than any of the others investigated thus far, Agrippa knew how to cultivate friendships with Rome. He had been sent to the capital for this purpose and had a good amount of success. Josephus explicitly mentions friendships with Livia, Antonia, Drusus, and L. Pomponius Flaccus. He was the first in his family to receive a Roman *tria nomina* identifying a heritage of friendships developed in previous generations.[121] Agrippa only gained power by "cultivating" the friendship of emperors (*Ant.* 18.167–168, 289–300).[122] In his early career, Agrippa's reckless spending habits incurred great debts and almost forfeited his friendship with Tiberius (ὡς φιλίας μὴ ἁμάρτοι τῆς πρὸς Τιβέριον; *Ant.* 18.143–46; 151–167). Josephus recounts the, often devious, measures Agrippa attempted to get out of debt. When he fled the scene after taking a loan, Tiberius was informed and their friendship was imperiled (*Ant.* 18.163–164). He resorted to taking a loan from another lender, Antonia, paid off the debt and salvaged the relationship. Agrippa did not always target his "cultivation" in the proper direction. While Tiberius was still in office, Agrippa was overheard praying that God would, euphemistically speaking, "take Tiberius off the stage" so that Gaius could be emperor. Their driver overheard him say this and warned Tiberius who obviously

---

[119] Schwartz, *Agrippa I*, 44–45. Schwartz doubts the authenticity of Agrippa's Jewish piety throughout his monograph. Jensen appears more open to the possibility that Agrippa truly felt some warmth toward the Jewish faith even if he also enjoyed the Roman cults.

[120] Schwartz, *Agrippa I*, 41; he refers to E. Ciaceri, *Atti del Reale Istituto Veneto di Scienze, Lettere ed Arti* 76/2 (1916/17), 703, 707; Braund, *Friendly King*, 9–21; Bowersock, *Augustus and the Greek World*, 42–61.

[121] Braund, *Friendly King*, 44, 111; Schwartz, *Agrippa I*, 40. One inscription attests this name: *OGIS* 428.

[122] Schwartz, *Agrippa I*, 135

punished Agrippa for it (*Ant.* 18.168–169; cf. *War* 2.179–181 [with a different setting]). Agrippa intended to reiterate the advancement of his friendship with Gaius (ἐπὶ μέγα τῷ 'Αγρίππᾳ τῆς πρὸς Γάιον φιλίας), but this would have to wait until Tiberius had exited and Gaius took his place. Agrippa endured six grueling months in prison for the offense, but was granted Philip's tetrarchy upon Gaius' accession.

Though he had several political gaffs, Agrippa did acquire significant status. Agrippa's reputation for overspending had been a source of disdain earlier in his life, but he could also use it for political gain. In an important episode, Josephus describes a lavish banquet thrown by Agrippa to advance his friendship with Gaius (*Ant.* 18.289; cf. *Ant.* 18.289–300).

Αγρίππας δὲ ὁ βασιλεύς ἐτύγχανεν γὰρ ἐπὶ 'Ρώμης διαιτώμενος προύκοπτε φιλίᾳ τῇ πρὸς τὸν Γάιον μειζόνως καί ποτε προθεὶς δεῖπνον αὐτῷ καὶ πρόνοιαν ἔχων πάντας υ'περβαλέσθαι τέλεσί τε τοῖς εἰς τὸ δεῖπνον καὶ παρασκευῇ τοῦ εἰς ἡ'δονὴν φέροντος ω'ς μὴ ὅπως ἄν τινα τῶν λοιπῶν ἀλλὰ μηδ' αὐτὸν Γάιον πιστεύειν ποτε ἰσωθῆναι θελήσοντα οὐχ ὅπως υ'περβαλέσθαι τοσοῦτον ο' ἀνὴρ τῇ παρασκευῇ πάντας υ'περῆρεν καὶ τῷ τὰ πάντα ἡ Καίσαρος ἐκφροντίσας παρασχεῖν

"Meanwhile King Agrippa, who, as it happened, was living in Rome, advanced greatly in friendship with Gaius. Once he made a banquet for him with the intention of surpassing everyone both in the expenditure on the banquet and in provision for the pleasure of his guests. He was so successful that, to say nothing of the others, even Gaius himself despaired of equaling, much less surpassing it, if he should desire to do so. So far did this man surpass everyone in his preparations and in devising and providing everything for the emperor."

In doing so, he went beyond his own capacity and even Caesar's, extending himself to the point of danger he placed Gaius under obligation to reciprocate. Gaius recognized the noble traits of this benefactor (τήν τε διάνοιαν αὐτοῦ καὶ τὴν μεγαλοπρέπειαν; *Ant.* 18.291). Gaius desired not to be superseded in honor (φιλοτιμίαν), so he exerted much energy to please him (ἐπ' ἀρεσκείᾳ τῇ αὐτοῦ βιάζοιτο). Agrippa showed honor (τιμήν) and good will (πολλὴν εὔνοιαν), putting himself in harm's way (μετὰ κινδύνων) to provide this banquet (*Ant.* 18.292). Gaius needed something with which he might reciprocate (ὅτι χαρίζοιτ' ἄν αὐτῷ; *Ant.* 18.296). Agrippa did not ask for wealth or land, but instead that Gaius would refrain from placing his statue in the Jerusalem temple (*Ant.* 18.297–298). Agrippa's bold move, opportunely timed, forced Gaius' hand since he had put himself into a position in which he could not deny any request from the host. The favor was granted (χαριζόμενος), and the friendship cultivated (*Ant.* 18.301). After advancing the political ranks, Agrippa eventually earned the revered title "friend of Caesar."

Philo's story of Agrippa's visit to Alexandria explains the import of the title and the extent of honor deserved by Agrippa (*In Flaccum* 26–40). Returning from a visit to Gaius after receiving part of his father's kingdom,

3.4 Agrippa I

Agrippa was instructed to go through Alexandria on his way to Palestine. The Alexandrians felt that any honor granted to another had a resultant dishonor to them attached. Flaccus compelled the people to mock Agrippa, the newly appointed king. They ridiculed Agrippa by propping up a lunatic as king in the gymnasium and calling him Μάριν, the Syrian name for Lord (because Agrippa was Syrian by birth and ruled a good portion of Syria; *In Flaccum* 36–39). The offense to Agrippa mattered much because the one insulted had received Praetorian honours (*ornamenta praetoria*) from the Roman senate and was a friend of Caesar's (φίλον Καίσαρος καὶ ὑπὸ τῆς Ῥωμαίων βουλῆς τετιμημένον στρατηγικαῖς τιμαῖς ἐτόλμησαν; *In Flaccum* 40). Flaccus of Alexandria, himself also a newly appointed ruler, publicly treated Agrippa as a friend, but in reality attempted to undermine Agrippa's new authority as an offense to the Alexandrians (*In Flaccum* 30–32). In narrating the events, Philo considers Agrippa worthy of honor not only for being king, but also for being a member of Caesar's household (τις τῶν ἐκ τῆς Καίσαρος οἰκίας; *In Flaccum* 35). During different stages of his life Agrippa had been friends with the three emperors (Tiberius, Gaius, Glaudius), but he had also jeopardized these friendships at different times as well.

Agrippa had a turbulent relationship with Rome and the emperors. He grew up in close proximity to present and future emperors and their families. Such close proximity had both positive and negative impacts on his situation. On the one hand his ability to cultivate the emperor, something which began quite early in his life, helped him to move up the social ranks to the point of taking over the entire realm of his father (*Ant.* 18.167–168, 289–300). On the other hand, he knew first hand that the imperial family was just as human as any other and it appears that after attaining the extent of his father's kingdom he grew callous and apathetic toward fostering those friendships. Schwartz makes this case from two observations and a discussion of two confrontations which took place later in Agrippa's reign. (1) He did not return to Rome to develop his friendship with the new emperor Claudius. Abandonment of his previous practice expressed a lack of zeal to maintain the source of his power. (2) Minting coins with the title "the Great," which Agrippa proceeded to do for the duration of his career, elevated his status and is interpreted as an affront (to some extent) to Rome's power.[123] The two "clashes" which signal to Schwartz growing resentment of Rome are the "Tiberian conclave" and the "Third Wall" of Jerusalem (*Ant.* 19.338–342; *War* 2.218–219; 5.147–160; *Ant.* 19.326–327). Agrippa did not rebel against Rome but simply stopped working to strengthen his friendships in Rome. With no realm left for him to gain he seems to have lost interest in his imperial friendships.

---

[123] For this entire argument see, Schwartz, *Agrippa I*, 135–144.

3.4.3 Public Perception

Sentiments about Agrippa have polar extremes. At one point his spending habits earn him the reputation of frivolity and later as a magnanimous benefactor. He can be perceived as adhering to Judaism or being outright pagan. Inhabitants of a city can praise him as god or cheer his death and forget his benefits. Early in his life Agrippa had a reputation for irresponsible spending habits. He was mistrusted by some (*Ant.* 18.143–144, 160), and confirmed that reputation by perpetuating his debts. Josephus at times explains this as the generosity of his nature which later in life flowered into a good thing which endeared the people to him (*Ant.* 18.144). His best friends growing up had awful reputations for cruelty and wickedness, and some suggest that Agrippa was the instigator (Tacitus *Annals* 1.29, 76; Suetonius *Tib.* 52; Cassius Dio 57.13; 59.24.1).[124]

Josephus contrasts Agrippa from Herod I. He maligns Herod for constructing baths, theaters, and temples in foreign cities and not devoting any attention to his own region (something Josephus himself contradicts elsewhere). But Agrippa, who Josephus informs the reader also built in other countries, does not receive condemnation but commendation (*Ant.* 19.328–330).[125]

Ἐπεφύκει δ' ὁ βασιλεὺς οὗτος εὐεργετικὸς εἶναι ἐν δωρεαῖς καὶ μεγαλοφρονῆσαι ἔθνη φιλότιμος καὶ πολλοῖς ἀθρόως δαπανήμασιν ἀνιστὰς αὑτὸν εἰς ἐπιφάνειαν ἡδόμενος τῷ χαρίζεσθαι καὶ τῷ βιοῦν ἐν εὐφημίᾳ χαίρων κατ' οὐδὲν Ἡρώδῃ τῷ πρὸ ἑ'αυτοῦ βασιλεῖ τὸν τρόπον συμφερόμενος ἐκείνῳ γὰρ πονηρὸν ἦν ἦθος ἐπὶ τιμωρίαν ἀπότομον καὶ κατὰ τῶν ἀπηχθημένων ἀταμίευτον Ἕλλησι πλέον ἢ Ἰουδαίοις οἰκείως ἔχειν ὁμολογούμενος ἀλλοφύλων γέ τοι πόλεις ἐσέμνυνεν δόσει χρημάτων βαλανείων θεάτρων τε ἄλλοτε κατασκευαῖς ἔστιν αἷς ναοὺς ἀνέστησε στοὰς ἄλλαις ἀλλὰ Ἰουδαίων οὐδεμίαν πόλιν οὐδ' ὀλίγης ἐπισκευῆς ἠξίωσεν οὐδὲ δόσεως ἀξίας μνημονευθῆναι πρᾶος δ' ὁ τρόπος Ἀγρίππᾳ καὶ πρὸς πάντας τὸ εὐεργετικὸν ὅμοιον τοῖς ἀλλοεθνέσιν ἦν φιλάνθρωπος κἀκείνοις ἐνδεικνύμενος τὸ φιλόδωρον τοῖς ὁμοφύλοις ἀναλόγως χρηστὸς καὶ συμπαθὴς μᾶλλον

"Now King Agrippa was by nature generous in his gifts and made it a point of honour to be highminded towards gentiles; and by expending massive sums he raised himself to high fame. He took pleasure in conferring favours and rejoiced in popularity, thus being in no way similar in character to Herod, who was king before him. The latter had an evil nature, relentless in punishment and unsparing in action against the objects of his hatred. It was generally admitted that he was on more friendly terms with Greeks than with Jews. For instance, he adorned the cities of foreigners by giving them money, building baths and theatres, erecting temples in some and porticoes in others, whereas there was not a single city of the Jews on which he deigned to bestow even minor restoration or any gift worth mentioning. Agrippa, on the contrary, had a gentle disposition and he was a benefactor to all alike. He was benevolent to those of other nations and exhibited his generos-

---

[124] Schwartz, *Agrippa I*, 45.
[125] Richardson, *Herod*, 31 n. 41.

ity to them also; but to his compatriots he was proportionately more generous and more compassionate."

It was Herod who was evil and severe, and, worse than that, kinder to the Greeks than to the Jews (*Ant.* 19.329, 335). He did not make a single donation to any Jewish city worth mentioning (ἠξίωσεν οὐδὲ δόσεως ἀξίας μνημονευθῆναι)! But Agrippa was a truly generous man, equally liberal to all men. He was a benefactor to all and full of benevolence (πρὸς πάντας τὸ εὐεργετικόν; φιλάνθρωπος; *Ant.* 19.330, 328). He loved to reside at Jerusalem and never allowed the sacrifices to go undone (*Ant.* 19.331). Agrippa stands out for his gentleness and mildness rather than severity and anger. Indeed, Agrippa is worthy of the heights of status he has reached, and it was just of God to exclude Agrippa from the punishments made on Herod's descendents (*Ant.* 18.129).

In several ways Josephus presents Agrippa as a pious Jew. Tracing Agrippa's lineage to the Hasmonean family (eventually son of Mariamme and Aristobulos), Josephus places Agrippa as "the pinnacle of dignity and power."[126] Agrippa stands out in three particular episodes as a protector of the Jews (*Ant.* 19.278–291; 19.300–311; cf. 19.293, 331).[127] Jensen interprets Josephus as describing Agrippa as one who walked the line between allegiance to Rome and appeasement of Jews. He was not traditionally pious, but genuinely esteemed the religion of the people.[128] Schwartz considers Agrippa's piety as nothing more than political sagacity.[129] He knew that the longevity of his rule depended upon maintaining peace, so he took measures to ensure that his people saw him as pious (e.g., therefore he frequented the temple) and to prevent outsiders from tampering with the peace (e.g., he stopped the statue of Gaius). Schwartz would contest Josephus' statement that Agrippa "loved" to be in Jerusalem because he only rarely visited the holy city to check on its affairs. When Agrippa was in his region, and that was not all too often, he resided in Caesarea. Schwartz may be overstating his conclusion slightly. It seems that one can be simultaneously politically savvy and interested in the ancient faith. Agrippa most likely practiced in other cults (see discussion 3.4.5), but this does not rule out the possibility of him participating in Judaism.

---

[126] Jensen, *Antipas*, 84; *Ant.* 18.142.

[127] Jensen, *Antipas*, 84

[128] See Jensen, *Antipas*, 83–90. A. H. M. Jones takes Josephus at face value interpreting Agrippa's religion as traditional and devoted. A. H. M. Jones, *The Herods of Judaea* (Oxford: Clarendon Press, 1938), 309; in Schwartz, *Agrippa I*, 117 n. 37.

[129] Schwartz, *Agrippa I*, 116–130. Agrippa was not a "pious Jew of any sort." He did not return the region back to traditional Judaism ibid., 132. His "showy sacrifices" were just that and no more (*Ant.* 19.292–294, 331; *m. Sotah* 7:8; *Leviticus Rabbah* 3:5; compare Agrippa with others in *Leg.* 157, 294–297, 317–319; *War* 2.412–413; 5.563).

Others among his contemporaries thought quite well of him. Some people apparently had such a high view of Agrippa that they desired to worship him no longer as a man, but from that point on as a god (*Ant.* 19.344–346; Acts 12:21–23). The worship did not last very long because his death immediately followed. Josephus can even present this story as evidence of Agrippa's uprightness as he willingly accepts the lot of providence (19.346–350). Some inhabitants of Caesarea and Sebaste, however, celebrated his death (*Ant.* 19.356–361), forgetting the benefits conferred upon them by Agrippa (τῶν εὐποιιῶν αὐτοῦ λαθόμενοι τὰ τῶν δυσμενεστάτων ἐποίησαν) and acting generally in an ungrateful way to both Agrippa and Herod (τοὺς ἀχαριστήσαντας). It is instructive for this study that Agrippa can be heralded as a benefactor by Josephus and turned against in Caesarea by not adhering to the unwritten rules of benefaction upon his death. Agrippa and Herod I had been lauded as benefactors in life, but others interpreted their benefactions in a negative light.

3.4.4 Construction Projects

Not much mention of Agrippa's building activity can be found in Josephus, but in the primary section in which it is discussed the author identifies Agrippa as a benefactor of the highest regard (*Ant.* 19.326–328, 335–337). Josephus acknowledges Agrippa's hand in the construction of an impenetrable wall for Jerusalem which was made at great expense. A message to the emperor curtailed its construction and postulations of its identification in the archaeological record remain inconclusive.[130]

After Josephus shows Agrippa's kind disposition and reasonable nature (εὐεργετικὸς; μεγαλοφρονῆσαι; *Ant.* 19.328), he writes that Agrippa was a prolific builder in many regions (19.335). He focuses on Berytus where Agrippa built a theater, amphitheater, baths, and porticoes. Sparing no expense, he made them large and beautiful and christened their opening with extravagant gladiatorial games and music (*Ant.* 19.335–337).

Πολλοῖς δὲ κατασκευάσας πολλὰ Βηρυτίους ἐξαιρέτως ἐτίμησεν θέατρον γὰρ αὐτοῖς κατεσκεύασε πολυτελείᾳ τε καὶ κάλλει πολλῶν διαφέρον ἀμφιθέατρόν τε πολλῶν ἀναλωμάτων βαλανεῖα πρὸς τούτοις καὶ στοάς ἐν οὐδενὶ τῶν ἔργων στενότητι δαπανημάτων ἢ τὸ κάλλος ἀδικήσας ἢ τὸ μέγεθος ἐπεδαψιλεύσατο δ' αὐτῶν τὴν καθιέρωσιν μεγαλοπρεπῶς ἐν τῷ θεάτρῳ μὲν θεωρίας ἐπιτελῶν πάνθ' ὅσα μουσικῆς ἔργα παράγων καὶ ποικίλης ποιητικὰ τέρψεως ἐν δὲ τῷ ἀμφιθεάτρῳ πλήθει μονομάχων τὴν αὐτοῦ δεικνὺς μεγαλόνοιαν ἔνθα καὶ τὴν κατὰ πλῆθος ἀντίταξιν βουληθεὶς γενέσθαι τῶν θεωμένων τέρψιν ἑπτακοσίους ἄνδρας ἑπτακοσίοις μαχησομένους εἰσέπεμψεν κακούργους ὅσους εἶχεν ἀποτάξας εἰς τήνδε τὴν πρᾶξιν ἵν' οἱ μὲν κολασθῶσιν τὸ πολέμου δ' ἔργον γένηται τέρψις εἰρήνης τούτους μὲν οὖν πασσυδὶ διέφθειρεν

---

[130] Schwartz, *Agrippa I*, 140–144.

"He erected many buildings in many other places but he conferred special favours on the people of Berytus. He built them a theatre surpassing many others in its costly beauty; he also built an amphitheatre at great expense, besides baths and porticoes; and in none of these works did he allow either the beauty or the size to suffer by stinting on the expenses. He was also magnificently lavish in his provision at the dedication of them; in the theatre he exhibited spectacles, introducing every kind of music and all that made for a varied entertainment, while in the amphitheatre he showed his noble generosity by the number of gladiators provided. On the latter occasion also, wishing to gratify the spectators by ranging a number of combatants against each other, he sent in seven hundred men to fight another seven hundred. All these men were malefactors set aside for this purpose, so that while they were receiving their punishment, the feats of war might be a source of entertainment in peace-time. In this way he brought about the utter annihilation of these men."

Agrippa acts as other Hellenistic kings had by showcasing his wealth on luxuries for the people. Benefaction truly is the appropriate term for his projects. Inscriptions attached to building projects elsewhere confirm Agrippa's reputation as a benefactor through construction (see 3.4.6). Though Agrippa did not earn the same reputation as his grandfather for construction, he did contribute in many ways to construct new edifices or improve existing buildings.

3.4.5 Coins

In many ways Agrippa's coins express his passion for Rome and its rulers.[131] The imagery, messages, and quality combine to show how Agrippa kept imperial interests at the forefront of his thoughts. Agrippa followed Philip's lead in displaying images of the emperor and his family, in addition to some images of himself. In his second regnal year (Autumn 37–Autumn 38), Agrippa mimicked nearly exactly Gaius' *dupondii* in honor of his recently deceased brothers *Nero et Drusus Caesares*. The obverse reads ΒΑΣΙΛΕΥΣ ΑΓΡΙΠΠΑΣ with Agrippa wearing a diadem and the reverse has ΑΓΡΙΠΠΑ ΥΙΟΥ ΒΑΣΙΛΕΩΣ with Agrippa's son on horseback.[132] In the second coin from his second regnal year, Agrippa mimicked Gaius' sesterius with a portrait of Gaius on the obverse and his three sisters (Julia, Drusilla, and Agrippina) on the reverse.[133] These first two were minted in Paneas since Agrippa controlled no other mint in 37/38. Agrippa only

---

[131] On Agrippa's coins see, A. Burnett "The Coinage of King Agrippa I of Judaea and a New Coin of King Herod of Chalcis," in Bastien, Huvelin, Christol, and Gautier, *Mélanges de numismatique*, 25–38; Meshorer, *Jewish Coinage*, 78–80, 138–141; Meshorer, *Ancient Jewish Coinage*, 55–56; Jensen, *Antipas*, 201–202.

[132] Burnett 1, pl. 3, 1; = Meshorer, *Ancient Jewish Coinage*, 1. Burnett, "Coinage," 27.

[133] Burnett 2, pl. 3, 2; pl. 3, B = Meshorer, *Ancient Jewish Coinage*, 2. Burnett, "Coinage," 27–28. Cf. Burnett 7, pl. 3, 7 = Meshorer, *Ancient Jewish Coinage*, 7 which reads ΑΓΡΙΠΠΑ[and has a diademed head of Agrippa on the obverse and "[u]ncertain standing figures" on the reverse, Burnett, "Coinage," 31.

ruled Philip's tetrarchy as king at this point, and he contested further rule with Antipas. Perhaps this explains the aggressive imitation of the emperor's coinage and overt announcement of his relationship to Gaius. Burnett examines five coin types minted in the fifth regnal year (A.D. 40/41) which carry images of Gaius, Agrippa, Drusilla (Gaius' daughter), and Caesonia (Gaius' wife).[134] The first of these coins shows the pattern of these coins, namely a tribute to the emperor (or his family) and visible/verbal connection to Agrippa.[135] Its obverse reads ΓΑΙΩ[] ΚΑΙΣΑΡΙ ΣΕΒΑΣΤΩ ΓΕΡΜΑΝΙΚΙ[and has a "laureate head of Gaius, to left." The reverse reads ΝΟΜΙΣ ΒΑΣΛΕΩΣ ΑΓΡΙΠΠΑ and has "Germanicus in triumphal *quadriga*; in exergue."[136] A second example honors Agrippa with the title, "friend of Caesar."[137] It bears]ΑΓΡ – ΡΙΠΠΑ ΑΓΡΙΠΠ[with young Agrippa's head on the obverse and ΒΑΣ ΑΓΡΙΠΠ]Α ΦΙΛΟΚΑΙΣΑΡ with a crossed cornucopia on the reverse. Agrippa freely publicized his relationship to the emperor and the honors which he had received.

Under Claudius, the publicizing of such relationships and honors only increased and grew more specific. Three coin types fall into this category. The first has been reconstructed through combining seven specimens to read on the obverse: ΒΑΣ ΑΓΡΙΠΠΑΣ ΣΕΒ ΚΑΙΣΑΡ ΒΑΣ ΗΡΩ[ΔΗΣ].[138] It has King Agrippa and King Herod of Chalcis crowning Emperor Claudius with a wreath. Claudius "stands wearing a toga, *capite velato*." The reverse reads: ΟΡΚΙΑ ΒΑΣ ΜΕ ΑΓΡΙΠΠΑ ΠΡ(ος) ΣΕΒ ΚΑΙΣΑΡΙ[Α Κ(αι) ΣΥ]ΝΚΛΗΤΟΝ Κ(αι) ΔΗΜΟ ΡΩΜ ΦΙΛΙ Κ(αι) ΣΥΝΜΑΧΙ ΑΥΤΟΥ and has a "[w]reath enclosing clasped hands." Burnett translates: "sworn treaty of the great king Agrippa to Augustus Caesar, the Senate and the Roman People: his friendship and alliance."[139] He suggests that the coin refers to "the treaty made between Claudius and Agrippa in A.D. 41 confirming and enlarging his kingdom."[140] The second coin type reads ΤΙΒΕΡΙΟΣ ΚΑΙΣΑΡ ΣΕΒΑΣΤΟΣ ΓΕΡΜ with a "laureate head of Claudius" on the obverse and ΒΑΣΙΛΕΥΣ ΜΕΓΑΣ ΑΓΡΙΠΠΑΣ ΦΙΛΟΚΑΙΣΑΡ with a "[t]emple containing four figures" on the reverse.[141] Many interpretations have been suggested, but Burnett thinks the "conse-

---

[134] Burnett, 4–8; Burnett, "Coinage," 28–31.

[135] Burnett, 4, pl. 3, 4; Meshorer, *Ancient Jewish Coinage*, 2.

[136] Burnett, "Coinage," 28.

[137] Burnett 5, pl. 3, 5; Meshorer, *Ancient Jewish Coinage*, 4. This coin used to be ascribed to Agrippa II, but is now treated as coming from Agrippa I.

[138] Burnett 8, pl. 4, 8; Meshorer, *Ancient Jewish Coinage*, 5.

[139] First and Second Maccabees employ similar language several times (φιλίας καὶ συμμαχίας; 1 Macc 8:17, 20, 31; 10:16; 12:3, 8, 14, 16; 14:18, 40; 15:17; 2 Macc 4:11).

[140] Burnett, "Coinage," 32–35; Meshorer, *Ancient Jewish Coinage*, 55–57. For reference to the ὅρκιά and διάταγμα see *Ant.* 19.275; *War* 2.216.

[141] Burnett 10, pl. 4, 10a–b; Meshorer, *Ancient Jewish Coinage*, 8 and 9.

cration of the treaty [conferring the kingdom to Agrippa] in the Temple of Jupiter on the Capitolene" is the most likely signification.[142] One of the figures may be a pig which was sacrificed in the ceremony.[143] Acknowledging an event in a pagan temple,[144] offering pagan sacrifice, to show allegiance to the Roman emperor and his religion, certainly marks Agrippa as a unique minter among the Jewish kings of the first-century. By referring to an event in Agrippa's political career that took place in a foreign land and neglecting local imagery and events, the king directs his attention and energy toward Rome. His near exact replication of several of Gaius' coins seems to say that he intended to impress the emperor rather than his constituents.

Considering the depth of Agrippa's allegiance to Rome, it is important not to neglect the political/religious tact he showed for the inhabitants of Jerusalem. Agrippa was preoccupied with Rome, but he respected the religious milieu in which he minted (aniconic in Jerusalem, but iconic in the north). The *prutah* minted in Jerusalem avoids an icon, but gets the message out that Agrippa is king (6th regnal year; A.D. 41/42). Its legend reads ΑΓΡΙΠΠΑ ΒΑΣΙΛΕΩΣ and has a picture of a canopy (a sign of royalty). The reverse has three ears of grain symbolizing the fertility of the land of Israel.[145] Agrippa adeptly advanced his message without explicitly offending Jewish sensibilities. This coin enjoyed extensive circulation. It is unique among Agrippa's coins for not having an image or explicit reference to Rome.

3.4.6 Benefactions

Both literary and archaeological evidence attribute benefactions to Agrippa I. Josephus, as noted above, contrasts Agrippa with his grandfather Herod in that the latter was evil whereas the former was a liberal benefactor (*Ant.* 19.327–331, esp. 328). Josephus employs specific terminology of benefaction in this description (εὐεργετικὸς; ἐν δωρεαῖς καὶ μεγαλοφρονῆσαι; φιλότιμος; χαρίζεσθαι; τῷ βιοῦν ἐν εὐφημίᾳ χαίρων). He also refers to

---

[142] Burnett, "Coinage," 35–37; Suetonius *Claud* 25.5; *War* 2.216; followed by Meshorer, *Treasury*, 98; Jensen, *Antipas*, 201–202.

[143] Burnett is not completely certain about this identification. See Meshorer, *Ancient Jewish Coinage*, 248–249; Jensen, *Antipas*, 201–202; Schwartz, *Agrippa I*, 131.

[144] The practice of putting buildings on coins is particularly Roman (their fascination with building being expressed therein), Howgego, "Coinage and Identity," 4. Howgego identifies "Romanness" by this fact in Spain and among client kings including Herod Philip and Agrippa I. A. Burnett, "Buildings and Monuments on Roman Coins," in *Roman Coins and Public Life Under the Empire: E. Togo Salmon Papers II* (ed. G. M. Paul and Michael Ierardi; Ann Arbor: University of Michigan Press, 1999), 137–164, here 153–162; *RPC* 2.309.

[145] Jensen, *Antipas*, 202; Meshorer, *Treasury*, 96–98, 120.

practices noteworthy among benefactors (banquets, lavish gifts, extending oneself in generosity to the point of personal injury).[146] In the subsequent paragraphs Josephus elaborates upon some of these benefits. In Berytus he built a theater and amphitheater and funded spectacles and games, including gladiatorial competitions.[147] He had lavish parties and banquets, including a birthday celebration which was considered a pagan practice by some, but was also a mark of benefactors.[148] It seems that Agrippa intentionally operated as a benefactor among his people, and Josephus ascribes this terminology to his actions. Such generosity was a hallmark of Hellenistic kings (Aristotle, *Pol* 1310b34ff, 1286b10f; Polybius 5.11.6.). Toward the end of the first-century B.C. Greeks began to attribute the phrase "common benefactors" ('Ρωμαῖοι οἱ κοινοὶ εὐεργέται) to the Romans as a way of signifying their superiority and the uniqueness of the power/generosity they wielded.[149] By the time of Augustus and Julius Caesar the ascription moved from the collective Rome to individuals. Very few received this description, but it may be that Josephus approximates the unique terminology of "common benefactor" to Agrippa by claiming that he was πρὸς πάντας τὸ εὐεργετικὸν ὅμοιον τοῖς ἀλλοεθνέσιν ἦν φιλάνθρωπος (*Ant*. 19.330). Whether or not Josephus intended this nuance, he describes Agrippa as a benefactor whose penchant for delivering luxury goods in an effort to increase his public reputation certainly validates the description.

Several inscriptions confirm Agrippa's generosity and the use of the term benefactor to describe his actions. A few features stand out. Dedicatory inscriptions connected to Agrippa employ a more elevated vocabulary with "exaggerated" descriptions when compared to Herod I.[150] Benefaction inscriptions have been primarily found outside of his realm (e.g., Heliopolis, Athens). Specific reference to Agrippa's being φιλοκαῖσαρ, φιλορώμαιος, and εὐεργέτης surface regularly (e.g., *OGIS* 419, 420,[151] 425,[152] 428). In regard to the exaggerated language adopted in these inscriptions, Richardson highlights the frequent use of μέγας and κύριος (*OGIS* 418–

---

[146] See Danker, *Benefactor*, 45–6, 419–425; Danker, "Endangered Benefactor."

[147] Herod the King and Agrippa II did the same in Berytus (*War* 1.422; *Ant*. 20.211–212).

[148] *Ant*. 19.321; *m.Avodah Zarah* 1:3. Schwartz, *Agrippa I*, 133; E. E. Urbach, "The Rabbinical Laws of Idolatry in the Second and Third Centuries in the Light of Archaeological and Historical Facts," *IEJ* 9 (1959): 149–165, 229–245, 239–241; Schürer I. 346–348 n. 26.

[149] Erskine, "Common Benefactors."

[150] Richardson, *Herod*, 209–211.

[151] Agrippa I or II—Schwartz follows *OGIS* in ascribing it to Agrippa II, Schwartz, *Agrippa I*, 136 n. 125; Richardson links it with Agrippa I, Richardson, *Herod*, 210.

[152] *OGIS* links 425 to Agrippa II, but Richardson regards it as a reference to Agrippa I, Richardson, *Herod*, 210.

428).¹⁵³ Listing attributes such as pious, "friend of Caesar", "friend of Rome", and benefactor gives the impression that these inscriptions attempt to go over-the-top in expressing gratitude. Agrippa earned this gratitude in many areas outside of his realm. For example, Agrippa is included among the benefactors of Athens in an inscription thanking King Eumenes and his family for generosity (*OGIS* 428).¹⁵⁴

Ἡ βουλὴ ἡ ἐξ Ἀρείου πάγου καὶ
ἡ βουλὴ τῶν χ καὶ ὁ δῆμος Ἰου
λίαν Βερενείκην βασίλισσαν
μεγάλην Ἰουλίου Ἀγρίππα βασι
λέως θυγατέρα καὶ μεγάλων
βασιλέων εὐεργετῶν τῆς πό
λεως ἔκγονον διὰ τῆς προνοί
ας τοῦ ἐπιμελητοῦ τῆς πόλε
ως Τιβ(ερίου) Κλαυδίου Θεογένους
Παιανιέως

The council of the Areopagus and
The council of those and the people to
Julias Berenice the great queen
Daughter of Julius Agrippa the king
And granddaughter of the great
Kings, benefactors of the city
Through the provision/foresight
Of the epimeletes of the city
Tiberius Claudius Theogenous
Praise. (Author's translation)

Although Berenice receives the direct praise for benefiting the city she stands in a long line of benefactors. Agrippa, her father, is the explicit link between this great queen and the μεγάλων βασιλέων εὐεργετῶν who had done so much to improve Athens.¹⁵⁵ Agrippa receives recognition as one king among many benefactors of Athens, and in other inscriptions he receives individual recognition for being a friend of Caesar, friend of Rome, and benefactor. An inscription in Siʻa thanks Agrippa II, and recognizes Agrippa I as friend of Caesar, pious, and friend of Rome (*OGIS* 419):

---

¹⁵³ Richardson, *Herod*, 209–211.
¹⁵⁴ Getzel M. Cohen, *The Hellenistic Settlements in Syria, the Red Sea Basin, and North Africa* (Joan Palevsky Imprints in Classical Literature; Berkeley: University of California Press, 2006), 88; M. Holleaux, *Études d'épigraphie et d'histoire grecques* (6 vols.; Paris: Librarie d'Amerique et d'Orient Adrien Maisonneuve, 1952–1968), 2:127–147; S. B. Downey, *History of Antioch in Syria: From Seleucus to the Arab Conquest* (Princeton: Princeton University Press, 1961), 95 n. 42. *Editio Princeps*, Fränkel.
¹⁵⁵ Schwartz, *Agrippa I*, 132 n. 101. Harmand, *Le patronat sur les collectivités publiques*.

Ἐπὶ Βασιλέως μεγάλου Ἀγρίππα Φιλοκαίσαρος Εὐσεβοῦς καὶ Φιλορωμαι[ί]
ου τοῦ ἐκ βασιλέως μεγάλου Ἀγρίππα Φιλοκαίσαρος Εὐσεβοῦς καὶ"Φϊ
λορωμαίου Ἀφαρεὺς ἀπελεύθερος και Ἀγρίππας υἱός ἀνέθηκαν
To the great king Agrippa, friend of Caesar, pious and friend of Romans,
the son of the great king Agrippa, friend of Caesar, pious and friend of Romans
Apharus, a freedman, and his son dedicate [this] ... (Author's translation)[156]

Agrippa receives recognition at the Acropolis in Athens for benefactions (εὐεργεσίας) given to the city (*OGIS* 427):

[ὁ δ]ῆμος
[Βασι]λέα Ἡρώδην Εὐσεβῆ καὶ
Φιλοκαὶσαρα [ἀ]ρετῆς ἕνεκα
καί εὐεργεσίας.

"The people/
to Herod the pious (eusebes) King and friend of the Emperor/
because of his moral excellence (arete) and good works."[157]

Dittenberger identifies the Herod of this inscription as Agrippa I, but Richardson thinks it refers to Herod I for three reasons: (1) the use of "king" seems to be a special title for Herod, (2) the location in Athens has many inscriptions to Herod I, and (3) the description of the honorand resembles many others dedicated to Herod.[158] Richardson seems to draw too strong a conclusion from such slim evidence. Agrippa also had the title "king" granted to him (see, *OGIS* 418, 419, 420, 422; *SEG* 16.490). Josephus mentions the benefactions conferred on Athens by Agrippa and there are other inscriptions which confirm this (*OGIS* 428). The description in this inscription is general and short allowing that a number of honorands may be so described not simply Herod I. It seems best not to depart from Dittenberger on this inscription. If the inscription does refer to Agrippa I then it is clear evidence of his individual reputation as a benefactor in Athens.

One unique inscription thanking Agrippa (I or II?) for his role as patron of Heliopolis suggests that Agrippa was understood in such Roman terms outside of Palestine. The extant version of the inscription does not elaborate with sufficient detail to confidently ascribe the inscription to either our Agrippa or his son.[159] It stood with a bronze statue. This reconstruction comes from *IGLS* 6.2759 (cf. *ILS* 3.2.8957):[160]

---

[156] Thanks to Ron C. Fay for help in this translation.

[157] *OGIS* 427; cf. *SEG* 12 [1955] 150. Though it possibly refers to Agrippa I (Dittenberger), Richardson argues that it must refer to Herod the King, Richardson, *Herod*, 207–8. *Editio Princeps*, B. D. Merritt, *Hesperia* 21 (1952): 370 n. 14, c. im. Ph. Pl. 93, coll. IG II² 3441. Dated 27–4 B.C.

[158] Richardson, *Herod*, 207–208.

[159] Dessau argues that it refers to Agrippa I, but the editors of both *ILS* and *IGLS* refrained from a conclusion because there is not much evidence for the discussion. Dessau,

[----------*regi*]
magno Ag[*rip*]
pae pio Philocae
sare (sic) et Philoromaeo,
patrono col(oniae).,
pub(lice) fac(tum).
To the great king Agrippa, in honor, friend of Caesar, friend of the Romans, patron of the colony, (statue) erected at the expense of the city (Author's translation)

If the inscription honors Agrippa I then it can be concluded that outside of Palestine Agrippa had earned the reputation of patron, in addition to being recognized as a friend of Caesar and of Rome. He was honored with the erection of a statue to thank him for his generosity. Though the inscription is intriguing and suggestive it cannot be conclusively connected to Agrippa I. It is imprudent to take too much from the inscription, but it is at least possible that Agrippa I was understood as a patron of a city outside of Palestine.

Agrippa I took the trajectory of embracing Roman and Hellenistic culture, introduced to his family by his grandfather, to an extent unattested among those surveyed here. His thorough education in Rome created a person more comfortable among Gentiles than Jews. Early in his life, he began to cultivate strategic friendships with the imperial family, including three emperors, and he learned the lavish habits of those in the capital. He earned the title friend of Caesar, but came close to forfeiting it at several points. He frequently traveled back to Rome after receiving his own territory, but it appears that toward the end of his life he grew disenchanted with the emperor or simply realized that he had nothing more to offer. It is clear that Agrippa operated in Greco-Roman reciprocal terms with complete understanding of friendship and its obligations. It is also quite likely that he learned the more specific practices of benefaction and *patrocinium*. Commentators, both ancient and modern, differ in their assessment of Agrippa. He can be praised for piety or condemned for cruelty; honored for generosity or maligned for frivolity. It is instructive for our study that onlookers assess him through the category of benefaction. Josephus considers him a benefactor to all, but others refuse gratitude out of disrespect for his benefits. Josephus' description of Agrippa as a benefactor intro-

---

Geschichte der romische Kaizerzeit II/2 (1930): 791–792, n. 1. Eilers identifies the patron as Agrippa I, Eilers, *Roman Patrons*, 195.

[160] *Editio princeps*, O. Puchstein, *Jahrbuch* 16 (1901): 155. The French translation given reads: "Au grand roi Agrippa, pieuex, ami de César, ami des Romains, patron de la colonie, (statue) érigée aux frais de la cité." D. Braund, "Four Notes on the Herods," *CQ* 33.1 (1983): 239–242, 242; J. -P. Rey-Coquais, "Syrie romaine, de Pompée à Dioclétien," *JRS* 68 (1978): 44–73. Eilers briefly mentions Agrippa's role in Heliopolis, Eilers, *Roman Patrons*, 195.

duces a section which catalogues some building projects and events which establish his magnificence. Though not as many projects can be listed as his grandfather they are nevertheless significant in the mind of Josephus as truly deriving from a generous spirit. Agrippa's coins indicate his posturing toward Rome. In the majority of those discussed Agrippa connects himself to the emperor or his family. He specifically recalls the treaty which established his friendship and alliance with Rome and confirmed his possession of the kingdom which his grandfather previously held. Agrippa minted these coins first in Paneas then in Caesarea Maritima, but when minting for Jerusalem he avoided offensive images. Thus, the majority of his coins circulated in areas touched by the ministry of the apostles, including those which explicitly cite his friendship with Rome. Finally, both literary and archaeological evidence showed that Agrippa had a reputation as a benefactor, friend of Caesar, and friend of Romans. Josephus describes Agrippa I as a "benefactor to all" which approximates an ascription usually reserved for extraordinary rulers. In Caesarea, Peter describes the ministry of Jesus in similar terms (εὐεργετῶν καὶ ἰώμενος πάντας; Acts 10:38). Several inscriptions employ specific terminology to identify Agrippa with these titles. In regard to the inscriptions discovered in Athens it seems likely that Paul would have read them as he examined the city's statues closely (Acts 17:16–33). He would learn of Agrippa's reputation as a benefactor in a long line of benefactors. Friendship and benefaction dominate the categories discussed above, but it seems possible that Agrippa himself thought along *patrocinium* lines more than his Herodian predecessors. The inscription to Agrippa (I or II) describing him as city patron of Heliopolis, if connected to Agrippa I, gives evidence that he received this title.

3.5 Summary of the Personality Perspective

Hellenistic and Roman ideology definitely penetrated the Herodian family, and several of them operated or were viewed as benefactors. Herod I's attempt to set himself apart as a benefactor earned him an excellent reputation among outsiders, but many within Palestine did not look favorably upon his self-aggrandizing motivations. In inscriptions on monuments and artifacts, contemporaries describe Herod as a benefactor (*Ant.* 15.232–233; 16.209–212; "Stone Weight"; *OGIS* 415). Like the Hellenistic kings who had earned the name in the past, Herod lavished games, spectacles, and monumental buildings both in his realm and outside of it. But upon his death, Josephus and residents of Caesarea forsook the gratitude they had likely shown while he was alive and expressed contempt (*War* 1.400, 429–

430; *Ant.* 14.377–78; *War* 2.84–86; *Ant.* 17.191). His son, Herod Antipas, did not pursue the same level of construction projects, nor did he strongly desire elevation in the ranks of politics during his entire career. Antipas showed some signs of involvement in developing and maintaining friendships with Rome. He devoted a few projects in his realm (Tiberias, Sepphoris) and outside it (Athens) to Rome and its emperor. Josephus describes him as a benefactor in providing for those that came to inhabit the newly founded Tiberias (*Ant.* 18.36–38; *OGIS* 416, 417; *SEG* 16.488). But his affronts toward the Jews (e.g., building on unclean ground, killing John the Baptist) merited scorn from them (e.g., *Ant.* 18.101–129). Philip is a notable exception to the pattern of arousing hatred among the Jews. His region had less stringent Jews and a greater percentage of non-Jews so his attempts to cultivate friendships with Rome were not looked down upon (*War* 2.167–168; *Ant.* 18.27–28, 106–108). He refurbished Caesarea Philippi and its temple, and developed Bethsaida with a new temple in honor of Julia. He also connected himself to Rome on his coins and was the first of the Herodians to imprint images (including the emperor, his family, and Philip himself). A dearth of evidence (both literary and archaeological) prevents in-depth discussion of Philip as benefactor or patron. He had spent considerable time in Rome, but preferred his realm during his reign (e.g., *War* 2.14). He does seem to operate as a benefactor in reconstructing and renaming cities, but without explicit vocabulary this must remain tentative. Agrippa I capably balanced cultivation of Rome and the Jews, at least according to Josephus, but ultimately lost interest in impressing the emperor when he had nothing left to gain (*Ant.* 18.167–168, 289–300). Agrippa cherished the title friend of Caesar which was in peril, but maintained, at several points in his career (*Ant.* 18.143–146, 151–168, 289–300; *In Flaccum* 36–40). He was distinguished from his grandfather for having a beneficent character and for always acting as a benefactor both within and without his territory (*Ant.* 19.328–330, 335–337; *OGIS* 419, 428). One inscription also identifies him as a patron of Heliopolis (*IGLS* 6.2759; cf. *ILS* 3.2.8957). This would accord well with the fact that Agrippa I had spent more time than any of his Herodian predecessors in Rome and with Roman nobility. He could have been understood as "Roman" according to his populace. He certainly understood the intricacies of reciprocity, especially friendship, and functioned within them.

Each of those investigated in this personality perspective had reasonable adeptness in Hellenistic reciprocity. In the literary sources the ideology of friendship surfaces frequently as does benefaction. Patronage arises less often, but it does come up occasionally. All but Philip have the title benefactor employed to describe them at one point. Only Agrippa, possibly, has the title patron given to him. Philip's practice of meeting directly with the people provides an opportunity for the ideology of reciprocity to enter the lower classes. Public inscriptions would also have been on display, if not prominently in Galilee, at least in Jerusalem, Caesarea, Samaria, and outside of Palestine. These would tell of the benefits conferred by the Herodian family and give opportunity for an understanding of the practice to develop.

3.6 Conclusion

Foregoing the conclusions of cross-cultural analysis and attempting instead to investigate the historical *realia* of first-century Palestine challenges the use of sociological patron-client terminology and gives a more accurate perspective of the use of different modes of social interaction in the various regions. Since *patrocinium* was relatively absent (except, later, with Agrippa I) throughout the land, patron-client terminology potentially confuses the study of Palestine. One may be led to believe that Roman ways had taken control when in reality they had only created a veneer in many, but not all, areas. A better category of description would be the more general Greco-Roman idea of reciprocity. It does not necessarily entail all the intricacies of *patrocinium* in all situations, but admits other forms of interchange including friendship (*amicitia*) and benefaction while not excluding *patrocinium*. Verboven's study of patronage and *amicitia* shows how important friendship was in Roman society, and its terminology was often preferred over that of *patrocinium*.[161] D. Braund detects the same pattern which leads him to put forward the paradigm of the "friendly king" in place of "client king."[162] Friendship terminology was found in archaeological and literary evidence in several of our regions and deserves further investigation. Notions of friendship are especially pertinent to Lukan study because of his ubiquitous use of its terminology.[163]

The personality perspective demonstrated the level of Hellenization and Romanization among the Herodian kings and tetrarchs and highlighted how they more or less attempted to meet the ideals of Hellenistic kings. Herod I certainly extended himself in lavish benefactions, but when he was not properly reciprocated he stopped the practice (according to Josephus). In Jerusalem and outside of his realm, Herod had a reputation for being a benefactor and many used that title for him. He also earned the titles friend

---

[161] E.g., Verboven, *Economy*.
[162] Braund, *Friendly King*, 5–7, 23.
[163] Mitchell, "Greet the Friends," 246–248, esp. n. 79. Luke uses "friend" at least in: Luke 7:6, 34; 11:5, 6, 8; 12:4; 14:10, 12; 15:6, 9, 29; 16:9; 21:16; 23:12; Acts 10:24; 19:31; 27:3.

of Caesar, friend of Rome, and king. Josephus chastises Herod for his Hellenistic motivations even while he praises the beauty and grandeur of his creations. Antipas had less zeal for construction projects, but he did cultivate some strategic friendships with Rome. He also earned the title friend of Caesar, but not king. He apparently made less effort in construction projects, but both in his realm (e.g., Tiberias) and outside it (e.g., Cos, Athens) Antipas earned the reputation of being a benefactor. Philip and Agrippa I provide somewhat of a shift in the Herodian family being more overtly Romanized. Philip was the first to advertise his relationship with Rome through images on his coins. He also commemorated and exalted the emperor's wife by renaming a city and constructing a temple in her honor. Refurbishing and renaming Caesarea Philippi was another way that Philip showed his friendship and alliance with Rome. Very little evidence remains in the literary sources about Philip, so it is difficult to tell if he self-consciously attempted to function as a benefactor or patron. Agrippa I was the most thoroughly Romanized of the four leaders surveyed. He felt more at home in Rome (or Caesarea) than in Jerusalem, and deliberately mimicked Roman ways in his coins. He earned the reputation and title of both benefactor and patron in his realm and outside it (e.g., Tyre). He cultivated friendships with Rome, earning the titles friend of Caesar and friend of Rome, but seems to have lost interest in developing them later in life. Josephus praises Agrippa I for his generosity. He repeats the specific vocabulary of benefaction in this praise.

Differentiating the various regions and characters of first-century Palestine allows for more precision and confidence in examining the biblical text. The following chapters investigate Luke to see if he has indeed described the lives and teaching of Jesus and the earliest Christians in benefaction or *patrocinium* categories. Several passages have been adduced as examples of patron-client activity, so these will be the focus of attention.

Chapter 4

Reciprocity, *Patrocinium*, and Benefaction in the Sermon on the Plain (Luke 6:17–38)

Luke has received substantial treatment in studies of patrons, benefactors, and reciprocity. Many of these studies take the form of social-scientific or social-historical investigations. Often a brief citation of a passage from Seneca or an inscription from somewhere in the Roman empire serves as "background" to a passage or verse from Luke-Acts and a commentary follows on Luke's critique or embrace of certain cultural mores. This study attempts to push further by taking this particular aspect of Greco-Roman culture and thoroughly investigating its presence, absence, or alteration in first-century Palestine. Chapters two and three advance evidence which supports the presence of Hellenistic and Roman ways in certain areas of Palestine to greater and lesser extents. They attempt to clarify and specify regions and persons which have explicitly adopted benefaction or *patrocinium*, and also duly appreciate the importance of Jewish culture.

In one study of these relationships as they are described by Luke, Moxnes identifies the need for a more thorough exegesis of passages relevant to the discussion.[1] Moxnes' identification of this need invites the contribution of this book's next three chapters. It is the intent of the next three chapters to take the discussion of reciprocity, benefaction, and *patrocinium* deeper. Three passages which typically surface in these discussions will be treated: Luke 6:17–38; 14:1–24; 22:14–34. At the end of Harrison's work on the language of grace, he suggests that an investigation of "Jesus' searing critique of the hellenistic reciprocity and honour systems – as rendered in Luke's gospel (6:27–38; 14:12–14; 22:24–27) – requires attention." He suggests that Jesus perhaps teaches a replacement of the Hellenistic system with a "distinctly theological understanding of beneficence."[2] The present study takes up these three passages, but extends the limits of the passages to reflect and include their broader contexts. Limitation to three passages allows for a more extended treatment. I will focus on the specific contribution these passages make to a discussion of reciprocity, benefaction, and *patrocinium*. By examining literary, linguistic, and cultural material, it is

---

[1] Moxnes, "Patron-Client," 268.
[2] Harrison, *Language*, 352.

possible to discern if *patrocinium* or benefaction are present in Luke's presentation of Jesus. This is a necessary first step in the process of determining if Luke simply imports his own culture into his gospel or if he accurately situates Jesus in terms available to someone of Jesus' provenance.

Some scholars distance Luke's culture from Jesus' and insert comments to the effect that when Luke employs patrons or benefactors in his discussion he reflects his own culture rather than that of Jesus. The present study takes up this bifurcation.[3] Through its investigation of the cultures of Palestine it is hopefully apparent that in general Jews may have adopted these categories in conversation depending on their location and relationships. Benefaction and *patrocinium* had filtered through many areas of Palestine and likely became topics of conversation. Benefaction in particular had made inroads into Palestine not only among the Hellenistic leaders but also in the Jewish leadership of the Maccabean era. By the time of Jesus benefactions could be found in many areas of Palestine. Rather than taking up the criteria for identifying the authentic material related to the historical Jesus (e.g., multiple attestation, dissimilarity),[4] this study asks the broader question of historical plausibility. If it is found that Luke attributes to Jesus familiarity with reciprocity, benefaction, and *patrocinium*, is there reason to believe that this plausibly reflects a person in Jesus' social situation? Could a person like Jesus, as he is described in the four canonical accounts, have taken up these categories and referred to them in his own program? The point of the investigation is not to isolate specific sayings as authentic or inauthentic, but it is rather to question whether such a critique of benefaction and/or *patrocinium* by Jesus is plausible, and whether it "fits" with first-century Jewish social realities. It is also appropriate to identify differences between what Jesus may have intended with a certain phrase and what people from different backgrounds (e.g., Jewish villager, Hellenistic visitor, or Roman leader) may have conceived him to be saying. The focus here is on historical plausibility, the meaning of Jesus' teaching, and its reception by his original audiences.

The following three chapters break down into four main sections. The first begins by examining details which may shed light on Jesus' involvement with or awareness of benefaction and/or *patrocinium*. I thus seek to expand the cultural influences beyond Galilee and incorporate as much as possible of the relevant cultures Jesus likely encountered. The next three sections (section 4.2; ch. 5, ch. 6) follow roughly the same outline as one another. Each section exegetes individual passages in Luke. Each begins by identifying scholars who adopt benefaction, *patrocinium*, or reciprocity

---

[3] E.g., Braun, *Feasting*, 99; Rohrbaugh, "City," 141.

[4] E.g., Theissen and Winter, *Plausibilitätskriterium*; idem, *Plausible Jesus*; Theissen, "Historical Scepticism"; Freyne, *Galilee and Gospel*, 20–25; Jensen, *Antipas*, 47–48.

as an explanatory paradigm for the passage. It then identifies a starting and ending point for the passage, addresses relevant intertextual connections, and addresses the particular teaching of the passage. Before one can determine if Luke (mistakenly) imports *patrocinium* and benefaction into the teaching of Jesus, it must be determined if Luke in fact uses those categories at all. Literary, linguistic, and cultural analyses will clarify the presence or absence of these categories in Luke's writing. Brief references to redaction and source critical questions further clarify the specific content of Luke's presentation. The conclusions of each section attempt to connect the teaching with the material uncovered in chapters two and three. After determining if *patrocinium* and benefaction are in fact evident in Luke's writing, a case will be made that Luke does not import his culture into Jesus' teaching but instead it is concluded that a person of Jesus' provenance could have adopted the ideology (and sometimes terminology) present in Luke's writing. Evidence of Jesus' critique of benefaction, *patrocinium*, or reciprocity will be briefly summarized in the final section of each chapter and expanded upon in the final chapter.

4.1 Modes of Cultural Transmission in the Ministry of Jesus

Several details in the Gospels suggest potential circumstances under which Jesus could have become familiar with non-Jewish cultures in the areas both in and around Galilee. Details such as the occupation, relationships, or status of an individual whom Jesus encountered may have a role in developing a theological or instructional point, but often they arise without such an intention. They are often ancillary details which can be clues toward identifying people from whom Jesus learned. Travel through different regions also provides an opportunity for insight into different cultures. Descriptions of Jesus' ministry travels give insight into the possibility of his learning about the various ways that different peoples lived. These details give clues about the types of people and cultures that Jesus interacted with and show that his cultural influences were not limited to his Galilean upbringing.

The following paragraphs identify several details deemed relevant for understanding how Jesus learned of different cultures or ways of interacting. I will specifically be looking for avenues through which Jesus may have become familiar with *patrocinium*, benefaction, and/or reciprocity. Investigation begins with a survey of encounters and relationships Jesus had in his teaching ministry and travels. These paragraphs call attention to the cities which Jesus is said to have visited, recall the findings of the previous chapter, and argue that Jesus may have acquired an understanding of

4.1 Modes of Cultural Transmission in the Ministry of Jesus

different cultures while traveling. Following this, a survey of Jesus' awareness of Herodian rulers demonstrates another avenue through which he might have learned more specifically the Hellenistic and/or Roman ways of the elite. It has been shown in the previous chapter whether and to what extent each of the pertinent members of the Herodian family had adopted benefaction or *patrocinium*. This discussion provides a historically plausible reading of the ways in which Jesus learned of reciprocity, benefaction, and, to a lesser extent, *patrocinium*.

4.1.1 Evidence from Jesus' Travels and Encounters

Jesus had conversations and relationships with several people who lived in more Hellenistic locations or interacted with officials known to have been familiar with benefaction. A few conversations suggest that Jesus interacted with "Hellenists" who were at least Greek speakers and were perhaps culturally "Hellenistic." Inscriptions, coins, and papyri combine to suggest that Greek and Aramaic functioned as lingua franca in Palestine (see sections 2.2.3; 2.2.4), though "the Latin language played only a minor role."[5] S. E. Porter sets forth four passages which he suggests were originally spoken in Greek by Jesus (Mark 7:25–30/Matt 15:21–28; John 12:20–28; Matt 8:5–13/Luke 7:2–10; Mark 15:2–5/Matt 27:11–14/Luke 23:2–5/John 18:29–38).[6] He provides three reasons for this conclusion. (1) The audience in these episodes would perhaps not have known a Semitic language, or it would not have been their primary language. (2) The evangelists do not include an interpreter or offer the remark "which is interpreted." (3) The pace of the conversation, specifically between Pilate, the Jews, crowd, leaders, and Jesus, makes it unlikely an interpreter was present.

The first of these stories, Jesus' interaction with the Syrophoenician woman, is set in the region of Tyre (and Sidon)[7] and involves Jesus' distinction between Jews and outsiders (Mark 7:24–30; Matt 15:21–28). Mark describes her as a Ἑλληνίς and Συροφοινίκισσα τῷ γένει (7:26). She is definitely not a Hebrew since Jesus excludes her from the lost house of Israel (Matt 15:24). G. Theissen suggests that the "Hellenization" of this woman could be found in terms of culture and language. Josephus' comment on the Jewish resident who had become Greek in both language and

---

[5] Schnabel, *Mission*, 1.201–203.

[6] Stanley E. Porter, "Jesus and the Use of Greek in Galilee," in Meyers, *Galilee*, 123–154, 136. If Luke's version of the healing of the centurion's servant is original (Luke 7:2–10) it would not support this argument as well as Matthew's version (Matt 8:5–13) because the Jewish emissaries would likely have spoken Aramaic, ibid., 151.

[7] NA²⁶ excludes "and Sidon" from Mark 7:24 while retaining it in Matthew 15:21. Though the variant has strong external support in Mark (e.g., ℵ, A, B, 33) it is likely a harmonization.

soul indicates that such Hellenization was possible (*Apion* 1.178–180; see section 2.2.5 *Tyre*). It is likely that the Syrophoenician woman was a Greek speaker from a region heavily influenced by Hellenistic culture, but one cannot be certain how much of Hellenistic culture she embraced. In a few Gospel stories, Jesus interacts with others from the region of Tyre and Sidon who may have been similarly Hellenistic ([Matt 11:21–22]; Mark 3:8; 7:24, 31; Luke 6:17; [10:13–14]). Residents of Tyre expressed themselves in euergetistic inscriptions (*Ant.* 14.185–267), and identified some Romans as patrons of their city (M. Aemilius Scaurus; Ti. Iulius Alexander; *IGR* 3.1102; Eilers, *Roman Patrons*, C153). It is possible that Jesus saw an inscription honoring a benefactor or patron and he may have conversed about this while in the Tyrian home.

Among the crowds, many from the Decapolis also attended Jesus' teaching and benefited from his healing ministry (Matt 4:25; Matt 8:28–34//Mark 5:1–21; Luke 8:26–40). Though that region had a mixture of cultures it showed pockets of Hellenization with which Jesus may have become familiar when an onlooker approached Jesus for healing or explanation.[8] The Decapolis held many different cultures (e.g., Graeco-Macedonian, Arab, and Jewish), and several of them expressed Greco-Roman sentiments and specifically practiced benefaction (Mark 5:1–20/Matt 8:28–9:1/Luke 8:26–40; Mark 7:31). Monuments to Greco-Roman cults in a few of its cities (e.g., theaters, monumental gates, and temples in, e.g., Hippos, Gadara, and Scythopolis) highlight the extent of the Hellenization in some of its parts (see section 2.2.5 *Smaller Cities*). But eastern, "Arab", and Jewish cultures co-existed in the region so one should not assume that any and all persons Jesus faced in the region were Hellenistic. It was argued in the previous chapter that interregional trade increased in Capernaum during the time when Jesus counted it as his hometown (section 2.2.3 *Capernaum*). He would have encountered Gentiles (and Jews) from the Decapolis passing through his own city even without traveling to the Decapolis.

Some scholars tend to limit the possibility of an encounter between Jesus and Hellenism to a potential time in Sepphoris or Tiberias, but several other travel locations would certainly have offered a more thorough encounter with non-Jewish culture. Sepphoris, it has been shown, was less Hellenized than many scholars propose. Its government was Jewish; its theater and temples were finished after the era of Jesus; and its archaeological remains support Jewish religious observance (100 stone vessel fragments, twenty *miqvaoth*, no pig bones, Second Temple Jewish tombs; see section 2.2.3 *Sepphoris*). It did begin a process toward Hellenization in

---

[8] Lichtenberger, *Dekapolis*; Bowsher, "Decapolis"; Jensen, *Antipas*, 179; Ball, *Rome*, 181.

the time of Jesus, but during his years of ministry it was only in its Hellenistic beginnings. Tiberias was slightly further along on the path toward Hellenization, but it was not as thoroughly Hellenistic as some imagine (see section 2.2.3 *Tiberias*). Antipas' construction of Tiberias, and consequent residence in that location, may have started a process toward Hellenization around A.D. 18/19. Antipas' actions in the area were described as those of a benefactor and he had earned a reputation as a benefactor outside of his realm (*Ant.* 18.37–38; *OGIS* 416, 417; see section 3.2.6). Nevertheless, the city still contained indicators of Jewishness (stone vessels, a *miqveh*, and ossuaries). Jesus had followers from Tiberias (John 6:23). As Hellenization began in Tiberias Jesus would have grown familiar with Antipas and perhaps the ideology of benefaction. His followers from that region may have added further insight.

Jesus also had long term relationships with three disciples for whom Bethsaida was home (John 1:44; 12:21). That city had Hellenistic, Jewish, and even Roman cultural influences (Hellenistic fineware; [Jewish] limestone vessels; coins with imperial images, temple to Rome, Augustus, and Livia; see section 2.2.5 *Bethsaida*). Philip the tetrarch's efforts to show allegiance to Rome do not find parallels among the common people in the archaeological record. This is suggested by the relatively small distribution of Hellenistic fineware which would have been used by common people. However, Jewish revolt against Philip's Hellenization/Romanization program is also absent suggesting that Jews in this city accommodated the cultural intrusion to some extent. It is instructive that when "some Greeks" ("Ελληνές τινες)[9] come to Palestine they approach the disciples who hail from Bethsaida for information (12:21). Jesus may or may not have had contact with these Greeks, but the story reinforces the assessment of Bethsaida's culture given above. Jesus' relationship with the three disciples from Bethsaida would have afforded him the opportunity to learn of Hellenistic and Roman lifestyles. Philip the tetrarch's expressions of reciprocity (benefaction, *patrocinium*, or otherwise) could have become familiar to Jesus in his conversations with these disciples since Philip the tetrarch had a reputation for interacting with his people (*Ant.* 18.107; see section 3.3.3). Jesus' disciples may have been familiar with benefaction and/or *patrocinium* early in their lives and discussed these practices with Jesus while they ministered together.

Two well-known stories put Jesus into contact with Samarians whose cultural ties to Hellenism were highlighted in the previous chapter (John

---

[9] Whether these are Jews from the Diaspora, proselytes from the Greek-speaking world, God-fearers from the Decapolis, or simply curious Greek-speakers is not imperative for the argument of this section since all that needs to be proven is that some with more affinity toward Hellenistic culture interacted with Jesus. Carson, *John*, 435–436.

4:1–43; Luke 17:11–19; see section 2.2.5 *Samaria*). Debate surrounds the description of Sychar as a πόλις τῆς Σαμαρείας (John 4:5), but Hellenism had entered Samaria in both cities and villages so it is not necessary to prove that Sychar was a πόλις, in the technical sense, before one suggests that Jesus therein encountered Hellenism.[10] The Hellenization of Samaria before the time of Jesus brought a Greek style constitution, stadium, and temple. Renaming Samaria as Sebaste (Greek for *imperator*) shows Herod I's desire to connect himself to Rome (*Ant.* 15.296). Samaritans and their governors expressed themselves in terms of benefaction at times (*Ant.* 15.296–298; 12.258–261). Jesus encountered people from this culture in his teaching ministry. In John's episode Jesus has time to grow familiar with Samarian culture since he stayed two days before leaving again for Galilee (John 4:40, 43). He may have had opportunity to see the stadium or temple and likely knew of the purpose behind the city's renaming. Benefactions like these had been constructed in Samaria and Jesus may have discussed these buildings and messages as he proclaimed his own kingdom while traveling through Samaria.

Probably the most likely source, and definitely the most explicit, through which Jesus learned of benefaction and/or *patrocinium* would be two of the women mentioned in Luke 8:1–3 who financially supported his ministry. Mary and Joanna were women of means whose financial and political connections probably helped Jesus to become familiar with "the Herodian sphere of influence."[11] As Tiberias developed into an economic hub, Magdala (Tarichaeae) likely adjusted its fishing industry to suit a growing need. Mary probably earned her nickname while traveling, since one is less likely to be known by city of origin within that city. Sawicki suggests that this was business travel undertaken as Magdala increased its lake-related industries in connection with the construction of Tiberias.[12] Mary may have met Joanna while traveling to Tiberias where Joanna resided. Joanna was probably from Tiberias since her husband served Antipas who moved his capital to the new city. Whether Sawicki's recreation of this relationship's beginnings stands or falls is not the most important issue. In regard to Mary it is more important that she traveled (earning the nickname) and earned enough money to support Jesus. Sawicki infers that the traveling was business travel which allowed her to gain familiarity with elite and Hellenistic ways. For Joanna, her husband's occupation

---

[10] To my knowledge Zangenberg, "Samaria," is the latest in the debate about cities and villages in Samaria. He concludes that Samaria had Hellenistic and Jewish elements in both city and countryside, but cautions that archaeological investigation is still in the initial stages.

[11] Sawicki, *Crossing*, 133.

[12] Sawicki, *Crossing*, 133–135, 41–53.

(ἐπιτρόπου Ἡρῴδου), and therefore boss (Antipas), brought her into the inner circles of Galilean politics.[13] Joanna might have been the conduit through which Jesus learned of Antipas' feelings towards him and of how Antipas learned of the ministry of Jesus (Luke 9:7). Jesus' familiarity with the Herodian family will be discussed below, but here it is important to note that Jesus had plenty of time to discuss with Joanna their ways of living. He could have an insider's look at Antipas' motivations for constructing Tiberias and relocating its people (see section 3.2.6). The investigation of Antipas in the previous chapter yielded a few pertinent conclusions. Antipas did not build an international reputation as a benefactor to the same degree as his father, but he did attain this title in a few cities (*OGIS* 416, 417; *SEG* 16.488). Josephus ascribes this title (εὐεργέτης) to him for his construction of Tiberias (*Ant.* 18.37–38). Antipas functioned as a benefactor and friend (e.g., *Ant.* 18.101–105), but he allowed his relationship with Rome to taper off in the later years of his reign. If Antipas behaved as a benefactor (so, Josephus) or patron (an assumption not confirmed by textual or archaeological evidence), Joanna could have explained this to Jesus while she followed him. Antipas primarily operated as a benefactor and friend without intense, long-lasting interest in fostering a relationship with Rome (see section 3.2.2).

The Synoptics mention a visit to the area of Caesarea Philippi, a visit which would have developed Jesus' understanding of Hellenistic and Roman religion and culture (Matt 16:13–16; Mark 8:27–29; [Luke 9:18–20]; see sections 2.2.5 *Smaller Cities*; 2.2.6; 3.3).[14] Matthew describes the location as going εἰς τὰ μέρη Καισαρείας τῆς Φιλίππου, while Mark identifies it as εἰς τὰς κώμας Καισαρείας τῆς Φιλίππου. The architectural main feature of the city was the temple dedicated to Caesar and Rome. While in the vicinity of this city Jesus would likely have learned of Herod I's construction of this tribute to Roman superiors along with Philip's recent refurbishment and the addition of his name to the city's title. Philip expressed his allegiance to Rome explicitly by building a temple to Livia-Julia in Bethsaida, putting images of the emperor and his family on coins (e.g., Augustus, Tiberius, Livia-Julia), and changing the city's name to honor the emperor (see sections 3.3.2, 3.3.4, 3.3.5).[15] Jesus would have learned of loyalty to Rome, both in the temple and the coins which Philip had just

---

[13] On the status of one whose spouse had such a position and the potential difficulties connected to her desire for joining Jesus see Green, *Luke*, 320–321.

[14] For this assessment of Caesarea Philippi, see, Freyne, *Jesus, a Jewish Galilean*, 54–56. On Caesarea Philippi, see, Schnabel, *Mission*, 1.253–254; section 2.2.5 *Smaller Cities*.

[15] See, Strickert, "Coins of Philip"; Jensen, *Antipas*, 198–200; Meshorer, *Jewish Coinage*, 76–77, 135–136.

minted. He would perhaps have seen some of the monumental constructions since the temple had been located in a spot visible from great distances.[16] Caesarea Philippi was probably the most overtly pro-Roman region that Jesus visited. He would likely have encountered the ethic of reciprocity and its specific forms, benefaction and *patrocinium*.

Jesus' visits to Jerusalem would have introduced him to benefaction ideology. It is debated how often Jesus actually went to Jerusalem (whether as a child or as an adult). It is debated how often Jesus would have visited Jerusalem because some contend that Galileans looked askance toward Jerusalem and its temple and therefore would not have adopted it as a pilgrimage site. This view has been called into question because increasingly scholars conclude that Galilee was more Jewish than Hellenistic, that a focus on stratigraphy decreases the evidence of tension between city and country, and that the repopulation of Galilee was likely of Judean immigrants.[17] There was little cultural or economic reason for animosity between Galileans and Jerusalem. A story relating the practice of Gamaliel, "one of the foremost contemporary authorities in Judaism," tells of him sitting with elders instructing the people of Upper and Lower Galilee on the steps of the temple (*t. Sanhedrin* 2.6).[18] It is plausible that the story of Jesus' family visiting the Jerusalem Temple as a child was a historical event (Luke 2:22–35), even if certain elements have historical difficulties connected to them (e.g., purification of the two rather than just the woman, naming the child after eight days).[19]

The Gospels indicate that Jesus visited Jerusalem prior to his Passion. John's Gospel differs with the Synoptics in his description of three journeys to Jerusalem by Jesus (John 7:2–10; 11:17–18; 12:12). D. A. Carson coordinates three mentions of Jerusalem in Luke's "travel narrative" with these three visits in John (Luke 9:51–53; 13:22; 17:11).[20] It is safer to conclude that Luke does not intend chronological and geographical precision in this travel narrative, and that he allows for different visits to Jerusalem during this general time period of Jesus' ministry. Luke collects stories with mention of Jerusalem to serve the theological purpose of highlighting the role Jerusalem will play in the ministry of Jesus. Events in this section typically do not take place in specific locations suggesting that geographi-

---

[16] Netzer, *Architecture of Herod*, 218–222.

[17] Jensen, *Antipas*, 5–7, provides a summary with sufficient bibliography.

[18] Dan Bahat, "Jesus and the Herodian Temple Mount," in Charlesworth, *Archaeology*, 300–308, 307.

[19] Green, *Luke*, 140–141.

[20] D. A. Carson, "Matthew," in *The Expositor's Bible Commentary* (vol. 8; ed. F. E. Gaebelein; Grand Rapids: Zondervan, 1984), 1–599, 408–409, in Schnabel, *Mission*, 1.257–258.

cal progression is not the main issue.²¹ E. J. Schnabel argues that Jesus had significant ministry in Jerusalem and Judea before his passion on three main grounds: (1) Jesus had relationships with people who showed him hospitality in Bethany which was less than two miles away (Luke 10:38–42; Matt 26:6–13/Mark 14:3–9/John 12:1–8). (2) Jesus had a relationship with someone who could provide him a donkey on short notice (Mark 11:3). (3) Jesus had a relationship with someone who could provide an upper room to enjoy his final meal (Mark 14:13–15).²² It seems quite likely that Jesus visited Jerusalem on several occasions before his passion. No cultural struggle prevented him from this action and each of the four gospels hints or explicitly claims that he made occasional visits. If the passion were his only visit to Jerusalem, an unlikely conclusion in my opinion, the understanding gained while on the visit would not have impacted his previous teaching. However, new understanding gained while on this trip to Jerusalem could have influenced his final teaching to his disciples, among which is a comparison to the benefactors of the Gentiles (Luke 22:24–30).

While in Jerusalem he would have seen large monuments dedicated to superiors and euergetistic inscriptions honoring those who had made various donations. Herod's elaborate Temple reconstruction had been motivated by a Hellenistic love of honor (φιλοτιμία; *Ant.* 15.271). His reputation as a benefactor is attested in the stone weight mentioned previously (see section 2.2.4; "Stone Weight"). He dedicated portions of the temple to various Roman superiors (e.g., Antony). The temple also contained at least one inscription commemorating a benefactor who had made its construction possible (*SEG* 1277; cf. 1 Macc 11:37; 14:26). Benefactors expressed themselves in other projects in Jerusalem as well (1 Macc 14:25–49; *SEG* 8.170). While in Jerusalem, Jesus would most likely have heard stories of Hasmonean, Herodian, and Hellenistic benefactors. Josephus offers some Jewish sentiment about Herod and those who followed his approach. He disapproves of Herod's penchant for taking honor for himself which properly belongs to God (*Ant.* 15.328–330; 16.153, 158). It is laudable to be generous, but ungodly to inappropriately take God's honor as one's own (*Ant.* 16.158–159; *War* 1.408–410). Jesus' understanding of benefaction would have developed further from these experiences and perhaps have given him a taste for the local response to such persons.

---

²¹ Schnabel, *Mission*, 1.257–258; I. H. Marshall, *The Gospel of Luke: A Commentary on the Greek Text* (NIGTC 3; Grand Rapids: Eerdmans, 1978), 152.
²² Schnabel, *Mission*, 1.259.

4.1.2 Evidence from the Herodian Family

Since the Herodian family stands out among others in Palestine in regard to Hellenization and Romanization, Jesus' knowledge of their ways of life suggests familiarity with the ideology of benefaction, *patrocinium*, and reciprocity in general. There is explicit evidence in the gospels that Jesus could have been familiar with Herod I, Archelaos, Herod Antipas, Philip the tetrarch, Herodias (and the other "Herod Philip"),[23] and some Herodians. Although Herod I died shortly after Jesus' birth, Jesus and his family definitely knew about him. Besides the grandiose monuments he constructed in Palestine, Herod had attempted to kill Jesus (Matt 2:13–15). Mary and Joseph probably heard initial details of the plan when the magi arrived (Matt 2:8–12), but more details of the story would have come over the years as different mothers discussed with one another (and Mary) their own tragic tale. The couple apparently knew Herod well enough that the angel did not need to elaborate or prove Herod's plan to kill their son (Matt 2:13). It seems likely that Jesus' parents and family would have recounted the story to Jesus when he was old enough to understand. Other stories about Herod would complement and fill out the description. His reputation as a benefactor in Jerusalem and outside of it was publicized in his construction projects and on inscriptions (see section 3.1; "Stone Weight"). Herod himself operated in a more eastern fashion as a benefactor and no evidence has surfaced which identifies him as a patron (see section 3.4.6). His relationship with M. Agrippa does indicate that he understood *patrocinium* even if he did not himself receive this title (*CIG* 3609; Nicolaus of Damascus, *FGrHist* 90 F 134). Herod I would likely have been the first benefactor Jesus' family encountered and the first example of the positive and negative aspects of that ideology. Jesus likely learned of benefaction in the early years of his life in conversations about Herod I.

Jesus' family was also aware of Archelaos who took over upon his father's death but was subsequently replaced by Rome because of ineptitude (*Ant.* 17.250–264, 286–297).[24] Joseph responded to news of Archelaos' reign by avoiding Judea and instead going to Galilee (Matt 2:19–23). Some see the debacle with Archelaos and Rome behind Jesus' parable of the pounds (Luke 19:11–15).[25] In the parable Jesus may simultaneously criti-

---

[23] I have adopted the scholarly concession which conflates the names given to Herodias' first husband as found in Mark 6:17 and *Ant.* 18.109. The concession resolves more issues than it raises, Gary A. Herion, "Herod Philip," *ABD* 3:160–161; David C. Braund, "Philip (Person)," *ABD* 5:310–312.

[24] Schnabel, *Mission*, 1.419.

[25] Schultz, "Jesus as Archelaus"; Freyne, *Galilee and Gospel*, 201. Green and Jeremias consider the parallels with the story of Archelaos as providing historical realism to

cize the Herodian family and the Jewish rulers (including the high priests) who gained their authority from Rome rather than from God. Jeremias sees in the tradition behind Luke's version a comparison to the unexpected return of Archelaos to destroy his detractors.[26] The shortness of Archelaos' reign (4 B.C. to A.D. 6), the youth of Jesus during his reign, and his distance from Galilee decreases the level of familiarity Jesus would have had with him.

Antipas, on the other hand, reigned for a long time (4 B.C. - A.D. 39), during the majority of Jesus' life, and within Jesus' Galilee. For these reasons he is the most immediately important political figure for Jesus. The Gospels relate several stories in which Jesus expresses sentiment about Antipas (Matt 8:20[?]//Luke 9:58[?]; Matt 11:7–8//Luke 7:25; 14:1–12//Mark 6:14–29//Luke 9:7–9; Mark 8:15; Luke 3:1, 18–20; [8:3]; 13:31–32; 23:6–16; cf. Acts 4:27). Luke's narrative provides the most details about Jesus' knowledge of Antipas.[27]

Luke lines up John's and Jesus' ministry with the tenures of Philip and Antipas (3:1). Darr has recently made the case that Luke follows the LXX "prophet-versus-king confrontation" motif in his depiction of Antipas.[28] He begins this motif by introducing the story of John's arrest and murder. This arrest and murder was apparently a widely known series of events since Josephus references it as one of Antipas' worst political mistakes (*Ant.* 18.116–119).[29] It makes sense then that the Gospel writers also relate the story, and for those disciples of Jesus who had come to him from discipleship under John this story would have been quite important (Matt 14:1–12//Mark 6:14–29//Luke 3:18–20). The killing of prophets surfaces a few times in Jesus' teaching and he may include Antipas' murder of John among these atrocities (Luke 11:47–50; 13:33–35; 20:9–18; cf. 6:22–23). For a first-century Galilean Jew, Antipas was an important figure whose treatment of purported prophets received public condemnation.

---

the story, Green, *Luke*, 678; Joachim Jeremias, *The Parables of Jesus* (London: SCM, 1985), 58–59. Cf. Craig Blomberg, *Interpreting the Parables* (Downers Grove: InterVarsity Press, 1990), 217–221; Brent Kinman "Parousia, Jesus, 'A-Triumphal' Entry, and the Fate of Jerusalem (Luke 19:28–44)," *JBL* 118 (1999): 279–294; Adelbert Denaux, "The Parable of the King-Judge (Lk 19,12–28) and Its Relation to the Entry Story (Lk 19,29–44)," *ZNW* 93 (2002): 35–57.

[26] Jeremias, *Parables*, 59. He sees such a difference in background that he postulates the existence of a different parable fused with Matthew's parallel parable of the talents (Matt 25:14–30).

[27] The following paragraphs on Antipas in Luke are dependent on Jensen, *Antipas*, 112–124.

[28] Darr, *Herod the Fox*, 142, 157; Jensen, *Antipas*, 115.

[29] Jensen, *Antipas*, 227–230.

Each of the synoptic gospels relate the story of Antipas's confusion about Jesus' identity and Luke uses the story to point forward to the encounter between Antipas and Jesus during his trial (Matt 14:1–2//Mark 6:14–16//Luke 9:7–9). Luke tells the reader that Antipas was confused (διαπορέω) and that he hoped to one day see (ἐζήτει ἰδεῖν αὐτόν) the prophet from Galilee. According to Luke it was not only Jesus who had knowledge of Antipas, but Antipas who had knowledge of Jesus. This is historically plausible since Jesus would have caused at least as much of a stir among the local population as John had, and our sources indicate that Antipas was agitated enough by John to inquire and intervene. Antipas's role as tetrarch was to keep local uprisings under control and generally to maintain peace in his region. A movement of hundreds (or thousands) led by Jesus would have required at least some investigation.

Antipas's curiosity took a sour turn when some Pharisees warned Jesus that the tetrarch desired to kill him (Luke 13:31–32). Some debate if Antipas actually threatened Jesus, if this was an invention of the Pharisees to get Jesus into the jurisdiction of the Sanhedrin, or if this was the invention of Luke to indict another Roman ruler. Darr, Hoehner, and Jensen conclude that the threat by Antipas was real, but also that it was used by the Pharisees to draw Jesus into Jerusalem so that the Sanhedrin might try him.[30] Jesus responded with a critique of Antipas's reign and a declaration of his intent to continue his God-ordained path despite the Pharisees' warning (13:33–35). Identifying Antipas as a fox (ἀλώπηξ) carries connotations of craftiness, destructiveness, and impotence (Epictetus, *Disc.* 1, 3, 7, 9; *bT Ber.* 61b; Song 2:15; Ezek 13:4).[31] A response by a Jewish Galilean prophet to a threat made by the tetrarch is also historically plausible considering the response made by John to Antipas's marriage to Herodias.

Luke adds to his description of Jesus' trial the encounter between Antipas and Jesus. Luke builds toward this meeting by anticipating the tetrarch's motivation for seeing Jesus earlier in his narrative (9:7–9; 13:31–32). For this reason, Antipas was very glad (ἐχάρη λίαν) about the meeting and hoped to see what he had been waiting for, namely a sign (ἤλπιζέν τι σημεῖον ἰδεῖν ὑπ' αὐτοῦ γινόμενον; 23:8). There is some question whether the story is historical or not, but Hoehner demonstrates that at the time of Jesus infractions were dealt with in the region in which they were committed and J. Nolland, J. A. Fitzmyer, and R. E. Brown have argued for a historical nucleus behind Luke's rendition.[32] It is not necessary to establish

---

[30] Hoehner, *Antipas*, 220; Darr, *Fox*, 175–6; Jensen, *Antipas*, 116.

[31] Jensen, *Antipas*, 117; Johnson, *Luke*, 218 (craftiness and slyness); Green, *Luke*, 536 (impotence); Darr, *Herod the Fox*, 144 (impotence).

[32] Hoehner, *Antipas*, 235–236 (follows Sherwin-White rather than T. Mommsen); Nolland, *Luke*, 1122; Fitzmyer, *Luke*, 1478–1480; R. E. Brown, *A Commentary on the*

the historical veracity of the details of Luke's story since it is only being argued in this section that Jesus had awareness of Antipas. Antipas's curiosity was partially satisfied when he finally met Jesus, but he was frustrated by Jesus' silence and decided to mock and return Jesus to Pilate uncondemned. Luke paints a portrait of Antipas awkwardly responding to the encounter by showing his confusion in dealing with Jesus' silence and Antipas' hesitancy to reach an absolute verdict (23:14–15).[33]

In light of the many explicit references to Antipas in Luke, scholars have proposed a few implicit references to the tetrarch which may add to the portrait of Antipas. Jesus may allude to Antipas (and his coins) by speaking of a reed shaking in the wind. Theissen's suggestion that the reed shaking in the wind refers to Antipas is followed by many exegetes (Luke 7:25; see section 3.2.5).[34] Antipas' coins issued in A.D. 19/20 to commemorate the foundation of Tiberias carry the image of a bowing stalk or reed. Antipas may have intended the symbol as a veiled sign of deference to Roman authority or he may have simply adopted this normal Jewish symbol for innocuous reasons. Theissen suggests that Antipas wavered between wives, capital cities, his view of John the Baptist, and political allegiances. Jesus seems to interpret the symbol in a negative light as a sign of acquiescence to foreign authority. Reed suggests that Jesus alludes to Antipas in indicating that foxes have holes and birds have nests (Luke 9:58).[35] Jesus refers to Antipas as a fox (Luke 13:31) and Antipas's early capital, Sepphoris, means "little bird" (*Zippori*) in Hebrew. Jesus has no home, but Antipas has a palace to enjoy in luxury. These allusions to Antipas could support the notion of Jesus' familiarity with Antipas. In these two episodes Jesus shaped his message in contrast to the lifestyle of Antipas.

Passion Narratives in the Four Gospels: Vol. 1. The Death of the Messiah: From Gethsemane to the Grave (New York: Doubleday, 1994), 785.

[33] Jensen, *Antipas*, 117–121. Jensen describes Antipas' role in the trial as passive, though Darr considers him "thoroughly wicked," *Darr, Fox*, 210. See also Brown, *Death*, 760–786, 671–672 (bibliography); K. Müller, "Jesus vor Herodes: Eine redaktionsgeschichtliche Untersuchung zu Lk 23,6–12," in *Zur Geschichte des Urchistentums* (ed. G. Dautzenberg, Josef Blank, Helmut Merklein, and Karlheinz Müller; Quaestiones Disputatae 87; Frieburg: Herder, 1979), 111–141, 114–116; M. L. Soards, "Tradition, Composition, and Theology in Luke's Account of Jesus Before Herod Antipas," *Biblica* 66 (1985): 344–364, 347–358; E. Buck, "The Function of the Pericope 'Jesus before Herod' in the Passion Narrative of Luke," in *Wort in der Zeit* (ed. W. Haubeck and M. Bachmann; K. H. Rengstorf Festgabe; Leiden: Brill, 1980), 165–178; P. Parker, "Herod Antipas and the Death of Jesus," in *Jesus, the Gospels, and the Church* (ed. E. P. Sanders; Honor of W. R. Farmer; Macon: Mercer, 1987), 197–208.

[34] Theissen, *Gospels*, 26–39; Freyne, *Galilee and Gospel*, 201; Schnabel, *Mission*, 1.238–239; John Reumann, "Archaeology and Early Christology," in Charlesworth, *Archaeology*, 660–682, 670–672.

[35] Reed, *Archaeology*, 138; Oakman, "Models," 119–120; Schnabel, *Mission*, 1.239.

Jesus was familiar with the tetrarch of his home-region, and this gave him opportunity to become acquainted with the ideology of benefaction, friendship, reciprocity, and (to a lesser extent) *patrocinium*. Luke's stories and allusions combine to suggest that Jesus formed his message, at least in part, in response to the rule of Antipas.[36] The critique was at least partly economic since he criticizes Antipas for living in luxury. I argued earlier that Antipas had lesser aspirations of attaining the status his father had attained (see esp. section 3.2.2). He did attempt to be viewed as a benefactor in the construction of Tiberias and some buildings outside of Palestine as well as in providing for the people settled in the newly founded city (*Ant.* 18.36–38). He built a reputation as a benefactor outside of Palestine, but this reputation was not as strong as his father's (*OGIS* 416, 417; *SEG* 16.488). Antipas also attained the status of "friend of Caesar" (cf. *Ant.* 18:27, 36). He knew how to navigate in the world of reciprocity, benefaction, and friendship.

There is less reason to think Antipas acted along *patrocinium* lines though it is not impossible. Extant sources do not adopt the language of *patrocinium* in reference to Antipas, so any ties between him and the practice can only be inferential (at best) or speculative (at worst). His zeal for Rome was not strong and he pursued little in the way of status promotion until his wife compelled him (*Ant.*18.240–255). Unlike others who desired to be promoted, Antipas did not lavish benefits upon his superiors or show strong signs of loyalty (in, e.g., coins, temples; see sections 3.2.4; 3.2.5). Despite this lack of zeal, Jews still viewed him as too pro-Roman, a sentiment which Jesus may have shared (see section 3.2.3).

To some extent Jesus may have lumped Antipas together with his father as points along the trajectory of Hellenistic values which threatened to dominate the culture. Herod I's Hellenistic love of honor which takes what properly belongs to God (namely glory and honor), might have been applicable for Antipas in the minds of many Jews. Josephus criticized Herod I's motivation as a benefactor for this reason (*Ant.* 15.328–330; 16.153, 158). He was indeed generous to the people, but in the process he violated God's law by embracing praise from others. The use of the title "Herod" to describe the Herodian family (except Philip) may be Luke's subtle way of lumping the leaders together.[37] In a culture controlled by the idea of "like father, like son" Jesus would have had good reason to assume the same motivation in Antipas as had been seen in Herod I.

The influence which Philip the tetrarch potentially had on Jesus and his early disciples has been touched upon intermittently in the previous pages so only a collection of pertinent factors will be presented here. Jesus

---

[36] Moxnes, *Economy*, 59; Freyne, *Galilee and Gospel*, 202–203.
[37] Schwartz, *Agrippa I*, 120 n. 50; cf. Brown, *Death*, 784–786.

probably grew in his understanding of Philip the tetrarch through his disciples who came from his tetrarchy (esp. Andrew, Peter, Philip). Philip the tetrarch loved to mediate for and adjudicate issues for his people as he made a circuit through his region (*Ant.* 18.106). This opens up the possibility that the disciples from Bethsaida would have known his *modus operandi* relatively well. Philip constructed some monumental buildings (e.g., temple to Livia-Julia; refurbished temple to Rome in Caesarea Philippi) and dedicated cities in honor of Roman superiors (e.g., Caesarea Philippi). He also showed loyalty to Rome through iconic coins and temples (see section 3.3.5). The possibility that Philip practiced Roman *patrocinium* exists, but his preference to remain in his own territory (which held him back from travel to Rome) does temper how far one can take the influence of Roman ways. No explicit evidence identifies Philip as a patron, so if one opts for this description it is purely inferential. Nevertheless, Jesus might have learned more about specifically Roman ways through Philip. It is more likely that Philip functioned as a benefactor considering the magnitude of his gifts and his Hellenistic influences.

Though fairly ambiguous, the references to Jesus' encounter with the "Herodians" offers another example of Jesus interacting with persons associated with the Hellenistic rulers. Before the first-century only Mark (3:6; 12:13) and Matthew (22:16) adopt the term. Some have postulated that the Gospel references to Herodians ('Ηρῳδιανοί; Matt 22:16; Mark 3:6; 12:13; [8:15 *v.l.*]) are anachronistic since the group only developed with Agrippa I or II.[38] This postulation does not seem likely. A beginning in the time of Herod I with a transfer of allegiance to Antipas upon Herod I's death seems more plausible. (1) Josephus adopts various descriptions to identify a group of Herod I's supporters (τῶν Ἡρώδου τινὲς ἐπιλέκτων [*War* 1.351]; τοὺς τὰ Ἡρώδου φρονοῦντας [*Ant.* 14.450]; τῶν Ἡρωδείων [*War* 1.319]). The last of these, Ἡρωδεῖοι, is the proper Greek form parallel to Ἡρῳδιανοί. (2) Herod I and Antipas had long careers (40 B.C.–4 B.C. and 4 B.C.–A.D. 39 respectively) in Palestine and therefore long time-frames in which to attract supporters. Agrippa I's propensity to stay out of Palestine, especially Judea and Galilee, leaves him less opportunity to attract support (see section 3.4.2). His relatively short reign (A.D. 37–44) also decreases the likelihood of such supporters (see section 3.4.3). Herod I held a wide-ranging authority for a long period and had a big reputation with which people would be more likely to connect themselves.[39] It seems more likely that the Herodians first supported Herod I (as Josephus intimates) and then joined Herod Antipas (as Mark and Matthew suggest).

---

[38] B. W. Bacon, "Pharisees and Herodians in Mark," *JBL* 39 (1920): 102–112, 109–112. Richardson disputes the view, Richardson, *Herod*, 260.

[39] Richardson, *Herod*, 259–260.

Many options have been posited for the identity of the synoptic Herodians. Meier limits his list of options to fourteen and chooses servants or courtiers of Antipas as the most likely option.[40] Since Ἡρῳδιανοί is not a proper Greek form, but is rather taken from the Latin *Herodiani*, parallels to three other similarly formed terms can be instructive. Καισαριανοί, Χριστιανοί, and Πομπειανοί each refer to adherents or partisans of the particular leader.[41] For this reason the most likely options among the fourteen listed by Meier would be courtiers, household servants, slaves, or "more generally all the supporters of Herod's regime."[42] Josephus' use of Ἡρῳδεῖοι to describe supporters of Herod I suggests that supporters connected themselves to the Herodian family before the time of Antipas and received or adopted a similar title (*War* 1.319). As confidants of Antipas the Herodians would likely have observed his Greco-Roman attitudes and manners, including reciprocity, benefaction, and *patrocinium*. The gospels portray them as in league with the Pharisees and Sadducees in a threat to Jesus' ministry (Matt 22:15–16; Mark 3:6; 12:13).

Excursus: *John Meier and The Historical Herodians*

Meier doubts the historicity of Herodians teaming up with Pharisees, but his arguments seem less conclusive than he suggests. (1) He claims the two references in Mark provide bookends to the narrative and thus reflect theological construction rather than historical *realia* (Mark 3:6; 12:13). It seems odd, however, to think that Mark would introduce characters into his story which are nowhere else found in the traditions as his bookends especially when he provides no elaboration of their identity. (2) Meier's second argument, that Pharisees would not have objected to Jesus' healing of the withered hand on the Sabbath because Jesus did nothing, seems to sterilize the moment too much. It may be that Pharisees would not have had legitimate grounds for objecting to Jesus because he took no action, but they may still have objected out of frustration or a sense of uneasiness. (3) Meier has an implicit argument as well which claims that since the political and religious dimensions of the Marcan debates so perfectly align with the identity of the Herodians Mark must have concocted their appearance. But it does not seem best to rule out the presence of certain characters in a story just because they frequently engaged in the sort of activity described in that story. Jewish religious leaders sometimes sided with the resident Greco-Roman leadership in order to achieve mutually beneficial ends (cf. Philo, *Legatio Ad Gaium* §261–329). Meier does not "in principle" dispute the notion that a group of Antipas's supporters identified as "Herodians" could have existed in the

---

[40] For bibliography and summary of the debate see, John P. Meier, "The Historical Jesus and the Historical Herodians," *JBL* 119 (2000): 740–746; H. H. Rowley, "The Herodians in the Gospels," *JTS* 41 (1940): 14–27; Constantin Daniel, "Les 'Hérodiens' du Nouveau Testament sont-ils des Esséniens?" *RevQ* 6 (1967): 31–53; idem, "Nouveaux arguments en faveur de l'identification des Hérodiens et des Esséniens," *RevQ* 7 (1970): 397–402; W. J. Bennett, Jr., "The Herodians of Mark's Gospel," *NovT* 17 (1975): 9–14.

[41] Meier, "Historical Herodians," 742; cf. Epictetus, *Disc.*, 1.19.19; 3.24.117; Appian, *Bellum civile* 3.82; Acts 11:26; 26:28.

[42] Meier, "Historical Herodians," 742.

first-century. If Josephus identifies a similar group of supporters of Herod I, then it does not seem incredible that Mark would identify a group in support of Antipas.

The Herodians may have been one conduit through which Jewish leaders developed their understanding of benefaction or *patrocinium* ideology since they seem to have conspired together occasionally. These lesser figures in the Herodian circle potentially contributed to Jesus' understanding of benefaction and *patrocinium*.

4.1.3 Summary

The preceding paragraphs attempt to show that Jesus was likely exposed through various people and travels to the ideology of reciprocity and specifically benefaction and, to a lesser extent, *patrocinium*. It was argued that Jesus had relationships or conversations with several people who had first-hand knowledge of these practices. During his travels through various areas Jesus would have seen monuments, coins, and inscriptions which told of this Greco-Roman way of life. Benefaction supersedes *patrocinium*, just as Hellenism supersedes Romanism, in the majority of regions and persons he encountered. The one explicit location where *patrocinium* was practiced was Tyre where Jesus encountered the Syrophoenician woman. An ethic of reciprocity had taken form before his day and it manifested itself specifically in benefaction usually and, sporadically, in *patrocinium*.

This and the following two chapters examine three passages which have been set forth as proceeding from a critique against reciprocity, benefaction, or patronage (6:17–38; 14:1–24; 22:14–34). The study asks several questions: (1) Does the ideology of reciprocity present itself in the passage? (2) Can a more specific form of reciprocity, namely benefaction or patronage, be detected through specific vocabulary or other clues? Does the vocabulary or context allow for specification or is such specification unwarranted speculation? (3) How important is this ideology in the teaching of Jesus? Is a different ideology (e.g., kinship, honor-shame, OT fulfillment, or covenant) more important for the argument? That is to say, is there a better explanatory paradigm for the episode than the ideology of reciprocity, benefaction, or patronage? (4) Would it have been possible for a Jew from Galilee, like Jesus, to adopt the ideology or ideologies discovered in Luke's writing?

4.2 The Sermon on the Plain (Luke 6:17–38)

Several portions of Luke's "sermon on the plain" have been described as critiques of the Hellenistic reciprocity system, benefaction, or *patrocinium*. J. R. Harrison includes Luke 6:17–49 among three important passages which describe Jesus' critique of Hellenistic reciprocity and benefaction.[43] He postulates that Luke replaces typical reciprocity with a theologically grounded form of beneficence. F. Bovon finds reciprocity and perhaps some benefaction in Luke's narrative. He suggests that Hellenistic benefaction (*Wohltäter*; *bienfaiteur*) may be a key to understanding the healing of the man which precedes the sermon (Luke 6:10). Following this, Jesus presents "a new form of reciprocity, with its roots in God."[44] The reciprocity envisioned is "simultaneously antithetical and analogous to human reciprocity; the Christian God remains kind toward ungrateful and evil people (v. 35)."[45] Bovon suggests, though, that the Hellenistic system is not the only background relevant for this form of reciprocity since he finds examples of the same in the Hebrew Bible (Isa 27:8; Exod 18:11; Gen 37:32).[46] J. B. Green argues that patronage had penetrated Mediterranean culture thoroughly and brought with it a high potential for exploitation. In each parallel statement of Luke 6:27–38 Jesus calls his audience to resist the normal practice, found in Mediterranean patronage, of giving in order to receive a return. In this way Jesus challenges the "patronal ethic characteristic in the peasant village" and commands instead "boundary redefinition and ideal benefaction."[47] D. A. deSilva suggests that God supersedes the "high water mark" of the ideal benefactor, giving to the ungrateful, when he in fact gives to his outright enemies (Luke 6:35). God offers public benefactions as well as personal patronage.[48] B. Malina and R. Rohrbaugh suggest that the term "Lord" (6:49) indicates that Jesus becomes patron of the clients who identify him with this title. Their description of patronage in Roman Palestine appears to be an attempt at describing *patrocinium* rather than simply sociological patron-client relationships.[49]

H. Moxnes argues that Luke critiques *patrocinium* and benefaction in the context of this sermon. He identifies the "reversal speech in 6:20–26"

---

[43] Harrison, *Language*, 352.

[44] Bovon, *Luke*, 1.237, 241; idem, *Evangelium*, 1.276; idem, *Luc*, 1.269 n. 35. Cf. Danker, *Luke*, 33–34; van Unnik, "Die Motivierung," 284–300; Charles H. Talbert, *Reading Luke: A Literary and Theological Commentary* (Macon: Smyth & Helwys, 2002), 77–79. Nolland disputes this reading, Nolland, *Luke*, 1.298–299, 303.

[45] Bovon, *Luke*, 1.237.

[46] Bovon, *Luke*, 1.242–243 n. 80.

[47] Green, *Luke*, 270–271; idem, *Theology of Luke*, 114–115. L. T. Johnson considers the teaching to have rejected the "logic of ancient reciprocity (and benefaction)", Johnson, *Luke*, 108–109.

[48] deSilva, *Honor, Patronage*, 129–131. This offer is given in a public and universal way even though individuals will join him in a personal patronage relationship.

[49] Malina and Rohrbaugh, *Social-Science Commentary*, 251, 388–390. They offer no primary source documentation or bibliographic reference for their statement that *patrocinium* flourished in Palestine during the early empire.

as a benefaction of God aimed at the poor.[50] The solution to the unequal distribution of wealth and exploitative patron-client relations is Luke's presentation of God as benefactor who redistributes wealth (1:52–53; 6:20–26), and the ethic of almsgiving which characterizes the new community.[51] Mention of debts in Luke (e.g., 6:34; 7:41–42; 12:58–59; 16:1–9) leads Moxnes to suggest that patron-client relationships began when a poor person, living in the village (periphery), needs a loan from a rich person living in the city (center).[52] The rich become patrons and the poor become clients. Jesus functions as a broker when God's power to heal works through him (6:19).[53] Moxnes identifies many teachings on *patrocinium* in Luke's narrative. Nevertheless he concludes that Luke does not describe the historical system of *patrocinium* in first-century Palestine but rather the situation of Luke's culture which, he implies, is a more or less western Greco-Roman society.[54] He offers no argument for the statement.

It is apparent that Luke's sermon on the plain has been understood in relation to reciprocity, benefaction, and patronage. The following exegesis investigates this conclusion, and attempts to decipher which, if any, of the aforementioned readings should be accepted. Whether *patrocinium* and/or benefaction are present in Luke's writing is first investigated. A comparison with the conclusions of chapters 2 and 3 of this book is then set forth to determine if a person of Jesus' provenance or an audience such as is described by Luke in the narrative could have interpreted Jesus in terms of *patrocinium* or benefaction.

4.2.1 Introductory Summary (6:17–19)

Literary Context

Luke's "Sermon on the Plain" should be held together from 6:17–49, admitting slight shifts in thought, and read in conjunction with the preceding and following narratives. Most commentators maintain verses 17 and 49 as the beginning and ending limits of the passage.[55] A few scholars have sug-

---

[50] Moxnes, *Economy*, 20; idem, "Patron-Client," 257–258; Johnson, *Luke*, 111. This coordinates with Jesus' program announced in 4:16–19. Cf. Lull, "Benefactor," 289 who lists this speech as a benefaction.

[51] Moxnes, *Economy*, 74, 119–122, 132–134. The program ends the patron-client system through advocating giving without expectation of reciprocity.

[52] Moxnes, "Patron-Client," 254; idem, *Economy*, 73.

[53] Moxnes, "Patron-Client," 258–259. Jesus' making "friends" of tax-collectors and sinners refers to his taking these lowly persons as clients. Moxnes cites 6:34, but intended 7:34.

[54] Moxnes, "Patron-Client," 256–257.

[55] E.g., Leon Morris, *Luke* (TNTC; Downers Grove: InterVarsity, 1988), 138–149; J. R. Nolland, *Luke 1–9:20* (WBC 35a; Dallas: Word, 1989), 273–311; Fitzmyer, *Luke I-IX*,

gested different points where the sermon ends and a new context begins (6:36, 37, 39). For example, εἶπεν δὲ καὶ παραβολὴν αὐτοῖς seems to suggest the start of a new section since it sounds as if a new teaching section will be introduced (6:38). But Tannehill shows that similar phrases are used elsewhere in Luke to expand upon teaching previously mentioned (5:36; 12:16; 13:6; 21:29).[56] It is best to view those three potential breaks in the sermon (6:36, 37, 39) as transitions in thought within the same context and sermon.[57] Luke provides a transition with the selection of the twelve (6:12–16) which precedes the opening lines of the sermon. He then introduces the sermon and the audience making clear that a new setting is in view (6:17). Luke's "introductory summary" recounts Jesus' previous actions and the message which follows (6:17–19).[58] A new section begins with the completion of the teaching (ἐπλήρωσεν πάντα τὰ ῥήματα αὐτοῦ) and a journey to Capernaum (7:1). The three verses which some scholars mark as slight transitions (6:36, 37, 39) should be understood as indicating movement within the main message of the sermon.

The sermon should be read as a whole, but it should not be cut off from the preceding and following narratives. Rather, the sermon needs to be understood in light of its literary context. Jesus' selection of apostles (6:12–16) clarifies a portion of the audience. Jesus called together a large number of disciples and selected twelve from this number (καὶ ἐκλεξάμενος ἀπ' αὐτῶν δώδεκα; 6:13). He addresses the twelve along with crowds of disciples and a multitude of people (πλῆθος πολὺ τοῦ λαοῦ) in the sermon (6:17). Insight from narratives prior to the selection of the apostles will be given below. The narrative which follows the sermon is also pertinent (esp. 7:1–10). Jesus' teaching on discipleship with reference to reciprocity in the sermon is followed by his encounter with a centurion who operates along the lines of reciprocity as well. It will be shown below how the sermon fits as a transition between the previous teaching stories and this story of the centurion and his servant.

625–646; Marshall, *Luke*, 236–275; R. C. Tannehill, *Luke* (Abingdon NTC; Nashville: Abingdom, 1996), 113–123; Bock, *Luke*, 1.548–628; Green, *Luke*, 260–281; Johnson, *Luke*, 105–112; Alan Kirk, "Some Compositional Conventions of Hellenistic Wisdom Texts and the Juxtaposition of 4:1–13; 6:20b–49; and 7:1–10 in Q," *JBL* 116.2 (1997): 235–257; idem, "'Love Your Enemies,' The Golden Rule, and Ancient Reciprocity (Luke 6:27–35)," *JBL* 122.4 (2003): 667–686.

[56] Tannehill, *Luke*, 37–38.

[57] The commentaries tend to identify these verses as transitions within the longer sermon. Johnson and Kirk point to 6:35. Morris, Tannehill, R. H. Stein (*Luke* [NAB; Nashville: Broadman, 1992], 205–210) identify 6:36 as such a transition. Bovon, Nolland, Marshall, Bock, and Green consider 6:38 to be a transition verse.

[58] Bock, *Luke*, 1.548.

4.2 The Sermon on the Plain (Luke 6:17–38)

Several variant readings surface in the section, but none of them severely alters the text. In 6:31 some MSS add words (καὶ ὑμεῖς; καλὰ) before ποιεῖτε probably in an attempt at harmonization with Matt 7:12. Several important MSS support the reading καὶ ὑμεῖς ποιεῖτε (ℵ A D L W Θ Ξ Ψ f^{1,13} 33), while other relatively insignificant MSS have καλὰ ποιεῖτε (r^1 vg^{mss} sy^s). External evidence, however, cannot outweigh the point that it seems obvious that scribes have attempted to harmonize the text with its Synoptic parallel.[59] A second variant reading comes in 6:35 where either confusion over the meaning of ἀπελπίζοντες or a simple case of dittography caused some scribes to write μηδένα rather than μηδέν.[60] External evidence (*v.l.* has only ℵ W Ξ *pc* sy^{s,p} in support) and the obvious explanation for the *varia lectio* combine in favor of the NA^{27} reading. Other variant readings in the passage harmonize with Synoptic parallels, improve the literary quality, or do not affect the meaning. For these reasons no others will be addressed here and the text of NA^{27} will be adopted as it is.

For the sake of clarity the sermon and its context have been broken down into three main sections (6:17–19; 20–26; 27–38). Each section will be examined in regard to literary, linguistic, and cultural matters. This will focus attention on relevant evidence from each section. The last of these three sections (6:27–38) has been the subject of more extended discussion in regard to reciprocity, benefaction, and patronage, so this section will be dealt with in more detail. Full treatment of each detail in the text is impossible and unnecessary. Exegesis of these passages will instead focus on information and details relevant to reciprocity, benefaction, and patronage.

Luke prefaces the sermon on the plain with a description of the audience and an "introductory summary"[61] of Jesus' ministry (Luke 6:17–19). Following directly upon the selection of the twelve, Jesus descends to a level place (ἐπὶ τόπου πεδινοῦ; 6:17). Gathered with him were a large crowd of his disciples (ὄχλος πολὺς μαθητῶν αὐτου) and a multitude of the people (καὶ πλῆθος πολὺ τοῦ λαοῦ) from Judea and Jerusalem and from Tyre and Sidon. These had come out to hear and to be healed (οἳ ἦλθον ἀκοῦσαι αὐτοῦ καὶ ἰαθῆναι; 6:18). The healing ministry of Jesus was already flourishing (4:31–37, 38–39, 40–41; 5:13–16, 17–26; 6:6–11). Luke's prefatory remark serves as both summary of previous ministry and as introduction to the sermon and current healing activity. Luke has a penchant for such summaries (e.g., 4:14–15, 31–32, 40–41).[62] J. A. Fitzmyer suggests that the focus in Luke is on the teaching of Jesus and the listening of the audience;

---

[59] Metzger, *Textual Commentary*, 141.
[60] Nolland, *Luke*, 292, 299–300; Metzger, *Textual Commentary*, 141.
[61] Bock, *Luke*, 1.548.
[62] Fitzmyer, *Luke*, 1.622; Bock, *Luke*, 1.548; Nolland, *Luke*, 1.275.

mention of miracles is simply a carry-over from his Marcan source.[63] But such a bifurcation does not seem appropriate. Luke emphasizes healings throughout his two volumes and uses such healings as one parallel between Jesus and his apostles (e.g., Luke 5:17–19; Acts 5:14–15).[64] Luke actually adds more terminology to emphasize those healings that cannot be found in Mark (or Matthew; Mark 3:10 [θεραπεύω]; Matt 4:24 [θεραπεύω]; θεραπεύω and ἰάομαι in Luke 6:18 [2x]; 19; see 4.2.1 *Linguistic*). The sermon lines up with the "hearing/listening" aspect of the introductory summary while Luke quickly mentions the healing ministry Jesus performed in the summary itself. Luke situates this passage following the selection of the twelve and mentioning the group of disciples to identify this section as teaching on discipleship.

Linguistic Evidence

Luke emphasizes the universal scope of Jesus' healing and appeal in ways which resemble descriptions of benefactors. In describing the healings which Jesus performed just before selecting the twelve, Mark mentions that Jesus healed many (πολλοὺς), which compelled the whole group (ὅσοι; 3:10) of sick people to try to touch him. Matthew does not specify the extent of Jesus' healings, but simply states that Jesus healed them (ἐθεράπευσεν αὐτούς; 4:24). Luke expands these descriptions when he twice repeats that "all" (πᾶς) those who came to him were healed (6:17, 19[2x]).

Danker considers this editorial change highly significant to Luke and adds the parallel in Acts 5:16 as two examples of "public outreach."[65] Danker finds many examples of benefactors being described in such terms.[66] For example, a decree from around A.D. 9 identifies the birth of Augustus as the beginning of "the good and common fortune of all" since Augustus was "benefactor of all" (*SEG* 4.490 ll. 8–9; cf. *IGSK* 3.82.7–8; Danker, *Benefactor*, 33.32–42).[67]

---

[63] Fitzmyer, *Luke*, 1.622. Supporting a Marcan source behind Luke's summary are Bovon, *Luke*, 1.212; Johnson, *Luke*, 106; Bock, *Luke*, 1.548–549; Heinz Schürmann, *Das Lukasevangelium: Kommentar zu Kap. 1,1–9,50* (2 vols.; 2nd ed.; HThKNT 3; Freiburg im Breisgau: Herder, 1982), 1.323; Tim Schramm, *Der Markus-Stoff bei Lukas: Eine literarkritische und redaktionsgeschichtliche Untersuchung* (SNTSMS 14; Cambridge: Cambridge University Press, 1971), 113–114.

[64] Bock, *Luke*, 1.564–565; cf. Stein, *Luke*, 196; Tannehill, *Narrative Unity*, 2.6.

[65] Danker, *Benefactor*, 336–339.

[66] Danker, *Benefactor*, nos. 17, 33, 41, 42, 51.

[67] *Editio princeps* W. H. Buckler, "An Epigraphic Contribution to Letters," *Classical Review* 41 (1927): 119–121, 119.

Ἐπειδὴ ἡ θείως διατάξασα τὸν βίον ἡμῶν πρόνοια σπουδὴν εἴσεν ἐνκαμένη καὶ φιλοτιμίαν τὸ τεληότατον τῶι βίωι διεχόσμησεν ἀγαθὸν ἐνενχαμένη τὸν Σεβαστόν ὅν εἰς εὐεργεσίαν ἀνθρώπων ἐπλήρωσεν ἀρητῆς ὥσπερ ἡμεῖν καὶ τοῖς μεθ' ἡμᾶς σωτῆρα χαρισαμένη τὸν παύσαντα μὲν πόλεμον κοσμήσοντα δὲ εἰρήνην ἐπιφανεὶς δὲ ὁ Καῖσαρ τὰς ἐλπίδας τῶν προλαβόντων εὐανγέλια πάντων ὑπερέθηκεν οὐ μόνον τοὺς πρὸ αὐτοῦ γεγονότας εὐεργέτας ὑπερβαλόμενος ἀλλ' οὐδ' ἐν τοῖς ἐσομένοις ἐλπίδα ὑπολιπὼν ὑπερβολῆς ἦρξεν δὲ τῶι κόσμωι τῶν δι' αὐτὸν εὐαγγελίων ἡ γενέθλιος ἡμέρα τοῦ θεοῦ
Whereas Providence that orders all our lives has in her display of concern and generosity in our behalf adorned our lives with the highest good: Augustus, whom she has filled with arête for the benefit of humanity, and has in her beneficence granted us and those who will come after us a Savior who has made war to cease and who shall put everything in peaceful order; and whereas Caesar, when he was manifest, transcended the expectations of all who had anticipated the good news, not only by surpassing the benefits conferred by his predecessors but by leaving no expectation of surpassing him to those who would come after him, with the result that the birthday of our God signaled the beginning of Good News for the world because of him.[68]

The decree declares several noble characteristics of Providence, namely foresight (πρόνοια), zeal (σπουδὴν), and honor (φιλοτιμίαν). The emperor is of similar character since the decree recognizes that he has been filled with honor (ἐπλήρωσεν ἀρητῆς). It also offers a few titles to describe both the deity and the emperor. Notably it describes Augustus as benefactor (εἰς εὐεργεσίαν; εὐεργέτας; cf. ll. 46–47) and generous savior (σωτῆρα χαρισαμένη; cf. l. 45) who brought good news of peace to all (τὸν παύσαντα μὲν πόλεμον κοσμήσοντα δὲ εἰρήνην ἐπιφανεὶς ... εὐαγγέλια πάντων). The decree emphasizes that Augustus did not restrict his generosity to the people of his own realm, but extended generosity to all.

Luke also shapes his narrative to fit a "words match deeds" form which commonly described the generosity of benefactors. Mark and Matthew each state only one time that this episode involved healing (Mark 3:10 [θεραπεύω]; Matt 4:24 [θεραπεύω]), but Luke repeats the idea three times using two different terms (θεραπεύω; ἰάομαι; Luke 6:18 [2x]; 19). Luke connects the healing activity of Jesus to his teaching activity (Luke 6:18–19). By connecting these activities, Luke adopts the "words match deeds" description of benefactors.[69] This was a common way to describe the lifestyle of the benefactor as is attested in literary (Homer *Iliad*, 9.443) and archaeological sources (e.g., *Choix d'inscriptions de Delos* 20.6–8//CIG 3655//IG 11.4.562).[70] This decree from the third century B.C. honors Apol-

---

[68] Danker, *Benefactor*, 217.
[69] Danker, *Benefactor*, 339–343; idem, *Luke* 2nd ed., 31–32, 34.
[70] Félix Durrbach, *Choix d'inscriptions de Délos* (Subsidia Epigraphica 6; New York: Hildesheim, 1976), 20.6–8; 42.4–5. Cf. Danker, *Benefactor*, 12.26–31 (= *SIG* 762), 17.14–16 (= *OGIS* 339), 20.15–16 (= *IG* 2.621). Ἔδοξεν τῆι βουλῆι καὶ τῶι δήμωι Ἰέαρχος Προχλείους εἶπεν ἐπειδὴ Ἀπολλόδωρος ἀνὴρ ἀγαθὸς ὢν διατελεῖ περί τε τὸ ἱερὸν καὶ τὴν πόλιν τὴν Δηλίων καὶ ποιεῖ ἀγαθὸν ὅ τι δύναται καὶ λόγωι καὶ ἔργωι

lodorus of Cyzique.⁷¹ Apollodorus earned the titles of proxenos and benefactor from the people of Delos as well as the privileges attached to those honors.⁷² He is identified as a good man (ἀνὴρ ἀγαθός) who has done good (ποιεῖ ἀγαθόν) in word and deed (λόγωι καὶ ἔργωι), so he is praised (ἐπαινέσαι) for his honor and good will (αὐτὸν ἀρετῆς καὶ εὐνοιας ἕνεκα) and received the titles of *proxenos* and benefactor of the temple, the people, and the city (πρόξενον δ' εἶναι καὶ εὐεργέτην τοῦ ἱεροῦ καὶ τοῦ δήμου; προξένοις καὶ εὐεργέταις τῆς πόλεως; cf. *SIG* 105, 106). By depicting Jesus as a healer of all and as a person whose great words match great deeds, Luke follows a pattern of describing benefactors.

It must be admitted, however, that these two descriptors are rather general and no other explicit linguistic evidence ties this activity to benefaction explicitly. Recipients of benefactions may have heralded their benefactors as expressing their generosity to all and as people whose words match deeds, but these descriptions alone do not demand that one read the description of Jesus exclusively within the category of benefactor. There also is nothing explicit in the text which links Jesus' activity to *patrocinium*. Terms which may indicate *patrocinium* are absent from the introductory summary (e.g., κηδεμονία, πατρωνεία, and προστασία; κηδεμών, πάτρων, πατρώνης, προστάτης; πατρωνεύω; κλίενς and πελάτης; ἐπιτροπή). Μαθητής is the only relational term in the short paragraph. The general nature of the descriptors of Jesus' ministry means that one should not overconfidently describe Jesus as a benefactor from this short paragraph alone. Luke may intend to compare Jesus to Israel's previous prophets who had healing and teaching ministries. Before inaugurating his healing ministry Jesus referred to the healing ministries of Elijah and Elisha (Luke 4:25–27). Elijah had been sent to heal the widow from Sidon (4:26) which may prepare for Jesus' healing of Sidonians in the present passage (6:17–19). Jesus begins to cleanse people (5:12–16), making the connection to El-

---

τοὺς ἐντυγχάνοντας ἑαυτῶι Δηλίων ἐπαινέσαι μὲν αὐτὸν ἀρετῆς καὶ εὐνοιας ἕνεκα πρόξενον δ' εἶναι καὶ εὐεργέτην τοῦ ἱεροῦ καὶ τοῦ δήμου τοῦ Δηλίων Ἀπολλόδωρον Ἀπολλωνίου Κυζιχηνὸν αὐτὸν καὶ ἐχγόνους καὶ εἶναι αὐτοῖς πολιτείαν ἐν Δήλωι καὶ ἀτέλειαν πάντων καὶ προεδρίαν καὶ γῆς καὶ οἰκίας ἔγχτησιν καὶ πρόσοδον πρὸς τὴμ βουλὴν καὶ τὸν δῆμον πρώτοις μετὰ τὰ ἱερὰ καὶ τἆλλα ὅσαπερ τοῖς ἄλλοις προξένοις καὶ εὐεργέταις τῆς πόλεως δέδοται παρὰ Δηλίων ἐπιμελεῖσθαι δ' αὐτῶν τὴμ βουλὴν τὴν ἀεὶ Βουλεύουσαν καὶὑπηρετεῖν ἐάν του δέωνται ἀναγράψαι δὲ τόδε τὸ ψήφισμα τὴμ μὲμ βουλὴν εἰς τὸ βουλευτήριον τοὺς δὲ ἱεροποιοὺς εἰς τὸ ἱερόν

⁷¹ Durrbach, *Délos*, 29–30.

⁷² Proxenos is sometimes thought to be a term denoting *patrocinium*, but this is not true. Eilers, *Roman Patrons*, 110–113. On the meaning of proxenos see, C. Marek, *Die Proxenie* (Europäische Hochschulschriften 3.213; Frankfurt am Main, Bern, and New York: Peter Lang, 1984); F. Gschnitzer, "Proxenos," in *Real-Encyclopädie der classischen Altertumswissenschaft* (ed. A. Pauly, G. Wissowa, and W. Kroll; Stuttgart, 1894–1980), suppl. 13 (1973): 629–730.

isha's cleansing ministry explicit (ἐκαθαρίσθη; 4:25), before summarizing his ministry as a cleansing ministry following the sermon on the plain (λεπροὶ καθαρίζονται; 7:22). If Luke intended a comparison to Greco-Roman benefactors he did not do so to the exclusion of Jewish prototypes.

Cultural Matters

Different audiences may have interpreted Jesus' actions and teachings differently. It is important, therefore, to recall the descriptions of the cultures of Palestine and Syria from the previous chapter. Luke mentions four locations from which Jesus' audience derived, Jerusalem, Judea, Tyre, and Sidon. Judea is perhaps to be taken as a general reference to the entire Palestinian area (cf. Luke 4:44; 5:17).[73] Luke does not in this passage identify the home-towns of the twelve who also audited this sermon, but other evidence suggests that they derived from Galilee or Philip's tetrarchy (e.g., Philip, Andrew, Peter, James; John 1:44; 12:21).[74] A reminder of the cultural make-up of these areas, and specifically of their participation in reciprocity, benefaction, or patronage, should be offered.

To some extent the four mentioned locations (Jerusalem, Judea, Tyre, and Sidon) had been Hellenized and had even participated in benefaction and *patrocinium*, but the Hellenization of each region must be differentiated. Jerusalem and Judea had endured several different Hellenistic and Roman rulers from the Hasmonean to the post-revolt era. Adoption of the Greek language by "the common residents of Jerusalem" between 40 B.C. and A.D. 70 is one facet of the lasting effect of Hellenization (see section 2.2.4; *Ant.* 20.262–265).[75] Greek education, entertainment (hippodrome, games, amphitheater), and architecture (theater, temple, gymnasium) also support the notion of Hellenization in Jerusalem. The study also revealed that Herod and others employed benefaction ideology. Inscriptions identify Herod as a benefactor and other residents also as benefactors (Meshorer, "Stone Weight"; *SEG* 1277; *SEG* 8.170; B. Isaac, "Donation"). *Patrocinium* was only argued for indirectly through a combination of noticing Roman influences (e.g., architecture, style), relationships (e.g., Herod and Antony or Augustus), and honoring of those relations in public (e.g., Antonia fortress). No explicit evidence suggests the adoption of *patrocinium* in Jerusalem. Rather the culture was largely indebted to Judaism. Archaeological and literary evidence support a strong influence of Jewish culture in

---

[73] Bock, *Luke*, 1.564; Marshall, *Luke*, 242; Fitzmyer, *Luke*, 623; Bovon, *Luke*, 213; J. M. Creed, *The Gospel According to St. Luke* (London: Macmillan, 1965), 89; Josef Ernst, *Das Evangelium nach Lukas* (RNT 3; 5th ed.; Regensburg: Pustet, 1977), 212.

[74] Schnabel, *Mission*, 1.265–269. Not all the disciples are accounted for in regard to places of origin.

[75] Sterling, "Judaism," 273; Van Der Horst, "Greek," 154–174.

Jerusalem (chalk vessels, *miqvaoth*, burial tombs, and absence of pig bones; *War* 1.648–55; *Ant.* 17.146–63). Judaism had a more significant role in forming the worldview of most people in Jerusalem, Judea, and Galilee (see sections 2.2.3 *Summary*; 2.2.4; 2.2.5 *Tyre*).

Galilee attests less Hellenization than Jerusalem but the presence of Jewish culture was just as strong (see section 2.2.3). In each village and city investigated the presence of the four major Jewish identity markers stood out (chalk vessels, *miqvaoth*, burial tombs, and absence of pig bones). Bethsaida had a mixture of Jewish (e.g., limestone vessels) and Greco-Roman archaeological remains (iconic coins, temple to Livia-Julia; see section 2.2.5 *Bethsaida*). Since Josephus makes no mention of revolt against the Hellenistic practices it seems reasonable to conclude that to a certain degree residents of Bethsaida were less stridently opposed to Hellenism than other Jewish groups (e.g., as in the golden eagle incident; *War* 1.648–55). The investigation undertaken in the second chapter emphasized strong adherence to Judaism in Galilee and Jerusalem, with significant adherence in Bethsaida. Cultural indebtedness to Judaism was the bedrock of Galilee and Jerusalem, and by extension Judea. A primary locus of influence would have been the Torah and OT tradition. It is pertinent therefore to evaluate Jesus' teaching in light of this Jewish background.

Tyre and Sidon had a different cultural make-up which allows for the interpretation of Jesus' message and actions in light of benefaction and *patrocinium* (see section 2.2.5 *Tyre*). Tyre was significantly Hellenized. Josephus comments that even a Jewish resident of Tyre (at the time of Aristotle) could be Greek in both language and soul (*Apion* 1.178–180). Literary and archaeological evidence suggest that its residents understood benefaction and patronage. Caesar made a decree, which was placed in Tyre and Sidon, that announced the relationship of benefaction, friendship, and *suffragium* which existed between Rome and the Jewish residents of those areas (*Ant.* 14.190–195). He apparently assumes that the residents understand the inner-workings of these types of relationships. An inscription made in honor of M. Aemilius Scaurus recognizes him as patron of Tyre (*IGR* 3.1102). Patronage was sought by the city itself (rather than by the patron) which indicates that the city understood this relationship and its obligations (cf. Eilers, *Roman Patrons*, C153). Tyre and Sidon were more Hellenized than Jerusalem or Galilee, and have explicit evidence of *patrocinium* which is lacking in those two Jewish areas. Jerusalem, Bethsaida, Tyre, and Sidon have evidence of benefaction. Galilee had no evidence of benefaction. The audience of the sermon on the plain may therefore have interpreted its message in different ways. In the following exegesis potential points where different members of the audience may have interpreted differently will be identified.

Conclusion

The introductory summary with which Luke prefaces the sermon on the plain presents the audience to whom Jesus speaks and mentions a few actions (e.g., healings, exorcisms) which may have been variously interpreted by different auditors. Those from Judea, Jerusalem, and Galilee, being more indebted to Jewish culture probably would have interpreted Jesus' healing actions in terms of its previous prophets (e.g., Elijah, Elisha). Luke seems to indicate this connection by introducing Jesus' healing ministry with reference to these Jewish prophets (Luke 4:25–27). There may have been a few from Jerusalem who interpreted Jesus' actions in line with benefactors. Jerusalemites had seen great men arise, do great things, and receive the honorary title of εὐεργέτης (e.g., 1 Macc 14:25–49; 2 Macc 4:2; *War* 4.145–146; 5.536; 2.538). They would also have seen inscriptions heralding other benefactors in Jerusalem (e.g., Herod I; an anonymous Jew from Rhodes [*SEG* 1277]). Those from Tyre and Sidon perhaps held the categories of benefaction and *patrocinium* in a more important place in their worldview. As Jesus performed miraculous healings they may have interpreted him as a benefactor who brought salvation through physical healing. It is also possible that as they witnessed Jesus' generosity they considered that he might make a good patron of their cities. Tyre had asked M. Aemilius Scaurus to be patron after a series of great deeds, and these Tyrians may have considered Jesus a good candidate to be their city's patron. It should be noted, however, that in Eilers' study of inscriptions and literary evidence of patrons of Greek cities, Hellenistic people from the east did not use the title *patronus* to describe non-Romans. It is unlikely that Jesus would have been sought as a *patronus* unless he were understood as a Roman. No linguistic evidence in the text links Jesus' healing to *patrocinium*, nor are there substantial grounds for understanding benefaction in the background to the exclusion of Jewish interpretations of the healings. It does not appear, therefore, that Luke intentionally cast this scene in explicit benefactor or patron imagery. If Luke did not intentionally adopt *patrocinium* or benefaction ideology in this introductory summary it is less likely that he intentionally adopted these ideologies in the subsequent teaching episode. The absence of these ideologies from the description aligns with the conclusions of chapters 2 and 3 of this book since it was demonstrated that *patrocinium* and benefaction were not prominent in the specific places mentioned (Galilee, Jerusalem, Tyre and Sidon), if they were present at all.

4.2.2 Blessings and Woes (6:20–26)

Literary Context

The sermon begins with a series of four blessings and four woes set in parallel structure (6:20–26).[76] The introductory blessing and woe contrast the present situation of the poor (ὁ πτωχός; 6:20) and rich (ὁ πλούσιος; 6:24). In both instances Luke employs a present active verb to describe how the respective individual receives recompense. The poor are recompensed through reception of the kingdom of God (ὑμετέρα ἐστὶν ἡ βασιλεία τοῦ θεοῦ) and the rich are recompensed in their present comfort (πέχετε τὴν παράκλησιν ὑμῶν). Two subsequent blessings and woes entail future recompense indicated by the switch to future active or passive verbs (6:21, 25). The hungry will be satisfied (χορτασθήσεσθε) and the weeping will laugh (γελάσετε; 6:21). Those who are filled now will hunger (πεινάσετε) and those who laugh now will weep and cry (πενθήσετε καὶ κλαύσετε; 6:25). The final blessing and woe receive a lengthier explanation as Jesus compares present disdain or praise with the reception of true and false prophets respectively (6:22–23, 26). Those who are hated (μισέω), excluded (ἀφορίζω), reproached (ὀνειδίζω), or have their name denounced (ἐκβάλλω τὸ ὄνομα ὑμῶν ὡς πονηρὸν) are blessed and should leap for joy since they receive the same treatment as the prophets (6:22–23). They receive a great reward in heaven in response (μισθὸς ὑμῶν πολὺς ἐν τῷ οὐ'ρανῷ). Those who are well-spoken of by all need to be warned that the false-prophets received a similar reception (6:25).

Each blessing and woe is attached to an attendant reciprocal action among which a few implicitly derive from God. Three of the blessings and two of the woes allude to divine reciprocity although the allusions are slight. The poor receive the kingdom of God which is a reciprocation God grants; this seems logical since God has ultimate authority over his own kingdom (6:20b). God gives satisfaction to the hungry (χορτασθήσεσθε; 6:21); the passive voice hints that this satisfaction comes from God. God reciprocates with a reward in heaven for those that are mistreated on account of the Son of man (6:23); again the logic is that only God can grant treasure in heaven. Allusions to God's reciprocation of the wicked are less clear, but it does seem to be implied by the future tense verbs (πεινάσετε; πενθήσετε; κλαύσετε; 6:25) that a negative consequence from God awaits those who currently have privilege. Because of these allusions to God's re-

---

[76] Green, *Luke*, 266–268; Johnson, *Luke*, 111; Bovon, *Luke*, 1.224–229; idem, *Lukas*, 298–306; idem, *Luc*, 291–299; Tannehill, *Luke*, 114–116; Plummer, *Luke*, 179; Marshall, *Luke*, 244; Talbert, *Theological Commentary*, 71–73.

ciprocation several scholars refer to this section as teaching a type of "divine reversal."[77]

Linguistic Evidence

There is no technical terminology in the beatitudes and woes section of this sermon which evinces notions of benefaction or *patrocinium* (6:20–26). In order to include this section as a benefactor/patron teaching section scholars have typically appealed to the notion that benefactors/patrons provided "reversal" for their clients of the sort offered by Jesus in his beatitudes and woes. After describing the section in terms of a "divine reversal" Lull and Moxnes compare this reversal with the types of reversals brought about through the generosity of benefactors (see section 4.2.1 *Cultural*).[78]

P. Spilsbury, in a discussion of Josephus, suggests that μισθός may come close to signaling a benefit.[79] Luke's use of the term in 6:23 may be considered a comparable setting where μισθός might similarly evince a benefaction context. Spilsbury is reluctant to claim too much from the word by itself, and this is prudent since the term arises in many Jewish contexts which do not have benefactor/patron ideology in view (e.g., Gen 15:1; 29:15; 30:18).[80] Luke uses μισθός in other contexts to indicate wages (Luke 10:7) or payment (Acts 1:18).[81] In light of the common ways that μισθός is used in the LXX and in Luke-Acts it seems likely that Luke intends no special benefaction meaning with its use here.

The absence of technical benefactor or patron vocabulary should make one cautious about describing this passage primarily in benefaction or patronage categories.

---

[77] The term is from Johnson, *Luke*, 106–108. Cf. Green, *Luke*, 265; idem, *Theology*, 113–115; Moxnes, *Economy*, 20, 74, 119–122, 132–134; Esler, "Review," 231; Bock, *Luke*, 1.576; Bovon, *Luke*, 1.225; Tannehill, *Luke*, 230; York, *Last*, 55–62; Klaus Koch, *The Growth of the Biblical Tradition: The Form-Critical Method* (New York: Scribner, 1969), 17–18; Charles H. Talbert, *Reading Luke-Acts in Its Mediterranean Milieu* (NovTSupp 107; Leiden: Brill, 2003), 170–171; idem, *Reading Luke: A Literary and Theological Commentary* (Macon: Smyth & Helwys, 2002), 171; Parsons, *Luke*, 122; Nelson, *Leadership*, 86–93.

[78] E.g., Lull, "Servant-Benefactor," 289; Moxnes, "Patron-Client," 257–258; Moxnes, *Economy*, 20, 74, 138.

[79] P. Spilsbury, "God and Israel in Josephus: A Patron-Client Relationship," in *Understanding Josephus: Seven Perspectives* (ed. S. Mason; Sheffield: Sheffield Academic Press, 1998), 172–192, 186–187, 190. On μισθός see Zahn, *Lukas*, 292; J. Piper, *Love Command*, 162–170.

[80] Neither Lust nor BAGD list a meaning of μισθός as "benefit" in patron-client or benefactor relationships. They list, "hire, pay, wages, reward, earnings" (Lust, 1996, 2.307) and "remuneration for work done, pay, wages; recognition (mostly by God) for the moral quality of an action, *recompense*" (BAGD, 653).

[81] Johnson, *Luke*, 107.

Cultural Matters

The beatitudes and woes section of the sermon has some parallels in Greco-Roman and Jewish literature and thus can speak into both cultures. K. Koch charts the development of the beatitude in Greece and the Near East and finds reason to distance the NT beatitude from the Greek form. Beatitudes developed in Greece independently of the development of the OT beatitude. Greek beatitudes lack a motive clause, which is found in OT literature suggesting that NT beatitudes have modified OT rather than Greek predecessors. Greek beatitudes seem to have had no influence over the form of intertestamental and NT beatitudes.[82] Furthermore, beatitude lists like those found in the sermon on the plain are infrequent.[83] It is more common to find a beatitude standing alone (e.g., Luke 14:15; Rev 1:3; 14:13; 16:15; 19:9; 20:3; 22:7, 14),[84] than to find a list of beatitudes as in the sermons on the mount and plain. This is especially true of Greek and Egyptian beatitudes, but in Hellenistic Jewish literature beatitudes began to be compiled together (e.g., Sir 25:7–11; Tob 13:14–16). Some beatitudes are coordinated with woes (e.g., *2 En.* 52; *1 En.* 103:5; *2 Bar.* 10:6; Eccl 10:19[LXX]; *Did.* 1:5), though this combination is lacking in the OT (apart from Eccl 10:19 LXX).[85] Most beatitudes in the OT take a similar form. A person (not a thing or state) is blessed then the reason for the blessing is given "via a relative clause, a participial phrase, or a ὅτι clause that refers to the blessed in the third person."[86] Beatitudes can also be found in the

---

[82] Koch, *Growth*, 18. For a more detailed survey of beatitudes in ancient cultures see Jacques Dupont, "'Béatitudes' égyptiennes," *Bib* 47 (1966): 185–222, esp. 185–192. Dupont provides a similar study on Egyptian beatitudes. He has compiled many beatitudes from ancient Egypt, and suggests that some similarities exist between those beatitudes and the type that formed in ancient Israel. The form of the evangelists' beatitudes, however, is distinct from the Egyptian form and shares more affinity with the OT and intertestamental type.

[83] Bock, *Luke*, 1.572.

[84] Bovon, *Luke*, 1.222; Bock, *Luke*, 1.572; Koch, *Growth*, 17. J. Dupont identifies several stand-alone beatitudes in Egypt, often at gravesites, Dupont, "Béatitudes." He builds primarily upon P. Humbert, *Recherches sur les sources égyptiennes de la littérature sapientiale d'Israël* (Mémoires de l'Université de Neuchâtel 7; Neuchâtel: Université de Neuchâtel, 1929); H. O. Lange, *Das Weisheitsbuch des Amenemope, aus dem papyrus 10,474 des British Museum* (Copenhagen: A.F. Høst & søn, 1925); Norman de Garis Davies, Seymour de Ricci, and Geoffrey Thorndike Martin, *The Rock Tombs of El-Amarna* (Archaeological Survey of Egypt 18; London, Boston: Egypt Exploration Fund, 1903). Dupont concludes that the beatitudes of the evangelists are closer to the OT beatitudes in form, content, and purpose than the potential Egyptian parallels Dupont, "Béatitudes," 222.

[85] Koch, *Growth*, 17.

[86] E.g., Ps 1:1; 2:12; 34:8; 40:4. Bock, *Luke*, 1.572; Robert A. Guelich, *The Sermon on the Mount* (Waco: Word, 1982), 63; Fitzmyer, *Luke*, 1.632–633.

second person (e.g., Deut 33:29; Ps 127:2[LXX]; Eccl 10:17; Isa 32:20).[87] The beatitude developed from simple trust in God towards an "eschatological hope," especially as they were adopted in apocalyptic literature (e.g., *1 En.* 99:10–15; *2 Bar* 10:6–7; cf. Isa 30:18; 32:20; Dan 12:12).[88] God's recompense overturns the current tribulation. Green refers to the "topos of transposition" found in Jewish and Greco-Roman literature as the best explanatory paradigm for the blessings and woes.[89] This *topos* refers to status reversal,[90] the exaltation of the lowly and humbling of the proud, which can be seen in several texts, including, the story of Coriolanus (Dionysius of Halicarnassus *Roman Antiquities*, books 7–8; Dionysius *Ant Rom* 7.66.1; 6.22–90), and frequently in Luke (1:46–55; 14:7–24; 16:19–31; 18:9–14; 22–24).[91] D. L. Balch discusses this topos and emphasizes that Luke's Mediterranean audience, rather than Jesus' original Palestinian audience, would have had these Greco-Roman authors and stories in mind when hearing Luke's narrative. They would have considered the philosophers' debates about this disparity and considered Jesus' message in light of these philosophical discussions (*Ant Rom* 72.3–78.1; 79.1–3).[92] Considering the strength of Jewish culture in Jesus' Galilee this suggestion is important. If Jesus adopts the topos of transposition it would have derived from Jewish scriptures, but his audience (Tyrians? Sidonians?) may have interpreted his sayings through the lens of the Greco-Roman predecessors.

On account of the presence of status reversals (i.e., the "topos of transposition") in Greco-Roman literature and because benefactors are said to bring blessings of such reversals upon their recipients, some have suggested that Jesus functions as a benefactor in the pronouncement of this re-

---

[87] Bock, *Luke*, 1.572; Marshall, *Luke*, 248; Bovon, *Luke*, 1.222; Koch, *Growth*, 18.

[88] Koch, *Growth*, 17; Guelich, *Sermon on the Mount*, 64–65; Talbert, *Theological Commentary*, 71–73; Bovon, *Luke*, 1.222; Bock, *Luke*, 1.572.

[89] Green, *Luke*, 264–265. He follows John O. York, *The Last Shall Be First: The Rhetoric of Reversal in Luke* (JSNT 46; Sheffield: JSOT Press, 1991); Robert Alter, *The Art of Biblical Narrative* (New York: Basic Books, 1981), 95; Gerald Prince, *Narrative As Theme: Studies in French Fiction* (Lincoln: University of Nebraska Press, 1992), 3–4; David L. Balch, "Rich and Poor, Proud and Humble in Luke-Acts," in *The Social World of the First Christians: Essays in Honor of Wayne A. Meeks* (ed. L. Michael White, and O. Larry Yarbrough; Minneapolis: Fortress Press, 1995), 214–233; George W. E. Nickelsburg, "Riches, the Rich, and God's Judgment in 1 Enoch 92–105 and the Gospel According to Luke," *NTS* 25 (1979): 324–344; Koch, *Growth*, 17–18.

[90] On "status reversal" as a theme see Talbert, *Reading Luke-Acts*, 170–171; Talbert, *Reading Luke*, 171.

[91] Cf. *Panegyricus* 167–168, 112; *Archidamus* 66–68, 9–10; *On the Peace* 24; *Areopagiticus* 2–5; *1 En.* 58:2; 99:10; *2 En.* 42:11, Ps 1:1, Prov 8:32–36, Dan 12:12; Tob 13:15–16, *2 Bar.* 10:6–7.

[92] Balch, "Rich and Poor," 223. Balch follows Alexander Fuks, *Social Conflict in Ancient Greece* (Jerusalem: Magness Press, 1984).

versal.⁹³ Since one expression of a benefactor could be seen in providing for the incapable, it is argued, the reversal of fortunes offered by God in the blessings and curses should be understood as one of God's benefits (6:20–26). D. J. Lull offers a slight parallel from Dio Chrysostom.⁹⁴ In the narrative Dio assures his audience that Zeus keeps virtuous kings alive into old age, but if they perish prematurely Zeus has blessing for them in the form of everlasting praise among men (Dio Chrysostom *Or.* 2.77–78). The virtue of the king prolongs his reign or assures him of postmortem blessing. The contexts and content of Dio's reversal and that declared by Jesus are significantly different. Jesus describes the toppling of the rich and the exaltation of the poor whereas Dio details the typical blessing received by the rich (long life) and the default blessing Zeus offers if the king does not enjoy the typical blessing (lasting reputation). Jesus announces the overturning of societal norms, whereas Dio reiterates societal expectation. There is, however, some similarity in the fact that virtue is rewarded in the present or future in both cases. Zeus, the benefactor, provides a reward at the end of life, or during life by extending it, for his loyal subjects.⁹⁵ Perhaps Jesus' audience from Tyre and Sidon, and a few from Jerusalem, interpreted his pronouncement in light of the benefits of a benefactor, but this was likely not Jesus' primary frame of reference. Though Lull and Moxnes contend that benefactors often brought similar reversals to their clients neither of them offers sufficient documentation from the ancient literary or archaeological sources to support the claim. Lull's reference to Dio Chrysostom (above) is the closest he comes to showing a benefactor giving a reversal, and Moxnes only references Danker who himself does not include reversals in the lists of benefactions offered by benefactors in any of his three major works on the subject.⁹⁶

---

⁹³ D. J. Lull, "The Servant-Benefactor as a Model of Greatness (Lk 22:24–30)," *NovT* 28 (1986): 289–305, 289 n. 5; Moxnes, "Patron-Client," 257–258; Moxnes, *Economy*, 20, 74, 138. Lull and Moxnes both refer to Danker's works on benefactors for cross-reference, but Danker does not include this section of Luke in any of his discussions of benefaction in the works these scholars reference.

⁹⁴ Lull, "Servant-Benefactor," 301.

⁹⁵ Lull, "Servant-Benefactor," 301.

⁹⁶ Moxnes refers to the first edition of Danker's Proclamation series commentary (*Luke*, 1976), 6–17, but in the first edition Danker does not include a section on reversals nor mention reversals among the benefactions in his benefactor section. Danker does provide a section entitled "Reversal of Fortunes" (pages 47–57) in the second edition of that commentary. However, he does not establish "reversals" as benefactions, but rather as demonstrations of Luke's ability to speak to a Greco-Roman audience. His reference to the reversal in Luke 6:20–26 supports this point (according to Danker, *Luke*, 2ⁿᵈ ed., 54). Danker does not reference reversals as benefactions in *New Age*, *Benefactor*, or *Luke* (1ˢᵗ or 2ⁿᵈ ed.). Nor does he refer to Luke 6:20–26, 27–38 in any section on benefactions. Danker does mention the pattern "words match deeds" (see section 4.2.2) for benefactors

4.2 The Sermon on the Plain (Luke 6:17–38)

The parallels which can be found in (Hellenistic) Jewish literature were most likely a stronger influence on Jesus. Galilee was deeply indebted to Jewish culture, as can be determined from both archaeological and literary evidence (see section 2.2.3). Hellenistic education may have been undertaken in Jerusalem, but the same cannot be said for Galilee (see section 2.2.4; *Ant.* 12:239–241). Therefore, neither Jesus nor his Galilean followers would have had extended exposure to Hellenistic writings (and beatitudes) in an academic setting. However, many of the second temple Jewish writings were not averse to Greek language, philosophy, or pedagogy which suggests that Jewish culture had adapted to the dominant Hellenistic culture to some degree (e.g., Sir 39:1–4; Philo; 4 Macc, Eupolemes).[97] The presence of similar beatitudes in Hellenistic Jewish literature (e.g., Sir 25:7–11; *2 En.* 42:6–12; 52; Tob 13:14–16[LXX]; *2 Bar.* 10:6–7) provides an important parallel for Jesus' beatitudes and woes in Luke.[98] Sirach 25:7–11 has verbal and structural parallels with Jesus' beatitudes:[99]

ἐννέα ὑπονοήματα ἐμακάρισα ἐν καρδίᾳ καὶ τὸ δέκατον ἐρῶ ἐπὶ γλώσσης ἄνθρωπος εὖ 'φραινόμενος ἐπὶ τέκνοις ζῶν καὶ βλέπων ἐπὶ πτώσει ἐχθρῶν μακάριος ὁ συνοικῶν γυναικὶ συνετῇ καὶ ὃς ἐν γλώσσῃ οὐκ ὠλίσθησεν καὶ ὃς οὐκ ἐδούλευσεν ἀναξίῳ ἑαυτοῦ μακάριος ὃς εὗρεν φρόνησιν καὶ ὁ διηγούμενος εἰς ὦτα ἀκουόντων ὡς μέγας ὁ εὑρὼν σοφίαν ἀλλ' οὐκ ἔστιν ὑπὲρ τὸν φοβούμενον τὸν κύριον φόβος κυρίου ὑπὲρ πᾶν ὑπερέβαλεν ὁ κρατῶν αὐτοῦ τίνι ὁμοιωθήσεται

"I can think of nine whom I would call blessed, and a tenth my tongue proclaims: a man who can rejoice in his children; a man who lives to see the downfall of his foes. Happy the man who lives with a sensible wife, and the one who does not plow with ox and ass together. Happy is the one who does not sin with the tongue, and the one who has not served an inferior. Happy is the one who finds a friend, and the one who speaks to attentive listeners. How great is the one who finds wisdom! But none is superior to the one who fears the Lord. Fear of the Lord surpasses everything; to whom can we compare the one who has it?" (NRSV)

---

and God as the example of the "Supreme Benefactor" in reference to 6:27–38, 35, 46–49; ibid., 34.

[97] Collins, "Cult," 38–61.

[98] Bock, *Luke*, 1.572; Bovon, *Luke*, 1.221–222; Guelich, *Sermon on the Mount*, 65–66; Talbert, *Theological Commentary*, 73.

[99] For the sake of comparison I work from the Greek rather than Hebrew, Syriac, or Latin texts. For modern assessments of the MSS evidence and difficulties consult Friedrich Vinzenz Reiterer, Renate Egger-Wenzel, Ingrid Krammer, Petra Ritter-Müller, and Lutz Schrader, *Zählsynopse zum Buch Ben Sira* (Fontes et subsidia ad Bibliam pertinentes 1; Berlin: De Gruyter, 2003); Pancratius Cornelis Beentjes, *The Book of Ben Sira in Hebrew: A Text Edition of All Extant Hebrew Manuscripts and a Synopsis of All Parallel Hebrew Ben Sira Texts* (VTSupp 68; Leiden: Brill, 1997); Patrick W. Skehan and Alexander A. Di Lella, *The Wisdom of Ben Sira: A New Translation with Notes* (AB 39; New York: Doubleday, 1987), 51–63.

Sirach employs μακάριος and cognates to describe the person who is blessed by God (Sir 25:7, 8, 9; Luke 6:20b, 21, 22); Sirach always translates μακάριος for אשר.[100] The ultimate means to attain God's blessing is through fearing him which Sirach equates with wisdom.[101] Sirach provides structural parallels to Luke's beatitudes in the use of a list of beatitudes and in the structure of the individual beatitude. Each beatitude identifies a blessing (μακάριος) then describes the blessed one with an articular participial phrase (e.g., ὁ συνοικῶν; ὁ διηγούμενος; ὁ εὑρών; 25:8, 9, 10; cf. Luke 6:21[οἱ πεινῶντες; οἱ κλαίοντες]) or relative clause (ὃς εὗρεν φρόνησιν; 25:9).

Tobit 13:14–16 LXX[102] provides other verbal, structural, and thematic parallels with Jesus' blessings and curses:

ἐπικατάρατοι πάντες οἱ μισοῦντές σε εὐλογημένοι ἔσονται πάντες οἱ ἀγαπῶντές σε εἰς τὸν αἰῶνα χάρηθι καὶ ἀγαλλίασαι ἐπὶ τοῖς υἱοῖς τῶν δικαίων ὅτι συναχθήσονται καὶ εὐλογήσουσιν τὸν κύριον τῶν δικαίων ὦ μακάριοι οἱ ἀγαπῶντές σε χαρήσονται ἐπὶ τῇ εἰρήνῃ σου μακάριοι ὅσοι ἐλυπήθησαν ἐπὶ πάσαις ταῖς μάστιξίν σου ὅτι ἐπὶ σοὶ χαρήσονται θεασάμενοι πᾶσαν τὴν δόξαν σου καὶ εὐφρανθήσονται εἰς τὸν αἰῶνα ἡ ψυχή μου εὐλογείτω τὸν θεὸν τὸν βασιλέα τὸν μέγαν
Cursed are all those who hate you, all those who love you forever will be blessed, rejoice and exult over the sons of the righteous since they will be gathered together and will bless the Lord of the righteous. O, those who love you will rejoice in your peace. Blessed are all those who grieve over your afflictions, since in you they will rejoice forever, witnessing all your glory and they will be glad. My soul, bless God the great king!

A few verbal parallels can be found in Tobit's employment of several words which Luke also adopts in the sermon (μισέω [Tob 13:14; Luke 6:22]; χαίρω [Tob 13:15, 16; Luke 6:23]; μακάριος [Tob 13:15, 16; Luke 6:20–22]). Structurally, Tobit's combination of blessings and curses parallels Luke's combination of blessings and woes. Tobit also uses the structure of blessing, articular participial phrase, and reward (e.g., μακάριοι, οἱ ἀγαπῶντές σε, χαρήσονται ἐπὶ τῇ εἰρήνῃ; Tob 13:15) which is found in Luke's beatitudes (μακάριοι, οἱ πεινῶντες νῦν, χορτασθήσεσθε; Luke 6:21). Thematically, Tobit and Luke expect God to reward and punish

---

[100] Jan Liesen, *Full of Praise An Exegetical Study of Sir 39, 12–35* (JSJSupp 64; Leiden: Brill, 1999), 150.

[101] Jeremy Corley, *Ben Sira's Teaching on Friendship* (Brown Judaic Studies 316; Providence: Brown Judaic Studies, 2002), 25 n. 97, 113, 217, 222, 226, 227; Skehan and Di Lella, *Ben Sira*, 342.

[102] I work here from Rahlf's version, for a more sophisticated approach to the various Greek versions along with the Aramaic and Hebrew, see Joseph A. Fitzmyer, *Tobit* (CEJL; Berlin: Walter de Gruyter, 2003), v-vii, 313–317; Stuart Weeks, "Some Neglected Texts of Tobit: The Third Greek Version," in *Studies in the Book of Tobit: A Multidisciplinary Approach* (ed. Mark Bredin; Library of Second Temple Studies 55; London: T & T Clark, 2006), 12–42.

people according to their earthly activity. Current affliction will be turned into joy when God intervenes for his people. For Tobit this intervention appears to be this-worldly, i.e., in the restoration of Jerusalem which his offspring may enjoy (13:16a),[103] while for Jesus (in Luke) it is the kingdom of God and eschatological reward.[104] By depicting the overturning of present situations, so that the afflicted will one day flourish, Tobit utilizes the "topos of transposition." The verbal, structural, and thematic parallels between these Hellenistic Jewish beatitudes and Luke's beatitudes suggest that a Galilean Jew would likely have been more indebted to this cultural expression than to Greek or Egyptian beatitudes.

The relationship of the beatitudes to earlier Jewish scripture is also pertinent (e.g., Isa 61:1–3; 29:18–20; 40:29–31).[105] The beatitudes and woes have a parallel in Isa 61:1–3. Commentators point out that this sermon appears to be a public version of a similar message given in synagogues.[106] The obvious predecessor is the Nazareth sermon (Luke 4:16–30) wherein Luke depicts Jesus announcing the fulfillment of Isa 61:1–3 (and Isa 58:6–10). Verbal and conceptual parallels tie the sermons from Luke 4 and 6 together with Isa 61:1–3 and 58:6–10. The opening announcement of the kingdom message that good news comes to the poor (οἱ πτωχοί) has its parallel in the first beatitude in which Jesus declares a blessing on the poor who belong to the kingdom of God (4:18; 6:20; Isa 61:1). Shortly after the sermon on the plain John receives reassurance that the message of good news to the poor has in fact been preached (7:22). Jesus goes on to bless the hungry and weeping (6:21). These two show up together in Isa 58:6–7, 9–10 in reference to God's ideal fast.[107] The passage alludes to the (eschatological) Sabbath year, and Jesus' announcement of blessing on these

---

[103] Stefan Beyerle, "'Release Me to Go to My Everlasting Home...' (Tob 3:6): A Belief in Afterlife in Late Wisdom Literature?" in *The Book of Tobit Text, Tradition, Theology: Papers of the First International Conference on the Deuterocanonical Books, Pápa, Hungary, 20–21 May, 2004* (ed. Géza G. Xeravits and József Zsengellér; JSJSupp 98; Leiden: Brill, 2005), 71–88, 85–86; József Zsengellér, "Topography as Theology: Theological Premises of the Geographical References in the Book of Tobit," in Xeravits and Zsengellér, *Tobit*, 188+plates I-Iv, 182; Richard Bauckham, "Tobit as a Parable for the Exiles of Northern Israel," in Bedin, *Tobit*, 140–164, 151–152; Carey A. Moore, *Tobit: A New Translation with Introduction and Commentary* (AB 40A; New York: Doubleday, 1996), 277–282.

[104] Guelich, *Sermon on the Mount*, 65–66.

[105] Bovon, *Luke*, 223–224; Eduard Schweizer, *The Good News According to Luke* (Atlanta: John Knox Press, 1984), 122.

[106] Bovon, *Luke*, 1.223; Sloan, *Jubilary Theology*; Johnson, *Luke*, 111; Bock, *Luke*, 1.574–575; Creed, *Luke*, 91; Danker, *New Age*, 81; York, *Last*, 97–98.

[107] Danker, *New Age*, 85.

groups perhaps signals the inauguration of that hope (see section 4.2.3 *Cultural*).[108]

Another parallel between Luke's depiction of Jesus and Jewish prophets can be seen in the use of woes (οὐαί; 6:24–26). Israel's prophets employed "woes" upon the people (whether Hebrew or Gentile; e.g., Hos 7:13; 9:12; Amos 5:16, 18; 6:1 LXX). The practice is especially prominent in Isaiah (1:4, 24; 3:9, 11; 5:8, 11, 18, 20, 21, 22; 10:1, 5; 17:12; 18:1; 24:16; 28:1; 29:1, 15; 30:1; 31:1; 33:1). Habakkuk pronounces woes (οὐαί) upon those who plunder other nations for their own gain (Hab 2:6–11). Isaiah pronounces woes (οὐαί) upon the ungodly rich who deprive the people of Israel (Isa 5:8–23).[109] In Luke, Jesus employs this pronouncement (οὐαί), common among Israel's prophets, in his rebuke of the rich. Imitation of Jewish prophetic forms and language, in addition to allusions to Israel's scriptures, helps to show that the sermon had a Jewish tenor and continuity with Jewish prophetic speech. The use of forms and language familiar to the Jewish prophets supports the notion that Luke's Jesus presents his critique in Jewish terms. It is instructive that Danker concludes similarly. One would expect Danker to highlight the importance of the benefactor motif in the section since he has written extensively on the topic and even describes Jesus as the benefactor par excellence in his writings. But Danker does not mention the benefactor motif as pertinent to this section of the sermon (6:20–26) in his commentaries or monograph. He instead emphasizes the parallels with the Jewish prophets and, especially, their declaration of woes upon the unjust rich.[110] The beatitudes and woes were likely intended, by Luke, to be interpreted along the lines of Jewish prophets rather than Greco-Roman benefactors and patrons. This does not, however, exclude the possibility that some from Jesus' audience (e.g., Tyre, Sidon, Jerusalem) interpreted him as a benefactor (or *patronus*, though this is less likely because Jesus was not Roman) who brought reversal to the needy.

Conclusion

If the *topos* of transposition can be found in both Jewish and Greco-Roman literature then one need not resort to a primarily Greco-Roman interpretation of the passage. Since the Jewish scriptures provide a closer parallel to the beatitudes in both form and content it seems that the (Hellenistic) Jew-

---

[108] Bock, *Luke*, 1.404–411. Thomas D. Hanks offers several reasons for understanding Isa 58 as an interpretation of Lev 25 to which Bergsma adds the conclusions of M. A. Fishbane. Thomas D. Hanks, *God So Loved the Third World* (trans. James C. Dekker; Maryknoll: Orbis, 1983), 99–102; cf. Bergsma, *Jubilee*, 195–198; Michael A. Fishbane, *Biblical Interpretation in Ancient Israel* (Oxford: Clarendon Press, 1985), 304–307.

[109] Johnson, *Luke*, 108; Danker, *Luke*, 91; idem, *New Age*, 83–84.

[110] Danker, *New Age*, 80–84.

ish background should be deemed more important. With only indirect references to benefactors performing the types of "reversals" depicted in the beatitudes (Dio Chrysostom *Or.* 2.77–78) one should only cautiously suggest that Luke portrays Jesus as a benefactor while proclaiming these beatitudes and woes. Therefore, it is not prudent to limit the interpretation of the passage to benefaction (much less *patrocinium*). The conclusions in chapters 2 and 3 of this book (see section 2.2.3) suggest that Jesus was more aware of Jewish predecessors and patterns. It is therefore more likely that he self-consciously functioned as a Jewish prophet in line with his predecessors. It is less likely that he thought of himself as either a benefactor or patron in the telling of the beatitudes, even though this does not rule out his adopting this stance elsewhere. This conforms to Luke's presentation in this section since he does not adopt *patrocinium* or benefaction terminology and does not fill the writing with material which must be understood primarily in those categories. Nevertheless, those from Tyre and Sidon, or even Jerusalem, may have interpreted the sayings along the lines of benefaction without this being Jesus' original frame of reference.

4.2.3 Loving Enemies (6:27–38)

Literary Context

Whereas Luke prefaces the previous section with a statement which identifies the audience as his disciples (εἰς τοὺς μαθητὰς αὐτοῦ ἔλεγεν; 6:20), he prefaces the present section with a statement from Jesus which seems to broaden the audience to all auditors ('Ἀλλὰ ὑμῖν λέγω τοῖς ἀκούουσιν; 6:27). "Those who hear" (6:27a) reiterates Luke's introductory statement that people had come out to hear Jesus (οἳ ἦλθον ἀκοῦσαι; 6:18).[111] A strong division between this middle section (6:27–38) and the previous section (6:20–26) is unwarranted; a few verbal and conceptual parallels suggest a continuous line of thought. Those who conform to Jesus' expectations are said to receive a great reward (μισθὸς ὑμῶν πολύς; ὁ μισθὸς ὑμῶν πολύς; 6:23, 35). Repetition of the idea that a person in the new community may be "hated" (μισέω) can be found in both sections (6:22, 27). Resilience when others hate, exclude, persecute, and mistreat is a common theme to both (6:22, 27–29). The introductory phrase of the middle section ('Ἀλλὰ ὑμῖν λέγω) does not signal a strong break from the previous section, but rather reminds the audience to listen and pay attention.[112] Luke transitions from a description of the new community Jesus creates

---

[111] Green, *Luke*, 270–271.
[112] Green, *Luke*, 269; contra Evans, *Luke*, 333. Similar phrases are used elsewhere in the LXX and NT without signifying a new audience, setting, or message: Josh 6:18; Mark 9:12–13; John 10:26; 1 Cor 6:8; 2 Cor 12:14.

into a description of the manner of life which the new community must adopt.[113] A mixture of rich and poor auditors appears to be addressed as well. Some among this audience apparently were of some means since they had both ἱμάτιον and χιτών and were the object of begging (6:29–30).[114] They also could do good (ἀγαθοποιέω) and lend (δανίζω) to others which suggests they had at least some excess. Those who were hated (μισέω), cursed (καταράομαι), mistreated (ἐπηρεάζω), and struck on the face (τύπτω) were likely of the lower social class since one would not normally treat an elite person in these ways. Descriptions of the ill-treatment experienced by those in the new community also preprares the reader for subsequent stories in Luke-Acts where disciples receive this sort of treatment (e.g., Luke 12:4; Acts 5:40; 21:32; 23:2–3).

Luke's repeated use of parallel statements draws out the contrasts intended in the instructions (6:27–38).[115] Luke begins with four statements with parallel form and focus (6:27–28). Present imperative verbs (ἀγαπᾶτε; καλῶς ποιεῖτε; εὐλογεῖτε; προσεύχεσθε) give command to treat generously one's adversaries. Apart from the first of the parallel phrases each of the adversaries is described with the use of a present participle (τοῖς μισοῦσιν; τοὺς καταρωμένους; τῶν ἐπηρεαζόντων; cf. τοὺς ἐχθρούς). Luke emphasizes that the adversary is not simply a generally harmful person but one who specifically mistreats the auditor by repeating the second person plural (ὑμῶν or ὑμᾶς) in each parallel statement.

He continues the theme of responding with generosity to mistreatment with a second group of three parallel statements (6:29–30). Three present active participles introduce three persons whose treatment of the audience member is negatively interpreted (τῷ τύπτοντί; τοῦ αἴροντός; τοῦ αἴροντος). Again he emphasizes the personal injury experienced by the auditors by repeating the second person singular three times (σε; σου; σά). Three different case endings for the second person make the importance of the personal injury incurred stand out.[116] In each of the three instances Luke uses a verb with imperatival force to identify the appropriate response (πάρεχε; κωλύσῃς; ἀπαίτει). Within the three parallel statements Luke inserts παντὶ αἰτοῦντι to broaden the group to include not only those who undertake negative actions (6:30a). This insertion follows a similar pattern as the previous three parallel statements by adopting a present participle to describe the adversary (παντὶ αἰτοῦντί), repeating the second person singular (σε), and employing an imperatival verb in reference to the appropriate response (δίδου).

---

[113] Green, *Luke*, 269.
[114] Green, *Luke*, 271.
[115] Bovon, *Luke*, 231.
[116] Parsons, *Luke*, 27–29.

A third group of three parallel statements contrasts between the practice of Jesus' followers and the practices of sinners (6:32–34). The form of these parallels is not quite as consistent as the previous two groups of parallel statements, but the contrast is still apparent. The three statements begin with subordinating conjunctions (εἰ; ἐὰν; ἐὰν) followed by verbs with subjunctival force (ἀγαπᾶτε; ἀγαθοποιῆτε; δανίσητε) which present the hypothetical action of the audience member. A participial phrase from the same root word or a relative clause describes the type of person hypothetically involved on the receiving end of the generous action (τοὺς ἀ γαπῶντας; τοὺς ἀγαθοποιοῦντας; παρ' ὧν ἐλπίζετε λαβεῖν). Luke presents Jesus as questioning the action by thrice repeating ποία ὑμῖν χάρις ἐστίν. He then follows with a rationale explaining how these actions (ἀγαπᾶτε; ἀ γαθοποιῆτε; δανίσητε) do not deserve commendation because even sinners perform the same actions toward the same types of people. Sinners love those who love them and lend to those from whom they anticipate an equal return (τὰ ἴσα).

Excursus: Defining τὰ ἴσα

The meaning of τὰ ἴσα is difficult to isolate. Two of the most recent scholarly commentaries on Luke arrive at a similar conclusion on the meaning of the term. Klein considers τὰ ἴσα to have a double meaning, "1) das Ausgeliehene 2) eine entsprechende Gegenleistung."[117] Bovon discusses the major options debated among scholars.[118] These include: 1) in accordance with Jewish law, lending to a brother with the expectation of only receiving the same amount (no interest) in return (Exod 22:25; Lev 25:35–37; Deut 23:21); 2) the original sum plus interest; 3) it is not a question of the accruing of interest but rather of the difference between "lending" (Leihen) and "giving" (Schenken), men lend but Christians give; 4) the term does not refer to the concrete sum, but to the same kind of thing in return ("die gleiche Dienstleistung");[119] 5) a double meaning which includes the financial matter and a critique of human reciprocity generally ("die Gegenseitigkeit kritisiert [ἵνα ἀπολάβωσιν τὰ ἴσα]: die menschliche χάρις [oder τὸ ἀνταπόδομα]"). Bovon prefers the fifth option.

Each parallel statement offers insight into the motivations of the giver. He gives in expectation of a return of equal value because he recognizes in the recipient the capacity to reciprocate.

A fourth group of four parallel statements gives admonitions to the audience on how they ought to live (6:37–38a). The first two parallel statements contain negative commands through present active imperative verbs (κρίνετε; καταδικάζετε). God responds to abstenance from judging and condemning by not judging or condemning the obedient (κριθῆτε; καταδι

---

[117] Klein, *Lukas*, 258 n. 60.
[118] Bovon, *Lukas*, 317–318; cf. Bock, *Luke*, 1.600–601; Marshall, *Luke*, 263; Plummer, *Luke*, 187.
[119] Marshall, *Luke*, 263.

κασθῆτε). The passive voice in both instances indicates that God is the agent of the action. Luke presents Jesus commanding his audience to forego judging and condemning with the negative particle (μή), but ensures God's certain response to their obedience by adopting a double negative (οὐ μή). The following two parallel statements are positive commands. The same form, minus the negative particles, is used in these second two commands. Present active imperative verbs dictate the action to be taken (ἀπολύετε; δίδοτε) while future passive verbs (ἀπολυθήσεσθε; δοθήσεται) indicate God's response to obedience.[120] A fifth parallel statement with similar form (ᾧ γὰρ μέτρῳ μετρεῖτε ἀντιμετρηθήσεται ὑμῖν) comes after an explanatory expansion (6:38b).

The four groups of parallel statements are broken up by three explanatory and transitional comments (6:31, 35–36, 38). Each comment is explanatory in the sense that it develops the thought of the previous group of parallel statements and transitional in that it prepares for the subsequent group of parallel statements.[121] The "Golden Rule" is the first of these comments (6:31). The first set of parallel statements concern a response to negative treatment. Stating the Golden Rule in positive terms goes one step further. One does not simply "avoid unfair treatment that one might not wish for oneself" but proactively treats others in the manner which they would like to receive.[122] Bock mentions twelve parallels to the rule from Jewish, Greek, Roman, and Chinese cultures (*b. Sab.* 31a; Sir 31:15; Tob 4:15; *TestNaph* 1.6; *Letter to Aristeas* 207; Philo, *Hypothetica*, 7.6; *Targ Ps. Jonathan* on Lev 19:8; *2 En.* 61:2; Herodotus 3:142; Isocrates *Nicocles* [*Cyprians*] 49, 61; Seneca *Ben.* 2.1.1; Confucius *Analects*, 15.23). The Golden Rule, because it is positively stated and directed at others, is the most forceful of the similar statements.[123] Because of its positively stated form and directedness toward others, the command seems closest to Lev 19:18 (ἀγαπήσεις τὸν πλησίον σου ὡς σεαυτόν; LXX).[124] Bovon contends

---

[120] Marshall, *Luke*, 266–267; Bovon, *Luke*, 1.242; idem, *Lukas*, 324–325; idem, *Luc*, 316–317; Tannehill, *Narrative Unity*, 1.130; idem, *Luke*, 120–121; Plummer, *Luke*, 189–190; Bock, *Luke*, 607–608; Talbert, *Theological Commentary*, 77–78; Victor H. Prange, *Luke* (People's Bible Commentary; Saint Louis: Concordia, 2004), 71–72; A. R. C. Leaney, *A Commentary on the Gospel According to St. Luke* (Harper's New Testament Commentaries; New York: Harper, 1958), 138; Lagrange, *Luc*, 197.

[121] Green, *Luke*, 272–275; (only 6:35–36) Bock, *Luke*, 1.602–604; Marshall, *Luke*, 263–267.

[122] Bock, *Luke*, 1.596; Green, *Luke*, 272–273; Fitzmyer, *Luke*, 1.639–640; Marshall, *Luke*, 262; Tannehill, *Luke*, 118–119.

[123] Bock, *Luke*, 1.596–597; Nolland, *Luke*, 298; cf. Fitzmyer, *Luke*, 1.637–638; Marshall, *Luke*, 262; Schürmann, *Lukasevangelium*, 1.349.

[124] Johnson, *Luke*, 109; Bock, *Luke*, 1.596; Betz, *Sermon*, 514; Kirk, "Love Your Enemies," 670; Leaney, *Luke*, 137.

that Judaism picked up the idea from Hellenistic philosophy, but he makes no argument and cites only Diogenes Laertius (1.36; ca. A.D. 200–500) who wrote much later than the NT.[125] The subsequent comments about loving others suggest that the Leviticus passage may have been in the background (6:32, 35). The next section (6:32–35) thus expands upon the preceding (6:27–31).

In 6:35–36 Luke summarizes the second group of parallel statements (6:32–34) by repeating the main verbs of those statements (6:35a) and offering a theological rationale for the new way of life (6:35b–36).[126] The love of enemies appears as the general call to action, which governed both the first and second sections (6:27–31, 32–34), so it is repeated in the first position (ἀγαπᾶτε τοὺς ἐχθροὺς ὑμῶν; 6:35a). The following two verbs come directly from the second section (6:32–34) with subsequent reiteration of them intended to expand upon the type of approach to enemies Jesus expects of his followers (ἀγαθοποιεῖτε καὶ δανίζετε; 6:35a). With this way of life in mind he offers a theological rationale for how his people will live (6:35b–36). Rather than receiving recompense for their actions by directing their generosity towards those who can repay, the Christian directs his generosity toward those that cannot repay in the hope that God will reciprocate with reward in the future and in imitation of God's own manner of directing generosity.[127]

Luke 6:38b has less transitional force than the previous two summary statements (6:31, 35–36), but it seems to expand in summary fashion upon the teaching of its adjacent context (6:37–38a) and of the previous two sections (6:27–31, 32–36).[128] Luke culminates this section through the use of an expressive image, measuring wheat at market. The same sort of measure adopted by the individual will be employed by God in response. Luke anticipates a good measure being adopted by Jesus' followers and in response God gives an abundant measure to his children. Thus, the image of a storeowner filling the fold of his garment, shaking the seed so as to let it settle, pressing it together to make room, and carefully continuing to create a cone above the edge of the garment shows the abundance of God's blessing to be poured out in this life and in the life to come upon those that fol-

---

[125] Bovon, *Luke*, 1.244.

[126] Bock, *Luke*, 1.602–604; Fitzmyer, *Luke*, 1.640; Marshall, *Luke*, 263–265; R. Bultmann, *Die Geschichte der synoptischen Tradition* (Göttingen: 1958), 100; cf. Nolland, *Luke*, 1.299.

[127] Green, *Luke*, 273–275; Johnson, *Luke*, 112; Bovon, *Luke*, 1.234–239; Bock, *Luke*, 1.602–604; Talbert, *Theological Commentary*, 76–79; Nolland, *Luke*, 1.298–299; Fitzmyer, *Luke*, 1.639.

[128] Johnson, *Luke*, 115–116; Green, *Luke*, 275; Bovon, *Luke*, 1.243–244; Nolland, *Luke*, 1.301; Tannehill, *Luke*, 120–121.

low Jesus' commands.¹²⁹ Generosity toward others who cannot reciprocate is repaid from God's abundance.

Linguistic Matters

This critical section of Jesus' sermon (6:27–38) carries several terms which sometimes evince reciprocity, in general, or benefaction, in particular. The general (social historical) category of reciprocity found more specific expression in Hellenistic, Roman, and Jewish cultures (see sections 2.1; 2.2) which makes it difficult to isolate one specific background from which Jesus may have derived his adoption of reciprocity. It seems most likely, given the indebtedness of Galilee to Jewish thought, that Jesus would have developed thoughts on reciprocity in line with (Hellenistic) Jewish culture. In light of the vocabulary adopted it seems likely that a Hellenistic Jewish version of reciprocity lies in the background of Luke's comments (ἀπαιτέω; ἀπέχω; ἀπολαμβάνω; ἀπελπίζω; χαρὶς; μισθὸς; cf. ἀντιμετρηθήσετα), and it is possible that a critique of benefaction (καλῶς ποιεῖτε; ἀγαθοποιέω; ἀχάριστος; χρηστός; χάρις) was also intended.¹³⁰ No vocabulary connected to *patrocinium* in particular has been identified in this section (6:27–38).

G. B. Philipp argues that the preposition ἀπο- frequently signals the presence of reciprocity in ancient contexts.¹³¹ ᾿Αποδιδόναι, ἀπόδοσις, and ἐ ναποδεικνύναι repeatedly surface in reciprocity and benefaction contexts and often deserve to be rendered "to return" or "return" as in response to benefaction.¹³² For example, a decree honoring Eumenes II and his brother Attalos (175/174 B.C.) identifies the two as benefactors in need of being reciprocated by the people (*OGIS* 248):

---

¹²⁹ Marshall, *Luke*, 267; Bock, *Luke*, 1.608; Bovon, *Luke*, 1.242; Green, *Luke*, 275; Johnson, *Luke*, 113–114.

¹³⁰ For the Jewish idea of "measure for measure" see Beate Ego, "God's Justice: The 'Measure for Measure' Principle in 2 Maccabees," in *The Books of the Maccabees: History, Theology, Ideology* (ed. Géza G. Xeravits and József Zsengellér; JSJS 118; Leiden: Brill, 2005), 141–154, esp.142–148.

¹³¹ G. B. Philipp, "Kritzeleien eines erleichterten Lehrers auf einem hölzernen Buchdeckel," *Gymnasium* 85 (1978): 151–159, 157; Wolfgang Stegemann, "The Contextual Ethics of Jesus," in Stegemann, Malina, Theissen, *Social Setting*, 45–61, 58–59.

¹³² Harrison, *Language*, 40–4, 51, 55. Inscriptions include: Michel, 982; decree of Piraeus from 217/216 B.C. with translation by Harrison, *Language*, 40; *SEG* XXIV 1100; *IG* XII(9) 899; *IG* VII(2) 4133; *SEG* XI 948. Moxnes identifies Luke as exemplary in his understanding of reciprocity terminology (ἀνταπόδομά, ἀνταποδοῦναί, ἀνταποδοθήσεται; Luke 14:12–14), Moxnes, *Economy*, 129–130; cf. Lukas Bormann, *Recht, Gerechtigkeit und Religion im Lukasevangelium* (Studien zur Umwelt des Neuen Testaments 24; Göttingen: Vandenhoeck & Ruprecht, 2001), 142, 144–145, 147–148.

4.2 The Sermon on the Plain (Luke 6:17–38)

In order, therefore, that the People may appear foremost in the returning of a favour (ἐγ χάριτος ἀποδόσει) and be conspicuous in honouring those benefiting (εὐεργετοῦντας) the People and its friends voluntarily and in committing the goodness of their deeds to eternal memory (ἀίδιος μνήμην) ... (trans. Harrison, *Language*, 41)

Ἀπο- prefixed reciprocity can be seen in Hellenistic Jewish texts as well (e.g., Sir 30:6; 3:31; 32:2).[133] In describing the benefit of raising a son in godliness, Sirach claims that even in death the father will not lose honor because his son continues his legacy. In particular the son reciprocates both good and bad treatment of the father while he was living (Sir 30:4–6).

ἐναντίον ἐχθρῶν κατέλιπεν ἔκδικον καὶ τοῖς φίλοις ἀνταποδιδόντα χάριν
"He has left behind him an avenger against his enemies, and one to repay the kindness of his friends." Sir 30:6 (NRSV)

The ἀπο- prefix again is adopted to indicate reciprocity.[134] Doubling the prefix by adding ἀντί- increases the likelihood of reciprocity in this text since ἀντί- is also frequently found in reciprocal situations (cf. ἀντὶ μετρηθήσετα; 6:38).[135]

Luke's use of several terms prefixed by ἀπο-may suggest that reciprocity is in view (e.g., ἀπαιτέω; ἀπέχω; ἀπολαμβάνω; ἀπελπίζω; cf. ἀντὶ μετρηθήσετα). These terms are not those commonly identified in reciprocity and benefaction contexts (e.g., ἀποδιδόναι, ἀπόδοσις, and ἐναποδεικνύναι), but the ἀπο-prefix often suggests this background. Nevertheless, the specific terms adopted by Luke more frequently indicate demand for return of things which rightfully belong to one (ἀπαιτέω; Herodotus 1.2; 5.35), payment for work done or return for a loan (ἀπολαμβάνω; Herodotus 8.137; *And*. 3.15), to keep away from (e.g., Il. 6.96.277) or have/receive ("payment") in full (ἀπέχω; Aeschines 2.50; Callimachus *Epigr.* 55), or to despair (ἀπελπίζω; Hyp Ath. 35; Plb. 1.19.2).[136] Ἀντιμετρέω means "to measure in return" (Ps. Lucian *Amor* 19; *Rhet Gr.* 1.523.12).[137] The combination of four ἀπο-prefixed terms, and a fifth ἀντί-prefixed term, suggests

---

[133] Harrison, *Language*, 110–111.

[134] Harrison, *Language*, 110–111.

[135] Harrison, *Language*, 51. Cf. *SEG* 11.948. "and also to give to him the front seats at the theatre and the first place in a procession and (the privilege of) eating in the public restivals which are celebrated amongst us and to offer willingly (χαρ[ιζομένους) all (the) honour (τιμὴν) given to a good and fine man in return for (ἀντί) the many (kindnesses) which he provided ... in order that those who confer benefits may receive favour (χαρὶν) in return for (ἀντί) love of honour ..."

[136] Spicq, *Lexicon*, ἀπελπίζω (156–158); BDAG, 100, asserts that context "demands the meaning, lend, expecting nothing in return (whether in kind or in other goods or services)." Ἀπέχω (162–168); BDAG, 102–103; Liddell, *Lexicon*, 175, 188, 205, 185.

[137] BDAG, 89, "measure in return."

that Luke may have intended to describe Jesus' teaching in terms of reciprocity, though the common use of these terms in wage/payment settings prevents one from being certain that reciprocity is in view.

One of the four ἀπό-prefixed terms (ἀπελπίζω) generates debate because etymylogically it seems to indicate reciprocity, but its usual meaning does not have reciprocity in view. Luke likely intends ἀπελπίζοντες to mean "hope for reciprocation" despite the fact that it has no parallel usage with this meaning in extant literature. The normal meanings of ἀπελπίζω, "to doubt" or "to despair", are not preferable in this context because the phrase the term summarizes (παρ' ὧν ἐλπίζετε λαβεῖν) and other uses of ἀπό for "return" prefixes (e.g., ἀπαίτει; ἀπολάβωσιν) in the paragraph make clear the focus on reciprocating activity.[138] *Exod. Rab.* 31 (91c), though late, may be a helpful parallel use of the term. "The one who lends money without demanding interest, God esteems this so highly in him that it is as if he had kept all the commandments."[139] Ἀπελπίζω should be understood in parallel with ἐλπίζειν λαμβάνειν and ἀπολαμβάνειν to refer to recompensation for generosity.[140] Other terminology that lacks the ἀπο- prefix (ἀμείβειν, ἀμοιβή, ἀντάμειψις, and ἐν μέρει), which commonly signals reciprocity often specifically in benefaction contexts, does not surface in our passage.[141]

---

[138] Bovon prefers the normal meaning and therefore translates the phrase "lend, without doubting at all," Bovon, *Luke*, 1.238; cf. Plummer, *Luke* (ICC; 1896), 188; Isa 29:19; 1 Clem 59:3; Sir 22:21; 27:21; 2 Macc 9:18. Some suggest emending the text to read ἀντελπίζοντες or ἐπελπίζοντες, Théodore Reinach "Mutuum date, nihil inde sperantes," *Revue de études grecques* 7 (1894): 57–58; Hubert Pernot, "Une correction à Luc VI,35," *Comptes rendus de l'Académie des inscriptions et belles-lettres* (1929): 277–280. The adopted reading above has support in Theodore Zahn, *Das Evangelium des Lukas: Ausgelegt* (1st-2nd ed.; Kommentar zum Neuen Testament 3; Leipzig/Erlangen: Deichert, 1913), 292 n. 63; Johnson, *Luke*, 109; cf. Nolland, *Luke*, 1.299–300. Fitzmyer contends that the normal meaning "scarcely suits the context here." He instead translates, "looking for nothing in return," with reference to J. H. Moulton and G. Milligan, *The Vocabulary of the Greek Testament* (London: Hodder and Strougton, 1930), 56; cf. Godet, *Luke*, (1875),1.326; Creed, *Luke*, (1930),95; Marshall, *Luke*, 264; Fitzmyer, *Luke*, 1.640; Schürmann, *Lukasevangelium*, 355 n. 90.

[139] Cited in Spicq, *Lexicon*, 158 n. 8.

[140] Hans Klein, *Das Lukasevangelium* (Kritisch-exegetischer Kommentar über das Neue Testament 1.3; Göttingen: Vandenhoeck und Ruprecht, 2006), 258 n. 62; Bock, *Luke*, 1.602; Spicq, *Lexicon*, 1.158; idem, *Agapè dans le Nouveau Testament analyse des textes* (Etudes Bibliques; Paris: Gabalda, 1958), 1.111; E. Klostermann, *Das Lukas-Evangelium* (2nd ed.; Tübingen, 1929), 82 (citing a parallel in *Exod. Rab.* 31 [91c]); M. J. Lagrange, "Néhémie et Esdras," *RB* 3 (1894): 561–585; 4 (1895): 193–202, 196–197; idem, *Luc*, 195; Godet, *Luke*, (1875),1.326; Creed, *Luke*, (1930),95; Marshall, *Luke*, 264; Fitzmyer, *Luke*, 1.640; Schürmann, *Lukasevangelium*, 355 n. 90.

[141] *I. Delos* IV 1521; *OGIS* 248 (trans. Harrison 41). Cf. *SIG* 3.800; *SEG* XIV 1100; *IG* XII(9) 899.

4.2 The Sermon on the Plain (Luke 6:17–38)

Χαρὶς and μισθὸς may be interpreted under the general (social historical) category of reciprocity. Bovon suggests that χαρὶς and μισθὸς are indicative of reciprocity as seen in Hellenistic Jewish texts (e.g., Sir 12:1).[142] Elsewhere in the Hellenistic world the importance of χαρὶς in reciprocity contexts is clearly evident (e.g., *CEG* 326, 227; *Mem.* 4.3.15; cf. 332, 275; see section 2.1.1).[143] Harrison's work showcases the importance of χαρὶς in reciprocity in Greco-Roman and Hellenistic Jewish cultures.[144] Μισθὸς has not been the subject of such extended study and its general use in Hellenistic Jewish literature as reward, wages, and payment prevents one from identifying reciprocity from this term alone (see section 4.2.1 *Linguistic*). However, in conjunction with several other terms and in a context of reciprocity one may have more reason to include μισθὸς in a list of reasons to suggest that reciprocity is in view.

A few terms suggest an interpretation of this instruction in terms of benefaction (καλῶς ποιεῖτε; ἀγαθοποιέω; ἀχάριστος; χρηστός; χάρις). Two terms closely related to εὐεργεσία surface in the narrative (καλῶς ποιεῖτε; ἀγαθοποιέω).[145] Kirk, following Dihle, identifies a common theme in Hellenistic texts of kings (benefactors) offering their benefits to others, but receiving evil in return:[146] Βασιλικὸν καλῶς ποίοντα κακῶς ἀκούειν. In Hellenistic Jewish literature καλῶς ποιέω is sometimes employed without a clear expression of benefaction in view (e.g., Lev 5:4; 1 Macc 12:18, 22; 2 Macc 2:16; Jer 4:22). In other places, however, an interpretation along benefaction lines does seem appropriate (e.g., Gen 32:13; Est 8:18[LXX]). In Est 8:12–24 (LXX) King Artaxerxes is commended for being a gracious benefactor (τῶν εὐεργετούντων χρηστότητι) who does good for his people (καλῶς ποιήσετε).[147] The author expects the recipients to respond with gratitude but they refuse and instead plot against their benefactors (ἣν εὖ 'χαριστίαν οὐ μόνον ἐκ τῶν ἀνθρώπων ἀνταναιροῦντες ἀλλὰ καὶ τοῖς τῶν ἀπειραγάθων κόμποις ἐπαρθέντες). Luke's use of this phrase (καλῶς ποιεῖτε) may have been intended to indicate benefaction. The combination of this term with other terms which come in benefaction contexts adds to the possibility that benefaction is in view.

Ἀγαθοποιέω was unknown in the papyri before the time of the NT. Its meaning must be derived, therefore, from the *Letter of Aristeas* (242) and

---

[142] Bovon, *Luke*, 237. Cf. Zahn, *Lukas*, 292.

[143] Gill, Postlethwaite, and Seaford, *Reciprocity*, 108–118; Harrison, *Language*, passim.

[144] Esp. Harrison, *Language*, 50–53, 128–133, 140–144, 179–183, 194.

[145] One may also compare εὖ ποιεῖν and εὐποιΐα which do not surface in Luke, but were common in benefaction inscriptions (cf. Prov 3:27–28; Sir 12:1; 14:7, 11, 13; *Ep Jer* 1:63; Heb 13:16; Danker, *Benefactor*, no. 19 = *IGR* 3.739). Danker, *Benefactor*, 325.

[146] Kirk, "Love Your Enemies," 681 n. 72; Dihle, *Regel*, 45.

[147] Danker, *Benefactor*, 45, 299–301.

the LXX (Num 10:32; Judg 17:13; Tob 12:13; 1 Macc 11:33; 2 Macc 1:2; cf. *T. Benj.* 5:2; 1 Pet 2;14, 15, 20; 3:6, 17; 4:19; 3 John 11).[148] The uses of this term in the LXX do not seem usually to come in benefaction contexts. Several uses arise in covenant/legal contexts which argues against benefaction and *patrocinium* which are extralegal arrangements (e.g., Num 10:29–34; 2 Macc 1:2). At other times it seems to be generally used to describe good things expected from God's hand (Judg 17:7–13; Zeph 1:12) or good things done by man (Tob 12:11–15; Sir 42:14).

In 1 Macc 11:32–36, however, there is reason to consider its use in benefaction terms.[149] King Demetrius ratified the relationship he had with the Jews, whom he considered friends (φίλος), by doing good (ἀγαθοποιέω) to them. He praises them for having εὔνοια and being δίκαιος and reciprocates (χαρίς) their loyalty with good deeds. The language of reciprocity coupled with laudatory adjectives (εὔνοια, χαρὶς, δίκαιος) and friendship language (φίλος) suggests that a benefactor/beneficiary relationship is in view.

Although I have not discovered the exact term (ἀγαθοποιέω) in a benefaction inscription, grammatically similar uses do arise and the term was known in the Greco-Roman world (*OGIS* 54.14–20).[150]

Χαιρέστρατος εἶπε Λεονίδεν ἐάν τις ἀποκτένει ἐν τὸν πόλεον hὸν 'Αθεναῖοι κρατῶσι τὲν τιμορίαν ἔναι καθάπερ ἐάν τις 'Αθεναίον ἀποθάνει ἐπαινέσαι δὲ ἀγαθὰ hόσα ποιεῖ περὶ 'Αθεναίος Λεονίδες
Rejoice troops: Leonides said if anyone kills the mighty Athenians in the war the honor (to him) will be just as if any Athenian died, to praise all the good which Leonides the Athenian has done (Author's translation)

A second benefactor was noted for doing good (*OGIS* 167, ll. 17–26).[151] The decree praises the benefactor for his efforts on behalf of the city. He

---

[148] Ceslas Spicq, *Theological Lexicon of the New Testament* (trans. and ed. James D. Ernest; Peabody: Hendrickson, 1994), 1.1–4. The term is absent from literary sources before the first-century, and I have only discovered the term in one inscription (before the third century) which comes from the time of Trajan. See Adam Lajtar, *Die Inschriften von Byzantion Teil I. Die Inschriften* (Bonn: Habelt, 2000). He identifies an epitaph for the deceased Thracian, Marcus Cincius Nigrinus who lived during the time of Trajan, identified as being ἥρως ἀγαθοποιός (*SEG* 671; Lajtar, S31). Μᾶρκος Κίνκιος Νιγρεῖνος στράτιώτης χώρτης ἐνδεκάτης ὀρβανῆς ἥρως ἀγαθοποιός. "Bei der Bezeichnung ἥρως ἀγαθοποιός druckt sich die Glaube an die Macht der Toten zu schaden und zu nutzen, aus. Der verstorbene Marcus Cincius Nigrinus hat nur zum Guten beigetragen."

[149] Danker, *Benefactor*, 301.

[150] *Editio Princeps* H. G. Lolling, Sitzungsberichte preussischen Akad. Wiss. (Berlin, 1888), 241 n. 13.

[151] *Editio Princeps* A. Boeckh, *Corpus Inscriptionum Graecarum*, Berlin, 1828ff, 2691 c d e; cf. II page 473. Ἀρταξέρξευς βασιλεύοντος Μαυσσωλλου ἐξαιθραπεύοντος ἔδοξε Μυλασεῦσι ἐκκλησίης κυρίης γενομένης καὶ ἐπεκύρωσαν αἱ τρεῖς φυλαί τοὺς

has done well in word and deed (καὶ λόγωι καὶ ἔργωι) and earned the title of benefactor of the city (τὰ ἱερὰ Ἀναθήματα καὶ τὴμ πόλιν καὶ τοὺς εὖ 'εργέτας τῆς πόλεως). The decree describes his efforts as "doing good things" (ἀγαθὰ ποιήσαντος).[152]

Luke's use of the term ἀγαθοποιέω may have been intended along the lines of benefaction as in 1 Macc 11 or the approximations of the term in some inscriptions (*OGIS* 54; 167). At times the term appears related to εὐ 'εργεσία which suggests that Luke depicts Jesus as being familiar with benefaction ideology (6:32, 35). It is not necessary, however, to see in this term alone the ideology of benefaction since it could be used in Hellenistic Jewish writings with only a general meaning ("to do good") or in covenant contexts which rule out the extralegal benefaction and *patrocinium*.

A few terms which frequently arise in benefaction inscriptions also arise in the narrative (χάρις; ἀχάριστος; χρηστός). Χάρις and related terms (e.g., ἀχάριστος) were used on all sides of the benefactor exchange (see ch. 2). The generous giver could be described as χάρις or his recipient could respond appropriately with χάρις or inappropriately with ἀχάριστος. Harrison provides many examples of this practice. For example, after displaying his generosity to the Athenians and being recognized in a decree, Demosthenes critiques the ungrateful response of Aeschines harshly (Demosthenes *On the Crown*, 118–120).[153] The decree praises (ἔπαινος) Demosthenes for honor (ἀρετή) and good works (καλοκαγαθίας), but Demosthenes finds fault with Aeschines whom he condemns for not accepting gifts but indicting the gratitude shown by the decree.

Τὸ λαβεῖν οὖν τὰ διδόμεν' ὁμολογῶν ἔννομον εἶναι τὸ χάριν τούτων ἀπὸ δοῦναιπαρανόμων γράφει ὁ δὲ παμπόνηρος ἄνθρωπος καὶ θεοῖς ἐχθρὸς καὶ βάσκανος ὄντως ποῖός τις ἂν εἴη πρὸς θεῶν οὐχ ὁ τοιοῦτος
"Acceptance of gifts you admit to be legal; gratitude for gifts you indict for illegality. In Heaven's name, what do we mean by dishonesty and malignity, if you are not dishonest and malignant?" (C. A. Vince, LCL)

The decree praises Demosthenes as a benefactor whose generosity was properly received by the council and he was crowned in response. Demosthenes signals Aeschines' failure to appreciate proper reciprocity (τὸ χάριν τούτων ἀποδοῦναι) because he had claimed that it was unlawful (παρανόμων). Demosthenes puts Aeschines' actions on par with an enemy, claiming that Aeschines' actions have nullified the distinction between the

---

Πελδέμω παῖδας παρανομήσαντας ἐς τὴν εἰκόνα τὴν Ἑκατόμνω ἀνδρὸς πολλὰ καὶ ἀγαθὰ ποιήσαντος τὴμ πόλιν τὴμ Μυλασέων καὶ λόγωι καὶ ἔργωι ἀδικεῖν καὶ τὰ ἱερὰ Ἀ ναθήματα καὶ τὴμ πόλιν καὶ τοὺς εὐεργέτας τῆς πόλεως

[152] Danker no. 19; *IGR* 3.739 (8.30.85–105).

[153] Cf. Danker, *Benefactor*, 338–339. See also Danker, *Benefactor*, 1; Jost Benedum, "Griechische Arztinschriften aus Kos," *ZPE* 25 [1977]: 265–276, 265–270.

ungrateful enemy (ἐχθρός) and the grateful recipient. It is implied that the one who is ungrateful should also be understood as an enemy.

Some Greco-Roman philosophers on reciprocity had instructed others against halting generosity in the face of ingratitude, but most persisted to teach that one ought to identify and pursue worthy recipients (e.g., Seneca *Ben.* 3.1.3; 3.6.1–2; 3.7.1; 4.34.3; Herodotus 5.90; Cicero *Duties* 1.15.47).

Si sciam ingratum esse, non dabo beneficium. At obrepsit, at imposuit: nulla hic culpa tribuentis est, quia tamquam grato dedi. "Si promiseris," inquit, "te daturm beneficium et postea ingratum esse scieris, dabis an non? Si facis sciens, peccas, das enim, cui non debes date; si negas, et hoc modo peccas: non ads ei, cui promisisti."
"If I know that a man is ungrateful, I shall not give him a benefit. Yet if he has tricked me, if he has imposed upon me, no blame attaches to the giver because I made the gift supposing that the man would be grateful. 'Suppose,' you say, 'that you have promised to give a benefit, and later have discovered that the man is ungrateful, will you or will you not bestow it? If you do knowingly, you do wrong, for you give to one to whom you ought not to give; if you refuse, you likewise do wrong – you not give to one to whom you promised to give.'" (LCL; Seneca *Ben.* 4.34.2–3)

Seneca offers two hypothetical situations and in both cases deems it wrong to give to an ungrateful person. In the first scenario he will not intentionally give a benefit to one with a reputation of ingratitude. In the second scenario he sets a hypothetical trap in which he may be in error either for refusing a promise or for benefiting an ingrate. However, Seneca is not caught by the trap and insists that he made the promise in good conscience, expecting that the man was of thankful disposition, but feels no reservation for withholding the benefit when the new information of his ingratitude is presented (4:34.4–4:35.1–3). Jesus urges his followers to supersede this ethic by benefiting those with reputations of ingratitude. This ingratitude should not dissuade generosity even if the reputation of ingratitude is fully recognized before the benefit is given. He commands his followers to avoid calculating reciprocity when considering benefits. Instead they are commanded to give to everyone including the incapable of reciprocity, the ungrateful to reciprocity, and the outright enemy (6:27, 30, 35).

Jewish writers were also familiar with the category of the ungrateful sometimes using ἀχάριστος in benefactor contexts and sometimes without reference to benefaction (4 Macc 9:10; Wis 16:29; Sir 18:18; 29:16; 29:25; cf. 2 Tim 3:2).[154] Sirach 29:16 seems to describe an incorrect response (ἀχάριστος) to a benefactor's generosity. The ungrateful person (ἀχάριστος) abandons (ἐγκαταλείπω) his savior/rescuer (ῥυσάμενον). Savior

---

[154] See also Philo *Opif* 169.3; *Sac* 58.1; *Immut* 48.8; 74.2; *Heres* 226.11; 302.3; *Jos* 99.3; *Mos* 1.58.4; *Spec* 1.284.2; 2.115.5; *Virt* 166.1; *Legat* 60.2; 118.6; *QGen* 1.96.3; *QEx* 2.49a.3; *Sacr* 57–8; *Mut* 52–53; *Som* 2.224. Harrison, *Language*, 123–125. I did not find any uses of ἀχάριστος in Palestine in the papyri.

is frequently a title of benefactors while allegiance and gratitude were the expected responses (see section 2.1).[155] The one who shows ingratitude does so by abandonment. But just after this passage Sirach appears to use ἀχάριστος in a non-benefactor context (Sir 29:24–27). Sirach describes the paltry existence (ζωὴ πονηρὰ) of the guest who must submit to play the role of servant who serves drinks (ξενιεῖς καὶ ποτιεῖς) to others but is not thanked (εἰς ἀχαριστα) in response. The guest does not belong among the higher class of benefactors or patrons since the owner of the home speaks down to him (ἐπὶ τούτοις πικρὰ ἀκούσῃ) by referring to him derogatorily as a πάροικε who must make room for more honored guests (δόξης ἐπεξένωταί μοι). Jewish writers apparently used ἀχάριστος in both benefactor and non-benefactor contexts.

Jewish writers used χαρὶς and cognates in reciprocal and non-reciprocal contexts, but Philo appears to use the word-group as one component in recasting his Jewish faith in Hellenistic terms. Philo provides an example of a Hellenistic Jewish author who likely reinterpreted the OT covenant into a Greco-Roman form of benefactor relationship (*Quod Deus* 104–108; *Leg All* 3.14; *Jos* 249; *Som* 2.176–178; *Mut* 39–40, 52, 58.).[156] In his reinterpretation of the covenant (unmerited election by God), Philo describes a relationship which functions on the basis of merit, arête, and virtue while forbidding God's generosity (χαρὶς) for the ungrateful (e.g., *Sacr* 57–8; *Mut* 52–53; *Som* 2.224). Grace is restricted to the worthy (ἄξιος). Philo seems to have been impacted by Greco-Roman beneficience since benefactors would not benefit the unworthy or those "who might not respond worthily" (e.g., Seneca *Ben.* 2.18.5; 3.12.4; 4.27.4–5; 4.34.2; 5.20.6–7; 5.22.2–3; 6.4.5–6; see section 2.1).[157] His thought derives from the Greco-Roman world rather than the OT because he claims that the ἄξιος somehow attracted God's χαρὶς. Meriting God's χαρὶς does not take place in the OT (see section 4.2.2 *Cultural*).[158]

Kindness (χρηστός) was also a mark of benefactors. Two examples demonstrate this fact. Danker describes a decree made to honor Nikeratos, son of Papias, for the kindness (χρηστότης) he had shown the city of Olbia (*SIG* 730, ll. 20–29; first-century B.C.).[159] Nikeratos received a gold crown,

---

[155] Danker, *Benefactor*, 324–325.
[156] This paragraph is a summary of Harrison, *Language*, 122–124.
[157] Harrison, *Language*, 125.
[158] Harrison, *Language*, 125.
[159] Danker, *Benefactor*, 325; *Editio princeps* Wilhelm Goett, *Gottingische gelehrte Anzeigen* (1903), 796. M. Rostovtzeff, *The Social and Economic History of the Hellenistic World* (2 vols; 2nd ed.; rev. by P. M. Fraser; Oxford: Oxford University Press, 1972), 2.776. ὥστε ἐπὶ τούτους ὁ δῆμος αἰφνίδιον συμφορὰν θεασάμενος τῆς πόλεως ἀπὸ βεβλημένης ἀγαθὸν πολείτην καλεπῶς μὲν ἤνεγκεν τὸ πένθος αὐτοῦ διὰ τὴν χρηστότητα X ἐπαχθῶς δὲ διὰ τὴν τοῦ θανάτου ὠμότητα δεδόχθαι οὖν τῆι βουλῆι καὶ τῶι δήμωι

state funeral, and the honorary title of benefactor for his generosity to the city (in defending it to his death). In approximately 48–47 B.C., Kallistos, was honored by a decree for his χρηστός toward the city of Knidia (*SIG* 761, ll. 1, 10–18).[160] Kallistos received commendation as a good and noble man (ἀνὴρ καλὸς κἀγαθός). He therefore earned the honor of being recognized as proxenos and benefactor (πρόξενον καὶ εὐεργέτην) of Amphictyonus and Delphi. He was known for his kindness and largesse (χρηστότητα καὶ μεγαλοψυχίαν). Decrees often use χρηστός to describe the noble character of the benefactors they seek to honor. In some Greek philosophy imitation of the character of the gods was important.[161] If the god is merciful (χρηστός) the man ought also to be merciful.

The combination of adjectives found in Luke 6:35–36 (χρηστός; οἰκτίρμων) can also be found in Hellenistic Jewish texts which may hint at a benefaction context though this is less certain and is not consistent (Ps 68:17 LXX; Ps 111:4–5 LXX; cf. Ps 24:6–7 LXX; 68:17 LXX; 105:1–5, 46 LXX; 118:39–68, 77, 156 LXX; 144:7–9 LXX; Col 3:12).[162] These adjectives (χρηστός; οἰκτίρμων) are sometimes combined to describe God, man, or the human-divine relationship. In Ps 68 (LXX) the Psalmist cries for rescue from his enemies. Several times he describes God as Savior and himself as in need of salvation (68:1, 14, 15, 19, 29). Benefactors often offered rescue to their clients and were described as saviors for this activity so it is possible that the translator of the Psalm has benefaction in mind in his translation. Indicators of reciprocity may add to the suggestion that benefaction is in view (ἀνταπόδοσις; 68:23; ἀντιλαμβάνομαι; 68:30). It is possible that benefaction lies behind the translator's work though it is pos-

---

ὅπως ἐπιφανεστέρας τύχηι παρὰ πάντας τῆς ταφῆς τὸ μὲν σῶμα αὐτοῦ εἰσχομισθῆναι εἰς τὴν πόλιν πρὸς τὴν χαθήχουσαν κηδείαν Χ κλεισθῆναι δὲ τὰ ἐν τῆι πόλει ἐρ γαστήρια μελανΧειμονῆσαι τε τοὺς πολείτας καὶ παρέπεσθαι τῇ ἐξφορᾷ ἅπαντας ἐν τάξει στεφανωθῆναί τε αὐτὸν ὑπὸ τοῦ δήμου ἐπὶ τῆς Χ ἐκκομιδῆς Χ χρυσῷ στεφάνῳ ἀνασταθῆναι τε αὐτοῦ Χ καὶ ἀνδριάντα ἔφιππον ἐν ᾧ ἂν τόπῳ Χ οἱ προσήκοντες αὐτοῦ βούλωνται καὶ ἐπιγραφὴν δοῦναι τήνδε ΧΧΧ ὁ δῆμος Νεικήρατον Παπίου τὸν ἀπὸ προγόνων εὐεργέτην ὄντα καὶ πλεῖστα τῆι πόλει κατορθωσάμενον ἀγαθά Χ ἀρετῆς ἕνεκα καὶ εὐεργεσίας τῆς εἰς αὐτόν

[160] Danker, *Benefactor*, 325–326. Δόγμα τῶν Ἀμφικτιόνων ἐπεὶ Κάλλιστος Ἐ πιγένους Κνίδιος ἀνὴρ καλὸς κἀγαθός ... ὥστε καὶ κατὰ κοινὰν καὶ κατ' ἰδίαν φίλον καὶ ξένον καὶ εὐεργέτην ἑαυτὸν ἀποδεδειχέναι τῶν Ἑλλήνων καὶ ταῦτα πάντα πράττων διατετέλεκεν καὶ πόλεις καὶ ἰδιώτας σῴζων χωρὶς Κιρραίων δεομένων ἀμοιβῆς τε καὶ δαπάνης ὥστε τὴν χρηστότητα καὶ μεγαλοψυχίαν αὐτοῦ παρὰ πᾶσι γεγονέναι διάδηλον τύχηι τῆι ἀγαθῆι δεδόχθαι τοῖς Ἀμφικτίοσιν ἐπαινέσαι τε Κάλλιστον Ἐπιγένους Κνίδιον ἐφ' ἅι ἔχων εὐνοίᾳ διατελεῖ πρόσξτε τὰς Ἑλληνίδας πόλεις καὶ τὸ Ἀμφιχ τιονιχὸν σύστημα καὶ εἶναι αὐτὸν πρόξενον καὶ εὐεργέτην καὶ τοὺς ἐξγόνους αὐτοῦ τοῦ τε συνεδρίου τῶν Ἀμφιχτιόνων καὶ τῶν ἄλλων Ἑλλήνων ...

[161] Epictetus 2.14.12–13; cf. Danker, *New Age*, 150; Bock, *Luke*, 1.604 n. 52.
[162] Bock, *Luke*, 1.603; K. Weiss, TDNT 9:487; Plummer, *Luke*, 189.

sible that a more general expression of seeking God's rescue and resting in his reciprocating the enemy may be just as likely.

Themes and vocabulary from Psalm 111 (LXX) demonstrate the comprehensibility of Luke's writing in a Hellenistic Jewish context without explicit connection to benefaction. The psalm begins with a blessing (μακάριος) upon the one who fears the Lord and delights in his commands (Ps 111:1). The blessed one is described as merciful (ἐλεήμων), compassionate (οἰκτίρμων), and just (δίκαιος; 111:4). The compassionate one (ὁ οἰκτίρμων) receives blessing (χρηστός) from God because he has lent generously (κιχράω; 111:5). Bad news does not dissuade him, since he knows that in the future he'll triumph over his enemies (ἐχθρός; 111:7–8). He distributes freely and gives to the poor (ἐσκόρπισεν ἔδωκεν τοῖς πένησιν; 111:9). His horn will be exalted (ὑψωθήσεται) in glory (111:9). Apart from adjectives which were sometimes used for benefactors there is no verbal or conceptual indication in this text which suggests that benefaction is in view. The adjectives which describe the blessed man appear simply as descriptions of a person who trusts in God while living justly and generously.

This investigation finds no vocabulary typically connected to *patrocinium* in 6:27–38 (e.g., κηδεμονία, πατρωνεία, and προστασία; κηδεμών, πάτρων, πατρώνης, προστάτης; πατρωνεύω; κλίενς and πελάτης; ἐπιτροπή; πίστις, φίλος). A lack of specific vocabulary warrants caution towards the suggestion that Luke or Jesus utilize patron-client relationships to describe discipleship in this section. If Jesus attacks the Roman patronal system (e.g., Green) in this short section he does so indirectly and without reference to the specific language of that system. The use of language which falls within Hellenistic Jewish discussions of right living suggests that he specifically addresses those familiar with Hellenistic Jewish culture and its corruptions.

Cultural Matters

In regard to this subsection (6:27–38) scholars have proposed both Greco-Roman (Kirk, Dihle, Green, Harrison, Moxnes, Lull) and (Hellenistic) Jewish (Bock, Johnson, Bovon) modes of interaction as plausible frameworks through which one might better understand the message. Greco-Roman reciprocity and benefaction have been suggested in light of reciprocal and benefaction vocabulary (section 4.2.1 *Linguistic*), but also because of the logic of the argument. Jewish prophetic calls to repentance and imitation of God have been identified as pertinent to understanding the subsection in light of the language, structure, and themes of the subsection. Each framework (Greco-Roman reciprocity; Hellenistic Jewish prophetic call to repentance) will be taken in turn in order to assess whether Luke interprets Jesus' message in terms of either background or whether Jesus' audience likely interpreted his message in terms of Greco-Roman or Jewish modes of interaction. It will be argued that while some of Jesus' audience (e.g., those from Tyre, Sidon, and Jerusalem) may have interpreted him in line with Greco-Roman reciprocity/benefaction, he more likely built from a Jewish prophetic call to repentance based on the fulfillment of Sabbath/Jubilee expectation.

Luke 6:27–38 receives the most attention of any subsection in the sermon in discussions of reciprocity, patronage, and benefaction, so its contents and teaching will be investigated to see if it falls within either the general (reciprocity) or specific (benefaction, *patrocinium*) categories. A. Kirk's work on reciprocity and the Golden Rule focuses on this subsection of the sermon.[163] Kirk enters the debate about the Golden Rule and reciprocity. Following the discussion introduced by A. Dihle and examined subsequently by P. Hoffmann, P. Ricoeur, J. Wattles, J. Topel, A. E. Harvey, and H. D. Betz, among others,[164] scholars discuss whether the "love command" (6:27, 35) conflicts with the Golden Rule (6:31) because the latter seems to be based on reciprocity and the former seems to dismiss reciprocity.

To some scholars the Golden Rule seems to suggest the calculation of future reciprocations in the consideration of generosity.[165] Offer the type of generosity to others you hope to receive (through reciprocity). The love command seems to refute the calculation of reciprocity by directing generosity toward those who are predisposed against reciprocating. The one who hates you is not expected to return a favor of equal kind but nevertheless Jesus commands his people to be generous. Dihle suggests that the Golden Rule is best understood as a descriptive rather than prescriptive teaching;

---

[163] Kirk, "Love Your Enemies," 667–686.

[164] Kirk, "Golden Rule," 267–273. Dihle, *Goldene Regel*; Paul Hoffmann, *Tradition und Situation: Studien zur Jesusüberlieferung in der Logienquelle und den synoptischen Evangelien* (Neutestamentliche Abhandlungen 28; Münster: Aschendorff, 1995), 19–22, 41–42; cf. Fitzmyer, *Luke*, 1.639–640; Paul Ricoeur, "The Golden Rule: Exegetical and Theological Perplexities," *NTS* 36 (1990): 392–97; Jeffrey Wattles, *The Golden Rule* (New York: Oxford, 1996); John Topel, "The Tarnished Golden Rule (Luke 6:31): The Inescapable Radicalness of Christian Ethics," *TS* 59 (1998): 475–485; A. E. Harvey, *Strenuous Commands: The Ethic of Jesus* (London: SCM; Philadelphia: Trinity, 1990), 100, 107–115, 206; Hans Dieter Betz and Adela Yarbro Collins, *The Sermon on the Mount: A Commentary on the Sermon on the Mount, Including the Sermon on the Plain (Matthew 5:3–7:27 and Luke 6:20–49)* (Hermeneia; Minneapolis: Fortress Press, 1995); Reinhold Merkelbach, "Über eine Stelle im Evangelium des Lukas," *GrB* 1 (1973): 171–175, 171.

[165] Rudolph Bultmann, *History of the Synoptic Tradition* (trans. John Marsh; Oxford: Blackwell, 1963), 103; Josef Fuchs, "Die scheierige goldene Regel," *Stimmen der Zeit* 209 (1991): 773–781, 773; Heinz Schürmann, *Das Lukasevangelium* (vol. 1 *Kommentar zu Kap. 1,1–9,50*; HTKNT 3; Freiburg: Herder, 1969), 351.

4.2 The Sermon on the Plain (Luke 6:17–38)

society functions under the principle of reciprocity, but Jesus offers the love command to counteract this practice.[166] Two problems cripple Dihle's conclusion: (1) the absence of contrastive conjunctions following the Rule which would introduce a critique of the Rule in subsequent teaching;[167] (2) the presence of the imperative (ποιεῖτε; 6:31) in the Rule which signals a prescriptive rather than descriptive teaching.

P. Hoffmann, J. A. Fitzmyer, and R. Horsley, sharing a similar view with one another, find a critique of the Golden Rule in the subsequent (non-reciprocal) love commands.[168] "Luke creates tension between the two perspectives, the intent being that the former verses critique and surpass the latter."[169] Luke retains the reciprocal teachings in order to grab the attention of audience members who participated in reciprocity regularly. Tension builds as they see their own thoughts (in the reciprocal teachings of 6:30, 31, 36) contrasted to Jesus' non-reciprocal teachings (6:27a, 28b, 35c, 32–34, 29). This conclusion has two central flaws as well: (1) Hoffmann begins with the suggestion that the reciprocal and non-reciprocal teachings were separated in Luke's sources with the implication that this reduces their tension. He suggests that the original source(s) held the reciprocal teachings in a collected set in the same context as the collected set of non-reciprical teachings. The tension identified in Luke, however, is not ultimately resolved by suggesting the two were originally separate since they would have created tension whether intertwined (as in Luke) or in separate lists (as in the purported sources). (2) Hoffmann cannot adequately account for the imperative of the Golden Rule.[170]

J. Wattles and J. Topel attempt to distance the Rule's relationship with the ethic of reciprocity. They claim, in different ways, that the reciprocity of the Rule far exceeds Jewish and Greco-Roman forms of reciprocity to the extent that it is closer to "love your enemies" than reciprocity. Wattles focuses on the intiative oriented component of the Rule; it is not concerned with receiving in return as much as in initiating actions toward another. The distance between the Rule's teaching and reciprocity, in Wattel's interpretation, is only created by his limited definition of reciprocity. With a broader definition of reciprocity, developed from Jewish and Greco-Roman sources, the distance between reciprocity and an initiative orienta-

---

[166] Dihle, "Goldene Regel," *RAC* 11 (1981): 930–940, 931.

[167] Merkelbach overcomes this problem by emending the text, adding contrastive conjunctions. Merkelbach, "Evangelium," 171–175; in Kirk, "Love Your Enemies," 668.

[168] Hoffmann, *Tradition*, 19–22, 41–42; Fitzmyer, *Luke*, 1.639–640; Horsley, *Spiral of Violence*, 266; idem, "Ethics and Exegesis: 'Love Your Enemies' and the Doctrine of Non-Violence," *JAAR* 54 (1986): 3–31, 19.

[169] Kirk, "Love Your Enemies," 668.

[170] Kirk, "Love Your Enemies," 668–669.

tion shrinks.¹⁷¹ Topel takes a different approach. He suggests that the Rule so far surpasses Jewish and Greco-Roman forms of reciprocity, in its reorientation from self to the other, that it becomes "unique and 'non-reciprocal.'"¹⁷² Topel, though successfully showing the Rule's connection to Jewish and Greco-Roman reciprocity, has not succeeded in putting the Rule into a different class of teachings. Similarity with Sir 31:15a and Seneca *Ben.* 2.1.1 shows its compatibility with Hellenistic Jewish and Greco-Roman teachings on reciprocity: νόει τὰ τοῦ πλησίον ἐκ σεαυτοῦ; "Judge your neighbors feelings by your own" NRSV); Seneca *Ben.* 2.1.1 "sic demus, quomodo vellemus accipere; "let us so give as we would wish to receive".¹⁷³

Other scholars (Betz, cf. L. Schottroff, Nolland, Theissen)¹⁷⁴ suggest that the Golden Rule and/or love command are best understood in terms of reciprocity. According to Betz Luke attempts to rationalize Jesus' radical call to love enemies (6:27–30) in the subsequent paragraph (6:31–35) by translating that call into Greco-Roman reciprocal terms. Maxims of the type Jesus pronounces in the Rule were often created to "counteract the cycles of retaliation and counterretaliation" in Hellenistic ethical and religious dialogue.¹⁷⁵ Kirk follows Betz in identifying reciprocity as an interpretive aid, but challenges his view that the Golden Rule conforms to standard statements in Hellenistic religion. He finds Luke's "persistently contrarian attitude" toward reciprocity (especially in the use of χάρις) as a major point which distinguishes Luke's thoughts from typical Hellenistic moral reasoning.¹⁷⁶

In his resolution of the conflict Kirk appeals to notions of reciprocity, friendship, patronage, and benefaction inherent in the Greco-Roman world. Both the love command and the Golden Rule can be read within an ethic of reciprocity. Building on the work of the scholars summarized above (Dihle, Hoffmann, Wattles, Topel, and Betz) he resolves the apparent contradiction. To begin he clarifies his working definition of reciprocity since an ambiguous definition of the idea leaves the interpreter bereft of the specificity necessary to distinguish different types of relationships. After all, nearly all types of relationships involve a form of reciprocity at some

---

¹⁷¹ Kirk, "Love Your Enemies," 671.

¹⁷² Kirk, "Love Your Enemies," 671.

¹⁷³ Kirk, "Love Your Enemies," 671–672.

¹⁷⁴ Betz, *Sermon*, 591–600; Louise Schotroff, "Gewaltverzicht und Feindesliebe in der urchristlichen Jesustradition," in *Jesus Christus in Historie und Theologie* (ed. Georg Strecker; Tübigen: Mohr-Siebeck, 1975), 197–222, 214–215; Nolland, *Luke*, 1.293–296; Gerd Theissen, *Social Reality and the Early Christians* (trans. Margaret Kohl; Minneapolis: Fortress, 1992), 122–131, 149–151. Kirk, "Love Your Enemies," 672–673 n. 27.

¹⁷⁵ Kirk, "Love Your Enemies," 672.

¹⁷⁶ Kirk, "Love Your Enemies," 672–673.

level.[177] Borrowing from M. Sahlins and N. Z. Davis[178] he distinguishes three forms of (social-historical) reciprocity: general (gift), balanced (sale), and negative (coercion; see sections 2.1.1; 2.1.2). General reciprocity may be undertaken between friends, benefactors, or patrons and their friends or clients. It is open ended generosity wherein the recipient normally reciprocates the favor through a complementary gift or a show of gratitude through loyalty or public acclaim. In self-interest a person's generosity incites an obligation to assist in times of need in the recipient, but this self-interest does not negate the altruistic motives of most givers. Balanced reciprocity stipulates conditions of the exchange beforehand with details of a sufficient return clarified in advance. Self-interest is expected in both parties of the exchange. Negative reciprocity is purely self-interested in that it takes from another without expectation of reciprocation.

Kirk develops a case that Jesus' teaching on reciprocity mirrors the attempts of Hellenistic authors to salvage reciprocity while amending its inherent problems.[179] In Hellenistic culture Greeks believed that one helped one's friends and not one's enemies (e.g., Hesiod *Op.* 342, 354).[180] But this maxim did not satisfy everyone since retaliation was not perceived as virtuous by some (e.g., Aeschulus *Oresteia*). Moreover, the application of reciprocity in its straightforward sense often proved unsettling to Hellenistic philosophers and attempts to liberate society from rigid adherence to reciprocity often surfaced. "It searched for a rationally grounded and autono-

---

[177] Kirk, "Love Your Enemies," 673–677.

[178] Sahlins, *Stone Age Economics*, 198; Natalie Zemon Davis, *The Gift in Sixteenth-Century France* (The Curti Lectures; Madison: University of Wisconsin Press, 2000), 129; A. W. Gouldner, "The Norm of Reciprocity," in *Friends, Followers, and Factions: A Reader in Political Clientelism* (ed. Steffen W. Schmidt, J. C. Scott, C. Landi, and L. Guasti; Berkeley: University of California Press, 1977), 28–43, 31; Julianne Pitt-Rivers, "The Kith and the Kin," in *The Character of Kinship* (ed. Jack Goody; Cambridge: Cambridge University Press, 1973), 89–105, 100.

[179] Dihle, *Goldene Regel*, 45; Betz, *Sermon*, 288, 306; Dieter Zeller, *Die weisheitliche Mahnsprüche bei den Synoptikern* (FB 17; Würzburg: Echter Verlag, 1977), 53–58; Schotroff, "Gewaltverzicht," 204–205.

[180] Mary W. Blundell, *Helping Friends and Harming Enemies: A Study in Sophocles and Greek Ethics* (Cambridge: Cambridge University Press, 1990), 26–31; Lionel Ignacius Cusack Pearson, *Popular Ethics in Ancient Greece* (Stanford: Stanford University Press, 1962), 87, 120–121, 130, 136; Kenneth James Dover, *Greek Popular Morality in the Time of Plato and Aristotle* (Berkeley: University of California Press, 1974), 183–184; John T. Fitzgerald, "Friendship in the Greek World Prior to Aristotle," in Fitzgerald, *Greco-Roman Perspectives on Friendship*, 13–34, 32; David L. Balch, "Political Friendship in the Historian Dionysius of Halicarnassus, *Roman Antiquities*," in Fitzgerald, *Greco-Roman Perspectives on Friendship*, 123–144, 143; cf. Prange, *Luke*, 69–71.

mous basis for ethics, and, correspondingly, focused less on establishing balance and rectification in the empirical world than on cultivation of one's internal state."[181] This involved overcoming passion and desires to the point of "benefiting others without calculations of return."[182] Jesus' teaching which advocates giving without expectation of return and loving one's enemies fits in with "the tradition of development and innovation within common reciprocity ethics."[183] Kirk's solution to the apparent problem between the Golden Rule and the Love Command has been commended in general even while reservations about some details persist.[184]

Isolated from the surrounding co-texts this subsection appears to address Hellenistic reciprocity, suggests awareness of benefaction, but does not contain specific vocabulary connected to *patrocinium*. Luke has Jesus begin the subsection with a challenge to negative reciprocity (6:27–30). Negative reciprocity is self-seeking and finds its worst manifestation in enemies, thieves, and persecutors. The Hellenistic expectation would be to respond to this negative reciprocity with retaliation, but Jesus instead challenges his audience to respond with a good deed (6:27). The description employed (καλῶς ποιεῖτε) approximates εὐεργεσία which has been discussed previously as a highly significant term for a benefaction (see sections 2.1.3; 2.1.4).[185] Jesus continues with six concrete examples of good deeds which respond to negative reciprocity with generalized reciprocity. He calls his audience to bless those who curse, pray for those who persecute, not retaliate when struck, give the undergarment to the one who has stolen the outer garment, give to all who ask, and do not demand back that which has been taken (6:28–30).[186] Each example includes an acute instance of negative reciprocity responded to by dramatic beneficence.

---

[181] Kirk, "Love Your Enemies," 680–681.

[182] Kirk, "Love Your Enemies," 681; Dihle, *Goldene Regel*, 103–104, 45, 64–69; idem, "Goldene Regel," 935–936; Wattles, *Golden Rule*, 33–36; Betz, *Sermon*, 305–306; Harvey, *Strenuous Commands*, 98; Christopher Gill, "Altruism or Reciprocity in Greek Ethical Philosophy?" in Seaford, Gill, Postlethwaite, *Reciprocity*, 315–327.

[183] Kirk, "Love Your Enemies," 681.

[184] E.g., Zeba A. Crook, "Reflections on Culture and Social-Scientific Models," *JBL* 124.3 (2005): 515–520. Crook critiques Kirk's use of Sahlins' model of reciprocity since it grows out of investigation of primitive society which did not persist into the Roman imperial era. He also points out some inappropriate uses of specific terminology in Kirk's analysis (e.g., friend, gift, favor, benefactor, and patron-client). Kirk recently responded to Crook's criticism in Alan Kirk, "Karl Polanyi, Marshall Sahlins, and the Study of Ancient Social Relations," *JBL* 126.1 (2007): 182–191. In this article he defends the use of Sahlins by emphasizing the need to appreciate the complexity of his models. He in turn criticizes Crook for flattening this complexity.

[185] Danker, *Benefactor*, 324.

[186] deSilva, *Honor, Patronage*, 146; Danker, *New Age*, 85–86; Nolland, *Luke*, 1.295–298. Cf. Sirach 20:15.

4.2 The Sermon on the Plain (Luke 6:17–38)

The Golden Rule which follows does not undermine this radical call to subvert negative reciprocity with beneficence since it addresses initial rather than reciprocal actions (6:31). The Golden Rule plays into discussions of reciprocity since its language corresponds to the language of responding in kind to an action. Luke has Jesus switch focus from the responder to the initiator of the action. His instruction appears to undermine self-interest as a motivation by inverting the focus from responding appropriately to acting generously. Rather than telling his disciples how to respond to good benefits, he instructs his disciples on how to initiate good benefits (6:31–35). The rule "transforms the principle of acting prudentially in order to elicit beneficial returns (*do ut des*) into a rule of thumb for how one should act in the first place toward others, shifting focus from oneself to the other."[187] The Rule thus progresses the thought of the sermon from responding to negative action with positive action (6:27–30) to initiating positive action toward those incapable of reciprocating in kind (6:31–35). This does not contradict the earlier call to love enemies with an ethic of normal reciprocity, but rather offers his audience an approach to initiating actions. The attempts by Dihle and Merkelbach to understand the Rule as subsequently negated in Jesus' Love Command should not be accepted.[188] They cannot adequately account for the imperative in the Rule (ποιεῖτε) and the teaching actually fits within a stream of new thoughts on reciprocity prevalent in the first-century. Rather than calculating future reciprocity, Jesus calls his hearers to initiate by treating others as they would desire to be treated.

Luke has Jesus expand upon the initiative oriented Golden Rule by providing three examples of persons to whom lending or giving shows no great beneficence (6:32–34). In the first two examples Jesus presents a person that currently treats one well and hence has earned a reputation for good deeds. In the Hellenistic world such a person would be a prudent target of reciprocity since expectation of proper returns would be high (see section 4.2.1 *Linguistic*). Luke's choice of a near synonym of εὐεργεσία (i.e., ἀγαθοποιέω) suggests, again, familiarity with benefaction ideology (6:32, 35; *OGIS* 54.15; *OGIS* 167). The use of present participles indicates the current activity and/or reputation of the person (τοὺς ἀγαπῶντας; τοὺς ἀγαθοποιοῦντας). Such a reputation ensures the giver that he might confidently expect a return on his favor (παρ' ὧν ἐλπίζετε λαβεῖν). The thrice repeated question, ποία ὑμῖν χάρις ἐστίν, points out that such behavior does not deserve the description of beneficence (χάρις) since even those

---

[187] Kirk's summary of Wattles, *Golden Rule*, 58, 65–67; Topel, "Golden Rule," 484; and Harvey, *Strenuous Commands*, 100, 107–115, 206; Kirk, "Love Your Enemies," 671–672.

[188] Contra Dihle, *Goldene Regel*, and Hoffmann, *Tradition und Situation*.

not worthy of that description (e.g., οἱ ἁμαρτωλοί) can so act. It shows no remarkable generosity to give to one from whom one expects to receive an approximately equal response. The first two examples emphasize that initiative should be taken regardless of the worthiness of the recipient while the last example shifts focus slightly to warn against self-preservation motivated giving. Here Luke has Jesus depart from at least one Hellenistic Jewish predecessor. Sirach 12:1–6 commends generosity toward the devout since this will be recompensed either by the devout himself or by God. But he forbids generosity toward the evil since they will use the gift to strengthen their attack against the giver.

ἐὰν εὖ ποιῇς γνῶθι τίνι ποιεῖς καὶ ἔσται χάρις τοῖς ἀγαθοῖς σου εὖ ποίησον εὐσεβεῖ καὶ εὑρήσεις ἀνταπόδομα καὶ εἰ μὴ παρ' αὐτοῦ ἀλλὰ παρὰ τοῦ ὑψίστου οὐκ ἔσται ἀ γαθὰ τῷ ἐνδελεχίζοντι εἰς κακὰ καὶ τῷ ἐλεημοσύνην μὴ χαριζομένῳ δὸς τῷ εὐσεβεῖ καὶ μὴ ἀντιλάβῃ τοῦ ἁμαρτωλοῦ εὖ ποίησον ταπεινῷ καὶ μὴ δῷς ἀσεβεῖ ἐμπόδισον τοὺς ἄρτους αὐτοῦ καὶ μὴ δῷς αὐτῷ ἵνα μὴ ἐν αὐτοῖς σε δυναστεύσῃ διπλάσια γὰρ κακὰ εὑρήσεις ἐν πᾶσιν ἀγαθοῖς οἷς ἂν ποιήσῃς αὐτῷ ὅτι καὶ ὁ ὕψιστος ἐμίσησεν ἁμαρτωλοὺς καὶ τοῖς ἀσεβέσιν ἀποδώσει ἐκδίκησιν

"If you do good, know to whom you do it, and you will be thanked for your good deeds. Do good to the devout, and you will be repaid – if not by them, certainly by the Most High. No good comes to one who persists in evil or to one who does not give alms. Give to the devout, but do not help the sinner. Do good to the humble, but do not give to the ungodly; hold back their bread, and do not give it to them, for by means of it they might subdue you; then you will receive twice as much evil for all the good you have done to them. For the Most High also hates sinners and will inflict punishment on the ungodly." (NRSV)

Sirach grounds his instruction on the character of God; God hates sinners so those who refuse generosity to sinners imitate the Most High (ὁ ὕψιστος). Parallel vocabulary in both texts (Luke 6:27–38; Sir 12:1–6) suggests common topics of discussion and perhaps a critique by Luke of Hellenistic Jewish forms of reciprocity. Sirach is concerned about those who do good (εὖ ποιῇς; εὖ ποίησον; πᾶσιν ἀγαθοῖς οἷς ἂν ποιήσῃς αὐτω), about the proper treatment of enemies (τοῦ ἁμαρτωλου; ἀσεβεῖ; τοῖς ἀσεβέσιν), and about the attitude of God (ἐμίσησεν ἁμαρτωλοὺς καὶ τοῖς ἀσεβέσιν ἀποδώσει ἐκδίκησιν) who is referred to as the Most High (παρὰ τοῦ ὑψίστου; ὁ ὕψιστος). Gratitude returns (χάρις; ἀνταπόδομα;) to the one who gives to the godly. Luke contrasts this message sharply. He insists instead that generosity toward those who will be expected to reciprocate does not consistute graciousness (χαρὶς), nor does it imitate the character of the Most High (ὑψίστος). Rather, by giving to those who cannot repay, even outright enemies (ἐχθρός), one imitates God who is kind to the ungrateful and the evil (αὐτὸς χρηστός ἐστιν ἐπὶ τοὺς ἀχαρίστους καὶ πον ηρούς).

4.2 The Sermon on the Plain (Luke 6:17–38)

Luke has Jesus attack the calculation of worthy recipients of benefits, and offer instead the example of God who benefits those who have reputations for not reciprocating and in fact have made themselves unworthy through evil deeds (6:32–36). Those who have earned a reputation for ingratitude do not typically deserve the beneficence of the benefactor (so Sirach 12:1–6; Seneca *Ben.* 1.1.13; 4.10.5–11.2; 4.28.5; 1.1.9–13; 1.2.5; 1.10.4–5). But Jesus goes beyond this approach. He exhorts his audience to benefit enemies and others without expectation of human reciprocity (6:35). Repetition of the commands to benefit (ἀγαπᾶτε; ἀγαθοποιεῖτε; δανίζετε) found in the previous three verses emphasizes the generous mindset toward the ungrateful which Jesus commends. It seems likely that Luke intends to contrast the typical Hellenistic (Jewish) motivation with his new paradigm. Rather than choosing for benefits those who love or do good to you, Luke instructs his audience to benefit enemies (τοὺς ἐχθροὺς). Rather than identifying those who are capable of reciprocity, Luke has Jesus urge lending to others without expectation of return (μηδὲν ἀπελπίζοντες).[189]

Luke presents two theological grounds upon which his audience might be assured that this course of action will not be in vain (6:35). First, rather than being rewarded by a simple human response the one who chooses incapable recipients receives a more valuable response from God. God offers a great reward to the one who so acts (ὁ μισθὸς ὑμῶν πολύς). Second, though on a human level social status will actually be compromised through neglect of the normal patterns of reciprocity, God offers a greater privilege, admission into his family (fictive kinship). The hope in human-human reciprocity is an increase in honor through acquiring a relationship with a social superior or in being lauded as beneficent in public. In human-divine reciprocity one ultimately receives a much better connection through attachment to God as one of his sons (ἔσεσθε υἱοὶ ὑψίστου). God reciprocates the benefit offered to the incapable human. One may lose honor through the sacrifice of one's reputation in society (6:22), but in the process gain the greater honor of association with God.[190]

Luke presents God with some of the same qualities of a noble benefactor (χρηστός; οἰκτίρμων; see section 4.2.3 *Linguistic*), and his followers should express the same characteristics in following Jesus' instruction. Luke ascribes an important adjective to God which surfaces frequently in

---

[189] Danker, *New Age*, 86; idem, *Luke*, 33–34; Marshall, *Luke*, 263–264; Bovon, *Luke*, 1.237–238, 241; idem, *Lukas*, 1.276; idem, *Luc*, 1.269 n. 35; van Unnik, "Die Motivierung," 284–300; Malina and Rohrbaugh, *Social Science Commentary*, 250–251; Talbert, *Theological Commentary*, 77–79; Prange, *Luke*, 69–71; Tannehill, *Luke*, 116–120; idem, *Narrative Unity*, 1.129–130; Lagrange, *Luc*, 196–197; Plummer, *Luke*, 189.

[190] deSilva, *Honor, Patronage*, 32.

benefaction inscriptions to denote the exemplary character of the benefactor (6:35). Χρηστός was a term used to describe the nature of benefactors. Χρηστός (or χρηστότης) can indicate "the quality of beneficence" (Philo *Virt.* 160; Josephus *Ant.* 8.214) which a benefactor displays in generosity.[191] It is possible that the reversal of fortunes offered in the sermon deserve mention as a benefit, though this possibility is diminished by the lack of explicit examples of the practice by benefactors. Ingratitude was considered a deplorable offense, but the noble benefactor was not dissuaded by this response. God's generosity to ὁ ἀχάριστος puts him in the category of such benefactors. With this description Luke continues his critique of those who seek worthy recipients of benefactions. God is generous to those who have proven records of neglecting reciprocity. Not only that, but he benefits the evil person whose poor reputation extends beyond a mere neglect of reciprocity.

Concrete examples of the reward offered to those that follow Jesus' instructions clarify the fact that it is God who is responsible for reciprocating the generosity of these disciples (6:37–38). Five divine passives and an explanatory proverb explain the response that God will shower upon the obedient.

Καὶ μὴ κρίνετε, καὶ οὐ μὴ κριθῆτε· καὶ μὴ καταδικάζετε, καὶ οὐ μὴ καταδικασθῆτε. ἀπολύετε, καὶ ἀπολυθήσεσθε· δίδοτε, καὶ δοθήσεται ὑμῖν· μέτρον καλὸν πεπιεσμένον σεσαλευμένον ὑπερεκχυννόμενον δώσουσιν εἰς τὸν κόλπον ὑμῶν· ᾧ γὰρ μέτρῳ μετρεῖτε ἀντιμετρηθήσεται ὑμῖν

"Judge not, and you will not be judged; condemn not, and you will not be condemned; forgive, and you will be forgiven; give, and it will be given to you. Good measure, pressed down, shaken together, running over, will be put into your lap. For with the measure you use it will be measured back to you." (ESV)

Repetition of divine passives in the text indicates God's hand in reciprocating. The solitary third person plural (δώσουσιν) in the proverb can be taken either as a divine plural or a reference to angelic assistance in the dissemination of God's benefits.[192] The statements express God's ability to reciprocate with benefits that far surpass those which humans may offer. These include both requital from negative threats (judgment, condemnation) and the offer of positive blessings (forgiveness, gifts). The list of concrete responses God offers highlights the superiority of looking to God for reciprocity rather than toward humanity who can only offer responses in kind.

---

[191] Danker defines the term as having "the ability to extend oneself in the interests of others beyond the requirements of duty or office." Danker, *Benefactor*, 325–326; see no. 19, 17.3–4; cf. *OGIS* 504.10; 505.12; 507.8; *SIG* 730.18–27; 761.12–13.

[192] Bovon, *Luke*, 1.242–243 n. 79. Marshall claims it is a "rabbinic periphrasis for the name of God" (CD 2.13; H. Braun, *Qumran und das Neue Testament* [Tübingen: Mohr Siebeck, 1966], 1.88f; Strack and Billerbeck, 2.221), Marshall, *Luke*, 267.

4.2 The Sermon on the Plain (Luke 6:17–38)

Human actions are paralleled by divine reactions (judge – judged; condemn – condemned; forgive – forgiven; measure – measured); in kind these are balanced reciprocations (the same thing is being exchanged in each instance). The two verses thus are similar to balanced reciprocity. God reciprocates with a similar gift to the one who offers a gift.[193] Since, however, the two parties (God and man) have different social statuses, and the gifts, though similar in name (forgive, forgiven), are dissimilar in magnitude, this exchange may be closer to general reciprocity.[194]

Luke follows the sermon with an illustration of the type of reciprocity Jesus urged (7:1–10). For those that give generously God will bring recompense. In the final portion of the sermon Jesus declares the importance of obeying his teaching (6:46–49). A person cannot simply profess his authority (κύριε κύριε) without following his teaching (6:49). In the subsequent pericope the centurion becomes a prime example of a person who properly respects Jesus' authority. In Capernaum, several Jews approach Jesus with a request to reciprocate the generosity of a Gentile soldier (7:2–3). They identify him as being worthy (ἄξιός) of a benefaction, in this case healing (διασώσῃ) for his servant, even though the centurion himself denies his worthiness (ἱκανός εἰμι; 7:4–6). The centurion, apparently recognizing in Jesus a more important figure, humbles himself below the evaluations of his Jewish emissaries. Luke's addition of friends (φίλος) as brokers for the centurion supports the notion that Hellenistic reciprocity underlies the story. Brokers and mediators often intervened on behalf of their benefactors as part of the obligation of gratitude.[195] Jesus hears of the centurion's confidence in his power. This confidence leads the centurion to forbid Jesus to continue his journey. He is confident that a word spoken from a distance will heal his valuable servant (7:6–8). Jesus marveled (ἐθαύμασεν) over the faith of the centurion and the healing is accomplished (7:9–10). Though friendship and faith can be components of patronage relationships they do not demand that reading (see section 2.1.3). Φίλος can refer to clients (*cliens*), or a normal friendship relationship. Πίστις can be the Greek equivalent of *fides* which was often employed in *patrocinium*, but it can also be used in non-Roman contexts to refer to faith or loyalty.[196] Since the centurion was most likely not a Roman, but rather a part of Antipas'

---

[193] Gary Stansell, "Gifts, Tributes, and Offerings," in Stegemann, Malina, Theissen, *Social Setting*, 349–364, 355–356.

[194] For distinguishing balanced and general reciprocity in contemporary scholarship see below the discussion about Sahlins and Stegemann and Stegemann. Crook, *Conversion*, 56–58.

[195] Green, *Luke*, 286; Garnsey and Saller, *Roman Empire*, 149. Cf. Moxnes, *Economy*, 64–65, who adopts the socio-historical term "patron" to describe the centurion whose clients function on his behalf as did other "agents" in Greco-Roman reciprocity.

[196] Crook, "Loyalty," 167.

troops, one need not read into these two terms the presence of *patrocinium* (see section 2.2.3 *Capernaum*). It is confusing for Moxnes to identify the centurion as a patron. He does not adequately differentiate the socio-historical from Roman meanings of "patron." If he intends the Roman rather than socio-historical meaning of patron, as in *patrocinium*, then he is probably in error on historical, archaeological, and literary grounds.[197] It is more likely that the centurion understood his relationship to the Jewish elders in terms of Hellenistic reciprocity and perhaps benefaction rather than *patrocinium*. The episode tells of a Gentile performing righteous acts on behalf of Jewish elders and receiving recompense from God in the form of a benefaction (healing [διασῴζω] of the servant).[198]

Hellenism had likely influenced the language, government, and economics of the cultures of many members of this audience (esp. Tyre and Sidon), but Judaism had a more significant role in forming the worldview of most people in Jerusalem, Judea, and Galilee (see sections 2.2.3 *Summary*; 2.2.4; 2.2.5 *Tyre*). The investigation undertaken in the second chapter emphasized strong adherence to Judaism as can be seen in both archaeological and literary evidence. Cultural indebtedness to Judaism was the bedrock of Galilee and Jerusalem, and by extension Judea. A primary locus of influence would have been the Torah and OT tradition. It is pertinent therefore to evaluate Jesus' teaching in light of this Jewish background.

Taking the sermon (6:20–49) as a whole and recognizing its position as the continuation of the preceding narratives, the sermon regains a Jewish flavor which hints at the fulfillment of Jubilee and Sabbath (year) expectation.[199] A few verbal indicators signal for the reader that Luke situates Je-

---

[197] Moxnes, "Patron-Client," 241–242; idem, *Economy*, 59–60.

[198] Understanding this as a benefaction are Danker, *Benefactor*, 403; idem, *Luke*, 12, 34; deSilva, *Honor, Patronage*, 125–126 n. 9.

[199] More extensive treatment of this topic may be found in Robert B. Sloan, *The Favorable Year of the Lord: A Study of Jubilary Theology in the Gospel of Luke* (Atlanta: Scholars Press, 1977); Donald W. Blosser, "Jesus and the Jubilee (Luke 4:16–30): The Year of Jubilee and Its Significance in the Gospel of Luke" (PhD diss., St. Andrew's University, 1979); Sharon H. Ringe, "The Jubilee Proclamation in the Ministry and Teachings of Jesus: A Tradition-Critical Study in the Synoptic Gospels and Acts" (PhD diss., Union Theological Seminary, 1981); Gabriel Kyo-Seon Shin, *Die Ausrufung des endgültigen Jubeljahres durch Jesus in Nazaret eine historische-kritische Studie zu Lk 4,16–30* (Bern: Peter Lang, 1989); Michael Prior, *Jesus the Liberator: Nazareth Liberation Theology (Luke 4. 16–30)* (Sheffield: Sheffield Academic Press, 1995); M. Rese, *Alttestamentliche Motive in der Christologie des Lukas* (Studium zum Neuen Testament 1; Gütersloh: Mohn, 1969). For the most current discussion of the history of Jubilee interpretation from the OT to Qumran see, John Sietze Bergsma, *The Jubilee from Leviticus to Qumran: A History of Interpretation* (VTSupp 115; Leiden: Brill, 2007), 1–18; John Howard Yoder, *The Politics of Jesus* (Grand Rapids: Eerdmans, 1972), 36–37,

sus' teaching in Jewish terms. It is instructive that Luke compares the reception of the prophets with those who have been hated for righteousness. It seems quite probable that Luke intends his audience to understand these as Jewish prophets because of his use of "their fathers" (οἱ πατέρες αὐτῶν) to describe the antagonists (6:23).[200] The following comparison of those who are well treated with the reception of the false prophets also should be understood as a reference to Jewish false prophets for the same reason (οἱ πατέρες αὐτῶν; 6:26).[201] Luke follows a macarism form which has been demonstrated to be thoroughly Jewish even though macarisms found some expression in Greco-Roman literature. The form of Luke's macarisms demonstrates his dependence on Jewish rather than Greco-Roman predecessors (section 4.2.2 *Cultural*). The combination of οἰκτίρμων and χρηστός as adjectives to describe God has been identified in many (Hellenistic) Jewish texts (see below, section 4.2.3 *Conclusion*).

A slight verbal link to Israel's covenant can be found in the use of οἰκτίρμων to describe God (6:36). The term and its cognates are common in the LXX in his covenant self-description (Exod 33:19; 34:6; Deut 4:31; cf. Neh 9:17, 19, 28, 31; 1 Kings 8:50). The call to be compassionate as God is compassionate continued in Jewish thought (*Tg. Ps.-J Lev* 22:28; *Mek. Exod.* 15:2; *Sipre Deut.* 11:22).[202] More work is needed on the translation of חֶסֶד from OT to LXX. Since many argue that חֶסֶד could be translated "loyalty" and should therefore be rendered πίστις in Greek it is interesting that it is usually translated ἔλεος (213/245 times). The LXX translation of a Hebrew loyalty word (i.e., ἔλεος) was not used at this point in Luke to describe God's character. Rather one has the typical translation of רַחוּם in οἰκτιρμός.[203] Perhaps Luke intends a more direct allusion to God's covenant character rather than an allusion to loyalty in general.

Luke places the sermon in the context of Jewish culture by adopting familiar forms and language as the Jewish prophets. The form of the bless-

---

41; Charles A. Kimball, *Jesus' Exposition of the Old Testament in Luke's Gospel* (JSOT 94; Sheffield: JSOT Press, 1994), 28–29, 97, 104, 113.

[200] Green, *Luke*, 268 (refers to Neh 9:26; Ezek 2:1–7; Acts 7:52); Bovon, *Luke*, 1.226; Bock, *Luke*, 1.582 (refers to Luke 11:47–51; Acts 7:51–52; Jer 2:29–30; 11:18–21; 20:2; 26:8–11, 20; 37:15–16; 38:4–6); Plummer, *Luke*, 181; Marshall, *Luke*, 255; Danker, *New Age*, 83 (refers to Jeremiah, Ezekiel, and Amos as persecuted prophets); Johnson, *Luke*, 107. Contra Douglas R. A. Hare, *The Theme of Jewish Persecution of Christians in the Gospel According to St. Matthew* (Cambridge: Cambridge University Press, 1967), 116–117.

[201] Green, *Luke*, 268 (Jer 5:12–13; 6:13–15; Mic 2:11); Johnson, *Luke*, 108 (Acts 13:6; LXX Jer 6:13; 33:7, 8, 11, 16; 34:9; 35:1; 36:1, 8; Zech 13:2); Bock, *Luke*, 1.585–586 (Jer 5:31; 14:13–16; 23:9–15, 27–28; Ezek 22:23–31; Isa 30:10; Mic 2:11); Marshall, *Luke*, 256–257; Fitzmyer, *Luke*, 1.637; Plummer, *Luke*, 183; Danker, *New Age*, 84.

[202] Nolland, *Luke*, 1.300.

[203] For discussion of חֶסֶד in the OT see, Crook, "Loyalty," 172–174.

ings and woes alludes to the blessings and curses of the Deuteronomic law (see section 4.2.2 *Linguistic, Cultural*; 4.2.3 *Linguistic, Cultural*). Those who follow God's/Jesus' instruction will be blessed, but those who disobey the instruction will be cursed. Verbal connection to this event comes when Jesus commands his followers to bless those who curse (εὐλογεῖτε τοὺς καταρωμένους ὑμᾶς; 6:28).[204] The LXX translator of Deuteronomy adopts εὐλογία and κατάρα to describe the blessings and curses.[205] Since Luke situates Jesus' sermon on a plain rather than mountain, thus foregoing the potential allusion to Moses' ascent of Sinai, the reader does not receive the full imagery connected to the giving of the law (Exod 19:20–23:33; Deut 4:44–26:19).[206] This lack of mountain imagery coupled with the use of woes (a commonplace among Israel's prophets) leads Johnson to suggest that Luke pictures Jesus like Moses the prophet more than Moses the law-giver (as in Matthew; Acts 3:22).[207]

The linguistic investigation of each subsection has identified several parallels between Jesus' sermon and Jewish culture. The parallel between the beatitudes and woes and Isa 61:1–3 has been noted (see section 4.2.2 *Cultural*).[208] Commentators note the parallels between this sermon and the message begun in the Nazareth synagogues.[209] In the Nazareth sermon (Luke 4:16–30) Jesus announces the fulfillment of Isa 61:1–3 (and Isa 58:6–10). Verbal and conceptual parallels tie the sermons from Luke 4 and 6 together with Isaiah 61:1–3 and 58:6–10.[210] The use of woes ties Jesus and Jewish prophets together (οὐαί; 6:24–26; Hos 7:13; 9:12; Amos 5:16, 18; 6:1 LXX). Isaiah stands out among the prophets in his use of woes (1:4, 24; 3:9, 11; 5:8, 11, 18, 20, 21, 22; 10:1, 5; 17:12; 18:1; 24:16; 28:1; 29:1; 29:15; 30:1; 31:1; 33:1). Luke's use of forms and vocabulary common among Jewish prophets suggests that he intends his critique in reference to Jewish ideology. The only explicitly mentioned targets of critique in the sermon are Jewish false prophets, the Jewish fathers who persecute true prophets, and those who follow in the footsteps of either of these predecessors. This does not rule out the idea that Luke had other targets in mind for his critique, but it does increase the burden of proof placed on those who consider his primary target a group of people other than those explicitly mentioned.

---

[204] Johnson, *Luke*, 108, 111.
[205] εὐλογία Deut 28:2, 3, 4, 5, 6, 8, 12; κατάρα/ἐπικατάρατος Deut 27:15, 16, 17, 18, 19, 20, 21, 22, 23, 24, 25, 26; 28:15, 16, 17, 18, 19, 45.
[206] Johnson, *Luke*, 110; Nolland, *Luke*, 1.300.
[207] Johnson, *Luke*, 110–111; cf. Exod 19:20–23:33; Deut 4:44–26:19.
[208] Sloan, *Jubilary Theology*; Johnson, *Luke*, 111; Bock, *Luke*, 1.574–575; Creed, *Luke*, 91.
[209] Danker, *New Age*, 81.
[210] Bovon, *Luke*, 226; Green, *Luke*, 265; Danker, *New Age*, 81; Johnson, *Luke*, 111.

It seems likely that the Deuteronomic, Levitical, and Isaianic concepts which converge in the Sabbath and Jubilee release have informed the sermon on the plain and provide the basis for Luke's critique of Hellenistic reciprocity and the general disobedience of God's people. These concepts enjoyed a rich development in the OT prophets (Ezek, Jer, and Dan), historical writings (esp. 1–2 Kings, 1–2 Chron, and Ezra-Neh), DSS literature (4Q383–391; 11QMelch), and OT apocrypha/pseudepigrapha (*Jub*, *1 Enoch*, *ApocWeeks*, and *TestLevi*).[211] Luke provides several hints, both contextual and verbal, that he has in mind the fulfillment of the Sabbath/Jubilee expectation in the preaching and ministry of Jesus and the early Christian community. The most recent monograph devoted to the Jubilee suggests that the conflation of Isaiah 61 and 58 in Luke 4:17–19 so clearly demarcates a Jubilee fulfillment that he adopts it as evidence for the presence of Jubilee ideology in Isa 58:6–10. According to Bergsma, Jesus' use of the two passages (Isa 61:1–2; 58:6) in the Nazareth sermon constitutes one link in the "'jubilary' history of interpretation" of Isa 58.[212] Four main arguments support the notion that Jesus cast his instructions in terms of fulfillment of Sabbath/Jubilee in the sermon. These arguments are used to more precisely interpret Luke's teaching and the context for the sermon in order to establish the most important cultural and/or theological context for his presentation of Jesus. After this discussion it will be argued that Luke properly prioritizes the Hellenistic Jewish background in his description of Jesus, relegating potential connections to benefaction to secondary importance (see section 4.2.3 *Conclusion*).

(1) Luke introduces the fulfillment of Sabbath/Jubilee in the Nazareth sermon (4:16–21). By doing so he alerts the reader to look for the theme elsewhere in his two volumes. The hope announced in Isaiah 61:1–3 and Isaiah 58:6–10 was a combination of (eschatological) Sabbath and Jubilee years. J. D. W. Watts draws a few connections between the passages in both vocabulary and concepts.[213] He identifies several phrases in Isa 61:1–2 which recall the Jubilee instruction from Lev 25:10 (לִקְרֹא דְרוֹר; לַיהוָה שְׁנַת־רָצוֹן).[214] Emancipation of those who are trapped against their will is a

---

[211] For the full history of interpretation and development see Bergsma, *Jubilee*. Cf. M. de Jounge and A. S. van der Woude, "11QMelchizedek and the New Testament," *NTS* 12 (1965–66): 301–326; Merrill P. Miller, "The Function of Isa 61:1–2 in 11QMelchizedek," *JBL* 88 (1969): 467–469; Asher Finkel, *The Pharisees and the Teacher of Nazareth: A Study of Their Background, Their Halachic and Midrashic Teachings, the Similarities and Differences* (Arbeiten zur Geschichte des Spätjudentums und Urchristentums 4; Leiden: Brill, 1964), 155–158.

[212] Bergsma, *Jubilee*, 196, following Sloan, *Favorable Year*, 40.

[213] J. D. W. Watts, *Isaiah 34–66* (WBC 25; Waco: Word, 1987), 302–304.

[214] Ibid. Cf. John Goldingay, *Isaiah* (NIBC; Peabody: Hendrickson, 2001), 347. Goldingay adds the Sabbath year to the Jubilee as the location of such a proclamation. De-

conceptual link between the passages.²¹⁵ Jewish interpreters connected these passages as well (11QMelch).²¹⁶ Luke picks up the LXX translation of the pertinent phrases in Isa 61:1–2 which Watts suggests point to Sabbath/Jubilee expectation (דְּרוֹר; לִקְרֹא; לַיהוָה שְׁנַת־רָצוֹן; κηρύξαι αἰχμαλώτοις ἄφεσιν; κηρύξαι ἐνιαυτὸν κυρίου δεκτόν; Luke 4:18–19). Luke interprets the passages together. Luke differs from the LXX in slight ways. He has left out the phrase ἰάσασθαι τοὺς συντετριμμένους (Isa 61:1; Luke 4:18). Luke may have omitted the phrase because he would insert a similar phrase from Isa 58:6 (ἀπόστελλε τεθραυσμένους ἐν ἀφέσει).²¹⁷ Luke changes the verb from imperative to infinitive (ἀποστεῖλαι) in order to conform it to the structure and grammar of his quotation. He exchanges κηρύξαι for καλέσαι (Isa 61:2; Luke 4:19). In his citation of the passage Jesus preached Luke conflates the texts of Isa 61:1–2 and Isa 58:6. Jews connected these passages²¹⁸ and the possibility of connection through *gezerah shewah* (שָׁלַח; רָצוֹן appear in both Isa 58:5–6 and Isa 61:1–2) compels a few scholars to suggest a traditional source.²¹⁹ The importance of the Isaiah quote in the introductory sermon of Jesus and its Sabbath/Jubilee connection suggests that this Jewish construct may be more important than a Greco-Roman construct like benefaction or *patrocinium*.

(2) Several words found in the original Sabbath year instruction (Deut 15:1–11) come together in Luke-Acts to suggest that Luke has the fulfill-

---

litzch saw a link between Isa 58:6–14 and Jer 34:8–22 where the Jubilee Year was the subject of a scandal (reference in John Oswalt, *The Book of Isaiah 40–66* [NICOT; Grand Rapids: Eerdmans, 1998], 503). Oswalt connects the Isaianic passages ibid., 503 n. 49. He also notes the use of דְּרוֹר with the Jubilee Year in Lev 25:10; Jer 34:8; Ezek 46:17, ibid., 565 n. 19.

²¹⁵ Jeremiah also adopts the imagery of the Jubilee in his description of emancipation from exile (Jer 34:8, 15, 17). Watts, *Isaiah 34–66*, 301–302.

²¹⁶ No Targum exists for Isa 61, but the two passages may be linked through *gezerah shewah* (ἄφεσιν/ἀφέσει; שָׁלַח, רָצוֹן), Bock, *Luke*, 1.404–405. Bock argues that a traditional source lies behind Jesus' sermon and conflation. Cf. Sloan, *Favorable Year*, 39–41; Rese, *Christologie des Lukas*, 219. On 11Qmelch see, Bergsma, *Jubilee*, 282–294.

²¹⁷ Bock, *Luke*, 1.404–405.

²¹⁸ E.g., 11QMelch; Bergsma, *Jubilee*, 194–203; M. H. Tannenbaum, "Holy Year 1975 and Its Origin in the Jewish Jubilee Year," *Jubilaeum* 7 (1974): 63–79, 65; C. Westermann, *Isaiah 40–66: A Commentary* (Old Testament Library; trans. D M. G. Stalker; Philadelphia: Westminster, 1969), 337.

²¹⁹ J. A. Sanders, "Isaiah in Luke," in *Luke and Scripture: The Function of Sacred Tradition in Luke-Acts* (ed. C. A. Evans and J. A. Sanders; Minneapolis: Fortress, 1993), 14–25, 21–25; D. L. Bock, *Proclamation from Prophecy to Pattern: Lucan Old Testament Christology* (JSOTSupp 12; Sheffield: JSOT Press, 1987), 317 n. 59; B. Violet, "Zum rechten Verständnis der Nazareth-Perikope Lc4[16-30]," *ZNW* 37 (1938): 251–271, 258–259; B. Chilton, "Announcement in Nazara: An Analysis of Luke 4:16–21," in *Gospel Perspectives* (vol. 2 *Studies of History and Tradition in the Four Gospels*; ed. R. T. France and D. Wenham; Sheffield: JSOT Press, 1981), 147–172, 162–163.

ment of this ideal in mind in description of the new community. Luke depicts Jesus giving instructions on lending practices to his people and employs the verb δανείζω which occurs in the OT nineteen times (6:34–35).[220] Six of eight Pentateuch uses of the verb refer or allude to Sabbath lending practices (Deut 15:6[2x], 8, 10; 28:12, 44). Another rare verb, ἀπαιτέω, refers to the demanding back of payment. It occurs only eight times in the OT, ten in the LXX, with two of those occurrences in Deut 15:2–3. In Deuteronomy 15 God's people were expected to lend to brothers without interest and to release the debt if not paid back after seven years. Jesus informs his people that it is no special godliness to lend to another expecting to receive back the same amount (τὰ ἴσα; Luke 6:34).[221] Rather, they are to follow the example of God, lending and never expecting anything in return. Luke has Jesus push beyond the Sabbath release (seven years), instructing his people to lend without ever expecting a return. A final peculiar term, ἐνδεής, signals that Luke has in mind the fulfillment of Sabbath hope in the Christian community. Deuteronomy describes the relief offered the poor if God's people follow his instruction on lending and release. The LXX employs ἐνδεής three times in the process (Deut 15:4, 7, 11).[222] Luke hints at one realization of this Sabbath hope when he describes the result of the new community (Acts 4:34–35). No needy (ἐνδεής) existed among them because of their generosity and the grace of God. This state did not exist for long since poverty persisted as a problem in the early church (e.g., Acts 6:1–2; 11:28–29). Lending differs from benefaction and/or *patrocinium* in the fact that it exchanges equal goods (grain for grain; money for money) whereas benefaction and *patrocinium* exchange large gifts for allegiance and public acclaim. Lending comes closer to balanced reciprocity (sale) than general reciprocity (gift). Jesus' instructions seem to move away from balanced reciprocity toward general reciprocity by negating the payback or expectation of equal exchange. Socio-historical patron-client relationships fall into the category of general reciprocity which may suggest putting this

---

[220] It occurs twenty three times in the LXX, with eight in the Pentateuch (Deut 15:6[2x], 8, 10; 28:12[2x], 44[2x]); Ps 36:21, 26; Prov 19:17; 20:4; 22:7; Isa 24:2 (2x); Neh 5:4; Sir 8:12 (2x); 20:15; 29:1, 2; 4 Macc 2:8; Wis 15:16. Lust, *Lexicon* (2003), 59.

[221] Controversy surrounding the meaning of the phrase, τὰ ἴσα, may be helped by accounting for the Sabbath year background of this passage. Bock (*Luke*, 1.601) mentions four options for the meaning of the phrase, and Bovon (*Luke*, 1. 237–238) mentions five (see section 4.2.3 *Literary*).

[222] Proverbs uses the term and its cognates most frequently (e.g., 3:27; 7:7; 9:4, 13, 16; 11:12, 16; 12:11; 13:25; 15:21; 18:2; 21:17; 24:30; 27:7; 28:16, 27). Outside of Proverbs the term is quite rare (e.g., Isa 41:17; Ezek 4:16–17; 12:16; Job 30:3). Its repetition in Deut 15 in a context of lending and release links its use there with its use in Luke-Acts.

teaching into that broad category.²²³ Putting the teaching into this socio-historical category would however create confusion because it may imply that Jesus understood his teaching in terms of *patrocinium*. The absence of *patrocinium* language cautions against ascribing *patrocinium* to Jesus' new teaching.

(3) Luke places Jesus' sermon just after three stories about Sabbath and fasting controversies (5:33–39; 6:1–5, 6–11), one of which includes a benefaction (6:9), and fills the sermon with language reminiscent of the Sabbath year. He subtly connects the stories with the sermon through shared language (ἀγαθοποιῆσαι; ἀγαθοποιῆτε; 6:9, 33, 35).²²⁴ It seems plausible to assume that Luke put these stories together to build toward Jesus' declaration of how Sabbath and Jubilee expectations would be fulfilled. Although he does not explicitly refer to the Sabbath or Jubilee, Jesus explains how these expectations become reality by teaching his disciples about release, freedom, and forgiveness. Jesus' declaration of the way his people will release debtors (forgive, do not retaliate) flows out of his announcement at the Nazareth synagogue that the Year of Jubilee and true Sabbath had arrived. This teaching continues when the disciples request instruction on prayer. Jesus repeats the call to release others from debts in that story (11:1–13). In the narrative context of other Sabbath instruction the reader expects elaboration on this subject which suggests that Jesus' instruction on reciprocity and generosity were intended primarily within the Jewish construct of Sabbath fulfillment rather than the Greco-Roman construct of benefaction or *patrocinium*.

(4) Compared to the other evangelists, Luke emphasizes controversies about healing on the Sabbath (6:7; 13:14; 14:3). By contrast the other synoptics have only the triple tradition story shared by Luke, and John has one fewer stories of a controversial healing on the Sabbath (Matt 12:9–14//Mark 3:1–6//Luke 6:6–11; John [5:1–17²²⁵;] 7:14–24; 9:1–23).²²⁶ Sabbath and release play an important role in Luke's narrative. Jesus' healing was likely intended to be interpreted in line with the release brought with Sabbath more than with the activity of a benefactor or patron. Jesus' Jew-

---

²²³ Moxnes, "Patron-Client," 266; Green, *Luke*, 273–275.

²²⁴ Ἀγαθοποιέω is an infrequent word in the LXX (Num 10:32; Tob 12:13; 2 Macc 1:2; Sir 42:14; Zeph 1:12) and NT (1 Pet 2:14, 15, 20; 3;6, 17; 4:19; 3 Jn 11). See section 4.2.2.

²²⁵ It is not until the end of the story that the reader finds out that the Jews persecuted Jesus because he did "these things on the Sabbath." It is not clear what "these things" refers to most explicitly, but earlier in the story the Jews had confronted the man for illegally picking up his bed on the Sabbath. John highlights this as the point of controversy.

²²⁶ John's stories are less explicitly focused on the legality of healing on the Sabbath than Luke's stories. In Luke's stories the Jews explicitly connect Sabbath law and healing in a direct question.

ish audience would have understood his actions as consistent with the arrival of Sabbath and Jubilee which brought with it the blessing of healings. This does not rule out the notion that some among his audience could have interpreted his actions in line with benefactors (e.g., those from Jerusalem) or even patrons (e.g., those from Tyre and Sidon). But Luke crafts Jesus' message and ministry more in line with the (Hellenistic) Jewish expectation of Sabbath/Jubilee.

From these various strands of evidence it seems that Luke presents Jesus challenging his audience by presenting the fulfillment of Sabbath and Jubilee expectations. Jesus introduced the time to realize the essence of the Sabbath and Jubilee expectation, namely uncalculating generosity. The realization of this promised reality (Sabbath/Jubilee) confronted the greedy, ungrateful, and evil practices which thrived among the people. Jesus addresses problematic components of the reciprocity ethic and instructs his disciples to forego calculations of reciprocity in favor of following the realization of the Jubilee/Sabbath. By casting his program in these terms Jesus fits into the Hellenistic Jewish tradition of awaiting the realization of Sabbath. By challenging components of the reciprocity ethic he teaches in a stream of Hellenstic Jewish and Greco-Roman thinkers who challenged reciprocity (e.g., Philo, Sirach, Seneca). Just as God promised to bless generous people by reciprocating their open-handed giving to each other (e.g., Deut 15:1–18; Lev 25:8–55), Jesus promises that God will bless those who do not evaluate the worthiness of recipients before being generous. God rewards the generous. However, one need not adopt this specific portion (Sabbath/Jubilee) of the exegesis to see that Jesus presents the way of discipleship in contrast to the ethic of reciprocity and benefaction which prevailed in certain parts of Palestine.

Conclusion

This subsection (6:27–38) has been analyzed in terms of reciprocity, benefaction, and patronage to see whether it was originally intended by Luke to be understood under those terms. The prevalence of reciprocity terminology (ἀπαιτέω; ἀπέχω; ἀπολαμβάνω; ἀπελπίζω; χαρὶς; μισθός; cf. ἀντὶ μετρηθήσεται) gives an initial indicator that reciprocity may be in view. Another phrase which corresponds with the logic of reciprocity furthers this suggestion (παρ' ὧν ἐλπίζετε λαβεῖν). Kirk's demonstration of the compatibility of a critique of typical reciprocity within a tradition of Hellenistic philosophers supports the notion that Luke here works with reciprocity categories (e.g., Sir 31:15; Seneca *Ben.* 2.1.1). Similarities in vocabulary and construction of argument suggest that he directly addresses a Hellenistic Jewish version of reciprocity (e.g., Sir 12:1–6).

Some terminology adopted in this subsection also can be found in benefaction contexts (καλῶς ποιεῖτε; ἀγαθοποιέω; ἀχάριστος; χρηστός; χάρις). These include both Greco-Roman (*OGIS* 54.14–20; *OGIS* 167, ll. 17–26; Demosthenes *On the Crown*, 118–120) and Hellenistic Jewish (Esth 8:12–24 LXX; 1 Macc 11:32–36) inscriptions and texts. Seneca instructed against generosity toward the ungrateful (Seneca *Ben.* 4.34.2–3; cf. Hesiod *Op.* 342, 354) and Sirach warned against giving to sinners (Sir 12:4–7). Philo suggested that beneficence should not be directed toward the ungrateful but ought to be directed toward the worthy (ἄξιος; e.g., *Sacr* 57–8; *Mut* 52–53; *Som* 2.224). The sermon's instruction to give specifically to those who cannot repay and have reputations of ingratitude based on the example of generosity found in God directly overturns these teachings. Luke builds a critique of both sides of Philo's position. On the one hand he claims that one ought to direct benefits to the ungrateful in following God. On the other hand he critiques the Jewish leaders in the following pericope (7:1–10) for identifying the centurion as ἄξιὸς. The centurion himself claims that he is not worthy (ἱκανός εἰμι; 7:4–6) of the benefit. A subtle critique against the Jewish leaders who attempt to earn the benefit may be in mind.

Description of God as χρηστός and οἰκτίρμων may be interpreted in light of benefactors who received similar description (*SIG* 730; *SIG* 761; Philo *Virt.* 160; Josephus *Ant.* 8.214), but it seems more likely that Luke drew from LXX descriptions of the covenant God (Ps 68:17 LXX; Ps 111:4–5 LXX). No vocabulary or thematic elements suggest the presence of *patrocinium* (e.g., κηδεμονία, πατρωνεία, and προστασία; κηδεμών, πάτρων, πατρώνης, προστάτης; πατρωνεύω; κλίενς and πελάτης; ἐπιτροπή; πίστις, φίλος). This does not rule out the possibility of some familiar with *patrocinium* (e.g., those from Tyre) from interpreting Jesus' teaching and actions in this light, but it cautions against making *patrocinium* the central interpretive grid for understanding the section. This assessment also holds for the healing of the centurion's servant (Luke 7:1–10). The centurion was likely not ethnically Roman and so was probably more influenced by Hellenistic practices. His generosity ought to be interpreted in light of benefaction rather than *patrocinium*. He probably intended his response to Jesus to be understood in the category of benefactors and clients.

It seems probable that Jesus' teaching was originally crafted in terms of Jewish scripture and expectations, especially the curses and blessings of law and the Sabbath and Jubilee. Luke compares correct and incorrect manners of life with the Jewish prophets and false-prophets with the expectation that his audience would find these a suitable and understood point of comparison. Luke earlier uses vocabulary consistent with Jewish prophets (e.g., οὐαί). Descriptions of God as οἰκτίρμων surface in covenant contexts (Exod 33:19; 34:6; Deut 4:31; cf. Neh 9:17, 19, 28, 31; 1 Kgs 8:50). Vocabulary and themes relate his instruction to the blessings and curses of the law (εὐλογεῖτε τοὺς καταρωμένους ὑμᾶς; Luke 6:28; Exod 19:20–23:33; Deut 4:44–26:19). He adopts language from the LXX instructions and prophecy about Sabbath and Jubilee (δανείζω; ἀπαιτέω; ἐνδεής; Deut 15:1–18; Lev 25:8–58; Isa 61:1–3; 58:6–10). It seems probable that Luke intends Jesus' directives about generosity to be interpreted in light of Sabbath and Jubilee generosity. One need not accept the specific concepts of Jubilee and Sabbath as the intended background in order to recognize the primarily Hellenistic Jewish context of this subsection of the sermon. The fact that many parallels can be drawn between this subsection and Jewish scriptures supports the overall notion that Luke has in mind Jewish practices including their understanding of reciprocity.

4.3 Conclusions for The Sermon on the Plain (Luke 6:17–38)

Three subsections (6:17–19, 20–26, 27–38) of the sermon on the plain have been examined in light of reciprocity, benefaction, and *patrocinium*. The goal of the investigation was to determine whether these provide the best explanatory paradigm for Luke's description of Jesus' actions and instructions. In the first subsection (6:17–19) Jesus performs healings and Luke prepares the reader for the subsequent teaching. Luke does not explicitly prioritize benefaction or *patrocinium* in the introductory summary, but literary, linguistic, and cultural matters suggest rather the importance of Jewish backgrounds. The importance of Jewish culture in Galilee and Jerusalem has been demonstrated from both archaeological and literary materials (see sections 2.2.3; 2.2.4). Luke properly prioritizes this background in his introduction of Jesus' ministry. Jesus' healings would have been interpreted by Galilean audience members in light of Jewish prophets who had come before (e.g., Elijah, Elisha). Luke does use some language which may have been intended to describe benefaction. Specific language is not used for *patrocinium*. It is possible that those from Jerusalem interpreted his actions with reference to benefactors who had contributed generously to their city and earned the title of εὐεργέτης (e.g., 1 Macc 14:25–49; 2 Macc 4:2; *War* 4.145–146; 5.536; 2.538; *SEG* 1277). Those from Tyre and Sidon may have seen in Jesus a candidate for patron of their city similar to M. Aemilius Scaurus. The absence of explicit *patrocinium* terminology suggests that this was likely not Luke's primary explanatory context, but it does not rule out the possibility that Tyrians and Sidonians interpreted Jesus as a potential patron. Tyrians and Sidonians would need to see Jesus as "Roman" to consider him a potential patron. This seems unlikely, so even the Tyrians and Sidonians probably would not have adopted the ideology of *patrocinium* in their interpretation of Jesus. Lack of specific benefactor terminology suggests that this was not Luke's exclusive explanatory paradigm and connection to previous Jewish prophets supports the notion that the Jewish background was of primary importance for Luke in addition to audience members from Galilee. This conforms to the findings of chapters 2 and 3 of this book where it was shown that Jewish culture was of primary importance in Galilee and Jerusalem with some expression of benefaction in Jerusalem and Tyre. A person of Jesus' provenance (and his Galilean audience) would have been aware of benefaction, and to a lesser extent *patrocinium*, but his primary interpretive paradigm would have been Jewish.

In the beatitudes and woes subsection of the sermon (6:20–26) Luke utilizes a topos of transposition which surfaces in Greco-Roman and Jewish contexts. The presence of this topos in both cultural contexts suggests that the subsection cannot be interpreted only in light of Greco-Roman reciprocity, benefaction, or patronage. The suggestion that Luke has Jesus offer a "reversal" similar to benefactors is not strongly supported from primary evidence since only Dio Chrysostom (*Or.* 2.77–78) has been cited as an example. Luke's presentation of Jesus' teaching fits quite well in the historical, cultural world constructed in chapters 2 and 3 of this book. It seems less likely that Jesus or Galilean audience members would have interpreted his message in line with benefactors since in Galilee benefaction is only rarely attested. Those from Tyre, Sidon, and Jerusalem may have interpreted his actions in terms of benefaction since benefactors functioned as such in those cities. The lack of explicit terminology and examples of this type of benefit decrease the likelihood that Luke intended benefaction as the primary explanatory paradigm and the plausibility that auditors from Tyre, Sidon, and Jerusalem would have interpreted the teaching as such. Similarity to Jewish beatitudes makes a Jewish cultural context Luke's most likely intended reference point; this aligns with the predominance of Jewish culture in first-century Galilee. The absence of linguistic evidence of *patrocinium* makes it extremely unlikely that Luke intended to describe Jesus' teaching in such terms. This conforms to the picture of Galilee and Jerusalem, no patrons could be found, developed in chapters 2 and 3 of this book.

The final subsection examined (6:27–38) contains evidence of reciprocity and hints of benefaction, but seems to derive more directly from Jewish prophetic announcements with perhaps a special reference to Sabbath/Jubilee fulfillment. Words common to reciprocity discussions do arise in the section (ἀπαιτέω; ἀπέχω; ἀπολαμβάνω; ἀπελπίζω; χαρὶς; μισθός; cf. ἀντιμετρηθήσεται). Similarities with Hellenistic Jewish discussions of re-

4.3 Conclusions for The Sermon on the Plain (Luke 6:17–38)

ciprocity seem closest to Luke's presentation (Sir 12:1–6). Terminology which has been discovered in benefaction contexts can also be found (καλῶς ποιεῖτε; ἀγαθοποιέω; ἀχάριστος; χρηστός; χάρις). It is possible that Luke intended to shape this section in terms of benefaction. Such shaping does not rule out the possibility that Jesus could have used such ideology because benefaction was present (though sparse) in Galilee and his travels (esp. to Jerusalem and Tyre) would have made him more familiar with this ideology. Teaching in terms of benefaction would have been easily interpreted by audience members from Jerusalem, Tyre, and Sidon. These three cities attest the practice of benefaction in archaeological and literary evidence (*OGIS* 54.14–20; *OGIS* 167, ll. 17–26; Demosthenes *On the Crown*, 118–120; Est 8:12–24 LXX; 1 Macc 11:32–36). Some of these terms arise in covenant contexts which suggest that they would not have been interpreted, at least not primarily, as references to benefaction by Jewish audience members (χρηστός and οἰκτίρμων; Ps 68:17 LXX; Ps 111:4–5 LXX). No terminology connected to *patrocinium* has been discovered in the section. This conforms to the findings of chapters 2 and 3 of the book since no practice of *patrocinium* was discovered in Galilee or Jerusalem (see sections 2.2.3; 2.2.4). This does not rule out the possibility that those from Tyre and Sidon interpreted Jesus' teaching and actions in light of *patrocinium*, since *patrocinium* was practiced in those cities (see section 2.2.5), but it must be admitted that this view cannot be substantiated with direct evidence. Luke's use of vocabulary and forms familiar among the Jewish prophets supports the notion that Jewish prophets and scripture were his primary descriptive paradigm (e.g., οὐαι; εὐλογεῖτε τοὺς καταρωμένους ὑμᾶς). Vocabulary and themes which resonate with Sabbath and Jubilee expectation suggest that Luke presents Jesus' program in terms of Sabbath/Jubilee fulfillment (δανείζω; ἀπαιτέω; ἐνδεής). It is possible that some audience members conflated notions of benefaction and Sabbath/Jubilee fulfillment in their interpretation of Jesus' actions. In this scenario Luke depicts the Sabbath as a time of "divine benefaction."[227]

---

[227] Braun, *Feasting*, 26–27.

Chapter 5

Reciprocity, Benefaction, *Patrocinium*, and Friendship at Table (Luke 14:1–24)

Many scholars have also included Luke 14:1–24 among a class of teachings aimed against reciprocity, benefaction, and/or *patrocinium*.[1] Some refrain from specifying the more particular forms of reciprocity (benefaction, *patrocinium*) and simply suggest that Jesus or Luke attack balanced or generalized reciprocity and/or the honor-shame system of the first-century.[2] Others specify benefaction and/or patronage as forms which Jesus or Luke addressed in their instruction. Green identifies the healing of the dropsical man (14:1–6) as a divine benefaction comparable to the healing in Luke 6:7–9. In the meals, the audience may choose between normal patterns of patronage (receive human rewards for human favors) or reciprocity from the Supreme Benefactor (divine rewards for human favors).[3] Danker suggests that Jesus' new instruction (14:12–14) be thought of under the category of benefaction since it involves generosity beyond the "in-group." Such action was commonplace among benefactors in the inscriptions he surveys.[4] With his power to heal Jesus functions as a benefactor to many (Luke 4:23; 4:33–40; 5:31; 6:18; Acts 10:38).[5] Hanson and Oakman move from a discussion of reciprocity to the specification of patronage as the proper paradigm through which Jesus (or Luke) casts his social pro-

---

[1] For general bibliography see Bovon, *Luc*, 410–411, 426–427, 441–443.

[2] Reciprocity = Harrison, *Language*, 352; Johnson, *Luke*, 226–227; John Paul Heil, *The Meal Scenes in Luke-Acts: An Audience Oriented Approach* (SBLMS 52; Atlanta: Scholars Press, 1999), 108; Douglas E. Oakman, "The Radical Jesus: You Cannot Serve God and Mammon," *BTB* 34 (2004): 122–129, 126; John H. Elliott, "Household and Meals Vs. Temple Purity Replication Patterns in Luke-Acts," *BTB* 21 (1991): 102–109. Honor-Shame = deSilva, *Honor, Patronage*, 31; Crossan and Reed, *Rediscovering*, 110. Neyrey adduces both, Jerome H. Neyrey, "Ceremonies in Luke-Acts: The Case of Meals and Table-Fellowship," in Neyrey, *Social World*, 361–387, 373–373, 379; cf. S. Scott Bartchy, "The Historical Jesus and Honor Reversal at the Table," in *The Social Setting of Jesus and the Gospels* (ed. Wolfgang Stegemann, Bruce J. Malina, and Gerd Theissen; Minneapolis: Fortress Press, 2002), 175–183, 179–183.

[3] Green, *Luke*, 547–548; idem, *Theology*, 114–116.

[4] Danker, *Benefactor*, 339.

[5] Bovon, *Luc*, 2.420–421.

gram (14:7–24).⁶ Through reference to Juvenal (*Satires* 5.12–25), they posit that patrons maintained the dependence of their clients by offering banquets. Jesus challenges the system by advocating invitations to those outside the social network. Moxnes takes a similar route. He begins with the general categories of honor-shame and reciprocity, but later specifies patronage and benefaction in his discussion of Luke 14:1–24.⁷ Luke does away with the patron-client system by establishing God as the ultimate patron and calling disciples to pursue a vertical generalized reciprocity (God repays). A. Mitchell critiques Moxnes, suggesting that since the terminology of patronage and benefaction does not surface in the narrative it should not be set forth as the mode of interaction. Instead, following upon the language of friendship and balanced reciprocity employed in the passages one may legitimately compare and contrast Jesus' teaching to prevailing notions of friendship and reciprocity in the culture of Jesus or Luke.⁸ The following investigation of Luke 14:1–24 agrees to an extent with Mitchell's critique and proposal, but does find some reasons to suggest benefaction as plausibly in the background. Again this study cannot provide an exhaustive exegesis of each passage, but will focus on teachings relevant to reciprocity, benefaction, and *patrocinium*.

Luke offers a fairly clear introduction to the section, but the nebulous character of its ending has made identifying the end more unclear than identifying its beginning. In 14:1 Luke presents a new scenario (meal) in a new location (the house of a ruler of the Pharisees) on a new day (one Sabbath). It is rather apparent that a new section begins here even though it certainly connects to previous pericopes. More difficulty arises with the section's ending. Two main options have been presented. (1) Many deduce that the meal introduced in 14:1 is an exclusive (Pharisee only or mainly) event to which crowds would not be invited. Therefore the presence of crowds in 14:25 signals a new story leaving the Pharisee meal to close at 14:24.⁹ (2) Others do not describe the meal in such closed terms and they see continuity of thought spanning all of chapter 14. These scholars thus

---

⁶ Hanson and Oakman, *Palestine*, 74–76.

⁷ Moxnes, *Economy*, 33–35, 109, 127–132; cf. Green, who follows Moxnes at many points, Green, *Luke*, 550–554; idem, *Theology*, 73, 116.

⁸ Mitchell, "Greet the Friends by Name," 246–247 n. 79; H. –J. Klauck, "Kirche als Freundesgemeinschaft? Auf Spurensuche im Neuen Testament," *Münchener theologische Zeitschrift* 42 (1991): 10–13.

⁹ Talbert, *Reading Luke*, 196; Smith, "Symposium"; idem, *Symposium to Eucharist*; Steele, "Symposium"; Braun, *Feasting*, 14; Heil, *Meal Scenes*, 97–113; Kyoung-Jin Kim, *Stewardship and Almsgiving in Luke's Theology* (JSNTSupp 155; Sheffield: Sheffield Academic Press, 1998), 184; Fitzmyer, *Luke*, 2.1060; Marshall, *Luke*, 591–592; Bovon, *Luc*, 2.465; idem, *Lukas*, 525; Plummer, *Luke*, 363; Talbert, *Theological Commentary*, 169, 171; Bormann, *Recht*, 298–300; Leaney, *Luke*, 214; Lagrange, *Luc*, 408.

choose to retain 14:1–24 together with 14:25–35.[10] The precise limits of the section do not dramatically influence the discussion of this thesis, however, since the reciprocity teaching falls within the first segment (14:1–24).[11] It must only be reiterated that a close relationship exists between the first segment and the previous and following pericopes. This close relationship influences the overall interpretation of the passage even if it does not have large bearing on the presence of reciprocity teaching itself. For the sake of space the following discussion will be limited to 14:1–24 while reference will be made to surrounding pericopes. The narrative breaks down easily into four smaller sections (14:1–6, 7–11, 12–14, 15–24) which will be addressed consecutively. In keeping with the structure of the previous analysis this study proceeds by investigating the literary context, linguistic evidence, and cultural matters before drawing evidence together into a conclusion.

5.1 Healing the Dropsical Man (14:1–6)

5.1.1 Literary Context

Luke repeats the pattern of a controversial healing on the Sabbath and the unique nature of the ailment (dropsy) introduces a theme which is expounded in the following parables (14:1–6). The repetition of three phrases signals the repetition of the Sabbath healing controversy motif. In the Sabbath controversies, Luke describes the audience as "watching closely" (παρατηρέω; 6:7; 17:20; 20:20; cf. Acts 9:24), presents the ailing person with the same phrase (καὶ ἰδοὺ; 7:37; 13:11; cf. 4:31–37), and introduces the controversy with similar terminology (ἔξεστιν τῷ σαββάτῳ; 6:2, 9; cf. 13:14). Those who are healed are "released" (ἀπολύω; 13:12; 14:4) in a manner akin to the Sabbath release announced in 4:18–19.[12] A Sabbath

---

[10] Rohrbaugh, "City," 137–138; Johnson, *Luke*; Nolland, *Luke*, 2.721; Robert J. Karris, "Poor and Rich: The Lukan Sitz im Leben," in *Perspectives on Luke-Acts* (ed. C. H. Talbert; Danville: Association of Baptist Professors of Religion, 1978), 112–125, 121 (14:1–33); J. L. Resseguie, "Point of View in the Central Section of Luke," *JETS* 25 (1982): 41–47, 46. Danker, *New Age*, 163–168 sees strong affinities between the passages (14:1–24; 14:25–35) and hesitates to separate too sharply.

[11] In light of the triple tradition (Matthew, Luke, *Thomas*) a discussion about the original form has developed. The difficulties are immense and Rohrbaugh suggests that Beare's conclusion might be accepted by many. He claims that the text is now so "mangled" that "it is no longer possible to tell in what form it was first uttered, or in what context." F. W. Beare, *The Gospel According to Matthew* (New York: Harper and Row, 1981), 432, in Rohrbaugh, "City," 138. For this reason a discussion of the "original" form will not be undertaken.

[12] Green, *Luke*, 546–548, esp. n. 121; Bovon, *Luc*, 2.421.

controversy about the healing is in view here, but it receives little elaboration or mention in the subsequent pericopes (14:7–24).

For this reason more attention has been paid recently to the nature of the ailment and its possible metaphorical import for those pericopes. W. Braun introduces the notion that dropsy (ὑδρωπικός) frequently surfaces in Greco-Roman literature as a metaphor for one whose insatiable appetite for wealth will eventually be their demise.[13] Just as a craving for water, if appeased, will eventually destroy the dropsical person, so the craving for wealth, if appeased, will destroy the avaricious person (Stobaeus *Florilegium* 3.10.45; 4.33.31; Plutarch *Moralia* 524A–D; Seneca *Ad Helviam* 11.3; Polybius 13.2.2; Horace *Epode* 2.2.146–149; Ovid *Fasti* 1.215–216). One example should be sufficient to express the point.

Διογένης ὡμοίου τοὺς φιλαργύρους τοῖς ὑδρωπικοῖς ἐκείνους μὲν γὰρ πλήρεις ὄντας ὕδρου ἐπιθυμεῖν ποτοῦ τοὺς τε φιλαργύρους πλήρεις ὄντας ἀργυρίου ἐπιθυμεῖν πλείονος ἀμφοτέρους δὲ Πρὸς κακοῦ ἐπιτείνεσθαι γὰρ μᾶλλον τὰ πάθη ὅσῳ τὰ ἐπιθῦ μούμενα πορίζεται

"Diogenes compared money-lovers to dropsies: as dropsies, though filled with fluid crave drink, so money-lovers, though loaded with money, crave more of it, yet both to their demise (κακοῦ). For, their desires increase the more they acquire the objects of their cravings." (Stobaeus *Florilegium* 3.10.45)[14]

Braun's thesis that the healing story is a *chreia* which receives elaboration in the vein of Hermogenes of Tarsus has not won universal assent,[15] but the general point that the dropsical healing has metaphorical import seems plausible.[16] The metaphorical import of dropsy thus leads into the following sections in which Jesus identifies the need for many from the audience to be healed of greed. In general, this pericope (14:1–6) provides another example of Jesus having favor on the poor (4:16–30; 6:20–21; 7:22; 16:20–22; 18:22; 19:8; 21:3).[17]

---

[13] Braun, *Feasting*, ch. 3.

[14] O. Hense, *Die Synkrisis in der antiken Literatur* (Lehmann: Freiburg, 1893), 419, in Braun, *Feasting*, 34.

[15] E.g., R. C. Tannehill, "Review of *Feasting and Social Rhetoric*," *Biblica* 77 (1996): 565.

[16] E.g., Green, *Luke*, 546–547; cf. Malina and Rohrbaugh, *Social Science Commentary*, 284. Esler disputes understanding dropsy as a metaphor for interpreting Pharisaical greed, and charges Braun with over-emphasizing the Greco-Roman background to the neglect of the Jewish background. P. F. Esler, "Review of *Feasting and Social Rhetoric*," *JTS* 49/1 (1998): 229–232. Bock refers instead to rabbinic references to dropsy as an indication of sexual sin (*b. Sab.* 33a), Bock, *Luke*, 2.1256.

[17] Esler, "Review," 231; idem, *Community*, 115–117, 164–200; Green, *Luke*, 546.

5.1.2 Linguistic Evidence

The lack of benefaction or *patrocinium* terminology in the episode calls into question the importance of these forms of reciprocity in the interpretation of this episode, but the lack of such a term does not rule out a first-century interpretation, by some audience members or readers, of the healing of the dropsical man as a benefit.[18] Common phrases and terms which arise frequently in benefaction and *patrocinium* contexts would be a clear indication that such practices were in view (e.g., εὐεργεσία, χάρις, κηδεμονία, πατρωνεία, προστασία, κηδεμών, πάτρων, πατρώνης, προστάτης, πατρωνεύω, κλίενς, πελάτης, ἐπιτροπή, cf. καλῶς ποιέω, ἀγαθοποιέω). The passage lacks these terms and instead makes allusions to Sabbath healing.

It is possible that through the connection with other Sabbath healings (6:6–11; 13:10–17)[19] some readers of Luke would have understood this healing as a benefit since those healings have verbal and contextual reasons to be understood as benefits from a new benefactor ("son bienfaiteur").[20] The healing of the man with the withered hand in 6:6–11, it was argued, could be understood as a benefaction. Luke uses a near synonym of εὐεργεσία, i.e., ἀγαθοποιέω, to describe the healing (6:9). Though these are not necessary terms in descriptions of benefactions they arise frequently in such circumstances (e.g., 1 Macc 11:32–36; *OGIS* 54.14–20; *OGIS* 167, ll. 17–26; see section 6.2.2). The response of gratitude toward God in the healing of the woman with the disabling spirit suggests that this act may have been interpreted as a benefaction (Luke 13:10–17). Her immediate response is to glorify God (13:13) and this glorification becomes public at the end of the story (13:17). Public acclaim for benefits is commonplace in benefaction inscriptions (e.g., *Benefactor* 28 = *SIG* 1173; *Benefactor* 29).[21] By paralleling this third Sabbath healing (14:1–6) with the previous two Luke perhaps hints that this, too, should be thought of as a Sabbath-benefaction bestowed by Jesus.[22] It is a one-time, extravagant benefit

---

[18] Recall Danker's statement above, "[T]he Graeco-Roman world had no technical generic expression for the civic-minded benefactor. Instead, literary writers and formulators of official documents drew on a vast stock of terms and phrases that functioned within a semantic field to denote and connote a person or group deserving of recognition." Danker, *Benefactor*, 43.

[19] Robert F. O'Toole, "Some Exegetical Reflections on Luke 13,10–17," *Bib* 73 (1992): 84–107; J. Duncan M. Derrett, "Positive Perspectives on Two Lucan Miracles," *Downside Review* 104 (1986): 272–287; Green, *Luke*, 543–44, 545, 547; Bovon, *Luke*, 1.203; Danker, *New Age*, 163; Esler, *Community*, 115–117; Bock, *Luke*, 2.1254–1255.

[20] Bovon, *Luke*, 204; idem, *Luc*, 421; van Unnik, "Motivierung."

[21] See P. Roussel, "Un nouvel hymne à Isis," *Revue des Études Grecques* 42 (1929): 136–168; Danker, *Luke*, 36. Cf. Otto Kern, *Die Inschriften vom Magnesia am Maeander* (Berlin: Speman, 1900; reprint de Gruyter, 1967), 105.23–24.

[22] Lull, "Servant-Benefactor," 289; Green, *Luke*, 548.

which comports closely with the description of a benefaction given in earlier chapters. Patrons typically gave gifts that were less extravagant and tended to be necessities which suggests that the generosity of a patron is not in view. In the absence of explicit vocabulary (not technical terms, but common benefaction language) and actions (e.g., public praise) it is best to conclude that the healing of the dropsical man may be a benefit, but it cannot be wholeheartedly endorsed as such. Similarities to previous benefits push in this direction without providing conclusive evidence. The construct of *patrocinium* does not work for this episode because of the nature of the gift, the lack of loyalty language, and the lack of specific vocabulary connected to the construct.

5.1.3 Cultural Matters

The cultural setting of the meal is somewhat ambiguous, but it seems probable that it is a thoroughly Jewish group. Scholars debate the meal's participants because it seems unlikely that an unclean dropsical man and a despised Jesus would be invited to dine with Jewish leaders who were consumed by purity concerns (see section 5.1.1). Green sets forth three descriptions of the diners. (1) The host is identified as a τινος τῶν ἀρχόντων [τῶν] Φαρισαίων (14:1) and those who joined him would be persons of similar status because meals were times of reinforcing status. (2) Since the host is a Pharisee it is unlikely that anyone other than Pharisees attended. He references the presence of scribes and Pharisees as a warrant/confirmation for this claim (14:3a). (3) In dining scenes the rules of purity are of prime importance and concern for status would have been a point of interest.[23] Green's first and third points seem on target. Luke appears to emphasize the presence of elite members of society by referring to the attainment of honor and advancement in society (e.g., in 14:7–11: τὰς πρωτοκλισίας; ἐντιμότερός; ἀνώτερον; δόξα ἐνώπιον πάντων; ὑψωθήσεται). The host is a leader of the Pharisees and scribes also attended the gathering (Luke 14:1). Saldarini has shown that scribes belonged to the upper class as well (Luke 14:3).[24] The text does not indicate if the dropsical man was wealthy or not, but the ailment does not in itself indicate a lower financial status. Herod I may have suffered from dropsy at the end of his life (*Ant.* 17.168–170; *War* 1.656).[25] The dropsical man in Luke 14:1–6 may well have been wealthy as the other members of the meal appear to be.

---

[23] Green, *Luke*, 545.

[24] Anthony J. Saldarini, *Pharisees, Scribes and Sadducees in Palestinian Society: A Sociological Approach* (Wilmington: M. Glazier, 1988), 241–276.

[25] Bock, *Luke*, 2.1256 n. 5.

Green's second point of description, however, seems too limited. The emphasis in Luke seems not to rest on Pharisees since that term falls from discussion after its first two mentions in the opening verses (14:1, 3). To claim that none other than Pharisees would attend a meal hosted by a Pharisee seems too constricted. The presence of outsiders in the home of a Pharisee for a meal is not unprecedented in Luke (7:36–40). In a meal described by Josephus Pharisees dine with others not of their group. Josephus describes a meal hosted by Hyrcanus in which he attempts to commend himself as righteous before Pharisees. Although Hyrcanus was not a leader of the Pharisees, Josephus emphasizes that he was an avid member of their group. The meal was attended by Pharisees, but also by Sadducees and a few corrupt men like Eleazar whose reputation for evil preceded him (*Ant* 13.288–296). It is also not unprecedented in Luke for a despised person like Jesus to be invited by a Pharisee to eat (7:36–50; 11:32–52). In the absence of specification of the dinner guests in the text itself it seems unwarranted to overly limit the constituents of the meal. The elite status of most members seems likely, but limitation to Pharisees seems overly restrictive.

Though all attendees were probably not Pharisees, it is likely that they were all Jews. A Sabbath meal was an occasion for fellowship with those of similar social and religious status.[26] A leader of the Pharisees likely would not have invited Gentiles to the meal for fear of contamination (cf. Gal 2:12–14).[27] Exclusivity in dining was a mark of Pharisees so they would likely not have had an open stance to others.[28] The "Jewishness" of the guests makes sense of the argument Jesus makes in defense of the healing. Reference to Jewish legal issues would have been less important, if important at all, to non-Jews. It seems likely that the meal was attended exclusively by Jews. Considering the importance of hospitality in Jewish culture, however, it is possible that an outsider (Gentile or lower social status) may have been admitted.[29] The claim that the meal takes place in Jerusalem is however unwarranted by the available evidence.[30] There is nothing in the text to identify the location as Jerusalem. If the leaders of the Pharisees were located in Jerusalem, then the presence of Jerusalemites

---

[26] Neyrey, "Ceremonies," 361–363, 364–365, 371–373; Bartchy, "Reversal at Table," 175–184.

[27] A list of those deemed inadmissible for table fellowship can be found in Schnabel, *Mission*, 1.214–215.

[28] Bartchy, "Table Fellowship," 174–179; Neyrey, "Ceremonies," 363–364 ("Pharisee haburah meal").

[29] Plummer, *Luke*, 354; H. B. Tristram, *Eastern Customs in Bible Lands* (London: Hodder and Stoughton, 1894), 36, 81; Oakman, "Countryside," 151, 163.

[30] Fitzmyer, *Luke*, 2.1040; Bock, *Luke*, 2.1256. Contra Ellis, *Luke*, 192; cf. Plummer, *Luke*, 353.

at the meal is possible. The text does not identify the place of origin of any guests.

5.1.4 Conclusion

In light of the ethnicity of the meal participants it seems probable that the healing of the dropsical man was interpreted primarily in light of Jewish predecessors. In the previous Sabbath healing (6:6–11) it was suggested that Elijah and Elisha were immediately available for comparison to Jesus' action because of their mention in the Nazareth sermon (4:22–30). By describing the healing as a "release" (ἀπολύω; 14:4) Luke alludes to Sabbath release. The setting of the story on a Sabbath makes this allusion more plausible. The reference to legal stipulations in the following verses (14:5–6) brings the Jewish context of the story into the foreground. This healing would have been interpreted in light of Jewish predecessors (perhaps, Elijah/Elisha) and as an expression of Sabbath release and legal challenge. It appears therefore that Luke intends to present this miracle primarily in line with Jewish predecessors, though there is some reason to suggest that benefaction may also be in view.

Luke's prioritization of Jewish predecessors, along with the possibility of a benefaction interpretation, conforms to the conclusions reached about the cultural make-ups of Galileans and Jerusalemites in chapters 2 and 3 of this book. The similarity of this healing to previous benefits makes it possible that it was understood as a benefit, especially by potential participants from Jerusalem. Luke does not explicitly mention any geographical or cultural outsiders which limits the extent to which this would be interpreted as a benefit. If people from Jerusalem were present they may have understood the healing as a benefit. Investigation of Jerusalem revealed the practice and knowledge of benefaction among some of its constituents (e.g., 1 Macc 14:25–49; 2 Macc 4:2; *War* 4.145–146; 5.536; 2.538; *SEG* 1277) which means that if a Jerusalemite were present at the meal he may have interpreted Jesus' healing as a benefaction. Those who interpreted the healing in this way would have seen in Jesus a superior benefactor to his predecessors (e.g., Herod I, Onias). He provides a benefit unparalleled by his predecessors. Nevertheless, lack of benefactor and patron vocabulary casts doubt on the intended meaning (by Luke) and primary interpretation of the healing as a benefit from a benefactor or patron. Lack of specific connection to patronage or benefaction would be particularly appropriate if the meal was set in Galilee because that region did not attest the practice of benefaction or patronage (apart from Herod I and Herod Antipas). Without the presence of geographical outsiders there is not a plausible individual who is explicitly mentioned for whom the primary interpretive paradigm for the healing would have been benefaction. Since the people seem to be

Jews, Jewish predecessors (e.g., Elijah/Elisha) would be a better paradigm for understanding the healing. Green puts the Jewish and Greco-Roman pieces together in suggesting that the healing of the dropsical man expresses the arrival of the Sabbath and Jubilee declaration of release. The Sabbath is thus a "day of divine benefaction for the needy."[31] This suggestion is plausible for guests from Jerusalem, but guests from Galilee probably would not have had benefaction as a primary interpretive paradigm.

5.2 Wedding Seat Arrangements (14:7–11)

5.2.1 Literary Context

Luke organizes Jesus' teaching into three successive stages (14:7–11, 12–14, 15–24). The three stages share similar themes though they are directed toward different persons at the meal (πρὸς τοὺς κεκλημένους; τῷ κεκληκότι αὐτόν; τις τῶν συνανακειμένων). It is implied in the third stage that each stage was overheard by the rest of the audience because one man who sat at table, but was not directly addressed, responds to Jesus' instruction ('Ακούσας; 14:12–14, 15) with a remark that draws from Jesus further elaboration. For this reason it seems likely that Luke does not present each stage of the teaching as only applicable to the individual addressed. Green further connects 14:7–11 with 14:12–14 on the basis of "language of invitation" (καλέω 14:7, 8, 9, 10, 12, 13; φωνέω 14:12; ἀντικαλέω 14:13) and structure:[32]

Verses 7–11	Verses 12–14
Jesus addresses his fellow guests	Jesus addresses his host
῎Ελεγεν δὲ .	῎Ελεγεν δὲ .
When you are invited to a meal ...	When you host a meal with guests...
ὅταν	ὅταν
Do not ... lest	Do not ... lest ... .
μὴ . μήποτε	μὴ . μήποτε
But when you are invited to a meal...	But when you host a meal with guests...
ἀλλ' ὅταν ...	ἀλλ' ὅταν ...
Then you will... because... .	Then you will... because... .
τότε ἔσται ... δόξα ... ὅτι	καὶ μακάριος ἔσῃ, ὅτι

---

[31] Green, *Luke*, 548.
[32] Green, *Luke*, 549–550; cf. Fitzmyer, *Luke*, 2.1043–1045; Nolland, *Luke*, 2.750; de Meeus, "Composition," 868; C. Cavallin, "'Bienheureux seras-tu ... á la résurrection des Justes': Le macarisme de Lc 14,14, " in *À cause de l'Évangile: Études sur les Synoptiques et les Actes* (FS J. Dupont; LD 123; ed. F. Refoulé; Paris: Cerf, 1985), 531–546, 538–539, 544; cf. Nolland, *Luke*, 2.748.

In this initial teaching section Luke has Jesus addressing the collected group of invited guests (πρὸς τοὺς κεκλημένους). He offers them instruction on how to approach the meal in a manner which will ultimately lead to glory (δόξα). Instruction comes by way of negative and positive example. In the negative example, a person enters the wedding feast and assumes a high position, but is shamed upon hearing that a more noble guest (ἐντιμότερός) has arrived to take the seat (14:8). Rather than retaining the highest seat, the ashamed guest must now take the lowest (τὸν ἔσχατον τόπον), assuming that by this point in the meal all intermediary seats had been taken (14:9). In the positive example, the guest enters the wedding feast and chooses the lowest seat (ὀν ἔσχατον τόπον; 14:10). Upon seeing this situation, the host invites the guest to join him at a higher place (προσανάβηθι ἀνώτερον) which leads to public glory (ἔσται σοι δόξα ἐνώπιον πάντων). In the interchange the host identifies the guest as φίλος (14:10). Jesus concludes the teaching segment with an aphorism (14:11). He summarizes his teaching and gives a theological interpretation to the message when he says that the person who initially desires the higher place (ὁ ὑψῶν ἑαυτὸν) will be humbled by God (ταπεινωθήσεται) and the person who initially takes the lower place (ὁ ταπεινῶν ἑαυτὸν) will be exalted by God (ὑψωθήσεται). Repetition of future passives (ταπεινωθήσεται; ὑψωθήσεται) indicates that God performs the humbling and exalting of those who take either course of action on earth.[33] Luke describes this teaching as a parable, and though the form of the section does not resemble a parable the addition of the wisdom saying (14:11) provides theological grounding and perhaps gives Luke reason to describe the whole as a parable.[34] This verse also moves the teaching from simple pragmatics (i.e., operate in this way to succeed in society) to the realm of spiritual reality (i.e., God rewards those who live humbly).[35]

5.2.2 Linguistic Evidence

Linguistic evidence reveals that this section (14:7–11) addresses honor-shame protocol and friendship. It is immediately apparent that honor and shame play a significant role in the understanding of this passage. Specific

---

[33] Fitzmyer, *Luke*, 2.1045, 1047; Nolland, *Luke*, 2.749; Tannehill, *Luke*, 229–230; idem, *Narrative Unity*, 1.109, 185; Leaney, *Luke*, 213; Lagrange, *Luc*, 401.

[34] Fitzmyer, *Luke*, 2.1045; cf. Marshall, *Luke*, 581; H. Flender, *St. Luke Theologian of Redemptive History* (London: SPCK, 1967), 81–82; Bovon, *Luc*, 2.427–428; Meynet suggests that verse 11 connects 7–10 and 12–14. R. Meynet, *Quelle est donc cette parole? Lecture "rhétorique" de l'évangile de Luc (1–9,22–24)* (Lectio Divina 99 A-B; 2 vols.; Paris, 1979), 1.45, 2.157.

[35] Plummer, *Luke*, 358; Fitzmyer, *Luke*, 2.1045, 1047; cf. Marshall, *Luke*, 583; Bovon, *Luc*, 2.427–428; Nolland, *Luke*, 2.749; Tannehill, *Luke*, 229–230; Plummer, *Luke*, 358.

vocabulary connected to honor and shame pervades the pericope. The double mention of first seats (πρωτοκλισία) introduces the topic of honor-shame. Selection of these seats may be unwise if someone more honorable (ἐντιμότερός; 14:8) joins the dinner. Shame follows (μετὰ αἰσχύνης) the dishonored as he moves toward the last and least-honorable seat (τὸν ἔσχατον τόπον κατέχειν; 14:9). A different approach to the banquet, selecting the last seat initially, leads to glory (δόξα; 14:10) and exaltation (ὑψωθήσεται; 14:11).

Appeal need not be made to Greco-Roman adoption of honor-shame since the language is prevalent in the LXX. Two passages in the LXX carry a similar teaching (Ezek 21:31; 17:24). Ezekiel describes the exaltation of the humble by God as well as the humbling of the exalted:

ἐταπείνωσας τὸ ὑψηλὸν καὶ τὸ ταπεινὸν ὕψωσας
Humbling the exalted and exalting the humble (Ezek 21:31 LXX)
ἐγὼ κύριος ὁ ταπεινῶν ξύλον ὑψηλὸν καὶ ὑψῶν ξύλον ταπεινὸν)
I am the Lord, the one who humbles the exalted tree and exalts the humbled tree (Ezek 17:24 LXX)

In Ezekiel, as in Luke, God takes credit for exalting and humbling those who stand in positions of humility and self-exaltation respectively. The honor-shame vocabulary employed in Luke 14:7–11 surfaces often in the LXX. Ἔντιμος as a description of (public) honor frequently arises in the LXX (Num 22:15, 17; Deut 28:58; Sir 10:19–20; Wis 18:12; Job 34:19; 3 Macc 2:9), and αἰσχύνη is likewise littered throughout the Greek OT in reference to (public) shame (1 Sam 20:30; 27:12; 2 Sam 19:4; 23:7; 1 Kgs 18:19, 25).[36] Hellenistic Jews had categories for discussing relative honor and shame at table.

One does not find explicit vocabulary connected to benefaction or patronage, but instead the only more specific vocabulary that surfaces in this section is the lone reference to a φίλος (14:10). It will be shown below (section 5.1.3), in reference to Plutarch, Agrippa, and the LXX, that questions of friendship were pertinent in banquet conversations. The banquet was a time for instigating or improving friendships. It is possible that φίλος is employed as a euphemism for *cliens* since that is one way in which it was used in the first-century. But a euphemistic reading does not seem appropriate in this context for two reasons. (1) Meals were times of balanced reciprocity wherein people of similar status gathered to solidify their positions (see section 5.2.3). One became indebted by the gift, but the debt did not subordinate him to the status of a client.[37] His debt is to return

---

[36] Honor words related to ἔντιμος (ἐντίμως; ἐντιμόομαι) occur 30 times while shame words connected to αἰσχύνη (αἰσχρῶς; αἰσχυντηρός; αἰσχύνω) occur 183 times, see LSJ.

[37] J. Nicols, "Patrons of Greek Cities, " 81–83; Eilers, *Roman Patrons*, 18; Crook, *Conversion*, 58; cf. Brunt, "Clientela," 386.

a gift of similar value to the host. (2) In the following pericope φίλος is grouped with terms which imply equal status (ἀδελφούς; συγγενεῖς σου; γείτονας πλουσίους; 14:12; see section 5.2.2). Inviting the friend up to a higher level suggests that he belongs in closer social proximity (and status) to the host. Linguistic evidence suggests that the ideology of patronage and benefaction was not the primary interpretive grid intended by Luke for this teaching section. Rather, he references the categories of honor-shame and friendship.

5.2.3 Cultural Matters

Honor-shame and friendship were common topics of conversation in the larger Hellenistic world as well as the Hellenistic Jewish world. In the Hellenistic world a dinner enjoyed around a *triclinium* would have had established positions of greater and lesser importance. Seats closer to the host had greater honor attached to them.[38] In discussions of this passage many scholars turn to Plutarch's *The Dinner of the Seven Wise Men* (*Septum sapientium convivium*) and specifically the saying which shows contempt for neighbors and host in the complaint against location (148F-149F).[39]

ὡς ὅ γε τόπῳ κλισίας δυσχεραίνων δυσχεραίνει τῷ συγκλίτῃ μᾶλλον ἢ τῷ κεκληκότι, καὶ πρὸς ἀμφοτέρους ἀπεχθάνεται

"a man that objects to his place at table is objecting to his neighbor rather than to his host, and he makes himself hateful to both" (149B; F. C. Babbitt LCL)

Thales, the voice of the advice, willfully assumes the lowest position (to show admiration for the lower?). Plutarch's *Table Talk* (*Quaestionum convivalium libri*) also describes a meal without prescribed seating in which late-coming noblemen were embarrassed by the seats left for them (*Quest. Conv.* 616C-F). The point of not prescribing seats in Plutarch's tale was the increase of equality and friendship which prescription of seats seems to speak against.

Debate about seat locations and the friend-making purpose of meals were natural topics of conversation at these events. The second portion of some meals, the symposium (συμπόσιον), mixed drinking and entertainment. In the philosophical world entertainment often involved "elevated" conversation such as ethical discourses (Athenaeus *Deipnosophists* 5.186a;

---

[38] Green, *Luke*, 550; Neyrey, "Ceremonies," 364; David B. Gowler, *Host, Guest, Enemy, and Friend: Portraits of the Pharisees in Luke and Acts* (Emory Studies in Early Christianity 2; New York: P. Lang, 1991), 248–249; Moxnes, *Economy*, 135; Bormann, *Recht*, 293–294; Plummer mentions Greek, Roman, Jewish, and Persian customs which make precision on which is the "highest" more difficult, Plummer, *Luke*, 356.

[39] Smith, *Symposium to Eucharist*, 254; Smith, "Table Fellowship," 621; Steele, "Symposium," 384; Braun, *Feasting, passim*; Talbert, *Theological Commentary*, 169–171; Malina and Rohrbaugh, *Social Science Commentary*, 286.

Aulus Gellius *Attic Nights* 15.2.3).[40] Two of the most common grounds upon which ethical arguments are made in regard to table are friendship and pleasure (Plutarch *Sept sap* 149B; Plutarch *Quaest. Conv.* 612D, 615F, 616C-F; Plato *Leg* 2.671C-672A).[41] Plutarch refers to τῷ φιλοποιῷ λέγ᾽ ὑμένῳ ... τῆς τραπέζης (Plutarch *Quaest. Conv* 612D). Disparaging comments against the one who does not appreciate his seat location and the potential embarrassment of a more honorable late-arriver certainly mirror the story Jesus tells in Luke. Although no mention is made of drinking, or of a "banquet" *per se* (φαγεῖν ἄρτον; 14:1), ethical instruction led by a preeminent guest to a selection of honored invitees and a noble host does share similarities with the symposium genre.[42]

Discussions about honor and shame around the table also took place in the Jewish world. Scholars who recognize this reality point to Proverbs 25:6–7; Sir 31:12–32:9; *Aboth de R. Nathan* 25; cf. *Leviticus Rabb.* 1 (fifth century A.D.).[43] "De telles leçons de bonne conduite n'étaient pas nouvelles dans la tradition juive."[44] Proverbs 25:6–7 LXX provides a succinct statement of Jewish opinion.

μὴ ἀλαζονεύου ἐνώπιον βασιλέως μηδὲ ἐν τόποις δυναστῶν ὑφίστασο κρεῖσσον γάρ σοι
τὸ ῥηθῆναι ἀνάβαινε πρός με ἢ ταπεινῶσαί σε ἐν προσώπῳ δυνάστου
"Do not make pretensions before the king, nor stand in the place of the powerful. For it is better for it to be said to you, 'Come up to me' than to be humbled in the presence of the powerful." (Author's translation)

It is best to enter a noble person's presence humbly and to be exalted by them than to take a higher position and be humbled. The author follows this advice by mentioning the potential of being shamed by a friend (σε ὁ νειδίσῃ ὁ σὸς φίλος; 25:8). Philo is also aware of symposia. He offers a critique which holds up the Therapeutae as maintaining a more noble meal practice. The Therapeutae exchange philosophical discourses on pleasure in favor of a discussion of the Jewish Law (*Vit. Cont.* 58–80).[45] Philo's disapproval of the symposium has support in the LXX which sometimes em-

---

[40] Smith, "Table Fellowship," 614; cf. Flender, *Theologian*, 81–82.

[41] Smith, "Table Fellowship," 619.

[42] X. de Meeus, "Composition de Lc. XIV et genre symposiaque," *Ephemerides Theologicae Lovanienses* 37 (1961): 847–870; Steele, "Symposium," 379; Smith, "Table Fellowship," 614; Neyrey, "Ceremonies," 377; Bovon, *Luc*, 2.427.

[43] E.g., Johnson, *Luke*, 226; Bartchy, "Table Fellowship," 179; Corley, *Public Meals*, 70; Fitzmyer, *Luke*, 2.1047; Green, *Luke*, 552; Plummer, *Luke*, 357–358; Amy-Jill Levine, "Second Temple Judaism, Jesus, and Women: Yeast of Eden," *BibInterp* 2 (1994): 8–33; Marshall, *Luke*, 581.

[44] Bovon, *Luc*, 2.429.

[45] Ross Kraemer, "Monastic Jewish Women in Graeco-Roman Egypt: Philo Judaeus on the Therapeutrides," *Signs* 14 (1989): 342–370, 343–344; Smith, "Table Fellowship," 615.

ploys the term (συμπόσιον) for a drunken party (Esth. 4:17; 7:7; 1 Macc 16:16; 3 Macc 5:16).

Expected etiquette at such symposia also appears to have been appreciated in Jewish culture. In the introduction to 2 Macc the author compares the labor of abbreviating a history to that of hosting a συμπόσιον (2:27). Both seek the gratitude of the recipients (ζητοῦντι τὴν ἑτέρων λυσιτέλειαν; διὰ τὴν τῶν πολλῶν εὐχαριστίαν), but after much difficulty. Other texts give further advice about the types of conversation to have or not have and the expectation of entertainment at such events (Sir 31:31; 32:1–9; 49:1). In a discussion of the blessings and problems of wine, Sirach suggests that when drinking at a symposium one should not reprove a neighbor, despise him when he is glad, nor make demands of him (μὴ ἐλέγξῃς; ἐξουθενήσῃς αὐτὸν ἐν εὐφροσύνῃ αὐτοῦ; ἐν ἀπαιτήσει; 31:25–31). Following this he instructs his audience to avoid speaking when music is provided (32:4). Those who are old may speak as they please, granted they do so with accuracy, but those who are young ought only to speak briefly, only when asked, and only two times (32:6–9). The community at Qumran also assessed social standing by seat location in meals resembling a symposium. Closer to the "anointed one of Israel" meant higher status. "Afterwards, [the messiah] of Israel [shall enter] and the heads of the [thousands of Israel] shall sit before him [ea]ch according to his importance, according to [his station] in their encampments and their journeys" (1 *QSa* 2:13).[46] The Gospels frequently depict the Pharisees' desire to have the places of honor at feasts (Matt 23:6; Mark 12:39; Luke 11:43; 14:7–8; 20:46; 23:5–7). Repetition of the term πρωτοκλισία signals Pharisaic desire to take the highest positions. These discussions do not take place at symposia (in the setting of the Gospel stories), but they express a sentiment toward Pharisaic priorities at such feasts.

The Hellenistic and Jewish discussion of honor-shame at banquets can be seen vividly in the practice of the Herodians. Herod I held a symposium with Hyrcanus which shows that the practice did not remain isolated among the Herodians but found its way into Jewish society (*Ant.* 15.175). A feast attended by Gaius and Agrippa, mentioned in the previous chapter, follows some of the protocol established in Plutarch (*Ant.* 18.289–301). In

---

[46] *Rule of the Congregation*, translated in Lawrence Schiffman, *The Eschatological Community of the Dead Sea Scrolls* (SBLMS 38; Atlanta: Scholars, 1989), 54; cf. Corley, *Public Meals*, 68. James C. VanderKam, *The Dead Sea Scrolls Today* (Grand Rapids: Eerdmans, 1994), 174–175; Bartchy, "Table Fellowship," 177; Talbert, *Theological Commentary*, 173. Burrows and Vögtle compare Luke 14 with the Qumran community as represented in the DSS. Millar Burrows, *More Light on the Dead Sea Scrolls; New Scrolls and New Interpretations* (New York: Viking Press, 1958), 91; Anton Vögtle, *Das Öffentliche Wirken Jesu auf dem Hintergrund der Qumranbewegung* (Freiburger Universitätsreden, N.F., Heft 27; Freiburg im Breisgau: Schulz, 1958), 12–13.

the episode Agrippa holds a feast to extend his friendship (προύκοπτε φιλίᾳ) with Gaius. Gaius, indebted, attempts to reciprocate Agrippa's many gifts. Agrippa refuses to directly improve his own station and instead requests dissolution of the plan to erect Gaius' statue in the temple. The request impresses Gaius and he grants it. Familiarity with symposia among the Herodian family finds another example in Mark's gospel (6:21–29). In his description of Herod's birthday feast Mark refrains from using the technical term for the event (συμπόσιον), but delays it until he describes the ordering of groups at the miraculous feeding in the following pericope (6:39).[47] Nevertheless, a few details in the narrative signal that a symposium takes place. The fact that Herodias' daughter and Herodias herself did not sit in the same room as Herod and his leading men follows the standard procedure of keeping men and women in separate quarters (6:22, 24, 25). Even though women could dine and assume the reclining posture at these meals they were excluded from taking part in the conversation (συμπόσιον).[48] Archaeological descriptions of Herod's palace at Machaerus suggest that he both held Greco-Roman symposia and women attended them (though in a separate dining room).[49] Crossan and Reed find further archaeological evidence for the meal scene in Luke 14:7–11. They suggest that a third century Dionysios Villa in Sepphoris with triclinium and room for dining can be brought to bear on the first-century by reference to Unit II (Meyers) and a similar Jewish villa which followed Roman practices.[50] The language of honor-shame, prevalent in the LXX, is adopted by several Hellenistic Jewish groups (e.g., Philo, Sirach, Qumran, Gospels, Herod I, Herod Agrippa I).

Jesus' instruction toward the Pharisees in this section (14:7–11) fits into the Hellenistic Jewish culture which discussed notions of honor-shame and friendship at meals. The point of identifying honor-shame discussions at Hellenistic Jewish symposia is to demonstrate the historical plausibility of Jesus' story. Several authors imply that the parable is wholly created by Luke whose culture adopted this grid (honor-shame) and way of life (symposia) while Jesus' did not. Braun's comments that "competition for positive peer appraisals" and "the soft currency of honour" were incredibly

---

[47] That Luke omits the double use of the technical term (συμπόσιον) in his version of the miraculous feeding has not been appreciated in studies postulating his use of the symposium genre. Mark twice repeats the term to describe the later meal scene (6:39).

[48] S. Stein, "The Influence of Symposia Literature on the Literary Form of the Pesah Haggadah," *JJS* 8 (1957): 13–44, 32ff; Corley, *Public Meals*, 69.

[49] B. Schwank, "Neue Fund in Nabatäerstädten und ihre Bedeutung für die neutestamentliche Exegese," *NTS* 29 (1983): 429–435; Corley, *Public Meals*, 68–69.

[50] Crossan and Reed, *Excavating Jesus*, ch. 3, esp. 111–113; James Strange, "Six Campaigns at Sepphoris: The University of South Florida Excavations, 1983–1989," in Levine, *Galilee in Late Antiquity*, 339–355.

important in Luke's culture suggest that Jesus did not think in such terms. He later suggests that the *klinium* is a "literary locale not to be converted into an actual historical representation without ado."[51] By proposing that reciprocity was critical in Luke's culture, Rohrbaugh implies that it was not so in Jesus'.[52] Again, Moxnes explicitly claims that Luke does not describe "the historical situation and the real expectations of patrons and brokers in first-century Palestine, but his own social system."[53] It has been shown that honor-shame and symposium etiquette were known in first-century Jewish culture even in Palestine. Sawicki admits this point, but thinks that a Galilean peasant could not have been sufficiently socially savvy to take part in such symposia discussions.[54] She therefore constructs a genealogy of Jesus that places him in a line of Judean nobles which had recently immigrated to Galilee. But Sawicki's efforts are unnecessary since non-elite conservative Jews at Qumran practiced something quite similar to the symposium. It is also possible that the Passover meal itself had affinities with the Hellenistic meal by the first-century.[55]

If knowledge of symposia etiquette was available in Palestine then Braun's accusation against Jülicher of placing too much importance on Proverbs and Sirach for the interpretation of Jesus' instruction is off-based.[56] To Braun, the Greco-Roman and especially Cynic sources are "the most instructive examples" for understanding this section of Jesus' teaching (14:7–11), but literary and archaeological evidence show that a first-century Jew in Palestine could have learned of the symposium in his local land or through native sources.[57] A first-century Galilean Jew could also readily cast a message within an honor-shame grid. Considering the prevalence of honor-shame and friendship discussions in Hellenistic Jewish sources it seems more plausible that Jesus shapes his message in light of

---

[51] Braun, *Feasting*, 99, 177.

[52] Rohrbaugh, "City," 141.

[53] Moxnes, "Patron-Client," 256.

[54] Sawicki, *Crossing*, 182.

[55] Corley, *Public Meals*, 68; Gordon J. Bahr, "The Seder of Passover and the Eucharistic Words," *NovT* 12 (1970): 181–202, 181, 190; Stein, "Symposia Literature," 13–44; Dennis E. Smith, "Social Obligation in the Context of Communal Meals: A Study of the Christian Meal in 1 Corinthians in Comparison with Graeco-Roman Communal Meals" (Th.D. diss., Harvard Divinity School, 1980), 178; G. H. R. Horsley, "Reclining at the Passover Meal," *NewDocs* 2.75.

[56] Jülicher, *Gleichnisreden*, 2.246–254; cf. Braun, *Feasting*, 61 n. 53. According to Braun, Jülicher "wrongly looked at Proverbs and Sirach for the most illuminating parallels."

[57] Braun, *Feasting*, 61 and n. 53. Smith admits that even the more skeptical Jesus scholars consider open table-fellowship a staple in the ministry of the historical Jesus. Smith, *Symposium*, 175, citing Bartchy, "Table Fellowship," in *DJG*, 796–800, 797–798; Crossan, *Historical Jesus*, 341–342. Smith himself does not endorse this idea fully.

Hellenistic Jewish predecessors (e.g., Prov 25:6–7; Sir 31:12–32:9) rather than Greco-Roman philosophers (Plutarch *Dinner* 148F-149F; *Quest. Conv.* 616C-F).[58] The theological aphorism attached to the end fits with Hellenistic Jewish depictions of God's actions toward the proud and humble respectively (Ezek 21:31 LXX; 17:24 LXX).

5.2.4 Conclusion

In this section, Luke does not shape Jesus' instruction on discipleship in comparison or contrast to benefaction or patronage. A lack of specific benefactor/patron vocabulary points in this direction. The absence of gifts or services which may have derived from a benefactor confirms that benefactors and patrons were not a paradigm addressed in this section. Those who espouse patronage and benefaction as background for other sections of Luke 14 properly omit reference to this section in their discussion.[59] In reference to honor-shame and friendship, Jesus instructs his would-be disciples to forego normal patterns of status seeking in favor of being reciprocated by God with exaltation. Luke has Jesus pitch his instruction in relation to honor-shame, and in passing reference friendship, to counteract the status-seeking nature of these Pharisees. Jesus seems to coordinate advice on human-human and human-God relationships. By choosing to put oneself in company with those of lower status the person is potentially shamed. But this shame turns to honor when the host publicly announces his improvement of status. Likewise the Pharisees ought to put themselves in the company of the lower social classes so that God might exalt them in the presence of men. Being promoted (ὑψωθήσεται) or demoted (ταπεινωθήσεται) by God follows in the same vein (14:11). According to Luke, Jesus turns what appears to be straightforward advice on navigating social situations into a theological message about how one receives glory from God.

5.3 Banquet Guest List (14:12–14)

5.3.1 Literary Context

Luke depicts Jesus directing a second section of teaching toward the host of the party (τῷ κεκληκότι αὐτόν; 14:12). The passage is connected to the

---

[58] Plummer, *Luke*, 356–357; Fitzmyer, *Luke*, 2.1047; Nolland, *Luke*, 2.749; Marshall, *Luke*, 583; Jeremias, *Parables*, 107; Bovon, *Luc*, 2.434; Malina and Rohrbaugh, *Social Science Commentary*, 285.

[59] E.g., Green, *Luke*, 549–552; Moxnes, "Patron-Client," 256, 264–265, 268; Danker references only 14:12–14 in regard to benefaction, Danker, *Benefactor*, 339.

previous pericope through linguistic and thematic parallels (see section 5.1.1), and it is connected to the following pericope (14:15–24) through linguistic and thematic parallels as well.[60] Repetition of the appropriate persons to invite (κάλει πτωχούς, ἀναπείρους, χωλούς, τυφλούς; 14:13; οὓς πτωχοὺς καὶ ἀναπείρους καὶ τυφλοὺς καὶ χωλοὺς εἰσάγαγε ὧδε; 14:21) connects the two pericopes. The setting of both pericopes is the provision of a banquet (ποιῇς ἄριστον ἢ δεῖπνον; 14:12; ἐποίει δεῖπνον μέγα; 14:16, cf. 24). The central theme which spans both pericopes (14:12–14, 15–24) is the proper persons to invite to dinners (ἄριστον; δεῖπνον; δοχὴν). In all three pericopes, Jesus offers a negative and positive example of how to approach feasting, in this section from the vantage point of the one who invites others. In the present section (14:12–14), Jesus challenges the widespread practice of inviting social equals to dinners because their reciprocal invitation will recompense the inviter (14:13). He then suggests his own approach through the positive example (14:14). By inviting those who cannot repay, the inviter leaves room for God to reciprocate at the resurrection of the just (ἀνταποδοθήσεται γάρ σοι ἐν τῇ ἀναστάσει τῶν δικαίων; 14:14). The future passive indicates that God provides the reciprocation.

5.3.2 Linguistic Evidence

Technical vocabulary adopted in benefaction and patronage contexts is not employed in this section (14:12–14), but the language of reciprocity (ἀντὶ καλέω; ἀνταπόδομα; ἀνταποδίδωμι) and friendship (φίλος) does surface. Luke adopts technical terms used in discussions of reciprocity (ἀντικαλέω 14:12; ἀνταπόδομα 14:12; ἀνταποδίδωμι[61] 14:14). These terms were familiar in Greco-Roman literature, but also arise frequently in Hellenistic Jewish sources. For example, ἀνταπόδομα can be found twenty-two times in

---

[60] Marshall, *Luke*, 587–588; Fitzmyer, *Luke*, 2.1052; Bovon, *Luc*, 2.443.

[61] Bovon, *Luc*, 2.435. Kloppenborg identifies similar terms, ἀποδοῦναι and παραδιδόναι, in labour contracts (*PCairZen* II 59182; *PKöln* III 144; *BGU* IV 1122) which, by their contractual nature, would not fit into the categories of patron-client or benefactor/client. John S. Kloppenborg, *The Tenants in the Vineyard: Ideology, Economics, and Agrarian Conflict in Jewish Palestine* (WUNT 195; Tübingen: Mohr Siebeck, 2006), 328 n. 185, 339. References are to (*BGU*) Herwig Maehler, ed., *Ägyptische Urkunden aus den Staatlichen Museen zu Berlin, Griechische Urkunden aus Hermupolis* (München: Saur, K G, 2005); (*PCairZen*) Campbell Cowan Edgar, ed., *Zenon papyri* (vol. 2.; Cairo: L'Institut français d'archéologie orientale, 1926); (*PKöln*) Bärbel Kramer, M. Erler, D. Hagedorn, Robert Hübner, and Michael Gronewald, eds., *Kölner Papyri* (Abhandlungen der Rheinisch-Westfälischen Akademie der Wissenschaften 7–8; Opladen: Westdeutscher Verlag, 1976).

the LXX with the meanings "repayment, requital, recompense, reward."[62] It is only used twice in the NT (Luke 14:12; Rom 11:9) and the second of these instances is a quote from the LXX (Ps 68:23 LXX). In light of the reciprocity language employed in the passage it is important to assess the social standing of potential invitees. This is important because reciprocity is defined in part according to whether it takes place between social equals (balanced reciprocity) or unequals (generalized reciprocity; see section 5.2.3). Several clues in the text signal that the potential exchange involves social equals exchanging gifts of relatively equal worth. Jesus' new invitation list includes those of lower social class who are chosen because of an inability to reciprocate equally.

The descriptions of the individuals identified initially as typical recipients of elite banquet invitations all come under the category of social equal (φίλος; ἀδελφούς; συγγενής; γείτονας πλουσίους).[63] Φίλος could be a euphemism for a client, but more often refers to a social equal.[64] Hanson and Oakman prefer the euphemistic use of φίλος, but this is not the best translation for this episode.[65] As noted above (see section 5.1.3), certain Greco-Roman authors sought various ways to maintain a feeling of equality at meals because of a desire to promote friendships (e.g., Plutarch *Dinner* 148F–149F; *Quest. Conv.* 616C-F; 612D). Meals were times for increasing and improving friendships, so Luke has Jesus mention the invitation of friends. Hesiod instructed his audience to only invite friends and leave others out of banquets (*Opus* 341–352, esp. 342, 354).[66] Without explicit evidence of a superior to inferior relationship, or the technical terminology of *patrocinium* (e.g., κλίενς or πελάτης), there is no justification in the text for understanding the friends mentioned as clients (inferior). This is especially true considering that meals were frequently idealized as times to promote equality rather than promote status differences. Ἀδελφούς and συγγενής may refer to fictive kin and kin relationships respectively,[67] but if both terms refer to actual family then they are of equal status with the host (i.e., no tensions or agonistic contests).[68] Ἀδελφούς may be used to strengthen the emotive connection between members of a similar social group (e.g., Christian "family"; Rom 16:14; 1 Cor 16:20; Phil 4:21; 1

---

[62] Lust, *Lexicon* (2003), 53. Ἀνταποδίδωμι is found ninety times in the LXX, but ἀντικαλέω cannot be found in the LXX.

[63] Bartchy, "Honor Reversal," 176; cf. Malina and Rohrbaugh, *Social Science Commentary*, 286.

[64] Eilers, *Roman Patrons*, 14–15; Mitchell, "Greet the Friends," 246–249; contra Hanson and Oakman, *Palestine*, 71; deSilva, *Honor, Patronage*, 95–98.

[65] Hanson and Oakman, *Palestine*, 75; cf. Parsons, *Luke*, 54.

[66] John T. Fitzgerald, "Friendship in the Greek World Prior to Aristotle," 32.

[67] Hanson and Oakman, *Palestine*, 75.

[68] Crook, *Conversion*, 56

Thess 5:26), or actual blood-family (e.g., Mark 3:32; Luke 8:20; Josh 2:18 LXX). Γείτονας πλουσίους is a description of one capable of returning a favor and is clearly not a social inferior.

Luke also makes clear that the meal and the reciprocation are of equal value. It is important to establish that the gifts exchanged are of equal value since this is a second component of differentiating between generalized (unequal gifts) and balanced (equal gifts) reciprocity. Jesus instructs the man not to invite someone to a dinner who will in turn invite him back (ἀντικαλέσωσίν; 14:12). The return invitation constitutes equal repayment of the favor (γένηται ἀνταπόδομά σοι; 14:12). If the parties are of equal status and the exchanged goods of equal worth then a situation of balanced reciprocity exists. The hypothetical situation to which Jesus contrasts his new way of functioning is a meal constituting balanced reciprocity.

Jesus' instruction, through Luke, in response to this situation of balanced reciprocity is to inculcate generalized reciprocity wherein a person invites others of lower social class who cannot reciprocate in kind. Two factors must be shown. First, it must be shown that the persons targeted for the generosity are of a lower social class. The text makes clear that these guests are of a lower social class (κάλει πτωχούς, ἀναπείρους, χωλούς, τυ φλούς). Each potential guest is marked by a socially stigmatizing condition or state.[69] Second, it must be shown that the targets cannot reciprocate. Indeed, the text emphasizes their inability to reciprocate (οὐκ ἔχουσιν ἀντα ποδοῦναί σοι; 14:14).[70] Rather than being reciprocated by enjoying a meal with social equals, the one who invites those who cannot reciprocate will be reciprocated by God (ἀνταποδοθήσεται; 14:14). God provides the return on the gift at the resurrection of the just (ἐν τῇ ἀναστάσει τῶν δικαίων; 14:14; cf. Ben Sira 48:11 Heb; 4Q548 1–2 ii 12–14; 2 Macc 7:23; Ps Sol 3, 9; Wis 5:1).[71] Luke has Jesus advocate a form of generalized reciprocity (see section 5.2.3).[72]

Scholars who espouse benefaction and patronage behind this section typically do so for three reasons. First, Moxnes and Green identify patron-client relations behind the form of reciprocity Jesus advocates because one specific form of generalized reciprocity is the patron-client relationship.[73] Since the disciples take the generous position, their generosity would imi-

---

[69] Moxnes, "Patron-Client," 256, 264–265; Green, *Luke*, 552–554; Johnson, *Luke*, 225; Plummer, *Luke*, 359; Fitzmyer, *Luke*, 2.1047–1048.

[70] Bovon finds in the reciprocity language reason to believe this is traditional material (non-Lukan). Bovon, *Luc*, 430.

[71] Danker, *New Age*, 165; Emile Puech, "Jesus and Resurrection Faith in Light of Jewish Texts," in Charlesworth, *Archaeology*, 639–659, 640, 643–645.

[72] Green, *Luke*, 552–554; Moxnes, "Patron-Client," 256–257; Stansell, "Gifts," 355–358, 360.

[73] Moxnes, "Patron-Client," 256–257, 265; Green, *Luke*, 552–554.

tate that of a patron. This approach to the text follows socio-historical categories and in the absence of technical vocabulary for *patrocinium* is confusing. Jesus does not specifically identify patrons or clients, nor was the language or practice of *patrocinium* prevalent in first-century Palestine (see section 2.5). Additionally, Moxnes mistakenly accuses Luke of describing his own culture, rather than the social *realia* of first-century Palestine. Although he gives no reasoning for this conclusion it seems that he draws this conclusion because he assumes that discussions of reciprocity at meals did not take place in first-century Palestine. This is erroneous as has been demonstrated above (see section 5.1.3).

Second, Hanson and Oakman suggest that the passage be understood as critiquing patronage because patrons often cultivated their clients through invitations to banquets (e.g., Juvenal *Satires* 5.12–25).[74] It is common to suggest that public euergetism (in the form of gifts of money [*largitiones*], entertainment, banquets [*epulae*], and public monuments) was an obligation of patrons, but this is not so in the Greek east of the Late Republic and early Imperial period. According to Eilers, patrons were "rarely materially generous toward the governed, and in the few cases when they were, we have no evidence to suggest that they were acting as the *patroni* of these cities, or that they were considered to be patrons because of their generosity."[75] Though patrons and clients sometimes offered banquets to express gratitude or to strengthen the bonds of loyalty other reasons exist for meals and other social relationships offered meals. It is not necessary to jump from the offer of a meal to the explicit relationship of patron-client (which intimates a link with Roman practices). Banquets can be categorized socio-historically as "gifts" which find expression in nearly all cultures and need not carry with them the specific language of patron-client with its attendant connection to Romanism (e.g., Gen 43:15–34; 1 Kgs 10:13; Dan 5:1, 17; Esth 2:18).[76] It would be better to forego the socio-historical category of "patron-client" in discussions of this passage because of the potential confusion with *patrocinium*.

Third, Danker suggests that Jesus advocates a new form of benefaction because he commands potential disciples to be generous beyond the "in-group."[77] It has been shown above that benefactors were known for generosity which included others outside of their social group (see section 3.4.2;

---

[74] Hanson and Oakman, *Palestine*, 74–76.

[75] Eilers, *Roman Patrons*, 98; contra Harmand, *Un aspect*, 145–146, 358–385.

[76] Stansell, "Gifts," 356–358; Neyrey, "Ceremonies," 371–373. Neyrey subsequently connects to socio-historical "patron-client" relationships which, like Hanson and Oakman, creates confusion with the Roman practice of *patrocinium*, Neyrey, "Ceremonies," 373–375.

[77] Danker, *Benefactor*, 339.

SEG 4.490 ll. 8–9; cf. *IGSK* 3.82.7–8; Danker, *Benefactor*, 33.32–42). In this reading, Jesus instructs potential disciples to function as benefactors who spread their generosity to those outside of their societal group. In the following pericope he intimates that God invites beyond the "in-group" (14:15–24). Reading this in tandem with 14:12–14 gives theological ground for the action advised by Jesus; give beyond the in-group and you will be a benefactor like God. Although benefactors built reputations for generosity outside of the "in-group" it seems to be an overstatement to claim that by advocating generosity beyond the "in-group" Jesus develops a new form of benefaction. It is possible that Luke had benefaction as a secondary explanatory paradigm. And, it is possible that some in the audience would be able to draw connections to other benefactors who built reputations for this type of generosity (e.g., Herod I in Athens; Herod Antipas in Cos and Delos). However, Luke does not adopt any technical verbiage which would make a connection to benefactors explicit. A connection to benefaction is thus slightly possible though not confirmable simply on the basis of the advocacy of generosity beyond the "in-group."

5.3.3 Cultural Matters

It was argued earlier (section 5.1.3) that the meal was attended primarily, and perhaps exclusively, by Jews. If Luke intends to accurately depict the social *realia* of first-century Palestine a nearly exclusive attendance by Jews limits the likelihood that Luke cast Jesus' instruction in response to *patrocinium* since Palestinian Jews of the first-century would have had limited exposure to this ideology. Luke could employ benefaction as an interpretive paradigm since this ideology could be found in Jerusalem (see section 2.2.4) and in the practices of the Herodian family (e.g., Herod I, Herod Antipas, Philip; see sections 3.1.1, 3.1.2, 3.1.3). Extending generosity outside of the "in-group" was one practice noted among benefactors. The lack of explicit terminology which would confirm the presence of benefaction in the passage, however, limits the extent to which this ideology should be brought into the scholarly discussion. It is more prudent to suggest the more general, socio-historical category of reciprocity since the special vocabulary of reciprocity is found in the passage. Jesus castigates attendees who practice balanced reciprocity and instead urges potential disciples to pursue a modified form of generalized reciprocity.

From the context it becomes clear that the host has chosen to invite his social equals, namely those who can pay him back in kind for the feast he now holds (ἀντικαλέσωσίν σε καὶ γένηται ἀνταπόδομά σοι; 14:12). Equal status distance and equivalent gifts exchanged suggest that balanced reciprocity is in view in Jesus' negative example (14:12).[78] For investigations of reciprocity earlier studies employed the categories of M. Sahlins,[79] but more recently a plea has been made for NT scholars to employ the categories of E. W. Stegemann and W. Stegemann.[80] Sahlins offers three categories of reciprocity (balanced, generalized, negative) which were differentiated by the social distance between the two parties and the motivation of the giver. E. W. Stegemann and W. Stegemann improve upon Sahlins with two better criteria: "the social status of the interlocutors" and "the nature of what is exchanged and how."[81] This model is more appropriate for Greco-Roman cultures since it attempts to describe a world where "kinship shares the stage with fictive kinship" and it has been developed from societies having a centralized political state.[82] In this new model, meals fall under the category of balanced reciprocity. Since status distance is at issue it is pertinent that if the recipients are expected and able to reciprocate with a relatively equal gift then they do not become "clients" of the host. In balanced reciprocity no remainder is left over once a gift has been reciprocated; a remainder creates a client because the client can never fully repay the patron for his generosity. This remainder is satisfied by expressions of allegiance and loyalty directed toward the patron. According to the Stegemanns' model, a banquet does not advance a patron-client relationship. It is instead undertaken between social equals with "mutual exchange of gifts with balanced value."[83] Jesus therefore critiques a system of

---

[78] On meals being situations of balanced reciprocity see Bartchy, "Table Fellowship"; Crook, *Conversion*, 56–58; Tannehill, *Luke*, 230; Braun, *Feasting*, 96. On the importance and symbolic meaning of meals see, Bartchy, "Table Fellowship"; Heil, *Meal-Scenes*; Smith, *Symposium to Eucharist*; Moessner, *Lord of the Banquet*; Neyrey, "Ceremonies"; Esler, *Community*, 71–109; Stansell, "Gifts," 356–358.

[79] Sahlins, *Stone Age Economics*. Moxnes, Oakman, and Elliott argue for generalized reciprocity in meals based on Sahlins' descriptions. Moxnes, *Economy*, 155; Douglas E. Oakman, *Jesus and the Economic Questions of His Day* (Lewiston/Queenston: Edwin Mellen, 1986), 169; Elliott, "Household and Meals vs. Temple Purity," 102–109. Note that each of these authors writes before the 1995 publication of Stegemann and Stegemann. Contextual clues or direct citation of Sahlins can be found in each of the three.

[80] Crook, "Reflections," 517–518; idem, *Conversion*, 56–58; Wolfgang Stegemann, "The Contextual Ethics of Jesus," in Stegemann, Malina, Theissen, *Social Setting*, 45–61, 58–59.

[81] Crook, *Conversion*, 56; E. W. Stegemann and W. Stegemann, *Urchristliche Sozialgeschichte: Die Anfänge im Judentum und die Christusgemeinden in der mediterranen Welt* (Stuttgart: Kohlhammer, 1995); ET *The Jesus Movement: A Social History of Its First-century* (trans. O.C. Dean, Jr.; Minneapolis: Fortress Press, 1999).

[82] Crook, "Reflections," 517. Sahlins built from societies which lacked a political state and kinship was the central institution.

[83] Crook, *Conversion*, 56–57.

5.3 Banquet Guest List (14:12–14)

balanced reciprocity wherein the wealthy offered banquets in order to be reciprocated by their guests with an equivalent gift.

Luke then depicts Jesus offering a positive example of the type of giving he demands of potential disciples (14:13–14). He advocates a form of generalized reciprocity wherein generosity flows to social un-equals who have reputations of being incapable of reciprocity. General reciprocity, of which the (socio-historical) patron-client relation is a specific example, is different than balanced reciprocity. The gifts are of unequal value and the people are of unequal status. The lack of balance ensures a long-term relationship because the receiver can only reciprocate through "homage, loyalty, political support, or information."[84] Patron-client exchanges fall under the category of general reciprocity where the gift itself cannot be reciprocated equally. The leftover deficit is repaid through loyalty, political support, and other forms of allegiance. In Jesus' instruction, however, the deficit is not repaid by loyalty to the human giver. Instead, God reciprocates the human-human generosity. In socio-historical terms, the giver does not become a patron, nor does the receiver become a client. God's intervention into the cycle of reciprocity prevents the response of loyalty and allegiance being offered to the generous host. This follows the Hellenistic Jewish pattern of God responding to both positive and negative actions which humans undertake for and against his people (e.g., Sir 12:1–6; see sections 4.2.2 *Linguistic, Cultural*).[85] Sirach 17:22–23 suggests that God reciprocates almsgiving toward those who cannot reciprocate.

ἐλεημοσύνη ἀνδρὸς ὡς σφραγὶς μετ' αὐτοῦ καὶ χάριν ἀνθρώπου ὡς κόρην συντηρήσει μετὰ ταῦτα ἐξαναστήσεται καὶ ἀνταποδώσει αὐτοῖς καὶ τὸ ἀνταπόδομα αὐτῶν εἰς κε φαλὴν αὐτῶν ἀποδώσει
"Alms are a like a seal (σφραγὶς) with him and [God] will protect a man's gracious ways like a maid (κόρη). After these things he will raise up and reciprocate them and he will reciprocate their recompense on their head." (Author's translation)

Just as Sirach recognized God's reciprocation for the generosity which men express toward those who cannot reciprocate, Luke has Jesus command potential disciples to give without expectation of human reciprocation so that God will reciprocate at the resurrection (14:14). Luke need not directly address *patrocinium* for his message to have radical application for a Gentile reader of his gospel. By undermining the general category of reciprocity and stealing away the central manner by which clients reciprocated their patrons' generosity (i.e., loyalty) Luke nullifies the possibility

---

[84] Stegemann and Stegemann, *Jesus Movement*, 36; Crook, *Conversion*, 57.
[85] More often in the LXX the ἀνταπόδομά of God is his intervention upon his enemies to give them the judgment they deserve (Ps 27:4; Ps 136:8; Joel 4:4, 7; Oba 1:15; Jer 28:6; Lam 3:64; Judith 7:15; 1 Macc 2:68).

of Jesus' followers continuing in normal patterns of *patrocinium*.⁸⁶ In Luke's description of his teaching, however, Jesus does not directly address *patrocinium*, but rather his message directly confronts the more general ideology of reciprocity.

5.3.4 Conclusion

The second teaching segment contrasts discipleship with reciprocity, friendship, and a new kind of benefaction. Discussions of friendship were natural at symposia which some suggest is the context of Jesus' instruction (see section 5.1.3). According to Luke, Jesus directly addresses the host of the party. He first addresses the assumption of reciprocity in meals. Jesus advances something different than either balanced or general reciprocity. He instructs his disciples to forego the balanced reciprocity system of inviting equals to banquets who can return the favor with a similar gift. He then teaches them to invite social un-equals to banquets emphasizing that they will not be able to reciprocate (οὐκ ἔχουσιν ἀνταποδοῦναί σοι; 14:14). The descriptions of these guests clarify that they are of a lower social class (κάλει πτωχούς, ἀναπείρους, χωλούς, τυφλούς).⁸⁷ The gift and the status distance between the two parties put this exchange into the general reciprocity category. The gift is too large to be repaid by the recipients. This would potentially create (socio-historical) clients out of the invitees, but Jesus does not stop there. He introduces God as the provider of the reciprocation that the invitees could not offer (ἀνταποδοθήσεται; 14:14). A return comes to the host through God's reciprocation. The double use of the divine passive tells the audience that God will definitely reciprocate.⁸⁸ Neither socio-historical nor Roman clientage begins. The host functions as a benefactor. In a kind of generalized reciprocity he gives outside of the "in-group," but he does not receive the attendant loyalty and honor. Like a benefactor the host gives a gift to people outside of his social group, who cannot repay his kindness, and thus leave open an imbalance. Some benefactors earned reputations for extending generosity beyond the "in-group" (e.g., Menas, Caesar Augustus, Antiochus of Kommagene, Tiberius Julius Alexander)⁸⁹ and Jesus advocates this sort of approach to would-be disciples. But unlike benefaction the host does not receive loyalty or public praise from the recipients because God balances the exchange by reciprocating.

---

⁸⁶ Green, *Luke*, 552–553.

⁸⁷ Bovon finds in the reciprocity language reason to believe this is traditional material (non-Lukan). Bovon, *Luc*, 430.

⁸⁸ Bock, *Luke*, 2.1267; Tannehill, *Luke*, 230; Nolland, *Luke*, 2.751; Marshall, *Luke*, 584; Fitzmyer, *Luke*, 2.1048; Talbert, *Theological Commentary*, 173.

⁸⁹ Danker, *Benefactor*, 336–337.

Luke does not use technical verbiage for benefaction or *patrocinium* and this conforms to the descriptions of social *realia* in first-century Palestine developed in chapters 2 and 3 of this book. First, it must be admitted that the description of the host's generosity as a benefit cannot be firm. It is only "generosity beyond the in-group" which signals a similarity with benefaction and specific terms which speak of benefaction are missing from the passage. No explicit verbiage of *patrocinium* can be found in this section which suggests that *patrocinium* is not the best explanatory paradigm for the passage. The use of φίλος in the passage may suggest that Greco-Roman or Hellenistic Jewish understandings of friendship are a more important paradigm.[90] Jesus calls his disciples to include outsiders into their friend group rather than attempting to scale the social ladder by befriending those of the upper classes. Hellenistic Jewish cultural patterns prevailed in Galilee and Jerusalem, with some practice of benefaction in Jerusalem of which traveling Galileans could have become aware. *Patrocinium* was not explicitly practiced in Galilee or Jerusalem. Luke attains an appropriate balance of Hellenistic Jewish cultural patterns in his description of the teaching, and the possibility of a benefaction interpretation corresponds with the small amount of benefaction practiced in those areas.

5.4 Refused Invitations and New Guests (14:15–24)

5.4.1 Literary Context

Instigated by a statement from one of his auditors, Jesus expands upon the previous pericope with a story (14:15–24). He addresses directly a man who dined with him (τις τῶν συνανακειμένων; 14:15), but the last verse of the section seems to indicate that Jesus intends to address all those who gather. Use of the plural pronoun (ὑμῖν) expands the audience from the single auditor to the whole group (λέγω γὰρ ὑμῖν ὅτι; 14:24). The difficulties of identifying the implied "I" of λέγω as well as the plural group addressed are well known.[91] It seems probable that the speaker is equivalent with the κύριος of the story since he was the last mentioned speaker and γὰρ provides a reason for his previous invitation of others. The implied "I" is not the servant since he does not throw the banquet nor does he have responsibility for refusing entry. It seems that Luke transitions from story to direct address by drawing the κύριος out of the story and into the ban-

---

[90] Mitchell, "Greet the Friends," 246–247, esp. n. 79.
[91] On this topic see Braun, *Feasting*, 121–128; Bovon, *Luc*, 2.455; Marshall, *Luke*, 590–591; Nolland, *Luke*, 2.758.

quet Jesus was addressing.[92] The breadth of the intended audience can also be seen in the fact that Luke patterns the story after the instruction Jesus had just given (i.e., 14:12–14). A man threw a great banquet (14:16; cf. 14:14:12) to which he invited many rich friends (14:16b–20; cf. 14:12). Upon their refusal to come he chooses to invite the same groups that Jesus had instructed the host to invite (πτωχούς, ἀναπείρους, τυφλούς, χωλούς; 14:21b; cf. 14:13). Jesus appears to expand upon the instruction that he had directly addressed to the the host and thus implicitly addresses both the questioner (τις τῶν συνανακειμένων; 14:15) and the host (τῷ κεκληκότι αὐτόν; 14:12) with the story. By bringing the κύριος of the fictional meal into the actual meal in which Jesus partook, Luke identifies Jesus as the κύριος and it seems likely that he intends to address all those who gather.[93]

The effect of linking the two pericopes (14:12–14, 15–24) together is to simultaneously teach about God's character and the human imitation of God.[94] In the first pericope (14:12–14) it is the host who is addressed and given advice on how to hold a dinner. His reward comes from God if he invites those who cannot reciprocate. The second episode (14:15–24) elaborates upon the previous episode with further instruction on how to hold a dinner. In this regard one may partially accept Braun's conclusion that the entire narrative (14:1–24) is about the "conversion" of the host. He suggests that the entire narrative (14:1–24) teaches that the insatiable greed of the host (symbolized in dropsy) is cured as the host learns to resist socially prescribed reciprocity (from men) and instead to await God's reciprocation. Braun presses the Greco-Roman background too far, however, in diminishing the importance of the messianic banquet and the description of

---

[92] Eta Linnemann, *Jesus of the Parables: Introduction and Exposition* (New York: Harper & Row, 1967), 90; James M. Dawsey, *The Lukan Voice: Confusion and Irony in the Gospel of Luke* (Macon, Ga.: Peeters, 1986), 16–17; Klaus Berger, *Die Amen-Worte Jesu: Eine Untersuchungen zum Problem der Legitimation in apokalyptik Rede* (BZNW 39; Berlin: de Gruyter, 1970), 89–91; M. Pesce, "Riconstruzione dell'archetipo letterario commune a Mt. 22,1–10 e Lc. 14,15–24," in *La Parabola degli invitati al banchetto dagli evangelisti a Gesù* (ed. J. Dupont; Brescia: Paideia, 1978), 167–236, 225–232; Nolland, *Luke*, 2.758; Marshall, *Luke*, 590–591 (reluctantly allows for this meaning).

[93] Plummer, *Luke*, 363; Nolland, *Luke*, 2.758; Linnemann, *Jesus*, 90; Green, *Luke*, 555.

[94] Nolland, *Luke*, 2.750–751; Tannehill, *Luke*, 232–234; Jülicher, *Die Gleichnisreden Jesu*, 2.416; F. Hahn, "Das Gleichnis von der Einladung zum Festmahl," in *Verborum veritas: Festschrift für Gustav Stählin zum 70 Geburstag* (ed. Otto Böcher and Klaus Haacker; Wuppertal: Theologischer Verl. Brockhaus, 1970), 73; Richard J. Dillon, *From Eye-Witnesses to Ministers of the Word: Tradition and Composition in Luke 24* (Analecta Biblica 82; Rome: Biblical Institute Press, 1978), 202 n. 133; Robert Walter Funk, *Language, Hermeneutic, and Word of God: The Problem of Language in the New Testament and Contemporary Theology* (New York: Harper & Row, 1966), 174; Jeremias, *Parables*, 45.

God in this pericope (see below section 5.3.3).⁹⁵ The intervening statement (14:15) alerts the reader that God's banquet must be kept in mind in the story. Eating bread in the kingdom of God links back to Luke 13:29 (ἀνακ λιθήσονται ἐν τῇ βασιλείᾳ τοῦ θεοῦ) and forward to Luke 22:16 (οὐ μὴ φάγω αὐτὸ ἕως ὅτου πληρωθῇ ἐν τῇ βασιλείᾳ τοῦ θεοῦ).⁹⁶ It is God's banquet that is shamed by a people fonder of their possessions and earthly relationships than him (14:15-24). He in turn invites others who have no such distractions. It becomes clear in the following pericope that following Jesus (and God) over earthly relationships must take precedence (14:25-27). Building his teaching with reference to the messianic banquet allows for a picture of God's invitation practice to be used for a point of comparison with the audience's invitation practice.⁹⁷ The host, and potential hosts, should imitate God who invites those who cannot reciprocate to his banquet.

Another piece of evidence suggesting that the host might see both himself and God in this episode (14:15-24) is the use of οἰκοδεσπότης.⁹⁸ The use of οἰκοδεσπότης to describe the host of this dinner may bring to mind two earlier pericopes. In Luke 12:39 οἰκοδεσπότης refers to the disciples who do not anticipate the arrival of the thief (Son of man). In 13:25 the οἰκοδεσπότης is Jesus who refuses entry to those who did not take the correct path.⁹⁹ Adopting this same term, for the third time in three chapters, the audience has reason to see both themselves and God in view. Like God, they must make new choices in regard to the invitations they send out. In this reading the host of the actual party finds reason to see himself in the host of the fictional banquet, and he is assured that the type of action Jesus demands of him is actually a godly manner of living. Other auditors would be warned to take similar action when they host their own banquets.¹⁰⁰

5.4.2 Linguistic Evidence

Patterned as it is after the previous section (14:12-14), this story (14:15-24) also can be read against the backdrop of reciprocity and, indirectly, a new kind of benefaction. This backdrop does not, however, derive from the use of explicit vocabulary connected to reciprocity, friendship, or benefac-

---

[95] E.g., Braun, *Feasting*, 7, 62, 116, 144; Esler, "Review," 232–233.

[96] Talbert, *Reading Luke-Acts*, 132.

[97] Esler, "Review of Braun, *Feasting*"; Talbert, *Reading Luke-Acts*, 132; Fitzmyer, *Luke*, 2.1054; Plummer, *Luke*, 360–361; Green, *Luke*, 555.

[98] Heil, *Meal Scenes*, 108–109.

[99] John H. Elliott, "Temple Versus Household in Luke-Acts: A Contrast in Social Institutions," in Neyrey, *Social World*, 211–240, 228; Fitzmyer, *Luke*, 2.1025; Bovon, *Luc*, 384–385; Marshall, *Luke*, 566.

[100] Green, *Luke*, 557–558; Tannehill, *Luke*, 232–234; Braun, *Feasting*, 119–126.

tion. It derives rather from assumed protocols underlying the invitation to dinner. Meals were times of balanced reciprocity and the first group of invitees would have been capable of following protocol (see section 5.3.3). Their refusal suggests another reason why a rich host should not invite those who can reciprocate, namely, they may publicly shame the host by not accepting his invitation. In response to the public shaming, the host expands his social group inviting those whose reputations for inability to reciprocate were well-known. It is possible that here the host functions as a benefactor who reaches beyond the "in-group" with his generosity (see section 5.2.2). It will be argued below that if benefaction is critiqued in the episode then it is not simply abandoned altogether, but transformed. Benefactors expected their generosity to be repaid by men with public praise, but Jesus advocates a benefactor-like generosity without expectation of public praise. In return, the benefactor receives commendation and reciprocation from God. However, without explicit vocabulary adopted in discussions of benefaction and *patrocinium*, interpreters should not too quickly identify these Greco-Roman cultural practices as the best explanatory paradigm for the episode. It is better for interpreters to refrain from specifying the specific form of reciprocity envisioned (benefaction or *patrocinium*) and instead to interpret the passage in terms of Hellenistic Jewish reciprocity and Hellenistic Jewish social group formation.

5.4.3 Cultural Matters

Once again a meal is a time for balanced reciprocity and there are clues in the text that this was the host's expectation as well. He invites rich guests who can respond in kind to his invitation. To highlight the elite status of these members Luke includes several clues.[101] The host throws a great banquet (δεῖπνον μέγα) and was able to host many (ἐκάλεσεν πολλούς; 14:16). He is rich enough to send a servant to invite the guests and each of their excuses involves a monetary transaction of some sort, though the first two more obviously involve richer persons. Buying fields and five pairs of oxen were the stuff of the elite. The purchase of fields was an atypical practice probably limited to the elite. Elite persons would likely live in the safer city limits and purchase fields outside of city walls for farming. In this scenario the wealthy function as absentee landlords.[102] A team of five

---

[101] Braun, *Feasting*, 73–80; L. Schotroff, "Das Gleichnis vom grossen Gastmahl in der Logienquelle," *Evangelische Theologie* 47 (1987): 192–211, 206; Marshall, *Luke*, 588–589; Talbert, *Theological Commentary*, 171–173; Bovon, *Luc*, 2.449; Tannehill, *Luke*, 234.

[102] Green, *Luke*, 560; Rohrbaugh, "City," 143; Braun, *Feasting*, 75; Luise Schottroff and Wolfgang Stegemann, *Jesus and the Hope of the Poor* (Maryknoll: Orbis Books, 1986), 101; Gildas H. Hamel, *Poverty and Charity in Roman Palestine, First Three*

oxen could work a farm of over one hundred acres.[103] Typical families farmed three to six acres per adult, so a farm of one hundred acres would have been sizable. Moreover, it may be assumed in the story that these are not the only oxen this invitee owns, a fact which would increase the size of his farm and wealth.[104] At least two of the guests would have been quite wealthy.

Taking a wife involved monetary exchange in the form of a dowry, though this invitee need not be wealthy to undertake the action.[105] Luke depicts Jesus addressing a different component of his social world (i.e., family) in his third example more than repeating the emphasis on financial matters. Braun's extended argument that the marriage is a financially motivated choice stretches the evidence.[106] He has mistakenly identified the monetary exchange with the consummation rather than the betrothal stage of marriage. He also does not provide evidence from Luke-Acts that women were considered "property" to be exchanged financially. In focusing on the financial component of marriage he neglects an important theme in Jesus' call to discipleship in Luke. That is, "family ties" cannot take precedence over following Jesus.[107]

The invitees are patterned after the rich from the previous pericope and stand in a position to reciprocate the meal. Their unified refusal would be a public act of shaming the host. Many Jewish banquets had a double invitation for one of two reasons (14:6–7).[108] (1) The host needed to know the number of guests so as to make proper arrangements, so the initial invitations allowed him to approximate this number. (2) The interval between

---

Centuries C.E. (University of California Publications 23; Berkeley: University of California Press, 1990), 151–152; Ramsay MacMullen, *Roman Social Relations: 50 B.C. to A.D. 284* (New Haven: Yale University Press, 1974), 3–7; Malina and Rohrbaugh, *Social Science Commentary*, 286.

[103] Green, *Luke*, 560; Eric R. Wolf, *Peasants* (Englewood Cliffs: Prentice-Hall, 1966), 19–35; Jeremias, *Parables*, 177; Rohrbaugh, "City," 143; Charles W. Hedrick, *Parables As Poetic Fictions: The Creative Voice of Jesus* (Peabody: Hendrickson Publishers, 1994), 154; Malina and Rohrbaugh, *Social Science Commentary*, 286.

[104] Green, *Luke*, 560; Moxnes, *Economy*, 57; Gowler, *Portraits*, 247; Rohrbaugh, "City," 143; Bailey, *Peasant*, 95–98; Jeremias, *Parables*, 177. Contra Fitzmyer, *Luke*, 2.1056.

[105] Rohrbaugh, "City," 142–143.

[106] Braun, *Feasting*, 75–79.

[107] Green, *Luke*, 559–560 n. 156; Nolland, *Luke*, 2.756; Bovon, *Luc*, 2.450–452; Talbert, *Theological Commentary*, 174–175.

[108] Rohrbaugh, "City," 140–141. He cites Esth 5:8; 6:14; Philo *Opif.* 78; *Lam. R.* 4:2 "None of them would attend a banquet unless he was invited twice." Cf. Green, *Luke*, 558; Kenneth E. Bailey, *Through Peasant Eyes: More Lucan Parables, Their Culture and Style* (Grand Rapids: Eerdmans, 1980), 94; Braun, *Feasting*, 102–103; Marshall, *Luke*, 587–588; Bovon, *Luc*, 2.449 n. 30; Nolland, *Luke*, 2.755.

invitations gave the invitee chance to calculate if he was able or desired to reciprocate. The interval allowed the invitee to examine the preparations undertaken by the host to see if they measured up to his standards. The invitees in Luke's story had the financial means to reciprocate, so they probably did not refuse the invitation for the reason of inability. By collectively refusing they imply that they do not find the meal or the host to be worthy of them and thus put themselves above the host in regard to status.[109]

Refusal by the rich compels the host to invite another group who cannot reciprocate. Luke repeats the descriptions of these new invitees and accurately situates them around the hidden places of society (14:22–23). Luke provides a fuller description of the class of people from the previous pericope who could not respond in kind (14:14). These invitees are described as ὁ πτωχός καὶ ἀνάπηρος καὶ τυφλός καὶ χωλός who live in ἡ πλατύς καὶ ἡ ῥύμη τῆς πόλεως and ἡ ὁδός καὶ φραγμός (14:21, 23). Living on the outskirts and hidden places of the city were those considered outsiders by those who lived in more visible locations.[110] In the previous episode (14:12–14) it was expressly the inability of the (hidden) poor to reciprocate which made them worthy candidates of an invitation. If the descriptions of their financial status and their marginalized locations did not communicate their inability to reciprocate, then the host's instruction to "compel" them to come to the party may reinforce this reality (ἀνάγκασον εἰσελθεῖν; 14:23).[111] An initial invitation to an extravagant meal would have provoked caution and resistance from a group of people incapable of reciprocating. They knew not to join such a meal since they could not meet the social obligation of reciprocity. For this reason the host must convince them of their welcome.[112] In the present episode the host abandons the societal expectation of reciprocity and "repudiate[s] the need for approval from his peers" by inviting those who cannot possibly reciprocate.[113] The poor understood this inability, likely leading them to refuse a casual invitation, and so needed to be compelled to join in the banquet.

---

[109] Rohrbaugh, "City," 141; Green, *Luke*, 559; Mary Douglas, *Risk and Blame: Essays in Cultural Theory* (London: Routledge, 1992), 85.

[110] Rohrbaugh, "City," 141–145; Braun, *Feasting*, 86–96; Green, *Luke*, 562.

[111] Braun, *Feasting*, 86–97, esp. 95–96; Rohrbaugh, "City," 144–145; Green, *Luke*, 562; Neyrey, "Ceremonies," 385.

[112] Contra Plummer, *Luke*, 362; George W. Clark, *Notes on the Gospel of Luke: Explanatory and Practical A Popular Commentary Upon a Critical Basis, Especially Designed for Pastors and Sunday Schools* (Philadelphia: American Baptist Publication Society, 1876), 335. Plummer and Clarke think that the poor would accept the invitation without hesitation.

[113] Green, *Luke*, 561; cf. Talbert, *Theological Commentary*, 173–176.

5.4 Refused Invitations and New Guests (14:15–24)

As in the previous pericope Luke has Jesus advocate a move away from balanced reciprocity and toward a generalized reciprocity with, perhaps, a new kind of benefaction. There are differences in the way this pericope describes the host, as opposed to the previous pericope (14:12–14), in light of the double-referent (God and man). The host reiterates that the first invitees would not enjoy the banquet (14:24). The new invitees could not reciprocate the dinner, but were forced to come. At the close of this section (14:15–24), however, Jesus does not explicate how it is that the host would be reciprocated. It seems likely that the initiatory statement (14:15) should be employed as an interpretive grid for the story. The story thus answers two questions simultaneously: Who is it that will enjoy a meal in the kingdom of God? What happens to reciprocity? Those who refuse the invitation of God will not enjoy his banquet. Persons too wrapped up in their possessions to desire the banquet and in this response shame the host, will not take part in the banquet of God. But the poor and marginalized will enjoy it. Persons without financial distractions and humbly awaiting God's invitation enter the banquet. On this level God functions as a benefactor reaching beyond the "in-group" and granting favors which cannot be reciprocated. There would be no qualms with God receiving loyalty and public praise, as benefactors ought to receive, for his favors, but the text does not make this explicit. On the human level, potential hosts are called to a new form of reciprocity. It is a reciprocity which does not take place between humans, but rather anticipates God's gift of access to his banquet for those that do not seek repayment on earth. This again takes the form of generalized reciprocity where the host invites those who cannot reciprocate in kind. He acts like a benefactor who grants favors to those outside the "in-group," but unlike a benefactor he receives no loyalty or public praise for his generosity. His reward comes from God.

Green argues that the host who invites outsiders does not become a benefactor or patron because by extending generosity to those incapable of reciprocity he abandons completely the world of reciprocal and patronal ethics.[114] Green's conclusion should be challenged for three reasons. First, incapacity to reciprocate is a hallmark of targets for *patrocinium*, benefaction, and even socio-historical patronage because this incapacity creates a repayment gap which is filled through loyalty and/or public praise. Targeting those who could not reciprocate was standard practice, though sometimes patrons and benefactors gave to others who could reciprocate tangibly to a certain (lesser) extent. Second, in this evaluation Green seems to deny a third possibility, namely that in his instruction Jesus neither adopts nor abandons reciprocal or patronal ethics, but instead transforms them into a new kind of benefaction or patronage. It is possible that in

---

[114] Green, *Luke*, 562.

Luke Jesus presents a new form of benefaction which gives generously to outsiders, but does not expect repayment of any kind (monetary or social). This approach to *patrocinium* or benefaction would have been unique, but philosophers on the subject of reciprocity offered many different approaches to reciprocity which did not fall into a standard pattern. Third, the positive use of εὐεργ- words in Luke and Acts (Luke 22:25; Acts 4:9; 10:38), without qualification or disclaimer, suggests that the category has not been abandoned completely. Luke freely describes the actions of Peter and Jesus using εὐεργεσία and εὐεργετέω which were nearly technical terms for benefaction.[115] If Luke has Jesus instruct his disciples in reference to benefaction then he transforms it from its typical form. Generosity flows beyond the in-group, but reciprocity for the deed will not be found in loyalty or public praise. Rather, reciprocity will come directly from God's invitation to the messianic banquet.

Moxnes' suggestion that this meal must be understood within a socio-historical patronage model should also be rejected.[116] He contends that "meals and food distribution ... are dominant forms of patronage in Luke-Acts" which leads him to suggest that patron-client relationships are the best grid through which to read the episode (14:15–24).[117] To suggest that meals and food distribution were popular forms of generosity bestowed by patrons upon clients is understandable in light of the *salutatio* (morning meal) which clients attended at the homes of their patrons. But beyond this simple meal it must be emphasized that patrons were not known for generosity (in general), especially in regard to giving banquets.[118] It is also erroneous to argue that when a person gives a meal they therefore function as a patron. Meals played many other roles in many other social relationships outside of the patron-client relationship (e.g., king, priest, governor, family).[119] Meals belong in the broader categories of gifts and honor-reversal, though they also fit into the more specific category of patron-client relationships. The gift of a banquet does not create a patron. In order to demonstrate Moxnes' suggestion it must be shown that a hierarchical relationship exists and that the return granted to the patron is loyalty or public praise. The first group of invitees in the final two pericopes (14:12–14, 15–24) were of the same social group and the text claims explicitly that they would have returned a meal rather than loyalty. The host does not ap-

---

[115] Neyrey overstates his case to claim that these were outright technical terms; Neyrey, "God, Benefactor and Patron," 471 n. 22. See Danker, *Benefactor*, 27; idem, *Luke*, 15; section 6.1.2.

[116] Moxnes, "Patron-Client," 268; cf. Hanson and Oakman, *Palestine*, 74–76; Rohrbaugh, "City," 137–147; Neyrey, "Ceremonies," 373–374, 385.

[117] Moxnes, "Patron-Client," 268.

[118] Eilers, *Roman Patrons*, 98.

[119] Neyrey, "Ceremonies," 362–373; Bartchy, "Honor Reversal," 178–180.

5.4 Refused Invitations and New Guests (14:15–24)

pear to be a patron. The second group of invitees was of a lower social status but God reciprocates on their behalf. They do not reciprocate the human host with loyalty. Again, the host does not function under the normal understanding of a patron. Furthermore, in order to avoid the error of confusing the socio-historical category of patron-client with the Roman category of *patrocinium* Moxnes must keep his model quite broad and clearly identify the difference between the two practices. He does not do the latter, and the former is problematic in that its broadness prevents specification and invites confusion. To claim that a patron-client relationship exists (per Saller) whenever persons are of different social statuses (asymmetrical), an exchange is made (reciprocal), and develops a long term relationship (relational) is unhelpful because such distinctions describe many relationships but do not add immensely to the description of the relationship under investigation (see section 2.1.2; 2.1.3).[120] If he intends to adopt a model which is more specific, and therefore closer to *patrocinium*, then he must identify vocabulary which was explicitly used in *patrocinium*. Since this vocabulary is lacking from the episode he cannot move closer to *patrocinium* in his definition of the patron-client relationship.

Another dimension to Luke's version of Jesus' teaching in light of honor-shame and reciprocity ought to be added. Since meals were times in which one identified their social group, the call to reorient invitations is also a call to reorient one's social group.[121] The hosts in both pericopes (14:12–14; 14:15–24) invited members of elite social groups made up of those that would solidify their social status. Jesus instructs them to adopt a new social group into their midst. This may not be a total abandonment of the former group if one follows Bock's interpretation of μὴ φώνει. He claims that the phrase derives from Semitic rhetorical idiom "not x ... but y" which means "not so much x ... but y." Jesus does not eliminate inviting certain richer or more familiar guests, but rules it out as a habitual practice.[122] Do not invite the rich exclusively. The call comports with the preceding pericope which instructed the invitee to initially put himself in company with the lower class at the banquet. Since seating arrangements were made according to social status the one who willingly sits in the lowest class identifies with that level of status. The invitee willingly associates with the lower status invitees, and in this pericope the host willingly asso-

---

[120] Eilers, *Roman Patrons*, 1–5; cf. Verboven, *Economy*, 2–9.

[121] Bartchy, "Honor Reversal," 176–177, 179–180; Green, *Luke*, 561–563; Esler, *Community*, 198; Neyrey, "Ceremonies," 364–371; Mary Douglas, "Deciphering a Meal," *Daedalus* 101 (1972): 61–81, 61; Elliott, "Temple Versus Household," 226–228.

[122] Bock, *Luke*, 2:1265; Plummer, *Luke*, 358; Marshall, *Luke*, 583; O. Betz, "φωνέω," *TDNT* 9:303.

ciates with lower status members of society by inviting them to dinner. In this call to forego rich friends (φίλος) and instead associate with the lowly, one is reminded of Jesus' making friends with tax collectors and sinners (φίλος τελωνῶν καὶ ἁμαρτωλῶν; Luke 7:34). He willingly put himself onto the same social level as these low-status people.

5.4.4 Conclusion

Luke elaborates upon the previous pericope with a story instigated by an auditor at the meal. If Luke intends the statement of the auditor (μακάριος ὅστις φάγεται ἄρτον ἐν τῇ βασιλείᾳ τοῦ θεοῦ; 14:15) to be the grounds for the final statement Jesus makes in this section (ἀνταποδοθήσεται γάρ σοι ἐν τῇ ἀναστάσει τῶν δικαίων; 14:14) this suggests that God responds to the human invitation of the poor to a banquet with invitation to the divine banquet. Jesus had instructed his audience to resist inviting those who could invite in return. He instead teaches them to invite those who cannot invite in return but rather to await God's invitation to eat bread in the kingdom of God. To an extent God reciprocates in kind (meal for meal), but on another level his return far outweighs the original favor. Jesus then elaborates upon this teaching by presenting a story about a fictional host whose rejection by his social equals drives him to compel those who cannot reciprocate to his banquet.

As an elaboration of the previous pericope (14:12–14) this episode (14:15–24) shares the possibility that reciprocity and benefaction may be appropriate interpretive grids for the teaching section, but also that *patrocinium* and socio-historical patronage are not proper explanatory paradigms for the section. It is primarily the connection to the previous episode which suggests these interpretive grids since the specific vocabulary of reciprocity, benefaction, and *patrocinium* are absent from the pericope. It is possible that a slight allusion to benefaction is present in the generosity extended to those beyond the in-group, but this is not sufficient to suggest that benefaction is a primary paradigm of interpretation. In the episode Jesus encourages would-be followers to invite those who cannot reciprocate. On account of the social norm of reciprocity these may need to be compelled, but this is in fact what God has done for the same social group. It is implied, because of the introductory and concluding statements (μακάριος ὅστις φάγεται ἄρτον ἐν τῇ βασιλείᾳ τοῦ θεοῦ; 14:15; γεύσεταί μου τοῦ δείπνου; 14:24) that those who extend generosity beyond the in-group will be reciprocated by God through an invitation to his banquet. Through inviting outsiders to meals this act of generosity extends the social group and overturns the societal norm of reciprocity.

Neither *patrocinium* nor socio-historical clientage begins with these poor invitees. The language of *patrocinium* is absent from the narrative, so

5.4 Refused Invitations and New Guests (14:15–24)

it is unwise to inject that cultural framework into the discussion. Luke does not depict Jesus directly teaching against *patrocinium* nor advocating it as a model for discipleship. The socio-historical category is also insufficient to explain Jesus' model of discipleship. Although a type of general reciprocity is advocated, the remainder left over when the poor invitees cannot reciprocate the meal is not resolved by the attribution of public praise or loyalty. Rather, God reciprocates the generous and resolves the gap which remained when the poor could not reciprocate the meal. The one who follows Jesus' example does not become a patron, though his generosity imitates the type of generosity described in socio-historical patron-client relationships. The absence of *patrocinium* ideology in the episode suggests that the adoption of the socio-historical category of patron-client is potentially confusing. In order to avoid the mistake of adopting *patrocinium* ideology as an explanatory paradigm it is best to avoid the socio-historical category of patron-client in interpretation of this passage. That socio-historical category, it has been suggested, does not adequately account for the instruction Jesus gives which is a further reason to reject its use for explaining the passage. It is best to confine interpretation to the socio-historical category of reciprocity and if attempting a historically more specific category the ideology of benefaction may be appropriate to a small extent.

Luke has appropriately adopted reciprocity as an interpretive paradigm, left open the possibility of benefaction as an interpretive framework, and kept out *patrocinium* in the episode. Without the language of benefaction and *patrocinium* it is imprudent to suggest that Luke directly attacks those specific practices. It seems possible that he presents Jesus' instruction as a new form of benefaction. Danker's reference to benefaction in the previous pericope, on account of generosity beyond the in-group, is suggestive, but this lone connection is not substantial enough to demand reading this pericope primarily or largely in terms of benefaction. Benefaction could be found in Jerusalem (see sections 2.2.4; 3.1), but was not prevalent in Galilee (see sections 2.2.3; 3.2). In light of the complete absence of *patrocinium* vocabulary, Moxnes' suggestion that the gift of a meal signals the operation of a patron should not be preferred. Meals functioned in various ways and were gifted in various social settings. More specificity in vocabulary and description of the scenario (e.g., relation of host to guests, response of guests) is required to support Moxnes' suggestion. Again Luke correctly avoids *patrocinium* in his description of Jesus' teaching. These practices were not found in Galilee or Jerusalem, nor were they explicitly practiced by the Herodian leaders of those areas. It is therefore unlikely that *patrocinium* or benefaction were the primary explanatory paradigm adopted by Jesus or his auditors in the instruction. Reciprocity seems quite likely as an interpretive paradigm, and this paradigm developed in both Greco-Roman and Hellenistic Jewish worlds.

5.5 Conclusions for the Table Discussion (Luke 14:1–24)

In the absence of necessary vocabulary and the proper setting for the identification of patron-client relationships it seems best to suggest that the social program outlined by Luke matches more closely with a combination of reciprocity, friendship, and, to an extent, benefaction. Apart from the potential use of φίλε/φίλος to designate a client, the passage does not have specific vocabulary connected to patronage or benefaction. Instead of jumping directly to these more specific forms of reciprocity it is prudent to assess the pericopes in terms of the more general notions of honor-shame and reciprocity and, when moving toward specificity, friendship. The language of reciprocity is present (e.g., ἀντικαλέω 14:12; ἀνταπόδομα 14:12; ἀνταποδίδωμι). Mitchell suggests that Luke "sought an extension of friendship across social lines in his community" more "than the creation of a new kind of patronage."[123] Expanding one's social group to include others from different (lower) social levels was one part of the call to follow Jesus. Similar to benefactors, they should grant favors to those outside of the in-group. Those who host parties were instructed to do so without reference to the human ability to respond in kind. However, unlike normal benefaction, they should not look for human reciprocity but await the reciprocity of God. In this approach they imitate God who has likewise extended favors across status lines and made company with people of lower social classes. They will also be imitating Jesus who had granted a benefaction to the man with dropsy in the first pericope of this section. This man would have been socially an outsider on account of his condition, but Jesus heals him.

In the vicinity of Galilee and Samaria it is historically plausible that Jesus taught in terms of reciprocity, friendship, and benefaction. It was shown in the previous chapter that these modes of interaction had taken root in these areas, although the presence of *patrocinium* was not discovered. Luke's depiction of this teaching, therefore, does not necessarily derive from his own social location and culture as Moxnes and others suggest. These episodes could just as easily stem directly from an encounter between the purported audience of the narrative and Jesus' recognition of ungodly components in that culture. As one encountering Hellenism and traces of Romanism in his home region, Jesus, like a

---

[123] Mitchell, "Greet the Friends," 246–247 n. 79.

prophet, would likely have formed a response. In this episode he responds with instructions to those on the giving and receiving end of favors. He does not completely abandon notions of reciprocity, but recasts them in relationship to God the ultimate benefactor and reciprocator. He instructs would-be disciples to follow his path of changing one's social group (friends) to include the lower status, giving to those outside the in-group who cannot repay in kind (benefaction), without expecting loyalty or public praise. Reciprocity comes from God through invitation to the messianic banquet at the resurrection of the just.

Chapter 6

Benefaction and *Patrocinium* at The Last Supper (Luke 22:14–34)

Luke's version of the Last Supper (Luke 22:14–34) has been interpreted in terms of both patronage and benefaction by several scholars. Many authors have entered the discussion and given various proposals as to the contrast or comparison Luke presents Jesus making to the kings and benefactors of Luke 22:14–34.[1] The majority of interpreters consider a strong contrast to be in view. Jesus mentions kings and benefactors as negative examples of leadership and authority, and the disciples must be mindful to take a different course. Y. S. Ahn considers "servant-benefactor" (from Lull) an appropriate description of Jesus' new way insisting, contra Lull, that benefactors serve as anti-types to the new teaching.[2] Nelson and Tannehill think that Jesus critiques the category of benefaction because it entails a response of public honor.[3] Following Nelson, Tannehill concludes that it is not "doing good" (i.e., being a "benefactor") which is outlawed, but doing good for the sake of gaining public honor.[4] Green takes a similar tack but

---

[1] A helpful review of literature on the passage can be found in Nelson, *Leadership*, 15–22; cf. Heil, *Meal-Scenes*, 166 n. 1 (oddly he omits Nelson in this initial footnote, but interacts with his work often throughout the section). Billings provides the most recent monograph, Bradly S. Billings, *Do This in Remembrance of Me: The Disputed Words in the Lukan Institution Narrative (Luke 22:19b–20): An Historico-Exegetical, Theological and Sociological Analysis* (LBS 314; London and New York: T & T Clark, 2006). After Nelson's work several authors wrote monographs on this section and its contents. P. J. Fitzpatrick, *In Breaking of Bread: The Eucharist and Ritual* (Cambridge: Cambridge University, 1993); Joel B. Green, *The Death of Jesus: Tradition and Interpretation in the Passion Narrative* (WUNT 33; Tübingen: Mohr, 1988); Eugene LaVerdiere, *The Breaking of Bread: The Development of the Eucharist According to the Acts of the Apostles* (Chicago: Liturgy Training Publications, 1998); idem, *The Eucharist in the New Testament and the Early Church* (Collegeville: Liturgical Press, 1996); I. H. Marshall, *Last Supper and Lord's Supper* (Vancouver: Regent College, 2007). Cf. Jonathan D. Brumberg Kraus, "Symposium Scenes in Luke's Gospel with Special Attention to the Last Supper" (PhD diss., Vanderbilt University, 1991); Calvin K. Katter, "Luke 22:14–38: A Farewell Address" (PhD diss., The University of Chicago, 1993).

[2] Ahn, *Luke's Passion Narrative*, 161–168; cf. Nelson, *Leadership*, 29–32.

[3] Nelson, *Leadership*, 49; Tannehill, *Luke*, 318; Robert C. Tannehill, "What Kind of King? What Kind of Kingdom? A Study of Luke," *WW* 12 (1992): 17–22, 21.

[4] Tannehill, *Luke*, 317–318; Nelson, *Leadership*, 49.

works within the patron-client category. Following Moxnes, he suggests that Jesus transforms patron-client ideology by ruling out generosity which seeks reciprocation in honor.[5] Jesus critiques the whole system, not just its abusers, because the pattern of giving-for-honor had penetrated so deeply.[6] Within this position stand those who consider the whole system suspect (e.g., Green) as well as others who think that after a very thorough redefinition benefaction or patronage may be an appropriate category to describe discipleship (e.g., Danker; Moxnes; Nelson).

Other scholars consider the benefactor a more positive model. This position attests a range of opinions from Lull who thinks that benefactors serve with little qualification as role-models to Freyne who suggests a middle ground opinion which finds in Luke's redaction of Mark evidence of a more positive appraisal of benefaction that nevertheless needs thorough recasting. To Freyne, Luke's redaction of Mark 10:41–45 (Luke 22:24–27) shows signs of softening the harsh critique. Luke drops κατὰ as a (pejorative) prefix to κυριεύω and adds εὐεργέτης which carried some positive overtones.[7] Danker determines that the benefactor serves as a positive model because in many episodes Jesus operates in this role. The double-mention of εὐεργ- terms (Acts 4:9; 10:38) solidifies to Danker the idea that the benefactor category itself is not called into question in Luke 22 but only its abuse. Luke freely adopts this terminology without qualification elsewhere in his work which suggests that it was not the term (category) to which Luke was opposed. To Danker, however, generosity in the form of benefits often masked the reality of a tyrannical rule.[8]

Lull carries this trajectory of thought one step further. He provides the most extreme position in this group, offering an extended defense of his conclusion. To him the benefactor is an example which the disciples have not been following but should be. Lull's logic builds upon a central decision about the implied verb in 22:26a. Most would supply an imperative

---

[5] Moxnes, "Patron-Client," 261, in Green, *Luke*, 767 n. 87.

[6] Green, *Luke*, 767–768.

[7] Freyne, *Galilee and Gospel*, 199; idem, *Jesus*, 146–147; cf. Paul W. Walaskay, *'And So We Came to Rome': The Political Perspective of St. Luke* (Cambridge: Cambridge University Press, 1983), 36; Esler, *Community*, 208.

[8] Danker, *Benefactor*, 324; cf. 294, 322, 384, 404, 414, 420, 436, 484; no. 48; *OGIS* 527; *Editio Princeps* J. G. C. Anderson, *Journal of Hellenic Studies* 17 (1897): 411–413, no. 14; Ptolemy VIII (145–116 B.C.); cf. York, *Last*, 170–171; Esler, *Community*, 207–208. Danker follows Nock, "*Soter* and *Euergetes*," 2.720–735, 2.724–725. Evil rulers sometimes forced others to identify them as benefactors, e.g., Albinus (*Ant.* 20.253). Bock also hints at tyranny masked by public works with reference to 2 Macc 4:2, 3; 3 Macc 3:19; *War* 3.9.8; Bock, *Luke*, 2.1737.

(ἔσεσθε or ποιήσετε),⁹ turning Jesus' statement (ὑμεῖς δὲ οὐχ οὕτως) into a charge for the disciples not to follow in the path of the aforementioned leaders. Lull chooses an indicative (e.g., καλεῖσθε) which suggests that in fact the disciples are not following in the benefactors' path.¹⁰ The strong contrastive in 22:26b (ἀλλά) introduces a contrast not to the benefactors themselves (22:25), but to the disciples' failure to imitate them (22:26a). Jesus then proceeds to describe the type of benefaction the disciples should have been practicing but in fact were not (22:26b–27). Benefactors provide a positive model for discipleship which the disciples were not practicing but should have been. In Luke, Jesus transforms the category by describing this benefaction as servant-benefaction.

Several scholars connect this passage to patron-client relationships. Sloan follows a similar line of thought as Lull, freely acknowledging that Jesus and the disciples function as benefactor and clients respectively. He also connects Jesus' teaching to *patrocinium* and specifically cites the morning *salutatio* as a time when patronage expressed itself. He implies in this that the patronage Jesus contrasts his teaching to would have taken part in the *salutatio*.¹¹ Moxnes and Tannehill suggest that patrons often earned the title of benefactor and therefore this teaching section can be interpreted in reference to Roman *patrocinium*.¹² In the following investigation of Luke 22:14–34 the manner in which Luke employs the ideology of benefaction (positive/endorse; negative/adjust or throw-out) will be examined, and it will be determinied if in fact the ideology of *patrocinium* is a proper interpretive grid for the episode.

6.1 A Passover to Remember (22:14–23)

6.1.1 Literary Context

The setting for the meal plays a role in the type of discussion which may be expected in the last meal. Luke offers a situational reminder just before

---

⁹ E.g., Marshall, *Luke*, 812; Bock, *Luke*, 2.1737; cf. Nolland, *Luke*, 3.1062; Fitzmyer, *Luke*, 2.1411, 1417; Prange, *Luke*, 233; Leaney, *Luke*, 266, 269; Lagrange, *Luc*, 550; Heil, *Meal Scenes*, 184.

¹⁰ Lull, "Servant-Benefactor," 293–295.

¹¹ Sloan, "Reciprocity," 68. Sloan perhaps intends only to say that Luke's audience might have assumed this aspect of the relationship, but his description of the background material and the relationship between Luke's and Jesus' teaching makes this unclear. He claims that patronage pervaded Rome and the provinces which leaves open the possibility that he includes Palestine (or the province from which Luke hails).

¹² Moxnes, "Patron-Client," 260–261, 266; Tannehill, *Luke*, 317.

the Passover[13] scene begins. Jesus lodged on the Mount of Olives, but would venture inside the city gates to teach in the temple during the day (Luke 21:37–38). Jesus had been on the Mount of Olives for a little while and had made some trips into Jerusalem from this strategic hillside (19:28–40). From his vantage point on the hillside Jesus had a clear view of Herod's grandest benefaction to Israel, the temple. Already Luke has included several teachings aimed against the temple and its authorities (19:41–44, 45–48; 20:45–21:4, 5–9). The temple was also the location of one benefaction inscription discussed in the last chapter (*SEG* 1277; see section 2.2.4). Luke describes Jesus as spending multiple days in the vicinity of Jerusalem, teaching in the temple, before the Passover feast (Ἦν δὲ τὰς ἡμέρας ἐν τῷ ἱερῷ διδάσκων; 21:37).

The progression of Luke's narrative to this point has emphasized loyalty to leaders, perseverance in the midst of trials, a critique of current Greco-Roman authority and values (honor), and the delay before Jesus receives his own kingdom. As he approached Jerusalem people thought the kingdom of God was coming shortly, so Jesus told a parable about a nobleman going to receive a kingdom in a far country (19:11–27, 11–12). The parable may poke fun at Archelaos who traveled in vain to Rome to gain his father's kingdom after his death (19:13–14).[14] This nobleman/king actually gains his kingdom and divides the reward among his faithful servants (19:15–26). Those who expressed disloyalty to the nobleman received severe punishment (19:26–27). The following story shows Jesus assuming the role of king and being praised as such (19:28–40). People praise Jesus as he descends the Mount of Olives on his way to Jerusalem. He pronounces judgment on Jerusalem and portends its destruction (19:41–44, 45–48). He then teaches in the temple challenging the Jewish authorities (20:1–8). Another parable about a rich man, who takes time away from his business leaving others in charge, ends with an allusion to the temple

---

[13] Scholars dispute if the meal in fact was a Passover or if Luke has only added those elements for effect. Green, Kilpatrick, Marshall, and Bock argue for a Passover meal. Green, *Luke*, 757–758; Kilpatrick, *Eucharist*, 42; Marshall, *Last Supper*, 83–84; Bock, *Luke*, 2.1719; cf. Tannehill, *Luke*, 311–312; Ellis, *Luke*, 254; C. K. Barrett, "Luke xxii.15: To Eat the Passover," *JTS* 39 (1958): 28–47. Non-passover interpreters include: F. C. Burkitt and A. E. Brooke, "St Luke xxii 15, 16: What is the General Meaning?" *JTS* 9 (1907–8): 569–572; H. K. Luce, *The Gospel According to S. Luke* (Cambridge: Cambridge University Press, 1933), 328–329.

[14] Schultz, "Jesus as Archelaus"; Plummer, *Luke*, 437–438; Nolland, *Luke*, 3.911; Fitzmyer, *Luke*, 2.1234–1235; Marshall, *Luke*, 703–704; Wright, *Jesus and the Victory of God*, 632–633. Schultz claims that the connection to Archelaos is almost unanimous, Schultz, "Archelaus," 109. Two commentators deny the connection, Scott, *Hear Now the Parable*, 223; Bovon, *Luc*, 3.257–258. Denaux questions the connection. Denaux, "The Parable of the King-Judge," 53–54; idem, "The Parable of the Talents/Pounds," 430.

which symbolizes rejection of Jesus (20:9–18). Apparently near the temple Jesus remarks about the impending judgment on the scribes who seek the best seats in synagogues and feasts (20:45–47). He follows this with an observation about a humble and generous widow whose offering to the temple serves as an example of piety (21:1–4). Her example instigates comments about the temple which allow Jesus opportunity to tell of its coming destruction (21:5–28). In the destruction of Jerusalem the disciples who endure will gain their lives (ἐν τῇ ὑπομονῇ ὑμῶν κτήσασθε τὰς ψυχὰς ὑμῶν; 21:19). In the immediate context Jesus has apparently supportive crowds attending his teaching, but a satanically inspired opposition planning its assault (21:37–40; 22:1–6). Several discussions of authority-humility, leadership-service, loyalty-betrayal, honor-shame, and Jesus' kingdom in contrast to the Greco-Roman kingdom precede the Passover discussion and prepare for its contents.

Luke has woven together a coherent narrative picturing Jesus in discussion with his disciples with the reversal motif at center. The Passover meal begins when the hour arrives and Jesus and his disciples recline with him at the table (22:14). He offers a reinterpretation of the Passover significance, replacing the story of the Exodus (Deut. 26:5–11) with an interpretation based upon his coming death (Luke 22:14–20). Mention of his death leads into a discussion of his betrayal. One among the twelve will prove disloyal and in fact will play an instrumental role in his demise (22:21–23). Naturally, personal defenses against disloyalty turn to personal professions of allegiance to Jesus and relative positions in his entourage. The disciples dispute who among them is the greatest, but Jesus challenges their understanding of greatness (22:24–27). Utilizing the reversal motif, he offers his own life as the model for a service-oriented type of greatness. Indeed, loyalty in the midst of trials results in the greatness the disciples desired. Jesus overturns normal notions of greatness and then offers precisely what the disciples had desired as reward (22:28–30). Immediately, Jesus turns to Peter to warn that Satan will attempt to sift all of the disciples. He comforts Peter that he has prayed for the apostle's faith and encourages him to strengthen the rest who struggle when he turns. Peter's allegiance will falter, but not forever (22:31–34). Each of these paragraphs (22:14–20, 21–23, 25–27, 28–30, 31–34) deserves further attention as each is relevant to a discussion of patrons, benefactors, reciprocity, and loyalty. This discussion breaks the meal and teaching into two larger components (22:14–23, 24–34). The first two paragraphs belong together (14–20, 21–23) as they involve a discussion of correct and incorrect responses to Jesus' role as benefactor. The latter three paragraphs (24–27, 28–30, 31–34) belong together because they involve instruction on a new form of benefaction with its attendant roles for the disciples.

In regard to 22:14–23, it is important to discuss the disputed longer reading in which Jesus gives new meaning to the Passover symbols. Debate still continues as to whether the shorter or longer reading should be preferred.[15] Codex Bezae and a few minor MSS omit 22:19b–20 from the section leaving the Passover elements relatively unexplained and avoiding the difficulty of two cups (cup, bread, cup). With essentially only one major manuscript in favor of the shorter reading (D; it), the external evidence of the longer reading pushes strongly in its favor. The longer reading being the more difficult reading adds to its weight.[16] Billings has recently made a thorough defense of the longer reading which combines internal and external evidence with a unique contribution as to the derivation of D. The social situation of early Christians in Lyons put them into danger of accusations of cannibalism and strange sexual rituals ("Thyestean Banquets" and "Oedipodean Intercourse"). He proposes that this persecution compelled the D scribe, or his exemplar, to omit the potentially hazardous evidence of cannibalism and the drinking of human blood.[17] Billings' sociological explanation of the derivation of D adds another dimension to the strength of the longer reading.

6.1.2 Linguistic Evidence

Linguistic and thematic elements in this section suggest that Luke presents Jesus as a benefactor. If the longer reading is original then two sides of a benefit given by a benefactor may be detected in the paragraph. First, benefactors increased their reputations by extending themselves to the point of suffering. This pattern is so prevalent that Danker developed the term "endangered benefactor" to describe the action.[18] For example, of Akornion, benefactor of Dionysopolis, it is said that he "shrinks from no danger in his determination to accomplish whatever might be advantageous

---

[15] Billings gives the most current review of the matter in Billings, *Institution Narrative*, 4–20.

[16] Bock, *Luke*, 2.1722; Tannehill, *Luke*, 313–314; Nolland, *Luke*, 3.1041; Fitzmyer, *Luke*, 2.1387–1388; Marshall, *Luke*, 799–803; Jeremias, *Words*, 139–159; Heinz Schürmann, *Traditionsgeschichtliche Untersuchungen* (Düsseldorf, 1968), 159–192. Earlier scholars favored the shorter reading. E.g., Plummer, *Luke*, 496; Klostermann, *Lukasevangelium*, 207; Creed, *Luke*, 263–264; B. S. Easton, *The Gospel According to St. Luke* (Edinburgh, 1926); 321; Leaney, *Luke*, 72–75.

[17] Bradly S. Billings, "The Disputed Words in the Lukan Institution Narrative (Luke 22:19b–20): A Sociological Answer to a Textual Problem," *JBL* 125.3 (2006): 507–526; idem, *Institution Narrative*.

[18] Danker, "Endangered Benefactor"; cf. Danker, *Benefactor*, 417–435 ("Endangered Benefactor"), 322–323.

to the city."[19] Lysias provides another example. A dispute over the worthiness of Andocides to receive public acclaim leads Lysias to the following piece of reasoning.

Ἀλλὰ Λακεδαιμόνιαι γὰρ ἐν ταῖς πρὸς αὐτοὺς συνθήκαις ἐπεμελήθησαν Ἀνδοκίδου ὅτι ἔπαθον ἀγαθόν τι ὑπ' αὐτοῦ ἀλλ' ὑμεῖς ἐπεμελήθητέ γε αὐτοῦ; ἀντὶ ποίας εὐεργεσίας; ὅτι πολλάκις δι' ὑμᾶς ὑπὲρ τῆς πόλεως ἐκινδύνευσεν;
"Yet it may be said that the Lacedaemonians, in the agreements made with them, took care of Andocides because of some benefit that they had received from him; but did you take care of him? For what sort of good service? Because he has often risked danger because of you, in aid of the city" (Lysias, 6.40–41; W. R. M. Lamb)

Andocides earned the right to be identified as a benefactor because he extended himself to the point of self-endangerment on behalf of the city. By offering his life Jesus pushes this to its limit. Therefore terms which identify his suffering may suggest the endangered benefactor paradigm (τοῦ με παθεῖν; ὁ σῶμά μου τὸ ὑπὲρ ὑμῶν διδόμενον; ἐν τῷ αἵματί μου τὸ ὑπὲρ ὑμῶν ἐκχυννόμενον; τοῦ παραδιδόντος με; δι' οὗ παραδίδοται). By willingly subjecting himself to danger, Jesus acts as the "preeminent benefactor."[20]

Second, the benefit is memorialized in the last supper meal (εἰς τὴν ἐμὴν ἀνάμνησιν; εὐχαριστήσας; Luke 22:17, 19).[21] "Ingratitude is the cardinal social and political sin in the Graeco-Roman world, and failure to memorialize benefactions conferred by generous people is its flipside."[22] For this reason "remembering" words were important in inscriptions and decrees (cf. Acts 10:2, 31). For example, the prefect Tiberius Claudius Balbillus was honored as a benefactor by the inhabitants of Busiris, Egypt. In the decree they declare the benefits (τάς τούτου χάριτας καὶ εὐεργεσίας πλημύρουσα) they have enjoyed on account of the prefect's generosity and have inscribed these truths on a stone for all to remember.

...ἁρμόζει γάρ τὰς ἰσοθέους αὐτοῦ χάριτας ἐνεστηλειτωμένας τοῖς ἱεροῖς γράμμασιν αἰῶνι μνημονεύεσθαι παντί.
"Therefore it is appropriate that his god-like favors be inscribed in sacred letters for all time to remember."[23]

---

[19] Danker, *Benefactor*, no 12, pages 77–78; *Inscriptiones Graecae ad res Romanas pertinentes* 1.662.

[20] Danker, *Benefactor*, 321–323; Lull, "Servant-Benefactor," 299.

[21] Danker, *Benefactor*, 321–23, cf. nos. 13, 17, 52; Hengel, *The Atonement*, 1981, 6–15, 34–39. For acts of commemoration see Danker, *Benefactor*, 420, 436–7.

[22] Danker, *Benefactor*, 436–438.

[23] Trans. Danker, *Benefactor*, 225–226. *Editio princeps Quarterly Review* 19 (1819): 413, no. 38; cf. *The British Museum: Egyptian Antiquities* (vol. 2; London, 1836), 376–379. Danker, *Benefactor*, 35 = *OGIS* 666; *CIG* 4699; *IGR* 1.1110.

Recipients of benefits were expected to memorialize the benefit as an expression of gratitude. Memorializing a benefaction was thought to stimulate others to action as well. A memorial would result in the stimulation of the benefactor to more good works (*OGIS* 213.23–31; *Choix* 50.14–16; cf. Acts 24:2–4, 5–8). Luke's addition of remembering terms, not found in Matt or Mark, increases the likelihood that Luke presents Jesus as a benefactor. Jesus provides the model for greatness, a benefactor who gives all in service to others. He is a benefactor in the sense that he willingly endangers himself for the benefit of others. He provides his disciples with a ready way to memorialize his benefaction, which both proclaims their appreciation of the benefit and invites others to see the generosity of their benefactor.

One among the twelve, however, will not appreciate the benefaction or take part in memorializing it, but will rather offer the opposite of gratitude, namely disloyalty (22:21–23). Jesus has just described his benefaction (self-giving) and then given instruction on how to properly remember the deed. Luke chooses a strong contrastive (Πλὴν ἰδοὺ; 22:21), therefore, to highlight the improper and ungrateful response taken by the betrayer. Jesus instructs his disciples on how they may be loyal in light of the excellent benefit bestowed, but one among them will not be loyal and instead will shun the gift/benefit and the giver/benefactor. Luke inverts the order of these two paragraphs (institution then betrayal; rather than betrayal then institution in Matthew and Mark). He highlights the generous act of the benefactor which makes the ignominious betrayal stand in stark relief. Those familiar with patterns of reciprocity would quickly recognize in Judas one who did not properly respond to the benefit. Though even this betrayal does not fall outside of God's will (ὅτι ὁ υἱὸς μὲν τοῦ ἀνθρώπου κατὰ τὸ ὡρισμένον πορεύεται), the betrayer still deserves a woe to be pronounced upon him (πλὴν οὐαὶ τῷ ἀνθρώπῳ ἐκείνῳ δι' οὗ παραδίδοται; 22:22). A discussion (συζητεῖν) ensues among the disciples over which of them might show such disloyalty. Each evangelist describes the disciples denying that they will be the perpetrators of the betrayal (Matt 26:21–25; Mark 14:18–21; John 13:21–26). This evolves into a question about who might be the greatest. It seems likely that disciples would attempt to distance themselves from the predicted betrayal to the point of saying that they were in fact furthest, i.e., the greatest. The natural progression from a small debate about who would betray Jesus escalates into a competition (φιλονεικία) for the highest spot of greatness (22:24–30).[24]

There is no explicit vocabulary in this section (22:14–23) connecting Jesus' actions or instruction to *patrocinium*. Without explicit vocabulary it

---

[24] Nelson, *Leadership*, 140–141; Fitzmyer, *Luke*, 2.1414–1415; Marshall, *Luke*, 810–811.

is unwise to move from describing Jesus as a benefactor to describing him as a patron at least in this subsection. Here Luke appropriately avoids the use of patron language because the constituents of the meal were likely more familiar with benefaction than patronage (see below, section 3.14.3). This is so because the twelve originated from Galilee and Philip's tetrarchy which attest some practice of benefaction but nothing explicit of *patrocinium* (see sections 2.2.3; 2.2.5).

6.1.3 Cultural Matters

As the Passover approached Jesus may have interacted with Jews from both Palestine and the diaspora (section 4.1.1), but once the meal commenced his audience was limited to the twelve from Galilee and Philip's tetrarchy. Passover, being one of the most important festivals on the Jewish calendar, attracted large numbers of pilgrims from the diaspora communities among whom some might have been exposed to benefactions of and inscriptions honoring Herod I and/or Antipas (in e.g., Athens, Si'a). It is probable that Jesus interacted with at least some of these visitors. Among those who came to hear Jesus in the temple it is plausible to include Greek speaking, hellenistically influenced Jews (Luke 21:38). John's Gospel gives this impression when Greek speaking Jews come looking for Jesus during the Passover (John 12:20).[25] Philip's ability to converse with them suggests an avenue through which Jesus could learn and instruct on Hellenistic ways of life (John 12:21; see section 3.2.1). Both Herod I and Antipas had reputations as benefactors in communities outside of Palestine (see sections 3.1.6; 3.2.6). It was argued in the previous chapter that Herod I may have intentionally aimed his benefactions toward those communities with large Jewish populations (see 3.1.4). Many of these Jews would have been familiar with the political situation in Palestine and perhaps taken note of Herodian ways. It seems likely that pilgrims would be among the crowds of people, of whom the scribes and priests were afraid, who attended Jesus (Luke 22:6). Combining the glorious yet offensive benefaction of the temple in Jesus' sight with the potential interaction with Hellenistic Jews on pilgrimage it seems reasonable that Jesus had benefactors on his mind as he entered his final week.

The meal itself, however, Jesus shared only with Jews from Galilee and Philip's tetrarchy which suggests benefaction, more so than *patrocinium*, as a plausible interpretive paradigm. It has been argued that the twelve hailed from Galilee and Philip's tetrarchy. The archaeological and literary

---

[25] Schnabel, *Mission*, 1.277–278, who follows R. Riesner, *Lehrer*, 412; "Hellenistic Jews from the Diaspora," in Ernst Haenchen, *John 2* (Hermeneia; Minneapolis: Fortress, 1984), 96.

investigation of those regions undertaken in the previous chapter determined that Galilee was predominately Jewish with only slight infiltration of benefaction ideology (esp. in Antipas; see section 2.2.3; 3.2.6). Philip's tetrarchy may have contained the practice of *patrocinium* but the sources do not make this explicit (see section 2.2.5). Considering Philip's aversion to travel (i.e., visit Rome) it was suggested that he probably did not participate in *patrocinium*. However, his expressions of affinity with the Roman imperial family (in coins and temples) may indicate that he was more familiar with Roman ways and thus *patrocinium* (see section 3.3.2). Philip's projects were interpreted primarily as expressions of a benefactor because of the lack of explicit connection to *patrocinium* drawn in the sources. Therefore, as one approaches the Passover meal it seems intrinsically more likely that Jesus would instruct his followers in terms of Hellenistic Jewish culture with Hellenistic benefaction a possible grid and Roman *patrocinium* a less likely though not impossible grid.

The conversations which preceded this meal likely included a discussion of the Herodian family and their attempts to be recognized as benefactors. The twelve had been with Jesus for a little time as he taught and more than once they discussed the central benefaction of Herod to Jerusalem, the temple (19:41–44, 45–48; 21:5–9). As Jesus journeyed to Jerusalem the Herodian family had been a topic of conversation. Jesus alludes to Archelaos' failed attempt to gain the kingdom from Augustus (Luke 19:13–14). Within the larger narrative section (9:51–19:44) Jesus critiqued Herod Antipas as well during a discussion of the kingdom of God (13:22–35, 31–32; cf. 9:57–62, 58). Jesus comments on the temple twice prior to this last meal (19:45–46; 21:5–9), according to Luke's gospel. It had apparently been an important topic of conversation indicating that a reference to it again in this passage would not be far-fetched. The temple stood as an important symbol for Israel, but also as the grandest reminder of Herodian rule in Jerusalem. As the Passover celebration approached, and conversations developed about preparing the sacrifice, it is quite likely that the corruption of the temple by the Herodian family of "benefactors" arose.

Luke's description of the ministry of Jesus to this point suggests the importance of Jewish matters but also keeps the Hellenistic leadership in close view. Luke retains this balance when describing the Passover meal. He emphasizes Jewish matters but also provides a critique of the Hellenistic leadership. A closer examination of the way Luke shapes the meal supports the suggestion that he accurately depicts cultural *realia* of first-century Palestine.

According to Luke, Jesus and the twelve enjoy a Passover meal together which naturally gives rise to Jewish cultural matters. The question of whether the meal was in fact a Passover or not, historically speaking, has long perplexed scholars and cannot be addressed in this book.[26] For our purposes it is sufficient to show that Luke portrays the event as a Passover and that the content of the ensuing conversation fits within this context. The aim of this part of the book is to first identify Luke's presentation of events and subsequently to question whether this "fits" with first-century life in Palestine. In three steps Fitzmyer argues that the Synoptic evangelists, especially Luke, depict the meal as a Passover.[27] First, "the disciples clearly prepare for a meal to be eaten at sundown" which coincides with the night of Passover's beginning (Nisan 15; Luke 22:1, 7–14). Second, authorities arrest Jesus that night and eventually kill him before the next day (still Nisan 15) is through (Luke 22:39, 47–54). Third, this day (Nisan 15) is designated as ἡμέρα ἦν παρασκευῆς καὶ σάββατον ("the day of prepration, the day before the Sabbath"; Luke 23:54). Thus, the day is a parasceve (day before the Sabbath), that is Friday.

"Remembering" was an important aspect of the Passover celebration (Exod 12:14; Deut 16:3; *m. Pesah* 10:5).[28] It is important to identify the connection between Passover and remembering because of Danker's suggestion that "remembering" connects to benefaction ideology. Passover began as a time of remembrance. Exodus 12:14 describes the meal as a memorial (זִכָּרוֹן; μνημόσυνον LXX). In the Deuteronomic description of the Passover the biblical author highlights the importance of remembering. Deuteronomy 16:1–8 emphasizes the importance of remembering by identifying remembrance as the purpose of the meal (16:3). The MT employs a

---

[26] Fitzmyer, *Luke*, 2.1378–1382; Harold W. Hoehner, *Chronological Aspects of the Life of Christ* (Grand Rapids: Zondervan, 1977), 65–93; Anthony J. Saldarini, *Jesus and Passover* (New York: Paulist Press, 1984); S. S. Kim, "The Christological and Eschatological Significance of Jesus' Passover Signs in John 6," *BibSac* 164 (2007): 307–322; J. B. Green, "Preparation for Passover (Luke 22:7–13," in *The Composition of Luke's Gospel Selected Studies from "Novum Testamentum"* (ed. David E. Orton; Brill's Readers in Biblical Studies 1; Leiden: Brill, 1999).

[27] Fitzmyer, *Luke*, 1378.

[28] Mark G. Steiner, "The Covenantal Significance of Remembrance As It Is Used in Luke 22:19" (S.T.M. thesis, Concordia Seminary, 1988); Bock, *Luke*, 2.1725–1726; Leaney, *Luke*, 268; Green, *Luke*, 762; idem, *Death of Jesus*, 201–203; Barth, *Lord's Supper*, 12–13. F. G. Carpinelli finds remember words in cultic settings which leads him to conclude that εἰς τὴν ἐμὴν ἀνάμνησιν (22:19) speaks of Jesus' memorial (as opposed to someone else's) in which he ordains a "cultic memorial." He finds that "a divinely elected mediator providing a cultic memorial so that others may have expiation before God is a feature of ancient Jewish piety, and thus, is available to Luke as an interpretive principle for Jesus' relations to God" (1 *Enoch* 15:21–25; *Jub* 6:10–14; 17–31). Francis Giordano Carpinelli, "'Do This as My Memorial' (Luke 22:19): Lucan Soteriology and Atonement," *CBQ* 61 (1999): 74–91. This suggestion need not be taken up in this dissertation since it is concerned with the salvific implications of the subsequent meal and not directly with the topic of benefaction/patronage.

purpose particle (לְמַעַן) to emphasize the purpose of the meal as remembering God's rescue of Israel from slavery (Deut 16:3). The LXX adopts a ἵνα plus aorist passive subjunctive to translate the purpose clause (ἵνα μνησθῆτε; 16:3 LXX). The centrality of remembrance to the purpose of Passover indicates that Danker's ascription of a benefaction context to Luke's use of "remembrance" (εἰς τὴν ἐμὴν ἀνάμνησιν) cannot be disconnected from the Passover context.

Although Passover was an important Jewish ceremony, Hellenistic cultural elements have been identified in the Last Supper meal. Commentators on Luke's Last Supper compare its contents to symposia, farewell addresses, and table fellowship generally.[29] These types of dining have implications for the expected conversation which would ensue. Luke accomplishes a "relatively seamless discourse" in the adoption "of the literary form of the farewell address ... set within a Passover meal constructed along the lines of a Greco-Roman symposium."[30] Barth notes that Passover meals by this point had taken on many elements of the Greek symposium.[31] Symposia had as a central point of conversation the evaluation of honor and shame at table. Farewell addresses afforded times to discuss last words and to appoint successors. These two topics intertwine in Jesus' message at the table (22:14–34).[32] The topic of honor-shame at table had already been broached earlier in Jesus' ministry (14:1–24). A connection to symposia was also entertained in the interpretation of that passage. The topic had not dropped out of view as Luke draws Jesus' ministry to a close. In a nearby pericope Luke depicts Jesus warning his disciples of the tendency of scribes to choose the places of honor at meals (20:46). In his Last Supper instruction he instructs them not to recline, but instead to assume the position of the servant and stand up to minister to the recliners (22:27). Honor-shame, the conferral of benefits, and implementation of successors were natural topics at symposia, in farewell addresses, and in table-fellowship generally. By weaving these three dining conventions into

---

[29] Smith, *Symposium*, 253–272, esp. 262–266; W. S. Kurz, "Luke 22:14–38 and Greco-Roman and Biblical Farewell Addresses," *JBL* 104.2 (1985): 251–268; Neyrey, *Passion*, 7–8; Kraus, "Symposium Scenes"; Danker, *Benefactor*, 344–345; Evans, *Luke*, 321; David Lenz Tiede, *Luke* (Augsburg Commentary on the New Testament; Minneapolis: Augsburg, 1988), 377; Katter, "Luke 22:14–38"; Talbert, *Mediterranean Milieu*, 129–131; idem, *Reading Luke*, 206–211; Francois Bovon, *Luke the Theologian* (trans. Ken McKinney; Allison Park: Pickwick, 1987), 379–383; Bock, *Luke*, 2.1719.

[30] Green, *Luke*, 756.

[31] Markus Barth, *Rediscovering the Lord's Supper: Communion with Israel, with Christ, and among the Guests* (Atlanta: John Knox, 1988), 10, in Green, *Luke*, 756 n. 37.

[32] Green, *Luke*, 766; Tannehill, *Luke*, 311–320; Kurz, "Farewell Address," 251–268; Nelson, *Leadership*, 97–119; Talbert, *Theological Commentary*, 233, 234–235.

the narrative Luke provides a very logical situation for discussions of honor-shame, reciprocity, and benefaction to occur.

The Jewish and Hellenistic cultural influences discovered in the meal appear to work in tandem as Luke reinterprets the Passover meal in reference to Jesus. Luke reinterprets the symbolic import of the Passover elements. The bread is reinterpreted to refer to his "offered body" (τὸ ... διδόμενον; 22:19).[33] Luke's narrative does not develop a substitutionary sacrificial interpretation of Jesus' death, but Jesus does extend himself to the point of death for the sake of (ὑπὲρ ὑμῶν) his disciples.[34] Luke's text does not indicate the manner of Jesus' death in the breaking of bread,[35] but "'[g]iving one's body' is potent as an image for giving one's life (in battle) for the sake of one's people."[36] Luke reinterprets the cup as blood of the new covenant (22:20). The blood is given on behalf of Jesus' disciples (τὸ ὑπὲρ ὑμῶν ἐκχυννόμενον). "Pouring out" blood symbolizes a "violent death and sacrifice" (Gen 4:10–11; 9:6; Lev 4:18, 25, 30; Deut 19:10; Isa 53:12; 59:87; Ezek 18:10).[37] Covenants were often ratified by blood (cf. Exod 24:8; Zech 9:11), so Jesus offers blood to ratify the new covenant (Jer 31:31–34; cf. 1 Cor 11:24–25; 2 Cor 3:6).[38] Luke refers to Jesus' death without making explicit how this death functions on behalf of others. Luke does not explicitly develop the meaning of ὑπὲρ ὑμῶν (22:19, 20), but elsewhere in Luke-Acts Jesus' death is tied to the forgiveness of sins (Luke 24:44–47; Acts 5:30–31; 10:39–43; 13:26–39). Through connection to the salvific event of the exodus Luke implies that Jesus' death will also have salvific value for others. Thus, the death has some beneficial and perhaps salvific force if not explicit expiatory value.[39]

If the previous healings deserve the description "Sabbath benefactions" then Jesus' action in this episode may appropriately be termed "Passover

---

[33] Bock, *Luke*, 2.1724.

[34] Joel B. Green, *The Death of Jesus: Tradition and Interpretation in the Passion Narrative* (WUNT 33; Tübingen: Mohr, 1988); idem, *Recovering the Scandal of the Cross: The Atonement in New Testament and Contemporary Contexts* (Carlisle, U.K.: Paternoster, 2004); idem, *Luke*, 761, but cf. 763–764; Nolland, *Luke*, 3.1054. Bock hesitatingly brings substitution and sacrifice language into his interpretation because of Acts 20:28, but distances himself from this connection as he progresses, Bock, *Luke*, 2.1724–1725; cf. Fitzmyer, *Luke*, 2.1401.

[35] Marshall, *Last Supper*, 86; Green, *Luke*, 761.

[36] Green, *Luke*, 761; cf. Nolland, *Luke*, 3.1054 (refers to Thucydides 2.43.2).

[37] Green, *Luke*, 762–763.

[38] Marshall, *Luke*, 806; Plummer, *Luke*, 499; Bock, *Luke*, 2.1727–1728; Green, *Luke*, 762 (refers to *Targum Onqelos* and *Targum Pseudo-Jonathan* on Exod 24:8); Douglas J. Moo, *The Old Testament in the Gospel Passion Narratives* (Sheffield: Almond Press, 1983), 302.

[39] Cf. Bock, *Luke*, 2.1725–1726; Plummer, *Luke*, 498; Green, *Luke*, 762; Barth, *Lord's Supper*, 12–26.

benefaction." Benefactors provided salvation for others frequently by extending themselves to the point of self-endangerment. Jesus takes this course to its extreme by giving his life on behalf of his disciples. This death will later be connected with the forgiveness Jesus offers to his followers. Benefactors were often noted for granting forgiveness and amnesty (e.g., *SIG* 495.165–189; *OGIS* 90; Danker nos. 29, 43; section 2.1.2).[40] Though Luke does not in this text connect Jesus' death on behalf of others with forgiveness he does make this connection in subsequent stories. As a benefactor Jesus' death provides amnesty for others. Such acts of beneficence would then be memorialized in some way. Typically this occurred through an inscription of some sort, but Luke reinterprets the well-known Passover as the proper event to memorialize Jesus' salvific act on behalf of others. God had provided for the release and salvation of his people from Egypt, and now in the new covenant Jesus provides for the release and salvation of his people. His people express gratitude for this generosity through a memorial meal. Thus, Jesus' self-sacrifice on behalf of others constitutes a Passover benefaction.

6.1.4 Conclusion

In the literary context which precedes the narrative under investigation (22:14–23), Luke gives reason to believe that Jesus and his apostles discussed benefactors (e.g., the Herodian family) and their benefactions (e.g., temple) as they made their way to Jerusalem (Luke 13:22–35, 31–32; cf. 9:57–62, 58; 19:13–14, 41–44, 45–48; 21:5–9). Luke describes the group making preparations for the Passover meal which he then narrates. His use of remembering language (ἀνάμνησις) and the description of Jesus extending himself to the point of self-endangerment were two components commonly identified in descriptions of benefactors (*SIG* 762. 32–33; Lysias, 6.40–41; *OGIS* 666; *OGIS* 213.23–31; *Choix* 50.14–16). No language connecting this story to *patrocinium* can be found. By reinterpreting his death in terms of the Passover Luke implies that Jesus' death will have salvific effect for his people. He extends himself to the point of self-endangerment in order to provide salvific benefit for others (ὑπὲρ ὑμῶν). One of the benefits of this death, described in subsequent stories, is that his people will enjoy forgiveness of sins (Luke 24:44–47; Acts 5:30–31; 10:39–43; 13:26–39). Benefactors often earned their reputations in part because they could offer amnesty and forgiveness to others (e.g., *SIG* 495.165–189; *OGIS* 90; Danker nos. 29, 43). Thus, Luke presents the Last Supper primarily in terms of Jewish matters but in a few details gives reason to interpret the event in terms of benefaction. Joining this Hellenistic description

---

[40] Danker, *Benefactor*, 394–396.

with the obvious Jewish cultural setting of Passover leads to the suggestion that Luke presented Jesus' death as a "Passover benefaction." This corresponds well with the discoveries made in chapters 2 and 3 of this book for Galilee and Jerusalem. Jews from Galilee and Jerusalem held Jewish culture in a primary position, but could be conversant in benefaction because of a few inscriptions and benefactions as well as the practice of certain Herodian leaders. As a first-century Galilean who had visited Jerusalem and certain regions influenced more by Hellenism, Jesus would have been familiar enough with benefactors to situate his teaching against this ideology. Likewise, Jesus' self-sacrifice on behalf of others could have been interpreted by some of his disciples as the action of a benefactor.

6.2 Leaders and Disciples (22:24–34)

6.2.1 Literary Context

As the story progresses the disciples increasingly distance themselves from identification as "the betrayer" to the point that they enter a debate (φιλονεικία) about who of them might be considered the greatest (22:24).[41] Jesus responds by referencing the hierarchy which prevails among the Gentiles (22:25–27) and contrasting this with greatness and leadership in the kingdom of God (22:28–30). A challenge to Peter's faith and assurance of his resolve contrast with the description of the disloyal betrayer and provide a positive example of the proper way to respond to Jesus' benefaction (22:31–34).

Since scholars tend to separate 22:24–27 from 22:28–30 a point about the relationship of these two paragraphs (22:24–27, 28–30) is in order. Some disconnect the first paragraph from the second,[42] but this is not best. Lull and Nelson offer reasons to consider the two as a unity. Nelson provides both verbal and conceptual connections between 22:24–27 and 22:28–30. Terms for leadership and authority fall in both paragraphs and the discussion of location at table also comes in both.[43] In this category he lists οἱ βασιλεῖς, κυριεύουσιν, οἱ ἐξουσιάζοντες, εὐεργέται, ὁ ἡγούμενος, ὁ ἀνακείμενος, διατίθεμαι, διέθετό, βασιλείαν, τῇ βασιλείᾳ, θρόνων, and κρίνοντες. He offers similar lists of subordinates and relative greatness. Lull notes a syntactical construction which connects the two (ἐγὼ δὲ . εἰμι;

---

[41] Contra Nolland, *Luke*, 3.1064. Following Nelson, *Leadership*, 140–141; Fitzmyer, *Luke*, 2.1414–1415; Marshall, *Luke*, 810–811.

[42] E.g., Marshall, *Luke*, 810–818; Creed, *Luke*, 268; Lagrange, *Luc*; Ernst Lohmeyer, *Evangelium des Markus* (Göttingen: Vandenhoeck and Ruprecht, 1959).

[43] Nelson, *Leadership*, 3–4, 236–239.

ὑμεῖς δέ ἐστε).⁴⁴ Scholars sometimes suggest distance between the paragraphs because of the overall messages each conveys. It is sometimes said that the first paragraph denounces leadership in favor of service and the latter commends leadership.⁴⁵ This strong division however does not stand as Nelson has demonstrated.⁴⁶ Jesus presents a new form of leadership which serves. Jesus combines leadership and service in his own life and commends this to his disciples in both paragraphs. It is best to consider the two paragraphs as a joint statement addressing the central issue of greatness.

The question of Luke's sources for this subsection of the narrative (22:24–30) deserves attention because conclusions on the topic of sources influence the interpretation. The intent of this section of the book is to determine Luke's particular message. Freyne's conclusion that Luke redacts directly from Mark 10:41–45 leads him to conclude that Luke has softened the critique against the Gentile leaders.⁴⁷ Lull objects to the "consensus view" about benefactors in part because they mistakenly import into Luke the (purportedly) more pejorative sense of κατακυριεύω from Mark 10:42 into Luke's use of κυριεύω (22:25; see section 6.1.2).⁴⁸ Neyrey and Soards focus primarily on redactional clues in their respective evaluations of Luke's passion narrative.⁴⁹ Redactional differences between Luke and his sources reveal, to Neyrey and Soards, the theology of Luke. The two most

---

⁴⁴ Lull, "Servant Benefactor," 299–300; cf. Nelson, *Leadership*, 4.

⁴⁵ E.g., Creed, *Luke*, 268; cf. Marshall, *Luke*, 814; Bernd Kollmann, *Ursprung und Gestalten der frühchristlichen Mahl Feier* (Göttingen: Vandenhoeck and Ruprecht, 1990), 222–223.

⁴⁶ Nelson, *Leadership*, 236–239; cf. G. Schneider, *Evangelium*, 2.451; Fritz Rienecker, *Das Evangelium des Lukas* (Wuppertaler Studienbibel 2; Wuppertal: R. Brockhaus, 2005), 504; Soards, *Passion*, 52; Jacques Dupont, "Le logion des douze trônes (Mt 19,28; Lc 22,28–30)," *Bib* 45 (1964): 355–392, 380; Xavier Léon-Dufour, "Le testament de Jésus selon Luc," in *Le partage du pain eucharistique selon le Nouveau Testament* (Parole de Dieu; ed. Xavier Léon-Dufour; Paris: Seuil, 1982), 266–284, 273; Frank J. Matera, *Passion Narratives and Gospel Theologies: Interpreting the Synoptics Through Their Passion Stories* (New York: Paulist Press, 1986), 162; Günther Baumbach, *Das Verständnis des Bösen in den synoptischen Evangelien* (Berlin: Evangelische Verlagsanstalt, 1963), 193; Eugene LaVerdiere, *Luke* (New Testament Message 5; Wilmington, Delaware: Michael Glazier, 1980), 260–261; Robert C. Tannehill, "A Study in the Theology of Luke-Acts," *ATR* 43 (1961): 195–203, 200; Plummer, *Luke*, 500.

⁴⁷ Freyne, *Galilee and Gospel*, 199.

⁴⁸ Lull, "Servant-Benefactors," 290–291.

⁴⁹ Jerome Neyrey, *The Passion According to Luke: A Redaction Study of Luke's Soteriology* (New York: Paulist, 1985); Marion L. Soards, *The Passion According to Luke: The Special Material of Luke 22* (JSNTSup 14; Sheffield: JSOT, 1987).

pertinent potential sources are Mark 10:41–45 (cf. Luke 22:24–27) and Matthew 19:28 (cf. Luke 22:28–30).[50]

Scholars disagree about Luke's dependency on Mark 10:41–45, but it seems best to conclude that Luke has not drawn directly from Mark but rather the two drew from a similar tradition.[51] Vocabulary and form are the two major foci of the discussion. Vocabulary similarities sometimes can be used in favor of Lukan dependency on Mark since there is agreement on approximately 57% of the words (Mark 10:41–45 and Luke 22:25–27). But more often vocabulary argues against dependency since many of the words are insignificant conjunctions, pronouns, or articles and verbal agreements are often different in form.[52] In regard to form, it can be shown that the two pericopes have a very similar structure with an introduction (Mark 10:41; Luke 22:24), example and teaching (Mark 10:42–44; Luke 22:25–26), and christological conclusion (Mark 10:45; Luke 22:27). The setting which provokes the discussion, the contrasted ways of greatness, and the "structural center" of the stories (οὐ ... ἀλλὰ) also support the notion of similarity in form.[53] However, Luke typically follows Mark's order of pericopes so the location of this pericope stands out (from Judean/Perean ministry before Jerusalem in Mark to Jerusalem at the Last Supper in Luke). Luke apparently transposes the pericope. The oddity of such a transposition indicates to Jeremias that Luke does not follow Mark because Luke does not typically transpose from his sources.[54] Nelson concludes that form and

---

[50] The side-by-side charts offered by Nelson for the two passages are quite helpful, Nelson, *Leadership*, 124, 174.

[51] Those who posit Mark as a source include: Soards, *Passion*, 42; J. A. Bailey, *The Traditions Common to the Gospels of Luke and John* (NovT Sup 7; Leiden: Brill, 1963), 35; Augustin George, *Études sur l'œuvre de Luc* (SB; Paris: Gabalda, 1978), 193; A. Loisy, *L'Évangile selon Luc* (Paris: Nourry, 1924), 515–516; R. Pesch, "The Last Supper and Jesus' Understanding of His Death," *Bible Bhashyam* 3 (1977): 58–75, 64; Danker, *New Age*, 221. See Nelson, *Leadership*, 126 n. 8 for many others. Those who deny Mark as a source include: Eduardo Arens, *The ΗΛΘΟΝ-Sayings in the Synoptic Tradition* (Orbis Biblicus et Orientalis 10; Göttingen: Vandenhoeck and Ruprecht, 1976), 126; Ernest Best, *Disciples and Discipleship: Studies in the Gospel According to Mark* (Edinburgh: Clark, 1986), 148; Ernst, *Evangelium*, 592; Virgil P. Howard, *Das Ego Jesu in den synoptischen Evangelien: Untersuchungen zum Sprachgebrauch Jesus* (Marburg: Elwert, 1975), 231; Vincent Taylor, *The Passion Narrative of St. Luke* (SNTSMS 19; Cambridge: Cambridge University Press, 1972), 62–63; see Nelson, *Leadership*, 127 n. 15 for more.

[52] Nelson, *Leadership*, 125–128. He prefers Soards' numbers, Soards, *Passion*, 42, 31, over those of Ernst, *Evangelium*, 592.

[53] Sydney Page, "The Authenticity of the Ransom Logion (Mark 10:45b)," in *Studies of History and Tradition in the Four Gospels* (GP 1; ed. R. T. France and David Wenham; Sheffield: JSOT Press, 1980), 137–161, 148.

[54] Joachim Jeremias, *The Eucharistic Words of Jesus* (NTL; 3rd ed.; trans. N. Perrin; London: SCM Press, 1966), 98; Nelson, *Leadership*, 128. Luke 6:18–19; 8:19–21 are the

language differences argue against dependence of Luke on Mark, but the similarity in structure and subject lead to the conclusion that Luke and Mark may have built from the same (or a related) source.[55]

Similar disagreement surrounds Luke's dependency on Matthew 19:28, and here it seems that the texts of Luke and Matthew derive from Q.[56] Although only slight connection can be made between Matt 19:28a–b and Luke 22:28–30a, there is enough verbal similarity between 19:28c and 22:30b to suggest a parallel. Similar vocabulary includes καθήσεσθε ἐπι, θρόνων/θρόνου, τὰς δώδεκα φυλὰς, κρίνοντες, and τοῦ Ἰσραήλ. The teaching context seems similar even though the settings differ. In Matthew Peter asks about the recompense the disciples will receive for leaving all to follow Jesus and in Luke Jesus grounds the reception of authority on their allegiance to him. Since Q is a sayings source transposition of the saying from one setting (the story of the rich young ruler in Matt) to another (Last Supper in Luke) does not count against a common source. Nelson concludes that they do derive from a common source because of strong similarity in language which includes important vocabulary. He suggests that the space of non-agreement, Luke 22:29–30a, might hold details of Luke's interpretation of Q.[57] Luke 22:24–30 does not directly depend on Mark or Matthew for its content but it seems likely that he shares a common source in the two pertinent sections.

6.2.2 Linguistic Evidence

This subsection contains many terms which are important to define because of their use in reciprocity and benefaction contexts. Important terms will be taken in the order in which they arise in the narrative and will be grouped according to the verses in which they appear.

The disciples do not seem too far removed from the scribes who aspire for higher status at meals (22:24). Indeed, the topics of honor-shame and status remain at the forefront of the conversation. Φιλονεικία surfaces in discussions of honor-shame and is sometimes translated as "competition for honor." It does not always have negative connotations, but can mean friendly competition, "a more or less neutral exercise in social sport," or "seulement rivalité" (e.g., Aelian *VH* 1.24).[58] But in the NT, LXX, Philo,

---

only other two transpositions to this point. Smith favors a transposition at this point Smith, *Symposium*, 256, 264.

[55] Nelson, *Leadership*, 131.

[56] Richard A. Horsley, "Jesus and Galilee: The Contingencies of a Renewal Movement," in Meyers, *Galilee*, 57–74, 69–70; Reed, *Archaeology*, 176, 209.

[57] Nelson lists several who agree with this claim. Nelson, *Leadership*, 174–176, 179.

[58] Nelson, *Leadership*, 115; BAGD, 860; M. –J. Lagrange, *Évangile selon Saint Luc* (8th ed.; Paris: Gabalda, 1948), 549 which each refer to F. Field, *Notes on the*

and Josephus the predominant meaning is a negative form of debate. Paul contends that his churches will not be φιλόνεικος (1 Cor 11:6). Its five uses in the LXX are all negative (Ezek 3:7; Prov 10:12; 2 Macc 4:4; 4 Macc 1:26; 8:26). Of sixty-seven uses in Philo and Josephus only three are non-negative (Philo *Det.* 45; *Spec. Leg.* 4.111; Josephus *Ant.* 15.290).[59] As the disciples debate their relative positions Luke negatively characterizes their competition as misguided to the point that Jesus must provide correction. The disciples compete over who appears to be the greatest (τὸ τίς αὐτῶν δοκεῖ εἶναι μείζων). Δοκέω indicates a question of appearances which Jesus will address shortly.[60] Most take the comparative μείζων in a superlative sense emphasizing that Luke twice repeats the word in the subsequent explanation (22:26, 27).[61] The fact that Luke repeats the term in Jesus' instruction suggests that he portrays Jesus directly responding to the debate over which of the disciples might be considered μείζων (22:24). The disciples essentially ask who will sit in the highest seat.

Three terms (κυριεύω; εὐεργέτης; καλοῦνται) from 22:25 prove significant in the interpretation of the entire subsection (22:24–34). Luke's use of κυριεύω (cf. ἐξουσιάζω) avoids the difficulty of interpreting the prefixed verbs (κατακυριεύω; cf. κατεξουσιάζω) adopted by Mark (Luke 22:25; Mark 10:42). It is not certain whether κατακυριεύω carries a pejorative tone in all of its uses.[62] Some have adduced a pejorative flavor to the prefixed verb,[63] but the same cannot be said of the un-prefixed verb in Luke.[64]

Translation of the New Testament: Being the Otium Norvicense (Pars Tertia) (Cambridge: University Press, 1899), 75–76.

[59] Nelson, *Leadership*, 142–143.

[60] Plummer, *Luke*, 501; Marshall, *Luke*, 811; Fitzmyer, *Luke*, 2.1416; Nolland, *Luke*, 3.1064.

[61] E.g., Nolland, *Luke*, 3.1064; Stein, *Luke*, 548–549; Fitzmyer, *Luke*, 2.1416; Bock, *Luke*, 2.1736 n. 5 (citing Blass, Debrunner, Funk, §244); Nelson, *Leadership*, 146.

[62] Lull, "Servant-Benefactor," 290–291; Kenneth W. Clark, "The Meaning of [kata]kyrieuein," in *Studies in New Testament Language and Text: Essays in Honour of George D. Kilpatrick on the Occasion of His Sixty-Fifth Birthday* (ed. J. K. Elliott; NovTSup 44; Leiden: Brill, 1976), 100–106, 104; Kenneth Willis Clark, *The Gentile Bias, and Other Essays* (NovTSup 54; Leiden: Brill, 1980), 207–212. Lull ("Servant-Benefactor," 291 n. 18) identifies an interesting chronological aspect of Bauer's lexicon. It is not until Danker took primary editorial responsibilities (BAGD) that the pejorative sense of κατακυριεύω was included. Such is not the case in the fifth edition of Bauer's *Wörterbuch*. In the LXX, κατακυριεύω usually describes either man's dominion over the earth and its beasts (Gen 1:28; 9:1; Num 32:29; Sir 17:4) or God's rule (Num 32:22; Ps 71:8; 109:2; Jer 3:14).

[63] E.g., Freyne, *Galilee and Gospel*, 199; Green, *Luke*, (implied) 767–768; Bock, *Luke*, 2.1737; Johnson, *Luke*, 344.

[64] Green, *Luke*, 767–768; Esler, *Community*, 208; Walaskay, *Political Perspective*, 36; Bock, *Luke*, 2.1737; Johnson, *Luke*, 344 (though his translation "dominate them" does not seem to remove the negative connotations of the prefixed verb).

One should not bring over the possible pejorative use from Mark into Luke. Luke describes kings who lead and others who exercise authority without intending a negative connotation within the verb (κυριεύουσιν) and participle (οἱ ἐξουσιάζοντες) themselves. According to Luke, Jesus intends a critique of Gentile (ἔθνος) leadership,[65] but this does not come out explicitly in this introduction of the kings (22:25).[66] In Luke, Jesus presents the kings of the Gentiles as a foil to which he will offer his own definition of greatness wherein he presents a more direct critique.

The presence of εὐεργέτης makes 22:14–34 a natural candidate for discussions of benefactors and patrons. The term, which arises in the LXX, Josephus, Philo, and throughout the Greco-Roman world, is usually translated "benefactor", but Danker is quick to provide two caveats. First, εὐ᾽εργέτης is not a technical term for benefactor because there was no technical terminology for this ideology.[67] Second, εὐεργέτης need not be present for a person to be described as a benefactor. "The title of this book, Benefactor, therefore has no single referent in Greek or Latin. It denotes rather a depth-structural reality that breaks into various thematic patterns and comes to linguistic expression in numerous modes and forms."[68] With those disclaimers in mind the term (εὐεργέτης) does frequently arise when authors or inscribers intend to identify a benefactor. Danker lists several examples, of which many have already been adduced in the previous chapter (e.g., *Sammelbuch* 8299; Danker, no. 31; *SEG* 8232; *OGIS* 90; *CIG* 3.4697; *SIG*[3] 372; *OGIS* 267; *OGIS* 75–78; Josephus *Ant.* 17.243; see section 2.1.2). Although the term "benefactor" (εὐεργέτης, σωτήρ, ἀνήρ ἀγαθός) sometimes comes in tandem with "patron" (κηδεμών, πάτρων, πατρώνης, προστάτης; section 2.1.4) the parallel does not necessarily imply equivalence.[69] It is inappropriate to jump from the use of εὐεργέτης to a description of patron-client relationships with the implication that *patrocin-*

---

[65] It is unclear to what Jesus refers in his use of ἔθνος, but this does not detract from the critique. Luke uses ἔθνος to describe nations and Gentiles. Fitzmyer compares it to 12:30 and 18:25 where he finds a reference to "pagans" or "heathens." Only one plural use of ἔθνος can be found in Luke-Acts which includes both Israel and the other nations (Luke 24:47), so it seems best to favor "Gentiles" at this point. Fitzmyer, *Luke*, 2.1416. Cf. Stein, *Luke*, 549.

[66] Nelson, *Leadership*, 148; Freyne, *Galilee and Gospel*, 199; Bock, *Luke*, 2.1737; Johnson, *Luke*, 344; Esler, *Community*, 208; Walaskay, *Political Perspective*, 36; Green, *Luke*, 767–768.

[67] Danker, *Benefactor*, 323–324; contra Neyrey, "God, Benefactor and Patron," 471 n. 22.

[68] Danker, *Benefactor*, 27.

[69] E.g., Eilers, *Roman Patrons*, ch. 4, 184–185; J. Nicols, "Civic Patronage in Ancient Rome," (Department of History, University of Oregon, typescript, 1995), 11; Bowditch, *Horace*, 15.

ium is in view.⁷⁰ In the inscriptions which Eilers surveys Greeks in the east use many labels for foreign benefactors (e.g., εὐεργέτης, πρόξενος, σωτήρ), but it is only the Romans for whom they transliterate the title πάτρων.⁷¹ This suggests that Greeks in the east did not fully embrace the title, but saw in it something foreign and particularly Roman.⁷² After Augustus "patron" decreased as a title for the emperor and senators in the east while it dramatically increased in the West (see sections 2.1.2; 2.1.3).⁷³ Ἐυεργέτης remained popular in the east during this time, while "patron" was used five times more frequently in the West than in the East.⁷⁴ For this reason, and the fact that Luke employs only benefaction terms, it is preferable to use benefaction ideology and language in description of this verse (22:25).⁷⁵

Luke seems to use εὐεργέτης without an inherent critique of those who have the title within the term itself. Some scholars suggest instead that Luke uses the title sarcastically to speak of tyrants who mask their tyranny with over-the-top generosity (e.g., Danker, Luce, Nock). Whether Luke uses εὐεργέτης sarcastically or not depends on three factors. First, scholars who claim that Luke rebukes the ascription of this title to the Gentile rulers tend to cite examples of tyrants who were lauded as benefactors (e.g., Albinus, Ptolemy II).⁷⁶ Indeed, "benefactor" would not describe the unani-

---

⁷⁰ E.g., Moxnes, "Patron-Client," 261; cf. Green, *Luke*, 767 n. 87. Neyrey does not specifically address Luke 22:25, but generally equates patron and benefactor throughout his latest article, Neyrey, "God, Benefactor and Patron."

⁷¹ Including "150 specific examples ... in the epigraphy and literature of the late Republic and early empire." Eilers, *Roman Patrons*, 17–18. The only Herodian example is Agrippa I which postdates the ministry of Jesus (*IGLS* 6.2759; cf. *ILS* 3.2.8957). Eilers, *Roman Patrons*, 195.

⁷² Eilers, *Roman Patrons*, 18; cf. John Nicols, "Patrons of Greek Cities in the Early Principate," *ZPE* 80 (1990): 81–108, 81–82. Nicols cites this as widely recognized among classicists. He claims that in the east "εὐεργέτης" or "σωτήρ" appear four times for each instance of "patron" in epigraphical sources. With Tiberius this pattern changed. Hellenistic titles were dropped, but εὐεργέτης remained among the Hellenistic titles adopted for Roman emperors.

⁷³ Nicols, "Patrons of Greek Cities."

⁷⁴ Nicols, "Patrons of Greek Cities, " 83.

⁷⁵ Johnson, *Luke*, 344; Danker, *Benefactor*, 323–324; Bock, *Luke*, 2.1737; Fitzmyer, *Luke*, 2.1416–1417; Plummer, *Luke*, 501.

⁷⁶ The following have been adduced as examples of men/tyrants desiring to be called benefactors with the commentator who identified the man in parenthesis. Albinus in Josephus *Ant.* 20.253 and Security officials in Hieropolis in A.D. 100 (Danker, *Benefactor*, 294); Ptolemy II (Luce, *Luke*, 333; Danker, *New Age*, 348); cf. kings generally without tyrannical undertones in Dio Chrysostom *Or.* 66.2; 75.7–8 (Nock, "Soter and Euergetes," 2.724–725). Self-proclamation as a benefactor was common among both the tyrannical and the benevolent. "Autobiographical" inscriptions in which the rich broadcasted their generosity were quite common (e.g., *OGIS* 383; *IGR* 3.159; *SIG* 814), Danker, *Benefactor*, 42–44.

mous opinion others held of many rulers who had the title ascribed to them. It was demonstrated in the previous chapter, however, that benefactors often earned the title from their subordinates through generosity, and the title did not always, or even usually, mask tyranny (section 2.1.2). One cannot simply draw a connection between a few tyrannical "benefactors" and the benefactors which Jesus presents without other evidence which points in this direction. Second, scholars bring Mark's tone of doubt about the legitimacy of the rulers' claims (Mark 10:42–45) into Luke's narrative (Luke 22:25). Mark refers to the kings as the "so-called" (οἱ δοκοῦντες) kings, and the tone tells of kings who describe themselves as authoritative but in fact are not (Mark 10:42). In describing Luke 22:25, some scholars suggest that these benefactors are not in fact generous but have only described themselves in this way. They suggest that Luke implies the use of οἱ δοκοῦντες as well. But, in the absence of this description (οἱ δοκοῦντες) one should not carry over Mark's doubt about the legitimacy of the claims made about these rulers. In order to determine Luke's intended meaning one should not bring Mark's tone of doubt into Luke's teaching section. Third, scholars who suggest a sarcastic tone interpret καλοῦνται as a reflexive middle rather than passive.[77] These leaders call themselves benefactors, but the people do not agree. However, in line wth many commentators (and most English translations), the passive voice is preferable to the middle. In favor of the passive voice is the fact that of all middle-passive forms of καλέω in Luke-Acts connected to personal nouns (thus capable of the reflexive voice) all are passive.[78] Strong contextual clues would be necessary to depart from Luke's pattern of choosing the passive voice with καλέω. If the passive is preferred then it is others who describe the leaders as benefactors rather than the leaders who describe themselves. Thus, they have earned the title through some extent of generosity. It seems that Jesus uses εὐεργέτης without explicit negative connotations in the term itself. This explains the unqualified use of εὐεργ- terms in Acts. If the category of benefactor itself were objectionable then one would expect a qualifier or

---

[77] Middle/reflexive: Plummer, *Luke*, 501; Green, *Luke*, 768 n. 90; Tannehill, "Kingdom," 21; Creed, *Luke*, 268; Klostermann, *Lukasevangelium*, 211; Danker, *Benefactor*, 294, 484 n. 178; Fitzmyer, *Luke*, 2.1411, 1416–1417. Passive: Bock, *Luke*, 2.1737; Heil, *Meal-Scenes*, 165, 183–184 n. 49; Nelson, *Leadership*, 153–154; Marshall, *Luke*, 812 (uncertain); Nolland, *Luke*, 2.1064, Tannehill, *Luke*, 317; Lull, "Servant-Benefactor," 295–296. Lull claims that the passive is the majority opinion of commentators and English translations, Lull, "Servant-Benefactor," 293. He finds this to be an odd pattern since the passive voice weakens the case of those who claim that benefactor is used as a negative foil for Jesus' program (the consensus view).

[78] 11 texts of 33 total uses of καλέω; Luke 1:60; 6:15; 8:2; 10:39; 19:2; 22:3; Acts 1:23; 7:58; 13:1; 15:22, 37. Nelson, *Leadership*, 153.

explanation when Luke uses the category to describe the activity of the apostles (εὐεργεσία; Acts 4:9) and Jesus (εὐεργετέω; Acts 10:38).[79]

Since Luke provides a contrast to the normal patterns of Gentile rulership in the following verse (22:26) it is important to discuss the precise nature of that contrast. Critical to this discussion is the implied verb to be supplied for the introductory phrase (ὑμεῖς δὲ οὐχ οὕτως). Most scholars supply an imperative (ἔσεσθε or ποίησετε),[80] charging the disciples to avoid the ruling practices of the Gentile leaders. Lull selects an indicative (e.g., καλεῖσθε); Luke thus chastises the disciples for not imitating the Gentile leaders in certain ways.[81] An indicative verb creates a descriptive rather than prescriptive statement. To Lull, the strong contrastive in 22:26b (ἀλλά) contrasts the behavior of the disciples with Jesus' description of Gentile benefactors as a critique. Though Lull's thesis is intriguing, it has not won support from many.[82] When Lull introduced his controversial re-reading of this passage a consensus held that the implied verb in this phrase (ὑμεῖς δὲ οὐχ οὕτως) had imperatival force. In this scenario Jesus commands his audience to reject the ways of kings and benefactors. Nelson argues at length against this proposal and concludes that though οὐ expects an indicative, the indicative has imperatival force. He builds his case by grouping the categories of persons (greatest/leaders/one who reclines; youngest/servant/servant Jesus) and showing that Jesus has contrasted the two categories. By putting himself into the latter category Jesus commends that group and he must have an opposing group with which to contrast.[83] According to Luke, Jesus contrasts his way with the kings and benefactors of the world.

Two terms for loyalty (διαμένω; πίστις) and one for the distribution of authority (διατίθεμαι) help describe the reasoning for granting the disciples authority in the kingdom (22:28–34). Διαμένω can mean "remain" or "continue" in a normal temporal sense (Luke 1:22), but it often carries the meaning of "to remain loyal" in the midst of trials. For example, in Sirach 22:23 the author parallels διαμένω with πίστιν κτῆσαι which indicates the

---

[79] Freyne, *Galilee and Gospel*, 199; idem, *Jesus*, 146–147; Green, *Luke*, 768–769.

[80] E.g., Marshall, *Luke*, 812; Bock, *Luke*, 2.1737; Heil, *Meal Scenes*, 184.

[81] Lull, "Servant-Benefactor," 293–295.

[82] Nelson, *Leadership*, 131–136; idem, "The Flow of Thought in Luke 22:24–27," *JSOT* 43 (1991): 113–123. Scholars may see that Lull's argument has not been adopted in the lack of reference to it in subsequent major commentaries. For example, the commentaries by Bock, Stein, and Nolland (cf. Talbert, Tannehill, Malina and Rohrbaugh) do not mention the article or make much of the potential issue. Nevertheless, Lull's reading provides valuable insights about the culture and provocative challenges to the consensus view.

[83] Nelson, *Leadership*, 131–136; idem, "Flow of Thought in Luke 22:24–27," 113–123.

6.2 Leaders and Disciples (22:24–34)

meaning "faithful to him" in hard times.[84] The prefix (δια) often adds a durative sense to verbs in Koine Greek with a few commentators suggesting that even apart from πειρασμός the term indicates faithfulness through difficulties (Schwierigkeiten).[85] Following his comments on the distribution of power in the kingdom, Jesus addresses Peter and the jeopardization of his faith (πίστις; 22:31–34). Πίστις arises frequently in benefaction and *patrocinium* contexts to denote the allegiance maintained by clients with their superiors (section 2.1.3). Spicq identifies many uses of the term including legal guarantee (*P.Cair.Zen.* 59355, 102, 127; *P.Ryl.* 28, 187), "plighted faith" (*P.Mert.* 32, 2), and "complete loyalty" (*P. Abinn.* 59, 17; 1 Tim 1:5).[86] Fifty-nine uses in the LXX as the "stereotypical rendition of derivatives of אמן" have been translated "faith, faithfulness, honesty" (Deut 32:20; Ps 32:4 LXX; Prov 12:22).[87] The term is in no way unique, therefore, to benefaction and *patrocinium* contexts, though it is quite familiar in those settings.

It is difficult to identify the proper meaning of διατίθεμαι, but it seems that "confer" is the best choice. The verb frequently arises in covenant contexts typically with other covenant vocabulary. At times it stands alone in the LXX as the translation of covenant language.[88] The manuscript witness (at Luke 22:29) mirrors this translation tendency as a few carry διαθηκην (A Θ 579 *pc* sy^h). If a strong notion of covenant were present in this passage this would diminish or perhaps rule out benefaction ideology since by definition benefits are voluntary and not legally prescribed. It is not necessary, however, to see in the simple use of διατίθεμαι the covenant connection especially since specific covenant vocabulary is not coupled with it (cf. Acts 3:25).[89] The use of the verb to describe both Jesus' relation

---

[84] Cf. 12:15; 22:23; 27:4; 40:17; 44:11; *Diodor* 14.48.4; Ignatius, *Trall.* 12.2. See, Nelson, *Leadership*, 182–185; cf. Plummer, *Luke*, 502.

[85] A. T. Robertson, *A Grammar of the Greek New Testament in the Light of Historical Research* (Nashville: Broadman Press, 1934), 562–563; James Hope Moulton and Wilbert F. Howard, *A Grammar of New Testament Greek* (vol. 2.; *Accidence and Word-Formation*; Edinburgh: Clark, 1986), 268–269, 300–302; Willibald Bösen, *Jesusmahl, eucharistisches Mahl, Endzeitmahl ein Beitrag zur Theologie des Lukas* (Stuttgarter Bibelstudien 97; Stuttgart: Katholisches Bibelwerk, 1980), 138; Nelson, *Leadership*, 184 n. 43; William Hendriksen, *The Gospel of Luke* (Edinburgh: Banner of Truth Trust, 1979), 979; Plummer, *Luke*, 502.

[86] Spicq, *Lexicon*, "πίστις" 110–116.

[87] Lust, *Lexicon* (2003), 493. There are eighty-eight uses of πιστεύω and seventy-five of πιστός.

[88] In the LXX, 76 of 87 instances (87%) occur with διαθήκη. Sometimes even without διαθήκη the verb means to make a covenant (1 Chron. 19:19; 2 Chron 5:10; 7:18; Ezek 16:30), Nelson, *Leadership*, 200.

[89] It may be important that Jesus uses covenant language earlier in the discussion (22:20), but it must be emphasized that he does not repeat that language at this point.

to God and Jesus' relation to his disciples makes the other two main meanings (to covenant, to will) awkward and not preferable. It would be unique in the NT to describe Jesus' relationship to God as a covenant, and it would be slightly odd to need Jesus' death to bequeath the kingdom as in a will (but, cf. Heb 9:16, 17).[90] By default and in light of the context, "confer" seems to be the most appropriate translation.[91] It would not alter the meaning greatly to choose "bequeath" over "confer" since benefactors often granted authority to subordinates at their deaths (e.g., Herod I).

No vocabulary specific to *patrocinium* arises in this passage. Terms identifying patrons, clients, the nature of that relationship, or the objects exchanged are absent. In the absence of technical vocabulary it is best to restrict the interpretation of the passage, and description of its cultural setting, to benefaction and reciprocity.

6.2.3 Cultural Matters

This subsection of Luke has garnered attention in discussions of *patrocinium* and benefaction especially in regard to how these ideologies relate to the conferment of kingdoms. It is often assumed that patrons distributed, often from obligation, kingdoms to their clients. This assumption has been recently overturned. In Roman culture the distribution of kingdoms was called *suffragium*.[92] In Hellenistic culture, benefactors conferred kingdoms on their clients. In Jewish culture the conferment of kingdoms was the prerogative of God which human authorities sometimes usurped. The following paragraphs elaborate these points.

In a recent investigation of over 150 inscriptions and literary pieces on the subject, Eilers demonstrates that the conferment of kingdoms fell into the category of *suffragium* rather than *patrocinium* among the Romans.[93] He suggests that the modern error of attributing the conferment of kingdoms to the hands of patrons results from a misunderstanding of Roman *patrocinium* and the mistaken blending of Roman and modern Western notions of patronage. As he discusses the nuances necessary in

---

[90] Those who consider the transaction as similar to bequeathing in a will include: Fitzmyer, *Luke*, 2.1419; Irénée Fransen, "Cahier de Bible: Le baptême de sang (Luc 22,1–23, 56)," *BVC* 25 (1959): 20–28, 25; Jacob Jervell, *Luke and the People of God* (Minneapolis: Augsburg, 1972), 79; Klostermann, *Lukasevangelium*, 212; K. Kuhn, "New Light on Temptation, Sin and Flesh in the New Testament," in *The Scrolls and the New Testament* (ed. Krister Stendahl; London: SCM Press, 1958), 94–113, 112; William S. Kurz, *Farewell Addresses in the New Testament* (Zacchaeus Studies New Testament; Collegeville: Liturgical, 1990), 64; Lull, "Servant-Benefactor," 301; Rienecker, *Lukas*, 504; Schneider, *Lukas*, 2.451; Tannehill, "Study," 202.

[91] Nelson, *Leadership*, 198–205.

[92] Eilers, *Roman Patrons*, 3–4.

[93] Eilers, *Roman Patrons*, esp. 1–18.

understanding Roman *patrocinium* he distinguishes several forms of contemporary (modern Western) patronage for which the Roman world had a similar practice which did not fall under the category of *patrocinium*. Among these practices is the distribution of kingdoms to worthy rulers. Modern westerners call "patronage" the practice of appointing someone special authority in public service, and the Romans practiced such appointing as well. But they never called the parties involved *patronus* and *cliens* respectively, nor did they refer to the practice as *patrocinium* or *patronatus*.[94] The conferment of kingdoms in Roman culture was called *suffragium*. No evidence assumes that patrons were expected to provide *suffragium* for *cliens*, nor that those who provided *suffragium* were referred to as *patroni*.[95]

Many have said previously that Jesus functions as a patron because patrons doled out offices for clients as part of that relationship. This is mistaken for two reasons. First, the vocabulary of *patrocinium* is lacking from Luke. Benefaction vocabulary is present, but the vocabulary of benefaction should not be assumed to be synonymous with the language of *patrocinium*.[96] Second, patrons in the Roman world did not confer kingdoms upon clients as an expression of *patrocinium*. If Luke intended to present Jesus rebuking or following a Roman system he would have needed to adopt the language of *suffragium*, but he has not. *Patrocinium* is an incorrect category through which to interpret Jesus' conferment of authority in the kingdom.

Eilers' work confirms the earlier work of Braund who argues that the Roman world preferred the ideology of friendship to *patrocinium* in discussions of the distribution of power.[97] Classicists frequently comment on the relative absence of "client" language in the ancient sources. Braund notices a trend in the sources to prefer the use of friendship terminology over that of client terminology. Braund, and others, interpret the absence of client language to the sympathy of patrons for their subordinates. In attempting to reduce the potentially shameful result of being known as a "client" (read: subordinate), patrons adopted the language of social equals, i.e., friendship. In order to maintain good standing with their superiors, "client-kings," as they are commonly referred to, were obliged to cultivate and sustain friendships with their superiors (φιλίας; *Ant*. 15.162, 189). Thus, Braund prefers the moniker "friendly king" over "client-king." The broader category of friendship is preferable to the more limiting category

---

[94] Eilers, *Roman Patrons*, 3–4.

[95] Eilers, *Roman Patrons*, 4.

[96] Contra Neyrey, "God, Benefactor and Patron," 471 n. 22; Malina and Rohrbaugh, *Social Science Commentary*, 316.

[97] Braund, *Friendly King*, 5–7, 23; cf. Verboven, *Economy*.

of *patrocinium*.⁹⁸ Eilers notices the same absence of "client" terms in the ancient sources, but explains this absence differently. He argues that client language is absent not because it was potentially shameful, some clients inscribed their status as a point of honor on their epitaphs,⁹⁹ but because it was not the social relationship through which kings received kingdoms. The broader category of friendship is preferable because the category of *patrocinium* is historically inaccurate. Both authors agree that *patrocinium* is poorly chosen for the further reason that it is potentially confused with the sociological concept of patron-client.¹⁰⁰ The broader, Hellenistic category of benefaction is appropriate in discussions of the conferment of kingdoms.

Benefactors conferred kingdoms on their subordinates. One benefaction that benefactors might bestow upon a subordinate was the conferment of a kingdom. This was seen in Augustus' granting of Herod authority over Palestine and the title of king (*Ant.* 15.109, 189–193; 14.280; *War* 1.226; 2.215). These local rulers could be granted a place of authority, without being granted the title of "king." For example, it is widely known that Antipas never earned the title of "king", despite his attempt to gain it, though he did receive a realm over which he might rule (*Ant.* 18.242–245; section 3.2.2). The story of Archelaos traveling to Rome to receive a kingdom is another example of a local ruler approaching his benefactor in order to obtain the conferment of a kingdom ('Αρχελάῳ δὲ τὴν βασιλείαν χαριζόμενος; *Ant.* 17.188; 17.230–239). Archelaos later lost the trust of Rome and was deposed. It is possible that Jesus used familiarity with these political figures in order to cast his own vision of the kingdom.

To refer to benefactors and benefaction is historically more accurate than to refer to *patrocinium* when discussing the conferment of kingdoms. Luke's use of εὐεργέτης to describe those in authority over the Gentile kings corresponds with the language of benefaction. It is inappropriate to draw into the discussion notions of *patrocinium* since this vocabulary is absent. The adoption of *patrocinium* by Jesus to describe the conferment of kingdoms would have been historically inaccurate. This mistake would have been excaberated by the fact that *patrocinium* was not discovered in Galilee or Jerusalem in the early first-century. If Luke had ascribed to Jesus the use of *patrocinium* language he would have presumably imposed

---

⁹⁸ Verboven arrives at a similar conclusion, but he focuses on sociological patron-client relations for the rest of his study. He laments the confusion which arises from the indiscriminate use of sociological and Roman patron-client language. Verboven, *Economy*, 9–12.

⁹⁹ Eilers, *Roman Patrons*, 15–16.

¹⁰⁰ Braund, *Friendly King*, 5–7, 23; Eilers, *Roman Patrons*, 3–5; cf. Verboven, *Economy*, 9–11, 50.

6.2 Leaders and Disciples (22:24–34)

his own culture upon Jesus'. Jesus' use of benefaction language does not encounter these two problems. By employing εὐεργέτης rather than κηδεμών, πάτρων, πατρώνης, or προστάτης, Luke refers to the Hellenistic system of benefaction rather than Roman *patrocinium*. It was shown (see section 2.1.2) that Roman authorities were described as "common benefactors" ('Ρωμαῖοι οἱ κοινοὶ εὐεργέται) by the Hellenistic, eastern constituents of the empire. Palestine, being in the east, would have adopted this verbiage in description of Rome as well (e.g., Lysimachus *SIG*^{3} 372; Eumenes *OGIS* 267; Ptolemy III *OGIS* 75–78), although those regions in Palestine more heavily influenced by Judaism would have had more important paradigms for describing outsiders. The conferment of kingdoms could be understood in the first-century eastern empire under the Hellenstic category of benefaction. The role of the benefactor was "fundamental to the Greek conception of a king" (Aristostle *Pol* 1310b34ff, 1286b10f; Polybius 5.11.6).[101] Benefaction was detected in Jerusalem in both literary and archaeological evidence (see section 2.2.4). Luke adopts the correct category to describe the conferment and he has not imposed (erroneously) a practice which did not exist in first-century Palestine (i.e., *patrocinium*).

Granting kingdoms in Jewish culture was solely the prerogative of God. Throughout the LXX God puts leaders on thrones and takes them down according to his own reasons and for his own purposes (1 Sam 10:24; Prov 8:15–16; Dan 2:37–38; 5:21; Sir 10:4; 17:17; *Ep. Arist.* 224; Isa 41:2–4; 45:1–7; Jer 27:5–6; Rom 13:1–7; cf. 1 *Enoch* 46:5; 2 *Apoc. Bar.* 82:9; *Ant.* 6.131; *War* 2.140).[102] Usurping this role of God would have been a grave sin. It is therefore startling when Luke declares Jesus' authority to grant positions of importance in the kingdom.[103] Jesus' claim to have a kingdom flows with earlier suggestions to this end as well as development of this theme in the rest of Luke's two volumes (Luke 1:32–33; 19:11–27, 28–40; 22:69; 23:42; Acts 2:33–36). Luke claims that God has granted Jesus authority, implicitly because of Jesus' loyalty to God. The comparative καθὼς perhaps includes both the action (conferment of kingdom) and the basis (loyalty) though this may stretch its capacity.

The structure of authority appears similar to the sort of hierarchy attested in benefaction contexts. Jesus gains authority on account of his allegiance to the supreme authority, God. His faithfulness is rewarded.

---

[101] Erskine, "Common Benefactors," 71.

[102] James D. G. Dunn, *Romans 9–16* (WBC 38b; Waco: Word, 1988), 761; W. Schrage, *Die Christen und der Staat nach dem Neuen Testament* (Gütersloh: Güterslohr, 1971), 14–28; J. Friederich, W. Pöhlmann, and P. Stuhlmacher, "Zur historischen Situation und Intention von Röm 13:1–7," *ZTK* 73 (1976): 131–166, 145–146.

[103] Fitzmyer, *Luke*, 1418–1419; A. George, "La royauté de Jésus selon l'évangile de Luc?" *ScEccl* 14 (1962): 57–69.

Similarly, the apostles' allegiance to Jesus throughout his life is reciprocated by the granting of authority. Loyalty leads to advancement in the kingdom. As Herod I demonstrated his loyalty to Antony (before Augustus) and his general pattern of being loyal to his superiors, with the result that he was granted kingly rule over Palestine (*Ant.* 15.189–193; see sections 3.1.1; 3.1.2), so Jesus grants authority to his disciples who have expressed loyalty to him during his life. There is similarity in the fact that loyalty leads to the conferment of a kingdom. There is a difference, however, in the origin of that authority. In Jewish culture only God possessed the authority and right to confer kingdoms. Jesus recognizes this authority in his critique of the benefactors and kings of his day. He critiques those benefactors and kings, in part, for assuming God's role as distributor of authority.

6.2.4 Conclusion

In Luke, the competition for honor affords Jesus the opportunity to present a two-fold critique of persons of high status and also a two-fold counter-proposal of greatness in his new community (22:24). The apostles adopt this Hellenistic way of thinking at least in part and Jesus responds with a two-fold critique. According to Luke, Jesus first critiques the manner of leadership undertaken by these kings. Then he critiques the source of their authority. I suggest that Luke first presents the two examples (kings and benefactors) and then offers a short rebuttal to each in the subsequent paragraphs. The critique of kings (22:25a) comes in 22:26–27 and the critique of benefactors (22:25b) can be found in 22:28–30.

Luke depicts Jesus denouncing the typical Hellenistic conception of status and growing in honor by reminding his audience of how they operate and offering a counter-example in his own lifestyle (22:25a, 26–27). Jesus proposes that the greatest in his community will forego high-status positions and instead adopt lower status positions and functions (22:26b–27). In a society in which increased age corresponded with increased status the call to adopt a position like the youngest corresponds to a willing denial of status.[104] Jesus commands his disciples to be like the youngest (γινέσθω ὡς ὁ νεώτερος; 22:26). The highest status person willingly assumes the position of lowest rank. He adds to this a command that those who lead ought to be like servants (ὁ ἡγούμενος ὡς ὁ διακονῶν). Kings rule and their authority in the ancient world often went unquestioned. Their social position gained for them the privilege to be waited upon constantly by teams of servants. But Jesus' community functions differently. Those who lead willingly take the low function of service. They deny the normal

---

[104] See Nelson, *Leadership*, 36–43.

6.2 Leaders and Disciples (22:24–34)

pattern of ruling others in order to serve them. According to Luke, rather than exercising rule over others in order to be publicly recognized as such, Jesus instructs the disciples willingly to take a humble manner of leading.

To ensure that the topic of greatness has not been abandoned, Luke has Jesus offer a second comparison (22:27). In this comparison he blends status and authority in both his critique and his counterproposal. His rhetorical question expects to receive the commonplace answer (τίς γὰρ μείζων). Those who are greatest in the world's eyes are those who recline at the table rather than those who serve (22:27a). But Jesus has redefined true status and authority in his own life. He willingly adopts the position of servant and thus offers a new model of greatness and leadership. He willingly adopts the lowest status and acts as a servant. Some debate surrounds this self-description since he stands as the teacher and thus high-status person at the table. There is no explicit service, it is sometimes argued, mentioned in the passage. But Jesus' description of his self-sacrifice and his distribution of the Passover meal may qualify as acts of service.[105] It is this mixture of leadership (presiding over the meal; instructing others) and service (sacrifice; serving) which transforms the nature of leadership from leading to gain prominence, privilege, and power to instead serving others humbly, through persecution, and awaiting God's reciprocation.

The second point of contrast Jesus makes, according to Luke, is with the benefactors who stand in authority over the kings of the Gentiles (22:28–30). Scholars generally assume that οἱ βασιλεῖς and οἱ ἐξουσιάζοντες refer to the same group of people, but it seems possible that this is not necessarily so. Jesus responds to a discussion of greatness as he has several times in Luke's gospel already. A mood of jockeying for greater status pervades and with that an awareness of various steps up the social ladder. There are a few clues elsewhere in Luke-Acts that suggest familiarity with the Greco-Roman hierarchy and the pattern of superiors granting positions of authority upon their subordinates. (1) Luke situates his narrative in Greco-Roman history with reference not only to local rulers (e.g. Herod I, Herod Antipas, Agrippa I, Agrippa II), but also the emperors of the day (e.g., Augustus [2:1], Tiberius [3:1]; cf. additional mentions of "Caesar" not found in other Gospels 23:2; Acts 17:7; 25:8, 10, 11, 12, 21; 26:32; 27:24; 28:19). In the three chronological locators in the opening chapters Luke mentions not only the superior but at least one subordinate (1:5; 2:1–2; 3:1). In the latter two, one finds the emperor and his local governors or tetrarchs mentioned. (2) When describing the trials of Jesus and Paul, Luke includes facts about different jurisdictions and demonstrates awareness of various levels of authority. After failing to find worthy cause for accusa-

---

[105] For the former view see Sloan, "Reciprocity," 63–64. For the latter view see Lull, "Servant Benefactor," 298.

tion and learning of Jesus' Galilean origins, Pilate sends Jesus to Herod, tetrarch of Galilee, for further interrogation (Luke 23:4–7). Luke mentions the succession of Festus after Felix and then includes details about trial in Jerusalem or before Caesar (24:26; 25:9–12).[106] (3) The parable about the nobleman going into a far country to receive a kingdom resembles the statements Jesus makes in this passage (19:11–27). Recall that Josephus describes the distribution of Herod's kingdom to Archelaos as a benefaction (χαριζόμενος; *Ant.* 17.188). Luke apparently was aware of the bestowal of kingdoms by benefactors upon people of noble (εὐγενής; Herodian?) birth. In the Lukan passage Jesus' critiques stem primarily from the fact that the Herodian ruler-to-be had gained his position from human authority rather than God's authority. Precisely the same critique appears to be in view at 22:24–30. These clues do not unquestionably affirm the suggested reading of 22:25, but they at least open up the possibility of a rebuke of the Greco-Roman hierarchy.

With that background in mind it seems possible that Luke presents three steps on this social ladder in his rebuke of Gentile authority (22:25). There are common-folk Gentiles who stand at the bottom rung (τὸ ἔθνος). Above them are the kings who rule over them (οἱ βασιλεῖς). Above the kings are those in authority who are called benefactors (οἱ ἐξουσιάζοντες... εὐ᾽εργέται καλοῦνται). The referent of the second αὐτῶν would thus not be the Gentiles, but the kings who rule over the Gentiles (22:25b). These authority figures are called (καλοῦνται) benefactors in part because they dole out positions of authority, namely kingship. Being in a position to grant kingdoms increased one's social status. It thus placed a person on a higher rung. On top of this social ladder stood the emperors who had granted Herodian authority (including kingship) in Palestine for much of Jesus' life (e.g., Augustus, Tiberius). Erskine demonstrates the prevalence of "common benefactors" as a description of Rome by people living in the east (section 2.1.2).[107]

The regional and personality investigations in chapters 2 and 3 of this book demonstrate the plausibility that a first-century Jew from Galilee could have understood such relationships and language. For example, Josephus' description of Agrippa I in similar terms (πρὸς πάντας τὸ εὐερ᾽γετικὸν ὅμοιον τοῖς ἀλλοεθνέσιν ἦν φιλάνθρωπος [*Ant.* 19.330]) demonstrates that a first-century Jew from Palestine could adopt this terminology (section 3.4.6). Herod Antipas was described as a benefactor in Tiberias and a visit to Jerusalem would expose a Galilean to Herod I or his benefac-

---

[106] It may be worth mentioning that in the subsequent paragraph Jesus singles Peter out as a leader among the other disciples which implies a sort-of hierarchy. In light of the preceding text (22:24–27) this would be a service-based hierarchy.

[107] Erskine, "Common Benefactors."

6.2 Leaders and Disciples (22:24–34)

tions (see sections 2.2.3; 2.2.4; 3.1; 3.2). The common people recognized these leaders as having ultimate authority and would describe them as benefactors as a form of public praise.[108] The accolade ("common benefactor") attested allegiance among the Gentiles toward the emperor or his vice-regents. The people showed loyalty to these benefactors in order that they might be looked upon favorably as well. Luke need not import his own cultural influences to present Jesus' teaching in terms of benefaction because they existed to a certain degree in first-century Palestine.

According to Luke, Jesus counters this situation with his theologically focused hierarchy (22:28–30). He begins by emphasizing the loyalty his disciples have shown toward him. He emphasizes their counter-cultural allegiances by placing ὑμεῖς in the first position. The Gentiles show allegiance to the emperor and his kings, but the disciples have shown allegiance to Jesus. Διαμένω can carry connotations of loyalty and allegiance though even its normal usage gets at the point of saying that they have chosen his path over against the easy way of compromise (section 6.1.2). Luke emphasizes that Jesus has been the recipient of the loyalty by repeating the first person pronoun six times in the three verses (μετ' ἐμοῦ; μου; μοι; μου; μου; μου; 22:28–30).[109] They have not shown loyalty to the Gentile kings and authority figures, but have instead directed their loyalty toward Jesus. In response to such loyalty Jesus assumes the position of benefactor and grants benefactions.

In this role, he will confer onto the disciples a kingdom, a position at his table, and authority to judge the twelve tribes of Israel (22:29–30). Since authority to grant kingdoms in the Jewish world starts and stops with God, the Gentile kings are in error for thinking that they can confer kingdoms upon one another. But by assuming this authority, Jesus also departs from the Jewish pattern. He claims to have received authority from God to grant authority to others. He effectively replaces the Greco-Roman hierarchy of his day with a theological hierarchy wherein God grants him authority and he grants the apostles authority in the kingdom of God. Mirroring the social hierarchy presented in 22:25, Luke has Jesus suggest a new theological hierarchy consisting of the father, himself, and his disciples (22:29). Luke connects 22:28 and 22:29 with a consecutive καί bringing the first verse in as the grounds for the action in the next.[110] Because of the loyalty the dis-

---

[108] A widely cited example describes Augustus: "Divine Augustus Caesar, son of a god, imperator of land and sea, the benefactor and savior of the whole world." David C. Braund, *Augustus to Nero: A Sourcebook on Roman History. 31 BC –AD 68* (London: Crook Helm, 1985), §66.

[109] Cf. Plummer, *Luke*, 502; Marshall, *Luke*, 816; Fitzmyer, *Luke*, 2.1418; S. Brown, *Apostasy and Perseverance in the Theology of Luke* (AnBib 36; Rome: Biblical Institute, 1969), 62–74.

[110] Nelson, *Leadership*, 198; Lull, "Servant-Benefactor," 301.

ciples have shown to Jesus, he reciprocates by conferring a kingdom on them. He had received a kingdom from the father, implicitly because of his loyalty in the midst of trials. Now he imitates the father's action from his authoritative position. Καθώς in this passage carries both causal and comparative nuance. Jesus receives a kingdom from the father and thus can bestow a kingdom on the disciples.[111] But his action also resembles his father in kind. The father takes the highest position, having authority to bestow a kingdom upon Jesus. He functions as a benefactor who grants kingdoms upon those who show loyalty. Likewise, Jesus functions as a benefactor who bestows a kingdom upon those who show loyalty to him. The disciples had desired at the beginning of their discussion to attain the type of positions and status held by kings and benefactors. Jesus provides the positions they desired by giving them a kingdom. But they do not, like Herod and others, gain this position through loyalty to the Greco-Roman benefactors (typically the emperor), but instead through loyalty to the true benefactors, God and Jesus.

In Luke, Jesus further elaborates upon the subject of status by explaining the status-elevating result of the conferral of his kingdom (22:30). At table the disciples argued over relative status, who seemed to be the greatest, which would naturally take the form of table locations and dinner invitations. Jesus connects the conferral of kingdoms with invitation to the ultimate table event. The ἵνα-clause shows the result of the conferral of the kingdom. Because the disciples have received a kingdom they can sit at Jesus' table in his kingdom. He potentially replaces a desire among the disciples to sit at the local Palestinian kingdom table, or perhaps he simply reorients their priorities to value the Messianic table over earthly tables. To further emphasize the superiority of this table and the relative status and position granted in this transaction Luke adds the second clause (καὶ καθήσεσθε ἐπὶ θρόνων τὰς δώδεκα φυλὰς κρίνοντες τοῦ Ἰσραήλ). Not only will they receive a place at the Messianic table, but they will also receive thrones upon which they may judge (κρίνοντες)[112] the twelve tribes of Israel. Authority has not been cast aside, but instead it has been recast in

---

[111] In favor of causal, Nelson identifies Lagrange, *Luc*, 551 Jürgen Roloff, *Apostolat – Verkündigung – Kirche: Ursprung, Inhalt und Funktion des kirchlichen Apostelamtes nach Paulus, Lukas und den Pastoralbriefen* (Gütersloh: Mohn, 1965), 188; Ingo Broer, "Das Ringen der Gemeinde um Israel: Exegetischer Versuch über Mt 19,28," in *Jesus und der Menschensohn: Festschrift für A. Vögtle* (ed. R. Pesch and R. Schnackenburg; Freiburg: Herder, 1975), 148–165, 150. In favor of the comparative, Nelson identifies G. Schneider, *Das Evangelium nach Lukas* (Ökumenischer Taschenbuchkommentar zum Neuen Testament 3/1–2; Gütersloh: Mohn, 1977), 2.451; Marshall, *Luke*, 816; Nelson, *Leadership*, 199.

[112] Whether κρίνοντες carries rule, condemnation, or other overtones in this use is not pertinent to the discussion.

6.2 Leaders and Disciples (22:24–34)

terms of service and Jesus' authority. They will not receive status or authority through allegiance to the Greco-Roman and Herodian leadership, instead they will receive status and authority by continuing in loyalty to Jesus. The status and authority Jesus offers supersedes that of the Greco-Roman and Herodian leadership because it involves the kingdom, table, and thrones of God. The disciples should not call "benefactors" those who stand above the Gentile kings because that is not the hierarchy they ought to care about. Jesus objects to the normal practice of calling those who rule over the kings "benefactors" because it assumes the wrong hierarchy (22:25). Rather, they ought to stay focused, as they have already shown (22:28), on the theological hierarchy wherein God and Jesus sit atop the ladder as benefactors and those who show loyalty to them may receive a kingdom.

Though Luke does not directly mention any specific kings or benefactors it would be plausible that for Jesus to have some from the Herodian family and/or an emperor past or present in mind. Being in Jerusalem, with the temple overwhelming the landscape and conversations of most residents, would have made Herod I a topic of conversation. His grandest monument stood in part as a tribute to his benefactors as well as a plea to be regarded as a benefactor himself among the Jerusalemites. Augustus had granted Herod authority as king over all the land (*Ant.* 15.109, 189–193; 14.280; *War* 1.226; 2.215; section 3.1.2) and Herod reciprocated appropriately in many different construction projects (see sections 3.1.4, 3.1.6). His son Antipas might also have been a topic of conversation among the disciples (and pilgrims) since he had recently reconstructed Tiberias and had a reputation in Galilee and the diaspora as a benefactor (see sections 3.2.4, 3.2.6). With Tiberias, Antipas attempted to express loyalty to his own benefactor (Tiberius) and to establish himself as a benefactor among the local population (e.g., *Ant.* 18.37–38). Tiberius had confirmed his position as tetrarch and the loyal recipient reciprocated appropriately. Jesus' disciples from Philip's territory may have been immediately drawn to think of their local governor. It is possible that Philip began his constructions in honor of Livia-Julia at precisely the time Jesus and his disciples ventured into Jerusalem (see sections 3.3.4, 3.3.5, 3.3.6). Philip honored the benefactor (Julia's husband Augustus) who gave him his position of authority through coins and temples (sections 3.3.4, 3.3.5).

If Luke uses βασιλεύς in its technical sense then only Herod I is a plausible candidate. Only he attained this precise title. The others attempted to gain this honor, but failed to receive it. Another argument in favor of Herod I is the fact that he did rule some "Gentile" areas as king. Iturea, Gaulanitis, Trachonitis, Idumea, and Samaria may have been considered non-Jewish by different factions in Palestine and Herod's rule may have been thought of as kingship of the Gentiles. Freyne considers Antipas (or Pilate) as good candidates because of the critique of the local rulers found in Acts 4:26–27.[113] If Tiberias were thought of as well-endowed with Gentile residents this would bolster his candidacy, but since only small numbers of Gentiles resided in the new city this argument should not be used (see section 2.2.3 *Tiberias*). Without explicit mention of a specific person it seems best to conclude that he makes a general critique of Gentile rulers.

Following his explanation of the new sort of functions Jesus' disciples ought to pursue (service) and the new source of authority and status (loyalty to God and Jesus), another concern for the allegiance of Jesus' disciples allows Luke opportunity to reinforce the importance of staying loyal to Jesus (22:31–34). In Luke, Jesus prefaces his prophecy of Peter's stumbling with assurance that his loyalty will return and he in turn can solidify the loyalties of the others. Jesus warns the apostle that Satan desires to sift the group (ὑμᾶς τοῦ σινιάσαι; 22:31). Apparently through trials Satan hopes to undermine their faith. Jesus assures the apostle that he has prayed for the perseverance of his faithfulness (ἵνα μὴ ἐκλίπῃ ἡ πίστις σου; 22:32a). After his brief stumble, Peter should turn to strengthen the resolve of the others (στήρισον τοὺς ἀδελφούς σου; 22:32b). Luke's addition of this preface to the story of Peter's denial illuminates his theme of loyalty in the midst of trials. When Peter endures trials in Acts it becomes clear that Jesus' prayer has been heard (Acts 5:18; 12:3). Since loyalty leads to exaltation in Jesus' kingdom and a position of authority over the tribes of Israel, Peter's allegiance earns him an important spot in the new community.

6.3 Conclusions for the Last Supper (Luke 22:14–34)

Many scholars have interpreted Luke 22:14–34 in terms of benefaction and *patrocinium*. It is appropriate to use the category of benefaction for its interpretation (e.g., Lull, Green, Freyne, Danker, Ahn), but inappropriate to interpret in terms of *patrocinium* (e.g., Sloan, Moxnes, Tannehill). Luke presents Jesus following the pattern of a benefactor extending himself to the point of self-endangerment for the sake of (ὑπὲρ ὑμῶν) benefiting his clients (*SIG* 762; Lysias 6.40–41). Jesus' self-endangerment, by interpreting it in terms of the Passover sacrifice, potentially carries salvific effect. His death may be interpreted as a Passover benefit. Elsewhere in Luke, the

---

[113] Freyne, *Galilee and Gospel*, 199–200. Freyne partially builds a case for Antipas based on a historical reconstruction of Antipas' reputation for ruthlessness. In light of Jensen's more tempered analysis of Antipas (e.g., Jensen, *Antipas*, 251–259), one may consider Freyne slightly overconfident in his assertion.

death of Jesus is related to the provision of forgiveness and amnesty, two benefactions provided by benefactors (e.g., *SIG* 495.165–189; *OGIS* 90; Danker nos. 29, 43). Those who recognize this benefaction properly respond by memorializing it (ἀνάμνησιν). Remembering words were important in benefaction inscriptions because this was one form of gratitude and reciprocity (*OGIS* 666; *OGIS* 213.23–31; *Choix* 50.14–16; cf. Acts 24:2–4, 5–8; 22:14–23). The betrayer's disloyalty is set in stark contrast to the generosity of the benefactor. Such ingratitude was a cardinal sin. The betrayal stands out as a publicly shameful expression of ingratitude from which the disciples are quick to distance themselves.

When a contest for honor (φιλονεικία) instigates a response by Jesus he provides a description of a new form of benefaction and leadership for his disciples (22:24–34). Luke uses κυριεύω and εὐεργέτης without explicit negative connotations initially (22:25). He does not use the potentially pejorative prefixed form κατακυριεύω, nor does he insert a qualifier (e.g., οἱ δοκοῦντες) to inform his audience that he intends sarcasm in identifying the "benefactors." His critique of those categories comes in the following explanation (22:26–30). Ἐυεργέτης was a commonly ascribed term for benefactors in the ancient world, even if it was not a technical term (*Sammelbuch* 8299; Danker, no. 31; *SEG* 8232; *OGIS* 90; *CIG* 3.4697; *SIG*³ 372; *OGIS* 267; *OGIS* 75–78; Josephus *Ant*. 17.243). Ἐυεργέτης is not a synonym for *patronus* (contra Neyrey), and, furthermore, there is no explicit vocabulary of *patrocinium* found in the entire section. The unqualified use of εὐεργεσία and εὐεργετέω in Acts 4:9 and 10:38 suggests that it is not the category of "benefactor" which is critiqued but its improper adoption (cf. Danker, Freyne, Lull).[114] Luke's critique of benefactors and kings is two-fold. First, Jesus critiques the manner of leadership expressed by the kings. Rather than ruling, Jesus' disciples must serve. In this they imitate Jesus, the greatest among them who serves. Second, Jesus critiques the source of Gentile authority and the hierarchy which follows. Rather than adopting the hierarchy of his day with the emperor on top and Herodian or Roman leaders on the second tier, Jesus presents a new hierarchy with God on top, Jesus as a mediator, and the apostles on the third rung. From this new hierarchy the disciples receive honor as they had hoped to gain, but from a different source (God rather than society) and in a different society (Jesus' table rather than earthly tables). They receive this honor precisely because they have been loyal to Jesus in the midst of trials. This contrasts with the loyalty others showed toward Herodian and Roman leaders. It is expected that the disciples will persist in this loyalty,

---

[114] Gardner's argument that Onias III held the title εὐεργέτης while maintaining his reputation as zealous for the law, i.e., upstanding Jew, may be relevant at this point. Gardner, "Jewish Leadership," 330–332.

and when they falter Jesus' intercession will strengthen them. By imitating Jesus who extended himself to the point of self-endangerment as an act of service, the disciples follow the endangered benefactor model provided by Jesus (cf. Danker). In this respect the disciples function as benefactors though without salvific benefits to provide.

It is inappropriate to interpret this passage in terms of *patrocinium* for several reasons. First, the specific vocabulary of *patrocinium* is absent from the episode. Without specific terminology it cannot be determined that Jesus adopts *patrocinium* as an interpretive paradigm. Second, *patrocinium* is not the proper category through which Romans understood the distribution of kingdoms. *Suffragium* was the category employed to speak of conferring kingdoms. Third, Greeks in the east properly differentiated the use of various terms reserving the title *patronus* to Romans. No ruler in Palestine, before Agrippa I, has been connected to this title in archaeological or literary sources. Fourth, Greeks in the east often referred to their Roman rulers as "common benefactors" ('Ρωμαῖοι οἱ κοινοὶ εὐεργέται). Even if the language of *patrocinium* were appropriate in this context, which is unlikely, Erskine has shown that Greeks in the east preferred to employ categories familiar to them (e.g., benefactor) in praising their Roman leaders. Therefore the language of benefaction is more appropriate in discussing the rule experienced by Jesus and the twelve in Palestine. A first-century Jew living in the Roman east would have preferred the language of benefaction over *patrocinium* in describing his overlords. He may have referred to a specific Roman as *patronus*, but would not have referred to a non-Roman with this term. However, even a Roman would preferably be referred to as a benefactor rather than *patronus* since this terminology was more familiar in the east.

Therefore Luke appropriately prioritizes Jewish matters and when venturing outside of Judaism prefers benefaction ideology. A first-century Jew from Galilee would have held Jewish matters in a position of first importance but travels and communication would have made him aware of benefaction ideology. Like other non-Romans in the east, Jesus would likely not have referred to Herod I, Antipas, or other Hellenistic rulers as patrons unless he considered them to be Romans. The portrait of the Last Supper painted by Luke corresponds quite well with the historical *realia* of first-century Palestine.

Utilizing the sociological/anthropological category of patron-client is not preferable because of the potential confusion it creates between the sociological and historical (Roman) practice. Sociological patrons appoint persons for public office. Roman *patroni* were not obligated to appoint persons, and if ever they did appoint someone to office Romans would not employ *patrocinium* or *patronatus* to describe the transaction. Sociological

6.3 Conclusions for the Last Supper (Luke 22:14–34)

patron-client relations are ubiquitous because of the generalized definition of the term. But Roman *patrocinium* was not ubiquitous being reserved solely for description of certain Romans and certain Roman relationships. Unless the modern author painstakingly differentiates between sociological and Roman *patrocinium* in discussing biblical episodes, confusion between the two will be created. Sloan provides an example of a modern author who falls into this confusion by not recognizing the difference. He includes the partaking of the morning *salutatio* as a component of *patrocinium* to which Jesus contrasts his teaching.[115] Not only was the *salutatio* not confined to *patrocinium* contexts,[116] but, more importantly, Sloan implies that Luke assumes that Jesus and the twelve partook in the *salutatio*. This is historically inaccurate and confuses the culture of Palestine with the culture of the Western Roman Empire. A further point of confusion arises from the neglect of differentiating the sociological and Roman practices. Some scholars suggest that Luke presents Jesus as teaching in terms of patrons and clients (sociological). Another scholar will suggest that patrons and clients (Roman) did not exist in first-century Palestine. The conclusion will be drawn that Luke erroneously ascribes teaching in terms of patron-client (unqualified) to Jesus because patron-client (Roman) did not exist in first-century Palestine. Clarity is needed. *Patrocinium* did not exist in first-century Palestine as far as our sources claim. Sociological patron-client relationships exist essentially in all cultures in all times, so it may be reasonably assumed that they existed in first-century Palestine. Jesus does not use the language of *patrocinium* in any of the instructions given in Luke's gospel. Therefore, Luke has not erroneously attributed a discussion of *patrocinium* where it did not exist. Jesus does speak of asymmetrical, long-term, reciprocal relationships (sociological patron-client). Luke has not erroneously attributed a discussion of sociological patron-client relationships to Jesus because these were present in Jesus' Palestine.

---

[115] Sloan, "Reciprocity," 68.

[116] Eilers, *Roman Patrons*, 8; Yakobsen, *Elections*, 72–73; H. Flower, *Ancestor Masks and Aristocratic Power in Roman Culture* (Oxford: Oxford University Press, 1996), 217–220; Q. Cic. *Comment. pet.* 34–35; Sall. *Cat.* 28.1–3; Cic. *Cat.* 1.9, *Sull.* 18, 52; Plut. *Cic.* 16.2. Attendance at the *salutatio* did not make one a client. Although clients were expected to attend *salutatio*, others besides clients attended.

Chapter 7

Conclusion

Luke-Acts has been interpreted in terms of patrons-clients and benefactors by many scholars. This was a natural inference since patrons, clients, and benefactors could be found throughout the Roman empire and had definitely made inroads into early Christianity by the second century. At the end of Moxnes' work on patrons-clients and discipleship in Luke-Acts, he calls for closer investigation of this topic.[1] Moxnes' call was taken up in this book.

Social historians have developed the category "patron-client" to describe relationships in both Roman society and other cultures throughout the world. The category derives from Roman culture, but recent classical studies have called for a redefinition in light of the Roman practice of *patrocinium* from which the socio-historical category developed. This study focuses on the Roman practice (*patrocinium*) rather than on the socio-historical category (patron-client). It was hoped that by focusing on the Roman practice confusion with the socio-historical category may be averted and clarification of the socio-historical category may be offered. A correlated danger inheres in the use of the socio-historical category without clarification of its difference from the Roman category when discussing Roman Palestine. By proposing the presence of patron-client relationships one infers that Roman culture had infiltrated Palestine in the first-century. It is necessary therefore to describe the culture of Palestine and to differentiate between socio-historical "patron-client" and Roman *patrocinium* so as not to imply the presence of a culture which (it was demonstrated in chapters 2 and 3) had not pervaded Palestine thoroughly.

7.1 *Patrocinium* and Benefaction in First-Century Palestine

Chapter two brought recent classical studies to bear on the definitions of patronage and benefaction. Many socio-historical (e.g., Eisenstadt and Roniger, Garnsey and Saller, Gellner and Waterbury) and exegetical (e.g., Neyrey, Moxnes, Green, deSilva, Ahn) studies rely heavily on outdated

---

[1] Moxnes, "Patron-Client," 268.

works of classicists such as Mommsen, Badian, Gelzer, Syme, von Premerstein, and Harmand. In the past decade several studies of *patrocinium* have appeared (e.g., Eilers, Verboven, Nicols, De Rossi). These new studies clarify the historical *realia* of *patrocinium* in the first-century.

Several findings prove important for this study. (1) *Patrocinium* describes a specific relationship which Romans recognized as distinct from other relationships (e.g., *suffragium, amicitia*) and manners of life (e.g., benefaction, reciprocity). Eilers' suggestion that social historians have misunderstood the Roman patron-client relationship when constructing their socio-historical patron-client relationship has been confirmed. By using "patron-client" to describe any asymmetrical, reciprocal, and long-term relationship (including, lord-vassal, landlord-tenant, professor-assistant, literary patron-author, socially unequal friends) social historians strip *patrocinium* of its distinctiveness and alter its original meaning. It originally referred to a relationship wherein patrons provided primarily legal aid for clients, but eventually morphed to include many forms of protection and financial help. Social historians make a further error when reinterpreting Roman society with the errant socio-historical patron-client relationship. In particular it must be emphasized that *patrocinium* is different from literary patronage and *suffragium* (appointments to office).[2] (2) *Patrocinium* differs from benefaction in that *patrocinium* identifies a relationship between *patronus* and *cliens* whereas benefaction describes a quality of generosity. Patrons were often generous but generosity was not expected of patrons. Patrons supplied their clients with goods, but these were primarily legal protection and general defense of the community. Benefactors provided lavish gifts such as stadia, gymnasia, and games. (3) *Patrocinium* did not enter the Roman east until the second century B.C., and it sharply declined in A.D. 11/12 in peregrine communities of the east because of a regulation enacted by Augustus. *Patrocinium* returned in the Trajanic period but had transformed and had become quite similar to benefaction. (4) Only Romans received the title of *patronus* from either Greeks or Romans; the title was not bestowed upon non-Romans. Available evidence demonstrates that only Romans received the title of *patronus*. Greeks in the east often adopted Hellenistic categories for Roman authorities, especially the phrase "common benefactors" ('Ρωμαῖοι οἱ κοινοὶ εὐεργέται). (5) Both patrons and benefactors could be viewed positively or negatively by others. Augustus perhaps forbid foreign communities from bestowing the title *patronus* because of the possibility that evil recipients might exploit the fact that clients could not take them to court (e.g., Dionysos Halicarnassus 2.10.3; Cicero *Verrines* 2.2.114, 154). Several benefactors attempted to mask their truly tyrannical nature by lavish expenditures (e.g., Albinus, Ptolemy II).

---

[2] Eilers, *Roman Patrons*, 3–4.

Following these clarifications on the nature of *patrocinium* and benefaction in the first-century an investigation was made into the culture of first-century Palestine. This investigation came in two parts: (1) regional and (2) personality perspectives. Several criteria were set forth by which either *patrocinium* or benefaction might be confidently identified (section 2.1.4). For *patrocinium* four criteria were given: high level of Romanization; "Roman" individual as potential patron; direct verbal evidence (πατρωνεία, προστασία, πάτρων, κλίενς and πελάτης); and interaction conforms with descriptions of *patrocinium* elsewhere. For benefaction five criteria were offered: significant Hellenization; written sources intended for locals detailing practice; epigraphical mention of practice; known benefactors in proximity of local culture; concepts from the "common stock" of phrases and semantic fields (e.g., εὐεργεσία, εὐεργέτης, σωτήρ, χάρις, φιλοτιμία, εὖ 'χαριστέω, ἀνήρ ἀγαθός). With these criteria an investigation of several regions (Galilee, Jerusalem, Philip's tetrarchy, Tyre, Sidon, Caesarea Maritima) and several personalities (Herod I, Herod Antipas, Philip, Agrippa I) was undertaken.

The regional perspective provided opportunity to differentiate various appropriations or non-appropriations of *patrocinium* and benefaction in the first-century. In Galilee neither Roman nor Hellenistic influence dominated the culture. Rather, material remains suggest a concerted effort to maintain Jewish distinctives (limestone/ chalk vessels, *miqvaoth*, Jewish burial, lack of pork bones, Hasmonean coinage). This was true in villages (Cana, Nazareth, Capernaum) as well as cities (Tiberias, Sepphoris). Some Hellenistic influence was identified in Tiberias (monumental structures – stadium, palace, gate complex; education – paideia; Greek language; a few Hellenistic inhabitants) and Capernaum (city plan), but Jewish culture outweighed this influence. No euergetistic inscriptions were found in any village or city of Galilee (see section 2.2.3 *Summary*). Hellenism had a stronger hold in Jerusalem than in Galilee (Greek language, availability of Greek education, monumental structures), but Jewish culture still was dominant (chalk vessels, *miqvaoth*, burial tombs, and absence of pig bones; *War* 1.648–55; *Ant.* 17.146–63). Hellenization expressed itself in benefaction in both literary (*Ant.* 15.189–190; 1 Macc 14:25–49; *War* 4.145–146) and archaeological sources ("Stone Weight"; *SEG* 1277; 8.170). Romanization was not very pronounced (few Roman inhabitants) in Jerusalem which corresponds with a lack of explicit *patrocinium* in the city. Romanization was more pronounced in Caesarea Maritima where Herod I built a Temple to Roma and Augustus, forum, baths, theater, hippodrome, wall, promontory palace, and an amphitheater which generally followed Roman rather than Near Eastern architectural techniques. He named the city and a few of the construction projects in honor of the emperor (*War* 1.156, 414).

7.1 Patrocinium and Benefaction in First-Century Palestine 327

The Roman prefect and Roman soldiers were part of the non-Jewish population of the city (*Ant.* 18.55–64; *War* 2.169–175). Euergetistic inscriptions can be found in Caesarea Maritima (*AE* 1963 no. 104). There is no explicit evidence of *patrocinium*, but the presence of Romans, including the prefect, makes the practice of *patrocinium* possible. Samaria was a Hellenized city ("Greek style" constitution in Sebaste; Sebaste named in honor of emperor; stadium, games; *Ant.* 14.408; 15.296; *War* 1.299, 166) which likely understood benefaction (*Ant.* 12.258–261; 15.298). A temple dedicated to Rome and Augustus illustrates the Roman influence and makes *patrocinium* a possibility even though *patrocinium* is not explicitly mentioned in the sources. Philip's tetrarchy requires a complex explanation because of the various influences (section 2.2.5 *Smaller Cities*). The influences of Hellenism and Romanism were strongly felt before the time of Philip (public institutions; temples to Augustus, Rome, Livia-Julia; iconic coins; Greco-Roman cult). But some villages remained strongly tied to Judaism (Gamla – Jewish coins, synagogue, *miqveh*; Bethsaida – limestone vessels, but iconic coins). Benefaction is possibly mentioned in a few sources (*War* 2.117–118; *Ant.* 18.1–10). *Patrocinium* is possible because of the Roman influences, but is not explicitly mentioned in the sources. Tyre was strongly influenced by Hellenism (*Apion* 1.178–180; cf. Mark 7:24–30) and has the only explicit πάτρωνα mentioned close to our time period (M. Aemilius Scaurus; 63–61 B.C.; *IGR* 3.1102). Josephus mentions expressions of benefaction (*Ant.* 14.185–267). *Amicitia* and *suffragium* were also attested in this passage from Josephus. Coin distributions suggest that Tyre, however, did not overtly Hellenize Galilee.

Four members of the Herodian family were investigated in the personality perspectives in order to determine if they practiced (or were interpreted as practicing) benefaction or *patrocinium*. Herod I understood benefaction and friendship, and he navigated his potential misstep with Augustus in accordance with the proper social codes (*Ant.* 15.109, 193–196; naming of cities and monuments for Roman superiors; *Ant.* 16.150–159). Herod was a friend of Rome (φιλορώμαιος; *War* 1.194; *Ant.* 14.137), and known as a benefactor in Jerusalem and outside of Palestine (*Ant.* 15.232–233; 16.209–212; "Stone Weight"; *OGIS* 415). Romanization was slight for Herod I and he was not identified as a *patronus* in the sources. Herod Antipas was also known as a benefactor (*Ant.* 18.36–38; *OGIS* 416, 417; *SEG* 16.488), though to a lesser extent than his father. Though he had been educated in Rome (*Ant.* 17.20), Antipas had little in the way of ambition to attain status with Rome (*War* 2.181–183; *Ant.* 18.240–255). It follows that *patrocinium* is not connected to Antipas in the sources. Philip maintained connections with Rome (iconic coins, dedicated temples, renamed Caesarea Philippi), but did not travel frequently to Rome to strengthen his relationships. He may have learned of *patrocinium* while being educated in Rome (*Ant.* 17.20; *War* 1.602). Along with a dearth of evidence on Philip there is no explicit indication of benefaction or *patrocinium* explicitly in the sources. It was suggested that Philip likely preferred benefaction because of imitation of his father, renaming of cities (in Hellenistic fashion), and neglect of visits to Rome. Philip possibly practiced *patrocinium* considering his education in Rome and freedom in connecting himself to Rome on coins, with temples, and in the renaming of cities (Caesarea Philippi). Agrippa I is the first Herodian ruler who is explicitly identified as a *patronus* in the sources (*IGLS* 6.2759; cf. *ILS* 3.2.8957). Agrippa preferred Rome to Palestine and took measures to ensure that he spent more time in that city than in the area he governed. He cultivated friendships with Rome and the emperors (*Ant.* 18.143–146, 151–168, 289–300; *In Flaccum* 36–40). He built a reputation as a benefactor (*Ant.* 19.328–330, 335–337; *OGIS* 419, 428). Three of the four Herods (Herod I, Antipas, Agrippa I) whom we investigated had reputations as benefactors explicitly in the sources. Only Agrippa I is explicitly identified as a patron in the sources.

7.2 Patrons, Benefactors, and Discipleship in Luke 6:17–38; 14:1–24; 22:14–34

Chapter four began by recognizing the tendency of scholars to interpret Luke-Acts in reference to reciprocity, benefaction, and patronage. Building upon the conclusions of the previous two chapters, the first major section of the chapter identified various avenues through which a first-century Galilean Jew may have learned of these modes of interaction. Both personal interactions and travels through different regions would have provided opportunity for Jesus, as he is presented in the canonical gospels, to receive an education in Greco-Roman culture. Several ancillary details in these accounts suggest that he was exposed to benefactors and benefactions, and perhaps the ideology of *patrocinium*. This was the first step in establishing historical plausibility for various episodes in Luke's gospel. Several passages have been identified as locations of a critique of reciprocity, benefaction, or patronage in the gospel. Three of these passages were then investigated in turn (Luke 6:17–38; 14:1–24; 22:14–34).

According to Luke 6:17–38, Jesus critiques an ethic of reciprocity that had found its way into Jewish and Greco-Roman society. He specifically implicates the (Jewish) false-prophets for wrongly adopting reciprocity as an ethic, but his teaching moves outward to include a broader spectrum. The vocabulary and concepts Luke adopts in the passage definitely speak of reciprocity (ἀπαιτέω, ἀπέχω, ἀπολαμβάνω, ἀπελπίζω, χαρὶς, μισθὸς, cf.

ἀντιμετρηθήσετα) and hint as well at benefaction (πᾶς 6:17, 19[2x]; καλῶς ποιεῖτε, ἀγαθοποιέω, ἀχάριστος, χρηστός, χάρις; public outreach *SEG* 4.490; words match deeds *CIG* 3655). Jesus' healing, as narrated in Luke 6:7–9, could have been interpreted as a benefit by persons from Tyre or Jerusalem, since those cities had known benefactors and benefactions; Luke's use of ἀγαθοποιέω to describe the healing corroborates this reading. Jesus' positive proposal includes the institution of an idealized Sabbath and Jubilee approach to generosity. Jewish thinkers critiqued reciprocity and benefaction for wrong motivations including the notion of taking honor that only belongs to God and being generous only in appearance but not in reality (cf. 4 Macc 9:10; Wis 16:29; Sir 18:18; 29:16; 29:25; Sir 30:6; 3:31; 32:2). Luke's description of Jesus' teaching falls into the broader Hellenistic Jewish practice of critiquing reciprocity. Such critique was available inside and outside of Palestine, so its presence in this context need not necessarily indicate that Luke has imported his own culture onto the episode. Indeed, those among the audience who had more familiarity with Hellenistic philosophy (perhaps Tyrians or Jerusalemites) could have understood Jesus critique the practice of looking for "worthy" candidates for generosity (παρ' ὧν ἐλπίζετε λαβεῖν; 6:34, 35). His theological ground for generosity sounds similar to balanced reciprocity, but because of the social location and superior response by God it is better categorized as generalized reciprocity. In Luke, Jesus calls his people to imitate God who responds to negative reciprocity with generalized reciprocity (6:35–36). They ought also to look to heavenly reciprocation from God rather than earthly reciprocation from man. Rather than calculating reciprocity, the follower of Jesus ought to approach giving from the stance of open-handed, uncalculating generosity which is in keeping with the ideal of the Sabbath and Jubilee release. Since there is no language of *patrocinium* or auditors heavily influenced by Roman culture, it is confusing to adopt the socio-historical category of "patron-client" for interpreting this passage.

Luke's use of reciprocity in the episode, along with some evidence of benefaction and no evidence of *patrocinium*, conforms to the prevailing cultural mix of Galilee, Jerusalem, Judea, and Tyre. In chapters 2 and 3 of this book it was demonstrated that Jewish culture dominated Galilean life with only hints of benefaction ideology entering toward the latter part of Jesus' life (i.e., with Antipas' erection of Tiberias). Jerusalem and Tyre had experienced some benefaction (esp. in Herod I) though the former was still dominated by Judaism. Tyre had at least one patron prior to the time of Jesus, but non-Romans in the east reserved that title for Romans so it is unlikely that they would have sought in Jesus a new patron. Luke presents Jesus in categories appropriate for a first-century Jewish Galilean.

In Luke 14:1–24 new forms of reciprocity, friendship, and benefaction replace normal patterns which existed among the audience. In the first episode (14:1–6), Jesus begins by healing the man in what may have been intended by Luke to be understood as a benefit, if it is compared to the other Sabbath healings (ἀγαθοποιέω in 6:6–11; cf. 13:10–17). Without specific vocabulary (εὐεργεσία, χάρις, καλῶς ποιέω, ἀγαθοποιέω) this cannot be determined conclusively. In the subsequent pericopes (14:7–11; 14:12–14; 14:15–24) Luke has Jesus challenge notions of reciprocity.

In the second episode (14:7–11), Jesus offers advice which fits well in Greco-Roman discussions of honor-shame "at table" (Plutarch *Dinner of Seven Wise Men* 148F-149F; *Quest. Conv.* 616C-F). However, one should not neglect the Jewish discussion of the same subject (Prov 25:6–7; Sir 31:12–32:9; *Aboth de R. Nathan* 25; Luke 14:7–11). Both cultures expressed status at table through seat location (e.g., Plutarch *Dinner of Seven Wise Men* 149B; 1 *QSa* 2:13; cf. Matt 23:6; Mark 12:39). Since Jews from lower classes participated in symposium like discussions, it is quite plausible that Jesus took part in a symposium-like discussion which instructed participants in the proper manner of pleasing men and God. If a particular form of reciprocity presents itself in this first section it must be that of friendship since there is no explicit vocabulary other than φίλος in the episode. Though some suggest that patrons gave banquets (e.g., Hanson and Oakman) we have affirmed Eilers' argument that this was not part of *patrocinium* (see section 5.2.2).[3]

In the third episode, Luke's Jesus instructs his audience to forego the normal practice of inviting social equals who could reciprocate in kind (14:12–14). Such a gift, of significant value and outside of his "in-group", may constitute a benefaction (e.g., Menas, Caesar Augustus, Antiochus of Kommagene, Tiberius Julius Alexander).[4] The generous giver in turn might be viewed as a benefactor who ought to receive loyalty from those who cannot reciprocate in kind. However, for those who invite people that cannot reciprocate God will step in to provide reciprocity. God offers a much better return on one's generosity than human recipients would be able to offer. Clientage does not begin because the giver does not expect reciprocity from the human recipient; that is, no socio-historical patron-client relationship begins between the human parties. God nullifies the response of loyalty given to humans by providing super-abundantly for the giver (Luke 14:14). He responds in kind (by offering a meal in return), but invitation to the divine banquet far outweighs the earthly banquet the host offers.

---

[3] Eilers, *Roman Patrons*, 98; contra Harmand, *Un aspect*, 145–146, 358–385.
[4] Danker, *Benefactor*, 336–337.

7.2 Patrons, Benefactors, and Discipleship in Luke 6:17–38; 14:1–24; 22:14–34

In the fourth episode, Luke depicts Jesus elaborating upon the notion of inviting those who cannot reciprocate (14:15–24). By blending the referents of God and man in the host of the party (e.g., οἰκοδεσπότης [12:39; 13:25]), potential disciples learn that they must follow the example of God who does not calculate ability to reciprocate in bestowing gifts. He rather offers benefactions to those outside the in-group (ὁ πτωχός καὶ ἀνάπηρος καὶ τυφλός καὶ χωλός), namely those who cannot reciprocate. Human hosts who imitate this action will find themselves reciprocated by God in an invitation to the Messianic banquet. They function as benefactors, offering benefits outside the "in-group," but do not receive the expected expressions of loyalty or praise from their human recipients. Their reciprocation comes from God. Clientage does not begin. In fact, the practice reorients the host's social group so that he now includes those of lower social status in his group. He makes "friends" with the lower class. The narrative as a whole (14:1–24) carries vocabulary important for reciprocity (ἀντικαλέω, ἀνταπόδομα, ἀνταποδίδωμι) and friendship (φίλος) along with some similarities to benefaction (e.g., generosity beyond the "in-group"). In the absence of specific vocabulary connected to *patrocinium* (κηδεμών, πάτρων, πατρώνης, προστάτης) it is probably best to exclude it from the discussion of the reciprocity herein envisioned. One stands on firmer ground by keeping the discussion under the general category of reciprocity and, when approaching specificity, friendship.

Luke presents Jesus primarily in terms prevalent in Hellenistic Jewish culture (reciprocity and friendship), secondarily as a benefactor, and not as a patron. This balance of cultures corresponds with the prevailing cultures of Galilee and Jerusalem. Several examples were culled to demonstrate that Jews from Palestine participated in symposium discussions about honor-shame and friendship. With a few benefactors as examples in and around Galilee, Jesus could have presented himself in contrast to their practice and expected his Jewish audience to understand the comparison. Since no patrons could be found in Galilee or Jerusalem it is historically accurate for Luke to omit reference to such a practice.

In Luke 22:14–34, Luke's Jesus offers a way of discipleship with reference to reciprocity and benefaction. The initial paragraph studied depicts Jesus as a benefactor who extends himself to the point of personal loss for the sake of his people (22:14–20). He offers his life for them as other benefactors had endangered themselves for the sake of their clients (e.g., *SIG* 762; Lysias, 6.40–41). He then provides an opportunity for his group to respond appropriately, namely in the form of memorializing the benefit (εἰς τὴν ἐμὴν ἀνάμνησιν; εὐχαριστήσας; Luke 22:17, 19). Those who memorialize the benefit function appropriately in the exchange and stimulate further benefits (*OGIS* 666; *OGIS* 213.23–31; *Choix* 50.14–16), while those who avoid memorialization insult the benefactor by showing disloyalty and ingratitude (e.g., Seneca *Ben.* 3.1.3; 3.6.1–2; 3.7.1; 4.34.3; Herodotus 5.90; Cicero *Duties* 1.15.47). The next paragraph highlights the error committed by the disloyal betrayer (22:21–23). He does not respond appropriately to the benefit through memorializing it (instead showing disloyalty), and the disciples scramble to disassociate themselves from this error. Patterns of reciprocity will be breached. The following episode shows that the majority of the disciples prefer to follow the normal pattern and indeed Jesus confirms that they thus far have done so (22:24–30). When Jesus contrasts his way of leadership with the prevailing pattern in his day, he instructs leaders to function as servants, the greatest to assume the lowest position, and those who desire increased status to express loyalty to Jesus rather than Gentile benefactors (μετ' ἐμοῦ, μου, μοι, μου, μου, μου; 22:28–30). God and Jesus function as benefactors who distribute kingdoms, a place at Jesus' table, and authority to judge for those that remain loyal to Jesus in the face of trials (cf. *Ant.* 15.109, 189–193; 14.280; *War* 1.226; 2.215; section 6.2.4). By imitating Jesus' endurance in trials and his consequent reception of a kingdom from God, the disciples expect to receive what they had hoped for (status, authority) but from a different source and in a different manner (from Jesus, for service, over Israel, at the Messianic banquet). The last episode recalls the topic of loyalty and Jesus takes measures to ensure the continued allegiance of Peter and the rest of the disciples as they enter trials (22:31–34).

Luke's use of Passover and benefaction ideologies to relate this episode fits with the cultures available among Galileans in Jerusalem. As Jesus and his disciples spent time in Jerusalem they would have had opportunity to discuss the monumental benefaction of Herod, the temple (Luke 21:37–38; 19:41–44, 45–48; 20:45–21:4, 5–9; *SEG* 1277). But benefaction would not eclipse the Passover in importance and so Luke appropriately does not diminish the importance of Passover. Luke does omit reference to *patrocinium* and this fits historical *realia* in two ways. First, *patrocinium* was not the relationship through which kingdoms were conferred in the early empire. Second, *patrocinium* was not prominent, if practiced at all, in Palestine. Again, Luke provides a plausible historical description of Jesus' teaching.

The three passages which have been investigated reveal a number of important conclusions. First, while reciprocity, friendship, and benefaction are common in both vocabulary and conception in Luke's description of Jesus' teaching, *patrocinium* was not detected. Though something similar to the socio-historical category of patron-client may be evident it is probably confusing to use this category heuristically since the Roman practice of *patrocinium*, which shares terminology (e.g., patron, client) with socio-historical patronage, is absent from these passages. Furthermore, Jesus was not considered "Roman" by his followers so they would not have identified him as a *patronus*. Second, in each of the passages studied there was ample reason to conclude that a person from Jesus' social location could plausibly converse about reciprocity, friendship, and benefaction as well as offer a critique of these practices. He had sufficient interaction with Hellenistic and Roman culture through individuals and through his travels to learn about benefaction, *patrocinium*, patrons, and clients. Other Jewish groups (Philo, Qumran, Josephus) undertook similar conversations so it should not be surprising if Jesus also did so (Philo *Vit. Cont.* 58–80; 1 *QSa* 2:13; *Ant.* 18.289–301; cf. Prov 25:6–7 LXX). Luke did not need to create these scenarios from his own experience to address a Gentile audience because it was quite possible for a first-century Jewish Galilean to attain this sort of knowledge and engage in this sort of critique. Third, in Luke Jesus approaches these forms of reciprocity in a manner which is reminiscent of contemporary Jewish practices (e.g., Proverbs 25:6–7 LXX). At the same time he departed in striking ways from others (e.g., Sir 12:1–6; Philo *Vit. Cont.* 58–80). He held God in the highest position of authority with exclusive rights to public praise and gratitude. God reciprocates those who decide to follow his example of generosity to those who cannot repay. He advocated a form of generosity that was truly generous rather than simply being a sale disguised as a gift (e.g., Philo *Cher* 122–123; see also *SEG* 9.948). Unlike other critics, however, Jesus did advocate memorializing his own benefaction. His self-giving should be remembered by his disciples and those who show disloyalty will receive just punishment. Loyalty must be directed toward God and Jesus, otherwise it is misdirected.

7.3 Fulfillment of the Aims of Research

Five aims for this book were identified in the first chapter, and here I will provide in encapsulated form the fulfillment of each aim. First, life in Palestine had various cultural influences (Jewish, Hellenistic, Roman, and "Arab"), but in Galilee and Jerusalem – the two most important places for historical Jesus studies – the dominant cultural influence was Jewish. The influence of Hellenistic culture was stronger in Jerusalem with the practice of benefaction explicit in the archaeological and literary evidence. *Patrocinium* is only explicitly mentioned in Tyre nearly a century before the ministry of Jesus (61–63 B.C.). Greeks in the east preferred the Hellenistic language of benefaction to describe superiors and Augustus regulated against peregrine communities identifying leaders in terms of *patrocinium* at the end of his reign (A.D. 11/12).

Second, this means that the historical Jesus would have been more familiar with the Hellenistic category of benefaction and probably knew relatively little about *patrocinium*. What he did learn of *patrocinium* would have come primarily through Tyre, but Galilee and Tyre do not appear to have culturally influenced each other heavily.

Third, the early Christians heard a message partially cast in terms of benefaction, but also in relation to reciprocity (which had long been a part of Jewish discussions) and friendship. They learned a new kind of reciprocity in which God reciprocates those who give to persons who cannot reciprocate. When Christians adopt the language of *patrocinium* in the second century and later it must be remembered that *patrocinium* had morphed to become very similar to benefaction. This means that the link between Jesus' message about benefactors stood somewhat closer to what *patrocinium* began to describe in the second century.

Fourth, interpreters of Luke's gospel should default to reciprocity, friendship, and benefaction rather than *patrocinium*. Appropriately, Luke does not use the language of *patrocinium*, though he does use language and concepts related to benefaction sporadically (esp. Acts 4:9; 10:38).

Fifth, socio-historical interpreters should adjust their categories to correspond with developments in classical studies. They should be mindful that *patrocinium* did not have banquets, appointments to office, and generosity as inherent obligations of the relationship therefore the presence of these in Luke does not indicate a patron-client relationship. Since Palestine was not heavily Romanized and no explicit link to *patrocinium* can be made in the sources it is confusing to adopt the "Roman sounding" patron-client terminology for Palestine. Since "patron-client" implies specific actions (e.g., *salutatio*; legal defense) which did not obtain in first-century Palestine it is best to prefer rather the more general types of reciprocity (e.g., reciprocity, friendship, benefaction) which obtained in both Greco-Roman and Jewish culture. The language of benefaction is appropriate, but should not be thought overly important in the discussion since the evidence of benefaction in Palestine is also rather slim.

7.4 Prospects for Further Research

I have only studied three passages in Luke, but there are several others which are relevant to investigate including some in Luke (e.g., Luke 7:1–10; 17:11–19) and Acts (3:1–4:22, 10:34–48; 12:1–24). The last of these episodes potentially may involve an objection to *patrocinium* because Agrippa I had received this public honor. The other episodes have been interpreted in terms of benefaction and patronage and need further investigation to see if either of these paradigms is primary. It is also important to investigate a larger number of passages because of Danker's admonition that there is no technical vocabulary for benefactors.[5] The notion of "benefactor" developed from concepts and ideas collectively more than individually. A study compiling the various descriptions of Jesus' activity and personal qualities may substantiate Danker's conclusion, i.e., Jesus is benefactor par excellence. It would be beneficial to compare this with other explanatory paradigms (particularly comparison with OT personalities).

The examination of Philip's tetrarchy and Philip himself was admittedly limited on account of the dearth of primary and secondary resources. In light of Jensen's recent work on Antipas, Schwartz' monograph dedicated to Agrippa I, and several monographs devoted to Herod I, it seems justifiable to call for a focused study of Philip.[6] Strickert claims that one can hardly underestimate the importance of Philip on the NT because of the relationship between Galilee and his tetrarchy and the presence of several disciples from the tetrarchy.[7] The recent study by Wilson moves in this direction but only devotes one chapter to Herodian era Caesarea Philippi.[8] In regard to *patrocinium* it is especially important to examine the coin which reads κτίστης in connection with the use of κτίστης in *patrocinium*.[9] It has traditionally been interpreted as indicating the foundation of the city, but it is possible that a connection to *patrocinium* is implied because this term (κτίστης) sometimes replaced *patronus*.

Further investigations of historical sources which provide insight into the culture of the NT are needed in light of the recent developments in understanding *patrocinium* and benefaction. A study of benefaction in the LXX and intertestamental writings is needed. Crook declares that patron-client and benefactor-client relationships did not enter Israel before the NT period.[10] Osiek questions this claim and suggests that further research into the subject is needed.[11] It would be good to examine these claims further to see how early biblical and intertestamental Jewish authors incorporated, modified, or rejected Greek and Roman ways. Gardner recently began

---

[5] Danker, *Benefactor*, 43.
[6] Jensen, *Antipas*; Schwartz, *Agrippa I*; Japp, *Baupolitik Herodes'*; Kasher and Witztum, *King Herod*; Kokkinos, *Herodian Dynasty*; Lichtenberger, *Baupolitik Herodes*; Netzer, *Herod*; Richardson, *Herod*; cf. Hoehner, *Antipas*; Jones, *Herods*.
[7] Strickert, "Coins of Philip," 168.
[8] Wilson, *Caesarea Philippi*, 1–37.
[9] Strickert, "Coins," 182.
[10] Crook, *Reconceptualising*, 79.
[11] Osiek, "Review of Crook, *Reconceptualising*," 2.

closer investigation of the intertestamental writings,[12] and more is needed. A study of *patrocinium* in Josephus is also needed. Scholars adopt the socio-historical category to describe Josephus, but an investigation of *patrocinium* would be beneficial. Does Josephus indeed describe himself as patron of Galilean villages? If so, does Josephus consider himself to be Roman, or did the Galileans consider him to be Roman? Or, does Josephus desire to present himself as Roman to his Roman readers?

One of the findings of the second chapter was that Jewish leaders in the Maccabean era earned reputations as benefactors. It would be worth exploration to see if Jesus implicitly or explicitly critiques these Jewish leaders in regard to their acceptance of the title benefactor. Gardner shows how many of the Jewish leadership in the Maccabee era received the title of benefactor, and other honorary gifts, almost without reservation (Onias III – 2 Macc 4:1–2; 3:4–13; Simon Maccabee – 1 Macc 14:25–49; *Ant.* 13:214; John Hyrcanus I – *Ant.* 14.149–155; Aristobulus I – *Ant.* 13.318). At times they are said to have followed the law scrupulously but one wonders if John Hyrcanus' reception of a gold crown and a statue would have been viewed in such good light (*Ant.* 14.149–155).[13]

Several important terms in NT studies were also involved in Augustus' (purported) decree to halt ascribing public honors (e.g., πάτρων) to leaders of the peregrine communities into which Palestine's communities fit (e.g., σωτήρ, κτίστης, θεὸς). A person who received one of these titles in the peregrine communities of the east would be considered a usurper (Cicero *In Verrem* 2.2.114, 154). Σωτήρ is a title excluded for people in peregrine communities, but Luke adopts the title for God and Jesus (Luke 1:47; 2:11; Acts 5:31; 13:23).[14] Patron was excluded as a title in the peregrine communities of the east at the same time that Augustus himself abandoned the title *patronus* in favor of *pater patriae*.[15] The NT does not appear to use the language of *patrocinium*, but is quite enmeshed in father language. It would be interesting to compare the uses of father in the NT descriptions of God with those adopted by Augustus and subsequent emperors. Luke includes (e.g., σωτήρ, father) and excludes (e.g., patron, κτίστης) different titles which Augustus had ruled illegal for peregrine communities. What do Luke's inclusion and exclusion of different titles suggest for his overall stance toward Rome?

---

[12] Gardner, "Jewish Leadership." Cf. Philip F. Esler, ed., *Ancient Israel: The Old Testament in Its Social Context* (Minneapolis: Fortress Press, 2006).

[13] Gardner, "Jewish Leadership," 337–339, esp. n. 58.

[14] Ben Witherington III, "Salvation and Health in Christian Antiquity: The Soteriology of Luke-Acts in Its First-century Setting," in Marshall and Peterson, *Witness to the Gospel*, 145–166.

[15] Nicols, "Patrons of Greek Cities," 82–83.

This book provides the most extended examination of benefactors and patrons in first-century Palestine from both archaeological and literary evidence. As such it should provide a starting point for any of these new investigations. These new investigations will no doubt challenge and refine the conclusions reached in this book.

Bibliography

1. Reference Literature

Aland, Barbara, Kurt Aland, Johannes Karavidopoulos, Carlo M. Martini, and Bruce M. Metzger, eds. *Novum Testamentum Graece*. 27th rev. ed. Stuttgart: Deutsche Bibelgesellschaft, 1993.

Barker, E. *From Alexander to Constantine: Passages and Documents Illustrating the History of Social and Political Ideas 336 B.C.–A.D.337*. Reprint 1956. Lanham/New York: University Press of America, 1985.

Bell, H. Idris, ed. *The Abinnaeus Archive: Papers of a Roman Officer in the Reign of Constantine*. Oxford: Clarendon Press, 1962.

Braund, David C. *Augustus to Nero: A Sourcebook on Roman History. 31 BC–AD 68*. London: Crook Helm, 1985.

Brodersen, Kai, Wolfgang Günther, and Hatto H. Schmitt. *Historische griechische Inschriften in Übersetzung*. 3 Bände. Texte zur Forschung 59.68.71. Darmstadt: Wissenschaftliche Buchgesellschaft, 1992/1996/1999.

Cancik, Hubert, and Helmuth Schneider, eds. *Der neue Pauly: Enzyklopädie der Antike*. 15 vols. Stuttgart and Weimer: Metzler, 1996–2002. English: *Brill's New Pauly: Encyclopaedia of the Ancient World*. 20 vols. Leiden: Brill, 2001–.

Danker, Frederick W., Walter Bauer, William Arndt, and F. Wilbur Gingrich, eds. *A Greek-English Lexicon of the New Testament and Other Early Christian Literature*. Chicago: University of Chicago Press, 2000.

Edgar, Campbell Cowan. *Zenon papyri*. Vol. 2. Cairo: L'Institut français d'archéologie orientale, 1926.

Ehrenberg, Victor, and A. H. M. Jones. *Documents Illustrating the Reigns of Augustus and Tiberius*. 2nd ed. reprint, 1955. Oxford: Clarendon, 1976.

Fredrich, Carl Johann, and Friedrich Hiller von Gaertringen, eds. *Inschriften von Priene*. Berlin: Walter de Gruyter, 1968.

Freis, Helmut, ed. *Historische Inschriften zur Römischen Kaiserzeit: Von Augustus bis Konstantin*. 2. Aufl. Texte zur Forschung 49. Darmstadt: Wissenschaftliche Buchgesellschaft, 1994.

Guarducci, Margherita. *Epigrafia Greca: Caratteri e Storia della Disciplina La Scrittura Greca dale Origini all'età Imperiale*. Rome: Istituto Poligrafico Dello Stato, 1967.

Hornblower, Simon, and Antony Spawforth. *Oxford Classical Dictionary*. 3rd ed. Oxford: Oxford University Press, 1996.

Hunt, Arthur S., John de Monins Johnson, Colin H. Roberts, and Victor Martin, eds. *Catalogue of the Greek Papyri in the John Rylands Library at Manchester*. 4 vols. Manchester: University Press, 1911–1952.

Kent, J. H. *The Inscriptions 1926–1950*. Corinth: Results of Excavations VIII/3. Princeton: Princeton University Press, 1966.

Kern, Otto. *Die Inschriften von Magnesia am Maeander*. Berlin: Speman, 1900. Reprint Berlin: de Gruyter, 1967.

Kramer, Bärbel, M. Erler, D. Hagedorn, Robert Hübner, and Michael Gronewald. *Kölner Papyri*. Abhandlungen der Rheinisch-Westfälischen Akademie der Wissenschaften 7–8. Opladen: Westdeutscher Verlag, 1976.
Lajtar, Adam. *Die Inschriften von Byzantion Teil I. Die Inschriften*. Bonn: Habelt, 2000.
Lifshitz, Baruch. *Donateurs et fondateurs dans les synagogues juives: Répertoire des dédicaces grecques relatives à la construction et à la réfection des synagogues*. Cahiers de la Revue biblique 7. Paris: Gabalda, 1967.
Lolling, H. G.. Sitzungsberichte preussischen Akad. Wiss. Berlin, 1888.
Lust, J., Erik Eynikel, K. Hauspie, and G. Chamberlain, eds. *A Greek-English Lexicon of the Septuagint*. 2 vols. Stuttgart: Deutsche Bibelgesellschaft, 1992.
Lust, J., Erik Eynikel, and Katrin Hauspie. *Greek-English Lexicon of the Septuagint*. Stuttgart: Deutsche Bibelgesellschaft, 2003.
Maehler, Herwig, ed. *Ägyptische Urkunden aus den Staatlichen Museen zu Berlin: Griechische Urkunden aus Hermupolis*. München: Saur, K G, 2005.
Merton, Wilfred, H. I. Bell, B. R. Rees, A. C. Beatty, J. D. Thomas, C. H. Roberts, eds. *A Descriptive Catalogue of the Greek Papyri in the Collection of Wilfred Merton*. 3 vols. London: University of London, Institute of Classical Studies, 1948–1967.
Meshorer, Ya'akov. *Ancient Jewish Coinage. Volume 1: Persian Period Through Hasmoneans. Volume 2: Herod the Great Through Bar Kochba*. Dix Hills, N.Y.: Amphora Books, 1982.
–. *Jewish Coins of the Second Temple Period*. Tel Aviv: Am Hassefer, 1967.
–. *A Treasury of Jewish Coins from the Persian Period to Bar Kokhba*. Jerusalem: Yad ben-Zvi Press, 2001.
Metzger, Bruce Manning. *A Textual Commentary on the Greek New Testament*. 2nd ed. *A Companion Volume*. Deutsche Bibelgesellschaft, 1994.
Meyers, Eric M., ed. *Oxford Encyclopedia of Archaeology in the Near East*. 5 vols. Oxford: Oxford University Press, 1997.
Pilhofer, Susanne. *Romanisierung in Kilikien? Das Zeugnis der Inschriften*. Quellen und Forschungen zur Antiken Welt 46. München: Herbert Utz, 2006.
Preisigke, Friedrich, Friedrich Bilabel, and Hans-Albert Rupprecht. *Sammelbuch griechischer Urkunden aus Ägypten: herausgegeben im Auftrage der Wissenschaftlichen Gesellschaft in Strassburg*. Strassburg: K. J. Trübner, 1915; repr. 1955.
Rahlfs, Alfred. *Septuaginta; Id est Vetus Testamentum graece iuxta LXX interpres*. Stuttgart: Deutsche Bibelgesellschaft, 1979.
Skolnik, Fred, ed. *Encyclopedia Judaica*. 8 vols. Jerusalem: Encyclopedia Judaica, 1972.
Smallwood, E. Mary. *Documents Illustrating the Principates of Gaius, Claudius and Nero*. London: Cambridge University Press, 1967.
Strecker, Georg, and Udo Schnelle, eds. *Neuer Wettstein: Texte zum Neuen Testament aus Griechentum und Hellenismus*. 2 vols. Berlin: De Gruyter, 1996.
Strecker, Georg, ed. *Jesus Christus in Historie und Theologie*. Tübingen: Mohr-Siebeck, 1975.
Temporini, Hildegard, and Wolfgang Haase, eds. *Aufstieg und Niedergang der römischen Welt: Geschichte und Kultur Roms im Spiegel der neueren Forschung*. Part 2, *Principat*, 33.1. New York: de Gruyter, 1989.
Carmina epigraphica Graeca. Edited by Peter Allan Hansen. Texte und Kommentare 12.15. Berolini: de Gruyter, 1983.
Choix d'inscriptions de Délos. Edited by Félix Durrbach. Subsidia Epigraphica 6. New York: Hildesheim, 1976.
Corpus Inscriptionum Graecarum. Edited by August Böckh. Berlin: Reimer, 1828–1877. Repr. Hildesheim: Olms, 1977.

Corpus Inscriptionum Judaicarum. Edited by Jean-Baptiste Frey. 2 vols. Rome: Pontificio istituto di archeologia cristiana, 1936–1952. Vol. 1 republished with prolegomenon. Edited by Baruch Lifshitz. New York: Ktav, 1975.
Inschriften griechischer Städte aus Kleinasien. Österreichische Akademie der Wissenschaften and Universität zu Köln. Bonn: Habelt, 1972. Helmut Engelmann and Reinhold Merkelbach, eds. Vol. 1 *Die Inschriften von Erythrai und Klazomenai*, Teil 1 (Nr. 1–200). Vol. 3 Peter Frisch, ed. *Die Inschriften von Ilion*, 1975.
Inscriptions Grecques et Latines de la Syrie. Edited by L. Jalabert and René Mouterde. Beirut and Paris: Geuthner, 1929–1986.
Inscriptiones Latinae Selectae. Edited by Hermann Dessau. Berlin: Weidmann, 1892; repr. Chicago: Ares, 1979.
New Documents Illustrating Early Christianity. Edited by G. H. R. Horsley and S. R. Llewelyn. 9 vols. North Ryde, N. S. W.: Macquarie University, Ancient History Documentary Research Centre; Grand Rapids: Eerdmans, 1981–2002.
Orientis Graeci Inscriptiones Selectae: Supplementum Syllogoges Inscriptionum Graecarum. Edited by Wilhelmus Dittenberger. Vol. 1. Lipsiae: S. Hirzel, 1903.
Roman Provincial Coinage. Edited by A. M. Burnett, M. Amandry, P. P. Ripollés Alegre, and Marguerite Spoerri. 7 vols. British Museum Press with Bibliothèque Nationale: Paris, 1992–2006.
Sammlung der griechischen Dialekt-Inschriften. Edited by H. Collitz. 4 vols. Göttingen: Vandenhoeck and Ruprecht, 1884–1915.
Supplementum epigraphicum graecum. Leiden: Sijthoff; Amsterdam: Gieben, 1923– (suspended 1972–1975).
Sylloge inscriptionum graecarum. Edited by Wilhelm Dittenberger. 3rd ed. 4 vols. Leipzig: Hirzel, 1915–1924.
Demosthenes. Translated by C. A. Vince and J. H. Vince. Loeb Classical Library. Cambridge: Harvard University Press, 1926–1949.
Dio's Roman History. Translated by Earnest Cary. 9 vols. Loeb Classical Library. Cambridge: Harvard University Press, 1914–1927.
The Attic Nights of Aulus Gellius. Translated by John Carew Rolfe. 3 vols. Loeb Classical Library. Cambridge: Harvard University Press, 1946.
The Geography of Strabo. Translated by H. L. Jones. 8 vols. Loeb Classical Library. Cambridge: Harvard University Press, 1917–1930.
Hesiod, Homeric Hymns, Homerica. Translated by Hugh G. Evelyn-White. Loeb Classical Library. Cambridge: Harvard University Press, 1914, repr. 1995.
Josephus. Translated by H. St. J. Thackeray, L. H. Feldman, and R. Marcus. 10 vols. Loeb Classical Library. Cambridge: Harvard University Press, 1926–1965.
Lysias. Translated by W. R. M. Lamb. Loeb Classical Library. Cambridge: Harvard University Press, 1967.
Martial: Epigrams. Translated by D. R. Shackleton Bailey. Loeb Classical Library. Cambridge: Harvard University Press, 1993.
Philo. Translated by F. M. Colson, G. H. Whitaker, and R. Marcus. 10 vols. Loeb Classical Library. London: Heinemann, 1929–1962.
Plato. Translated by H. N. Fowler, W. R. M. Lamb, R. G. Bury, P. Shorey. 12 vols. Loeb Classical Library. Cambridge: Harvard University Press, 1914–1935.
Plutarch. Translated by F. C. Babbitt. Loeb Classical Library. Cambridge: Harvard University Press, 1949–1976.
Polybius: The Histories. Translated by W. R. Paton. 6 vols. Loeb Classical Library. Cambridge: Harvard University Press, 1922–1927.

Seneca: Moral Essays. Translated by John W. Basore. 3 vols. Loeb Classical Library. Cambridge: Harvard University Press, 1928–1932.
Suetonius. Translated by J. C. Rolfe. 2 vols. Loeb Classical Library. Cambridge: Harvard University Press, 1997–1998.
Tacitus: The Histories; The Annals. Translated by Clifford H. Moore and John Jackson. 4 vols. Loeb Classical Library. Cambridge: Harvard University Press, 1969.

2. Secondary Literature

Adan-Bayewitz, D., and M. Aviam. "Iotapata, Josephus, and the Siege of 67: Preliminary Report on the 1992–94 Seasons." *Journal of Roman Archaeology* 10 (1997): 131–165.
Ahn, Yong Sung. *The Reign of God and Rome in Luke's Passion Narrative: An East Asian Perspective.* Biblical Interpretation Series 80. Leiden: Brill, 2006.
Albright, W. F. "Review of Leroy Waterman, *Preliminary Report of the University of Michigan: Excavations at Sepphoris, Palestine, in 1931.*" *Classical Weekly* 31 (1938): 148.
Alcock, Susan E., ed. *The Early Roman Empire in the East.* Oxbow Monograph 95. Oxford, England: Oxbow Books, 1997.
Alexander, Loveday. *Acts in Its Ancient Literary Context: A Classicist Looks at the Acts of the Apostles.* Early Christianity in Context. New York: T & T Clark International, 2005.
–. *The Preface to Luke's Gospel: Literary Convention and Social Context in Luke 1.1–4 and Acts 1.1.* Cambridge: Cambridge University Press, 1993.
Alföldy, G. "Pontius Pilatus und das Tiberium von Caesarea Maritima." *Scripta Classica Israelitica* 18 (1999): 85–93.
Alter, Robert. *The Art of Biblical Narrative.* New York: Basic Books, 1981.
Ameling, W. "Lucius Licinius in Chios." *Zeitschrift für Papyrologie und Epigraphik* 77 (1989): 98–100.
Anderson, J. G. C. *Journal of Hellenic Studies* 17 (1897): 411–413.
Arav, Rami, and Richard A. Freund, eds. *Bethsaida: A City by the North Shore of the Sea of Galilee.* Vol 1–3. Kirksville, Mo.: Thomas Jefferson University Press and Kirksville: Truman State University Press, 1995, 1999, 2004.
Arens, Eduardo. *The ΗΛΘΟΝ-Sayings in the Synoptic Tradition.* Orbis Biblicus et Orientalis 10. Göttingen: Vandenhoeck and Ruprecht, 1976.
Arnal, William E. *Jesus and the Village Scribes: Galilean Conflicts and the Setting of Q.* Minneapolis: Fortress Press, 2000.
Arterbury, Andrew E. *Entertaining Angels: Early Christian Hospitality in Its Mediterranean Setting.* New Testament Monographs 8. Sheffield: Sheffield Phoenix, 2005.
Avery-Peck, Alan J., ed. *The Special Problem of the Synagogue.* Leiden: Brill, 2001.
Aviam, Mordechai. *Jews, Pagans and Christians in the Galilee.* Land of Galilee Studies 1. Rochester: University of Rochester Press, 2004.
Avigad, Nahman. *Discovering Jerusalem.* Nashville: Nelson, 1983.
Avi-Yonah, M. "The Foundation of Tiberias." *Israel Exploration Journal* 1 (1950–1951): 160–169.
Bacon, B. W. "Pharisees and Herodians in Mark." *Journal of Biblical Literature* 39 (1920): 102–112.
Badian, E. *Foreign Clientelae (264–70 B.C.).* Oxford: Clarendon Press, 2000.
Bagatti, Bellarmino. *Villaggi Cristiani di Galilea.* Jerusalem: Franciscan Printing Press, 1971.

Bagatti, Bellarmino, and Eugenio Alliata. *Excavations in Nazareth*. Jerusalem: Franciscan Printing Press, 1969.
Bahr, Gordon J. "The Seder of Passover and the Eucharistic Words." *Novum Testamentum* 12 (1970): 181–202.
Bailey, J. A. *The Traditions Common to the Gospels of Luke and John*. Novum Testamentum Supplement 7. Leiden: Brill, 1963.
Bailey, Kenneth E. *Through Peasant Eyes: More Lucan Parables, Their Culture and Style*. Grand Rapids: Eerdmans, 1980.
Bakhos, Carol, ed. *Ancient Judaism in Its Hellenistic Context*. Supplements to the Journal for the Study of Judaism 95. Leiden: Brill, 2005.
Ball, Warwick. *Rome in the East: The Transformation of an Empire*. London and New York: Routledge, 2000.
Barag, D. "Tyrian Currency in Galilee." *Israel Numismatic Journal* 6/7 (1982/83): 7–13.
Barkay, Rachel. *The Coinage of Nysa-Scythopolis (Beth-Shean)*. Jerusalem: Israel Numismatic Society, 2003.
Barrett, C. K. "Luke xxii.15: To Eat the Passover." *Journal of Theological Studies* 39 (1958): 28–47.
Barth, Markus. *Rediscovering the Lord's Supper: Communion with Israel, with Christ, and among the Guests*. Atlanta: John Knox, 1988.
Barton, Stephen C. *The Spirituality of the Gospels*. Peabody: Hendrickson, 1992.
Batey, Richard L. "Is Not This the Carpenter?" *New Testament Studies* 30 (1984): 249–258.
–. *Jesus and the Forgotten City: New Light on Sepphoris and the Urban World of Jesus*. Grand Rapids: Baker, 1991.
–. "Sepphoris: An Urban Portrait of Jesus." *Biblical Archeology Review* 18.3 (1992): 50–63.
Batten, Alicia. "God in the Letter of James: Patron or Benefactor?" *New Testament Studies* 50 (2004): 257–272.
Bauckham, Richard. *Gospel Women: Studies of the Named Women in the Gospels*. Grand Rapids: Eerdmans, 2002.
Baumann, Uwe. *Rom und die Juden: Die römisch-jüdischen Beziehungen von Pompeius bis zum Tode des Herodes (63 v.Chr. – 4 v.Chr.)*. Studia Philosophica et Historica 4. Frankfurt/Bern: Lang, 1983.
Baumbach, Günther. *Das Verständnis des Bösen in den synoptischen Evangelien*. Berlin: Evangelische Verlagsanstalt, 1963.
Beare, F. W. *The Gospel According to Matthew*. New York: Harper and Row, 1981.
Beck, Brian E. *Christian Character in the Gospel of Luke*. London: Epworth Press, 1989.
Beentjes, Pancratius Cornelis. *The Book of Ben Sira in Hebrew: A Text Edition of All Extant Hebrew Manuscripts and a Synopsis of All Parallel Hebrew Ben Sira Texts*. Supplements to Vetus Testamentum 68. Leiden: Brill, 1997.
Benedum, Jost. "Griechische Arztinschriften aus Kos." *Zeitschrift für Papyrologie und Epigraphik* 25 (1977): 265–276.
Bennett, W. J., Jr. "The Herodians of Mark's Gospel." *Novum Testamentum* 17 (1975): 9–14.
Benzinger, "Caesarea Nr. 9." Pages 1291–1292 in volume 3 (1899) of *Paulys Realencyclopädie der classischen Altertumswissenschaft*. Edited by G. Wissowa. 49 vols. Munich, 1980.
Berger, Klaus. *Die Amen-Worte Jesu: eine Untersuchung zum Problem der Legitimation in apokalyptischer Rede*. Zeitschrift für die neutestamentliche Wissenschaft und die Kunde der älteren Kirche 39. Berlin: de Gruyter, 1970.

Bergsma, John Sietze. *The Jubilee from Leviticus to Qumran: A History of Interpretation.* Supplements to Vetus Testamentum 115. Leiden: Brill, 2007.
Berlin, Andrea M. *Gamla 1: The Pottery of the Second Temple Period, The Shmarya Gutmann Excavations, 1976–1989.* IAA Reports 29. Jerusalem: Israel Antiquities Authority, 2006.
Berlin, Andrea M., and J. Andrew Overman, eds. *The First Jewish Revolt.* London and New York: Routledge, 2002.
Bernett, Monika. "Der Kaiserkult als Teil der politischen Geschichte Iudeas unter den Herodianern und Römern (30 v. − 66n. Chr.)." Habilitationsschrift, Munich, 2002.
—. "Zur politischen Zeitrechnung des Königs Agrippa II." Pages 25–37 in *Saxa Loquenter: Studien zur Archäologie Palästinas/Israels.* Edited by Cornelius G. Den Hertog, Ulrich Hübner, and Stefan Münger. Münster: Ugarit-Verlag, 2003.
Best, Ernest. *Disciples and Discipleship: Studies in the Gospel According to Mark.* Edinburgh: Clark, 1986.
Betz, Hans Dieter. *Nachfolge und Nachahmung Jesu Christi im Neuen Testament.* Beiträge zur historischen Theologie 37. Tübingen: Mohr, 1967.
—. *The Sermon on the Mount: A Commentary on the Sermon on the Mount, Including the Sermon on the Plain (Matthew 5:3–7:27 and Luke 6:20–49).* Hermeneia. Trans. Adela Yarbro Collins. Minneapolis: Fortress Press, 1995.
Bickerman, E. J. *Der Gott der Makkabäer: Untersuchungen über Sinn und Ursprung der makkabäischen Erhebung.* Berlin: Schocken Verlag, 1937.
—. *The God of the Maccabees: Studies on the Meaning and Origin of the Maccabean Revolt.* Studies in Judaism in Late Antiquity 32. Leiden: Brill, 1979.
Billings, Bradly, S. *Do This in Remembrance of Me: The Disputed Words in the Lukan Institution Narrative (Luke 22:19b–20): An Historico-Exegetical, Theological and Sociological Analysis.* Library of Biblical Studies 314. London and New York: T & T Clark, 2006.
—. "The Disputed Words in the Lukan Institution Narrative (Luke 22:19b–20): A Sociological Answer to a Textual Problem." *Journal of Biblical Literature* 125 (2006): 507–526.
Binder, Donald D. *Into the Temple Courts: The Place of the Synagogues in the Second Temple Period.* Atlanta: Society of Biblical Literature, 1999.
Blok, A. "Variations in Patronage." *Sociologische Gids* (1969): 365–378.
Blomberg, Craig. *Interpreting the Parables.* Downers Grove: InterVarsity Press, 1990.
Blosser, Donald W. "Jesus and the Jubilee (Luke 4:16–30): The Year of Jubilee and Its Significance in the Gospel of Luke." PhD diss., St. Andrew's University, 1979.
Blundell, Mary W. *Helping Friends and Harming Enemies: A Study in Sophocles and Greek Ethics.* Cambridge: Cambridge University Press, 1990.
Bobertz, Charles A. "The Role of Patron in the *cena Dominica* of Hippolytus' Apostolic Tradition." *Journal of Theological Studies* [NS] 44 (1993): 170–184.
Böcher, Otto, and Klaus Haacker, eds. *Verborum veritas: Festschrift für Gustav Stählin zum 70. Geburtstag.* Wuppertal: Theologischer Verl. Brockhaus, 1970.
Bock, Darrell L. *Luke.* Baker Exegetical Commentary on the New Testament 3. 2 vols. Grand Rapids: Baker Books, 1994.
—. *Proclamation from Prophecy to Pattern: Lucan Old Testament Christology.* Journal for the Study of the New Testament Supplement 12. Sheffield: JSOT Press, 1987.
Böhlemann, Peter. *Jesus und der Täufer: Schlüssel zur Theologie und Ethik des Lukas.* Cambridge: Cambridge University Press, 1997.
Böhm, Martina. *Samarien und die Samaritai bei Lukas: eine Studie zum religionshistorischen und traditionsgeschichtlichen Hintergrund der lukanischenSamarientexte und*

zu deren topographischer Verhaftung. Wissenschaftliche Untersuchungen zum Neuen Testament 2.111. Tübingen: Mohr Siebeck, 1999.
Boissevain, Jeremy. *Friends of Friends: Networks, Manipulators and Coalitions.* New York: St. Martin's Press, 1974.
Bolkestein, Hendrik. *Wohltätigkeit und Armenpflege im vorchristlichen Altertum: ein Beitrag zum Problem „Moral und Gesellschaft".* Utrecht: Oosthoek, 1939.
Bond, Helen K. *Pontius Pilate in History and Interpretation.* Society for New Testament Studies Monograph Series 100. Cambridge: Cambridge University Press, 1998.
Bormann, Lukas. *Philippi: Stadt und Christengemeinde zur Zeit des Paulus.* Supplements to Novum Testamentum 78. Leiden: Brill, 1995.
–. *Recht, Gerechtigkeit und Religion im Lukasevangelium.* Studien zur Umwelt des Neuen Testaments 24. Göttingen: Vandenhoeck and Ruprecht, 2001.
Bösen, Willibald. *Jesusmahl, eucharistisches Mahl, Endzeitmahl: ein Beitrag zur Theologie des Lukas.* Stuttgarter Bibelstudien 97. Stuttgart: Katholisches Bibelwerk, 1980.
Bossuyt, Philippe, and Jean Radermakers. *Témoins de la parole de la grâce: Actes des Apôtres.* 2 vols. Collection Institut d'études théologiques 16. Brussels: Institut d'études théologiques, 1995.
Bourdieu, Pierre. *Outline of a Theory of Practice.* Cambridge: Cambridge University Press, 1977.
Bovon, François. *Das Evangelium nach Lukas.* Evangelisch-Katholischer Kommentar zum Neuen Testament 3. 3 vols. Zürich: Benziger Verlag, 1989.
–. *L'Évangile selon Saint Luc.* Commentaire du Nouveau Testament 3. 3 vols. Genève: Labor et Fides, 1991.
–. *Luke the Theologian: Fifty-Five Years of Research (1950–2005).* 2nd rev. ed. Waco: Baylor University Press, 2006.
–. *Luke the Theologian.* Trans. Ken McKinney. Allison Park: Pickwick, 1987.
–. *Luke 1: A Commentary on the Gospel of Luke 1:1–9:50.* Hermeneia. Trans. Christine M. Thomas. Minneapolis: Fortress Press, 2002.
Bowditch, Phebe Lowell. *Horace and the Gift Economy of Patronage.* Classics and Contemporary Thought 7. Berkeley: University of California Press, 2001.
Bowersock, G. W. *Hellenism in Late Antiquity.* Cambridge: Cambridge University Press, 1990.
–. *Augustus and the Greek World.* Oxford: Clarendon Press, 1965.
Bowsher, Julian M. C. "Architecture and Religion in the Decapolis: A Numismatic Survey." *Palestine Exploration Quarterly* 119 (Jan-June 1987): 62–69.
Braun, H. *Qumran und das Neue Testament.* Mohr Siebeck: Tübingen, 1966.
Braun, Willi. *Feasting and Social Rhetoric in Luke 14.* Society for New Testament Studies Monograph Series 85. Cambridge: Cambridge University Press, 1995.
–. "The Use of Mediterranean Banquet Traditions in Luke 14:1–24." PhD diss., University of Toronto. 1993.
Braund, David C. "Four Notes on the Herods." *The Classical Quarterly* 33.1 (1983): 239–242.
–. "Philip." Pages 310–312 in vol. 5 of *Anchor Bible Dictionary.* Edited by David Noel Freedman. 6 vols. New York: Doubleday, 1992.
–. *Rome and the Friendly King: The Character of the Client Kingship.* London and Canberra: Croom Helm; New York: St. Martin's Press, 1984.
Bredin, Mark, ed. *Studies in the Book of Tobit: A Multidisciplinary Approach.* Library of Second Temple Studies 55. London: T & T Clark, 2006.
Brooten, Bernadette J. *Women Leaders in the Ancient Synagogue: Inscriptional Evidence and Background Issues.* Brown Judaic Studies 36. Chico: Scholars Press, 1982.

Brown, R. E. *Apostasy and Perseverance in the Theology of Luke*. Analecta Biblica Investigationes 36. Rome: Biblical Institute, 1969.

–. *A Commentary on the Passion Narratives in the Four Gospels*. Vol. 1. *The Death of the Messiah: From Gethsemane to the Grave*. New York: Doubleday, 1994.

Bruce, F. F. *The Gospel and Epistles of John*. Grand Rapids: Eerdmans, 1983.

Brunt, P. A. *The Fall of the Roman Republic and Related Essays*. Oxford: Clarendon Press, 1988.

Buckler, W. H. "An Epigraphic Contribution to Letters." *Classical Review* 41 (1927): 119–121.

Bultmann, Rudolf. *Die Geschichte der synoptischen Tradition*. Göttingen: 1958. ET *History of the Synoptic Tradition*. Trans. John Marsh. Oxford: Blackwell, 1963.

Burkitt, F. C., and A. E. Brooke. "St Luke xxii 15, 16: What Is the General Meaning?" *Journal of Theological Studies* 9 (1907–1908): 569–572.

Burrows, Millar. *More Light on the Dead Sea Scrolls: New Scrolls and New Interpretations*. New York: Viking Press, 1958.

Burrows, R. M., and P. N. Ure. "Excavations at Rhitsóna in Boeotia." *Annual of the British School of Athens* 14 (1907–1908): 226–318, plates vii-xv.

Caird, G. B. *The Gospel of Saint Luke*. Harmondsworth: Penguin Books, 1963.

Cancik, Hubert, Hermann Lichtenberger, and Peter Schäfer, eds. *Geschichte, Tradition, Reflexion: Festschrift für Martin Hengel zum 70. Geburtstag*. Tübingen: Mohr Siebeck, 1996.

Carpinelli, Francis Giordano. "'Do This as My Memorial' (Luke 22:19): Lucan Soteriology and Atonement." *Catholic Biblical Quarterly* 61 (1999): 74–91.

Carson, D. A. "Matthew." Pages 1–599 in *The Expositor's Bible Commentary*. Vol. 8. Edited by F. E. Gaebelein. Grand Rapids: Zondervan, 1984.

–. *The Gospel According to John*. Pillar New Testament Commentary. Grand Rapids: Eerdmans, 1991.

Cartledge, P., P. Garnsey, and E. Gruen, eds. *Hellenistic Constructs: Essays in Culture,History, and Historiography*. Hellenistic Culture and Society 26. Berkeley: University of California, 1997.

Case, Shirley Jackson. "Jesus and Sepphoris." *Journal of Biblical Literature* 45 (1926): 14–22.

Cassidy, Richard J., and Philip J. Scharper, eds. *Political Issues in Luke-Acts*. Maryknoll, N.Y.: Orbis Books, 1983.

Chancey, Mark A. "Galilee and Greco-Roman Culture in the Time of Jesus: The Neglected Significance of Chronology." Pages 173–187 in *The Society of Biblical Literature 2003 Seminar Papers*. Society of Biblical Literature Seminar Papers 42. Atlanta: Scholars Press, 2003, 173–87.

–. *Greco-Roman Culture and the Galilee of Jesus*. Society for New Testament Studies Monograph Series 134. Cambridge: Cambridge University Press, 2005.

–. "The Cultural Milieu of Ancient Sepphoris." *New Testament Studies* 47 (2001): 127–145.

–. *The Myth of a Gentile Galilee*. Cambridge: Cambridge University Press, 2002.

Charlesworth, James H., ed. *Jesus and Archaeology*. Grand Rapids: Eerdmans, 2006.

Charlesworth, James H., and Loren L. Johns, eds. *Hillel and Jesus: Comparative Studies of Two Major Religious Leaders*. Minneapolis: Fortress Press, 1997.

Charlesworth, James H., and Walter P. Weaver. *What Has Archaeology to Do with Faith?* Faith and Scholarship Colloquies. Philadelphia: Trinity Press International, 1992.

Chilton, Bruce, and Craig A. Evans, eds. *Authenticating the Words of Jesus*. New Testament Tools and Studies 28.1. Leiden: Brill, 1999.
Chiranky, G. "Rome and Cotys: Two Problems." *Athenaeum* 60 (1982): 461–481.
Chow, John K. *Patronage and Power: A Study of Social Networks*. Journal for the Study of the New Testament Supplement Series 75. Sheffield: Sheffield, Academic Press, 1992.
Ciaceri, E. *Atti del Reale Istituto Veneto di Scienze, Lettere ed Arti* 76/2 (1916/17).
Clark, George W. *Notes on the Gospel of Luke: Explanatory and Practical A Popular Commentary Upon a Critical Basis, Especially Designed for Pastors and Sunday Schools*. Philadelphia: American Baptist Publication Society, 1876.
Clark, Kenneth Willis. *The Gentile Bias, and Other Essays*. Supplements to Novum Testamentum 54. Leiden: Brill, 1980.
Clarke, Thomas E. *Above Every Name: The Lordship of Christ and Social Systems*. Woodstock Studies 5. Ramsey, N.J.: Paulist Press, 1980.
Cohen, Getzel M. *The Hellenistic Settlements in Syria, the Red Sea Basin, and North Africa*. Joan Palevsky Imprints in Classical Literature. Berkeley: University of California Press, 2006.
Cohen, Shaye J. D. "Women in the Synagogues of Antiquity." *Conservative Judaism* 34 (1980): 23–29.
Collins, John J., and Gregory A. Sterling, eds. *Hellenism in the Land of Israel*. Notre Dame: University of Notre Dame Press, 2001.
Colpe, C. "Caesarea 2." Page 1004 of Vol.1 of *Der Kleine Pauly*. Edited by J. Ziegler, W. Sontheimer, and H. Gärtner, Munich: Druckenmüller, 1964–1979.
Corbo, Virgilio. "Capernaum." Pages 866–869 in vol. 1 of *Anchor Bible Dictionary*. Edited by David Noel Freedman. New York: Doubleday, 1992.
–. "Nouveaux arguments en faveur de l'identification des Hérodiens et des Esséniens." *Revue de Qumran* 7 (1970): 397–402.
Corley, Jeremy. *Ben Sira's Teaching on Friendship*. Brown Judaic Studies 316. Providence: Brown Judaic Studies, 2002.
Cotton, Hannah, and Ada Yardeni. *Aramaic, Hebrew, and Greek Documentary Texts from Naḥal Ḥever and Other Sites: With an Appendix Containing Alleged Qumran Texts*. Oxford: Clarendon Press, 1997.
Cotton, Hannah, David J. Wasserstein, Jonathan Price, and Robert Hoyland, eds. *From Hellenism to Islam: Cultural and Linguistic Change in the Roman Near East*. Cambridge: Cambridge University Press, forthcoming.
Cotton, Hannah. "Josephus' Roman Audience? Josephus and the Roman Elites." Pages 37–52 in *Flavius Josephus and Flavian Rome*. Oxford: Oxford University Press, 2005.
–. "Roman Officials in Iudaea and Arabia and Civil Jurisdiction." Pages 23–44 in *Law in the Documents from the Iudean Desert*. Edited by R. Katzoff and D. M. Schaps. Leiden: Brill, 2005.
Creed, J. M. *The Gospel According to St. Luke*. London: Macmillan, 1965.
De Ste. Croix, G. E. M. "*Suffragium*: From Vote to Patronage." *British Journal of Sociology* 5 (1954): 33–48.
Cromhout, Markus. *Jesus and Identity: Reconstructing Judean Ethnicity in Q*. Matrix: The Bible in Mediterranean Context 2. Eugene: Cascade Books, 2007.
Crook, Zeba A. "BTB Readers Guide: Loyalty." *Biblical Theology Bulletin* 34 (2004): 167–177.
–. *Reconceptualising Conversion: Patronage, Loyalty, and Conversion in the Religions of the Ancient Mediterranean*. Beihefte zur Zeitschrift für die neutestamentliche

Wissenschaft und die Kunde der älteren Kirche 130. Berlin/New York: Walter de Gruyter, 2004.
—. "Reflections on Culture and Social-Scientific Models." *Journal of Biblical Literature* 124.3 (2005): 515–520.
Crossan, John Dominic. *The Historical Jesus: The Life of a Mediterranean Jewish Peasant*. Edinburgh: T & T Clark, 1991.
Crossan, John Dominic, and Jonathan L. Reed. *Excavating Jesus: Beneath the Stones, Behind the Texts*. New York: HarperCollins, 2001.
Crouzel, Henri. "La imitation et la 'suite' de Dieu et du Christ dans les premiers siècles chrétiens, ainsi que leurs sources gréco-romaines et hébraique." *Jahrbuch für Antike und Christentum* 21 (1978): 7–41.
Daley, Brian E. "Position and Patronage in the Early Church: The Original Meaning of 'Primacy of Honour.'" *Journal of Theological Studies* [NS] 44 (1993): 529–53.
Daniel, Constantin. "Les 'Hérodiens' du Nouveau Testament sont-ils des Esséniens?"*Revue de Qumran* 6 (1967): 31–53.
Danker, Frederick W. *Benefactor: Epigraphic Study of a Greco-Roman and New Testament Semantic Field*. St. Louis: Clayton, 1982.
—. "Bridging St. Paul and the Apostolic Fathers: A Study in Reciprocity." *Currents in Theology and Mission* 15 (1988): 84–94.
—. *Jesus and the New Age: A Commentary on St. Luke's Gospel*. Philadelphia: Fortress Press, 1988.
—. *Luke*. Proclamation Commentaries. 2nd ed. Rev. and enlarged. Fortress: Philadelphia, 1987.
—. "The Endangered Benefactor in Luke-Acts." Pages 39–48 in *The Society of Biblical Literature 1981 Seminar Papers*. Society of Biblical Literature Seminar Papers 20. Chico: Scholars Press, 1981.
Darr, John A. *Herod the Fox: Audience Criticism and Lukan Characterization*. Journal for the Study of the New Testament 163. Sheffield: Sheffield Academic Press, 1998.
—. *On Character Building: The Reader and the Rhetoric of Characterization in Luke-Acts*. Literary Currents in Biblical Interpretation. Louisville: Westminster/John Knox Press, 1992.
Dautzenberg, G., Josef Blank, Helmut Merklein, and Karlheinz Müller, ed. *Zur Geschichte des Urchristentums*. Quaestiones Disputatae 87. Freiburg: Herder, 1979.
Davies, Norman de Garis, Seymour de Ricci, and Geoffrey Thorndike Martin. *The Rock Tombs of El-Àmarna*. Archaeological Survey of Egypt 18. London, Boston: Egypt Exploration Fund, 1903.
Davies, Philip R., and Richard T. White, eds. *A Tribute to Géza Vermes: Essays on Jewish and Christian Literature and History*. Journal for the Study of the Old Testament 100. Sheffield, England: JSOT Press, 1990.
Davis, Natalie Zemon. *The Gift in Sixteenth-Century France*. The Curti Lectures. Madison: University of Wisconsin Press, 2000.
Dawsey, James M. *The Lukan Voice: Confusion and Irony in the Gospel of Luke*. Macon, Ga.: Peeters, 1986.
Day, Joseph W. "Interactive Offerings: Early Greek Dedicatory Epigrams and Ritual." *Harvard Studies in Classical Philology* 96 (1994): 37–74.
Degenhardt, Hans Joachim. *Lukas, Evangelist der Armen: Besitz und Besitzverzicht in den lukanischen Schriften: eine traditions- und redaktionsgeschichtliche Untersuchung*. Stuttgart: Katholisches Bibelwerk, 1965.

Deines, Roland. *Die Pharisäer: ihr Verständnis im Spiegel der christlichen und jüdischen Forschung seit Wellhausen und Graetz*. Wissenschaftliche Untersuchungen zum Neuen Testament 101. Tübingen: Mohr Siebeck, 1997.

–. *Jüdische Steingefässe und pharisäische Frömmigkeit: ein archäologisch-historischer Beitrag zum Verständnis von Joh 2,6 und der jüdischen Reinheitshalacha zur Zeit Jesu*. Wissenschaftliche Untersuchungen zum Neuen Testament 52. Tübingen: Mohr, 1993.

Deissmann, Adolf. *Light from the Ancient East: The New Testament Illustrated by Recently Discovered Texts of the Graeco-Roman World*. Grand Rapids: Baker, 1965.

de Jounge, M., and A. S. van der Woude. "11QMelchizedek and the New Testament." *New Testament Studies* 12 (1965–66): 301–326.

Denaux, A. "The Parable of the King-Judge (Lk 19,12–28, and Its Relation to the Entry Story (Lk 19,29–44)." *Zeitschrift für die neutestamentliche Wissenschaft und die Kunde der älteren Kirche* 93 (2002): 35–57.

Denti, M. "La scultura ellenistica delle regioni transpadane nel I secolo a. C.: problemi e prospettive di ricera." *Dialoghi di archeologia* 37 (1989): 9–26.

De Rossi, Filippo Canali. *Il ruolo dei 'patroni' nelle relazioni politiche fra il mondo greco e Roma in età repubblicana ed augustea*. Beiträge zur Altertumskunde 159. Munich: Saur, 2001.

Derrett, J. Duncan M. "Positive Perspectives on Two Lucan Miracles." *Downside Review* 104 (1986): 272–287.

DeSilva, D. A. *Honor, Patronage, Kinship and Purity: Unlocking New Testament Culture*. Downers Grove: InterVarsity Press, 2000.

–. "Patronage and Reciprocity: The Context of Grace in the New Testament." *Ashland Theological Journal* 31 (1999): 32–84.

Dessau, H. *Geschichte der römischen Kaiserzeit* II/2 (1930): 791–792.

Dever, William G. "The Impact of the 'New Archaeology' on Syro-Palestinian Archaeology." *Bulletin of the American Schools of Oriental Research* 242 (1981): 15–30.

Dihle, Albrecht. *Die goldene Regel: eine Einführung in die Geschichte der antiken und frühchristlichen Vulgärethik*. Studienhefte zur Altertumswissenschaft 7. Göttingen: Vandenhoeck and Ruprecht, 1962.

Dillon, Richard J. *From Eye-Witnesses to Ministers of the Word: Tradition and Composition in Luke 24*. Analecta Biblica 82. Rome: Biblical Institute Press, 1978.

Dothan, M. ed. *Ashdod I-II: The Second and Third Seasons of Excavations*. Atiqot, Eng. Ser. IX-X; Jerusalem, 1971.

Douglas, Mary. "Deciphering a Meal." *Daedalus* 101 (1972): 61–81.

–. *Risk and Blame: Essays in Cultural Theory*. London: Routledge, 1992.

Dover, Kenneth James. *Greek Popular Morality in the Time of Plato and Aristotle*. Berkeley: University of California Press, 1974.

Downey, S. B. *History of Antioch in Syria: From Seleucus to the Arab Conquest*. Princeton: Princeton University Press, 1961.

Downing, F. G. *Cynics and Christian Origins*. Edinburgh: T. & T. Clark, 1992.

Drinkard, Joel F., Gerald L. Mattingly, and Maxwell J. Miller. *Benchmarks in Time and Culture: An Introduction to Palestinian Archaeology*. Atlanta: Scholars Press, 1988.

Dundergerg, Ismo, Kari Syreeni, and Christopher Tuckett, eds. *Fair Play: Diversity and Conflicts in Early Christianity*: Essays in Honour of Heikki Räisänen. Leiden: Brill, 2002.

Dunn, James D. G. *Romans 9–16*. Word Biblical Commentary 38B. Waco: Word, 1988.

Dunston, A. J., ed. Essays on Roman Culture: The Todd Memorial Lectures. Toronto: S. Stevens, 1976.

Dupont, Jacques, ed. *La Parabola degli invitati al banchetto dagli evangelisti a Gesù*. Brescia: Paideia, 1978.
Dupont, Jacques. "'Béatitudes' égyptiennes." *Biblica* 47 (1966): 185–222.
—. "Le logion des douze trônes (Mt 19,28; Lc 22,28–30)." *Biblica* 45 (1964): 355–392.
Duthoy, R. "Le profil social des patrons municipaux en Italie sous le Haut-Empire." *Ancient Society: Journal of the Ancient History of the Greek, Hellenistic and Roman World* 15–17 (1984–1986): 121–154.
—. "Quelques observations concernant la mention d'un patronat municipal dans les inscriptions." *L'Antiquité Classique* 50 (1981): 295–305.
—. "Scénarios de cooptation des patrons municipaux en Italie." *Epigraphica* 46 (1984): 23–48.
—. "Sens et fonction du patronat municipal durant le Principat." *L'Antiquité Classique* 53 (1984): 145–156.
Dyson, Stephan L. "A Classical Archaeologist's Response to the 'New Archaeology'." *Bulletin of the American Schools of Oriental Research* 242 (1981): 7–14.
—. "From New to New Age Archaeology: Archaeological Theory and Classical Archaeology – A 1990s Perspective." *American Journal of Archaeology* 97 (1993): 195–203.
Easton, B. S. *The Gospel According to St. Luke*. Edinburgh, 1926.
Eck, W. *Die staatliche Organisation Italiens in der hohen Kaiserzeit*. Vestigia 28. Munich, 1979.
Edmondson, Jonathan, Steve Mason, and James Rives, eds. *Flavius Josephus and Flavian Rome*. Oxford: Oxford University Press, 2005.
Edwards, Douglas R., ed. *Religion and Society in Roman Palestine: Old Questions, New Approaches*. New York and London: Routledge, 2004.
Edwards, Douglas R., and C. Thomas McCollough, eds. *Archaeology and the Galilee: Texts and Contexts in the Graeco-Roman and Byzantine Periods*. Atlanta: Scholars Press, 1997.
Eilers, Claude. *Roman Patrons of Greek Cities*. Oxford Classical Monographs. Oxford: Oxford University Press, 2002.
Eisenstadt, S. N., and Luis Roniger. *Patrons, Clients and Friends: Interpersonal Relations and the Structure of Trust in Society*. Cambridge: Cambridge University Press, 1984.
Elliott, John H. "Household and Meals Vs. Temple Purity Replication Patterns in Luke-Acts." *Biblical Theology Bulletin* 21 (1991): 102–109.
Elliott, J. K., ed. *Studies in New Testament Language and Text: Essays in Honour of George D. Kilpatrick on the Occasion of His Sixty-Fifth Birthday*. Supplements to Novum Testamentum 44. Leiden: Brill, 1976.
Ellis, Earle E. *The Gospel of Luke*. The Century Bible. Grand Rapids: Eerdmans, 1961, reprint 1981.
Ernst, Josef. *Das Evangelium nach Lukas*. Regensburger Neues Testament 3. 5th ed. Regensburg: Pustet, 1977.
Erskine, Andrew. "The Romans as Common Benefactors." *Historia* 43 (1994): 70–87.
Erskine, Andrew, ed. *A Companion to the Hellenistic World*. Blackwell Companions to the Ancient World. Oxford: Blackwell, 2003.
Esler, Philip F., ed. *Ancient Israel: The Old Testament in Its Social Context*. Minneapolis: Fortress Press, 2006.
Esler, Philip F. *Community and Gospel in Luke-Acts: The Social and Political Motivations of Lucan Theology*. Society for New Testament Studies Monograph Series 57. Cambridge: Cambridge University Press, 1987.

–. "Review of Feasting and Social Rhetoric." *Journal of Theological Studies* 49.1 (1998): 229–232.
Evans, C. F. *Saint Luke*. Trinity Press International New Testament Commentary. London: SCM, 1990.
Evans, C. A., and J. A. Sanders, eds. *Luke and Scripture: The Function of Sacred Tradition in Luke-Acts*. Minneapolis: Fortress, 1993.
Feldman, Louis H. "How Much Hellenism in Jewish Palestine?" *Hebrew Union College Annual* 57 (1986): 83–111.
—."The Term 'Galileans' in Josephus." *Jewish Quarterly Review* 72 (1981–82): 50–52.
Feldmeier, Reinhard, and Ulrich Heckel, eds. *Die Heiden: Juden, Christen und das Problem des Fremden*. Wissenschaftliche Untersuchungen zum Neuen Testament 70. Tübingen: Mohr, 1994.
Ferrary, Jean-Louis. *Philhellénisme et impérialisme: aspects idéologiques de la conquête romaine du monde hellénistique, de la seconde guerre de Macédoine à la guerre contre Mithridate*. Bibliothèque des écoles françaises d'Athènes et de Rome 271. Rome: Ecole française de Rome, 1988.
Festugière, A. J. "'ΑΝΘ'"ΩΝ. La formule 'én echange de quoi' dans la prière grecque hellénistique." *Revue des sciences philosophiques et théologiques* 60 (1976): 369–418.
Field, Frederick. *Notes on the Translation of the New Testament: Being the Otium Norvicense (Pars Tertia)*. Cambridge: University Press, 1899.
Finkel, Asher. *The Pharisees and the Teacher of Nazareth: A Study of Their Background, Their Halachic and Midrashic Teachings, the Similarities and Differences*. Arbeiten zur Geschichte des Spätjudentums und Urchristentums 4. Leiden: Brill, 1964.
Fishbane, Michael A. *Biblical Interpretation in Ancient Israel*. Oxford: Clarendon Press, 1985.
Fitzgerald, John T, ed. *Greco-Roman Perspectives on Friendship*. Resources for Biblical Study 34. Atlanta: Scholars Press, 1997.
Fitzmyer, Joseph A. *The Gospel According to Luke: Introduction, Translation, and Notes*. Anchor Bible Commentary. 2 vols. Garden City: Doubleday, 1981.
–. *Tobit*. Commentaries on Early Jewish Literature. Berlin: Walter de Gruyter, 2003.
Fitzpatrick, P. J. *In Breaking of Bread: The Eucharist and Ritual*. Cambridge: Cambridge University, 1993.
Flender, H. *St. Luke: Theologian of Redemptive History*. London: SPCK, 1967.
Flower, H. *Ancestor Masks and Aristocratic Power in Roman Culture*. Oxford: Oxford University Press, 1996.
Foerster, Gideon. "Beth-Shean at the Foot of the Mound." Page 1471 in vol. 1 of *The New Encyclopedia of Archaeological Excavations in the Holy Land*. Edited by Ephraim Stern, Ayelet Leyinzon-Gilbo'a, and J. Aviram. Jerusalem: Israel Exploration Society & Carta, 1993.
Foster, Paul. "Educating Jesus: The Search for a Plausible Context." *Journal for the Study of the Historical Jesus* 4 (2006): 7–33.
France, R. T., and David Wenham, eds. *Studies of History and Tradition in the Four Gospels*. Gospel Perspectives 1–2. Sheffield: JSOT Press, 1980–1981.
Frankel, Rafael, Nimrod Getzov, Mordechai Aviam, and Avi Degani, eds. *Settlement Dynamics and Regional Diversity in Ancient Upper Galilee: Archaeological Survey of Upper Galilee*. Israel Antiquities Authority Reports 14. Jerusalem: Israel Antiquities Authority, 2001.
Fransen, Irénée. "Cahier de Bible: Le baptême de sang (Luc 22,1–23, 56)." *Bible et Vie Chretienne* 25 (1959): 20–28.

Frevel, Christian, ed. *Medien im antiken Palästina: Materielle Kommunikation und Medialität als Thema der Palästinaarchäologie*. Tübingen: Mohr Siebeck, 2005.
Freyne, Seán. *Galilee and Gospel: Collected Essays*. Wissenschaftliche Untersuchungen zum Neuen Testament 125. Tübingen: Mohr Siebeck, 2000.
–. *Galilee: From Alexander the Great to Hadrian 323 B.C.E. to 135 C.E.: A Study of Second Temple Judaism*. Notre Dame: University of Notre Dame Press, 1980.
–. *Jesus, A Jewish Galilean: A New Reading of the Jesus Story*. London: T & T Clark, 2004.
–. "The Geography of Restoration. Galilee-Jerusalem Relations in Early Judaism and Early Christianity." *New Testament Studies* 47 (2001): 289–311.
Friederich, J., W. Pöhlmann, and P. Stuhlmacher. "Zur historischen Situation und Intention von Röm 13:1–7." *Zeitschrift für Theologie und Kirche* 73 (1976): 131–166.
Fritz, Volkmar, and Philip R. Davies, eds. *The Origins of the Ancient Israelite States*. Journal for the Study of the Old Testament 228. Sheffield: Sheffield Academic Press, 1996.
Freeman, Philip, and D. L. Kennedy, eds. *The Defence of the Roman and Byzantine East: Proceedings of a Colloquium Held at the University of Sheffield in April 1986*. BAR International Series 297. 2 vols. Oxford: B.A.R., 1986.
Fuchs, Josef. "Die schwierige goldene Regel." *Stimmen der Zeit* 209 (1991): 773–781.
Fuks, Alexander. *Social Conflict in Ancient Greece*. Jerusalem: Magness Press, 1984.
Funk, Robert Walter. *Language, Hermeneutic, and Word of God: The Problem of Language in the New Testament and Contemporary Theology*. New York: Harper & Row, 1966.
Gal, Zvi, ed. *Eretz Zafon: Studies in Galilean Archaeology*. Jerusalem: Israel Antiquities Authority, 2002.
–. *The Lower Galilee During the Iron Age*. American Schools of Oriental Research Dissertation Series 8. Winona Lake: Eisenbrauns, 1992.
–. "The Lower Galilee in the Iron Age II: Analysis of Survey Material and Its Historical Interpretation." *Tel Aviv* 15–16 (1988–1989): 56–64.
Gardner, Gregg. "Jewish Leadership and Hellenistic Benefaction in the Second Century B.C.E." *Journal of Biblical Literature* 126.2 (2007): 327–343.
Garnsey, Peter, and Richard P. Saller, eds. *The Roman Empire: Economy, Society, and Culture*. Berkeley: University of California Press, 1987.
Gauthier, Phillipe. *Les cités grecques et leurs bienfaiteurs*. Paris: Boccard, 1985.
Gehrke, Hans-Joachim. "Patronus." Pages 154–156 in volume 5 (2004) of *Brill's New Pauly*. Edited by H. Cancik and H. Schneider. Leiden: Brill, 2004.
Gellner, Ernest, and John Waterbury, eds. *Patrons and Clients in Mediterranean Societies*. London: Duckworth, 1977.
Gelzer, Matthias. *The Roman Nobility*. Translated by Robin Seager. Oxford: Blackwell, 1969.
George, Augustin. *Études sur l'œuvre de Luc*. Sources bibliques. Paris: Gabalda, 1978.
–. "La royauté de Jésus selon l'évangile de Luc?" *Sciences Ecclesiastiques* 14 (1962): 57–69.
Gill, C., N. Postlethwaite, and R. Seaford, eds. *Reciprocity in Ancient Greece*. New York: Oxford University Press, 1998.
Gill, D. "Socrates and Jesus on Non-Retaliation and Love of Enemies." *Horizons* 18 (1991): 246–262.
Giovannini, Adalberto, and Marguerite Hirot. "L'inscription de Nazareth: Nouvelle Interprétation." *Zeitschrift für Papyrologie und Epigraphik* 124 (1999): 107–132.

Godet, F. *A Commentary on the Gospel of St. Luke.* 2 vols. Trans. E. W. Shalders and M. D. Cusin. Edinburgh: Clark, 1875.
Goett, Wilhelm. *Göttingische gelehrte Anzeigen.* 1903.
Goldingay, John. *Isaiah.* New International Bible Commentary. Peabody: Hendrickson, 2001.
Goldstein, Jonathan A. *1 Maccabees.* Anchor Bible 41. Garden City: Doubleday, 1976.
Goodman, Martin. *State and Society in Roman Galilee: A.D. 132–212.* Totowa, N.J.: Rowman & Allanheld, 1983.
Goody, Jack, ed. *The Character of Kinship.* Cambridge: Cambridge University Press, 1973.
Gowler, David B. *Host, Guest, Enemy, and Friend: Portraits of the Pharisees in Luke and Acts.* Emory Studies in Early Christianity 2. New York: P. Lang, 1991.
Grainger, John D. "Village Government in Roman Syria and Arabia." *Levant* 27 (1995): 179–195.
Green, Joel B. *Recovering the Scandal of the Cross: The Atonement in New Testament and Contemporary Contexts.* Carlisle, U.K.: Paternoster, 2004.
–. *The Death of Jesus: Tradition and Interpretation in the Passion Narrative* Wissenschaftliche Untersuchungen zum Neuen Testament 33. Tübingen: Mohr, 1988.
–. *The Gospel of Luke.* The New International Commentary on the New Testament. Grand Rapids, Mich: Eerdmans, 1997.
–. *The Theology of the Gospel of Luke.* New Testament Theology. Cambridge: Cambridge University Press, 1995.
Green, Joel B., Scot McKnight, and I. Howard Marshall, eds. *Dictionary of Jesus and the Gospels.* Downers Grove: InterVarsity Press, 1992.
Green, Joel B., and Michael C. McKeever. *Luke-Acts and New Testament Historiography.* IBR Bibliographies 8. Grand Rapids: Baker Books, 1994.
Gruen, Erich S., A. Bulloch, A. A. Long, and A. Stewart, eds. *Images and Ideologies: Self-Definition in the Hellenistic World.* Berkeley: University of California Press, 1993.
Gruen, Erich S. *The Hellenistic World and the Coming of Rome.* Berkeley: University of California Press, 1984.
Gschnitzer, F. "Proxenos." Pages 629–730 in *Real-Encyclopädie der classischen Altertumswissenschaft* suppl. 13 (1973). Edited by A. Pauly, G. Wissowa, and W. Kroll. Stuttgart, 1894–1980.
Guelich, Robert A. *The Sermon on the Mount: A Foundation for Understanding.* Waco: Word Books, 1982.
Gutman, Shmaryahu. "Gamla." Pages 459–463 in vol. 2 of *The New Encyclopedia of Archaeological Excavations in the Holy Land.* Edited by Ephraim Stern, Ayelet Leyinzon-Gilbo'a, and J. Aviram. Jerusalem: Israel Exploration Society & Carta, 1993.
Haas, Peter J., ed. *Recovering the Role of Women: Power and Authority in Rabbinic Jewish Society.* Atlanta: Scholars Press, 1992.
Haenchen, Ernst. *John 1–2.* Hermeneia. Minneapolis: Fortress, 1984.
Hamel, Gildas H. *Poverty and Charity in Roman Palestine, First Three Centuries C.E.* University of California Publications 23. Berkeley: University of California Press, 1990.
Hamm, D. "What the Samaritan Leper Sees: The Narrative Christology of Luke 17:11–19." *Catholic Biblical Quarterly* 56 (1994): 273–287.
Hands, Arthur Robinson. *Charities and Social Aid in Greece and Rome.* Aspects of Greek and Roman Life. Ithaca, N.Y.: Cornell University Press, 1968.

Hanks, Thomas D. *God So Loved the Third World*. Trans. James C. Dekker. Maryknoll: Orbis, 1983.
Hanson, K. C. "The Galilean Fishing Economy and the Jesus Tradition." *Biblical Theology Bulletin* 27.3 (1997): 99–111.
Hanson, K. C., and Douglas E. Oakman. *Palestine in the Time of Jesus: Social Structures and Social Conflicts*. Minneapolis: Fortress Press, 1998.
Hare, Douglas R. A. *The Theme of Jewish Persecution of Christians in the Gospel According to St. Matthew*. Cambridge: Cambridge University Press, 1967.
Harmand, L. *Un aspect social et politique du monde romain: Le Patronat sur les collectivités publiques des origins au Bas-Empire*. Publications de la Faculté des Lettres de l'Université de Clermont. 2nd serv. 2. Paris, 1957.
Harris, H. A. *Greek Athletics and the Jews*. Cardiff: University of Wales Press, 1976.
Harrison, James R. "Benefaction Ideology and Christian Responsibility for Widows," Pages 106–116 in volume 8 of *New Documents Illustrating Early Christianity*. Edited by G. H. R. Horsley and S. R. Llewelyn. 9 vols. North Ryde, N. S. W.: Macquarie University, Ancient History Documentary Research Centre; Grand Rapids: Eerdmans, 1981–2002.
–. *Paul's Language of Grace in Its Graeco-Roman Context*. Wissenschaftliche Untersuchungen zum Neuen Testament 2.172. Tübingen: Mohr Siebeck, 2003.
Haubeck, W. and M. Bachmann, eds. *Wort in der Zeit*. K. H. Rengstorf Festgabe. Leiden: Brill, 1980.
Harvey, A. E. *Strenuous Commands: The Ethic of Jesus*. London: SCM; Philadelphia: Trinity, 1990.
Hawthorne, Gerald F., ed. *Current Issues in Biblical and Patristic Interpretation*. Grand Rapids: Eerdmans, 1975.
Hedrick, Charles W. *Parables as Poetic Fictions: The Creative Voice of Jesus*. Peabody: Hendrickson, 1994.
Heil, John Paul. *The Meal Scenes in Luke-Acts: An Audience Oriented Approach*. Society of Biblical Literature Monograph Series 52. Atlanta: Scholars Press, 1999.
Heil, Christoph. *Lukas und Q: Studien zur lukanischen Redaktion des Spruchevangeliums Q*. Berlin: De Gruyter, 2003.
Hellegouarc'h, Joseph. *Le vocabulaire latin des relations et des partis politiques sous la République*. Paris: Les Belles lettres, 1963.
Hemer, C. J. *Luke the Historian*. Manchester: John Rylands University Library, 1977.
Hendin, David. "A New Coin Type of Herod Antipas." *Israel Numismatic Journal* 15 (2003–2006): 56–61.
Hendriksen, William. *The Gospel of Luke*. Edinburgh: Banner of Truth Trust, 1979.
Hendrix, H. "Benefactor/Patron Networks in the Urban Environment: Evidence from Thessalonica." *Semeia* 56 (1991): 39–58.
Hengel, Martin. *Judaism and Hellenism: Studies in Their Encounter in Palestine During the Early Hellenistic Period*. Philadelphia: Fortress Press, 1974.
–. *The "Hellenization" of Judaea in the First-century After Christ*. With Christoph Markschies. London: SCM Press, 1989.
Hense, O. *Die Synkrisis in der antiken Literatur*. Freiburg: Lehmann, 1893.
Herbert, S., and A. Berlin. "A New Administrative Centre for Persian and Hellenistic Galilee: Preliminary Report of the University of Minnesota Excavation of Kadesh." *Bulletin of the American Schools of Oriental Research* 329 (2003): 13–59.
Herion, Gary A. "Herod Philip." Pages 160–161 in vol. 3 of *Anchor Bible Dictionary*. Edited by David Noel Freedman. New York: Doubleday, 1992.

Hezser, Catherine. *Jewish Literacy in Roman Palestine*. Texte und Studien zum antiken Judentum 81. Tübingen: Mohr Siebeck, 2001.
Hirschfeld, Yizhar. "Tiberias." *Excavations and Surveys in Israel* 16 (1997): 35–42.
Hodder, Ian. *The Archaeological Process: An Introduction*. Oxford: Blackwell Publishers, 1999.
Hoehner, Harold W. *Chronological Aspects of the Life of Christ* (Grand Rapids: Zondervan, 1977.
–. *Herod Antipas*. Society for New Testament Studies Monograph Series 17. Cambridge: Cambridge University Press, 1972.
Hoffmann, Paul. *Tradition und Situation: Studien zur Jesusüberlieferung in der Logienquelle und den synoptischen Evangelien*. Neutestamentliche Abhandlungen 28. Münster: Aschendorff, 1995.
Holbl, G. *Geschichte des Ptolemäerreiches: Politik, Ideologie und religiöse Kultur von Alexander dem Grossen bis zur römischen Eroberung*. Darmstadt: Wissenschaftliche Buchgesellschaft, 1994. ET *A History of the Ptolemaic Empire*. New York: Routledge, 2001.
Holleaux, M. *Études d'épigraphie et d'histoire grecques*. 6 vols. Paris: Librarie d'Amerique et d'Orient Adrien Maisonneuve, 1952–1968.
Holum, Kenneth G., Robert L. Hohlfelder, and Roberta Blender Maltese, eds. *King Herod's Dream: Caesarea on the Sea*. New York: Norton, 1988.
Hordern, P., and N. Purcell. *The Corrupting Seas: A Study of Mediterranean History*. Oxford: Blackwell, 2000.
Hornblower, Simon, and Antony Spawforth, eds. *Oxford Classical Dictionary*. 3rd ed. rev. Oxford: Oxford University Press, 2003.
Horrell, D., ed. *Social Scientific Approaches to New Testament Interpretation*. Edinburgh: Clark, 1999.
Horsley, G. H. R. "Reclining at the Passover Meal." Page 75 in volume 2 of *New Documents Illustrating Early Christianity*. Edited by G. H. R. Horsley and S. R. Llewelyn. 9 vols. North Ryde, N. S. W.: Macquarie University, Ancient History Documentary Research Centre; Grand Rapids: Eerdmans, 1981–2002.
–. "The Inscriptions of Ephesos and the New Testament." *Novum Testamentum* 34.2 (1992): 106–168.
Horsley, Richard A. *Archaeology, History, and Society in Galilee: The Social Context of Jesus and the Rabbis*. Valley Forge: Trinity Press International, 1996.
–. "Ethics and Exegesis: 'Love Your Enemies' and the Doctrine of Non-Violence." *Journal of the American Academy of Religion* 54 (1986): 3–31.
–. *Galilee: History, Politics, People*. Valley Forge, Pa.: Trinity Press International, 1995.
–. *Jesus and Empire: Kingdom of God and the New World Disorder*. Minneapolis: Fortress Press, 2003.
Horsley, Richard A., and Neil Asher Silberman. *The Message and the Kingdom: How Jesus and Paul Ignited a Revolution and Transformed the Ancient World*. Minneapolis: Fortress Press, 1997.
Howard, Virgil P. *Das Ego Jesu in den synoptischen Evangelien: Untersuchungen zum Sprachgebrauch Jesu*. Marburg: Elwert, 1975.
Howgego, C. J., Volker Heuchert, and Andrew Burnett, eds. *Coinage and Identity in the Roman Provinces*. Oxford: Oxford University Press, 2004.
Humbert, P. *Recherches sur les sources égyptiennes de la littérature sapientiale d'Israël*. Mémoires de l'Université de Neuchâtel 7. Neuchâtel: Université de Neuchâtel, 1929.
Humphrey, J. H., ed. *The Roman and Byzantine Near East*. Journal of Roman Archaeology Supplementary Series 49. Vol. 3. Portsmouth: JRA, 2002.

Huvelin, H., M. Christol, and G. Gautier, eds. *Mélanges de numismatique: offerts à Pierre Bastien à l'occasion de son 75e anniversaire.* Wetteren, Belgium: Editions NR, 1987.
Ilan, Tal. *Lexicon of Jewish Names in Late Antiquity: Part I Palestine 330 B.C.E.–200 C.E.* Tübingen: Mohr Siebeck, 2002.
Isaac, B. "A Donation for Herod's Temple in Jerusalem." *Israel Exploration Journal* 33 (1983): 86–92.
Japp, Sarah. *Die Baupolitik Herodes' des Grossen: die Bedeutung der Architektur für die Herrschaftslegitimation eines römischen Klientelkönigs.* Internationale Archäologie 64. Rahden/Westf: Leidorf, 2000.
Jeanrond, Werner G., and Andrew D. H. Mayes, eds. *Recognising the Margins: Developments in Biblical and Theological Studies: Essays in Honour of Seán Freyne.* Blackrock, Co. Dublin: Columba Press, 2006.
Jensen, Morten Hørning. "Herod Antipas in Galilee: Friend or Foe of the Historical Jesus." *Journal for the Study of the Historical Jesus* 5 (2007): 7–32.
—. *Herod Antipas in Galilee: The Literary and Archaeological Sources on the Reign of Herod Antipas and its Socio-Economic Impact on Galilee.* Wissenschaftliche Untersuchungen zum Neuen Testament 2.215. Tübingen: Mohr Siebeck, 2006.
Jeremias, Joachim. *The Eucharistic Words of Jesus.* 3rd ed. Trans. N. Perrin. London: SCM Press, 1966.
—. *The Parables of Jesus.* London: SCM, 1985.
Jerusalem Post Staff (author). "Roman Stadium Found at Tiberius." *Jerusalem Post.* June 17, 2002.
Jervell, Jacob. *Luke and the People of God.* Minneapolis: Augsburg, 1972.
—. *The Theology of the Acts of the Apostles.* New Testament Theology. Cambridge: Cambridge University Press, 1996.
Johnson, Luke Timothy. *The Gospel of Luke.* Sacra Pagina 3. Collegeville: Liturgical Press, 1991.
Jones, A. H. M. *Cities of the Eastern Roman Provinces.* New York: Oxford University Press, 1998.
—. *The Herods of Judaea.* Oxford: Clarendon Press, 1938.
Joubert, Stephan. *Paul as Benefactor: Reciprocity, Strategy, and Theological Reflection in Paul's Collection.* Wissenschaftliche Untersuchungen zum Neuen Testament 2.124. Tübingen: Mohr Siebeck, 2000.
Judge, E. A. *Rank and Status in the World of the Caesars and St. Paul.* University of Canterbury, 1982.
—. *Social Distinctives of the Christians in the First-century: Pivotal Essays.* Ed. David M. Scholer. Peabody: Hendrickson, 2007.
—. "The Early Christians as a Scholastic Community." *Journal of Religious History* 1 (1960–1961): 4–15, 125–137.
—. "The Social Identity of the First Christians: A Question of Method in Religious History." *Journal of Religious History* 11 (1980): 210–217.
Jülicher, Adolf. *Die Gleichnisreden Jesu.* 2 vols. *1. Die Gleichnisreden Jesu im Allgemeinen 2. Auslegung der Gleichnisreden der drei ersten Evangelien.* Tübingen: Mohr, 1910.
Kahlefeld, H. *Der Jünger: eine Auslegung der Rede Lk 6, 20–49.* Frankfurt: Knecht, 1962.
Kariamadam, Paul. "Discipleship in the Lucan Journey Narrative." *Jeevadhara* 16 (1980): 111–130.

Karo, Georg. *Greek Personality in Archaic Sculpture*. Martin Classical Lectures 11. Cambridge: Published for Oberlin College by Harvard Univ. Press, 1948.
Karris, Robert J. *Luke, Artist and Theologian: Luke's Passion Account as Literature*. Theological Inquiries. New York: Paulist Press, 1985.
Käsemann, E. "Das Problem des historischen Jesus." *Zeitschrift für Theologie und Kirche* 51(1954): 125–152.
–. *Essays on New Testament Themes*. London: SCM Press, 1964.
Kasher, Aryeh, and Eliezer Witztum. *King Herod: A Persecuted Persecutor; A Case Study in Psychohistory and Psychobiography*. Berlin: Walter De Gruyter, 2007.
Katter, Calvin K. "Luke 22:14–38: A Farewell Address." PhD diss., The University of Chicago. 1993.
Katzoff, Ranon, and David M. Schaps. *Law in the Documents of the Judaean Desert*. Supplements to the Journal for the Study of Judaism 96. Leiden: Brill, 2005.
Katzoff, Ranon. "*Suffragium* in Exodus Rabbah 37. 2." *Classical Philology* 81.3 (1986): 235–240.
Kautsky, John H. *The Politics of Aristocratic Empires*. Chapel Hill: University of North Carolina Press, 1982.
Kee, H. C. "The Transformation of the Synagogue After 70 C.E.: Its Import for Early Christianity." *New Testament Studies* 36 (1990): 1–24.
Kennell, Nigel M. "New Light on 2 Maccabees 4:7–15." *Journal of Jewish Studies* 56 (2005): 10–24.
Kim, Kyoung-Jin. *Stewardship and Almsgiving in Luke's Theology*. Journal for the Study of the New Testament Supplement Series 155. Sheffield: Sheffield Academic Press, 1998.
Kim, S. S. "The Christological and Eschatological Significance of Jesus' Passover Signs in John 6." *Bibliotheca Sacra* 164 (2007): 307–322.
Kimball, Charles A. *Jesus' Exposition of the Old Testament in Luke's Gospel*. Journal for the Study of the New Testament 94. Sheffield: JSOT Press, 1994.
Kinman, Brent. "Parousia, Jesus, 'A-Triumphal' Entry, and the Fate of Jerusalem (Luke 19:28–44)." *Journal of Biblical Literature* 118 (1999): 279–294.
Kirk, Alan. "'Love Your Enemies,' The Golden Rule, and Ancient Reciprocity (Luke 6:27–35)." *Journal of Biblical Literature* 122.4 (2003): 667–686.
–. "Karl Polanyi, Marshall Sahlins, and the Study of Ancient Social Relations." *Journal of Biblical Literature* 126.1 (2007): 182–191.
–. "Some Compositional Conventions of Hellenistic Wisdom Texts and the Juxtaposition of 4:1–13; 6:20b–49; and 7:1–10 in Q." *Journal of Biblical Literature* 116 (1997): 235–267.
Klauck, Hans–Josef. "Kirche als Freundesgemeinschaft? Auf Spurensuche im Neuen Testament." *Münchener theologische Zeitschrift* 42 (1991): 10–13.
–. *Magic and Paganism in Early Christianity: The World of the Acts of the Apostles*. Trans. Brian McNeil. Minneapolis: Fortress Press, 2004.
Klein, Hans. *Das Lukasevangelium*. Kritisch-exegetischer Kommentar über das Neue Testament 1.3. Göttingen: Vandenhoeck and Ruprecht, 2006.
Kloppenborg Verbin, John S. "Dating Theodotos (*CIJ* II 1404)." *Journal of Jewish Studies* 51 (2000): 243–280.
–. *The Tenants in the Vineyard: Ideology, Economics, and Agrarian Conflict in Jewish Palestine*. Wissenschaftliche Untersuchungen zum Neuen Testament 195. Tübingen: Mohr Siebeck, 2006.
Klostermann, E. *Das Lukas-Evangelium*. 2nd ed. Tübingen: Mohr, 1929.

Koch, Klaus. *The Growth of the Biblical Tradition: The Form-Critical Method*. New York: Scribner, 1969.

Kokkinos, Nikos. *The Herodian Dynasty: Origins, Role in Society and Eclipse*. Journal for the Study of the Pseudepigrapha 30. Sheffield: Sheffield Academic Press, 1998.

Kollmann, Bernd. *Ursprung und Gestalten der frühchristlichen Mahlfeier*. Göttingen: Vandenhoeck and Ruprecht, 1990.

Kraemer, Ross. "Monastic Jewish Women in Graeco-Roman Egypt: Philo Judaeus on the Therapeutrides." *Signs* 14 (1989): 342–370.

Kraus, Jonathan D. Brumberg. "Symposium Scenes in Luke's Gospel with Special Attention to the Last Supper." PhD diss., Vanderbilt University, 1991.

Krause, Jens-Uwe. "Patrocinium I. Political." Pages 618–620 in *Brill's New Pauly* 10 (2007). Edited by H. Cancik and H. Schneider. Leiden: Brill, 2007.

Kremer, Jacob. *Lukasevangelium*. Neue Echter Bibel Neues Testament 3. Würzburg: Echter, 1988.

Krieger, Klaus-Stefan. *Geschichtsschreibung als Apologetik bei Flavius Josephus*. Text und Arbeiten zum neutestamentlichen Zeitalter 9. Tübingen: Francke, 1994.

Kuhnen, Hans-Peter, Leo Mildenberg, and Robert Wenning. *Palästina in Griechisch-Römischer Zeit*. Handbuch der Archäologie 2. 2 vols. Munich: C.H. Beck, 1990.

Kurz, William S. *Farewell Addresses in the New Testament*. Zacchaeus Studies New Testament. Collegeville: Liturgical, 1990.

–. "Luke 22:14–38 and Greco-Roman and Biblical Farewell Addresses." *Journal of Biblical Literature* 104.2 (1985): 251–268.

–. *Reading Luke-Acts: Dynamics of Biblical Narrative*. Louisville: Westminster/John Knox Press, 1993.

Kushnir-Stein, Alla. "An Inscribed Lead Weight from Ashdod: A Reconsideration." *Zeitschrift für Papyrologie und Epigraphik* 105 (1995): 81–84.

Kutscko, John. "Caesarea." Page 803 in vol. 1 of *Anchor Bible Dictionary*. Edited by David Noel Freedman. 6 vols. New York: Doubleday, 1992.

Lagrange, M. –J. *Évangile selon Saint Luc*. Études Biblique. 8th ed. Paris: Gabalda, 1948.

–. "Néhémie et Esdras. " *Revue Biblique* 3 (1894): 561–585; 4 (1895): 193–202.

Lämmer, Manfred. "Griechische Wettkämpfe in Galiläa unter der Herrschaft des Herodes Antipas." *Kölner Beiträge zur Sportwissenschaft* 5 (1976): 37–67.

Lange, H. O. *Das Weisheitsbuch des Amenemope, aus dem Papyrus 10,474 des British Museum*. Copenhagen: A.F. Høst & søn, 1925.

LaVerdiere, Eugene. *Luke*. New Testament Message 5. Wilmington, Del.: Michael Glazier, 1980.

–. *The Breaking of Bread: The Development of the Eucharist According to the Acts of the Apostles*. Chicago: Liturgy Training Publications, 1998.

–. *The Eucharist in the New Testament and the Early Church*. Collegeville: Liturgical Press, 1996.

Leaney, A. R. C. *A Commentary on the Gospel According to St. Luke*. Harper's New Testament Commentaries. New York: Harper, 1958.

Lee, Reuben Yat Tin. "Romanization in Palestine: A Study of Urban Development from Herod the Great to AD 70." *British Archaeological Reports International Series* 1180. Archaeopress: Oxford, 2003.

Lehmann, C. M., and K. Holum. *The Joint Expedition to Caesarea Maritima: Excavation Reports V: The Greek and Latin Inscriptions of Caesarea Maritima*. Boston: American Schools of Oriental Research, 1999.

Lémonon, J. P. *Pilate et le gouvernement de la Judée: Texts et monuments.* Études Bibliques. Paris: Gabalda, 1981.
Léon-Dufour, Xavier. *Le partage du pain eucharistique selon le Nouveau Testament.* Parole de Dieu. Paris: Editions du Seuil, 1982.
Lenski, Gerhard Emmanuel. *Power and Privilege: A Theory of Social Stratification.* New York: McGraw-Hill, 1966.
Levine, Amy-Jill. "Second Temple Judaism, Jesus, and Women: Yeast of Eden." *Biblical Interpretation* 2 (1994): 8–33.
Levine, Amy-Jill, Dale C. Allison, and John Dominic Crossan, eds. *The Historical Jesus in Context.* Princeton Readings in Religions. Princeton: Princeton University Press, 2006.
Levine, Lee I., ed. *The Galilee in Late Antiquity.* New York: Jewish Theological Seminary of America; Cambridge: Harvard University Press, 1992.
Levine, Lee I. *Judaism and Hellenism in Antiquity: Conflict or Confluence.* Seattle: University of Washington Press, 1998.
Lichtenberger, Achim. *Die Baupolitik Herodes des Grossen.* Abhandlungen des deutschen Palästinavereins 26. Wiesbaden: Harrassowitz Verlag, 1999.
–. *Kulte und Kultur der Dekapolis.* Abhandlungen des deutschen Pälastina-Vereins 29. Wiesbaden: Harrassowitz Verlag, 2003.
Lieberman, Saul. *Greek in Jewish Palestine: Studies in the Life and Manners of Jewish Palestine in the II-IV Centuries C.E.* New York: The Jewish Theological Seminary of America, 1942.
–. *Greek and Hellenism in Jewish Palestine.* Jerusalem: Bialik Institute, 1962.
Liesen, Jan. *Full of Praise: An Exegetical Study of Sir 39, 12–35.* Supplements to the Journal for the Study of Judaism 64. Leiden: Brill, 1999.
Lindemann, A. "Samaria und die Samaritaner im Neuen Testament." *Wort und Dienst* 22 (1993): 51–76.
–. *The Sayings Source Q and the Historical Jesus.* Bibliotheca Ephemeridum Theologicarum Lovaniensium 157. Leuven: University Press, 2001.
Lintott, Andrew W. "Cliens, clientes." Pages 450–452 in *Brill's New Pauly* 3 (2003). Edited by H. Cancik and H. Schneider. Leiden: Brill, 2003.
Linnemann, Eta. *Jesus of the Parables: Introduction and Exposition.* New York: Harper & Row, 1967.
Loffreda, Stanislao. *Recovering Capharnaum.* Jerusalem: Edizioni Custodia Terra Santa, 1985.
Lohmeyer, Ernst. *Evangelium des Markus.* Göttingen: Vandenhoeck and Ruprecht, 1959.
–. *Lord of the Temple: A Study of the Relation between Cult and Gospel.* Richmond: John Knox Press, 1962.
Loisy, A. *L'Evangile selon Luc.* Paris: Nourry, 1924.
Lomas, Kathryn, and Tim Cornell, eds. *Bread and Circuses: Euergetism and Municipal Patronage in Roman Italy.* London: Routledge, 2003.
Longenecker, Richard N., ed. *Patterns of Discipleship in the New Testament.* Grand Rapids: Eerdmans, 1996.
Luce, Harry Kenneth. *The Gospel According to S. Luke.* Cambridge Greek Testament for Schools and Colleges. Cambridge: Cambridge University Press, 1933.
Lull, David J., ed. *Society of Biblical Literature 1988 Seminar Papers.* Society of Biblical Literature Seminar Papers 27. Atlanta: Scholars Press, 1988.
Lull, D. J. "The Servant-Benefactor as a Model of Greatness (Lk 22:24–30)." *Novum Testamentum* 28 (1986): 289–305.

Mack, Burton L. *The Lost Gospel: The Book of Q & Christian Origins*. Shaftesbury, Dorset: Element, 1993.
MacLachlan, Bonnie. *The Age of Grace: Charis in Early Greek Poetry*. Princeton: Princeton University Press, 1993.
MacMullen, Ramsay. *Roman Social Relations: 50 B.C. to A.D. 284*. New Haven: Yale University Press, 1974.
–. *Romanization in the Time of Augustus*. New Haven: Yale University Press, 2000.
Magness, Jodi, and Seymour Gitin. *Hesed Ve-Emet: Studies in Honor of Ernest S. Frerichs*. Atlanta: Scholars Press, 1998.
Malina, Bruce. "Patron and Client." *Forum* 4 (1988): 2–32.
–. *Windows on the World of Jesus: Time Travel to Ancient Judea*. Louisville: Westminster/John Knox Press, 1993.
Malina, Bruce J., and Richard L. Rohrbaugh. *Social-Science Commentary on the Synoptic Gospels*. Minneapolis: Fortress Press, 2003.
Maoz, Z. U. "Banias." Pages 136–143 in vol. 1 of *The New Encyclopedia of Archaeological Excavations in the Holy Land*. Edited by Ephraim Stern, Ayelet Leyinzon-Gilbo'a, and J. Aviram. Jerusalem: Israel Exploration Society & Carta, 1993.
Marek, C. *Die Proxenie*. Europäische Hochschulschriften 3.213. Frankfurt am Main, Bern, and New York: Peter Lang, 1984.
Marguerat, Daniel. *First Christian Historian: Writing the "Acts of the Apostles"*. Cambridge: Cambridge University Press, 2002.
Marshak, Adam Kolman. "The Dated Coins of Herod the Great: Towards a New Chronology." *Journal for the Study of Judaism* 37.2 (2006): 212–240.
Marshall, I. H. *Luke: Historian and Theologian*. Exeter: Authentic Paternoster, 2006.
–. *Last Supper and Lord's Supper*. Vancouver: Regent College, 2007.
–. *The Gospel of Luke: A Commentary on the Greek Text*. New International Greek Testament Commentary 3. Grand Rapids: Eerdmans, 1978.
Marshall, I. Howard, and David Peterson, eds. *Witness to the Gospel: The Theology of Acts*. Grand Rapids: Eerdmans, 1998.
Martinez, Florentino Garcia, and Gerard P. Luttikhuizen, eds. *Jerusalem, Alexandria, Rome: Studies in Ancient Cultural Interaction in Honour of A. Hilhorst*. Leiden and Boston: Brill, 2003.
Mason, Hugh J. *Greek Terms for Roman Institutions: A Lexicon and Analysis*. American Studies in Papyrology 13. Hakkert: Toronto, 1974.
Mason, Steve, ed. *Understanding Josephus: Seven Perspectives*. Sheffield: Sheffield Academic Press, 1998.
Mason, Steve, Louis H. Feldman, and Christopher Begg, eds. *Flavius Josephus, Translation and Commentary*. Leiden: Brill, 2000–2003.
Matera, Frank J. *Passion Narratives and Gospel Theologies: Interpreting the Synoptics Through Their Passion Stories*. New York: Paulist Press, 1986.
Mattingly, Harold. *The Emperor and His Clients*. Sydney: Australasian Medical Pub. Co, 1948.
Mauss, Marcel. *The Gift: Forms and Functions of Exchange in Archaic Societies*. Trans. W. D. Halls. New York: Norton, 1967.
McCollough, C. Thomas. "The Roman Theater at Sepphoris: Monumental Statement of Polis at Play." Unpublished paper presented at the ASOR/AAR/SBL Southeastern Regional Meeting, Knoxville, Tenn., March 1998.
McKnight, Scot, and Grant R. Osborne, eds. *The Face of New Testament Studies: A Survey of Recent Research*. Grand Rapids: Baker Academic, 2004.

McLean, B. H. *An Introduction to Greek Epigraphy of the Hellenistic and Roman Periods from Alexander the Great Down to the Reign of Constantine (323 B.C.– A.D.337)*. Ann Arbor: University of Michigan Press, 2002.
McMahan, Craig Thomas. "Meals as Type-Scenes in the Gospel of Luke." PhD diss., The Southern Baptist Theological Seminary, 1987.
de Meeûs, X. "Composition de *Lc.*, XIV et genre symposiaque." *Ephemerides Theologicae Lovanienses* 37 (1961): 847–70.
Meier, John P. *A Marginal Jew: Rethinking the Historical Jesus*. The Anchor Bible Reference Library. 3 vols. New York: Doubleday, 1991–2001.
–. "The Historical Jesus and the Historical Herodians." *Journal of Biblical Literature* 119.4 (2000): 740–746.
–. "The Historical Jesus and the Historical Samaritans: What Can Be Said?" *Biblica* 81 (2000): 202–232.
Merkelbach, Reinhold. "Über eine Stelle im Evangelium des Lukas." *Grazer Beiträge* 1 (1973): 171–175.
Merritt, B. D. *Hesperia* 21 (1952): 370.
Meshorer, Ya'akov. "A Stone Weight from the Reign of Herod." *Israel Exploration Journal* 20 (1970): 97–98.
Meyer, B. *The Aims of Jesus*. London: 1979.
Meyers, Eric M., ed. *Galilee Through the Centuries: Confluence of Cultures*. Winona Lake, Ind.: Eisenbrauns, 1999.
Meyers, Eric M., and Ze'ev Weiss, eds. *Sepphoris in Galilee: Crosscurrents of Culture*. Winona Lake, Ind.: Eisenbrauns, 1996.
Meyers, Eric M., and Mark A. Chancey. "How Jewish Was Sepphoris in Jesus' Time?" *Biblical Archaeology Review* 26.4 (2000): 18–33.
Meyers, Eric M., and James F. Strange. *Archaeology, the Rabbis and Early Christianity*. London and Nashvillle: SCM and John Knox Press, 1981.
Meyers, Eric M. "Galilean Regionalism as a Factor in Historical Reconstruction." *Bulletin of the American Schools of Oriental Research* 221 (1976): 92–102.
–. "The Cultural Setting of Galilee: The Case of Regionalism and Early Judaism." In *Judentum: Allgemeines; Palästinisches Judentum*. Vol. 19.2.1 of *Aufstieg und Niedergang der römischen Welt*. Edited by Wolfgang Haase. Berlin: Walter de Gruyter, 1979.
Meynet, R. *Quelle est donc cette parole? Lecture "rhétorique" de l'évangile de Luc (1– 9,22–24)*. Lectio Divina 99 A-B. 2 vols. Paris, 1979.
Millar, Fergus. *Rome, the Greek World, and the East*. I: *The Roman Republic and the Augustan Revolution*. With Guy M. Rogers. Chapel Hill: University of North Carolina Press, 2002.
–. *Rome, the Greek World, and the East*. II: *Government, Society and Culture in the Roman Empire*. With Guy M. Rogers. Chapel Hill: University of North Carolina Press, 2004.
–. *Rome, the Greek World, and the East*. III: *The Greek World, the Jews and the East*. Ed. Hannah Cotton. Chapel Hill: University of North Carolina Press, 2006.
–. *The Emperor in the Roman World, 31 BC-AD 337*. Ithaca, N.Y.: Cornell University Press, 1977.
–. *The Roman Near East: 31 BC–AD 337*. Cambridge, Mass.: Harvard University Press, 1993.
–. *The Roman Republic and the Augustan Revolution*. Studies in the History of Greece and Rome. Chapel Hill: University of North Carolina Press, 2002.

Millard, A. R. *Reading and Writing in the Time of Jesus*. New York: New York University Press, 2000.
Miller, Merrill P. "The Function of Isa 61:1–2 in 11QMelchizedek." *Journal of Biblical Literature* 88 (1969): 467–469.
Miller, Stuart S. "Josephus on the Cities of Galilee: Factions, Rivalries and Alliances in the First Jewish Revolt." *Historia* 50.4 (2001): 453–67.
Minear, Paul S. "A Note on Luke xxii 36." *Novum Testamentum* 7 (1964): 128–134.
Mittelstaedt, Alexander. *Lukas als Historiker: zur Datierung des lukanischen Doppelwerkes*. Texte und Arbeiten zum neutestamentlichen Zeitalter 43. Tübingen: Francke, 2006.
Moessner, David P. *Lord of the Banquet: The Literary and Theological Significance of the Lukan Travel Narrative*. Minneapolis: Fortress Press, 1989.
Mommsen, T. *Römische Forschungen*. 2 vols. Berlin, 1864–1879.
Moo, Douglas J. *The Old Testament in the Gospel Passion Narratives*. Sheffield: Almond Press, 1983.
Moore, Carey A. *Tobit: A New Translation with Introduction and Commentary*. Anchor Bible 40A. New York: Doubleday, 1996.
Moors, Steveno Menno. "De Decapolis Steden en dorpen in de Romeinse proncicies Syria en Arabia." Diss., Rijksuniversiteit, Leiden, 1992.
Morris, Leon. *The Gospel According to John*. New International Commentary on the New Testament. Grand Rapids: Eerdmans, 1971.
–. *The Gospel According to St. Luke: An Introduction and Commentary*. The Tyndale New Testament Commentaries. Grand Rapids: Eerdmans, 1974.
Mott, S. C. "Greek Ethics and Christian Conversion: The Philonic Background of Titus II 10–14 and III 3–7." *Novum Testamentum* 20 (1978): 22–48.
–. "The Greek Benefactor and Deliverance from Moral Distress." PhD diss., Harvard University, 1971.
Moulton, James Hope, and George Milligan. *The Vocabulary of the Greek Testament Illustrated from the Papyri and Other Non-Literary Sources*. Grand Rapids: Eerdmans, 1930.
Moulton, James Hope, and Wilbert F. Howard. *A Grammar of New Testament Greek*. Vol. 2. *Accidence and Word-Formation*. Edinburgh: Clark, 1986.
Moxnes, Halvor. *Putting Jesus in His Place: A Radical Vision of Household and Kingdom*. Louisville and London: John Knox Press, 2003.
–. "The Construction of Galilee as a Place for the Historical Jesus – Part I, II." *Biblical Theology Bulletin* 31 (2001): 26–37, 64–77.
–. *The Economy of the Kingdom: Social Conflict and Economic Relations in Luke's Gospel*. Philadelphia: Fortress Press, 1988.
Müller, Paul-Gerhard. *Lukas-Evangelium*. Stuttgarter Kleiner Kommentar 3. Stuttgart: Verlag Katholisches Bibelwerk, 1984.
Murray, James A. H., Henry Bradley, W. A. Craigie, and C. T. Onions, eds. *The Oxford English Dictionary*. 2nd edition. Vol. 7. Oxford: Clarendon Press, 1989.
Nagy, Rebecca Martin, Carol L. Meyers, Eric M. Meyers, and Ze'ev Weiss, eds. *Sepphoris in Galilee: Crosscurrents of Culture*. Winona Lake: Eisenbrauns, 1996.
Nash, Robert N. "Luke 22:14–34." *Review and Expositor* 89 (1992): 397–401.
Nauta, Ruurd. *Poetry for Patrons: Literary Communication in the Age of Domitian*. Mnemosyne Supplement 206. Leiden: Brill, 2001.
Nelson, Peter K. *Leadership and Discipleship: A Study of Luke 22:24–30*. Society of Biblical Literature Dissertation Series 138. Atlanta: Scholars Press, 1994.

–. "Luke 22:29–30 and the Time Frame for Dining and Ruling." *Tyndale Bulletin* 44 (1993): 351–361.
–. "The Flow of Thought in Luke 22:24–27." *Journal for the Study of the Old Testament* 43 (1991): 113–123.
–. "The Unitary Character of Luke 22:24–30." *New Testament Studies* 40 (1994): 609–619.
Netzer, Ehud, with Rachel Laureys-Chachy. *The Architecture of Herod, the Great Builder*. Tübingen: Mohr Siebeck, 2006.
Neyrey, Jerome H., ed. *The Social World of Luke-Acts: Models for Interpretation*. Peabody, Mass.: Hendrickson, 1991.
Neyrey, Jerome, H. "God, Benefactor and Patron: The Major Cultural Model for Interpreting the Deity in Greco-Roman Antiquity." *Journal for the Study of the New Testament* 27 (2005): 465–492.
–. *The Passion According to Luke: A Redaction Study of Luke's Soteriology*. Theological Inquiries. New York: Paulist Press, 1985.
Nickelsburg, George W. E. "Riches, the Rich, and God's Judgment in 1 Enoch 92–105 and the Gospel According to Luke." *New Testament Studies* 25 (1979): 324–344.
Nicols, John. "Civic Patronage in Ancient Rome." Department of History, University of Oregon, typescript, 1995.
–. "Patrons of Greek Cities in the Early Principate." *Zeitschrift für Papyrologie und Epigraphik* 80 (1990): 81–108.
–. "Pliny and the Patronage of Communities." *Hermes* 108 (1980): 365–385.
–. *The Patronage of Communities in the Roman Empire*. Forthcoming.
Nigdelis, P. M. "'Ρωμαῖοι πάτρωνες και "αναγκαιότατοι καιροί" (παρατηρήσεις στην επιγραφή SEG 32.825 της Πάρου)." *Hellenika* 40 (1989): 34–49.
Nilsson, M. *Geschichte der griechischen Religion* II^2. Munich: 1961.
Nolland, John. *Luke*. Word Biblical Commentary 35A-C. 3 vols. Dallas: Word, 1989–1993.
Oakman, Douglas E. *Jesus and the Peasants*. Matrix: The Bible in Mediterranean Context. Eugene: Cascade, 2008.
–. "The Radical Jesus: You Cannot Serve God and Mammon." *Biblical Theology Bulletin* 34 (2004): 122–129.
Orton, David E., ed. *The Composition of Luke's Gospel: Selected Studies from "Novum Testamentum"*. Brill's Readers in Biblical Studies 1. Leiden: Brill, 1999.
Osiek, Carolyn. "The New Handmaid: The Bible and Social Sciences." *Theological Studies* 50.2 (1989): 260–278.
Oswalt, John. *The Book of Isaiah 40–66*. The New International Commentary on the Old Testament. Grand Rapids: Eerdmans, 1998.
O'Toole, Robert F. "Some Exegetical Reflections on Luke 13,10–17." *Biblica* 73 (1992): 84–107.
Overman, Andrew J. "Recent Advances in the Archaeology of the Galilee in the Roman Period." *Currents in Research: Biblical Studies* 1 (1993): 35–57.
Pao, David W. *Thanksgiving: An Investigation of a Pauline Theme*. New Studies in Biblical Theology 13. Downers Grove: InterVarsity Press, 2002.
Parente, F., and J. Sievers, eds. *Josephus and the History of the Graeco-Roman Period: Essays in Honour of Morton Smith*. Studia Post-Biblica 41. Leiden: Brill, 1994.
Parsons, Mikeal Carl, and Richard I. Pervo. *Rethinking the Unity of Luke and Acts*. Minneapolis: Fortress Press, 1993.
Parsons, Mikeal C. *Luke: Storyteller, Interpreter, Evangelist*. Peabody: Hendrickson, 2007.

Patrich, J. "Herod's Theater in Jerusalem—A New Proposal." *Israel Exploration Journal* 52 (2002): 231–239.
Paul, G. M., and Michael Ierardi. *Roman Coins and Public Life Under the Empire: E. Togo Salmon Papers II*. Ann Arbor: University of Michigan Press, 1999.
Pauly, August Friedrich von, Georg Wissowa, Wilhelm Kroll, and K. Witte, eds. *Paulys Real-Encyclopädie der classischen Altertumswissenschaft*. 49 vols. Stuttgart: Metzler, 1893–1963; Supplement, 1903–1978.
Pearson, Lionel Ignacius Cusack. *Popular Ethics in Ancient Greece*. Stanford: StanfordUniversity Press, 1962.
Pernot, Hubert. "Une correction à Luc VI,35." *Comptes rendus de l'Académie des inscriptions et belles-lettres* (1929): 277–280.
Pervo, Richard I. *Profit with Delight: The Literary Genre of the Acts of the Apostles*. Philadelphia: Fortress Press, 1987.
Pesch, R. "The Last Supper and Jesus' Understanding of His Death." *Bible Bhashyam* 3 (1977): 58–75.
Pesch, R., and R. Schnackenburg, ed. *Jesus und der Menschensohn: Festschrift für A. Vögtle*. Freiburg: Herder, 1975.
Petersen, Eugene, Adolf Hermann, and F. von Luschan. *Reisen in Lykien, Milyas und Kibyratis*. Reisen im südwestlichen Kleinasien 2. Vienna: Gerold, 1889.
Philipp, G. B. "Kritzeleien eines erleichterten Lehrers auf einem hölzernen Buchdeckel." *Gymnasium* 85 (1978): 151–159.
Phillips, Susan S., and Patricia E. Benner, eds. *The Crisis of Care: Affirming and Restoring Caring Practices in the Helping Professions*. Health Care Policy and Ethics. Washington, D.C.: Georgetown University, 1994.
Pickard, John. "Dionysus en Limnais." *The American Journal of Archaeology and of the History of the Fine Arts* 8.1 (Jan. – Mar. 1893): 56–82.
Pilch, J., ed. *Social Scientific Models for Interpreting the Bible: Essays by the Context Group in Honor of Bruce J. Malina*. Leiden: Brill, 2000.
Piper, John. *"Love Your Enemies": Jesus' Love Command in the Synoptic Gospels and in the Early Christian Paraenesis: A History of the Tradition and Interpretation of Its Uses*. Society for New Testament Studies Monograph Series 38. Cambridge: Cambridge University Press, 1979.
Pixner, Bargil. *Wege des Messias und Stätten der Urkirche: Jesus und das Judenchristentum im Licht neuer archäologischer Erkenntnisse*. 2nd ed. Giessen: Brunnen, 1994.
Plummer, Alfred. *A Critical and Exegetical Commentary on the Gospel According to St. Luke*. New York: Scribner's Sons, 1902.
Polanyi, Karl. *Primitive, Archaic, and Modern Economies: Essays of Karl Polanyi*. Garden City: Anchor Books, 1968.
Poon, Wilson C. K. "Superabundant Table Fellowship in the Kingdom: The Feeding of the Five Thousand and the Meal Motif in Luke." *Expository Times* (2003): 224–230.
Porath, Y., E. Yannai, and A. Kasher. "Archaeological Remains at Jatt." *Atiqot* 27 (1999): 1–78 and 167*–171*.
Porter, Stanley E. "Luke 17.11–19 and the Criteria for Authenticity Revisited." *Journal for the Study of the Historical Jesus* 1 (2003): 201–224.
Prange, Victor H. *Luke*. People's Bible Commentary. Saint Louis: Concordia, 2004.
Prince, Gerald. *Narrative as Theme: Studies in French Fiction*. Lincoln: University of Nebraska Press, 1992.
Prior, Michael. *Jesus the Liberator: Nazareth Liberation Theology (Luke 4. 16–30)*. Sheffield: Sheffield Academic Press, 1995.

Puchstein, Otto. *Jahrbuch des Kaiserlich Deutschen Archäologie Instituts* 16 (1901): 133–161.
Qedar, Shraga. "Two Lead Weights of Herod Antipas and Agrippa II and the Early History of Tiberias." *Israel Numismatic Journal* 9 (1986–1987): 29–35.
Quass, F. *Die Honoratiorenschicht in den Städten des griechischen Ostens: Untersuchungen zur politischen und sozialen Entwicklung in hellenistischer und römischer Zeit.* Stuttgart: Steiner Verlag, 1993.
Quincey, J. H. "Greek Expressions of Thanks." *Journal of Hellenic Studies* 86 (1966): 133–158.
Raban, Avner, and Kenneth Holum, eds. *Caesarea Maritima: A Retrospective After Two Millennia.* Leiden: Brill, 1996.
Rajak, Tessa. *Josephus: The Historian and His Society.* London: Duckworth, 2002.
Rappaport, Uriel. "Les juifs et leurs voisins à l'époque perse, hellénistique et romaine." *Annales: Histoire, Sciences Sociales* 5 (1996): 955–974.
—. "Phoenicia and Galilee: Economy, Territory and Political Relations." *Studia Phoenicia* 9 (1992): 262–268.
Raubitschek, A. E. "Epigraphical Notes on Julius Caesar." *Journal of Roman Studies* 44 (1954): 65–75.
Rawson, E. *Roman Culture and Society: Collected Papers.* Oxford: Oxford University Press, 1991.
—. "The Eastern Clientela of Cladius and the Claudii." *Historia* 22 (1973): 219–239.
Reed, Jonathan. *Archaeology and the Galilean Jesus: A Re-Examination of the Evidence.* Harrisburg, Pa.: Trinity Press, 2000.
Refoulé, F., ed. *À cause de l'Évangile: Études sur les Synoptiques et les Actes.* Festschrift J. Dupont. Lectio Divina 123. Paris: Cerf, 1985.
Reinach, Théodore. "Mutuum date, nihil inde sperantes." *Revue des études grecques* 7 (1894): 57–58.
Reiterer, Friedrich Vinzenz, Renate Egger-Wenzel, Ingrid Krammer, Petra Ritter-Müller, and Lutz Schrader. *Zählsynopse zum Buch Ben Sira.* Fontes et subsidia ad Bibliam pertinentes 1. Berlin: De Gruyter, 2003.
Rese, M. *Alttestamentliche Motive in der Christologie des Lukas.* Studium zum Neuen Testament 1. Gütersloh: Mohn, 1969.
Resseguie, J. L. "Point of View in the Central Section of Luke." *Journal of the Evangelical Theological Society* 25 (1982): 41–47.
Rey-Coquais, J. –P. "Paneas." Page 670 in vol. 2 of *The Princeton Encyclopedia of Classical Sites.* Edited by Stillwell, Richard, William Lloyd MacDonald, and Marian Holland McAllister. 2 vols. Princeton: Princeton University Press, 1976.
—. "Syrie romaine, de Pompée à Dioclétien." *Journal of Roman Studies* 68 (1978): 44–73.
Reynolds, J. M. "Review of Harmand, *Un aspect social et politique.*" *Revue belge de philology et d'histoire* 37 (1959): 1149–1151.
Richardson, Peter. *Building Jewish in the Roman East.* Waco: Baylor University Press, 2004.
—. *Herod: King of the Jews and Friend of the Romans.* Columbia: University of South Carolina Press, 1996.
—. "Religion, Architecture and Ethics: Some First-century Case Studies." *Horizons in Biblical Theology* 10.2 (1988): 19–49.
—. "What Has Cana to Do with Capernaum?" *New Testament Studies* 48 (2002): 314–331.

Ricoeur, Paul. "The Golden Rule: Exegetical and Theological Perplexities." *New Testament Studies* 36 (1990): 392–397.

Riedo-Emmenegger, Christoph. *Prophetisch-messianische Provokateure der Pax Romana. Jesus von Nazaret und andere Störenfriede im Konflikt mit dem Römischen Reich.* Novum Testamentum et Orbis Antiquus 56. Freiburg: Academic Press; Göttingen: Vandenhoeck and Ruprecht, 2005.

Rienecker, Fritz. *Das Evangelium des Lukas.* Wuppertaler Studienbibel 2. Wuppertal: R. Brockhaus, 2005.

Riesner, Rainer. *Jesus als Lehrer: eine Untersuchung zum Ursprung der Evangelien-Überlieferung.* Wissenschaftliche Untersuchungen zum Neuen Testament 7. Tübingen: Mohr Siebeck, 1981.

Ringe, Sharon H. "The Jubilee Proclamation in the Ministry and Teachings of Jesus: A Tradition-Critical Study in the Synoptic Gospels and Acts." PhD diss., Union Theological Seminary, 1981.

Robert, Jeanne, and Louis Robert. "Bulletin Épigraphique." *Bulletin Épigraphique* 83 (1970): 362–488.

Robertson, A. T. *A Grammar of the Greek New Testament in the Light of Historical Research.* Nashville: Broadman Press, 1934.

Rodgers, Zuleika, ed. *Making History: Josephus and Historical Method.* Journal for the Study of Judaism Supplement 110. Leiden: Brill, 2007.

Rogers, Guy. "The Gift and Society in Roman Asia: Orthodoxies and Heresies." *Scripta Classica Israelica: Yearbook of the Israel Society for the Promotion of Classical Studies* (Jerusalem) 12 (1993): 188–199.

Roloff, Jürgen. *Apostolat – Verkündigung – Kirche: Ursprung, Inhalt und Funktion des kirchlichen Apostelamtes nach Paulus, Lukas und den Pastoralbriefen.* Gütersloh: Mohn, 1965.

Roniger, Luis. "Modern Patron-Client Relations and Historical Clientelism: Some Clues from Ancient Republican Rome." *Archives Europeennes de Sociologie* 24 (1983): 63–95.

Rostovtzeff, M. *The Social and Economic History of the Hellenistic World.* 2 vols. 2nd ed. Rev. by P. M. Fraser. Oxford: Oxford University Press, 1972.

Rothschild, Clare K. *Luke-Acts and the Rhetoric of History: An Investigation of Early Christian Historiography.* Wissenschaftliche Untersuchungen zum Neuen Testament 175. Tübingen: Mohr Siebeck, 2004.

Rouland, N. *Pouvoir politique et dépendance personnelle dans l'Antiquité romaine: Genèse et rôle des rapports de clientèle.* Brussels: Latomus, 1979.

Roussel, P. "Un nouvel hymne à Isis." *Revue des études grecques* 42 (1929): 136–168.

Rowe, C. Kavin. "Luke-Acts and the Imperial Cult: A Way Through the Conundrum?" *Journal for the Study of the New Testament* 27.3 (2005): 279–300.

Rutgers, Leonard Victor, ed. *What Athens Has to Do with Jerusalem: Essays on Classical, Jewish, and Early Christian Art and Archaeology in Honor of Gideon Foerster.* Interdisciplinary Studies on Cultural Interaction in Antiquity 1. Leuven: Peeters, 2002.

Ryan, Rosalie. "The Women from Galilee and Discipleship in Luke." *Biblical Theology Bulletin* 15 (1985): 56–59.

Rowley, H. H. "The Herodians in the Gospels." *Journal of Theological Studies* 41 (1940): 14–27.

Safrai, Zeev. *The Economy of Roman Palestine.* London and New York: Routledge, 1994.

Sahlins, Marshall David. *Stone Age Economics.* Chicago: Aldine-Atherton, 1972.

Saldarini, Anthony J. *Jesus and Passover.* New York: Paulist Press, 1984.

–. *Pharisees, Scribes and Sadducees in Palestinian Society: A Sociological Approach.* Wilmington: M. Glazier, 1988.
Saller, Richard P. *Personal Patronage Under the Early Empire.* Cambridge: Cambridge University Press, 1982.
Sánchez, Héctor. *Das lukanische Geschichtswerk im Spiegel heilsgeschichtlicher Übergänge.* Paderborner theologische Studien 29. Paderborn: Ferdinand Schöningh, 2001.
Sanders, E. P., ed. *Jesus, the Gospels, and the Church.* In Honor of W. R. Farmer. Macon: Mercer, 1987.
Sanders, E. P. *Jesus and Judaism.* London: SCM, 1985.
–. "Jesus in Historical Context." *Theology Today* 50 (1993): 429–448.
Sawicki, Marianne. *Crossing Galilee: Architectures of Contact in the Occupied Land of Jesus.* Harrisburg, Pa.: Trinity Press, 2000.
Schiffman, Lawrence. *The Eschatological Community of the Dead Sea Scrolls.* Society ofBiblical Literature Monograph Series 38. Atlanta: Scholars, 1989.
Schmidt, Steffen W., J. C. Scott, C. Landi, and L. Guasti, eds. *Friends, Followers, and Factions: A Reader in Political Clientelism.* Berkeley: University of California Press, 1977.
Schmithals, Walter. *Das Evangelium nach Lukas.* Zürcher Bibelkommentare NT 3.1. Zürich: Theologischer Verlag, 1980.
Schnabel, Eckhard J. *Early Christian Mission.* Vol. 1 *Jesus and the Twelve.* Vol. 2. *Paul and the Early Church.* Downers Grove: InterVarsity Press, 2004.
Schneider, G. *Das Evangelium nach Lukas.* Ökumenischer Taschenbuchkommentar zum Neuen Testament 3/1–2. Gütersloh: Mohn, 1977.
Schottroff, Luise. "Das Gleichnis vom grossen Gastmahl in der Logienquelle." *Evangelische Theologie* 47 (1987): 192–211.
Schottroff, Luise, and Wolfgang Stegemann. *Jesus and the Hope of the Poor.* Maryknoll: Orbis Books, 1986.
Schrage, W. *Die Christen und der Staat nach dem Neuen Testament.* Gütersloh: Gütersloher Verlag, 1971.
Schramm, Tim. *Der Markus-Stoff bei Lukas: eine literarkritische und redaktionsgeschichtliche Untersuchung.* Society for New Testament Studies Monograph Series 14. Cambridge: Cambridge University Press, 1971.
Schultz, Brian. "Jesus as Archelaus in the Parable of the Pounds (Lk. 19:11–27)." *Novum Testamentum* 49.2 (2007): 105–127.
Schürer, Emil. *The History of the Jewish People in the Age of Jesus Christ (175 B.C.– A.D.135).* Edited by Géza Vermes and Fergus Millar. Edinburgh: Clark, 1973.
Schürmann, Heinz. *Das Lukasevangelium.* 2 vols. 2nd ed. Herders Theologischer Kommentar zum Neuen Testament 3. Freiburg im Breisgau: Herder, 1982.
–. "Der Jüngerkreis Jesu als Zeichen für Israel." *Geist und Leben* 16 (1963): 21–35.
–. *Traditionsgeschichtliche Untersuchungen.* Düsseldorf, 1968.
Scott, Bernhard. *Hear Now the Parable: A Commentary on the Parables of Jesus.* Minneapolis: Fortress, 1989.
Schwank, B. "Neue Funde in Nabatäerstädten und ihre Bedeutung für die neutestamentliche Exegese." *New Testament Studies* 29 (1983): 429–435.
Schwartz, Seth. *Imperialism and Jewish Society: 200 B.C.E. to 640 C.E.* Princeton and Oxford: Princeton University Press, 2001/2004.
–. *Josephus and Judaean Politics.* Leiden: Brill, 1999.
Schwartz, Daniel R. *Agrippa I: The Last King of Judaea.* Texte und Studien zum antiken Judentum 23. Tübingen: Mohr, 1990.

Schwarz, Günther. "'Αγαπᾶτε τοὺς ἐχθροὺς ὑμῶν: Mt 5,44a/Lk 6,27a (35a): Jesu Forderung kat' exochèn." *Biblische Notizen* 12 (1980): 32–34.
–. "Μηδὲν ἀπελπίζοντες." *Zeitschrift für die neutestamentliche Wissenschaft und die Kunde der älteren Kirche* 71 (1980): 133–135.
Schweizer, Eduard. *The Good News According to Luke.* Atlanta: John Knox Press, 1984.
Seaford, Richard. *Reciprocity and Ritual: Homer and Tragedy in the Developing City-State.* Oxford: Clarendon Press, 1994.
Segal, Arthur. *Hippos – Sussita: Fifth Season of Excavations and Summary of All Five Seasons.* Haifa: University of Haifa, 2004.
Segovia, Fernando F., ed. *Discipleship in the New Testament.* Philadelphia: Fortress Press, 1985.
Sevenster, Jan Nicolaas. *Do You Know Greek? How Much Greek Could the First JewishChristian Have Known?* Supplements to Novum Testamentum 19. Leiden: Brill, 1968.
Shanks, Michael, and Christopher Tiller. *Re-Constructing Archaeology: Theory and Practice.* Cambridge: Cambridge University Press, 1987.
Sheridan, M. "Disciples and Discipleship in Matthew and Luke." *Biblical Theology Bulletin* 3 (1973): 235–255.
Sherwin-White, A. N. *Roman Society and Roman Law in the New Testament.* Sarum Lectures 1960–1961. Oxford: Clarendon, 1963.
Shin, Gabriel Kyo-Seon. *Die Ausrufung des endgültigen Jubeljahres durch Jesus in Nazaret. Eine historisch-kritische Studie zu Lk 4,16–30.* Bern: Peter Lang, 1989.
Silberman, Neil Asher, and David B. Small, eds. *The Archaeology of Israel: Constructing the Past, Interpreting the Present.* Journal for the Study of the Old Testament 237. Sheffield: Sheffield Academic Press, 1997.
Skaard, Eiliv. *Zwei Religions-Politische Begriffe: Euergetes-Concordia.* Avhandlinger utgitt av Det Norske Videnskaps-Akademi i Oslo. Vol 2. Hist.-Filos. Klasse. 1931. No 2. Oslo: Jacob Dybwad, 1932.
Skehan, Patrick W., and Alexander A. Di Lella. *The Wisdom of Ben Sira: A New Translation with Notes.* Anchor Bible Commentary 39. New York: Doubleday, 1987.
Sloan, Ian. "The Greatest and the Youngest: Greco-Roman Reciprocity in the Farewell Address, Luke 22:24–30." *Studies in Religion* 22 (1993): 63–73.
Sloan, Robert Bryan. *The Favorable Year of the Lord: A Study of Jubilary Theology in the Gospel of Luke.* Austin: Schola, 1977.
Smallwood, E. Mary. *Philonis Alexandrini, Legatio Ad Gaium: Edited with an Introduction, Translation and Commentary.* Leiden: Brill, 1961.
–. *The Jews Under Roman Rule: From Pompey to Diocletian.* Studies in Judaism in Late Antiquity 20. Leiden: Brill, 1976.
Smith, Dennis E. *From Symposium to Eucharist: The Banquet in the Early Christian World.* Minneapolis: Fortress, 2003.
–. "Social Obligation in the Context of Communal Meals: A Study of the Christian Meal in 1 Corinthians in Comparison with Graeco-Roman Communal Meals." Th.D. diss., Harvard Divinity School, 1980.
–. "Table Fellowship as a Literary Motif in the Gospel of Luke." *Journal of Biblical Literature* 106.4 (1987): 613–638.
Snyder, H. Gregory. *Teachers and Texts in the Ancient World: Philosophers, Jews and Christians.* London: Routledge, 2000.
Soards, Marion L. *The Passion According to Luke: The Special Material of Luke 22.* Journal for the Study of the New Testament Supplement 14. Sheffield: JSOT, 1987.

–. "Tradition, Composition, and Theology in Luke's Account of Jesus before Herod Antipas." *Biblica* 66 (1985): 344–364.
Sperber, Daniel. *A Dictionary of Greek and Latin Legal Terms in Rabbinic Literature.* Ramat-Gan, Israel: Bar-Ilan University Press, 1984.
Spicq, Ceslas. *Agapè dans le Nouveau Testament analyse des textes.* Etudes Bibliques. Paris: Gabalda, 1958.
–. *Theological Lexicon of the New Testament.* Trans. James D. Ernest. Peabody: Hendrickson, 1994.
Spitzl, Thomas. *Lex Municipii Malacitani.* Vestigia 36. Munich: Beck, 1984.
Steele, E. Springs. "Luke 11:37–54–A Modified Hellenistic Symposium?" *Journal of Biblical Literature* 103.3 (1984): 379–394.
Stegemann, Ekkehard W., and Wolfgang Stegemann. *Urchristliche Sozialgeschichte: die Anfänge im Judentum und die Christusgemeinden in der mediterranen Welt.* Stuttgart: Kohlhammer, 1995. ET *The Jesus Movement: A Social History of Its First-century.* Trans. O. C. Dean, Jr. Minneapolis: Fortress Press, 1999.
Stegemann, Wolfgang, Bruce J. Malina, and Gerd Theissen, eds. *The Social Setting of Jesus and the Gospels.* Minneapolis: Fortress Press, 2002.
Stein, Robert H. *Luke.* The New American Commentary 24. Nashville: Broadman Press, 1992.
Stein, S. "The Influence of Symposia Literature on the Literary Form of the Pesah Haggadah." *Journal of Jewish Studies* 8 (1957): 13–44.
Steiner, Deborah Tarn. *Images in Mind: Statues in Archaic and Classical Greek Literature and Thought.* Princeton: Princeton University Press, 2001.
Steiner, Mark G. "The Covenantal Significance of Remembrance as It Is Used in Luke 22:19." S.T.M. thesis, Concordia Seminary, 1988.
Stendahl, Krister, ed. *The Scrolls and the New Testament.* London: SCM Press, 1958.
Stephanou, P. Ἐθνόμαρτυς Πλάτων ὁ Χίου Nov. 1956, 131.
Sterling, Gregory E. *Historiography and Self-Definition: Josephos, Luke-Acts, and Apologetic Historiography.* Supplements to Novum Testamentum 64. Leiden: Brill, 1992.
Stern, Ephraim, and Amihay Mazar. *Archaeology of the Land of the Bible: The Assyrian, Babylonian, and Persian Periods, 732–332 B.C.E.* Vol. 2. New York and London: Doubleday, 2001.
Stern, Ephraim, Ayelet Leyinzon-Gilbo'a, and J. Aviram, eds. *The New Encyclopedia of Archaeological Excavations in the Holy Land.* Jerusalem: Israel Exploration Society & Carta, 1993.
Stern, Menahem. *Greek and Latin Authors on Jews and Judaism.* Jerusalem: Israel Academy of Sciences and Humanities, 1974–1984.
Stewart, Z., ed. *Essays on Religion and the Ancient World.* 2 vols. Cambridge: Harvard University Press, 1972.
Strange, James F., Thomas R. W. Longstaff, and Dennis E. Groh, eds. *Excavations at Sepphoris.* Vol. 1: *University of Florida Probes in the Citadel and Villa.* Brill Reference Library of Judaism 22. Leiden: Brill, 2006.
Strickert, Frederick M. *Bethsaida: Home of the Apostles.* Collegeville: Liturgical Press, 1998.
Sweetland, D. M. "The Lord's Supper and the Lukan Community." *Biblical Theology Bulletin* 13 (1983): 23–27.
Syme, Ronald. *The Roman Revolution.* London: Oxford University Press, 1960.
Syon, Danny. "The Coins from Gamla: An Interim Report." *Israel Numismatic Journal* 12 (1992/1993): 34–55.

–. "Tyre and Gamla: A Study in the Monetary Influence of Southern Phoenicia on Galilee and the Golan in the Hellenistic and Roman Periods." PhD diss., Jerusalem, 2004.
Syon, Danny, and Shlomit Nemlich. *Gamla*. Qazrin, Israel: Golan Archaeological Museum, 2001.
Syon, Danny, and Z. Yavor. "Gamla 1997–2000." *Hadashot Arkheologiyot-Excavations and Surveys in Israel* 114 (2005): 2–5.
Talbert, Charles H., ed. *Perspectives on Luke-Acts*. Danville: Association of Baptist Professors of Religion, 1978.
Talbert, Charles H. *Reading Luke-Acts in Its Mediterranean Milieu*. Supplements to Novum Testamentum 107. Leiden: Brill, 2003.
–. *Reading Luke: A Literary and Theological Commentary*. Macon: Smyth & Helwys, 2002.
Talmon, Shemaryahu, Yigael Yadin, Carol A. Newsom, and Elisha Qimron. *Masada VI: Yigael Yadin excavations, 1963–1965: Final Reports: Hebrew fragments from Masada*. Jerusalem: Israel Exploration Society, 1999.
Tannenbaum, M. H. "Holy Year 1975 and Its Origin in the Jewish Jubilee Year." *Jubilaeum* 7 (1974): 63–79.
Tannehill, Robert C. "A Study in the Theology of Luke-Acts." *Ashland Theological Review* 43 (1961): 195–203.
–. *Luke*. Abingdon New Testament Commentaries. Nashville: Abingdon Press, 1996.
–. "Review of *Feasting and Social Rhetoric*." *Biblica* 77 (1996): 565.
–. "What Kind of King? What Kind of Kingdom? A Study of Luke." *Word and World* 12 (1992): 17–22.
Taylor, Joan E. "Pontius Pilate and the Imperial Cult in Roman Judaea." *New Testament Studies* 52 (2006): 555–582.
Taylor, Lily Ross. *Party Politics in the Age of Caesar*. Sather Classical Lectures 22. Berkeley: University of California Press, 1949.
Taylor, Vincent. *The Passion Narrative of St. Luke*. Society for New Testament Studies Monograph Series 19. Cambridge: Cambridge University Press, 1972.
Tcherikover, Victor. *Hellenistic Civilization and the Jews*. Philadelphia: Jewish Publication Society of America, 1959.
–. "Was Jerusalem a 'Polis'?" *Israel Exploration Journal* 14 (1964): 61–78.
Theissen, Gerd. "Historical Scepticism and the Criteria of Jesus Research: My Attempt to Leap over Lessing's Yawning Gulf." *Scottish Journal of Theology* 49 (1996): 146–175.
–. *The Gospels in Context: Social and Political History in the Synoptic Tradition*. Trans. Linda M. Maloney. Minneapolis: Fortress Press, 1991.
–. *Social Reality and the Early Christians*. Trans. M. Kohl. Minneapolis: Fortress Press, 1992.
Theissen, Gerd, and Dagmar Winter. *Die Kriterienfrage in der Jesusforschung: Vom Differenzkriterium zum Plausibilitätskriterium*. Freiburg: Novum Testamentum et Orbis Antiquus, 1997. ET. *The Quest for the Plausible Jesus: The Question of Criteria*. Trans. M. Eugene Boring. Louisville: Westminster, 2002.
Tiede, David Lenz. *Luke*. Augsburg Commentary on the New Testament. Minneapolis:Augsburg, 1988.
–. "The Kings of the Gentiles and the Leader Who Serves: Luke 22:24–30." *Word and World* 12 (1992): 23–28.
Topel, John. "The Tarnished Golden Rule (Luke 6:31): The Inescapable Radicalness of Christian Ethics." *Theological Studies* 59 (1998): 475–485.

Touloumakos, J. "Zum römischen Gemeindepatronat im griechischen Osten." *Hermes* 116 (1988): 304–324.
Tristram, H. B. *Eastern Customs in Bible Lands*. London: Hodder and Stoughton, 1894.
Tsafrir, Yoram, L. Di Segni, and Judith Green, eds. *Tabula Imperii Romani Iudaea-Palestina: Eretz Israel in the Hellenistic, Roman and Byzantine Periods; Maps and Gazetteer*. Jerusalem: The Israel Academy of Sciences and Humanities, 1994.
Tuchelt, Klaus. *Frühe Denkmäler Roms in Kleinasien: Beiträge zur archäologischen Überlieferung aus der Zeit der Republik und des Augustus*. Istanbuler Mitteilungen 23. Tübingen: Wasmuth, 1979.
Tuckett, C. M. *Luke's Literary Achievement: Collected Essays*. Journal for the Study of the New Testament 116. Sheffield: Sheffield Academic Press, 1995.
Tzaferis, Vassilios. *Excavations at Capernaum*. Winona Lake, Ind.: Eisenbrauns in association with Pepperdine University, 1989.
—. "Inscribed 'To God Jesus Christ': Early Christian Prayer Hall Found in Megiddo Prison." *Biblical Archeology Review* 33/2 (2007): 38–49.
van Unnik, W. C. "Die Motivierung der Feindesliebe in Lukas VI,32–35." *Novum Testamentum* 8 (1966): 284–300.
Urbach, E. E. "The Rabbinical Laws of Idolatry in the Second and Third Centuries in the Light of Archaeological and Historical Facts." *Israel Exploration Journal* 9 (1959): 149–165, 229–245.
Urman, Dan, and Paul Virgil McCracken Flesher, eds. *Ancient Synagogues: Historical Analysis and Archaeological Discovery*. 2 vols. Studia post-Biblica 47.2. Leiden: Brill, 1995.
Vaage, L. *Galilean Upstarts: Jesus' First Followers According to Q*. Valley Forge: Trinity Press International, 1994.
VanderKam, James C. *The Dead Sea Scrolls Today*. Grand Rapids: Eerdmans, 1994.
Verboven, Koenraad. "Review of Claude Eilers, *Roman Patrons of Greek Cities*." *Bryn Mawr Classical Review* 6.19 (2003).
—. *The Economy of Friends: Economic Aspects of* Amicitia *and Patronage in the Late Republic*. Brussels: Latomus, 2002.
Vermes, G. *Jesus the Jew*. London: Collins, 1973.
Veyne, Paul. *Bread and Circuses: Historical Sociology and Political Pluralism*. Trans. and abridged by Oswyn Murray and Brian Pearce. London: Penguin Press, 1990.
—. *Le pain et le cirque: Sociologie historique d'un pluralisme politique*. L'Univers historique. Paris: Seuil, 1976.
Vine, Victor E. "Luke 14:15–24 and Anti-Semitism." *Expository Times* (1991): 262–263.
Violet, B. "Zum rechten Verständnis der Nazareth-Perikope Lc4$^{16-30}$." *Zeitschrift für die neutestamentliche Wissenschaft und die Kunde der älteren Kirche* 37 (1938): 251–271.
Vögtle, Anton. *Das öffentliche Wirken Jesu auf dem Hintergrund der Qumranbewegung*. Freiburger Universitätsreden 27. Freiburg im Breisgau: Schulz, 1958.
Volkmann, Hans. *Res Gestae Divi Augusti: Das Monumentum Ancyranum*. Kleine Texte für Vorlesungen und Übungen 29–30. Berlin: De Gruyter, 1969.
Vom Brocke, Christoph. *Thessaloniki, Stadt des Kassander und Gemeinde des Paulus: Eine frühe christliche Gemeinde in ihrer heidnischen Umwelt*. Wissenschaftliche Untersuchungen zum Neuen Testament 125. Tübingen: Mohr Siebeck, 2001.
von Dobbeler, Axel, Kurt Erlemann, and Roman Heiligenthal, eds. *Religionsgeschichte des Neuen Testaments: Festschrift für Klaus Berger zum 60. Geburtstag*. Tübingen: Francke, 2000.

von Premerstein, A. *Vom Werden und Wesen des Prinzipats*. Abhandlungen der bayerischen Akademie der Wissenschaften, philologische-historische Abteilung 15. Munich, 1937.
Waddington, W. H., and Philippe Le Bas. *Inscriptions grecques et latines receuillies en Grèce et en Asie Mineure*. Vol. 3. 1870.
Walaskay, Paul W. *'And So We Came to Rome': The Political Perspective of St. Luke*. Cambridge: Cambridge University Press, 1983.
Wallace-Hadrill, Andrew. *Patronage in Ancient Society*. London and New York: Routledge, 1989.
Waterman, Leroy, et al. *Preliminary Report of the University of Michigan Excavations at Sepphoris, Palestine in 1931*. Ann Arbor: University of Michigan Press, 1937.
Wattles, Jeffrey. *The Golden Rule*. New York: Oxford, 1996.
Watts, J. D. W. *Isaiah 34–66*. Word Biblical Commentary 25. Waco: Word, 1987.
Webb, Robert L. "Book List: Books on the Historical Jesus." *Journal for the Study of the Historical Jesus* 5 (2007): 205–218.
Weill, R. "La Cité de David: Compte rendu des fouilles exécutées à Jérusalem sur le site de la ville primitive. Campaigne de 1913–14 [I-IV]." *Revue des études juives* 69 (1919): 3–85[I]; 70 (1920): 1–36 [II]; 149–179 [III]; 71 (1920): 1–45 [IV] + Plates.
Weissenrieder, Annette. *Images of Illness in the Gospel of Luke: Insights of Ancient Medical Texts*. Wissenschaftliche Untersuchungen zum Neuen Testament 164. Tübingen: Mohr Siebeck, 2003.
Welles, C. Bradford. *Royal Correspondence in the Hellenistic Period*. Repr. Chicago: Ares, 1974.
Westermann, C. *Isaiah 40–66: A Commentary*. Old Testament Library. Trans. D M. G. Stalker. Philadelphia: Westminster, 1969.
Wheatley, Alan Brent. "The Use and Transformation of Patronage in Early Christianity from Jesus of Nazareth to Paul of Samosata." PhD diss., University of California at Los Angeles, 1999.
White, L. Michael. *Social Networks in the Early Christian Environment: Issues and Methods for Social History*. Semeia 56. Atlanta: Scholars Press, 1992.
White, L. Michael, and O. Larry Yarbrough, eds. *The Social World of the First Christians: Essays in Honor of Wayne A. Meeks*. Minneapolis: Fortress Press, 1995.
Wiedemann, T. E. J. *Adults and Children in the Roman Empire*. London: Routledge, 1989.
Wilkins, P. I. "Legates of Numidia as Municipal Patrons." *Chiron* 23 (1993): 189–206.
Wilson, John Francis. *Caesarea Philippi: Basias, the Lost City of Pan*. London and New York: I. B. Tauris, 2004.
Winter, B. *Seek the Welfare of the City: Christians as Benefactors and Citizens*. First-century Christians in the Greco-Roman World. Grand Rapids: Eerdmans, 1994.
Winter, Bruce W., and Andrew D. Clarke, eds. *The Book of Acts in Its Ancient Literary Setting*. The Book of Acts in Its First-century Setting 1. Grand Rapids: Eerdmans, 1993.
Wolf, Eric R. *Peasants*. Englewood Cliffs: Prentice-Hall, 1966.
Wright, N. T. *Jesus and the Victory of God*. Minneapolis: Fortress Press, 1996.
Xeravits, Géza G., and József Zsengellér, eds. *The Book of Tobit: Text, Tradition, Theology: Papers of the First International Conference on the Deuterocanonical Books, Pápa, Hungary, 20–21 May, 2004*. Supplements to the Journal for the Study of Judaism 98. Leiden: Brill, 2005.
Xeravits, Géza G., and József Zsengellér, eds. *The Books of the Maccabees: History, Theology, Ideology: Papers of the Second International Conference on the

Deuterocanonical Books, Pápa, Hungary, 9–11 June, 2005. Supplements to the Journal for the Study of Judaism 118. Leiden: Brill, 2005.

Yadin, Yigael. *The Ben Sira Scroll from Masada*. Jerusalem: Israel Exploration Society, 1965.

Yakobson, Alexander. *Elections and Electioneering in Rome: A Study in the Political System of the Late Republic*. Stuttgart: F. Steiner, 1999.

Yoder, John Howard. *The Politics of Jesus: Vicit Agnus Noster*. Grand Rapids: Eerdmans, 1972.

York, John O. *The Last Shall Be First: The Rhetoric of Reversal in Luke*. Journal for the Study of the New Testament 46. Sheffield: JSOT Press, 1991.

Zahn, Theodor. *Das Evangelium des Lukas: Ausgelegt*. 1st–2nd ed. Kommentar zum Neuen Testament 3. Leipzig/Erlangen: Deichert, 1913.

Zangenberg, Jürgen, H. W. Attridge, and D. B. Martin, eds. *Religion, Ethnicity and Identity in Ancient Galilee: A Region in Transition*. Tübingen: Mohr Siebeck, 2007.

Zangenberg, Jürgen, Gabriele Fassbeck, Sandra Fortner, Andrea Rottlof, eds. *Leben am See Gennesaret: Kulturgeschichtliche Entdeckungen in einer biblischen Region*. Sonderbände der Antiken Welt. Mainz: Verlag Philipp von Zabern, 2003.

Zangenberg, Jürgen. *Frühes Christentum in Samarien: Topographische und traditionsgeschichtliche Studien zu den Samarientexten im Johannesevangelium*. Texte und Arbeiten zum neutestamentlichen Zeitalter 27. Tübingen: Francke, 1998.

Zeller, Dieter. *Die weisheitlichen Mahnsprüche bei den Synoptikern*. Forschung zur Bibel 17. Würzburg: Echter Verlag, 1977.

Author unknown. *Quarterly Review* 19 (1819): 413, no. 38.

Author unknown. *The British Museum: Egyptian Antiquities*. London. 2 (1836): 376–379.

Index of Ancient Sources

Greco-Roman Authors

Aristotle

Politeia

1310b24	313
1286b10	313

Cicero

In Verrem

2.2.114	41

Dio Chrysostom

De regno (Or. 1)

1.12–26	25

De regno II (Or. 2)

2.77–78	206

Diogenes

Epistles of Diogenes

8.11	1

Herodotus

Historiae
5.90	28

Josephus

Antiquities of the Jews

13.288–296	254
14.91	65, 86
14.122	126
15.21	70
15.189–190	103
15.193	127
15.271	97
15.290	304
15.298	111
16.158–159	129
17.20	137
17.188	316
18.27	90
18.28	114–115
18.36–38	79–80, 145, 179
18.106	152
18.118	140
18.164–165	156
18.240–255	144, 188
18.245	74
18.289	158
19.243	79–80
19.328–330	160–161, 165
19.330	166
19.335–337	162–163
20.264	94

Against Apion

1.178–180	120

Life

64–69	84

Jewish War

1.319	190
1.414–415	108
1.602	151
2.84–86	132
2.167–168	149
2.178–222	155
4.145–146	105

5.27	80	Suetonius	
Juvenal		*Divus Augustus*	
		60	81
Satirae			
5.12–25	249, 268	*Divus Claudius*	
		34	156
Lysias			
		Vitruvius	
6.40–41	292, 299		
		On Architecture	
Philo		5.1.1	82

*Quod deterius potiori
 insidari soleat*
45   304

Old Testament

De specialibus legibus
4.111   304

Plato		Exodus	
		12.14	296
Seventh Letter		*Leviticus*	
332–333	27	25.10	239–240
Plutarch		*Deuteronomy*	
		15.1–11	240–241
The Dinner of the Seven Wise Men		16.1–8	296–297
148F–149F	259, 264	*Esther*	
		8.12–14	219
Quaestionum Convivialum		*Proverbs*	
612D	260, 264	10.12	304
615F	260, 264	25.6–7	260
616–C–F	260, 264		
		Isaiah	
Polybius		58.6–7	209–210
		61.1–3	209, 238, 239
5.11.6	313		
		Ezekiel	
Seneca		3.7	304
		17.24	258
De beneficiis		21.31	258
1.1.8	34		
2.2.1	228	*Habakkuk*	
4.32.2–3	222	2.6–11	210
Stobaeus			
Florilegium			
3.10.45	251		

Index of Ancient Sources

New Testament

Matthew
2.13–15	184
22.15–16	190

Mark
6.21–29	262
7.24–30	177
8.22–25	117

Luke
4.17–19	239
5.17–19	196
7.1–10	75–76
7.24	139
8.1–3	180
13.31–33	139, 186
19.11–27	139
23.14–15	187

1 Cor
11.6	304

Apocrypha and Septuagint

Sirach
12.1-6	233-234, 271
17.22–23	271
22.23	308–309
25.7–11	204–205, 207–208
30.6	217
31.12–32.9	260, 264, 330
31.15	228
32.1–9	261

Tobit
13.14–16	208–209

1 Maccabees
11.32–36	220–221
14.25–49	104, 255

2 Maccabees
2.27	261
4.2	255
4.4	304

4 Maccabees
1.26	304
4.4	304
8.26	304

Dead Sea Scrolls

11QMelch	240

Rabbinic Literature

Baba Bathra
3b	132

Ta'anith
23a	132

Pesahim
10.5	296

Inscriptions

AE
1963 no. 104	109

CIG
3609	126, 184

IGLS
6.2759	153, 168–169

IGR
3.1102	121

OGIS
54	222, 252
75–78	313
90	299, 305
167	220–221, 252
213	293, 299
248	216–217
267	313
415	135
416	146

417	147	*SIG*	
419	166, 167–168	174	47–48
427	168	372	313
428	167	495	299
666	292, 299	761	224
		762	299
Sammelbuch		1173	252
8299	305		

SEG

Apostolic Fathers

1277	101		
4.490	197, 269	*1 Clement*	
8.170	102	19:2	1
16.488	147–148		

Index of Modern Authors

Ahn, Y. S. 286–287
Avigad N. 96

Ball, W. 83–84, 115–116, 127
Bartchy, S. S. 270
Batey, R. L. 55, 142
Billings, B. S. 290
Blok, A. 6
Bock, D. L. 21, 214
Bovon, F. 192, 213, 250
Braun, W. 251, 262–263, 274–275
Braund, D. C. 102, 103, 126, 127, 128, 134, 172, 311

Carson, D. A. 182
Chancey, M. A. 57, 77–78, 92
Crook, Z. A. 29, 32–33, 37–38, 47, 230, 335
Crossan, J. D. 19, 262

Daley, B. E. 1
Danker, F. W. 8, 25, 35, 198, 223–224, 248, 283, 291, 297
Darr, J. A. 185, 186, 187
deSilva, D. A. 19, 192, 324
Dihle, A. 226
Doran, R. 95

Eilers, C. 6–7, 41–42, 43–44, 201, 268, 306
Erskine, A. 39, 316, 322

Fitzmyer, J. A. 196, 227, 296
Fortner, S. 118
Freyne, S. 13, 16, 59, 91, 114, 287, 301

Gal, Z. 60
Gardner, G. 336
Goodman, M. 52–53
Green, J. B. 2, 10, 21, 192, 253, 279–280

Hanson, K. C. 21, 248–249, 266, 268, 330
Harris, H. A. 83
Harrison, J. R. 51, 174, 191–192
Hengel, M. 54
Hoffmann, P. 227
Horsley, R. A 60, 66–67, 82, 119, 227
Howgego, C. J. 56–57

Jensen, M. H. 12–13, 16, 60–61, 63–64, 161, 186
Joubert, S. 32–37

Kee, H. C. 75, 85–86, 142
Kirk, A. 219, 226, 243
Klein, H. 213
Kloppenborg, J. S. 265
Koch, K. 204

Lichtenberger, A. 95
Lull, D. J. 206–207, 286–288, 300, 301, 308

MacMullen, R. 39, 49–50, 59
Malina, B. J. 10
Mason, S. 51
Merkelbach, R. 231
Meshorer, Y. 133
Meyers, E. M. 16
Millar, F. 89
Mitchell, A. 26, 36, 172, 249, 266, 273, 284
Moxnes, H. 2, 20, 57–58, 174, 192–193, 249, 282–283, 287, 288, 324

Nelson, P. K. 3–4, 203, 286, 273, 293, 300, 301, 302–303
Neyrey, J. 10, 301
Nicols, J. 39–41

Oakman 10, 55, 248–249, 266, 268, 330

Peuch, E. 267
Philipp, G. B. 216
Piper, J. 203
Porter, S. 177

Reed, J. 13, 73–74, 262
Richardson, P. 66–67, 132, 144–145, 148, 166–167, 168

Sahlins, M. D. 9, 229, 270
Saller, R. P. 5, 8, 33, 43–44
Sanders, E. P. 86, 98
Sawicki, M. 19, 52–53, 55, 65, 98, 180, 263
Schnabel, E. J. 183
Schwartz, D. 128, 159, 161
Schwartz, S. 94
Seaford, R. 26

Sloan, I. 323
Soards, M. L. 301
Spilsbury, P. 203–204
Stegemann W. 270
Stegemann E. W. 270
Strange, J. F. 58
Strickert, F. M. 149, 153, 335

Talbert, C. H. 202
Tannehill, R. C. 194, 288
Taylor, J. E. 109
Theissen, G. 177–178

Van Wees, H. 28
Verboven, K. 5, 10, 33, 172, 312
Veyne, P. 4, 8, 11, 134

Zangenberg, J. 110–111

Index of Subjects and Key Terms

Agrippa I 20, 24, 53, 91, 98, 102, 125, 126, 138, 143, 144, 149, 173, 189, 306, 315, 316, 322, 328, 334, 335
Antipas 185, 186, 188, 255
Aphorism 257, 264
Archaelogy 13, 18, 57–59, 122
Archelaos 65, 112, 134, 137, 139, 141, 143, 146, 150, 151, 184, 185, 289, 295, 312, 316
Augustus 40–41, 152, 197, 295, 319, 333, 336

Banquets 156, 166, 249, 268, 275, 277, 279
Beatitudes 204–205
Benefaction 26, 44–49, 106, 151, 153, 165, 170, 219, 230, 231, 247, 255–256, 275, 279, 282, 284, 288, 289, 294, 296, 300, 311, 313, 320, 326, 329, 330, 335
Benefactor 4, 37–39, 125, 161, 233, 252, 285, 286–287, 295, 299, 300, 305–308, 314, 318, 319, 336
– endangered benefactor 166, 291–292, 299, 320, 322, 331
Broker 36, 197, 235

Chreia 251
Claudius 164
Client 45–46, 235, 258, 266, 311–312, 325, 326, 331
Codex Bezae 291
"Common Benefactors" 49, 170, 313, 316–317, 322, 325
Conversion 17, 25, 274
Χάρις 29–31, 46, 129, 134, 158–159, 162, 218–219, 221, 222–223, 231–232, 234, 312, 316, 328–329

Debt 2, 28, 29, 35, 37, 48, 63, 66, 156, 157, 160, 193, 199, 241, 242, 258
διατίθεμαι 309–310

Dining 253
Dionysios Villa 262
Discipleship (definition) 3–4
Dowry 277
Dropsy 250–251, 253, 274–275

Elijah 198, 201, 245, 255–256
Elisha 198, 201, 245, 255–256
Epigraphy 45
Εὐεργέτης 45, 48, 111, 138, 181, 197–198, 280, 287, 300, 305–307, 312–313, 321
Euergetism 7, 134, 230

Farewell Address 297
Friend 127, 128, 130, 136, 137, 138, 148, 156–157, 164, 169, 171, 172, 188, 193, 235, 235, 258–259, 260, 264, 266, 273, 284, 285, 311–312, 325, 327, 330, 331
φιλοτιμία 39, 52, 97, 183, 197

Gaius 163
Galilee 12–15, 55–56
– economics of 62–63, 141
– politics of 63–66
Games 170
Gift 241, 268, 271, 272, 279, 293, 333

Hellenization 51, 53–57, 71–72, 76–77, 78, 87, 93, 96, 112–113, 115, 119, 123–124, 131, 177, 199–200, 294, 326, 327, 329
Herod I 64, 70, 88, 255
Herodians 189–191
Historical Jesus 11–15, 23, 175, 262–264, 268, 284, 319, 324
Honor-shame 5, 34, 248, 253, 258, 261, 262, 264, 277, 286–287, 290, 297, 303, 330
Hospitality 254
Hyrcanus 254, 261, 336

Jerusalem 182, 256, 302, 326, 332, 333
Jewishness 61–62, 67, 68, 73–74, 84, 89, 91–92,.. 99, 106, 116, 121, 123, 165, 178–179, 200, 254, 322, 326
John the Baptist 136, 139, 140, 187
Jubilee 239–243, 247, 329

Κηδεμών 105, 151
Kinship (Fictive) 233, 270
Κτίστης 40, 45, 52, 107, 118, 235, 335, 336

Literacy 69
Livia-Julia 150, 153–154, 181
Loyalty (faith; πίστις) 5, 6, 28, 35, 45, 60, 70, 82, 94, 103, 105, 120, 127, 148, 158, 181, 189, 220, 229, 237, 258, 271, 285, 289, 290, 293, 308–309, 313, 317, 320, 321, 332
Luke (Gospel of) 22, 174–176
Luke (author) 175–176

Meals 21, 48, 62, 248, 253, 258, 259, 261, 262, 283, 294, 303, 305
Memorial 292–293, 295, 299, 321, 331–332

Numismatic evidence 116

Onias 255, 336

Passover 288–289, 295, 286, 300, 315, 320–321, 332
Pater patriae 40, 326
Patronage 4–5, 26, 37, 249, 272, 279, 280–281, 282–283, 305, 322–323, 325, 329, 332, 334
— literary 6, 7, 10, 43–44, 325
Patronus 5, 36, 49, 178, 189, 201, 210, 236, 268, 321, 322–323, 325, 333, 335
Patrocinium 24, 38–41, 44–49, 54, 103, 106, 109–110, 122–124, 125–126, 136, 141, 145, 150, 151, 153, 154, 171–173, 174–175, 177, 182, 184, 189, 191, 193, 198–199, 200, 201, 210–211, 220, 236, 241–242, 245–246, 248, 253, 255, 271–272, 279, 282–284, 288, 293–295, 305, 322–323, 324, 325, 327, 328, 329, 331, 332–333, 334
— terminology 51, 225, 230, 244, 252, 266, 268, 273, 275, 281, 282–284, 299, 305–306, 309, 310, 311, 313, 320, 321, 322–323, 324, 327, 333–334
Philip the tetrarch 20, 22, 32, 53, 66, 67, 92, 103, 106, 112, 113, 116, 117, 118, 122, 124, 125, 140, 143, 144, 164, 165, 171, 173, 179, 181, 182, 188, 189, 199, 294, 295, 326, 327, 335
Philo 260–261
Polis 73, 83, 84, 88, 90, 99, 107, 113, 114, 143, 152

Qumran Community 261

Reciprocity 27, 171–172, 174, 181, 215, 217–218, 226–231, 241, 244, 246–247, 248, 258–259, 265–267, 269, 270, 271, 272, 275, 278–279, 283, 284, 287, 303, 319, 323, 328–329, 330, 331
Redaction 302–303
Regionalism 16–17, 24, 52–53
Remember 296, 297, 299, 334
Reversal 203, 205–206, 246
Romanization 50, 53–57, 59, 65–66, 67, 71, 76, 85, 112–113, 131, 169, 268, 326, 333

Sabbath 239–243, 245, 247, 250–251, 254, 255, 298–299
Salutatio 6, 280, 288, 323, 334
Savior 36
Sepphoris 72–73
Socio-historical interpretation 15, 18, 23, 63–64, 322–323, 324–325, 334
Σωτήρ 4, 40, 41, 42, 44, 45, 52, 105, 111, 197, 305, 306, 326, 336
Substitutionary sacrifice 298
Suffragium 6, 43–44, 120, 200–201, 310–312, 325, 327
Symposium 249, 259–263, 286–287, 297–298, 331

Table 253, 256–257, 261, 275, 297, 318–319, 321, 330

- invitations to 257, 265, 274, 277–278, 281
Temple of Apollo 147
Temple of Jerusalem 289, 295
Tetrarch 143–144
Theodotus inscription 102

Therapeutae 260–261

Urbanization 69, 88

Woes 238